The Blue

D1454218

Blue Guide

THAILAND

Gavin Pattison and John Villiers

A & C Black · London

W W Norton · New York

First edition 1997
Published by A & C Black (Publishers) Limited
35 Bedford Row, London WC1R 4JH

© Gavin Pattison and John Villiers 1997
Maps and plans © A & C Black, drawn by Robert Smith
Illustrations © Jaideep Chakrabarti
'Blue Guides' is a registered trademark.

A CIP catalogue record of this book is available from the British Library.
ISBN 0-7136-3905-9

Published in the United States of America by
WW Norton and Company Inc.
500 Fifth Avenue, New York, NY 10110

Published simultaneously in Canada by
Penguin Books Canada Limited
10 Alcorn Avenue, Toronto
Ontario M4V 3BE
ISBN 0-393-31583-5   USA

The authors and the publishers have done their best to ensure the accuracy of all the information in Blue Guide Thailand however, they can accept no responsibility for any loss, injury or inconvenience sustained by any traveller as a result of information or advice contained in the guide.

Gavin Pattison is a freelance writer and journalist who has worked in Thailand, Cambodia, Indonesia and the Philippines. He has a Degree in Southeast Asian studies and language, and has explored the region very extensively. He is currently researching the forthcoming Blue Guide Indonesia.

John Villiers has a PhD in history from Cambridge University. He served in the British Council for twenty years, seven of them in Indonesia, until 1979, when he was appointed Director of the British Institute in Southeast Asia, a British Academy institute for research in Southeast Asian archaeology, history and anthropology, based for five years in Singapore and for three years in Bangkok. From 1991 to 1994 he was Southeast Asian editor of Macmillan's Dictionary of Art, to which he has also contributed several articles. He is a Fellow of the Royal Asiatic Society. He has lectured widely and published numerous books, papers and articles on the history of Southeast Asia and of the Portuguese empire in Asia. He is at present working on a biography of Vasco da Gama.

Cover photograph of a gilded gable on a *wat* in Bangkok by Kevin Morris/Corbis UK Ltd.
Title page illustration: Wat Phra Si Sanphet, Ayutthaya.
Drawings on p 67 adapted from *The Heritage of Thai Sculpture* by Jean Boisselier, Asia Books Co. Ltd, 1975; the plan on p 128 has been adapted from *A History of Wat Phra Chetuphon and its Buddha Images*, Siam Society, 1979.

The publishers invite readers to write in with comments, suggestions and corrections for the next edition of the Blue Guide. Writers of the most informative letters will be awarded a free Blue Guide of their choice.

Printed and bound by William Clowes Ltd, Beccles and London.

CONTENTS

Maps and Plans

INTRODUCTION

In this age of mass tourism and rapid communications even the most discriminating travellers tend to be unduly influenced in forming their opinions of a country of which they have no firsthand knowledge by what they hear from those whose impressions of it are derived from a single brief and hectic visit, usually confined to the capital and one or two well known resorts catering primarily for foreign tourists. The result of this is that, if subsequently they go to the country themselves, they tend to follow a similar itinerary. The lopsided view of the country which they thus acquire is distorted still further by the equally misleading and superficial accounts of it presented to them by the media. Of no country is this more true that Thailand. Few people travel further in Thailand than Bangkok, Patthaya, Phuket, Ko Samui and some of the other islands, and perhaps Chiang Mai and the Golden Triangle, and Thailand seldom features in the Western news except in connection with some sensational case of drug smuggling, murder, political unrest, corruption in high places, floods or some other natural disaster. Thailand also exemplifies, more obviously than most countries, the traveller's maxim that one should never judge a country or its people by the defects and shortcomings of its capital. Because Bangkok has the unenviable and, it must be admitted, not wholly undeserved reputation of being the sex capital of Asia, of having intolerably high levels of air and noise pollution, of suffering from virtually continuous traffic jams and frequent flooding, it is all too easy to dismiss it and by extension the whole of Thailand as dirty, difficult, dangerous and depraved. If this guide can help, by describing Thailand's outstanding areas of natural beauty and its most important monuments, many of them rarely visited by tourists, to remove some of these preconceptions and thereby create a better understanding of Thailand, the Thai people and Thai civilisation, it will have achieved its purpose.

Many areas of Thailand, notably the northeast (Isan), still have some way to go in catering for the increasingly sophisticated tastes and elaborate requirements of the modern tourist, but this makes them all the more interesting for the adventurous and independent traveller who is not afraid of occasionally having to rough it. At the same time, even in the most elegant and luxurious modern hotel in Bangkok there are numerous reminders of the richness, diversity and distinctiveness of Thai Buddhist civilisation and of the way in which it still informs almost every aspect of the daily life of almost every Thai. The Thais are a proud and independent people who have never been colonised and who remain devoted to their Buddhist religion, their monarchy and their traditional culture, and who still manage, if not to resist altogether the more pernicious effects of Western cultural influences and mass tourism, at least to modify and adapt them so that they can be accommodated more easily to the Thai way of life. At the same time, although it is a great mistake to assume that in this 'Land of Smiles', as the tourist brochures so often describe it, every smile you see on a Thai face betokens a state of happiness and contentment, still less of uncritical delight in your presence or in that of the millions of other foreign tourists in their country (sometimes, indeed, it denotes precisely the reverse), there is no doubt that most Thais manage to derive enjoyment from life (*sanuk*) without so great a reliance on the material props and aids that have come to be taken for granted in the West. Furthermore, they are almost invariably hospitable, good tempered, well mannered and courteous to foreign visitors, however much they dislike the way some of them behave. It is these qualities in the people as much as their gilded temples, their delicious food or the vibrant night life of their capital city that make travelling in Thailand so delightful and rewarding an experience and that more than compensate for any shortcomings in the provision they make for the comfort and convenience of tourists.

Acknowledgements

John Villiers's heartfelt thanks go to the two faithful friends who have accompanied him on many of his travels in Thailand: Ian Page, indefatigable explorer and photographer, passionate Khmerophile and Siamophile, and Nopporn Boonharn, who combines exceptional skills as a driver with an uncanny gift for discovering remote and fascinating places that do not appear on any map. Between them they have contributed more to this book than they will ever know.

Gavin Pattison would particularly like to thank Greg Hattingh, composer of pithy letters to the *Bangkok Post*, for his unceasing good humour as a travelling companion, and his wife Nee for putting up with piles of luggage in their tiny flat; Robert Mather at Wildlife Fund Thailand for his gratefully received contributions on Thailand's national parks and fauna, and his wife Noi for her unfailing hospitality in Chiang Khan; and Mike and Jip Parnwell who always found the time to give advice and assistance when needed. Jariyathon Soohoo in the TAT office in Khon Kaen provided much valuable information and worked hard to answer obscure requests. His grateful thanks are also due to Dusdee Vonnasuvon who first introduced him to the delights of Thai food many years ago, William Southworth for his archaeological advice, and Colin McQuistan.

Both authors owe an incalculable debt of gratitude to Gemma Davies for her patient and painstaking guidance and assistance at all stages in the preparation of this guide for the press.

Using the Guide

This Guide is in two parts. The first part gives practical and background information, the second comprises a series of routes which describe the country. Route summaries at the start of each chapter provide information on distances and road numbers. Excursions off the main routes are indicated by paragraphs beginning with ▶ and ending ◀. Information on hotels, restaurants and local transport is contained within the routes.

Abbreviations:
C century
km kilometre
m metre
Skt Sanskrit
T. Thanon (Road)

HIGHLIGHTS OF THAILAND

History, art and architecture

The history and art of the Thai kingdom of Sukhothai and of its successor Ayutthaya are magnificently exemplified in the ruins of four of their great cities—**Kamphaeng Phet**, **Si Satchanalai**, **Sukhothai** and **Ayutthaya**, which have been meticulously conserved and formed into historical parks. All four have museums in which are displayed notable examples of their sculpture and other works of art. A journey to Ayutthaya, by road or by river from Bangkok, can be conveniently combined with a visit to the royal palace of the early Chakri kings at **Bang Pa-in**, which contains several fine buildings in a variety of architectural styles set among beautiful lakes and gardens.

The architectural remains of Dvaravati and Sir Vijaya, two of the kingdoms that preceded the arrival of the Thais in the area, are few in number and chiefly of interest to specialists. On the other hand, there are numerous magnificent **Khmer monuments** dating from the period when the Khmer empire of Angkor held sway over much of northeast and central Thailand. The most important of these monuments in the northeast (Isan) are **Phimai** and **Phanom Wan** near Nakhon Ratchasima, and **Phanom Rung** and **Muang Tam** near Buri Ram. In central Thailand the principal Khmer monuments are **Muang Sing**, near Kanchanaburi, city of the Bridge over the River Kwae, and a group of temples in **Lop Buri**, which also contains several ruined but still impressive buildings dating from the time in the second half of the 17C when it was the summer capital of King Narai. **Preah Vihear**, known in Thai as Khao Phra Wihan, just over the Thai-Cambodian frontier in Cambodia, is the most dramatically situated of all Khmer monuments and has carving of exceptional quality, but in recent years it has often been difficult or impossible to visit. The carefully restored ruins of **Si Thep**, which was first a Mon and later a Khmer city, are also of considerable historical interest and are situated in an attractive and well-maintained historical park.

Although not even the most fervent of its admirers can claim that it is a beautiful city, **Bangkok**, together with its sister city of **Thon Buri**, has many splendid buildings, including the Grand Palace and Wat Phra Kaeo (Temple of the Emerald Buddha), Wat Arun (Temple of the Dawn), Wat Benchamabophit (Marble Temple), Wat Pho, with its colossal reclining Buddha image, Wat Saket and the Golden Mount, Wat Traimitr, an undistinguished temple, but containing a remarkable golden Buddha image, and Wat Suthat, as well as numerous more modest but no less interesting sights, such as Jim Thompson's House, the Suan Pakkad Palace, the Vimanmek Palace, the Royal Barge Museum and the canals (*khlong*) of Thon Buri, and, just to the north of the city and now virtually a suburb, the delightful town of Nonthaburi.

On the whole, Thai towns are somewhat lacking in charm and have few buildings of great architectural merit. Two exceptions within easy reach of Bangkok are **Ratchaburi** and **Phetchaburi**, which has two temples containing exceptionally fine wall paintings (see below) and where the royal palace of Phra Nakhon Khiri is also well worth visiting. In the north of Thailand, **Chiang Mai,** the kingdom's second city, is not only richly endowed with temples, many of them containing beautiful woodcarving and stucco decoration, but is also an attractive, well laid out town, blessed with an agreeable climate. Other outstanding monuments in the north include Wat Pa Sak and other ruined temples of **Chiang Saen**, a small town pleasantly situated on the bank of the Mekong where it forms the frontier with Laos, Wat Phumin in **Nan**, and the superb monastic complex of Wat Phra That Lampang Luang near **Lampang**.

Many of the finest religious monuments are in small towns and villages or in the depths of the countryside, as for example the numerous temples in the Burmese style with beautiful woodcarving to be found in and around **Mae HonG Son** and other places in the far northwest of the country. Also notable, for historical or architectural reasons or both, are the great *stupa* of Phra Pathom Chedi in **Nakhon Pathom**, the tallest and, although in its present from dating only from the 19C, one of the most ancient Buddhist foundations in Thailand, Wat Phra Si Ratana Mahathat in **Phitsanulok**, which houses one of the most revered and beautiful of all Thai Buddha images, and Wat Phra That Hariphunchai and Wat Cham Tewi in the tranquil and charming little town of **Lamphun**, the shrine of Phra Phutthabat (Buddha's Footprint) near **Saraburi**, Wat Phra Boromathat in **Chaiya**, and th mosques of **Pattani** and **Narathiwat**.

Temples in the capital containing specially fine wall paintings include Wat Benchamabophit, Wat Borom Niwet, Wat Chong Nonsi, Wat Pho, Wat Phra Kaeo, Wat Somanat Ratcha Wora Wihan, Wat Suthat and the Phutthasaiwan Chapel in the National Museum in Bangkok, and Wat Suwannaram and Wat Thong Thammachat in Thon Buri. In towns near Bangkok, there are important wall paintings in Wat Yai Intharam in Chon Buri, Wat Suwandararam in Ayutthaya, Wat Bangkae Yai in Samut Songkhram, and Wat Ko Keo Suttharam and Wat Yai Suwannaram in Phetchaburi. Temples with notable murals in the north of the country include Wat Phra Sing Luang in Chiang Mai, and Wat Phumin and Wat Nong Bua in Nan, and in the south Wat Matchimawat in Songkhla.

It is possible to gain a good idea of the splendours of these monuments without travelling to see them by visiting the Ancient City (**Muang Boran**) near Bangkok, where many of them have been skilfully reconstructed.

The **National Museum in Bangkok** has the largest and most comprehensive collection of sculpture of all the major schools that have flourished in the area, as well as many examples of Thai decorative arts, textiles, ceramics, woodcarving and metalwork, but in other cities and towns there are numerous smaller museums, most of them branches of the National Museum, with important collections. Of these the most notable are the splendid assembly of Khmer lintels and other architectural decorations in the **Phimai National Museum**, the display of Dvaravati stelae and prehistoric artefacts from Ban Chiang in the **Khon Kaen National Museum**, which is also rich in Khmer sculpture, the spectacular gold treasures in the **Chao Sam Phraya Museum** in Ayutthaya, and the remarkable collection of Hindu and Buddhist sculptures from the Sri Vijaya period in southern Thailand in the **Nakhon Si Thammarat Museum**.

Fairs and festivals

Colourful fairs, festivals, races and competitions take place in many Thai towns, many of them in association with Buddhist holy days or ancient animistic reli-

gious beliefs. They include the Thai New Year (Songkran) festival, which is cele-
brated all over the country, but with special enthusiasm in Chiang Mai, the
Royal Ploughing Ceremony in Bangkok (May), the rocket festival in Yasothon
(May), candle festival in Ubon Ratchathani (July), wax castle festival in Sakon
Nathon (October), Phi Ta Khon fair in Loei (June), and Chao Mae Lim Ko Nieo
festival after the Chinese New Year in Pattani, the elephant roundup in Surin
(November), buffalo races in Chon Buri (October), boat races and regattas in
Ang Thong, Nakhon Phanom, Nakhon Ratchasima, Nan, Pathum Thani,
Phichit and Surat Thani, vegetarian festivals in Trang and Phuket (October), a
banana festival in Kamphaeng Phet (September), lychee festival in Chiang Rai
(June), flower festival in Chiang Mai (February), sunflower festival in Mae
Sariang (November/December), silk fair in Khon Kaen (December) and many
more. Loi Kratong (Festival of Lights), the loveliest of all Thai festivals, is cele-
brated in November throughout the country.

National parks, islands and beaches

Some of the most beautiful country in Thailand, as well as the best opportunities for the observation of wildlife, is to be found in the **national parks**, of
which Doi Phukha, Phu Kradung, Khao Sam Roi Yot and Khao Yai are perhaps
the finest. Many national parks contain spectacular waterfalls, such as the
Erawan and Khlong Lan falls in the parks of the same name, and caves, such as
the Phraya Nakhon Cave in Khao Sam Roi Yot National Park and the Phra That
and Wang Badan caves in Erawan National Park. The country round Mae Hong
Son and Nan is of outstanding natural beauty.

Many of the **islands** off the coasts of the Gulf of Thailand, the South China
Sea and the Andaman Sea are deservedly famous for their magnificent beaches
and beautiful scenery. Among these are Ko Phuket, which is the largest and is an
internationally renowned holiday resort, the islands of the Chang Archipelago
National Park, Ko Samet, Ko Samui and its neighbours Ko Phangan and Ko Tao,
and the Phi Phi islands and nearby islands, several of which have beautiful coral
reefs. Krabi, on the mainland opposite Phuket, has several exceptionally fine
beaches, some fascinating caves in the surrounding hills and is as yet largely
unspoilt. On the mainland the most popular beach resort in the country, but
now, alas, by no means the most beautiful, is Phatthaya. Still relatively exclusive
are Hua Hin, which has royal connections, and nearby Cha-am. In the far south
of Thailand Songkhla is an attractive resort, Phangnga Bay has spectacular
limestone cliffs and caves, and the Surin and Similan archipelagos have the best
diving in Thailand.

JV

PRACTICAL INFORMATION

Tourist Information

General information about sights, hotels and transport is available from the government-run Tourism Authority of Thailand (TAT). This has offices in more than a dozen countries.

Australia: Level 2, National Australia Bank House, 255 George St, Sydney 2000, ☎ (02) 247 7549/0.

UK: 49 Albemarle St, W1X 3FE, ☎ 0171 499 767.

USA: 303 East Wacker Drive, Suite 400, **Chicago**, IL 60601, ☎ (312) 819 3990-5; 3440 Wilshire Blvd, Suite 1100, **Los Angeles**, CA 90010, ☎ (213) 382 2353-5; 5 World Trade Center, Suite 3443, **New York**, NY 10048, ☎ (212) 432 0433/5.

In **Thailand** the main office is at 372 T. Bamrung Muang, Bangkok 10100 ☎ (00662) 226 0072/85/98). There are 22 regional offices throughout the country, which are indicated with their addresses in the main text, and another at Don Muang Airport in Bangkok.

When to Go

Thailand has a tropical monsoonal climate, which is divided into a wet and a dry season. In most of the country, the wet season lasts from May to October, as the southwest monsoon brings warm moisture-laden air from over the Indian Ocean. From November to April, cool, dry air blows in from China, bringing pleasant weather to Thailand's north and northeast. However, the southern part of this air mass picks up moisture over the South China Sea, and between November and January this falls on Thailand's southern peninsula as the northeast monsoon. The southernmost provinces of Yala and Narathiwat are most affected.

Visiting Thailand in the wet season need not be a problem. Usually the rain comes in brief, heavy downfalls, and the sun reappears soon afterwards. In the northern hills, however, it can rain gently but persistently for seemingly endless hours. Travellers should be aware that some minor roads can become impassable in the wet season.

Most tourists come during the relatively cool, dry months of December, January and February, when the countryside is still lush from the earlier rains. Prices are at their highest at this time, and hotels in the popular destinations are often full, especially over Christmas and the New Year. There is a second tourist season during the months of July and August, when European holiday-makers fill the resorts.

Perhaps the best months to visit Thailand are October and November, between the end of the rains and the start of the tourist season. By March, temperatures are beginning to get unpleasantly high. April is generally the hottest month, especially on the Khorat Plateau in the northeast, where temperatures of 39°C are not uncommon and travel can be very uncomfortable. The plateau is also the driest part of the country and suffers from frequent droughts.

Passports and Formalities

A valid passport is needed to enter Thailand. Holders of British, USA, Canadian, and Australian passports, and the passports of more than 50 other countries may enter Thailand for up to 30 days without a visa; New Zealand passport-holders may stay for up to 90 days. Most other visitors may stay for 15 days. For longer visits, 60-day tourist visas are obtainable from any Thai embassy or consulate. Visa extensions for these are available from immigration offices around the country, but the 30-day entry permit is not extendable.

In in the **UK**, visas are available from the Royal Thai Embassy, 1/3 Yorkshire House, Grosvenor Crescent, London SW1X 7EP, ☎ 0171-259 5005 and from consulates in Birmingham, Cardiff, Glasgow, Hull and Liverpool; in the **USA** from the Royal Thai Embassy, 1024 Wisconsin Ave, Washington DC 20007, ☎ 202-944 3600, and from consulates in Atlanta (GA), Coral Gables (FL), Denver (CO), Honolulu (HI), Montgomery (AL), New Orleans (LA), and San Francisco (CA); and in **Canada** from the Royal Thai Embassy, 180 Island Park Drive, Ottawa, Ontario K1Y 0A2, ☎ 613-722 4444, and from consulates in Edmonton and Toronto.

Customs regulations
Luggage checks are usually fairly cursory on arrival, but they may be more thorough on departure. A litre of wine or spirits and 200 cigarettes can be brought in free of duty; permits are required for firearms, and all kinds of narcotic and pornography are prohibited. There are extremely severe penalties for possessing illegal drugs.

Antiques and works of art. The export of genuine antiques and of all images of the Buddha is forbidden without a licence from the Fine Arts Department. Information is available from the Bangkok National Museum.

Maps

Bartholomews and Nelles produce good general maps of Thailand to the scale 1:1,500,000, which are continually updated and widely available in the UK and Bangkok. Nelles also publishes an excellent map of Bangkok to the scale 1:15,000. Equally good is one to the scale 1:14,000 by Berndtson and Berndtson, which is available in Thailand from branches of DK Book House,, and shows some one-way streets.

In Thailand the Highways Department Club and Esso jointly produce a fairly accurate road map to the scale 1:1,600,000, which shows road numbers and is updated annually. The best road map for extensive touring is the bilingual Thailand Highways Map by Auto Guide Co., which is in atlas format to the scale 1:400,000. This also has street plans of every provincial capital, showing hotels, banks, *wat* etc. Older topographical maps produced by the military authorities to the scale of 1:250,000 are available from branches of DK Book House in Bangkok, Chiang Mai, Hat Yai and elsewhere.

Getting to Thailand

Air

There is a wide choice of flights from London to Bangkok, including non-stop services by British Airways, Thai Airways International (THAI) and Qantas. Several British charter companies fly to Phuket. In the USA, there are regular flights from Los Angeles, San Francisco and Seattle, and less frequent services from New York, Chicago and Atlanta. Bangkok is very well served by flights to most other Asian capitals, and several international carriers operate direct services to Chiang Mai, Hat Yai and Phuket from nearby countries.

Rail

A daily train service with comfortable sleeping berths operates from Butterworth in Malaysia to Bangkok (20 hrs), crossing the border at Padang Besar. A luxurious alternative is the Eastern & Oriental Express, operated by *Venice Simplon-Orient-Express*, which runs between Singapore and Bangkok with an excursion to the River Khwae Bridge at Kanchanaburi (c 52 hrs). Reservations can be made through travel agents.

Road

There are several road crossing points between Thailand and Malaysia. The main routes include road 4184 via Wang Prachan, road 4 via Sadao, road 410 via Betong, road 4057 via Waeng, road 4056 via Sungai Kolok; and the vehicle ferry across the estuary on the east coast between Ban Taba and Pengkalan Kubor. These border posts close at night, usually at about 18.00.

Share taxis and minibuses operate between Penang in Malaysia and Hat Yai, but at most other crossing points public transport stops at the border and the traveller is obliged to walk across and take local transport on the other side.

Roads to Laos, Burma and Cambodia are open, but in practice it is still difficult for foreigners to obtain permission to enter these countries by road from Thailand. The construction of the Friendship Bridge over the Mekong River between Nong Khai in Thailand and Vientiane in Laos has made overland entry into Laos more straightforward (see p 323–4): the Lao authorities operate a bus shuttle service from the frontier into Vientiane. It is also possible—but difficult to gain permission—to enter Laos by road from Chong Mek in Ubon Ratchathani province.

Sea

Entry by sea into southern Thailand from Malaysia is possible. There are daily **passenger boats** to Satun from Kuala Perlis on Malaysia's northwest coast.

Tour operators

A few of the many tour operators that offer holidays to Thailand are, in the UK: **Kuoni** ☎ 01233 211606, the main long-haul specialist; **Hayes and Jarvis** ☎ 0181 748 5050; **Bales Worldwide** ☎ 01306 885923, which offers both escorted tailor-made tours; **Trailfinders** ☎ 0171 938 3366, which specialises in discounted air fares and hotel accommodation; **Explore** ☎ 01252 344161, with tours and treks in small groups; **Abercrombie & Kent** ☎ 0171 730 9600, which specialises in luxury tours; **Indochina Travel** ☎ 0181 995

8280, which offers small group tours and tailor-made travel; **British Museum Tours** ☎ 0171 636 7169, **JMB Travel Consultants Ltd** ☎ 01905 425 628, and **NADFAS Tours** ☎ 0181 658 2308 for cultural tours led by experts.

Among similar tour companies and travel agencies in the US are **Abercrombie & Kent** ☎ (708) 954 2944; **Asia Pacific Adventures** ☎ (213) 935 3156; **Bolder Adventures** ☎ (303) 443 6789; **Eastquest** ☎ (212) 741 1688; **Myths & Mountains** ☎ (702) 832 5454; **Orientours Co. Ltd** ☎ (212) 838 8777; **Pacific Holidays** ☎ (212) 764 1977.

Money

The monetary unit is the **baht**, divided into 100 **satang**. There are coins of 25 and 50 *satang* (both very rare), and one, five and ten *baht*, and notes for 20, 50, 100, 500 and 1000 *baht*. Visitors can bring in any amount of foreign currency and *baht*. Exchange rates are listed in the *Bangkok Post*. Rates may vary slightly between banks.

Banks

The *Bangkok Bank, Siam Commercial Bank* and *Thai Farmers' Bank* are the largest and among the most efficient banks in Thailand, with branches throughout the country. Opening hours are usually 08.30–15.30, Mon–Fri (10.00–16.00 in Bangkok), but in busy tourist centres such as Phuket, Chiang Mai, and in the Silom, Sukhumvit and Khao San areas in Bangkok, many currency exchange counters open daily and for longer hours. Hotels will often change money, but usually at less favourable rates than the banks. At Don Muang Airport money counters stay open 24 hours.

Cheques, credit and debit cards

Travellers' cheques and Eurocheques are widely accepted by banks, although service can be slow in small provincial branches not used to dealing with them.

Visa and *Mastercard* can be used to obtain cash advances from banks and many ATMs, and are widely accepted in the better hotels and restaurants. *American Express* and *Diners Club* are less frequently accepted.

Accommodation

Thailand has a wide range of accommodation on offer to visitors, from luxury hotels, available in the main tourist centres such as Bangkok, Patthaya, Chiang Mai and Phuket, and developing commercial centres such as Hat Yai, Khon Kaen, Lampang and Nakhon Ratchasima, to more modest hotels, bungalow complexes, guest houses, houseboats, hostels, motels, and beachside huts, Guest houses generally provide very cheap, basic accommodation, often in traditional Thai style; some of them have restaurants/cafés attached. There are also ten YMCA and YWCA hostels in the kingdom. Spartan accommodation is available at many of Thailand's national parks, where camping is also frequently permitted. The Thailand Tourism Authority will provide listings of accommodation together with details of current rates. It is usually advisable to book in advance if you wish to stay at one of the first class hotels in any of the main resorts. There is a full list of hotels in Bangkok on p 107.

Travel in Thailand

Rail

The State Railway of Thailand runs an efficient service. One line runs from Bangkok to Chiang Mai, two lines to the northeast, one to the west, and one down the southern peninsula, dividing at Hat Yai to continue along each coast as far as the Malaysian frontier. A short line runs southwest from Bangkok to Samut Sakhon and Samut Songkhram.

Air-conditioned first-class sleepers are available on some trains, while most offer a choice between second-class sleepers and seats, and third-class seats. Food is available on express and rapid services. Sleepers and first- and second-class seats should be booked several days in advance, especially during holiday periods. A computerised booking system has been introduced at major stations, and this makes advance booking quick and simple. Bookings can also be made at many travel agents, but a surcharge will be levied. Timetables are usually available from the TAT, Hua Lamphong railway station in Bangkok, or from travel agents.

Bus

Both blue **air-conditioned** and cheaper orange **standard** buses operate between most major towns throughout the country. They travel fast, at times dangerously so, and are often crowded and uncomfortable, but remain the form of transport most widely used by Thais. The air-conditioned buses are greatly preferable: travellers are usually assured of a seat, which often reclines, leg-room is greater, and food is sometimes included. These buses also make fewer stops along the way.

Bus stations can be confusing, as destinations are generally displayed in Thai script only, but it is usually possible to find a porter or bus employee to help you find the correct bus. Tickets for non-air-conditioned buses can usually be bought on board, while those for air-conditioned services are numbered and must be bought in advance from a booth or ticket office,

In larger towns there are often several bus stations, each serving different destinations. Hotel staff will usually know which is the correct departure point. In some cases there may be no obvious station, simply a waiting area beside the road, but here local people can be very helpful.

A **warning**. Occasionally passengers, especially foreign tourists, are drugged and robbed on overnight buses, particularly on the popular southern routes to Phuket and Surat Thani. In most cases the tourist is befriended by a fellow-passenger, given some food or drink containing a strong sleeping potion, and then robbed.

Songthaeo and Samlo

Songthaeo ('two rows') are usually converted pick-up trucks with two parallel rows of seats in the back. In Bangkok's suburbs and large towns such as Khon Kaen, *songthaeo* operate on fixed routes and can be flagged down at any point on those routes. Elsewhere, as in Chiang Mai, they operate as a form of roving share-taxi: the driver will pick up passengers at any point and drop them off as he reaches their various destinations. In rural areas *songthaeo* may act as feeders for the main bus routes.

Samlo ('three wheels') may be either pedal or, like Bangkok's *tuk-tuk*, motorised tricycles with passenger seats. They come in many different shapes and sizes; those in Aranyaprathet are among the most stylish. It is necessary to agree the fare in advance with the driver. They are usually more expensive per kilometre than taxis, but may be faster and cheaper over short distances. They also provide a livelihood for a great many people, and can be fun to use. However, they cannot be recommended for comfort and they expose the passenger to the noise and exhaust fumes of the surrounding traffic.

Taxis

In Bangkok almost all taxis are now metered and are relatively cheap unless the traffic is exceptionally congested. In towns in the north and northeast, taxis are hard to come by except in Chiang Mai. In the far south, large old Mercedes-Benz cars are used as long-distance **share-taxis** between towns and provinces. More expensive than buses, they are generally much faster and more comfortable. However, they only leave when full, so there may be a long wait for passengers. The alternative is to charter several seats or the whole vehicle.

Private transport/rentals

The excellent road network makes driving in Thailand on the whole an agreeable experience. The chief drawbacks are the sometimes reckless driving and severe rush hour traffic congestion in the large towns, especially in Bangkok. On the other hand, country roads are often amazingly empty. Petrol is relatively cheap and widely available, and signposting, except on very minor roads, is clear and comprehensive, with road numbers marked and names of towns and villages given in both Thai and romanised script. An international driving permit is required. The speed limits are 60km hour in towns and 80km in the country.

Avis, Hertz and many local companies have offices in the main tourist centres and resorts, and offer a wide range of vehicles. Small **motorcycles** can be rented in many places, while more powerful machines can be found in such places as Phuket, Patthaya and Chiang Mai. Helmets are a legal requirement, although the law is widely flouted outside Bangkok. Several tourists are killed each year in motorcycle accidents, often through inexperience, drunkenness or sheer stupidity. Riders must be prepared to give way at all time to larger vehicles.

Bicycles can be rented cheaply in many places, including guest-houses, but are not recommended in busy towns. The ruins of old Ayutthaya, Sukhothai, Si Satchanalai and other sites where the monuments are widely scattered, and also the area around Chiang Khan, are ideal for cycling.

Air

Thai Airways International (THAI) operates a fairly extensive domestic network from its Bangkok hub. Timetables are frequently changed and it is advisable to book several days in advance to ensure a seat. Bangkok Airways has a smaller domestic network to several destinations not served by THAI, including Samui, Patthaya, Hua Hin and Loei.

Sea

There are regular ferry services to the most popular islands, such as Ko Samui and Ko Phangan, Ko Phi Phi and Ko Tarutao. To more distant islands, such as the Similans and the Surins, services may be limited at certain times of the year by the weather conditions.

Disabled Travellers

Almost no special provision is made for disabled people in Thailand, except in some international class hotels. Wheelchair users should note that cheaper hotels often have no lift. Pavement kerbs can be extremely high and the pavements themselves are usually too crowded and uneven for wheelchairs. Access to banks, post offices, *wat* and museums is frequently up a flight of steps, and public transport is ill-equipped for dealing with wheelchairs. However, these potential obstacles should not by themselves deter disabled visitors. Except in the best hotels, special diets can be difficult to arrange.

Health

The standard of medical care in Thailand is generally high. In the main towns hospitals are usually well-equipped and the staff are competent. Nevertheless, visitors are strongly advised to take out medical insurance that covers repatriation costs in case of serious illness.

Polio, tetanus, typhoid and hepatitis **vaccinations** are recommended but not mandatory. Visitors arriving from certain African and Latin American countries may be required to show a yellow fever certificate.

Malaria is a danger in parts of Thailand, and precautions should be taken. Some prophylactics can have severe side-effects if taken over a long period, so consult your doctor beforehand. Try to avoid being bitten by mosquitoes in the first place by using a repellant, wearing long sleeves, trousers and socks after dusk, and, where possible, sleeping under a mosquito net. Consult a doctor if you start to experience flu-like symptoms, as this may be the onset of malaria. Equally important, should you start to feel these symptons up to four weeks after you return home, tell your doctor you have been in a malarial area; people have died through misdiagnosis.

Rabies exists in Thailand, so any animal bite should be treated with the utmost care. A rabies vaccination before travelling will give you longer to get help should you be bitten.

AIDS is already widespread in Thailand and is likely to increase, although the available statistics are notoriously unreliable. Although most clinics and hospitals, even in the smallest towns, well understand the importance of using sterile medical instruments, it is a good idea to carry a personal supply of needles and syringes in case an injection is required,

Although Bangkok residents may tell you otherwise, **tap water** should not be drunk. Bottled water is available everywhere. Be careful of ice in drinks: hygenically produced ice cubes are generally safe, but be wary of odd-shaped chunks which have been chipped off a larger block. Fruit and salads washed with tap water are a potential problem, and locally made water-ices can also cause trouble, so stick to well-known brand names.

Food in Thailand is generally served freshly cooked and should not cause problems. However, mild diarrhoea may be experienced soon after arrival as the body's digestive system adapts to different bacteria.

Clothing

Light, loose cotton clothing is best. Sweaters are needed during the cool season evenings or if you are visiting mountainous areas and remote national parks. Remember always to dress modestly within the precincts of a temple (see Customs and Behaviour). Except on the most formal occasions, it is not necessary for men to wear a jacket and tie.

Electricity

The electric current is 220 volt AC throughout the country. Visitors carrying shavers, tape-recorders and other appliances should take an adaptor.

Embassies and Consulates

Australian Embassy: 37 T. Sathon Tai, ☎ (02) 287 2680.
British Embassy: 1031 T. Witthayu (Wireless Rd), ☎ (02) 253 0191, and a **consulate** at 54 Mu 2, T. Suthep, Chiang Mai ☎ (053) 222 571.
Canadian Embassy: 11th floor, Boonmitr Bldg, 138 T. Silom, ☎ (02) 237 4125.
US Embassy: 95 T. Witthayu (Wireless Rd), ☎ (02) 252 5040, and **consulates** at T. Wichayanon, Chiang Mai, ☎ (053) 252 629 and 35 T. Suphakit Chanya, Udon Thani, ☎ (042) 244 270.

Crime and Personal Security

The **Tourist Police** have offices adjacent to, or inside most TAT offices in Thailand, and have friendly English-speaking staff. In an **emergency**, call 1699 anywhere in Thailand (24 hrs).

Crime is not generally a problem for the tourist. However, pickpockets do hang around stations and work on buses, and travellers should be alert for bag-snatchers. Flaunting wealth is bound to attract unwelcome attention, and the sensible visitor would do well to wear little jewellery and to keep an eye on cameras and other valuables. Rooms in cheaper hotels often lock with a padlock; it is a good idea to travel with your own.

Violent crime is extremely rare, but smooth-talking con artists do sometimes manage to part gullible tourists from their money, especially in Bangkok. In recent years, the most common scam has involved persuading visitors to spend large amounts on gems, with the ridiculous claim that dissatisfied punters can later return the goods to the Thai Embassy in their home country and get their money back. Of course this is nonsense, as the Thai government exercises no control over private gem sales.

Sporting and Leisure Activities

Thailand offers a wide variety of activities, including some of the world's finest **diving** and **snorkelling** off the west coast of the southern peninsula. There is an ever-growing number of excellent **golf** courses throughout the country, with a particularly high concentration round the resorts of Hua Hin and Cha-am; **rock climbing** on the limestone in the south is becoming more popular, especially round Krabi, and there are plenty of **caves** to explore in the north near Mae Hong Son. There is also **flotilla sailing** in the magnificent scenery round Phuket, Krabi and Ko Phi Phi.

In northern Thailand, especially in the area around Chiang Mai and Chiang Rai, there are numerous **trekking** companies which arrange hikes of several days to visit villages of ethnic minorities. This is an extremely competitive business, and companies can be excellent or absolutely terrible. The best advice may be to talk to other, recently returned travellers. Many treks now include a day or more of elephant riding or rafting. More remote, and consequently less crowded trekking areas include Mae Hong Son, Nan, Thong Pha Phum in Kanchanaburi province, and Umphang near Mae Sot.

Thai boxing (see p 137), can be seen in Bangkok at different venues, notably at the Lumphini Stadium on Tuesday, Friday and Saturday and the Ratchadamnoen Stadium on the other four days of the week. Also well worth watching is the game of **takro** (see p 116).

Postal and Telephone Services

The Thai postal service is fairly efficient, although it is unwise to send valuable items through the system. Post offices in the main towns operate a poste restante service. To avoid filing errors, surnames should be very clearly written. Most post offices are open from Monday to Friday, 08.30–16.30, and Saturday, 09.00–12.00; some larger ones also open on Sunday mornings. Bangkok's central post office on T. Charoen Krung operates an efficient parcel-wrapping service.

The most reliable public telephones are the green card phones, which can be used for all domestic calls. Phone cards can usually be bought from a nearby shop or hotel. The older kiosks with red or blue phones are coin-operated and frequently out of order.

Post offices in most provincial centres have an international telecoms office attached, often upstairs and usually open daily from 07.00 to 22.00. Note that time in Thailand is GMT+7. In Bangkok, the telephone office next to the central post office on T. Charoen Krung is open 24 hours. At most offices, calls are operator-assisted at a fixed rate measured in 60-second units, but more modern offices have a computerised direct dial service with three different pay rates measured in 10-second units. These calls are 20 per cent cheaper from 21.00–24.00 and from 05.00–07.00, and 30 per cent cheaper from 00.00–05.00. International collect calls can be extremely expensive, as can international calls made from hotels, which generally add a surcharge.

News Media

The main English language newspapers in Thailand are the *Bangkok Post* and *The Nation*. The *Bangkok Post* tends to provide better coverage of international news, while *The Nation* contains more domestic news. *The Thailand Times* is a newer, inferior paper. *The International Herald Tribune* and other foreign papers are available in Bangkok and the major tourist resorts.

Short-wave radios can receive BBC World Service, Radio Australia and Voice of America programmes. Details of frequencies are printed in *Bangkok Metro Magazine* and *The Nation*. Virtually all national radio and TV is in Thai language. Many of the more expensive hotels, especially in Bangkok, Chiang Mai, Phuket and Hat Yai, have cable or satellite TV, with coverage from CNN, BBC or AusTV.

Film and Photography

The major international film manufacturers have developing facilities in Thailand. There are also many instant developing outlets. If you are taking still photographs it is likely that you will be free to shoot almost anywhere. However, cam-corders and video equipment are not allowed without special permission in Bangkok's Grand Palace and Wat Phra Kaeo complex (see p 120). Photography is also forbidden in some of the National Museums.

Public Holidays and Festivals

The following are fixed public holidays:

1 January	**New Year's Day**
6 April	**Chakri Day**, to commemorate the founding of the Chakri dynasty by Rama I in 1782
12–14 April (13–15 in the north)	**Songkran**, which until the 1940s was the traditional Thai New Year, is an old brahmanic ceremony originating in southern India. Today the festival involves merit-making, the building of sand *chedi* at the *wat*, the cleaning of Buddha images with lustral water and water-throwing to ensure abundant rain in the forthcoming rice-planting season
5 May	**Coronation Day**, to celebrate King Bhumibol's coronation in 1950, four years after his succession
12 August	**Queen Sirikit's Birthday**
23 October	**Chulalongkorn Day**, the anniversary of King Chulalongkorn's death in 1910
5 December	**King Bhumibol's Birthday**
10 December	**Constitution Day**, the anniversary of Rama VII's signing of the constitution in 1932, which replaced the absolute power of the king by a constitutional monarchy
31 December	**New Year's Eve**

The dates of the following **festivals** are decided by the royal astrologer or are tied to the lunar calendar:

Makkha Bucha (Magha Puja): held on the full moon of the third lunar cycle (mid-February to mid-March) to celebrate the time when, nine months after he had attained Enlightenment, the Buddha travelled to Rajgaha, capital of Magaha, and 1250 disciples came to pay homage to him.

Royal Ploughing Ceremony: held in May. An ancient brahmanic ceremony in which the king usually participates, It is held at Sanam Luang in Bangkok to mark the official commencement of the rice-planting season.

Wisakha Bucha (Visakha Puja or Wesak): held on the full moon of the sixth lunar cycle (mid-May to mid-June), the anniversary of the Buddha's Birth, Enlightenment and Death. A national holiday.

Asalaha Bucha (Asalaha Puja): held on the full moon of the eighth lunar cycle (mid-July or mid-August) to celebrate the First Sermon of the Buddha to his five disciples in the deer park at Sarnath after he attained Enlightenment.

Khao Phansa: held on the day after Asalaha Bucha to mark the beginning of the three month period known as *Phansa*, the Rains Retreat or Buddhist Lent, during which the monks go into retreat. Lenten candles are made to burn throughout the period. This tradition has evolved into a tourist attraction in some areas, especially Ubon Ratchathani, where a procession of enormous sculpted wax candles is paraded through the streets on floats.

Ok Phansa: held on the full moon of the 11th lunar cycle (October or November) to mark the end of Phansa.

Thot Kathin: a one month period from Ok Phansa to the full moon of the 12th lunar cycle (November or December). It is the custom to give new robes to monks at this time. The king presents new robes to the monks at Wat Arun, and this is followed by a procession of state barges (see p 148) on the Chao Phraya River.

Loi Krathong: held on the last day of Kathin, ie, the full moon of the 12th lunar cycle (November or December). This festival is not Buddhist in origin, although it occurs on a *wan phra* or day of worship, but is held to honour the water spirits. Lit candles, flowers, incense and coins are placed in miniature boats made of banana leaves (*krathong*), which are then launched after dark on the water. In Chiang Mai, where the festival is called Yi Peng, hot-air paper balloons are also launched into the sky.

In addition, **Chinese New Year** is very important in certain parts of Thailand, especially Nakhon Sawan, Phuket and Trang. **Muslim** festivals are celebrated by the large ethnic Malay population in the southern provinces of Narathiwat, Pattani, Satun and Yala. There are also dozens of colourful **local festivals** in all parts of the country. Some of the most popular are mentioned in the main text.   **GP**

Food and Drink

In Thai cooking indigenous ingredients and techniques are blended in a highly distinctive manner with elements borrowed from India, China, Malaysia, Vietnam, Laos, Japan and Portugal to create one of the world's most varied, most subtly flavoured and most delicious cuisines. All the ingredients are lightly cooked, usually by boiling (*tóm*), steaming (*nêung*) or stir-frying (*pàt*) in a wok. Dairy products are not used at all.

Thais attach great importance to the appearance of food and the way it is served, and every dish is designed to appeal as much to the eye as to the palate. The art of decorating dishes with fruit and vegetables carved into intricate shapes has been brought to a high level of refinement in Thailand and has always been associated with royalty. It is known to have been practised in the late 13C at the court of Sukhothai by Queen Nang Nopamat, consort of King Ramkhamhaeng, and it reached its zenith at the court of Rama II in Bangkok in the early 19C.

In a Thai meal there are traditionally no courses in the Western sense, and all the dishes are put on the table simultaneously. Moreover, Thais tend to eat whenever they feel hungry and at all times of the day and night, and this may account for the huge number of restaurants and food stalls in every town. In Bangkok alone there are thought to be at least 10,000 restaurants and 40,000 food stalls.

There are Chinese restaurants in all the main cities and towns, and Western food of a sort is available in most of the more expensive hotels throughout the country. In Bangkok and the larger cities there are French, Italian, Japanese, Indian, Korean and other foreign restaurants, as well as fast food centres such as McDonalds and Pizza Hut,

Table Manners

Except for sticky rice (see below), Thais eat most food with a spoon (*chón*) and fork (*sôm*), including meat, which is cut into small pieces before cooking. It is considered very bad manners to convey food to the mouth with a fork; the spoon alone should be used for this purpose. It is customary when eating a meal in company to start by eating a spoonful of rice on its own, and when a guest at a meal to leave some food on your plate and on the serving dishes to emphasise the superabundant generosity of your host.

Rice

The staple food of the Thais, as of most Southeast Asian peoples, is rice (*khâo*). The word *khâo* is frequently used in the general sense of 'food', and *kin khâo* ('eat rice') to mean 'have a meal'. Long-grain white rice is the variety preferred by most Thais and this may be eaten steamed (*khâo sǔei*—'beautiful rice') or fried (*khâo pàt*) with chicken (*kài*), crab (*pu*), pork (*mǔ*) or shrimps (*kûng*). In the north and northeast of Thailand and in Laos sticky or glutinous rice (*khâo nǐao*) is popular, and this is traditionally served in special baskets made of woven bamboo and is eaten by being rolled into small balls with the right hand. Mangoes with sticky rice (*khâo nǐao mamûang*) is a popular dish all over Thailand, as also is sticky rice and coconut roasted in a length of bamboo (*khâo lam*). Flour made with sticky rice is used in many dishes.

Noodles

Noodles, which were introduced from China, often take the place of rice, especially for light meals and snacks, and are always eaten with chopsticks (*ta kìap*). They may be made of rice flour (*kǔay tǐo*) or wheat flour (*ba mì*), wide or narrow, fried in soy sauce or boiled in soup, and accompanied by beancurd (*tofu*), vegetables (*pàk*), eggs (*kài*), peanuts (*tùa lisǒng*) or meat (*neúa*). Transparent or glass noodles (*wún sên*) are eaten in soup or in sweet dishes; a favourite delicacy is glass noodles baked with crab (*wún sên op pu*).

Herbs, Spices and Seasoning

The number of herbs and spices used in Thai cooking is enormous. Among the most commonly used are lemon grass (*takrai*), cardamom (*krawan*), cloves (*kanplu*), mint, sweet basil (*horapa*), spicy or 'holy' basil (*krapao*), coriander (*pàk chi*), of which the leaves, seeds and root are all eaten, garlic (*kratiam*), root ginger (*khing*), galingale (*kha*), which is a root similar to ginger but less piquant and with a slightly pink tinge, pepper (*prík thai*), tamarind (*makham*), turmeric (*kamin*) and chilli (*prik*). Though it is not true that chillies, which are thought to have been introduced into Southeast Asia from South America by the Portuguese, are an essential ingredient of all Thai food, they are used extensively in a wide variety of dishes. There are many kinds of chilli of differing shapes, sizes, colours and degrees of fieriness, the hottest being the small green ones popularly known as *prik ki nu* ('mouse-droppings chilli'). **Thai curries** (*kaeng*) are made either with red or green chillies. In the south of Thailand a mild Muslim Malay curry called *kaeng matsaman* made with chicken or beef and potatoes (*man faràng*) flavoured with cinnamon (*op cheuay*), cardamoms and peanuts is popular.

In traditional Thai cooking *nám pla*, a clear, pungent sauce made from fermented fish, is used instead of salt. At the table, it is usually served in a small bowl with pieces of chilli in it. Other ingredients used frequently in Thai cooking are *ka pi*, a paste made from small shrimps and finely ground rice, and oyster sauce (*nám man hoy*), which is chiefly used for cooking beef (*néua*). Soy sauce (*nám si yú*) is usually only served with Chinese food.

Soups

Thai soups are rich and nourishing and, if eaten with rice, make a satisfying meal in themselves. The most popular soup is *tom yam*, which is made with lime, mushrooms, lemon grass, chillies and other spices and herbs, to which are added shrimps, fish (*pla*), chicken, or pork. Another favourite soup is *tom kha kai*, of which the principal ingredients are pieces of chicken in coconut milk, galingale and lemon grass.

Vegetables

Vegetables are very lightly boiled or stir-fried, or not cooked at all. They include bamboo shoots (*nomai*), beansprouts (*tua ngok*), cucumber (*taeng kua*), eggplants (*makheŭa muang*), various forms of gourd (*buap*), lettuce (*pàk kat*), mushrooms (*hèt*), particularly black Chinese mushrooms, mangetout (*tua lantao*), morning glory (*pàk bûng*), which is usually eaten fried and served in a gravy, okra (*krachiap mon*), onions (*hua hom* or *ton hom*), peppers (*prik yuak*), taro (*peuak*), tomatoes (*makheua thet*), long green beans (*tùa fak yao*), mung beans (*tùa kaeo*), and many kinds of nuts (*tùa*).

Meat and Fish

Thais eat beef, pork, chicken and duck (*pèt*; duck cooked in lime is a special delicacy), but not mutton. Meat is often eaten in the form of satay, which is made by putting small pieces on a bamboo skewer and grilling them over charcoal, and is generally accompanied by peanut sauce. Thais also eat a great variety of freshwater and sea fish, among them catfish (*pla duk*) and squid (*pla meùk*), as well as crabs, prawns and shrimps.

Fruit

An enormous variety of fruit (*pŏnlamái*) is available in Thailand, including the following:

banana (*klûay*, all year). Often eaten fried or in coconut milk.

breadfruit (*sagai*, all year). A large rough skinned fruit tasting not unlike a potato.

coconut (*mapráo*, all year). The juice is drunk and the white flesh is eaten from the shell when young and when ripe is grated for use in cooking. The milk is made by soaking the grated flesh in water.

custard apple (*nóinà*, June to September). About the size of an orange with a rough green skin and sweet white flesh and black seeds.

durian (*durian*, May to July). A large fruit with a thick green prickly skin and a soft yellow flesh. It has a strong, pungent smell and flavour that many people find disagreeable, but others consider delicious.

guava (*faràng*, all year). About the size of a lemon. with edible green skin and white flesh with small brown seeds.

jackfruit (*khanún*, January to June). Large fruit with a rough green skin and sweet but rather leathery yellow flesh.

lime (*manao*, all year).

longan (*lamyai*, July to October). Small round fruit with brittle brown skin and flesh similar to the rambutan in taste and texture.

lychee (*linchì*, April to May).

mango (*mamûang*, March to June). Mango with sticky rice (*khao niao mamuang*) is a favourite dish (see above)

mangosteen (*mangkhút*, April to September). Small round fruit with a thick purple skin, which stains indelibly, and sweet white flesh in segments.

orange (*sôm*, all year).

papaya (*malako*, all year). Yellow-green fruit with succulent orange flesh and small black pips. Salad made of unripe green papaya, shrimp, chilli, sugar and other ingredients (*som tam*) is a popular dish.

pineapple (*sapporót*, all year).

pomelo (*sômo*, August to November). Large green citrus fruit with a pinkish-green flesh.

rambeh (*mafai*, april to May). Small yellow-red berries.

rambutan (*ngó*, June to September). Small fruit with a red, hairy skin and sweet white flesh.

rose apple (*chomphû*, April to July). Small red, pink or green fruit with apple-like taste and rather woolly texture.

sapodilla (*lamút*, July to September). Small brown fruit somewhat like a pear in taste and texture.

tamarind (*makham*, all year). Brown semi-circular pods. Sweet and sour varieties.

water chestnut (*kachap*, all year). Hard brown shell with two horns projecting from it.

water melon (*daengmoh*, all year).

Sweet Dishes

Thais are fond of sweet dishes (*khanom*), though these are more readily obtainable at food stalls and in coffee shops than in restaurants, where fresh fruit is usually served to end a meal. Thai sweets include glass noodles, tapioca, rice-flour dumplings, jelly cubes served in coconut milk and often coloured bright green or pink, miniature fruit (*luk chup*) made from mung bean paste and sugar, flavoured and dyed, custards, bananas in coconut milk, egg yolks sugared and shredded (*foi thong*), a dish said to have been introduced by the Portuguese, and sweed palm kernels (*luk tan cheuam*).

Drinks

Beer (*bia*) is the best alcoholic accompaniment to Thai food. There are three major brands of beer in Thailand—Kloster, Singha (pronounced Sing) and Amarit. Singha is the most popular, Kloster the most expensive. Many Thais and some foreigners like Thai rice whisky, of which the best known brand is Mekong, often mixing it with Coco Cola. A very pleasant wine is produced at the Château de Loei, owned by Chaijudh Karnasuta, the chairman of the Oriental Hotel, but most of the wine in Thailand is imported, chiefly from Australia, and is very expensive.

Non-alcoholic drinks include coffee (*kafe*; in southern Thailand, *kopi*). Both instant coffee and real coffee (*kafe thung*, 'bag coffee') are usually served with sugar and sometimes condensed milk already added, unless you ask for it without ('*mai sai namtan/nom*'). Tea is drunk either hot or iced, and both Thai and Chinese varieties are popular. Fruit juices are usually served with sugar and salt added, unless you ask for the salt to be omitted ('*mai sai kleua*'). Sugar cane juice (*nam oy*) is also a popular drink. It is not advisable to drink tap water or buy drinks with ice in them at road stalls. Bottled water is cheap and readily available almost everywhere in the kingdom.

Cookery Books

Thai cuisine has become extremely popular in the West in recent years, and many cookery books have been published to cater for the growing number of people who wish to cook Thai food for themselves. Among the best of these are:

Puangkram C. Schmitz and Michael J. Worman, *Practical Thai Cooking* (Tokyo, New York and London, 1985)

Hilaire Walden, *The Book of Thai Cooking* (London and New York, 1992)

JV

The Thai Language

The Thai or Siamese language, together with Lao, Shan and a number of other languages spoken by smaller ethnic groups in southern China (Yunnan and Hainan), northern Vietnam and northeast India belongs to the Tai family of languages (see p 44), which it has not yet been possible to classify with any certainty in any larger linguistic group, although some scholars believe it to be related to the languages of the Sino-Tibetan group. At an early stage in the southward migration of these Tai peoples, the culture and language of the Siamese Thais, particularly in central Thailand, became strongly influenced first by the Mons and then by the Khmers among whom they settled, and consequently a significant proportion of the vocabulary of modern Thai and some elements of its syntax derive from Mon and Khmer. The Thais also adopted the Buddhist religion of the Mons and the Khmers and, as a result of this, many words of Sanskrit and Pali origin entered the languge, at first through Mon and Khmer and later by direct borrowing from India and Sri Lanka. The elevated form of Thai known as Royal Thai (*ratchasap*), used only when addressing or referring to royalty, and the special vocabulary employed for addressing and referring to Buddhist monks contain many words of Sanskrit and Pali origin, as well as Khmer words that are not found in colloquial Thai, but are still current in modern Khmer.

Unlike Sanskrit and Pali and other Indo-European languages, Thai is a largely monosyllabic language, with no strict differentiation between parts of speech and so no affixes, case endings or other grammatical inflections, and this has meant that there is only a relatively limited number of combinations of sounds from which words can be formed. Consequently, like Chinese and other mono-syllabic languages, Thai has developed a system of tones as a means of distin-guishing between the many words of one syllable with identical sounds but different meanings (homonyms) that have arisen from this limitation. Moreover, the numerous polysyllabic words that Thai has borrowed from Sanskrit and Pali, and more recently from Arabic and European languages, also have tones attached to each syllable.

Some **Thai dialects** have as many as nine tones, but there are only five in the language now generally accepted as standard Thai, which is the Thai spoken in Bangkok and throughout most of central Thailand. These tones are usually defined as mid, level or neutral, rising, falling, high and low. Many words have entirely different, occasionally even contradictory, meanings according to their tone. For example, *ma* spoken with a level tone means 'come', with a high tone means 'horse' and with a rising tone means 'dog', *mai* with a high tone means 'wood', with a low tone means 'new', with a falling tone means 'not' or 'burn' and with a rising tone is the interrogative particle, while *glai* with a level tone means 'far' and with a falling tone means 'near'. It will be clear from these examples that in order to avoid misunderstandings the correct enunciation of tones is essential and it is therefore most important when speaking Thai not to indicate emotion, emphasis, negation or interrogation by tonal modulation, as this will distort the intrinsic tones of the words uttered.

The **Thai script**, although remarkably consistent and logical and bound by rules to which there are very few exceptions, is nevertheless of considerable complexity. It was supposedly invented in the late 13C by King Ramkhamhaneg of Sukhothai, who based it on Mon and Khmer versions of a South Indian script. It has 44 consonants for 21 consonantal sounds; every consonant belongs to one of three classes, and the class of the initial consonant of a word is one of the elements in that word that determines its tone. Another element that determines the tone of a word is the length of the vowel sound. There are 32 vowel signs or combinations of signs to represent 48 vowel sounds; every vowel sign or combi-nation of vowel signs has to be attached to a consonant and may be written before, after, above, below or even surrounding it on three sides. For words beginning with a vowel a special silent or zero consonant is used to which the vowel can be attached.

One major complication of the Thai script is that many letters and even entire syllables are silent, especially in words derived from Sanskrit and Pali, which are written as though they were still in those languages and had undergone no modification. For example, the name Nakhon Si Thammarat, is written as though it were Nagara Sri Dhammaraja, the three Pali words from which it is derived. Another difficulty is caused by the fact that some consonants are pronounced differently according to whether they occur initially or finally in a word: initial 'l' becomes 'n', 'b' becomes 'p', and 'd', 'ch', 'j' and 's' become 't'. Thus, Matchimawat can be and often is transliterated as Matchinawas, and the name of the king of Thailand is generally written Bhumibol, but is pronounced Phumiphon and, if transliterated letter for letter, would be spelt Bhumibala. These changes in the pronunciation of consonants also often affect the way in which Thais pronounce some foreign loan words in Thai. For example, the Central Department Store is known as 'Centran' and a bill is *bin* (or more usually *chek bin*). Learning to read Thai is still further complicated by the fact that written Thai does not require a space between words, there are no punctuation marks and no capital letters.

As a result of these anomalies, it is extremely difficult to devise a satisfactory or universally acceptable system of transliteration of Thai into the roman alphabet. A completely phonetic system of transliteration based on the orthography of a European language not only causes considerable divergences between the two scripts but results in many alternative spellings according to which European language is chosen as the model, while to transliterate letter for letter means that the spelling of many Thai words in the roman alphabet corresponds only approximately or not at all to their actual pronunciation.

There are numerous **Thai language courses** with cassettes now available, of which the Linguaphone Institute course by Manas Chitakasem and David Smyth and *Teach Yourself Thai* by David Smyth, published by Hodder and Stoughton, are the best. The Linguaphone course, however, is difficult and confusing to use, and *Teach Yourself Thai* is more practical and user-friendly. There is also a Thai cassette pack published by Berlitz and two courses with optional cassettes issued by the Europhone Language Centre, London—*Basic Thai plus Dictionary* by Sunthorn Kothbantan and *Simple Thai plus Dictionary* by Werachai Setthapun.

Still unquestionably the best book for learning to speak, read and write Thai without a teacher or accompanying cassettes is *The Fundamentals of the Thai Language* by Stuart Campbell and Chuan Shaweevongs, which has gone through several editions since it was first published in 1957. It is readily available in most bookshops in Thailand and is distributed in Britain by Bailey Bros and Swinfen, Warner House, Folkstone, Kent, in Australia by F.W. Cheshire Pty Ltd, 388 Little Collins Street, Melbourne, and in the USA by Paragon Book Gallery, 14 East 38th Street, New York NY 10016. Also recommended for a study of the basic elements of the language are *Thai in a Week* by Somsong Buasai and David Smyth, published by Hodder and Stoughton, and *Thai at your Fingertips* compiled by Lexus with David Smyth and Manat Chitakasem and published by Routledge. The latter work contains an English–Thai, Thai–English dictionary, a succinct reference grammar and a guide to pronunciation.

There are many good pocket phrase books, including Harrap's phrase book by David and Somsong Smyth, the BBC phrase book by Sanya Bunnag and the Lonely Planet phrase book by Joe Cummings. Lonely Planet have also published a phrase book of hill tribe languages by David Bradley. It covers Lahu, Lisu, Karen, Akha and Mien, all of which are tonal languages. Two useful pocket dictionaries, both more easily available in Bangkok than elsewhere, are the *Bua Luang Compact English–Thai Dictionary* and *Robertson's Practical English–Thai Dictionary*.

In this guide we have followed, with only a few modifications, the romanisation system formulated in 1954 by the Royal Institute in Bangkok and known as the RTGS (Royal Thai General System) for all place names and for religious, geographical and technical terms in the main text and in the glossary, as this is the system that has been adopted by the Thai authorities for all official publications and most (but unfortunately by no means all) road signs. The occasional exceptions include certain place names for which a variant spelling is more widely used (e.g. Mekong, not Mekhong). We have also followed the RTGS for personal names, except in those cases, notably some of the kings of the Chakri dynasty, in which the bearer of the name has adopted a different orthography. For the names and addresses of hotels we have generally used the spelling adopted by the hotels themselves, even if this diverges from the actual pronunciation. Non-Thai personal and place names we have left in the original language (e.g. Sri Vijaya, not Siwichai; Haripunjaya, not Hariphunchai, but Wat Phra That Hariphunchai). Most of the religious terms in the text and the glossary are given in Sanskrit, but we have sometimes used Pali terms when these have more general currency (e.g. Sangha, not Saṃgha; Theravada, not Sthaviravāda; *kinnara*, not *kiṃnara*).

In the list of useful words and phrases below and the section on food and drink we have used the same system, with only a few modifications to some words in an attempt to represent more nearly their actual pronunciation. The tone of each syllable is indicated thus: no mark = level tone, ´ = high tone, ` = low tone, ˇ = rising tone, ˆ = falling tone.

JV

Some useful words and phrases

In this brief vocabulary, the transliteration of words and phrases gives only an approximation of their sounds. On the other hand, an attempt has been made to achieve consistency with the transliteration adopted elsewhere in the guide, except in the case of some sounds that have been transliterated in the main text according to a more generally accepted but phonetically less accurate usage.

Greetings and civilities
One of the ways in which the Thai language can express politeness and deference is by the use of the two particles **kráp** and **kâ** or **ká** at the end of a sentence. Neither has any meaning in itself, but *kráp* is used only by male speakers, *kâ* by female speakers and *ká* by female speakers at the end of a question. For example:

pŏm yak ja klap bân kráp	I (male) want to go home
dìchǎn/chǎn mai chôp rán ahǎn ni kâ	I (female) don't like this restaurant
hông nám yù ti nai ká?	Where is the toilet?
pai nai?	general greeting (lit. 'where are you going?')
pai nai ma?	general greeting (lit. 'where have you been?')

pai tîo	reply to *pai nai?*
	(lit. 'I am just going around')
pai tîo ma	reply to *pai nai ma?*
	(lit. 'I have just been going around')
pen yangngai bâng	how are you?
sabai di lĕu	are you well?
sabai di	I am well.
sawàt di	hello, good morning, good evening etc.
la gòn	goodbye.
arai ná?	what did you say?
mai kao jai	I don't understand.
kòp khun (mâk)	thank you (very much)
khun chêu arai?	what is your name?
póm chêu	my name (male) is ....
đichán chêu	my name (female) is ....
mai pen rai	it doesn't matter, not at all,
	you're welcome.

Numerals

0	*soŏn*		
1	*nèung*	60	*hòk sìp*
2	*sŏng*	70	*jèt sìp*
3	*săm*	80	*paet sìp*
4	*sì*	90	*kao sìp*
5	*hâ*	100	*(nèung) róy*
6	*hòk*	101	*(nèung) róy nèung*
7	*jèt*	102	*(nèung) róy sŏng*
8	*pàet*	110	*(nèung) róy sìp*
9	*kâo*	111	*(nèung) róy sìp èt*
10	*sìp*	1000	*(nèung) pan*
11	*sìp èt*	3000	*săm pan*
12	*sìp sŏng*	10,000	*mèun*
13	*sìp săm*	50,000	*hâ mèun*
14	*sìp sì*	100,000	*saen*
15	*sìp ha*	700,000	*jèt saen*
16	*sìp hòk*	1,000,000	*(nèung) lán*
17	*sìp jèt*		
18	*sìp pàet*	1st	*tî nèung*
19	*sìp kâo*	2nd	*tî sŏng*
20	*yî sìp*	3rd	*tî săm*
21	*yî sìp èt*	4th	*tî sî*
22	*yî sìp sŏng*	5th	*tî hâ*
23	*yî sìp săm*	6th	*tî hòk*
30	*săm sìp*	7th	*tî jèt*
31	*săm sìp èt*	8th	*tî pàet*
32	*săm sìp sŏng*	9th	*tî kâo*
33	*săm sìp săm*	10th	*tî sìp*
40	*sì sìp*		
50	*hâ sìp*		

Telling the time

The Thai system of telling the time divides the day into four sections of six hours, each of which is known by a different name, as follows:

tî	midnight–06.00
cháo	06.00–12.00
{ *bài*	12.00–16.00
{ *yen*	16.00–18.00
tûm	18.00–24.00

midnight	*tîung keun*	midday	*tîung (wan)*
01.00	*ti nèung*	13.00	*bài mong*
02.00	*ti sŏng*	14.00	*bài sŏng mong*
03.00	*ti săm*	15.00	*bài săm mong*
04.00	*ti sì*	16.00	*bài sì mong*
05.00	*ti hâ*	17.00	*hâ mong yen*
06.00	*hòk mong cháo*	18.00	*hòk mong yen*
07.00	*jèt mong cháo*	19.00	*tûm nèung*
	or *mong cháo*		
08.00	*sŏng mong cháo*	20.00	*sŏng tûm*
09.00	*săm mong chăo*	21.00	*săm tûm*
10.00	*sì mong cháo*	22.00	*sì tûm*
11.00	*hâ mong cháo*	23.00	*hâ tûm*

Paradoxically, *hòk* ('six') *mong cháo* is earlier than *hâ* ('five') *mong cháo*.

An alternative way of counting the hours between 08.00 and 11.00 in Thai is as follows:

08.00	*pàet mong cháo*
09.00	*kâo mong cháo*
10.00	*sìp mong cháo*
11.00	*sìp èt mong cháo*

Half past the hour is expressed by adding the word *krêung* ('half') to the hour. For example:

05.30	*tî hâ krêung*
11.30	*hâ mong [cháo] krêung*
16.30	*bài sì mong krêung*

Minutes past the hour are expressed as hour + number + *nati* ('minutes')

There is no term to denote a quarter past or a quarter to the hour, which are both expressed as fifteen minutes. For example:

15.25	*bài săm mong yî sìp hâ nati*
22.10	*sì tûm sìp nati*
09.15	*săm mong (cháo) sìp hâ nati*

For minutes before the hour the word *ìk* ('further', 'more' is used), followed by the number of minutes + *nati* + the hour. For example:

08.45	*ìk sìp hâ nati săm mong cháo*
14.35	*ìk yî sìp hâ nati bài săm mong*
22.55	*ìk hâ nati hâ tûm*

The 24-hour clock is used in radio and television announcements, timetables etc; the word *naliga* is used for hours and *nati* for minutes. For example:

| 18.00 | *sìp pàet naliga* |
| 20.30 | *yî sìp naliga sám sìp nati* |

Days

wan day, *wan ní* today
prung ní tomorrow
mêua wan ní yesterday
wan jan Monday
wan angkan Tuesday
wan put Wednesday
wan paréuhat Thursday
wan súk Friday
wan săo Saturday
wan atít Sunday
wan phra Buddhist holy day
wan yút holiday
wan kêun pi mài New Year's Day
wan yút râtchakan public holiday
wan sŏngkran Sŏngkran Day (Thai New Year)
wan sáo atít weekend

Months

deuan month
deuan nâ next month
plai deuan the end of the month
deuan ní this month
tôn deuan beginning of the month
deuan gòn last month
klang deuan mid-month

mokgarakom January
gumpapan February
minakom March
maisăyon April
préutsapakom May
mítunayon June
karákadakom July
singhăkom August
gunyahyon September
tulakom October
préutsajìkayon November
tanwakom December

Notices

kâo in
òk out
tang kâo way in
tang òk way out
hâm pàn no admission
hâm kâo no entry
hâm jòt no parking
hâm klàp rót no turning
karuna tòt rong tao please remove your shoes
karuna gòt kring please ring
thanŏn soòan bùk kon private road
deung pull
plàk push
hâm ting kayà no litter

hâm tài rôop no photographs
hâm sòop burì no smoking
pròt ngîap silence please
sòp tăm inquiries
chán floor
lif lift, elevator
kêun up
long down
hóng nám toilet, rest room
sù kă toilet, rest room
burùt
chai } men
poôchai
satri
yïng } women
pôoyïng

Medical

rót payaban ambulance
kum gamnèut birth control
troòat lêuat blood test
hâng bai ya chemist, drug store
klinik clinic
hông klôt delivery room
tam fan dental surgery, dentist
jamnai ya dispensary
pâet ying doctor
nai pâet doctor (male)
tròoat sǎita eye test
rong payaban hospital
chìt ya injection
tròoat pàtsawá urine test
'X-ray' X-ray

Post and Telephone

tû jòtmai letter box
pátsadù parcel
ti tam gan praisani post office
long tabian registered mail
praisani yagon stamp
toralâik telegram
torasàp telephone
torasap tang klai long-distance telephone call
toô torasap sǎtaraná public telephone kiosk/booth
beu torasàp telephone number
samut beu torasàp telephone directory
tò extension

JV

Customs and Behaviour

Most Thais are devout Buddhists, and it is important not to do or say anything that might be interpreted as disrepectful of their **religion**. It is specially important to dress modestly in the precincts of a Buddhist monastery and to remove your shoes as you enter. For this reason, it is advisable to wear sandals or shoes without laces that can easily be slipped on and off when you are visiting monasteries or other Buddhist monuments. You should also remove your shoes if you are invited into a Thai home and as a general rule avoid displays of nudity in all public places.

Monks are treated with great respect. Women should take care never to touch a monk or even to stand near him, and never to hand anything to him directly. Monks are always given seats on buses, usually at the back. Many people also give up their seats on buses to children.

Images of the Buddha, whatever their condition, are sacred objects and you should not pose for a photograph in front of one, place it in an inferior position, treat it purely as an ornament, or show it any lack of respect. The export of Buddha images from the kingdom is prohibited without a special permit.

The Thai **monarchy** is held in great reverence, and any criticism of any member of the royal family should be avoided. Always stand up and remain silent whenever you hear the national anthem played (e.g. in cinemas or over a public address system). Take care never to step on a coin or banknote or a postage stamp with the king's head on it, always hand over banknotes with the king's head uppermost and place postage stamps on envelopes the right way up.

Thais believe that the feet are spiritually as well as physically the lowest part of the body and consider it extremely rude to point at anyone or anything with the foot, or even to sit with legs crossed and foot pointed. When sitting on the floor in a temple facing a Buddha image, you should always keep your feet to one side or beneath you.

The left hand is considered unclean and you should therefore try to avoid using it to eat food or to pass things to another person.

The head is considered to be the abode of the spirits and you should therefore refrain from touching Thais, even children, on the head.

When passing in front of somebody, particularly if he or she is seated, lower your body slightly as a mark of respect.

Thais exercise restraint and decorum in their personal relations, and demonstrations of affection in public are frowned upon, as are displays of anger. It is essential, therefore, in any argument or dispute to keep calm and not to raise your voice. Thais, when confronting any problem or difficulty, attach great importance to maintaining 'a cool heart' (*jai yen*) and quietly accepting the inevitable, an attitude which is summed up by their frequent use of the expression *mai pen rai* ('it doesn't matter', 'never mind').

Thais seldom shake hands, and their usual mode of greeting is the **wai**, in which both hands are placed together as if in prayer and raised close to the chest. The precise level to which the hands are raised depends upon the relative status of the two people concerned, but among social equals it is usually to about the height of the chin, accompanied by a slight bow. Since it is difficult for a foreigner to assess relative status with a Thai, it is generally wiser not to initiate a *wai*, particularly to a person younger than yourself or whom you think might consider himself to be of inferior social standing, but only to respond to a *wai* made to you.

JV

BACKGROUND INFORMATION

Geography

The kingdom of Thailand covers an area of 514,000 sq km (twice the size of the UK) and stretches 1600km from north to south and 780km from east to west. It can be divided broadly into six geographical regions.

The **Northern Highlands** comprise the mountain ridges and wide fertile valleys that extend south from the borders with Burma and Laos to about 17°N. In this region are the head-waters of the four major tributaries of the Chao Phraya River: the Ping, Wang, Yom and Nan, all of which run roughly parallel from north to south. The mountains in this region higher than 1000m originally supported montane broadleaf evergreen forest, with mixed deciduous and dry evergreen forest on the lower slopes. The valleys have long been cultivated, and increasing upland cultivation is now leading to deforestation of the higher slopes.

Stretching across northeast Thailand is the **Khorat Plateau**, bounded by the Phetchabun range in the west and the Dangrek mountains along the Cambodian frontier in the south. The plateau is now largely deforested, but some deciduous and evergreen forests remain on the less accessible fringes. The main rivers are the Chi and the Mun, which merge near Ubon Ratchathani before emptying into the Mekong. Much of this region suffers from low rainfall and a long dry season.

The immensely fertile **Central Plain**, the alluvial flood plain of the Chao Phraya River, where once there was freshwater swamp and monsoon forest, is now almost entirely under intensive rice cultivation.

The **Southeast Uplands**, to the southeast of Bangkok, are an extension of Cambodia and support moist evergreen forest.

Running south along the Burmese frontier to the Kra Isthmus are the **Tenasserim Hills**, which lie in the rain shadow of higher hills inside Burma. While semi-evergreen forest occurs on the higher elevations, much of the deciduous forest on the lower slopes has been cleared or degraded and replaced with bamboo and grasslands.

The **Southern Peninsula** to the south of the Kra Isthmus forms a distinct floristic and faunal boundary for many Indo-Chinese and Malesian species. An area of high rainfall, the peninsula was once covered in rain forest, but most of the lowlands have now been cleared for agriculture.

Flora and Fauna

Thailand stands at the centre of a biogeographic transition zone between the Sino-Himalayan region to the north and west, the Indo-Chinese region to the east and the Sundaic region to the south. The result is a tremendously diverse flora and fauna.

Thailand's **flora** comprises between 12,000 and 18,000 plant species, with 1200 endemics. About 3000 are fungi, 1000 are orchids, 600 are ferns and

500 are trees. Many endemic plant species have already become extinct, a further 100 are considered endangered and at least 1000 more are rare.

The major floristic habitat types in the country can be classified most simply as follows:

Lowland evergreen dipterocarp rain forest occurs at elevations below 1000m in areas with more than 2000mm of rainfall annually, evenly distributed throughout the year. This is found in the extreme south of the peninsula and is the most species-rich forest type in the country. Good examples can be found in the national parks of Thale Ban near Satun, and Budo-Sungai Padi near Narathiwat.

Seasonal moist evergreen forest is found throughout the rest of the peninsula and in the Chanthaburi pocket of the Southern Uplands. Typical of the peninsula are the forests of Khao Sok and Khao Luang national parks, while Khao Khitchakut national park in Chanthaburi province is a good example in the Southern Uplands.

Montane broadleaf evergreen forest occurs above 1000m in areas with more than 2000mm of rainfall annually, spread throughout the year. Mosses, ferns, rhododendrons and orchids are common, together with oaks and chestnuts. Such forest is found in Doi Inthanon and Phu Kradung national parks, and Phu Luang wildlife sanctuary.

Semi-evergreen monsoon forest, which once covered about 20 per cent of Thailand, occurs in areas of high, but strongly seasonal rainfall. Fine examples are Khao Yai, Kaeng Krachan and Nam Nao national parks.

Much of Thailand's once extensive **mixed deciduous monsoon forest** has been cleared for its valuable commercial species, such as teak. This type of forest receives less than 2000mm of rain each year and has an extended dry season when most trees lose their leaves. The best remaining natural teak forest is in Mae Yom national park, but this is threatened by proposed dam construction.

Dry dipterocarp forest is found in the north and east, especially along the rim of the Khorat Plateau, where poorer soils combine with a long dry season. Good examples of this open savannah-type forest can be found in Nam Nao national park and Phu Luang wildlife sanctuary.

Pine forests are found on sandy soils in the north and northeast at elevations between 400 and 1000m. The best are in Doi Inthanon and Phu Kradung national parks.

Scattered but spectacular **limestone formations** can be found in the southern peninsula, as at Khao Sam Roi Yot national park, and on islands off the southwest coast, such as those in Ao Phangnga Bay national park. There is more extensive karst in Mae Hong Son and Kanchanaburi provinces.

Almost all the **freshwater swamp forest**, once extensive along major rivers such as the Chao Phraya, has been cleared for irrigated rice cultivation, but small areas of peat swamp forest remain in Narathiwat province, especially in Pa Phru non-hunting area.

The **beach forest**, which fringes sandy mainland coasts and islands, has been heavily degraded by settlement and often also by tourism development. The **mangrove forest** has been heavily exploited for charcoal production and conversion to shrimp ponds. An estimated 50 per cent has been destroyed, and only six per cent lies in protected areas, such as Hat Chao Mai, Ao Phangnga and Tarutao national parks. **Sea-grass beds** are found along the southwest coast and provide feeding grounds for dugongs and turtles. The best examples are in Hat Chao Mai and Ao Phangnga national parks. **Coral reefs** occur on both east and west coasts. The most developed reefs are found off the west coast around islands lying in deep clear water. Islands closer to the mainland have broad reef flats. More than 180 coral species have been recorded on the west coast; the best remaining reefs are found in the Surin, Similan and Tarutao national parks.

Sadly, many of Thailand's **freshwater** ecosystems are badly degraded. Most large rivers have been dammed and many are severely polluted. Former marshes, such as Bung Boraphet near Nakhon Sawan, have been greatly reduced in size and degraded by drainage and land reclamation schemes. Remaining protected marshes include those in Khao Sam Roi Yot national park near Prachuap Khiri Khan and Thale Sap non-hunting area near Songkhla.

Significant **plantation** habitats include rubber, where once there was evergreen rain forest; coconut, found usually on sandy coastal soils; and teak, in former mixed deciduous forest. These and many other species are of great economic value. Dipterocarps such as teak, and other hardwoods such as rosewood are especially valuable, while indigenous rattans, orchids and fruit trees are of global importance. One of the best sites for wild **orchids** is Phu Luang wildlife sanctuary, where more than 200 species have been recorded. Mangroves provide spawning, nursery and feeding grounds for fish and prawns, while numerous wild plants are harvested for domestic or commercial consumption, for food, fuel and building materials. At least 450 plant species are used locally for medicinal purposes, and agriculture remains a mainstay of the nation's rural economy.

Nearly **300 mammal species** and more than **900 bird species** are found in Thailand, which lies across a boundary between two zoogeographic subregions, the Indochinese and the Sundaic. The former extends over the area north of the Kra Isthmus; the latter includes the southern Thai peninsula as well as Malaysia and parts of Indonesia and the Philippines. Thailand is also home to 1200 butterfly, 300 reptile, 2000 fish and 100 amphibian species.

The majority of Thailand's mammals are small; they comprise **insectivores**, **rodents** and **bats**. Among the 92 bat species is **Kitti's hog-nosed bat**, which weighs a mere two grams, is 30mm long, and daily eats food weighing two or three times its own body weight. Discovered in 1973 in a few limestone caves in Sai Yok national park in Kanchanaburi province, it is probably the world's smallest mammal.

Of the large mammals, Thailand's wild **Asiatic elephant** population has been drastically reduced by hunting and by the destruction of its habitat. There are now fewer than 2000 wild elephants and about 3000 domesticated elephants in the country. The largest wild populations are found in Huai Kha Khaeng and Thung Yai Naresuan wildlife sanctuaries, and in Kaeng Krachan, Nam Nao, Khao Yai, Pang Sida and Thap Lan national parks. In the southern peninsula, Khao Sok national park still has a sizeable population.The easiest place in Thailand in which to see elephants in the wild is probably Khao Yai.

Thailand's 36 **carnivores** include the clouded leopard, leopard and tiger, two bear and two wild dog species. It is estimated that fewer than 300 **tigers** remain, and perhaps a few more leopards. The tiger is prized for its bones and penis, which are used in traditional Chinese medicine, and for its skin. The **bears** too are probably seriously endangered as a result of the demand in Korea for their paws and gall-bladders. Sightings of any of these large carnivores are extremely rare.

Of Thailand's 18 **ungulates**, Schomburgk's deer is probably extinct, the last one having been clubbed to death by a drunk in 1938, and the Javan rhinoceros may also have been exterminated from the kingdom. The kouprey, Eld's deer and the Sumatran rhinoceros are extremely rare, if not already extirpated, and only a single population of wild water buffalo remains—in Huai Kha Khaeng wildlife sanctuary. There are occasional reports of Sumatran rhino sightings in Phu Khieo wildlife sanctuary, where an attempt has also been made to reintroduce a population of Eld's deer into the wild, and there have also been claimed sightings of kouprey in Pang Sida national park. The largest and most spectacular of the wild cattle is the gaur, which stands 2m high at the shoulder and weighs up to one tonne. Probably fewer than 1000 survive in Thailand, mainly in Huai Kha Khaeng and Phu Khieo wildlife sanctuaries and Khao Yai and Thap Lan national parks. Fresh spoors can often be seen in the morning around salt licks.

The 13 **primates** include the slow loris, macaques, langurs and gibbons. The beautiful morning chorus of gibbon song can still be heard in many of the kingdom's national parks.

Marine mammals include several species of dolphin and whale. The dugong was previously common in the sea-grass beds off the southwest coast around Trang, Satun and Phangnga, but is now rarely seen, as silt from tin mining has destroyed much of its habitat.

Thailand has an immensely rich and easily visible **avifauna**. Although most species can be found in protected areas, waterfowl are generally under-represented and some species such as vultures and cranes have become rare as a result of hunting and habitat loss. A programme to reintroduce the sarus crane is under way at Phu Khieo wildlife sanctuary. Easily seen forest birds include the noisy canopy-dwelling hornbill species. Among the rarest birds is Gurney's pitta, which is found in Khao No Chuchi non-hunting area in Krabi.

The most spectacular **amphibians** are the crocodiles and marine turtles. The salt-water crocodile and the false gavial have almost certainly been extirpated from the kingdom, while the last known remaining wild population of fresh-water crocodiles was recently found in Khao Ang Runai wildlife sanctuary in Chachoengsao. All four species of turtle found in Thai waters—the leatherback, the hawksbill, the green and the olive ridley—are endangered.

Thailand is also extremely rich in **insects**, and visitors to any protected area can easily observe many types of butterfly. The enormous Atlas moth and 200 species of hawk moth are also found here. Many of these and other Lepidoptera are now rare or endangered as a result of habitat destruction and degradation.

National Parks and Sanctuaries

In an effort to preserve Thailand's biological resources, a system of protected areas has been established since 1962, when the first national park, **Khao Yai**, was gazetted. The first wildlife sanctuary was created in 1965 at **Salak Phra**, and the first marine national park at **Tarutao** in 1974. About 13 per cent of Thailand (66,000 sq km) lies within national parks or wildlife sanctuaries, with an additional 24,000 sq km planned. Designated non-hunting areas cover a further 3500 sq km.

This mosaic of protected areas includes examples of most of Thailand's natural habitats, although lowland rain forests, mangroves, freshwater swamps and swamp forests are under-represented. Several protected areas are recognised as being internationally important: **Huai Kha Khaeng** and **Thung Yai Naresuan** wildlife sanctuaries together form a UNESCO World Heritage Site, and **Khao Yai** national park is an ASEAN Heritage Site. Sadly, many other areas are too small to permit the conservation of their present flora and fauna except in the short term, especially when surrounding lands are cleared for agriculture and there are no opportunities for species migration.

Wildlife sanctuaries are areas set aside specifically for the conservation of wildlife habitat. Visitors are not officially encouraged in these areas, although some sanctuaries are accessible to serious nature enthusiasts and study groups. There are now nearly 40 sanctuaries, of which the largest and best known are the adjacent **Huai Kha Khaeng** and **Thung Yai Naresuan** reserves, which together cover a great swathe of more than 6200 sq km across the provinces of Tak, Uthai Thani and Kanchanaburi.

National parks both play a conservation role and serve the recreational and educational needs of the population. Many have a visitor centre and provide simple accommodation, although facilities vary greatly between parks. In most, only a fraction of the total park is easily accessible; often this is the area around a particularly fine waterfall or cave system where the park headquarters and visitor accommodation are situated. There are now more than 110 national parks, ranging in size from 3000 sq km to less than 50 sq km. Some receive very few visitors because access is difficult or there is no accommodation.In others the accommodation is extremely limited or consists only of large dormitories, which must be rented in their entirety, thus making an overnight stay expensive. An alternative is to take a tent. Certainly, a visit to at least one park is highly recommended, but weekends and public holidays should be avoided if the intention is to observe the wildlife, as at these times parts of some parks become crowded and noisy. Some, especially those in more remote areas, are difficult to reach by public transport, and visitors are therefore advised to arrange their own transport.

A large number of parks are described in this guide in the hope of encouraging people to visit them. Thailand's natural environment is under siege from many sources, and the parks need all the support they can get. Since most are recent creations, all except four have human settlements within their boundaries, and despite receiving a high level of protection under the law, many parks suffer from continuing encroachment, illegal logging and poaching. Significant areas of many have been deforested.

Non-hunting areas (NHAs) have been established to protect certain species in specific areas. They are generally much smaller than parks and sanctuaries, providing protection to animals but not necessarily to the whole habitat. There are at present more than 30 NHAs in Thailand, but, since the principal threat to most species is loss or disturbance of their habitat, they are generally inadequate for effective conservation.

Several local conservation organisations, including Wildlife Fund Thailand, the Bangkok Bird Club and the Siam Society, organise regular field trips, which are advertised in the local press.

People of Thailand

The majority of Thailand's 60 million people belong to the **Tai** group of peoples (see p 44). Before the arrival of the Tais, Mons and Khmers already occupied parts of modern Thailand's territory. Today there are still several areas where **Mons** form the majority of the population, particularly in the southern part of the Central Plain, and in Ratchaburi province to the southwest of Bangkok, while **Khmer** speakers live chiefly along the Thai–Cambodian border in southern Isan (northeast Thailand). Isan also has a large **Lao**-speaking population.

Subsequently, Chinese, Vietnamese, and Malays have all settled in the territory, and in the northern hills are several more minorities or 'tribes' who have come from neighbouring countries to settle in Thailand. Most numerous of these are the **Karen**, who in recent times have entered Thailand from Burma, where they number several million, but who probably originated in Tibet or southwest China. Other groups include the Hmong, Lahu, Akha, Lisu and Mien. These people, easily recognised by their distinctive clothing, have retained unique cultural traits which set them apart from the Tai majority. Many, especially among the Hmong, are opium farmers.

The **Chinese** in Thailand, as in many Southeast Asian countries, have come to dominate urban business. However, their distinct identity only really becomes apparent at Chinese New Year, which is celebrated with exceptional vigour in Nakhon Sawan, Phuket and Trang. Whereas in Malaysia and Indonesia the economic power of the Chinese minority sometimes causes political unrest and divisions, the Chinese in Thailand have generally integrated well into Thai culture: many have married Thais, have changed their Chinese names to Thai names, and no longer speak Chinese.

There is a considerable **Vietnamese** community in northeast Thailand, most of whom came as refugees during the Vietnam War. Some, especially around Chantaburi and Trat, settled in Thailand in the early 20C. Many are Roman Catholics: Tha Rae, near Sakon Nakhon, has a large Vietnamese community and is the seat of a bishop.

The southernmost provinces of Narathiwat, Pattani, Satun and Yala all have large Muslim **Malay** populations. Arriving in these provinces fresh from Bangkok, the visitor will be struck, especially in the villages, by the number of mosques and Muslim cemeteries, the goats wandering in the streets, the Arabic newspapers and on the occasional billboard, and the Malay dress worn by both men and women.

Among the **Thais** themselves are numerous small sub-groups, including the Thai Yuan, Thai Lu, Thai Nua and Thai Phuan; most are found only in a few rural communities in northern Thailand, and make up only a tiny proportion of Thailand's total population.

GP

A BRIEF HISTORY OF THAILAND

Thailand before the Thais

The area covered by the modern state of Thailand, known until 1939 as Siam, is one of considerable ethnic diversity. The term Thai or Siamese is therefore primarily not ethnic, but political, denoting a subject of the king of Thailand, secondarily linguistic, meaning a speaker of the Thai language, and thirdly cultural, signifying a product of the culture to which the various ethnic groups that have formerly lived or live today in the region have all contributed. Somewhat confusingly, the term Tai is generally used to denote the various ethnically related peoples, among them the Shans, the Laos and the Siamese Thais, who, perhaps as early as the 7C, began a gradual process of migration into mainland Southeast Asia from southwest China and of whom the Siamese Thai branch now form the majority of the population of the kingdom of Thailand.

Archaeological excavations at several sites in northeast Thailand and in the Kanchanaburi area, especially those carried out in 1974 and 1975 at Ban Chiang near Udon Thani (see p 326), have revealed the existence of a people with an advanced Bronze Age culture that some scholars believe may date back to the 5th millennium BC. They were probably of Melanesian or Indonesian stock and they brought with them their animist religion, characterised by the worship of spirits of place and of the ancestors, and by a belief in the sacredness of high places, by settled agriculture based on the cultivation of rice and the use of domesticated animals, by pottery and by bronze and iron metallurgy.

Trading relations between the Indian subcontinent and Southeast Asia go back far into the prehistoric period, but the earliest evidence of Indian influence penetrating into the area in the wake of this trade dates from the 1C AD with the formation in mainland Southeast Asia, the Malay peninsula and the western islands of the Indonesian archipelago of states in which, apparently in order to legitimise their power, the rulers adopted Hinduism or Buddhism, together with Indian concepts of kingship, statecraft, law and administration, and forms of religious art and architecture derived from Indian models.

Among the earliest of these 'Indianised' kingdoms was the state called **Funan** by the Chinese chronicles. Funan grew up during the 1C in the valley of the Mekong in the area between Chaudoc and Phnom Penh. Its people were Indonesian and spoke an Austro-Asiatic language. According to the Chinese sources, Funan was founded by a brahmin from India called Kaundinya. The word Funan is the modern pronunciation of two characters formerly pronounced b'iu-nam, which the Chinese used to represent what they believed was the name of this kingdom, but it is thought was in fact the title of its rulers, *kurung bnam*, or 'king of the mountain', a title that was frequently used at that time by Indian rulers and later by rulers of Indianised states in Southeast Asia, and that has obvious connotations with Hindu and Buddhist cosmological ideas about Mount Meru, the abode of the gods and centre of the universe, as well as with more ancient animist beliefs in the sacredness of high places.

According again to the Chinese sources, Funan was replaced as the leading power in the Mekong valley by one of its vassals, the Khmer state of **Zhenla**, which was centred round Bassac in southern Laos. About the year 600, the ruler of Zhenla was Chitrasena or Mahendravarman ('Protected by the Great Indra'), whose inscriptions have been found in northeast Thailand, at Buri Ram and Surin. In the 8C and 9C Zhenla appears to have been divided between two rival dynasties, and their conflict was not resolved until 802, when Jayavarman II established his capital at Hariharalaya, on the Great Lake (Tonle Sap) in the Angkor region southeast of Siem Reap, and there initiated the cult of the *devarāja* ('the king who is god'), associated with the worship of Shiva in the form of a *linga* enshrined in a tower-sanctuary (*prasat*) at the summit of a temple-mountain. The temple-mountain, which was to become the predominant form of religious architecture throughout the Khmer world in Cambodia, Laos and Thailand, was sometimes built on the top of an actual mountain (e.g. Phanom Rung, see p 357), but was more usually only a formal representation in stone of a mountain. It was conceived not only as the centre of the capital and the realm of the ruler who built it, but also as a symbolic representation of the sacred mountain Mount Meru. The king was not a god-king, but the representative on earth of the *devarāja* whose cult he adopted, generally but not invariably Shiva, and thereby a universal monarch or *cakravartin*. Though the *devarāja* cult has long since disappeared, the idea of the king as a divinely sanctioned *cakravartin* has not, and many Hindu-Khmer monarchical concepts have been preserved to this day in the rituals of the Thai monarchy.

In the 6C, when Funan was being threatened by the rising power of Zhenla, the dominant people of central Thailand seem to have been the **Mons**, an ancient people, closely related to the Khmers, who probably settled in the region at about the same time as the Khmers. While under the rule of Funan, the Mons adopted Indian religion, chiefly Theravada Buddhism, unlike the predominantly Hindu Khmers. There appear to have been numerous small Mon states in the region, of which the most important was **Dvaravati**. Little is known about Dvaravati, and even its name occurs only once, in an inscription that refers to the 'Lord of Dvaravati'. Some scholars believe that it was a federation of Mon states rather than a single state, but the term is now applied to all Mon art and culture of this period in Thailand. The principal Mon-Dvaravati centres were U Thong, Lopburi, Khu Bua and Nakhon Pathom. In the north in the Lamphun area was the Mon kingdom of **Haripunjaya**, called Hariphunchai in Thai (see p 287). Haripunjaya is traditionally believed to have been founded in the late 7C by a group of holy men at whose invitation the Buddhist ruler of Lop Buri sent his daughter Cham Tewi with a large retinue of Mons to Lamphun to be the first ruler of the new state. These events, if they really occurred, probably took place in the 9C.

Dvaravati cities were usually oval and surrounded by one or two defensive moats. Later, these became rectangular, with earthen ramparts and gates. The most important surviving Dvaravati monument in Thailand is Phra Pathom Chedi in Nakhon Pathom (see p 153–4), and remains of Dvaravati monuments, built of brick and set on square, round or octagonal laterite platforms, have been found in central Thailand, notably at Si Thep (see p 344–5), and in the northeast at Nakhon Ratchasima (see p 348) and Kalasin (see p 333).

At about the time that Haripunjaya was founded, Dvaravati seems to have become politically, though not culturally, subject to the great maritime empire of **Sri Vijaya**, the capital of which is thought to have been at Palembang on the east coast of Sumatra and which at various times between the 7C and the 13C extended its rule over much of western Indonesia, the Malay peninsula and southern Thailand as far as the Kra Isthmus and other parts of the coast of the Gulf of Thailand. A number of important sculptures found in this area are ascribed to the Sri Vijaya period, but only scanty architectural remains have been discovered. In the early 11C the eastern part of the Mon realm fell under Khmer rule, while the western part was conquered by the Burmese King Anawrahta of Pagan (r. 1044–77). Haripunjaya also fell under Khmer hegemony in the 11C and was finally conquered at the end of the 13C by King Mangrai, ruler of the northern kingdom of Lan Na.

Between the 7C and the 11C the **Khmers** created a large and powerful empire, centred from 802 in the Angkor region and eventually covering all of modern Cambodia and much of what is now Thailand and Laos. They first penetrated into northeast Thailand at the end of the 6C. The earliest Khmer inscriptions in this area date from that period and the earliest Khmer monuments, such as Prasat Phumphon (see p 366), from the 7C. In the first years of the 11C, the usurper Suryavarman I, whose father was named Sujitaraja and is thought to have been king of Tambralinga (Nakhon Si Thammarat) in southwest Thailand, seized Lop Buri (see Rte 13) from its Mon ruler, thus bringing most of central Thailand within the Khmer realm. Suryavarman I was a Mahayana Buddhist, but he did not interfere either with the Hinduism of his Khmer subjects or the Theravada Buddhism of the Mons. Lop Buri became the chief centre of Khmer rule in central Thailand and the valley of the Chao Praya, and the name Lop Buri is traditionally used to designate all Khmer art or art inspired by Khmer models to be found in Thailand, even if outside the Lop Buri region or belonging to the period before or after Khmer rule in Lop Buri.

The Arrival of the Thais and the Foundation of Sukhothai

Throughout this period the **Tai** peoples had been gradually migrating southwards from their homeland in southern China, moving, like their predecessors, down the great river valleys of mainland Southeast Asia and settling among the Khmer, Mon and Burman populations whom they encountered on the way. By the 12C they had established several small states in Upper Burma (Shans), the Mekong valley (Laos) and the Chao Phraya valley (Thais). The most important of these early states was **Lan Na**, of which the successive capitals were Chiang Rai, founded by King Mangrai (see Rte 29), Chiang Mai founded in 1296, also by Mangrai in 1263 (see Rte 26), and Chiang Saen, on the west bank of the Mekong, founded in 1327 (see Rte 30). Lan Na retained a considerable measure of autonomy until the 18C, and Chiang Mai, which became the permanent capital after 1339, is still a major centre of northern Thai culture as well as being the second city of Thailand.

In the mid-13C, as Khmer power in central Thailand waned, the Thais moved further south to the headwaters of the Chao Phraya River, where at some time in the 1240s a Thai chief named Bang Klang Hao rebelled successfully against his Khmer suzerains and was crowned King Sri Indraditya of Sukhothai (see Rte 19). The new Thai state of Sukhothai is referred to in the Chinese sources of the late 13C as Siem (Siam), a name that occurs in earlier Cham, Khmer and Burmese inscriptions, where it denotes Tai slaves and mercenary soldiers. About 1279, Ramkhamhaeng, a younger son of Sri Indraditya, became king of Sukhothai and established it as one of the most powerful states in mainland Southeast Asia. According to the inscriptions, he achieved great territorial conquests and extended Thai rule as far as Lower Burma in the west, Laos in the east and the Malay peninsula in the south. He concluded a treaty of friendship with the Thai princes of Chiang Rai and Phayao in the north, which did much to assist the rise of Lan Na. Ramkhamhaeng is also credited with the invention of the Thai alphabet. Sukhothai is generally considered to be the cradle of Thai culture and civilisation, and Ramkhamhaeng is revered as the father of the Thai nation. During his reign Sukhothai and its subsidiary capitals of Si Satchanalai (see Rte 19), Phitsanulok (see Rte 21), and Kamphaeng Phet (see Rte 17) became centres of Buddhist art and learning. In both religion and art Sukhothai looked to Sri Lanka as the model, while retaining a uniquely Thai character.

After Ramkhamhaeng's death, his empire rapidly collapsed. In the north a number of small principalities that had formerly been subject to Sukhothai emerged as independent states, although some of them, notably Tak, soon exchanged the suzerainty of Sukhothai for that of Lan Na, while in the east both the Lao states of Luang Prabang and Vientiane asserted their independence, and in the south Suphan Buri also threw off Sukhothai rule. By the early 14C Sukhothai had dwindled into insignificance.

Ayutthaya

In 1351 a Thai prince of obscure origins named U Thong ('Golden Cradle') founded the city of Ayutthaya (see Rte 14) on a strategic site at the confluence of the Pasak and the Chao Phraya Rivers and was anointed king of a new Thai state, taking the regnal name of Ramathibodi. Under a succession of able and for the most part warlike rulers, Ayutthaya rose rapidly to become the most powerful state in central Thailand. Sukhothai was reduced to vassalage in 1378 and finally annexed in 1438, while Angkor was conquered in 1431/32, and the Khmers forced to abandon it as their capital soon after. Ayutthaya also pursued a policy of aggression against the Burmese, which led to almost continuous conflict over the next two hundred years and eventually in 1767 brought about its downfall. By the end of the 17C it had become so rich and powerful that it was considered by European writers to be, with China and the Indian state of Vijayanagar, one of the three greatest kingdoms in Asia and was often described as the 'Venice of the East'. The government of the kingdom was to a great extent modelled on that of Khmer Angkor, and in the early years of Ayutthaya's rise to ascendancy many of the court officials were drawn from the Khmerised aristocracy of Lop Buri and other former outposts of the Angkor empire. It was they who introduced at the court of Ayutthaya the special vocabulary based on Khmer and Sanskrit which is still in use today (see p 27–8).

In 1511 a small Portuguese force led by Afonso de Albuquerque captured Malacca, an important Muslim trading state on the west coast of the Malay peninsula, and from there sent envoys to Ayutthaya. In 1518 the Portuguese became the first European power to conclude a commercial treaty with Ayutthaya and to establish a permanent settlement there. During the 17C the Dutch, British and French all established trading relations with Ayutthaya. In 1678 a Greek adventurer named Constantine Phaulkon arrived in Ayutthaya in the service of the English East India Company and rapidly rose to become first minister of King Narai, whose pro-French inclinations he did much to encourage. A series of diplomatic missions between King Narai and Louis XIV was exchanged, and Jesuit missionaries were sent to Ayutthaya in a vain attempt to convert Narai to Catholicism. The death of King Narai in 1688 was followed by the fall and execution of Phaulkon and the expulsion of the Jesuit missionaries.

During the reign of Borommakot (1733–58) Ayutthaya reached the zenith of its power and influence, but in 1752 Alaungpaya, a Burman leader from Shwebo, gained recognition as king of Ava and founded the Konbaung dynasty, In 1757 he captured Pegu and in 1760 launched his first attack against Siam. In 1767, after almost eight years of war, Ayutthaya suffered the last and most terrible of all the many invasions to which it had been subjected by the Burmese. The Burmese sacked and looted the city so thoroughly that the court was compelled to abandon it and move almost 90km downstream to Thon Buri on the west bank of the Chao Phraya River near the estuary. Here in 1770 General Phraya Tak or Taksin, governor of Tak and commander of the Thai forces, who was the son of a Chinese father and a Thai mother, was proclaimed king.

The Chakri Dynasty

In 1782 Taksin, who had become prone to bouts of religious mania and acts of arbitrary and wanton cruelty, was declared insane and deposed on the orders of General Chaophraya Chakri, who shared the command of the Siamese army with his younger brother Chaophraya Surasi. Taksin is traditionally believed to have been executed by being placed in a velvet sack and beaten to death with sandalwood clubs in order that his executioners might avoid shedding royal blood, but there is no evidence for this. Another tradition has it that a substitute was beaten to death in his place and that Taksin was sent secretly to a palace near Nakhon Si Thammarat, where he lived until 1825. Chaophraya Chakri, who came of an old Ayutthaya noble family on his father's side, but whose mother was Chinese, ascended the throne as King Ramathibodhi and so became the founder of the Chakri dynasty. The title of Phra Phuttha Yotfa Chulalok was bestowed upon him posthumously, but he is generally known as **King Rama I**. The day of his accession, 6 April, is still kept as a public holiday, Chakri Day.

King Rama I

Rama I feared renewed Burmese attacks from the west, so one of his first acts was to transfer the capital of Bangkok, opposite Thon Buri on the east bank of the Chao Phraya River. He was also anxious to recreate in Bangkok as many of the glories of Ayutthaya as he could and accordingly undertook an ambitious programme of temple construction, making use of many of the statues and building materials salvaged from the ruins of Ayutthaya. The royal palace and most of the new buildings were erected on an artificial island on the bend of the Chao Phraya River and Khlong Lot called Ratanakosin ('Jewel of Indra'), from which the period and its art style takes their name. Here in the enclosure of the Grand Palace Wat Phra Kaeo was built as a shrine for the Emerald Buddha, which Rama I had seized during a campaign in Laos and which henceforth was to be the palladium of the Thai kingdom (see p 117–8).

Rama I continued the long struggle against the Burmese in a series of campaigns both in the peninsula and in Lan Na and the north. He encouraged the growth of trade with China. He reformed the Buddhist monkhood (*Sangha*), which had become corrupt and lax in discipline, and carried out a drastic revision of the laws of the kingdom, which resulted in the compilation of a new legal code known as the Three Seals Laws. He attempted also to rebuild the literary heritage of the Thais, much of which had been destroyed in the Burmese invasion, by rewriting many of the Thai chronicles, translating texts from Pali, Mon and Javanese, and composing the *Ramakien*, a Thai version of the great Indian epic the *Rāmāyaṇa*. This work has had a profound influence on all the arts in Thailand, and particularly on dance and drama, which draw on the *Ramakien* for much of their subject matter.

King Rama II
Rama I died in 1809 and was succeeded by his son Rama II, whose reign was on the whole peaceful, apart from a few minor clashes with the Burmese in the west and the Cambodians, Laos and Vietnamese in the east. Rama II himself seems not to have been greatly interested in government and to have allowed himself to be dominated by his ministers. Most of these belonged to a small group of interrelated noble families, whose influence the king tried unsuccessfully to curb by appointing members of his own family to supervise their activities. Rama II is chiefly remembered today as one of the greatest poets in the Thai language.

King Rama III
Rama II died in 1824 and was succeeded by his eldest surviving son Prince Chetsabodin, who took the regnal name of Phra Nangklao, but is generally known as Rama III. In his domestic policies Rama III was deeply conservative, as is shown by his restoration of Wat Pho in Bangkok (see p 128). In an attempt to preserve as much as possible of traditional Thai Buddhist culture and learning, he filled the temple with marble slabs on which were engraved inscriptions, some based on ancient texts and others on texts specially written for the purpose, dealing not only with religion and history, but with an immense variety of other subjects ranging from astrology and traditional medicine to botany and the art of war. The inscriptions are accompanied by illustrative sculptures and wall paintings.

In 1824 the British had gone to war with Burma, and the Thais were fearful that they might next attack Siam. For this reason, Rama III ordered the strengthening of the defences of the Chao Phraya River by putting across it a huge iron chain, to which every blacksmith in the kingdom had to contribute a number of links. At the same time, he tried to extend Siamese suzerainty over the Malay states on its southern borders. In 1825 Captain Henry Burney was sent by the governor-general of India to Bangkok to try to secure Siamese neutrality in the Anglo-Burmese conflict, to induce Siam to stop threatening British interests in the Malay states and to bring to an end the various discriminatory practices which hampered the trade of the British and other European powers in Siam. In the treaty that resulted from Burney's negotiations, Siam succeeded in maintaining its position in Pattani and other Malay states over which it had suzerainty, but had to make several major commercial concessions, including the creation of a single duty calculated according to the measurements of each cargo ship, which substantially reduced its tax revenues, and the abandonment of numerous royal monopolies.

Rama III pursued a more aggressive policy than his predecessor against his vassals in the east, especially the rebellious Lao leader, Chao Anu, ruler of Vientiane, who early in 1827, on the pretext of saving Bangkok from a British attack, seized Nakhon Ratchasima and then marched on to Saraburi. In retaliation, the Siamese invaded and totally destroyed Vientiane, and early in 1829 sent Chao Anu as a prisoner to Bangkok, where, after being put on public display for a few days, he died. During the next 20 years, the Siamese carried out a large-scale resettlement of Lao population across the Mekong in the Khorat Plateau, where no fewer than forty new tributary *muang* (principality) were created.

Rama III successfully adopted a similar policy towards Kedah, Pattani and his other rebellious Malay vassals in the south. In Cambodia he was able in a series of campaigns to reassert Siamese influence against the non-Buddhist Vietnamese, who during the 1830s had been interfering in Cambodia's dynastic politics and trying to gain control of the administration.

King Mongkut (Rama IV)

Rama III was succeeded in 1851 by his brother Mongkut, who had lived at Wat Bowon Niwet Wihan in Bangkok. He was a monk for most of the 27 years before he became king and in the 1830s had founded the Thammayutika sect (see p 70). However, during that time he had travelled widely and had acquired much Western learning. He was not only a considerable Pali scholar, but had an excellent command of French, English and Latin, and was keenly interested in science, particularly astronomy.

Early in 1855 the British sent Sir John Bowring, governor of Hong Kong, on a mission to Bangkok to negotiate a new commercial treaty, which would give them even more control over Siam's foreign trade. Under the terms of this treaty, which is known as the **Bowring Treaty**, all the Siamese government monopolies, except for the opium and alcohol monopolies and the lottery, were abolished, import and export duties were reduced, and British residents in Siam were given extraterritorial rights and their liability to tax was lessened. Siam thus once more sacrificed substantial sources of revenue in order to maintain good relations with the British, who were now threateningly present both in Burma and in the Malay peninsula.

Within ten years of the Bowring Treaty, similar treaties had been signed between Siam and the United States, France and several other states. The policy of King Mongkut and his government at this time was to safeguard Siamese independence by setting one Western power against another, and this they did with great skill. With regard to Britain, the Siamese also took advantage of the conflicting interests of the Foreign Office, the government of India and the Colonial Office in Malaya, while in their dealings with France they played the Quai d'Orsay off against the colonial government in Saigon. All this diplomatic activity was accompanied by trading agreements, which brought about important commercial changes, among them the rapid development of the port of Bangkok.

In domestic policy, the king, although he greatly desired to modernise his country and employed several foreign advisers to help him do this, realised the need to advance slowly and cautiously. Consequently, the internal reforms he initiated were few and modest. For example, he allowed the laws of the kingdom to be printed so that they would be more accessible to his subjects, he allowed his subjects to look at his face when he appeared in public, and he attempted to improve the conditions of slaves and to give women some freedom of choice in marriage, but he made scarcely any fundamental changes either in the law or in the administration.

King Chulalongkorn (Rama V)

In 1868 Mongkut's son, Chulalongkorn came to the throne. He was only 15 years old, but he had been well prepared for kingship by his father and had received an excellent education, some of it from his English governess Mrs Anna Leonowens, immortalised in the film *The King and I*, which is still banned in Thailand. For the first five years of his reign the government was in the hands of the regent Suriyawong, one of several members of the immensely powerful Bunnag family, who had been ministers in the previous reign. As soon as Chulalongkorn attained his majority, he continued the programme of reform and modernisation that his father had tentatively begun. He abolished slavery and the custom of prostration before the king, he established a Privy Council and a Council of State, to which he appointed those of his brothers and younger friends who supported his radical policies, and he instituted a series of financial reforms in an attempt to check corruption. These reforms encountered the implacable opposition of the old guard of officials (the *hua boran* or 'ancients') and caused the so-called Front Palace Crisis of 1875 led by his cousin Prince Wichaichan, which nearly cost the young king his throne. After this, both in Bangkok and the provinces, Chulalongkorn gradually replaced the ministers and officials he had inherited from the regency period by his brothers, many of whom had attended the school that he had established inside the royal palace.

In foreign policy, Chulalongkorn, like his father, had to perform a balancing act between France and Britain. British policy was generally aimed at preserving Siamese independence, although Britain did have designs on some Siamese territories in Burma and the Malay peninsula. Relations with France, however, became extremely strained and reached a critical point in 1893 when Siamese forces resisted French troops who had been sent into Laos to occupy the Lao territory to which they laid claim east of the Mekong. The French responded by forcing the defences at Paknam in the estuary of the Chao Phraya River and sending two gunboats up to Bangkok. The crisis which this incident precipitated was not finally resolved until the conclusion of two highly unequal treaties—one with the French in 1907 and the other with the British in 1909, under the terms of which Siam made further financial sacrifices and lost 176,000 square miles of territory, nearly half of the territory that had been under its suzerainty at the end of Rama III's reign.

King Chulalongkorn's legacy

When Chulalongkorn died on 24 October 1910, Siam was already a radically different country from the one he had begun to rule 42 years before. In the first place, it had shed most of its former vassal states in Laos, Cambodia and the

Malay peninsula and had assumed the frontiers that it has today. In agriculture, the cultivation of rice for export had developed dramatically since the Bowring Treaty had opened up the kingdom to international trade, and Siam was already, as it still is, a leading exporter of rice, principally to India and China. As a result of the abolition of slavery and corvée labour, the rural population had increased, and much new land had been brought under cultivation. These developments in turn led to an increase in the value of land and a consequent decay of village handicrafts as people earned money from growing rice and were enabled to buy imported goods. There was also a rapid increase in the Chinese population, as Chinese labour was brought in to do work that had formerly been done by Thais as corvée labour in the docks, the market gardens and the rice mills, on irrigation projects and elsewhere. Many of these Chinese later became prosperous merchants or entered government service. They married Thais and their children grew up speaking Thai as their first language. The vast majority of these Sino-Siamese families were settled in the towns, most of them in Bangkok.

In religion and education there had also been many important changes. Prince Wachirayanwarorot, who became leader of the Thammayutika sect and finally supreme patriarch, had instituted a reform of the Buddhist hierarchy and of Buddhist monasteries and schools, while secular education had been transformed by the foundation in 1898 of village schools throughout the country, using textbooks and following curricula devised by the Ministry of Public Instruction in Bangkok. These schools not only largely took over from the monasteries their traditional task of teaching basic literacy, but also for the first time introduced young Thais in the rural areas to Western science, mathematics and engineering. By this means too, Siam acquired a standard language (Bangkok or Central Thai) and a standard script in which to write it.

By 1910 Siam had a reformed, modernised bureaucracy, in which the old noble families had largely lost their supremacy and had been replaced by the brothers and sons of Chulalongkorn, many of whom had been educated in the West, and by members of the newly rich Sino-Siamese families

King Vajiravudh (Rama VI)

Chulalongkorn was succeeded by his eldest son by Queen Saowapha, Vajiravudh, who had been educated in England at Sandhurst and Oxford. Vajiravudh was a flamboyant personality, and his gifts were literary, theatrical and artistic rather than political, although he was not short of political ideas. He is perhaps best remembered today for having introduced a law requiring all Thais to bear surnames, many of which he himself coined. He was wildly extravagant; his coronation alone, which lasted for 13 days, cost a sum equivalent to eight per cent of the state budget for 1911.

Ostensibly in order to promote Siamese national unity and certainly in order to build up his own personal following, Vajiravudh created a somewhat bizarre paramilitary organisation called the Wild Tiger Corps (Sua Pa), to which he recruited members from the civil service and which already by 1912 had 4000 members. To this he later added a junior corps of Boy Scouts.

Vajiravudh also promoted sports and team games, particularly soccer. He encouraged mass education and was largely responsible for the foundation of Chulalongkorn University and the introduction of compulsory primary education for both boys and girls. He was strongly in favour of improving the social status of women and of monogamy. His literary endeavours ranged from translating parts of the *Rāmāyaṇa* into Thai verse to the composition and production of modern plays in Western style, in which his male favourites performed. He was also a prolific essayist and used the essay as a vehicle for the promulgation of his personal political philosophy and his concept of the Thai nation, founded on a common allegiance to nation, religion and monarch. In 1917 he replaced the old royal flag, which portrayed a white elephant on a red ground, by the present red, white and blue flag, in which the red stripes represent the Thai nation, the white stripes Thai Buddhism and the blue stripe the monarchy. His nationalism was also reflected in his wish to revoke the unequal treaties and free the economy of the kingdom from the domination of foreigners and in particular of the Chinese, to whom he was extremely hostile, describing them as the Jews of the East.

During the First World War, the majority of Thais, still smarting at the loss of Siamese territory to the French and British, tended to favour the Germans, but the king was anxious to maintain Thai neutrality. However, when the United States entered the war in 1917 and it became clear that the Germans were going to lose, he judged it expedient to support the Allies and in June 1918 even sent a token force to France. As a result of this gesture, between 1920 and 1926 Siam was able to renegotiate her unequal treaties with the Western powers, so that foreigners ceased to be exempt from the jurisdiction of Siamese courts and, apart from a few exceptions, Siamese autonomy over tariffs was fully restored.

King Prajadhipok (Rama VII), last absolute ruler of Siam
In his private life, Vajiravudh showed little interest in women and only married towards the end of his life. He died without male issue in 1925, leaving a mountain of debts and an inflated and incompetent bureaucracy, and was succeeded by Prajadhipok, his last surviving full brother and 76th of King Chulalongkorn's 77 children.

Prajadhipok, although not without ability, had not been prepared for kingship and probably did not want it. Like his predecessor, he had been educated in England, at Eton and the Woolwich Military Academy, and latterly at the École Supérieure de Guerre in France and had only returned to Thailand a year before succeeding to the throne, so that he had virtually no experience of government. His first act was to create a Supreme Council of State composed of five senior members of the royal family, including the scholarly Prince Damrong Rajanubhab, often called the 'father of Thai archaeology', thereby restoring some order to the royal finances, but at the same time reviving King Chulalongkorn's system of 'government by princes'. This made it difficult to introduce any constitutional changes, for which there was an increasing demand among urban intellectuals, in the legal profession and in the middle ranks of the army. Dissatisfaction with the government came to a head in the Great Depression of the early 1930s. This created numerous economic problems, including a catastrophic fall in the price of rice, on which the Siamese economy was largely dependent. On 24 June 1932, while Prajadhipok was on holiday playing golf at Hua Hin, a group of army officers and middle-level officials known as the Promoters, organised by a lawyer, Pridi Phanomyong, and an army officer, Luang Phibunsongkhram, both of whom had been educated in France, staged a coup and sent the king an ultimatum calling upon him to submit to a constitution. Prajadhipok accepted the terms of the Promoters' ultimatum so meekly that they sent him a second one apologising for the abrupt tone of the first. However, the king soon fell out with them, principally because of the ban they imposed on all political parties and the extreme socialist economic policies pursued by Pridi Phanomyong, and in 1935 he abdicated in favour of his 10-year-old nephew Ananda Mahidol, who was then a schoolboy in Switzerland.

Reactionary Forces

In December 1938, Luang Phibunsongkhram became prime minister. He was an admirer of Hitler and Mussolini, and his period of rule, which lasted until 1944, was marked by authoritarianism and strident nationalism. Within a month of taking office, he arrested 40 of his real or imagined opponents, among them members of the royal family and nobility, deputies of the National Assembly and rival army officers, on charges of conspiring against the government. Of these 18 were executed after a series of unashamedly political trials. In the first year of his government, Phibun also imposed on the Chinese a series of discriminatory laws and a greatly increased burden of taxation. In 1939, the name of Siam was changed to Thailand on the grounds that Siam was a foreign name forced upon the country by foreigners, whereas the name Thailand signified that the country belonged to the Thais rather than to the economically dominant Chinese.

After the fall of France in 1940, Phibun seized the opportunity of avenging the humiliating defeat that the Thais had received at the hands of the French in 1893 and invaded Laos and Cambodia. With Japanese mediation, he imposed a settlement by which substantial areas of Lao and Cambodian territory, including the Cambodian province of Siem Reap, which contains Angkor and which he renamed Phibunsongkhram, were ceded to Thailand.

In December 1941, at the same time as they attacked Pearl Harbour, the Japanese invaded Thailand at several points along the east coast and in the peninsula. The Thais at first resisted, but soon capitulated. Meanwhile, the British sent a force to Songkhla to attempt to stop the Japanese, but were held up by Thai border police; the Japanese continued their march south and captured Singapore. In January 1942, the Thai government concluded a military alliance with Japan and declared war on Britain and the United States. However, the Thai minister in Washington, Seni Pramoj, a cousin of the king, refused to deliver the declaration of war to the US government and in collaboration with the Americans set up a resistance movement called **Seri Thai** (Free Thai), while Pridi Phanomyong, who had been appointed regent for the absent king, also began secretly to organise resistance in Thailand.

At the end of the war Pridi repudiated the Japanese alliance, and in January 1946 an election was held, which resulted in the election of Pridi and the Seri Thai. A new consitition was drafted, and at the end of 1957 King Ananda returned to Thailand from Switzerland. Within six months of his return, the young king was found dead in the Grand Palace shot through the head with a pistol. Three palace servants were tried and executed, but the king's death has never been explained. Pridi was held responsible, either directly or indirectly, for the tragedy, resigned and went abroad, and the present king, Ananda's brother Bhumibol Adulyadej came to the throne as Rama IX.

These events were followed by a succession of short-lived governments overthrown by coups, until September 1957, when, after an election which Phibun had won only by more than usually flagrant coercion and vote-rigging, Field Marshal Sarit Thanit, who owed much of his wealth to skilful manipulation of the finances of the Government Lottery Bureau, organised a bloodless coup. Both Phibun and Sarit's other rival in the army, General Phao Siyanon, who was director-general of the Police Department and a notorious opium dealer, fled the country, and Sarit installed an interim government under a diplomat named Phote Sarasin. In October 1958, Sarit abolished the constitution, declared martial law and governed by decree through a Revolutionary Council.

Sarit died in 1963 and was succeeded by General Thanom Kittikachorn, who, with his deputy prime minister, minister of the interior and right-hand man, General Praphas Charusathian, remained in power till 1973. Thanom and Praphas continued Sarit's policies of ruthless suppression of all opposition, particularly if it seemed to have communist leanings, strong emphasis on law and order, morality and cleanliness, and, most important of all, strengthening the role of the monarchy as the apex of Thai society and the guardian of traditional Thai values. Like Phibun before them, both the Sarit and Thanom-Praphas governments relied heavily during the wars in Vietnam, Laos and Cambodia on American aid and military support to protect Thailand against the spread of communism from those countries.

Recent history

Partly as a result of this dependence on the USA, the period since 1960 has been marked by rapid industrialisation in Thailand, accompanied by a proportionate decline in the agricultural sector (from 73.9 per cent in 1960 to 55.6 per cent in 1980), a huge growth in population (from 14.5 million in 1937 to over 44 million in 1980 and over 56 million in 1996), the enormous and largely unregulated growth of Bangkok and to a lesser extent of some other towns such as Chiang Mai, Phitsanulok, Nakhon Ratchasima, Khon Kaen and Hat Yai, vast improvements in literacy and education at all levels, and the increasing assimilation of the Chinese minority into the Thai population. These changes have led in turn to a good deal of political turbulence and some erosion of traditional Thai Buddhist values.

In 1969 the Thanom-Praphas government issued a new constitution, which revived the bi-cameral legislature, with an elected lower house and an appointed senate, provided for in the constitution of 1932. Elections followed and Thanom was returned to power, but in 1971, concerned at the loosening of military control involved in this experiment in democracy, he dissolved Parliament, banned all political parties and reinstated a military regime. This time, however, the Thai people were no longer willing to accept without question that it was necessary to have a military government in order to safeguard national security, maintain law and order and protect the people against corrupt politicians. During 1973 there was a series of student demonstrations in Bangkok, culminating in a huge protest rally attended by as many as 500,000 people at Thammasat University and in the area round the Democracy Monument. Pridi Phanomyong had been one of the founders and subsequently rector of Thammasat University, and many of the students who shared his radical socialist views looked to him as their model. There were clashes with the police, but the army refused to intervene and were supported in this by King Bhumibol. Thanom was compelled to resign and leave the country, and a coalition government was formed, first under the leader of the Democrat party, Seni Pramoj, who had been Thai minister in Washington at the time of the invasion of Thailand in 1941, and then of his brother Kukrit Pramoj, who succeeded him as prime minister after only two weeks. Student unrest continued, and in October 1976 there were further and more violent demonstrations, especially at Thammasat University, in protest against Thanom, who had come back to Thailand in order to enter the monkhood. This time, the police and some of the right-wing students attacked the demonstrators at Thammasat University. Hundreds were killed or wounded and more than a thousand arrested, the army intervened to suspend the constitution and an even more authoritarian regime was imposed under an Administrative Reform Council led by Thanin Kraivichien, a lawyer of extreme right-wing views. Freedom of speech and of the press were curtailed and a curfew was enforced in Bangkok.

Thanin's government seems to have been too repressive even for the military, who forced him out of office in October 1977. General Kriangsak Chomanand then became prime minister, followed in 1980 by General Prem Tinsulanonda, who was backed not only by the army but also by many members of parliament and by the king. Prem remained in power until 1988, exercising a judicious blend of parliamentary and military government, sometimes jocularly known as 'premocracy'. He resigned in 1988, saying that the time had come for the prime minister to be chosen from among the elected representatives of the people in Parliament, and was replaced by a retired general named Chatichai Choonhavan. Chatichai's government was exceedingly corrupt even by Thai standards, and this, together with its attempts to reduce the political influence of the military, led in February 1991 to the commander in chief of the army, General Suchinda Kraprayoon staging a bloodless coup and installing a caretaker civilian government under Anand Panyarachun, In April 1992, however, Suchinda himself contrived to take over the office of prime minister, and this high-handed action caused widespread opposition. Only six weeks later, there were more demonstrations in Bangkok, which Suchinda crushed by force, leaving over 50 people dead and many more wounded. The king again intervened, publicly rebuking both Suchinda and the leader of the opposition, Chamlong Srimuang, the austere and devoutly Buddhist governor of Bankgok, in a television broadcast to the nation. Suchinda resigned and Anand was invited to form a new government. In September 1992 there were elections, which resulted in the formation of a coalition government under the premiership of Chuan Leekpai, the son of a fishmonger in Trang. Chuan's government bravely, though unsuccessfully, attempted to clamp down on corruption and survived until May 1995, when it was brought down by a scandal over land reform, and another election was called. This time the Chart Thai party led by Banharn Silpa-Archa won a majority of the seats, although none in Bangkok, where the votes of the electorate are less easily bought than in the rural areas. Banharn formed a seven-party coalition government, the stability of which seemed no more certain than any of its recent predecessors.

In June 1996, the voters of Bangkok again demonstrated their refusal to be bribed or browbeaten either by the political parties or by the military by electing as their governor the first ever independent candidate, **Pitchit Ratakul**. This election was also significant in that 43 per cent of the electorate voted, the highest percentage ever recorded in Bangkok. On 17 November 1996 a general election was held after a campaign marked by vote buying on a gigantic scale and the use of hired gunmen to intimidate both rival candidates and canvassers, especially in the north and northeast, and the New Aspiration Party (NAP) under its leader General Chavalit Yongchaiyudh was returned to office, narrowly defeating the Chart Thai party. Of the 37 MPs returned for Bangkok, only one was a member of the NAP.

JV

Chronology of Rulers

Kings of Funan

Kaundinya	1C AD
Fan Shiman	early 3C
Zhantan (Chandana)	c 357
Kaundinya-Jayavarman	478–514
Rudravarman	514–after 539

Kings of Zhenla

Bhavavarman I	c 550
Mahendravarman (Sitrasena)	c 600
Isanavarman I	before 615–after 635
Jayavarman I	645–681

Kings of Angkor

Jayavarman II	802–850
Jayavarman III	850–877
Indravarman I	877–889
Yasovarman I	889–900
Harshavarman I	c 900–922
Isanavarman II	922–928
Jayavarman IV	921 or 928–941
Harshavarman II	941–944
Rajendravarman II	944–968
Jayavarman V	968–1001
Udayadityavarman I	1001–1002
Jayaviravarman (usurper)	1002–1011
Suryavarman I	1002–1050
Udayadityavarman II	1050–1065 or 1066
Harshavarman III	1065 or 1066–1080
Jayavarman VI	1080–1107
Dharanindravarman I	1107–1113
Suryavarman II	1113–c 1150
Dharanindravarman II	c 1150–before 1160
Yasovarman II	before 1160–1165
Tribhuvanadityavarman	1165–1177
Cham invasion and period of anarchy	1177–1181

Jayavarman VII	1181–c 1220
Indravarman II	c 1220–c 1243
Jayavarman VIII	c 1243–1296 (abdicated)
Indravarman III	1296–1308
Indrajayavarman	1308–1327
Jayavarmandiparameshvara	1327–c 1353

Kings of Sukhothai

Sri Indraditya	?1240s–?1270s
Ban Muang	?1270s–?1279
Ramkhamhaeng	?1279–1298
Lo Thai	1298–1346 or 1347
Ngua Nam Thom	1346 or 1347
Mahathammaratcha I (Luthai)	1346 or 1347–?1368 or 1374
Mahathammaratcha II	?1368 or 1374–?1398
Mahathammaratcha III (Sai Luthai)	?1398–1419
Mahathammaratcha IV	1419–1438

Kings of Siam and Thailand

Ayutthaya

Ramathibodi	1351–1369
Ramesuan	1369–1370
Borommaratcha I	1370–1388
Thong Chan	1388
Ramesuan (second reign)	1388–1395
Ramaratcha	1395–1409
Intharatcha I	1409–1424
Boromaratcha II	1424–1448
Borommatrailokanat (Trailok)	1448–1463 (in Ayutthaya)
	1463–1488 (in Phitsanulok)
Borommaratcha III (Intharatcha)	regent in Ayutthaya, 1463–1488;
	king, 1488–1491
Ramathibodi II	1491–1529
Borommaratcha IV	1529–1533
Ratsada	1533–1534
Chairatcha	1534–1547
Yot Fa	1547–1548
Khun Worawongsa (usurper)	1548
Chakkraphat	1548–1569
Mahin	1569
Maha Thammaratcha	1569–1590
Naresuan	1590–1605
Ekathotsarot	1605–1610 or 1611
[Si Saowaphak	?1610–1611]
Song Tham (Intharatcha)	1610 or 1611–1628
Chettha	1628–1629
Athittayawong	1629
Prasat Thong	1629–1656

Chai	1656
Suthammaratcha	1656
Narai	1656–1688
Phra Phetratcha	1688–1703
Sua (Suriyentharathibodi)	1703–1709
Thai Sa (Phumintharatcha)	1709–1733
Borommakot (Borommathammikarat)	1733–1758
Uthumpon	1758
Suriyamarin (Borommaratcha V)	1758–1767

Thon Buri

Taksin	1767–1782

Bangkok (Ratanakosin): Chakri Dynasty

Phra Phuttha Yotfa (Rama I)	1782–1809
Phra Phuttha Loetla (Rama II)	1809–1824
Phra Nangklao (Rama III)	1824–1851
Mongkut (Rama IV)	1851–1868
Chulalongkorn (Rama V)	1868–1910
Vajiravudh (Rama VI)	1910–1925
Prajadhipok (Rama VII)	1925–1935 (abdicated)
Ananda Mahidol (Rama VIII)	1935–1946
Bhumibol Adulyadej (Rama IX)	1946–

Children of King Bhumibol and Queen Sirikit

Princess Ubon Ratana (b 1951)
Prince Vajiralongkorn (b 1952)
Princess Sirindhorn (b 1955)
Princess Chulaborn (b 1957)

Kings of Lan Na (Chiang Rai, Chiang Mai, Chiang Saen)

Mangrai	1259–1317
Chai Songkhram	1317–1318
Saen Phu	1318–1319
Khrua	1319–1322
Nam Thuam	1322–1324
Saen Phu (second reign)	1324–1328
Kham Fu	1328–1337
Pha Yu	1337–1355
Ku Na	1355–1385
Saen Muang Ma	1385–1401
Sam Fang Kaen	1401–1441
Tilokaratcha	1441–1487
Yot Chiang Rai	1487–1495
Muang Kaeo	1495–1526
Ket Chettharat	1526–1538
Thao Chai	1538–1543
Ket Chettharat (second reign)	1543–1545
Chiraprapha (queen)	1545–1546

Setthathirat of Lan Xang	1546–1551
Thao Mae Ku (queen)	1551
Mekuti of Nai	1551–1564
Wisutthithewi (queen)	1564–1578
[Burmese suzerainty	1578–1775]

Chao (Princes) of Chiang Mai

Kavila	1775–1781 (in Lampang)
	1781–1813 (in Chiang Mai)
Thammalangka	1813–1821
Kham Fan	1821–1825
Phutthawong	1825–1846
Mahawong	1846–1854
Kavilorot	1856–1870
Intanon	1870–1897
Suriyawong	1901–1911
In Kaeo Nowarat	1911–1939

HINDU AND BUDDHIST RELIGION AND ICONOGRAPHY

Early Indian Religion

The word **Hindu** was originally a geographical term used by the Persians and the Greeks to refer to the inhabitants of the Indus Valley. Between 2000 and 1200 BC the nomadic Indo-Aryan people migrated into India from the north-west, settling first in the Punjab and subsequently throughout northern India. Their language was Sanskrit, an Indo-European language that ceased to be spoken during the first millennium BC and survived only in their sacred texts and esoteric priestly rituals. The earliest of these texts are the four **Vedas** ('Body of Knowledge'), of which the first and most important is the *Rig Veda*, a compilation of hymns of praise to the ancient Aryan gods. The other three *Vedas* are slightly later and are concerned with the correct performance of sacrifices. Today, Hindus call their religion not Hinduism, but *sanātana dharma* ('eternal religion') or *vaidika dharma* ('religion of the *Vedas*'). The Indo-Aryans also introduced the caste system as a means of maintaining their authority over the conquered peoples. The highest caste was the priestly caste of the **brahmans** or brahmins (*brāhmaṇa*). As they alone possessed the secret knowledge that enabled them to perform the complicated sacrificial rites correctly and were thus the sole intermediaries between mankind and the gods, they acquired enormous social and political influence.

Most of the Vedic gods were personifications of natural forces, some of them adopted by the Indo-Aryans from the Indus valley civilisation that had flourished in northern India before they arrived. They included their tutelary god Indra, wielder of the thunderbolt (*vajra*), Surya, the sun god, Agni, the god of fire, Rudra, the god of storms, and Varuna, the god of rain and waters. All these gods were believed to dwell on the sacred mountain Mount Meru, the axis of the universe, under the presidency of Indra. The Vedic religion also took other religious ideas from the animist beliefs and fertility cults of the Indus valley civilisation, such as the belief in the principle of male vitality and divine procreative energy symbolised by the phallus (*liṅga*) and its female counterpart the *yoni*, and the cult of the *nāga* or serpent deity, who was both guardian of the treasure believed to be locked in the earth and a beneficent water spirit.

After the *Vedas* several other texts were compiled. These included the *Brāhmanas*, which are concerned with the effects of ritual sacrifices on the balance of moral forces, the *Upaniṣads*, which are collections of the metaphysical teachings and ascetic practices of the forest-dwelling sages (*ṛṣis*), and the *Purāṇas*, which recount various creation myths and legends of the gods. During the first millennium BC and the first two centuries AD, the *Mahābhārata* and the *Rāmāyaṇa*, the two great epics of ancient India, were compiled in Sanskrit from a miscellany of ancient folk tales, myths and legends. These texts provided an important part of the scriptural basis from which the central tenets of both

Hinduism and Buddhism were to evolve, as well as much of their iconography and a great wealth of narrative material for their art.

Brahman and Trimūrti

By the middle of the first millennium BC two main strands had emerged in Indian religious thought. The first of these stemmed from the idea that every thought and action sets in motion a chain of cause and effect. The second was the related belief in reincarnation or metempsychosis (*samsāra*). According to this belief, death is only an interlude in the cycle of birth and rebirth to which all living creatures are subject and which is dictated by the inexorable law of *karma* (literally, 'act', 'deed'), whereby the fruits of every action have a cumulative effect, so that the form of each individual's reincarnation is determined by the degree of merit attained in previous lives, and each successive reincarnation is therefore either a reward or a punishment. This belief in *samsāra* and *karma* provides a justification for the caste system, as birth into a low caste is held to be the result of misdeeds committed in a previous life. Only the attainment of true knowledge can bring release (*mokṣa*) from the bondage of *samsāra* and oneness with the single, unqualified, indefinable and absolute reality or *brahman*.

As a result of the emergence of these ideas the gods ceased to be thought of merely as the objects of ritual sacrifice and came to be seen as manifestations of the uncreated and eternal *brahman*. Consequently, although the multiplicity of deities gives Hinduism the appearance of being a polytheistic religion, in essence it is not so, because all the gods, together with everything else in the universe, are believed to be aspects of *brahman*. This belief in turn brought about the rejection both of the authority of the *brāhman* priests with their esoteric rituals and of the rigidities of the caste system, and led to the formation of numerous new sects, from which two new religions, Jainism and Buddhism, were later to evolve, in a way similar to that in which Christianity evolved from Judaism. *Brahman*, which is a neuter word in Sanskrit, came to be personified as Brahma, and Brahma, together with Vishnu and Shiva, formed the trinity of gods (*Trimūrti*) that were thought to be closest to the essential *brahman*. These three have remained the principal gods of Hinduism to this day. Devi or Mahadevi ('Great Goddess'), the dynamic aspect of Shiva, is also believed to incorporate all the qualities of the *Trimūrti*, and paying devotion to her is considered to be equivalent to worshipping all three gods together.

Brahma, Creator of the Universe and Dispenser of the *Vedas*, has four arms and four faces, denoting universal sovereignty. His attributes are a rosary, a water-pot and a book. His consort (*śakti*) is Vac or Sarasvati, goddess of speech and bestower of intelligence, and his mount (*vāhana*) is the wild goose (*haṁsa*), symbol of the pilgrim soul.

Vishnu, the Pervader, is the preserver and maintainer of order in the universe, god of the home and of love and emotion, and for many Hindus he is the supreme deity. One of his names is Ah, the first letter of the Sanskrit alphabet and the symbol of creation. He also has four arms and he wears a crown signifying his universal sovereignty. In painting he is usually depicted as blue, denoting infinite space. His attributes are a conch (*sankha*), representing his role as the origin of existence, a discus (*cakra*), which stands for the cosmic mind, a club (*gada*), which signifies his power over time, and a lotus (*padma*), representing the universe which Brahma brings into being. His consort is Lakshmi or

Sri, who personifies good fortune and abundance. His *vāhana* is the part-eagle, part-human Garuda, king of the birds and enemy of the *nāgas*. Vishnu has ten human and animal incarnations (*avatāras*), who appear on earth as saviours in periods of decline or danger. The three most important of these are Rama, Krishna and the historical Buddha. His animal *avatāras* include the fish Matsya, the tortoise Kurma, the boar Varaha, the man-headed lion Narasimha and the horse-headed man Kalki, who is Vishnu's future *avatāra*. A popular subject in Khmer art frequently depicted on the lintels of Khmer temples in Cambodia and Thailand is Vishnu before the dawn of creation lying in a deep trance on the cosmic serpent Ananta. From his navel rises a lotus flower, on which sits Brahma, who is about to create the universe. Another popular creation myth associated with Vishnu and frequently illustrated on Khmer lintels is the story of the Churning of the Ocean of Milk to produce both the goddess Lakshmi and the nectar of immortality (*aṁrta*), by means of using the serpent king Vasuki as a rope and the sacred mountain

A 14C bronze statue of Vishnu from Sukhothai. It is now in the National Museum, Bangkok

Mandara as a churning pole placed on the back of Kurma, Vishnu's tortoise *avatāra*. This also explains why Kurma is often depicted in Hindu cosmography supporting the world on his back. Stories of Rama from the *Rāmāyaṇa* epic and of Krishna from the *Bhāgavata Purāṇa* and other texts provide a rich and varied source of material for sculpture, painting and the performing arts in Thailand, as elsewhere in the Hindu and Buddhist world.

Shiva, whose name means the Auspicious One and was originally an epithet applied to Rudra, is both Destroyer and Recreator, and Lord of the Cosmic Dance (Nataraja), in which he destroys the universe and after which Vishnu rests and begins the process of creation over again. He has 1008 names, titles, epithets and forms, and many attributes, including a trident (*triśūla*). He is generally portrayed with a vertical third eye in the middle of his forehead, the matted dreadlocks of the ascetic and a skull and crescent (*candrakapala*) in his headdress. At an early date his cult was assimilated with pre-Vedic fertility cults of the *liṅga*, the *yoni* and the bull, and he is often represented as a *liṅga*, the axis of the universe, sometimes with his face carved on the shaft (*mukhaliṅga*). His *vāhana* is the white humped bull popularly known as Nandi or Nandin. His consorts are Devi, known in her kindly aspect as Parvati or Uma, and in her fierce and terrifying aspect as Durga or Kali, together with Ganga, the deified River Ganges. Ganesha, the elephant-headed son of Shiva, is the god of knowledge and the destroyer of obstacles. His attributes are an elephant's goad, a noose and a bowl, from which he takes sweetmeats with his trunk. His mount is a rat. Shiva also has another son, Skanda or Karttikeya, the eternally youthful god of war, whose mount is a peacock.

All these gods have characteristic adornments, postures and, most importantly, gestures (*mudrās*), which play an important part in their iconography. Shiva and Vishnu, for example, are often shown making the gesture of dispelling fear (*abhaya mudrā*) with one of their hands.

The Life of the Buddha and the Foundation of Buddhism

About 566 BC a prince named Siddhartha or Sarvarthasidda ('He whose Purpose is Accomplished'), later to be known as Gautama and the **Buddha** ('Enlightened One') was born, a prince of the Shakya clan of Kapilavastu, who ruled a small state in the foothills of the Himalayas near the borders of modern Nepal. The name Shakya accounts for his also being known as Shakyamuni ('Sage of the Shakyas'). His conception took place miraculously when his mother, Queen Mahamaya (whose name is also an epithet of Devi) saw in a dream a white elephant holding a white lotus in its trunk enter her right side. After a ten months' pregnancy, she went into the Lumphini Garden, where she grasped a *śāl* tree, which bent down and caused her child to emerge painlessly. She died seven days later.

The miracles and prophecies surrounding the birth convinced Siddhartha's father that his son was destined to be a great leader. He therefore kept him in the palace and carefully shielded him from all unpleasant influences and experiences. One day, however, the prince escaped and had four symbolic encounters, with a beggar (personifying poverty), an old man (old age), a sick man (illness) and a corpse (death). He was so disillusioned by this experience that, then aged 30, he abandoned the court, left his wife and child and went into the forest to lead the life of a mendicant. He exchanged his clothes with a huntsman, his horse died of grief. He became a wandering ascetic and subjected himself to many fasts and privations in order to exterminate all desire and so achieve complete liberation from suffering. In the course of his wanderings he attracted to himself five disciples, who practised the same austerities as he. After five years he realised that such extremes of asceticism could not provide him with the solution he sought and that he was about to die, so he ate a meal. This so horrified his five disciples that they abandoned him. Now entirely alone, Gautama went to Bodh Gaya and there on the night of the May full moon, seated beneath a peepul tree, henceforth to be known as *bodhi* ('enlightenment tree'), he finally understood that his true self was not bound to the endless cycle of suffering and rebirth, but existed outside it, beyond pain and pleasure, space and time, life and death, and so attained Enlightenment. He was then aged 35. Shorty after this, he went to the Deer Park at Sarnath near Benares, where he found the five disciples who had previously deserted him, and preached his First Sermon to them. These five became the first members of the *Saṁgha*, Sangha or Buddhist monkhood. The Buddha himself laid down a set of rules for a monk's daily life, his spiritual exercises and other duties.

There followed a ministry of 45 years, during which the Buddha wandered throughout the kingdoms of Magadha and Kosala preaching and performing many miracles, some of which are favourite subjects in Thai art. About 486 BC at Kushinagara in Bihar he died aged eighty of food poisoning. Having already at his Enlightenment eliminated all the causes of rebirth, he had become an *arahat* ('worthy one') and so passed into *nirvāṇa* (*Mahāparinirvāṇa*), a blissful state of non-existence or re-absorption into the Absolute, similar to the Hindu *mokṣa*. The Thais, among others, date this event and consequently the beginning of the Buddhist era to the year 543 BC.

After achieving **Enlightenment**, the Buddha had ceased to exist in the strict sense of that word, and had become omniscient and transcendental , and in this respect there is clearly a similarity between the Buddhist concept of *nirvāṇa* and the Hindu concept of *brahman*. However, whereas Hinduism teaches that humans have a permanent essence (*ātman*), which will ultimately be reunited with the Absolute, Buddhism denies this permanent reality and teaches that *nirvāna* means literally what it says, a blowing out or extinction, like the snuffing out of a candle flame, and that, before the attainment of this state, there are six states that may follow *samsāra*—god, demi-god or titan, human, wandering ghost, animal or dweller in hell. Buddhism also rejects the Hindu idea of caste, and, like Jainism, may be seen as essentially a reformist movement within Hinduism, in which all human beings are enjoined to show compassion to one another and to help each other obtain merit.

A corollary of the belief in the *Mahāparinirvāṇa* of the historical Buddha was the belief that he was one of an infinite number of previous and future Buddhas, omniscient and transcendent, who had appeared on earth to preach the true doctrine, and that he had either never been born or had always existed. In other words, he was transformed from being simply a great spiritual teacher into a god. Although images of the Buddha theoretically do not represent a god or a transcendental being, but a human being who embodies Buddhist doctrine, with time the honouring, the commissioning and the making of Buddha images have all come to be seen as important ways of making merit (Thai, *tham bun*), only exceeded by building and endowing an entire monastery. Even today the casting of bronze images of the Buddha is generally only carried out in monasteries and is accompanied by elaborate rituals, spiritual exercises and meditations carried out by the monks, while the bronzesmith pays homage to the spirit of his teachers, makes offerings to the guardian deities of the place, and exorcises evil influences from his tools, the moulds and the metal by sprinkling them with holy water.

Theravada, Mahayana and Vajrayana

After the death of the Buddha, his teachings were spread by the *Sangha*, committed to memory and gradually systematised in a series of four great councils. At length there emerged a definitive body of doctrine, and this was written down in the first century AD in Pali, one of the Prakritic or popular languages derived from Sanskrit, in Sri Lanka, which had been in the 3C BC the first country outside India to adopt Buddhism. This Pali canon forms the basis of the **Theravada** ('Doctrine of the Elders'), the form of Buddhism practised today in Sri Lanka and in Burma, Thailand, Laos and Cambodia. It is called the Three Baskets (Sanskrit, *Tripiṭaka*; Pali, *Tipiṭaka*) because it is divided into three sections, dealing respectively with discipline and the monastic code of rules, the discourses of the Buddha, and the ideas and concepts implicit in his teachings.

The fundamentals of Buddhist teaching are embodied in the Four Noble Truths: that all human life is suffering; that this suffering is caused by desire for unreal, transitory things; that the suppression of desire brings an end of suffering and the attainment of *nirvāṇa*; and that this suppression can be achieved by following the Noble Eightfold Path or Middle Way—right speech, right livelihood, right action, right effort, right mindfulness, right concentration, right opinion and right intention—through various spiritual exercises designed to bring about control over the mind and a capacity for deep meditation. The Noble Eightfold Path can best be followed within the discipline of the monastic life.

Probably as early as the 1C AD, a form of Buddhism known as the Mahayana or Greater Vehicle developed in southern India. The **Mahayana Buddhists** rejected the Theravada ideal of withdrawing from the world and living as a monk in order to attain *nirvāṇa* in as short a time as possible and they used the pejorative term Hinayana ('Lesser Vehicle') to describe the Theravada doctrine and the teachings of other sects that continued to follow earlier Buddhist traditions. Instead, they postulated the existence of *bodhisattvas*, beings 'whose essence is enlightenment' or 'intended for enlightenment', in other words who have achieved enlightenment, but have foregone the bliss of *nirvāṇa* and stayed behind in order to help others to achieve it. The mediation of the *bodhisattvas*, not unlike that of the Christian saints, is believed to help the individual to circumvent the inexorable law of cause and effect and thereby to achieve *nirvāṇa*, which thus ceases to be thought of simply as extinction and is transformed into a kind of paradise. Among the most popular *bodhisattvas* in Southeast Asian Buddhism are Avalokiteshvara ('the Lord who looks down with Compassion'), also known as Lokeshvara ('Lord of the World'), who carries an image of Amitabha, the transcendental Buddha of the northern region of the universe, in his headdress; Prajnaparamita ('Perfection of Wisdom'), a feminine *bodhisattva* who is sometimes thought of as the spiritual mother of all Buddhas and is the philosophical aspect of Avalokiteshvara's assistant, Tara, the Saviour; and Maitreya ('the Benevolent One'), who dwells in the Tushita Heaven and is the Buddha of the future. The historical Buddha himself was believed to have been a *bodhisattva* in his 550 previous existences, and it is these that provide the subject matter for the *jātakas* or birth tales, which are frequently illustrated in the wall paintings in Thai temples. The last ten lives, known in Thai as *Thotsachat* or *Sip chat*, are the most often illustrated, and of these the last of all, the *Vessantara jātaka* (Thai, *Mahachat*, 'Great Life'), the life of the supremely charitable Prince Vessantara is the most popular.

Contemporaneously with the Mahayana doctrine, a form of Buddhist practice developed that took its ideas from a group of texts known as **tantras**, which explain various esoteric religious rites, and meditational and yogic techniques, some of them of an erotic nature, and describe the incantations (*dharanīs* or *mantras*), ritual gestures (*mudrās*) and magical diagrams used to assist visualisation (*maṇḍalas*) with which they were linked. These practices, like the disciplines of the monastic life on which the Theravada places such emphasis, are thought by their adepts to be a means of attaining *nirvāṇa* more rapidly. Tantrism had long been a feature of early Indic religious beliefs and practices; in its Buddhist manifestation it is known as Vajrayana, because its practitioners have adopted as their symbol the *vajra*, the thunderbolt of Indra, a source of elemental energy that destroys all delusions and opens the way to enlightenment. In Tantric Buddhism the Supreme or Adi Buddha, who, as a result of religious practices has attained complete emptiness (*śūnyatā*), is known as Vajrasattva ('Being of the Thunderbolt'). From his meditations sprang the five *Jinas* or Conqueror Buddhas, each of whom represents a direction: Akshobya (east), Ratnasambhava (south), Amitabha (west), Amoghasiddhi (north) and Vairocana (centre or zenith). From the five *Jinas* in turn emanated other deities, who personify certain aspects, some of them terrifying, of the Buddha and his *Dharma*. That there were Tantric elements in early Khmer Mahayana Buddhism is shown by the presence of relief carvings of the Buddha Vajrasattva and of the *Jina* Buddhas in some Khmer temples in Cambodia and Thailand, notably at Phimai (see p 353).

The first **Buddhist missionaries** in Southeast Asia are traditionally believed to have been sent by the Emperor Ashoka, who ruled over the powerful Maurya empire in northern and central India from c 273 to c 232 BC, but the first reliable evidence for the presence of either Buddhism or Hinduism anywhere in Southeast Asia is no earlier than the 2C AD. It was during this period that Indian religions, Indian moral concepts, Indian ideas of government and statecraft and Indian art forms spread into Southeast Asia. The Khmers of Angkor adopted Hinduism and to a lesser extent Mahayana Buddhism, which in the reign of the fervently Buddhist Jayavarman VII (1181–c 1220) was the state religion. By this time Buddhism was virtually extinct in the land of its origin, and the Buddha had become identified as the ninth *avatāra* of Vishnu. By the time of the Thai conquest of Angkor in 1431/32 they seem to have become chiefly Theravada. Mahayana Buddhism was the predominant religion practised in Sri Vijaya, while the Mons in the Chao Phraya basin and Lower Burma and the Burmese of Pagan for the most part adopted the Theravada doctrine. It was chiefly from the Mons and the Burmese rather than directly from India that the Thais took their Theravada Buddhism and the other Indian elements in their culture as they moved southwards into mainland Southeast Asia. After the foundation of the Thai kingdom of Sukhothai and the establishment of Theravada Buddhism as its state religion, successive Thai rulers in Sukhothai and Ayutthaya looked to Sri Lanka as the land where Theravada Buddhism represented most nearly the teachings of the Buddha himself, although it is from the Khmers that the Thais have taken most of their concepts of kingship. Thai influence was largely responsible for the introduction of Theravada Buddhism into Laos and Cambodia. Today over 90 per cent of the people of Thailand consider themselves to be Theravada Buddhists, and the *Sangha* occupies an important place in Thai society and education. There are small minorities of Christians (about 100,000), chiefly confined to Thais of Chinese or Vietnamese origin, and of Muslims (about 1 million), particularly in the southern provinces, where many of the population are Malays.

Buddhist Iconography

The earliest representations of the Buddha were symbolic. For example, his **Birth** was represented by a flowering lotus, his **Enlightenment** by a *bodhi* tree, the **First Sermon** by a wheel, sometimes with a deer beneath it, and his **Māhaparinirvāṇa** by a *stūpa* (Thai, *chedi*), the funerary or reliquary monument derived from the early Indian burial mound, which is now an essential element in every Thai temple complex. These symbols have remained a prominent feature of Buddhist iconography ever since. Later, depictions of the Buddha himself and of scenes from his Life were rendered with varying degrees of realism in free-standing and relief sculptures and in mural and manuscript paintings, and a complex iconography developed. Among the most frequently illustrated episodes are the **Great Renunciation**, when Prince Siddhartha decides to become a wandering ascetic and bids farewell to his sleeping wife and son in the palace; the **Great Departure**, when he rides away, accompanied by Indra, depicted in green, and Brahma, who carries a monk's robes and alms bowl, his horse's hooves held up by celestial creatures to prevent them making a sound that might wake the palace guards; and the **Cutting of the Hair**, when he cuts off all his hair with a sword to symbolise his severance of worldly ties and his adoption of the life of an ascetic, after which his hair ceases to grow. Another popular scene shows him, after five years of extreme mortification, during which he reduces his food to a single grain of rice a day, being approached by Indra with a three-stringed lute. One string is so loose that it makes no sound when plucked, and the third string is so taut that it snaps, but the middle string is stretched to just the right degree and produces a beautiful sound when Indra strikes it. Gautama understands that the middle string represents the Middle Way, the way of moderation, and that this alone will lead to understanding and enlightenment, and so he ends his fast and accepts a meal prepared for him in a golden bowl by a rich noble lady called Sujata, who, seeing him surrounded by rays of light, thinks he is a god. Among the most popular of all subjects in Thai Buddhist art are the **Buddha in meditation** being sheltered from the rain by the hood of the *nāga* king Mucalinda and raised up from the flood by his coils, and the **Buddha's victory over Mara**, when, seated under the *bodhi* tree at Bodh Gaya in deep meditation, he is assailed by the evil tempter Mara, his daughters and his army of demons, and when Dharani, the earth goddess, bears witness to his good deeds by wringing out of her hair the lustral water that contains all his merits. The gesture (*mudrā*) most frequently used in Thai Buddha images is that of calling the earth to witness (*bhūmisparśa mudrā*), which symbolises this victory over Mara and is therefore often called the *Māravijaya mudrā*. Other popular subjects include the Buddha's First Sermon; his Ascent into the Tavatimsa Heaven to convert his mother and his Return from there accompanied by Indra and Brahma; the Taming of the Nalagiri Elephant sent by his cousin and rival Devadatta to crush him; his last Meal; his Death and Obsequies; and the Distribution of the Relics.

The iconography of images of the Buddha, like that of Brahmanic deities, has to follow certain precise specifications regarding their physical features, dress, adornments and attributes, postures and gestures. Furthermore, since every image is sacred and imbued with supernatural powers, being not only a portrait of the historical Buddha, but also a representation of Buddhist doctrine, the sculptor, who is always anonymous, does not attempt to produce a lifelike human figure, but tries to reproduce as exactly as possible an idealised model of the Buddha as a great man or *mahāpuruṣa*, who, having attained Buddhahood as a result of merit gained in previous existences, has become a universal ruler or *cakravartin*. The *mahāpuruṣa* is distinguished by 32 primary and 80 secondary auspicious marks or signs (*lakṣaṇa*), which are described in the early Sanskrit and Pali texts. Some of these, such as the acute sense of taste and the soft hands and feet, cannot, of course, be portrayed except symbolically, but others have been represented with varying degrees of literalism in different periods, such as the projecting heels, the arms like an elephant's trunk and reaching down to the knees, the fingers of equal length, the nose like the beak of a parrot, the chin like a mango, the mole between the eyebrows (*ūrṇā*), the elongated ear-lobes, the protuberance on the head (*uṣṇīṣa*) like a royal turban, with a flame or a jewel issuing from it, and the golden glow of the skin like bronze, which shines through the robe and makes it appear transparent (this is usually rendered by gilding or by the indication of the edge of the robe by incised lines and by the absence of any draperies, and occasionally by a nimbus or halo surrounding the whole body). Some of the iconographic features commonly found in Thai Buddha images are not mentioned in the ancient texts, for example, the clockwise direction of the curls of the hair and the elongated ear lobes denoting the Buddha's abandonment of princely adornments after the Great Departure.

Various ways of draping the monastic robes (trīcivara)

1. }
2. } *antaravāsaka*

3. }
4. } *uttarāsaṅga*
5. }

6. }
7. } *sanghāti*

All three of the **garments** worn by Buddhist monks—the undercloth (*antara-vāsaka*), the robe (*uttarāsaṅga*) and the shawl (*sanghātī*), known collectively as the *trīcivara*—play an important part in Buddhist iconography, as do certain princely adornments associated with the royal Birth of the Buddha or with the idea of him as a *cakravartin*, such as crowns and diadems, earrings, necklaces, jewelled belts, armlets and anklets.

In Thailand the Buddha is always portrayed in one of **four positions**—seated, standing, walking or reclining. The reclining position is only used to represent the Buddha at the moment of passing into *Mahāparinirvāṇa*, while freestanding images of the walking Buddha do not occur before the Sukhothai period in the 13C. The majority of Buddha images of all periods in Thailand

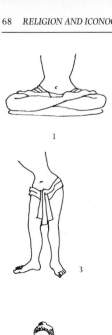

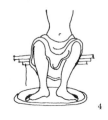

1. *padmāsana, vajrāsana*

2. *tribhaṅga*

3. *paryankāsana, virāsana*

4. *pralambapādāsana,*
   bhadrāsana

1. *vitarka mudrā*

2. *abhaya mudrā*

3. *dharmacakra mudrā*

4. *bhūmisparśa (māravijaya)*
   mudrā

5. *dhyāna mudrā*

6. *vara mudrā*

are in a seated yogic posture (*āsana*), usually the *virāsana* or *paryankāsana* (hero position), or the *vajrāsana* (adamantine position), also known as the *padmāsana* (lotus position), or occasionally the so-called European position (*bhadrāsana* or *pralambapādāsana*), with both feet on the ground and legs apart, as if seated on a throne.

The gestures of the hand (*mudrās*) are also of special significance in Buddhist iconography. The six most important of these are the *abhaya mudrā* (bestowing protection, dispelling fear), the *dhyāna mudrā* (meditation), the *vara* or *varada mudrā* (bestowing charity), the *vitarka mudrā* (teaching, reciting doctrine), which in some images, notably those of the Dvaravati school, is performed with both hands, in which case it refers to the Descent from the Tavatimsa Heaven, the *dharmacakra mudrā* (setting the Wheel of the Law in motion), and, as we have already seen, by far the most frequent, the *bhūmisparśa mudrā* (calling the earth to witness).

Changes and variations in the treatment of these iconographic features—*lakṣaṇas*, dress and adornments, *āsanas* and *mudrās*—provide one of the principal means by which Buddhist sculpture can be dated and classified.

The Sangha

It is customary for every Thai male, including members of the royal family, to become a monk one or more times in his life for at least three months (though nowadays it is often less), preferably before he marries, so that he can gain merit for his parents as well as himself, and generally during the season of *Phansa* or Buddhist Lent (July to September), which is the rainy season, when the monks have to stay in the temple and may not go on pilgrimage. Novices (*nak*), who cannot be admitted to the monkhood before the age of eight, must declare their faith in the Three Jewels (the Buddha, his Doctrine [*Dharma*] and his Order [*Sangha*] and the Ten Abstentions (from murder, theft, unchastity, untruth, fermented drink, eating after noon, dancing and singing, ornaments, comfortable beds, and touching money). The abstention from murder includes all living creatures, even mosquitoes and other insects, but does not forbid the eating of meat or fish, since these are already dead. One way in which a Buddhist can show compassion for all living creatures and so make merit is to buy a small bird (or sometimes a fish or a turtle) in a cage and release it; the fact that the bird has been caught specifically for this purpose and will no doubt be caught, caged and sold again does not appear to reduce the merit of the act of releasing it.

On the day of his ordination, the novice's head is shaved, he is dressed in white and, carrying a stick of incense, a candle and a lotus flower, he is carried in procession to the temple, where he is provided with the articles he is permitted to possess as a monk. Originally these were only an alms bowl, three garments (*trīcivara*), which must be either red or yellow, a belt, a razor, a needle and a water filter. To these were added later an umbrella, a fan, a wooden toothpick, sandals, a staff and a rosary. In early times, monks were only permitted to eat food that was given to them, to wear garments that had been discarded as rubbish, to live under trees and to use no medicines except cow's urine. They were expected to lead a wandering life of preaching and teaching, and settled life in a community was at first confined to the rainy season, when it became difficult to wander and the monks would dwell in groups of small huts, such as are used for the monks' living quarters (*kuti*) in many monasteries to this day. Monks of the Aranyika or Forest sect still lead the life of a pilgrim or a hermit in the forest or in caves, with no shelter other than a large yellow umbrella, and only move into a temple during *Phansa*.

At the age of twenty the novice can become a full monk and he then has to observe no fewer than 227 monastic rules, which he must recite every full moon at a special ceremony. In modern Thai Theravada there are two sects, the Mahanikai and the rather stricter Thammayutika. The latter was founded by King Mongkut in the 1840s and is based on a monastic discipline he followed when he was a monk at Wat Bowon Niwet in Bangkok before coming to the throne. Women cannot be admitted to the *Sangha*, but they can become nuns. They wear white robes, shave their heads and observe the Ten Abstentions.

The monk's day begins with his walk through the streets with his alms bowl. He is not begging for food, but giving people the opportunity to gain merit by giving him food. The giving of food to monks is indeed one of the principal ways in which a Buddhist can make merit. The rest of the day is devoted to prayer and meditation, study of the sacred texts, the performance of various ceremonies ranging from funerals to the inauguration of new businesses and the blessing of new houses, participation in Buddhist festivals and teaching. Until modern times Buddhist monasteries provided the only education for the people, and to this day, although the state now provides education for all, many monks are still active teachers and are consulted on a wide variety of practical local problems.

The Hindu Gods and Animist Spirits in Thai Buddhism

Hindu deities and many Brahmanic practices have been retained in Thai Buddhism, most notably in the coronation rites of the kings of Thailand and other royal ceremonies, and many of the fundamental features of Hindu cosmography have been incorporated into Buddhist cosmography. Rama has been adopted as a regnal name or part of it by many of the kings of Sukhothai and Ayutthaya and by all nine kings of the Chakri dynasty, and the *Ramakien*, the Thai version of the *Rāmāyaṇa*, plays an essential role in Thai religious art and in Thai literature. The shrine of Erewan, the three-headed elephant mount of Indra, in Bangkok is one of the most popular shrines in Thailand, and thousands of offerings are made there every day (see p 140).

The Thais have also retained many of the ancient animist beliefs and practices which they brought with them when they first migrated into Southeast Asia, and they still pay respect to the spirits (*phi*) of the ancestors and the spirits of place, who live in hills, springs, trees and caves and who protect their houses, shops, villages and cities. Some of these spirits are malign and have to be mollified and appeased with offerings. Spirit houses in the form of a miniature Thai dwelling house or a temple building are set on a pillar in front of most houses and public buildings to provide accommodation for the spirits that have been disturbed by the construction of the building and for those who will act as its guardians, and every time improvements are carried out to the building the spirit house has to be improved commensurately. Offerings of incense, candles, flowers, fruit and food are placed in the spirit houses every day. Actors, dancers and musicians make offerings to the *phi* before every performance, and the performances themselves are often commissioned by people in thanksgiving to the spirit for some favour granted. Drivers buy garlands of sweet scented jasmine and marigolds made by women and children at the side of the road and known as *malai*, and hang them in their cars to give protection against accidents. The primary purpose of tattooing, which, though in decline, is still customary among many Thai men, is to ward off evil spirits and ensure good fortune. None of these beliefs and practices is deemed to be superstitious or to conflict with Buddhism; on the contrary they are inextricably interwoven with it. For example, the ordination of monks is often preceded on the previous evening by a ceremony called *bai sii* in which the soul of the ordinand is summoned up by a medium specialising in rites of passage.

JV

THE ARTS IN THAILAND

Classification of Art Styles

The standard system of classification and periodisation of art styles in Thailand is that devised in 1926 by HRH Prince Damrong Rajanubhab, the father of Thai archaeology. This system uses the names of the kingdoms that at different times have flourished in different parts of Thailand to denote different art styles. It has been widely adopted by museums thoughout the world and is still followed by many scholars. However, in 1977, the distinguished Thai art historian, Dr Piriya Krairiksh proposed an alternative system in which the art styles are classified in the first instance under the three dominant ethnic groups in the area covered by modern Thailand—Mons, Khmers and Thais—and subdivided according to the areas in which each of these three groups has been dominant at different times—central, northeast, north, etc. The art of peninsular Thailand is classified separately. The main disadvantage of Prince Damrong's system is that the exact location and extent of the kingdoms after which the styles are named is not always known, and of Dr Piriya's scheme that the art of any area is not necessarily always produced by the ethnic group then dominant in that area, so that the occurrence of objects in the style of an ethnic group does not invariably correspond to the area defined by it, and that conversely objects in divergent styles may occur within a single geographical category. In this guide Prince Damrong's classification system has been followed, but the reader's attention is drawn in the text to the anomalies and inconsistencies created by both systems.

The Thai Temple

The correct meaning of the Thai word **wat** or **phutthawat**, which is usually translated loosely as 'temple', is a Buddhist monastery, but many Buddhist temples in Thailand are described as *wat* even though they have no monastic community attached to them. The Thai *wat* properly so-called generally consists of several buildings in a walled enclosure that together make up the monastic complex.

The central edifice of the *wat* is the reliquary monument. This may be in the form of a tower-sanctuary (*prang*), the form of which is derived from the tower-sanctuary of the Khmer temple (*prasat*), built above a cella or shrine, or of a *stūpa*, a virtually solid, dome-shaped structure ultimately derived from the burial mounds of ancient India and known in Thai as a *chedi*. The *chedi* or *prang* may contain relics of the Buddha or of his possessions (e.g. parts of his robes), Buddha images or other reminders of him, such as votive tablets or representations of the *bodhi* tree or the Wheel of the Law. Many *chedi* built today are merely copies of earlier *chedi* and do not contain any relics.

The **chedi** is generally raised on a series of circular, octagonal or redented platforms, usually in groups of three representing the three worlds (*Traiphum*) of Buddhist cosmology, separated by mouldings and set on a square base. This base is often in the form of a terrace wide enough to allow room for ritual circum-

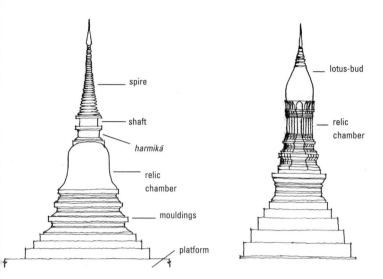

Sri Lankan-style bell-shaped chedi

Sukhothai 'lotus-bud' chedi

ambulation of the monument. Standing on the uppermost platform is the *chedi* proper or relic chamber, of which there are many variations, but which is usually in the form of a bell-shaped circular or many-sided dome, sometimes redented and sometimes with an entrance porch at each of the four cardinal points. Some *chedi*, particularly in northern Thailand, have only a very small bell-shaped element or lack it altogether, and consist instead of a series of cube-shaped structures of gradually diminishing size set one upon the other to form a stepped pyramid, with rows of Buddha images in niches at each level. Above the relic chamber is the *harmikā*, which is thought to represent the throne of the Buddha. This is generally box-shaped, but often continues the redentation of the relic chamber below. Above the *harmikā* is a shaft, often enclosed by a balustrade of short columns or ornamented with relief carvings, and above this again a tapering ringed conical spire. In *chedi* of the Sukhothai period, the bell element is sometimes replaced by a tall, tiered and redented shaft on which is set a finial in the form of a lotus bud tapering up to the ringed spire. Especially in northern Thailand, where Burmese influence is strong, a gilded multi-tiered parasol of Burmese origin known as a *chat* (Burmese, *hti)* is often placed on top of the spire.

The *prang* in its more strictly Khmer form, as at Phimai and Phanom Rung, consists of an ogival tower standing on a raised redented platform. The cella containing the relic or image is in the lower part of the tower, which generally has a single entrance on the east side with a *maṇḍapa* or antechamber, and above this is a series of tiers decorated at the corners with inward-sloping antefixes and progressively diminishing in size up to a *kalaśa* (pitcher) finial. In the Thai adaptation of the Khmer model the square platform is surmounted by three platforms representing the three worlds of Buddhist cosmology (*Traiphum)*. Above these is

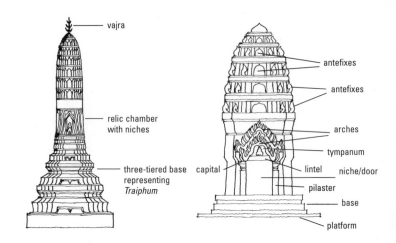

Khmer-style prang   **Khmer prasat**

the relic chamber, which has niches at the four cardinal points containing figures of guardians or Buddha images. On top is the distinctive *prang* tower shaped like a corn-cob, usually with six levels or storeys, each representing one of the Buddhist heavens and decorated with antefixes and small pediments. At the summit is a seven-pronged finial ornament representing the thunderbolt (*vajra*) of Indra, president of the 33 gods dwelling on Mount Meru.

Since both the *chedi* and the *prang* also represent Mount Meru, the axis of the universe and abode of the gods, they often contain other architectural and ornamental features symbolising other aspects of Hindu-Buddhist cosmology. The most obvious of these are the **nāgas**, the serpent deities that guard the waters and the subterranean treasures, which are frequently represented on antefixes, roof-ridges, gables and balustrade; the mounts of the different gods and a host of other celestial creatures that dwell in the different heavens, such as *garuḍas*, *kinnaris* and *kinnaras*, and *narasiṁhas* also often occur. Smaller versions of the central *prang* or *chedi* are sometimes set at the corners of the uppermost terrace to form a quincunx recalling the five peaks of Mount Meru.

The enclosure of the Thai *wat* also usually contains several rectangular assembly halls with multiple tiled roofs. The most important and most sacred of these is the ordination hall (**ubosot** or *bot*). The *ubosot* can be easily identified because it faces east and is surrounded by eight *bai sema*. These are leaf-shaped stone slabs or occasionally stone pillars placed at the cardinal and sub-cardinal points to demarcate the boundaries of the consecrated precincts. Beneath each one is buried a *sema* stone or *luk nimit*, and a ninth *luk nimit* is buried inside the *ubosot*, either in the centre or under the principal Buddha image. Double or triple *bai sema* denote either that the *ubosot* is a royal foundation or that it has been consecrated more than once. Similar in form to the *ubosot* is the *wihan*, which can serve various functions, but is chiefly used for gatherings of monks or of laity and contains the principal Buddha images of the *wat*. Some larger Thai temple complexes have more than one *wihan*. The *wihan* is less sacred than the *ubosot* and is not surrounded by *bai sema*. Many *wat* also have one or more open-sided study or preaching halls called *sala kan parian*, with porches at either end and pillars supporting a tiered and gabled roof.

Both *prang* and *ubosot* may be surrounded by a roofed gallery (**rabiang**), either enclosed with walls or open on one side like a cloister and containing rows of Buddha images. There are usually gateways or **gopuras** set in the galleries at the four cardinal points to give access to the central area. In Khmer temples these galleries represent the range of mountains that encircle Mount Meru at the centre of the universe, and this idea of the entire temple complex as a symbolic representation of the cosmos in architectural form is often carried further by the creation of ponds or moats within the temple precincts to represent the cosmic oceans, and by the wall that usually surrounds the entire rectangular temple complex and symbolises the boundary of the universe.

Several other smaller buildings are also often found within the *wat* enclosure. These may include one or more **mondop** or pavilions, often open-sided and surmounted by a multi-tiered wooden roof with a slender spire, enshrining a sacred object such as a Footprint of the Buddha, *Buddhapāda* (Thai: *Phutthabat*); a **ho trai**, a scripture repository or library in which the sacred Buddhist texts are

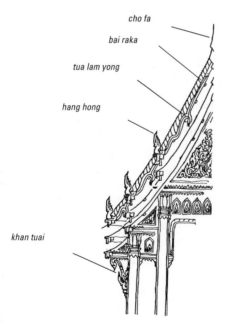

cho fa
bai raka
tua lam yong
hang hong
khan tuai

The roof of a Thai temple

(adapted from the work of the late
Professor Jote Kalayanamitr.)

housed and which is sometimes built on stilts over water in order to protect the texts from insects and vermin; and a belfry (**ho rakhang**). The monks' living quarters (**kuti**) are generally composed of a collection of plain wooden or white-washed brick buildings, sometimes located outside the *phutthawat*.

Styles of Religious Architecture and Sculpture

Mon-Dvaravati

Although the art of Dvaravati bears some superficial resemblances to the Gupta and post-Gupta art of central and western India, it is quite distinctive and original in style. Mon sculptors were on the whole better at relief carving in stucco and terracotta than at working with stone, perhaps because the stone that they chiefly used was a brittle schistous limestone, which shatters easily. This may also account for the rather stiff and ponderous treatment of the figures and for their rigid symmetry and frontality.

Dvaravati Buddha images are usually standing, with an asexual body. The

robe, which is without pleats, covers one or both shoulders, and the bottom of the undergarment (*antaravāsaka*) is below the hem of the outer (*uttarāsaṇga*), which forms a prominent U-shaped ridge. The belt is suggested by a slight bulge at the waist. The back is smooth and featureless, suggesting that the images were designed to be placed against a wall. The facial features are fleshy and rather coarse, with a wide flat nose and thick lips, the eyebrows heavily ridged and meeting at the centre. The curls of the hair are conical and the *uṣṇīṣa* terminates in a large conical

Mon-Dvaravati Buddha head 7C–8C

knob. Standing images of the Buddha, and more particularly of *bodhisattvas* and Hindu deities, are often slightly flexed, sometimes in the full *tribhaṅga* pose. The *mudrā* of both standing and seated images is usually the *vitarka mudrā*, in the case of the former often with both hands, an iconographic feature which does not occur in Indian art and only occasionally elsewhere in Southeast Asia. Seated images are usually in the *vīrāsana*, or occasionally the *pralambapādāsana* position. Images of the reclining Buddha are extremely rare.

The meditating Buddha raised above the flood by the *nāga* king Muchalinda and sheltered from the rain by his sevenfold hood is a favourite subject, as it is of Khmer Buddhist sculpture.

Dvaravati bronze images are in the same style as those in stone, but much rarer. They are often gilded and have eyes inlaid with copper or tin.

Dvaravati artists also produced relief carving in stucco and terracotta, and occasionally in stone, illustrating the Life of the Buddha and *jātaka* tales. One favourite subject of Dvaravati stone reliefs, which is found nowhere else in Southeast Asia in that period, is traditionally known as the Buddha on Panasbati. The Buddha is portrayed standing or sitting on a mythical bird-like creature, surrounded by an aureole and usually flanked by two figures holding ceremonial fly-whisks, who are thought to be either Indra and Brahma or, more probably, two *bodhisattvas*.

Another form of Buddhist sculpture which, although found in India, in Southeast Asia is peculiar to Dvaravati, is the **Wheel of the Law**. These were placed on tall columns in temple enclosures. They are often highly decorated on

both sides and have figures of deer at the base—a reference to the Buddha's First Sermon in the Deer Park at Sarnath.

The sculptors of the northern Mon kingdom of **Haripunjaya** made Buddha images in stucco and terracotta as well as stone and bronze. The style of Haripunjaya images owes much to their Dvaravati antecedents, but they have numerous distinctive features, notably the half-smiling lips, sometimes surmounted by a moustache indicated with a single incised line, downcast eyes and arched eyebrows meeting in the centre, sharply pointed curls of hair, a smooth conical *uṣṇīṣa*, and the robe covering both shoulders.

Mon-Haripunjaya Buddha head, 13C

Very little remains of **Dvaravati architecture** apart from the square laterite base of Chedi Chula Pathom near Nakhon Pathon and the recently excavated foundations of the monuments of the inner city of Si Thep (see p 344). The temple architecture of the northern Mon kingdom of Haripunjaya is principally represented by the two remarkable *chedi* at Wat Cham Tewi in Lamphun (see p 289–90). One of these, which dates from the mid-12C, is in brick and is decorated with stucco images of the standing Buddha, the other, which was rebuilt in the early 13C, is in laterite, with niches decorated with stucco and containing statues of the standing Buddha in terracotta.

Sri Vijaya

Between the 8C and 13C much of southern Thailand and the Malay peninsula came under the influence, if not the political control, of Sri Vijaya, the great maritime commercial empire which had its centre on the east coast of Sumatra, and the term Sri Vijaya is therefore often used to designate the art of southern Thailand throughout this period, whatever its style. However, there were four distinct phases in the art of the Peninsula before the advent of the Thais during the 13C. From the **3C to the 5C**, before the rise of Sri Vijaya, commercial contacts with India led to an early adoption of Mahayana Buddhism and strongly Indianised art forms in the area, and this is evident in the Buddhist bronze sculpture and clay votive tablets. From the **5C to the 8C** southern Thailand was divided into numerous small states, of which those at the head of the Gulf of Thailand were predominantly Mon, so that Mon influence is clearly apparent. From the **8C to the 11C** both Sri Vijaya and central Java were ruled by the kings of the Shailendra dynasty, and this led to the appearance of Indo-Javanese elements in the art of southern Thailand. **After the 11C**, as Sri Vijaya's power waned, the Khmers in central Thailand, although they never brought the Peninsula under their rule, exercised increasing influence in the south, and this change is reflected in the art produced in this region. With the extension of Sukhothai rule as far as Nakhon Si Thammarat in the **late 13C and early 14C**, the art of southern Thailand lost many of its distinctive characteristics and became virtually indistinguishable from the art of Sukhothai.

Relatively few **Sri Vijaya Buddha images** are known. Most of them are small bronze statuettes showing strong central Javanese influence and through this north Indian (Pala and Gupta) influences, and they may indeed have been imported from Java. They are all seated in the *vajrāsana* position and most of them are in *dharmacakra mudrā*. The famous Buddha of Grahi from Wat Wieng at Chaiya, near the Bay of Bandon, now in the National Museum, Bangkok (see illustration on p 126), which is inscribed in Khmer with a date that was first interpreted as being equivalent to 1183, but is now more generally thought to be 1291, and shows the Buddha in *bhūmisparśa mudrā* sheltering under the *nāga* king Mucalinda, is in a curious mixture of styles that makes it quite unlike anything else ascribed to the Sri Vijaya school: the *nāga* is Khmer in style; the Buddha's *mudrā*, the draperies of the *uttarāsanga*, and the wide pleats of the *sanghāti*, which is placed, instead of the flap of the *uttarāsanga*, over the left shoulder, are reminiscent of early Sukhothai sculpture, while the pointed curls and the smooth hemispherical *uṣṇīṣa* with an ornament bordered with flames at its base, although they do occur in one other bronze Buddha image from Chaiya, are highly unusual features.

Sandstone and bronze images of two-, four- or eight-armed **bodhisattvas**, particularly of Avalokiteshvara, are more numerous, larger and of finer quality. The bronze images are usually richly ornamented, as for example the two lovely bronze Avalokiteshvara torsos from Chaiya that are now in the National Museum in Bangkok. The stone images, on the other hand, are without any adornments apart from the antelope skin worn over the left shoulder. They are generally clad in a long sarong-like garment known as a *paridhāna*, covering the legs and tied at the waist with a tiger skin.

The large number of **votive tablets** made of unbaked clay carrying representations of the Buddha or Avalokiteshvara and with Sanskrit inscriptions written in Old Javanese or North Indian script that have been found in the Peninsula and the Gulf of Thailand demonstrates the wide diffusion of Mahayana Buddhism in this area during the Sri Vijaya period.

Sri Vijaya Brahmanic statues are usually of sandstone, occasionally of limestone and only rarely of bronze. They have been found over a wide area, ranging from Takua Pa in the south to two sites near Prachin Buri (Dong Si Maha Pot and Dong Lakhon) in the north. Most of them are four-armed figures of Vishnu, and their style and iconography owe much to Central Javanese models. The stone images are carved fully in the round and often carry a club and a sphere representing the earth or other attributes in their upper hands attached to a circular nimbus behind them in an attempt—in most cases vain—to prevent breakage of the upper arms and the feet. They wear long *paridhānas* and a variety of headdresses. Their faces have a serene and slightly remote expression and the necks are finely modelled, sometimes with the Adam's apple indicated. Some Shiva images and Shaivite *mukhaliṅgas* and figures of Skanda, Ganesha, Surya and other Brahmanic deities that belong to the Sri Vijaya period have been found in various places in southern Thailand. Some of them show Pallava or Chola influence from south India, but they are on the whole of inferior quality.

Little remains in Thailand or elsewhere of the architecture of the Sri Vijaya period and most of what there is either so ruined, consisting of little more than earth mounds, brick foundations and a few stone pillars, thresholds and door frames, or so altered by later reconstruction that it is difficult to imagine how they must have originally appeared. Wat Kaeo and Wat Long, two temples at Chaiya belonging to the early Sri Vijaya period (see p 381), were sensitively restored in the 1980s and may perhaps be regarded as typical.

Khmer-Lop Buri

The name of Lop Buri, which became the chief centre of power of the Khmer empire of Angkor in central Thailand from the early 11C, has been loosely applied to all Khmer and Khmer-inspired art produced anywhere in Thailand, even if it occurs outside the Lop Buri region and belongs to a period before or after Khmer domination in the area.

Khmer art styles in Cambodia are classified according to the monuments that principally exemplify them, as follows:

Style of Phnom Da (c 540–c 600)
Style of Sambor Prei Kuk (c 600–
   c 650)
Style of Prei Kmeng (635–c 700)
Style of Kompong Preah (c 700–
   c 800)
Style of Kulen (c 825–c 875)
Style of Preah Ko (c 877–c 893)
Style of Bakheng (after 893–c 927)
Style of Koh Ker (921–c 945)

Style of Pre Rup (947–965)
Style of Banteay Srei (967–c 1000)
Style of the Khleangs (c 965–1010)
Style of Baphuon (c 1010–c 1080)
Style of Angkor Wat (c 1100–
   c 1175)
Style of Bayon (c 1180–1230)

Between the 7C and the 9C Khmer art in Thailand combined stylistic features derived from Dvaravati models with elements characteristic of pre-Angkor Khmer styles found in Cambodia. From the 10C to the early 13C much of the sculpture and architecture, especially in the northeast, seems actually to have been the work of Khmer artists or produced directly under the supervision of Angkor. As the power and influence of Angkor ebbed in the later 13C and throughout the 14C, a more distinctive Khmer-Lop Buri style emerged.

7C. The earliest **Khmer or Khmer-inspired sculptures** found in Thailand are the relief carvings on three of the sandstone lintels which form an essential part of the structure and the architectural decoration of almost all Khmer temples. They come from two temples in the Chanthaburi area and are in the Sambor Prei Kuk style of the early 7C, decorated with floral pendants, *garuḍas* seizing *nāgas*, and, at either end, *makara* heads disgorging arches. Two are still in situ and one is in the National Museum in Bangkok. Only slightly later are the lintels from Prasat Khao Noi near Aranyaprathet (see p 191), which are in the Sambor Prei Kuk or early Prei Kmeng style and are decorated with a variety of motifs, including floral pendants, medallions, *haṅsas*, *garuḍas* and *makaras* at either end, and a similar lintel originally from Wat Sa Kaeo, Phibun Mungsahan and now at Wat Supatnaram Wora Wihan, Ubon Ratchathani. Of about the same date is the beautiful free-standing sandstone figure of a female deity discovered in Aranyaprathet and now in the Suan Pakkad Palace in Bangkok (see p 143). Another important early lintel, which has unfortunately been badly shattered, comes from Prasat Phumphon, near Surin, the earliest more or less intact Khmer monument in Thailand. It is in the Prei Kmeng style of the late 7C and is decorated with medallions and floral pendants with leogryphs at either end. It is now in the Phimai National Museum, where many of the finest lintels of all periods from Khmer temples in Thailand can be seen beautifully displayed in a new gallery specially built for them (see p 355).

Late 7C to 9C. The earliest Khmer bronze sculptures so far discovered in Thailand are the remarkable group of Mahayana Buddhist figures found at various sites on the Khorat Plateau and in the south of Buri Ram province, and now scattered among various private collections and museums, including the National Museum in Bangkok. Some of the figures are cast in a bronze alloy with an unusually high silver content. Ranging in date from the late 7C to the mid-9C and in height from less than 3cm to over 3m, they consist of images of the Buddha standing in the manner of Mon-Dvaravati images with both hands in *vitarka mudrā*, and of two or four-armed Avalokiteshvara and Maitreya *bodhisattvas* in the pre-Angkor Kompong Preah style that also show some Sri Vijaya influence. Some of the *bodhisattvas* are in a slightly flexed posture and nearly all are represented as youths wearing the elaborate chignon and the short *sompot* round their hips tied at the waist with a bow that denote the ascetic, although some are clad in a *paridhāna*. Some have a diadem ornamented with flowers and a conical headdress or *mukuṭa* reminiscent of 9C Javanese sculpture.

Among the finest pieces of sculpture in the whole history of Southeast Asian religious art are the remarkable group of **8C sandstone figures** of four-armed Brahmanic deities found at Si Thep, which are now in the National Museum in Bangkok (see p 124). Neither Mon nor wholly Khmer in style and execution, they have elements of both. The beautifully proportioned life-size or larger than life-size figures are carved with an extraordinary grace and feeling for movement. The sculptors, with a magnificent disregard for the friability of the stone, have portrayed the youthful gods standing in the *tribhaṅga* posture, their arms joined at the shoulder without any supporting arches or crosspieces and, in the case of one image thought to represent Krishna, with the left arm uplifted. Their faces are flat-nosed and thick-lipped and have a quality at once sensuous and refined. They have cylindrical or polygonal mitres, beneath which their hair falls in ringlets over the nape of their necks and, most unusually, they wear round their hips and thighs a short loincloth with a pleated flap in front.

10C to 14C. Khmer political control and cultural influence was strongest between the 10C and the 13C, so most of the great temples, such as Phimai and Phanom Rung, that were built on the Khorat Plateau and elsewhere in the northeast, date from this period. They were adorned with magnificent carved sandstone lintels and other architectural decorations, of which some are still in situ but most are now in the National Museum in Phimai. Those from Prasat Phimai are perhaps both the most beautiful and technically the most accomplished. Represent- ations of Hindu deities, particularly of Vishnu mounted on Garuda or asleep on the cosmic serpent Ananta, and of Shiva and Uma riding the bull Nandi, and scenes from the *Rāmāyaṇa* predominate.

Khmer-Lopburi
Buddha head, 13C

The statues of this period are on the whole less notable, though some of the images of the Buddha crowned and in royal attire, both in sandstone and bronze, are of high quality. Some of these crowned images show the Buddha standing in *abhaya mudrā*, in others he is seated in meditation protected by the *nāga* king Mucalinda. In the latter, the three heads on either side of the sevenfold hood of the *nāga* are usually turned inwards towards the head in the centre, unlike Dvaravati statues of the same subject, in which the head is turned outwards. The Buddha's robe usually covers both shoulders. The face is square with thick lips and straight eyebrows joining above the flat, wide nose. The *uṣṇīṣa* is conical and decorated with lotus flowers and roundels, and his diadem has a band in the centre with a lozenge motif and more roundels. The Buddha carries princely ornaments, including long pendant earrings, a necklace with a medallion on the chest, armlets and a jewelled belt.

The bronze and sandstone sculpture of the late 12C and early 13C is virtually indistinguishable both in style and subject matter from the sculpture in the Bayon style that was being produced in Cambodia and Champa at the same time. It consists chiefly of figures of the Buddha sheltered by the *nāga* king, of Avalokiteshvara seated against a stela, and of *dvārapālas* and guardian lions. Much of it is rather coarse and heavy, as, for example, the radiating Avalokiteshvara from the 13C temple of Muang Sing near Kanchanaburi in the far west of the Khmer empire, a monument which is also almost wholly lacking in any architectural decoration (see p 159). At its best, however, the sculpture of this period, as, for example, the presumed portrait statues of Jayavarman VII, one of which was made for Phimai, is of great distinction. The architectural decoration is notable chiefly for its repetitiveness and lack of originality, with the exception of the stucco carving, of which the little that remains in anything like its original state, as, for example, at Phra Prang Sam Yot, Lop Buri (see p 196), is of high quality. Also of exceptional refinement and elegance are the small bronze objects made during this period—statuettes of deities, some of them Tantric in character, fittings for chariots and palanquins, bells and lamps.

We have already noted that the earliest Khmer monument in Thailand to survive more or less unaltered is Prasat Phumphon, near Surin, which dates from the second half of the 7C (see p 366), and also that most of the Khmer monuments in the northeast were built between the 10C and the 13C. The majority of these consist either of a single tower on a T-shaped platform, or three towers on a rectangular platform, or five towers on several platforms. However, from the late 11C temples on a far more elaborate plan began to be built, as, for example, at Phimai, Phanom Wan and Phanom Rung. The reign of the Mahayana Buddhist Jayavarman VII was marked by the construction throughout the Khmer empire of many so-called 'hospitals' (*arogyasālā*) and resthouses (*dharmasālā*), as well as the building of new temples and the conversion of existing ones to Buddhist use.

In the late 13C and 14C, as the power of Angkor in central and northeast Thailand dwindled, Khmer stylistic influences became weaker. However, it was during this period that, perhaps because the kings of Sukhothai and Ayutthaya were anxious to assert their legitimacy as heirs of the rulers of Angkor, the Thai *prang*, a type of tower-sanctuary shaped somewhat like a corn-cob and modelled closely on the Khmer tower-sanctuary or *prasat*, became a prominent feature of Thai temples, and has remained so ever since.

The chief building material used by the Khmers in the earlier period was brick, later replaced by laterite, with sandstone extensively employed for lintels, pediments, door frames, colonnettes and other surfaces to which decorative carving could be applied. Carving was also sometimes applied to brick surfaces after the bricks had been put in place and then coated with stucco. A vegetable glue was used instead of mortar to bind bricks together, nor was mortar used for sandstone, large pieces of which were sometimes held together by the insertion of iron pins.

Sukhothai

Sukhothai is generally considered to be the cradle of Thai civilisation and its sculpture and architecture to be among the finest achievements of Thai art. Although the Sukhothai period saw the emergence of the first truly and distinctively Thai art style and the creation of two wholly original religious art forms—the lotus-bud *chedi* in architecture and the walking Buddha image in sculpture—yet Sukhothai art owes much not only to Mon and Khmer models, but also to Sri Lanka, to which the Thais of Sukhothai looked as the centre of orthodox Theravada Buddhist and Buddhist art forms.

The **sculpture** of the Sukhothai period consists chiefly of images of the Buddha in bronze, sometimes gilded, and in stuccoed brick or laterite, the latter often in relief. It is marked by a tendency towards stylisation and idealisation arising from the sculptors' desire to reproduce as exactly as possible the features described in the ancient Pali texts as marking the great man, or *cakravartin*, as well as certain other features traditionally attributed to the historical Buddha. Sukhothai artists were also the first to portray the Buddha in all four attitudes (*iriyāpatha*)—walking, standing, seated and reclining.

The head of the Sukhothai Buddha is surmounted by an *uṣṇīṣa*, above which is a flame-like finial (*rasmi*) symbolising his radiance; the hair has small conical curls and comes to a point in the centre of the forehead; the face is oval, with steeply arched eyebrows meeting above the nose, which is shaped like a parrot's beak; the eyes are lowered under heavy lids; the mouth is small with curving, faintly smiling lips; the neck has three lines incised under the chin. The body is asexual and without musculature, with exaggeratedly broad shoulders and a very narrow waist, the arms are sinuous and long like the trunk of an elephant, the fingers are of almost equal length, the heels project behind. The right shoulder is usually bare, and, as with the Buddha of Grahi (see above), the *sanghāṭī*, rather than the flap of the *uttarāsanga*, is draped over the left shoulder,

reaching to the navel and ending in a pleated fish-tail. The belt, if represented at all, is indicated only by a shallow groove or incised line. Standing images, however, sometimes have both shoulders covered and wear a broad belt with a flap in front in low relief.

The great majority of the **seated Buddha images** are in *vīrāsana*, with the right hand in *bhūmisparśa mudrā*, while standing Buddha images are more often shown with the right hand in *abhaya mudrā*, and walking images in *vitarka mudrā*. Images of the Buddha sheltered by the *nāga* king are rare in the Sukhothai period and found only in stucco reliefs, as at Wat Chedi Chet Thaeo in Si Satchanalai (see p 242). Images of the Buddha in *dharmacakra mudrā* are unknown. Reclining Buddha images rest on their right side. The larger standing Buddha

Sukhothai seated Buddha, 14C

images are more commonly in high relief than free-standing, although the Sukhothai period saw the production of numerous large free-standing statues known as the Eighteen Cubit Buddha or Phra Attharot, such as that at Wat Saphan Hin, on the west side of Sukhothai (see p 236). In some *wat*, either in the *wihan* or in a separate *mondop*, colossal images of the Buddha in each of the four attitudes are to be found, sometimes as high as nine metres.

Large images of **Hindu deities** were made in the Sukhothai period for use in court ceremonies and rituals performed by *brāhman* priests. These are similar in style to the Buddha images, but are sumptuously clad in royal attire, with a *mukuta* crown and an intricately decorated *paridhāna* with layers of flaring pleats on either side. Images of Shiva and Harihara often have the Brahmanic thread tied with a *nāga's* head on the left shoulder.

The **Buddha's Footprint** was much revered by the Thais of Sukhothai, and representations of it were closely modelled on the original Footprint on the summit of Adam's Peak in Sri Lanka. They are often adorned with the 108 auspicious signs and the Wheel of the Law.

Architectural decoration was chiefly in stucco, although terracotta and glazed ceramics were also used to some extent for smaller decorative features. Apart from the Buddha images placed in niches or carved in relief on the walls of Sukhothai monuments, the most notable of these decorations are those that surround the bases of some important *chedi*, such as the procession of praying disciples round the central *chedi* of Wat Mahathat in Sukhothai and the stuccoed laterite figures of elephants, usually only their foreparts, in niches round the bases of several *chedi* in Sukhothai, Si Satchanalai and Kamphaeng Phet. The idea of surrounding a *chedi* with elephants was probably inspired by the elephants at Anuradhapura in Sri Lanka. Friezes of walking Buddhas occur on the *harmikās* of some Sukhothai *chedi*, for example at Wat Chang Lom in Si Satchanalai, which also has free-standing elephants surrounding the base (see p 242).

The plan of the capital city of Sukhothai and the other cities of the Sukhothai kingdom closely followed Khmer models and paid due attention to traditional Buddhist cosmology. Likewise, the disposition of the different buildings in the Sukhothai *wat*—*chedi*, *ubosot*, *wihan* and the rest—generally also followed the same cosmological precepts. Stylistically, however, there was great variety among different buildings and even different parts of the same building in a temple complex. The *ubosot* and the *wihan* as well as the monks' living quarters were usually made of wood, especially during the early Sukhothai period, so all that remains of them today are their laterite or brick foundations and some of the pillars that supported the roofs. However, the *chedi*, the most important building in the *wat*, was made of laterite or brick and took a wide variety of forms. The bell-shaped *chedi* found in many Sukhothai temples is derived from Sri Lankan models, while the square *chedi* is of Mon inspiration, and the lotus-bud finial above the relic chamber, of which the central *chedi* of Wat Mahathat in Sukhothai is the best known example, is Sukhothai's own original contribution to temple architecture in Thailand. Sometimes the *chedi* is replaced by a *prang* or tower-sanctuary of Khmer type, especially in *wat* built in the Sukhothai period on the site of an earlier Khmer foundation, such as Wat Phra Si Ratana Mahathat at Chaliang near Si Satchanalai (see p 239).

Lan Na

Lan Na and the other early Thai states in northern Thailand produced a very distinctive style of Theravada Buddhist art. Lan Na art is generally divided into two periods—the earlier Chiang Saen style, which shows traces of Pala influence, probably transmitted via Pagan in Burma, and the later Chiang Saen or Chiang Mai style, which is closer to the indigenous style developed contemporaneously in Sukhothai and shares with it some characteristics of Sri Lankan art, especially during the reign of King Tilokaratcha in the second half of the 15C, when there was direct contact between Lan Na and Sri Lanka. These terms are used because, although the city of Chiang Saen did not become the capital of Lan Na until 1327, there is some evidence to suggest that the first truly Thai images of the Buddha were made by Thai settlers in the Chiang Saen region, perhaps as early as the 11C.

Lan Na seated Buddha, 13C

Lan Na sculpture. As in Sukhothai, bronze was the preferred medium of Lan Na sculptors, and sculpture in stone is rare, although fine work in stucco and terracotta was also produced, and Lan Na woodcarving, which made use of the abundant supplies of teak available from the forests of northern Thailand, although little survives earlier than the 18C, was of the highest quality. The Buddha seated in *vajrāsana* on a lotus base and making the *bhūmisparśa mudrā* is the most frequent type, and only a few standing, walking and reclining Buddha images and statues of Brahmanic deities exist. Some features of the early Buddha images indicate the possibility of influences from nearby Haripunjaya and from Sukhothai as well as from Pala art. Buddha images in the **Chiang Saen style** are characterised by a hemispherical *uṣṇīṣa* set on large curls and surmounted by a bulbous ornament shaped like a lotus-bud. The face is rounded, with arched, clearly separated eyebrows, lowered eyes, a sharp nose and small, somewhat fleshy mouth. The body has broad shoulders and a narrow waist. The whole of the right breast, which is well-rounded, is uncovered, and the flap of the robe (or *sanghātī*) is short, ending above the left breast. There is usually no belt, and the top of the *antaravāsaka* is merely outlined at the waist to indicate the transparency of the Buddha's robe and the radiance of his skin.

Buddha images of the later or **Chiang Mai period** are generally more stylised and closer to Sukhothai or Lao types. The Buddha is seated in the *vīrāsana* position, the *uṣṇīṣa* is surmounted by a flame, the face is more oval and has a slightly supercilious expression, the body is slimmer, and the flap of the robe is much longer and ends near the navel.

Some Lan Na Buddha images are crowned and richly adorned and gilded, and these are taken to represent the Buddha disguised as a king humbling the heretic King Jambupati. Lan Na artists also made very fine gilded metal votive objects, figures of sacred animals, reliquaries, and miniature representations of shrines, as is shown by the collection of such objects found in 1960 at Hot and now

Lan Na seated Buddha,
13C–14C

displayed in the National Museum in Bangkok. They also excelled at making votive objects in crystal and semi-precious stones, and it has been suggested that the Emerald Buddha (see p 117–8) may be the work of a Lan Na sculptor. On stylistic grounds alone, however, this seems unlikely.

Some of the stucco and terracotta relief sculpturs of Lan Na are exceptionally fine. Notable examples include the exquisite stucco figures of praying deities on the laterite walls of the base of the *chedi* of Wat Chet Yot, Chiang Mai (see p208), the stucco and terracotta decorations and figures of the standing Buddha and of deities in niches in the square *chedi* of Wat Pa Sak, Chiang Saen (see p 298) and the superb stucco figures on the base of the *ho trai* of Wat Phra Sing Luang in Chiang Mai (see p 277).

Lan Na temple architecture demonstrates a great variety of styles, and influences from Sukothai and Ayutthaya, Laos, Burma and Sri Lanka can sometimes all be discerned in different buildings in the same temple complex. The *ubosot, wihan, ho trai* and other monastic buildings are often made of wood taken from the teak forests that once covered much of northern Thailand and are characterised by their low walls or open sides and sweeping, multi-tiered roofs with wooden tiles and much ornately carved wooden decoration. These are either set on low walls or, if the building is open-sided, supported on short columns. In later temple complexes the wooden structures usually stand on brick or laterite bases, often adorned with stucco decoration, as on the *ho trai* of Wat Phra Sing in Chiang Mai (see p 277). The wooden monastic buildings of Wat Phra That Lampang Luang, southwest of Lampang (see p 267), are among the finest in northern Thailand and also contain much fine stucco decoration, including a magnificent gilded *ku* enshrining the principal Buddha image. Temples in the Burmese style are distinguished by the multi-tiered pyramidal towers, symbolising Mount Meru and decorated with intricate fretwork, that surmount their roofs. *Chedi* are sometimes in the form of a tiered pyramid on a square base with niches at each level, a type derived from Mon Haripunjaya, as for example at Wat Pa Sak, Chiang Saen, but more commonly have round or octagonal bell-shaped domes of Sri Lankan type, sometimes gilded or covered with sheets of gilded bronze and standing on a high redented base. The 15C *chedi* of Wat Chet Yot is copied directly from the famous Mahabodhi temple at Bodh Gaya in northeast India, while the 16C brick *chedi* of Wat Rampoeng outside Chiang Mai closely resembles a Chinese pagoda.

U Thong (Suphan Buri, Sankhaburi and Early Ayutthaya)

The kingdom of Ayutthaya was founded in 1351 by U Thong, whose name has been given to a town near Suphan Buri to the west of Ayutthaya and to a school of art that flourished in the Chao Phraya basin, and in particular in Suphan Buri and Chai Nat provinces, during the century preceeding the foundation of Ayutthaya and the first fifty years after it. The three phases that have been distinguished in the art of this style have been designated U Thong A, B and C or, in

Early U Thong seated Buddha, 13C

Piriya Krairiksh's classification, Suphan Buri, Sankhaburi and Early Ayutthaya.

U Thong sculpture consists almost entirely of bronze images of the Buddha seated in *vīrāsana* and making the *bhūmisparśa mudrā*, though a few early pieces in sandstone and stucco are known. Images in the **U Thong A** style of the second half of the 13C continue the tradition of Khmer-Lopburi art and also have features which seem to derive from Mon Haripunjaya. They have no flame above the *uṣṇīṣa*, the curls of the head are small and conical, there is a band below the hairline, and the eyebrows are straight and meet above the nose. The flap of the robe over the left shoulder is long and ends in a straight line. The proportions of the body are such that the width between the knees is only slightly less than the height. Images in the **U Thong B** style, dating from the late 13C to the mid 14C, are distinguished from those in the Suphan Buri style by the tall, stylised flame above the *uṣṇīṣa*, which is ringed round the base with lotus-petals, the even smaller curls, and the narrower proportions of the body.

Late U Thong seated Buddha, 14C–15C

Images in the **U Thong C** or early Ayutthaya style date from the foundation of Ayutthaya to the mid-15C. They closely follow the Sukhothai tradition, with a more oval face than Sankhaburi images, the *sanghātī* extending as far as the navel and ending in a fish-tail, and with fingers of unequal length, but they retain the band below the hairline and the unsmiling expression of Khmer-Lopburi and U Thong A images.

At the beginning of the **Ayutthaya period** proper in the mid-15C, there was a resurgence of Khmer influence as a result of Ayutthaya's conquest of Angkor in 1431/32. However, Ayutthaya sculptures seem to have attempted to avoid both what they saw as the excessive realism of Lopburi art and the exaggerated deference to the exact words of the ancient texts that marks much Sukhothai sculpture, and tried to achieve a new spirituality and purity based on classical perfection of form and technical excellence. The sculpture is chiefly bronze, with some sandstone, stucco and wood. The use of carved wood was chiefly confined to temple doors and pediments, and many of the finest of these wood sculptures were destroyed in the sack of Ayutthaya by the Burmese in 1767. The great majority of the images are of the Buddha seated in *bhūmisparśa mudrā*, but standing images in a variety of *mudrās*, and reclining images, often of colossal size, are also commonly found. Most of the features characteristic of U Thong C sculpture are retained. The curls of the hair are small and the *uṣṇīṣa* is surmounted by a flame ornament. The eyes are lowered beneath prominent lids and arched eyebrows, the lips are faintly smiling and surrounded by a ridge or incised line, which in stone images represents a moustache. The robe of the seated images is generally draped in the Sukhothai style, leaving the right shoulder bare, while on the standing images it covers both shoulders, as in Khmer-Lopburi sculpture. Some Ayutthaya images are draped in the Chinese manner, with the right shoulder bare except for a small flap brought forward from the back. The bases of the images become taller and more elaborate and sometimes contain depictions in relief of scenes from the Life of the Buddha.

In the reign of Prasat Thong in the mid-17C, when the Khmer kingdom of Cambodia again fell under Thai suzerainty, there was a revival of the carving of stone images in the Khmer style, though in these images the Buddha continued to be portrayed with a distinctively Thai oval face and a flame *uṣṇīṣa*. Figures of Shiva, Vishnu and other Brahmanic deities, as well as of *garuḍas*, *haṁsas*, lions and other animals, were also made in this period, in bronze, wood, stone or stucco.

From the mid-17C to the end of the Ayutthaya period in 1767, there was a great increase in the making of crowned images of the Buddha in royal attire, wearing tall, tapering headdresses, elaborate jewellery, including wing-like ornaments behind the ears, and robes with incised decoration. Much of this ornamentation appears to have been copied from the ceremonial dress worn by the kings of Ayutthaya at their coronations.

During the Ayutthaya period the **architecture** of the various buildings of the *wat* had already acquired most of the features that today are still essential elements in their design. These included a bell-shaped *chedi* or Khmer-style *prang*, and a *wihan* and *ubosot* with multi-tiered, low-sweeping and overlapping tiled roofs, and richly decorated triangular gables framed by barge boards in the form of *nāgas* adorned with flame-like *bai raka* ornaments and surmounted by *cho fa* finials. The roof would be supported outside the hall on square or round columns, usually with lotus capitals. There would often be porches at front and rear, with similar roofs, gables and columns, and the whole edifice would stand on a platform curved like the sides of a boat, possibly symbolising the voyage of the faithful across the sea of life towards *nirvāṇa*. Although before the 15C both *ubosot* and *wihan* were usually open-sided halls, by the mid-Ayutthaya period they generally had walls with thin slits pierced in them to admit light, although the interior pillars still bore most of the weight of the roof. Later, thicker walls were built that could take the weight of the roof and permit windows to be made. Sometimes these windows had lancet arches, said to have been introduced into Ayutthaya by the Persians and Europeans. Doors and window shutters were decorated with carved wood or lacquer, mother-of-pearl and glass mosaic inlay. The precinct of the *ubosot* was marked by *bai sema*, each one covered in a canopy, and temple buildings were often surrounded by galleries containing rows of Buddha images.

Ratanakosin

Both the sculpture and the architecture of the Ratanakosin period have generally remained faithful to the traditions of the later Ayutthaya period right up to the present day. In the early years of this period, relatively few new **Buddha**

images were commissioned, and instead a concerted attempt was made in the reign of Rama I to preserve and restore as many as possible of the images that had survived the sack of Ayutthaya in 1767 and to assemble them in Bangkok. It is thought that about 1200 Buddha images were rescued in this way. It was done partly as a practical means of providing suitable images speedily for the new monasteries that were being built in the capital, partly in order to collect together the merit accumulated in those images, and partly to contribute to the legitimisation of the new dynasty as the spiritual as well as the political heirs of Ayutthaya. Those new images that were made, whether cast in bronze, carved in wood or constructed of stucco over brick, strictly followed the orthodox artistic and iconographic traditions of Ayutthaya. Buddha images in royal attire, with elaborate jewellery, decorated robes and tall, tapering headdresses, continued to be made in large numbers, and there was also some widening of the iconographic range of Buddhist sculpture. For example, Rama III commissioned a series of statues, of which 34 were made and are now in Wat Phra Kaeo in Bangkok (see p 120), to illustrate the 40 most important events in the Life of the Buddha, and in the National Museum in Bangkok there is a group of 29 miniature statues from the same period illustrating events in the Buddha's Life. With the accession to the throne of King Mongkut in 1851, Western artistic ideas began to make themselves more strongly felt, and sculptors began trying to humanise Buddha images by making them more naturalistic and eliminating such supernatural attributes as the *uṣṇīṣa*. This tendency was associated with a revival of interest in the Graeco-Roman Gandhara style of 1C–3C India. There was also an increasing interest in sculptures of disciples, *riṣis*, notable Buddhist monks such as Phra Malai, Brahmanic deities, *dvārapālas*, *kinnaris* and other mythical creatures.

In **architecture**, with one or two notable exceptions, such as Wat Sala Loi in Nakhon Ratchasima (see p 349), there has been an even more slavish adherence to Ayutthaya models. Throughout the Ratanakosin period up to the present day, temples have almost invariably been constructed with a bell-shaped *chedi*, often tiered and redented, or a Khmer-style *prang*, and an *ubosot* and *wihan* of a conventional Ayutthaya type. Only in the decoration is a measure of deviation from strict orthodoxy sometimes apparent. Some temples, for example, show Chinese influence, and Chinese decorative motifs and pieces of Chinese ceramic are used to ornament them, and there is a general tendency to apply elaborate and sometimes garish decoration in the exterior of temple buildings, with much coloured glass mosaic inlay and ornately carved wooden gables. This tendency is well illustrated in the *ubosot* of Wat Phra Kaeo in Bangkok (see p 117), which houses the Emerald Buddha, and, in a different style, the great *prang* of Wat Arun in Thon Buri (see p 148), both of which are covered in exceptionally sumptuous decoration, but are entirely orthodox in plan.

Wall painting

Largely as a result of the ravages of warfare and of the climate, and especially of damage from water coming through leaking roofs, very few wall paintings earlier than the end of the 18C have survived, although one fragment, in the crypt of Wat Ratchaburana in Ayutthaya (see p 206), dates back to the 15C. However, the painting of religious scenes has always been considered an act of merit similar to the making of a Buddha image, and wall paintings also have a didactic purpose, so even the humblest *wat* will generally be decorated inside, and sometimes outside as well, with murals portraying scenes from the Life of the Buddha, from the *jātaka* tales, particularly the last ten (*Totsachat*), or from the three worlds (*Traiphum*) and 31 levels of existence of Buddhist cosmology.

For the same reasons, mural painters follow iconographic conventions almost as strict as those observed by the sculptors. These conventions extend to the placing of certain scenes on particular walls. For example, episodes from the *jātakas* are generally painted on the lower part of the lateral walls of the *wihan* and are surmounted by rows of celestial beings in the upper part, while the Buddha's Victory over Mara is traditionally depicted on the east wall above the entrance, and cosmological scenes are to be found on the west wall behind the principal Buddha image.

In the scenes portraying religious subjects, divine, human and animal figures, architecture and landscape are all portrayed in a flat, stylised manner, and there is no diminution of size to convey the idea of horizontal distance. Instead, an aerial perspective is used in which every object in every scene is painted in the same minute detail, so that it is as if the whole scene were being viewed from above. Succeeding episodes are presented as if they are happening simultaneously, only separated from each other by zigzag lines, or by buildings, rocks or areas of landscape, and there is much use of decorative foliage, flowers, birds and animals, painted in a more naturalistic manner and often showing Chinese influence. The depiction of celestial, royal and other exalted characters, with their graceful attitudes and serene facial expressions, is always highly formal and stylised, whereas the figures and buildings in the scenes from daily life painted at the edges of the main scenes are portrayed with greater realism and sometimes no little humour. The wall paintings of Lan Na temples are generally in a more informal and naturalistic style and often contain lively and charming scenes of daily life and customs in northern Thailand.

By the reign of King Mongkut, Western influence had brought about a greater degree of naturalism in Thai mural painting, and the use of perspective and shading, which was often combined with the traditional aerial perspective, as for example in the murals at Wat Phra Kaeo in Bangkok (see p 120). At the same time, although traditional religious subjects still predominated, there were more depictions of scenes from both village and court life, including the person of the king himself. Khrua In Khong, a monk who was court painter to King Mongkut, is generally credited with having first introduced Western techniques and Western subject matter into Thai mural painting, although he had never travelled outside Thailand. His work is to be seen in several temples, notably Wat Bowon Niwet, where King Mongkut was a monk before coming to the throne. In the reign of King Chulalongkorn, these Western influences became more pronounced, as more Thai artists studied under Western teachers in the newly established art schools. The most influential of these teachers was the Italian Corrado Feroci, who came to Thailand in the early 1930s and lived there until his death in 1962, adopting the Thai name of Silpa Bhirasri. Today, the best Thai mural painters create a judicious blend of styles, using traditional Thai techniques and conventional Buddhist iconography for the depiction of religious subjects and a more naturalistic Western style for portraying scenes of daily life.

In the Ayutthaya period pastel colours on a white or cream background were generally used, although in many cases these pale tones may be the result of fading. Most of the colours were made from locally available materials, such as indigo, cinnabar, soot and white clay, with gold leaf used only for highlighting. During the 19C mural paintings became more sumptuous and their detail more elaborate. Painters made increasing use of gold set against a dark background and of tempera colours imported from China, which gave them a more varied palette.

The **traditional technique** is first to apply a series of washes to the wall to remove the salt from it, and then to lay several priming coats composed of white chalk bound with a solution of boiled tamarind seeds. The priming coats are sealed by one or more further washes in pale colours. The design is drawn in outline in ochre or black and the tempera pigments applied when the priming is dry, and not as in European fresco painting when it is still wet. This technique, since it does not permit the colour to penetrate deep into the priming, tends to reduce the durability of the painting.

Decorative Arts

The Thais lavish as much skill and attention on the design and decoration of objects of all kinds in all manner of materials, ranging from lacquered wood musical instruments to ivory elephant howdahs and from paper kites to silver betel sets, particularly those that have a ceremonial or religious function, as they do on the casting of a bronze Buddha image or the building of a *wat*, and many of the decorative motifs derive from Hindu and Buddhist originals.

Basket making

The Thais use basketry, woven from bamboo, rattan and other materials, to make both utensils for daily use and ceremonial objects. In southern Thailand the stems of the *yan lipao* vine, which grows in great quantities in that area, are polished and woven to make containers such as rice-baskets and betel-

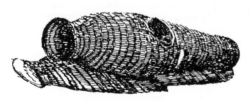

An example of the type of bamboo woven shrimp trap found in all regions of Thailand (c 70–80cm long)

boxes, trays, and increasingly, as a result of the support for this craft given by Queen Sirikit, handbags and other fashion accessories.

Ceramics

Ceramics have been made in Thailand since **prehistoric times**. The earliest cord-marked pottery found at Ban Chiang and other sites near Udon Thani in northeastern Thailand (see p 327) dates from the fourth millennium BC, while the production of painted wares in the same area seems to have begun about 1200 BC, and the well known red-on-buff wares were manufactured there from the 3C BC until the 3C AD. During the Dvaravati period from the 7C to the 11C, unglazed pottery and terracotta figurines and architectural ornaments were made in the Mon kingdoms of Dvaravati and Haripunjaya, and the fine earthenware that has been found at the Sri Vijaya site of Sathing Phra belongs to the same period. During the 11C and 12C Khmer ceramics, predominantly green-and brown-glazed stonewares, were produced at various sites on the Khorat Plateau, particularly in Buri Ram province.

In the **Thai kingdom of Sukhothai** the main centres of ceramics production were kilns near the city of Sukhothai itself and at Si Satchanalai. It was previously believed that these kilns were set up by Chinese potters brought to Sukhothai at the end of the 13C, but recent archaeological research has revealed that they were established 50 or more years before this and that Chinese potters are unlikely to have been involved. The earliest Sukhothai wares were unglazed, but later glazes of various colours were introduced, including celadon, accompanied by finely incised underglaze decoration.

In the **Ayutthaya period**, production of ceramics at Sawankhalok and Si Satchanalai continued, with occasional interruptions, until the early 17C. Perhaps the most characteristic of the later Sukhothai wares are those with a pale grey or green slip on which motifs of fish, flowers or geometric patterns are painted. Ceramic architectural ornaments, such as finials, tiles and balustrades, were also made in large quantities at least from the mid-14C. After the prohibition of overseas trade by the Ming emperors in China in the 14C, a flourishing export trade developed in Thai ceramics, chiefly to Indonesia and the Philippines.

In the north of Thailand, early kiln sites have been discovered at Kalong, Paan, San Kamphaeng, Phayao and Lamphun. These sites reveal that both monochrome and decorated wares similar to those produced in Sukhothai were being manufactured in Lan Na from about 1300. However, the production of ceramics in Lan Na remained on a small scale, partly because the ready availability of teak made the production of ceramic building materials unnecessary and partly because there was no export trade in these northern wares.

The technique of making the multi-coloured overglazed enamel wares known as *bencharong* was developed in China in the 15C, and the export of these wares to Ayutthaya began in the late 16C. Gilded *bencharong* wares called *lai nam thong* were also made for the exclusive use of royalty. *Bencharong* ceased to be made in China after the revolution of 1912, but its manufacture has recently been revived in Thailand.

Gold, silver and niello

Gold and silver objects dating back to the 8C have been found at various sites in central Thailand, the northeast and the peninsula. Gold and silver have been used over the centuries to make an enormous variety of objects, including votive plaques and reliquaries, jewellery, ceremonial bowls and trays, betel sets, domestic utensils and the miniature trees (*bunga mas* and *bunga perak*) given as tribute to the Thai kings by Malay rulers.

The skills of the goldsmiths of Ayutthaya are demonstrated by the spectacular 15C treasure found in Wat Ratchaburana and other Ayutthaya temples and now housed in the Chao Sam Phraya National Museum in Ayutthaya (see p 209). It includes several pieces of extremely fine filigree work. Gold is also used for the crown and elaborately jewelled robes which the king presents to the Emerald Buddha for each season of the year. Today, the goldsmiths of

Phetchaburi, some of whom are Chinese, are noted for the quality of the jewellery and other objects that they make from gold mined locally at Bang Saphan near Prachuap Khiri Khan.

The most accomplished silversmiths in Thailand are considered to be in Chiang Mai, where some 500 silversmiths are said to have fled from Burma after the capture of Pagan by the Mongols in 1284, and the work of the Chiang Mai silversmiths shows a strong Burmese influence. Bangkok, where many of the smiths are Chinese, and Nakhon Si Thammarat are also important centres. Until recently silver was obtained by melting down Indian and Chinese coins. The objects are generally decorated with repoussé work, which requires the use of almost pure silver, or with niello. Designs include all the traditional Hindu and Buddhist motifs, mythical animals, lotus petals and other floral and vegetal motifs, flames (*kranok*) and diaper patterns.

Niello is thought by some scholars to have been introduced into Thailand by the Portuguese, but it is more likely that it was first brought from Persia to Southeast Asia by Indian merchants. It is a form of decoration in which a design is engraved or etched on to a piece of gold or silver and the incisions are filled with a black amalagam composed of lead, copper and silver, which is annealed with the gold or silver by heating and is then filed smooth and polished. More intricate detail is added by the incision of fine lines. It is used to decorate all manner of objects from teapots to large pieces of furniture such as the throne in the Chakri Mahaprasat Hall in the Grand Palace in Bangkok (see p 122) on which the king sits to receive ambassadors when they present their credentials. Nakhon Si Thammarat is the leading centre of niello production in Thailand, and the museum of Wat Mahathat there contains a notable collection of silver and niello work.

Lacquer

The art of making lacquer may have been brought from China by the first Tai immigrants, but the earliest surviving pieces in Thailand are no older than the Ayutthaya period. Also of Chinese origin is the technique of gilding black lacquer (*lai rod nam*) by painting a solution of gamboge on to the lacquer as a resist (similar to the use of wax in batik-making) and then applying gold leaf with a wad of cotton-wool to those parts of the design which are to be gilded. It was brought to a high pitch of excellence by Thai craftsmen in the 18C and 19C. The technique lends itself to the composition of panoramic scenes in the manner of mural painting, in which human figures, birds and animals are depicted against an elaborate background of floral and vegetal motifs, frequently showing Chinese influence. Scenes from the Life of the Buddha and the *Ramakien* are very popular. As the gilding of a sacred object is considered to be a specially meritorious act, *lai rod nam* is used chiefly to decorate Buddhist manuscript chests and cupboards, and doors and window shutters in temple and palace buildings. The walls of the lacquer pavilion in the Suan Pakkad Palace in Bangkok (see p 143) are decorated with gilded lacquer work of quite extraordinary elegance and refinement.

Manuscript painting

Thai manuscripts are written either on palm leaf or on paper in folding books, and both types are frequently illustrated. The earliest surviving examples of palm leaf manuscripts date from the 16C. They were used almost exclusively for Buddhist texts and were written on long thin strips of dried palm leaf, usually about 6 x 60cm, and the text and decoration were either inscribed in ink or by means of incisions into which a lamp-black paste made of soot was rubbed to darken the lines. The strips were then bundled together and tied together by means of two strings threaded through holes at either end. The outer leaves were often lacquered and gilded, and sometimes the bundles were placed between boards of carved and inlaid wood, mother-of-pearl or ivory. In the monasteries the manuscripts were kept in decorated cabinets, and the libraries (*ho trai*) in which the cabinets were placed were frequently built over water to protect them from the attacks of termites.

Paper books were used for both Buddhist and secular texts and for official documents and correspondence. The paper was made from the bark of a bush known in Thai as *khoi* (*Steblus asper*). Like the palm leaf manuscripts, the outer leaves of the books were often decorated with lacquer and gilding, and they were generally stored in decorated wooden boxes.

The subject matter of Thai illustrated manuscripts includes the three worlds of Buddhist cosmology (*Traiphum*), divination, treatises on animals (particularly elephants, because of their symbolical and semi-religious significance and the reverence accorded to the so-called white elephant), *jātaka* tales, particularly the last ten (*Totsachat*), the story of the visits of Phra Malai to Heaven and Hell, and other Buddhist themes, though stories from the Life of the historical Buddha are relatively rare. Among notable illustrated manuscripts dealing with purely secular themes are the pencil drawings now in the British Library, London, of Thai dancers and actors and contemporary events done by Bun Khong for his British employer, James Low, in the 1820s.

Mother-of-pearl inlay

The complicated technique of decorating objects made of wood or rattan with mother-of-pearl inlay (*hoi fai*) obtained from the translucent pink and green shell of the turban snail, which is indigenous to the Gulf of Thailand, dates back at least to the 6C AD. Traces have been found in pieces of stucco on a Dvaravati monument at Khu Bua near Ratchaburi and on some Sri Vijaya and early Lan Na Buddha images. However, it seems that not until the late Ayutthaya period did it begin to be used extensively for the decoration of doors and window shutters, manuscript cupboards and chests, screens, ceremonial containers for gifts and offerings, monks' alms bowls, betel boxes, wooden book covers, musical instruments and other objects. Motifs include Buddhist scenes, Hindu deities, mythical birds and animals, lotus buds and other floral and vegetal motifs, and flames (*kranok*). The National Museum in Bangkok and the Suan Pakkad Palace in Bangkok contain important collections of mother-of-pearl objects, most of them dating from the 19C. Other notable examples of mother-of-pearl inlay include the throne in the Dusit Hall of the Grand Palace in Bangkok, the 108 auspicious signs on the feet of the Reclining Buddha in Wat Pho, Bangkok, the doors of Wat Phra Si Ratana Mahathat, Phitsanulok, and the three pairs of doors from Wat Borom Phuttharam, Ayutthaya, now in Bangkok, one pair in

Wat Benchamabophit, one in Wat Phra Kaeo and the third made into the doors of a manuscript cupboard in the National Museum.

Textiles

Traditional Thai textiles are almost invariably make of silk or cotton and, although there have always been marked differences between textiles made for the court and those produced for daily use in the villages, both materials are used for both types and at their best demonstrate equally great weaving skills and an impressive variety of techniques and designs. The cultivation and harvesting of cotton, the breeding and gathering of silkworms, reeling, spinning, weaving and dyeing have traditionally been carried out by the women, the role of the men being confined to making the looms, shuttles and other equipment. Until recently in the rural areas all women were taught to weave in early childhood by their female relations, and patterns were handed down from generation to generation. Certain weaves, patterns and colours, and certain garments were associated with different religious ceremonies, both Buddhist and animist, particularly those surrounding the ordination of monks, and with birth, marriage and other rites of passage, or denoted rank, status or occupation. There were also clear differences of pattern and style between different regions and ethnic groups. Only 50 years ago it was still possible in rural Thailand to tell the ethnic origin of any Tai woman from her *phasin*, the ankle-length tubular skirt then universally worn, and the sash or wrap known in northern Thailand as *pha sabai* and in the northeast as *pha biang* that she carried over her shoulder or used to cover her breasts, while the equally universal daily wear for men in the rural areas was the *pha sarong*, the male equivalent of the *phasin*, with a brightly coloured check pattern for young men and a darker check for older men. But, except among the hill tribes, these associations and distinctions are rapidly disappearing, as more and more Thais wear clothes made from factory-produced textiles or have adopted Western dress.

The range of colours produced from **vegetable and insect dyes** is relatively limited and includes red and pink (chiefly derived from shellac, sappanwood and betel nut), yellow (from turmeric, mangosteen sap, night-flowering jasmine and jackfruit wood), green (from wild almond and pineapple leaves), black (from ebony berries and pepper root), brown (from mangrove and cutch wood), orange (from henna and annatto leaves and seed pods) and blue (from indigo leaves). Garments of indigo-dyed cotton are commonly worn by both men and women for working in the fields. Before the discovery of aniline dyes, monks' robes were dyed with yellow dye obtained from the jackfruit tree, and the dye was fixed by dipping the robes beforehand in a preparation of cow dung, mud and various plant extracts.

There are many ancient superstitions concerning the preparation and use of these vegetable dyes. For example, the presence near the vats of a monk or a pregnant or menstruating woman is said to affect the strength of the dyes; dyeing cannot be carried out on Buddhist holy days; and the fixatives (mordants) must be prepared in silence.

The textiles are woven on a frame loom and many patterns are used, including plain weaves, float-weaves and twill weave, supplementary weft (*khit* or *muk*), tapestry weave and tie-dye or *ikat* (*matmi*). Gold and silver brocades and silk embroidered with jewels is made for court costumes or ceremonial wear.

The courts of Sukhothai and Ayutthaya imported Chinese silk, and in the 17C and 18C printed cottons and silk and cotton *patolas* (double *ikat*) Thai-inspired patterns were made in India especially for the Thai market and brought into the kingdom by Muslim merchants. In the late 17C King Narai of Ayutthaya imported velvet from France.

In 1948 **Jim Thompson**, an American intelligence officer in the Office of Strategic Services who had settled in Thailand after the Second World War (see p 142), revived the moribund silk-weaving industry in Bangkok by founding the **Thai Silk Company** to manufacture and sell Thai silk. His venture began to pay off when the company was invited to provide the costumes for the Broadway production of *The King and I*, and Jim Thompson's shop in Bangkok at the northeast end of T. Suriwong is still one of the best as well as one of the most expensive Thai silk shops in the capital.

Queen Sirikit has been largely responsible for another remarkable revival in the production of traditional textiles. In 1976 she founded **Support**, an organisation for the promotion of Thai arts and crafts and in particular hand-woven textiles, and, in order to help prevent the disappearance of traditional Thai costume, she has devised, with the assistance of a group of designers and historians of dress, five costumes for wear on different occasions at different times of day, each one consisting of a *phasin* and a blouse made of Thai silk in traditional patterns. These have proved to be an enormous success and are now widely worn by women all over Thailand.

Woodcarving

Although wood is only used rarely for the carving of Buddha images, it is a favourite medium for figures of deities and mythical creatures such as *garudas* and *kinnaris*, as well as for architectural decoration, furnishings in religious buildings, and objects used in religious ceremonies. Thai houses of all kinds, from simple peasant dwellings to royal palaces, have traditionally been made of wood, especially in the north where until recently teak was available in abundance. Moreover, teak is easy to carve and more resistant to termites and the effects of the climate than most wood, so it has always been extensively used for architectural decoration for grander buildings, both in temples and palaces. Roof superstructures, gables (*na ban*) and the finials that surmount them (*cho fa*), the leaf-shaped ornaments (*bai raka*, see cover illustration), side finials (*hang hong*) and bottom finials (*hang pla*) on bargeboards (*pan lom*), the brackets (*khan thuai*) supporting the eaves, doors and window shutters, ceilings and interior wall panels all provide woodcarvers with opportunities to display their skills. In the north of Thailand the supports at each end of the roof ridge are often extended to form a V-shaped structure known as a *kalae*, and these are now sometimes carved and applied to the roof ridge separately as a purely ornamental feature. The furnishings of the temple, such as shrines (*ku*), the *mondop*-like structures known as *busabok*, which are used to place above thrones or to house sacred images and relics, pulpits (*thammat*), altars and pedestals for images, frames for votive tablets, and scripture cabinets and boxes, are also usually made of carved wood, sometimes decorated with lacquer, gilding, glass mosaic or mother-of-pearl inlay, ivory or niello work. Equally elaborate and richly decorated are the carved wooden objects associated with royal ceremonies and processions and with court life, such as thrones, palanquins, howdahs, carriages and barges (see p 148), and crematory urns (*kot*, usually made of sandalwood), the constructions on which they are placed (*meru*), and the carriages which transport them to the place of cremation (see p 126). So highly is the art of the woodcarver esteemed that kings themselves have been known to practise it: two of the wooden doors of Wat Suthat in Bangkok (see p 130) are said to have been carved by King Rama II.

Until recent times, Thais of all classes led most of their domestic lives, both waking and sleeping, on the floor, and even the grandest houses were therefore only sparsely furnished. Chairs and beds were virtually unknown before the mid-19C, and furniture consisted only of couches, chests and cabinets for storage, mirrors and low tables. During the reign of King Mongkut, the upper classes began to adopt European styles and habits, and Thai woodcarvers responded to this development by making furniture which mixed traditional Thai and Western designs and motifs. For example, early Thai chairs were made to the same design as couches, with a sloping panel forming the back and a very wide seat; they are consequently quite remarkably uncomfortable.

With the destruction of so much of Thailand's forests, wood is now a scarce and valuable commodity, large-scale woodcarvings are beyond the means of all but the very rich, and even traditional Thai houses with steeply pitched roofs with wooden gables are becoming rare.

Drama, Dance and Music

Puppet theatre

The most ancient form of dramatic art in Thailand is probably the shadow puppet theatre. Like the shadow theatre of Indonesia (*wayang kulit*) and other Southeast Asian countries, its origins are obscure, but, since it has been used since early times as a vehicle for the dramatisation of the great Indian epics, the *Mahābhārata* and the *Rāmāyaṇa*, it seems likely that it was introduced into the region from India along with other elements of Indian culture.

The most important form of Thai shadow theatre, now unfortunately almost extinct, is the **nang yai**, which was originally performed only at the courts of Ayutthaya and Bangkok and has a repertoire derived almost exclusively from the *Ramakien*, the Thai version of the *Rāmāyaṇa*. In the *nang yai*, as in the *wayang kulit*, flat, two-dimensional puppets with their faces in profile or half-profile, made of intricately cut and painted buffalo or cow hide, are manipulated behind a white cloth screen, which is lit from behind so that the shadows of the puppets fall on it. However, the *nang yai* has several features that distinguish it from the *wayang*. In the first place, the puppets are much larger, sometimes as tall as two metres, and their limbs are not articulated. They are cut into a roughly circular shape and do not always represent a single character, but may show two warriors fighting or a pair of lovers, or even a complete scene, such as Rama riding in his chariot, with a background of trees or rocks. Secondly, the puppeteers do not narrate the story as in the *wayang*, but instead move both behind and in front of the screen, dancing to the musical accompaniment, which is provided by an orchestra known as **piphat**, and at the same time manipulating the puppets on two poles, one held in each hand. The narration is provided by two singers, who sit among the musicians with their backs to the audience. The *piphat* orchestra consists of oboes (*pi*), xylophones, gongs, cymbals and other metallophones, and drums, and the music is based not on the octave scale, but on a seven-note whole-tone scale.

A less courtly form of Thai shadow theatre is the **nang thalung**, which requires a group of some ten players, including the puppeteers, the narrators and the orchestra. *Nang thalung* is found only in southern Thailand, chiefly in Phatthalung province. The puppets are much smaller than *nang yai* puppets, ranging in height from 15 to 50cm, and are made of translucent calf hide painted in brilliant colours. Unlike the static *nang yai* puppets, the limbs of the *nang thalung* puppets can be articulated, and some of them are cut in full-face form. The repertoire includes not only episodes from the *Ramakien*, but also stories borrowed from the Western cinema and from **likai**, a form of folk opera developed in the 19C. There are several clownish and grotesque characters, and much of the humour is obscene. One clown character, for example, has an index finger shaped like a phallus.

Once as popular at court as the *nang yai* but now rare is the **hun krabok** puppet theatre. *Hun krabok* are not shadow puppets but, like the Indonesian *wayang golek*, three-dimensional puppets mounted on wooden rods and operated from below by means of a complicated arrangement of strings. Their movements are copied from the Thai classical dance-drama (*lakhon*), and in form and features they are exact replicas of the masked *khon* dancers (see below), with heads made, like *khon* masks, of painted and lacquered papier mâché, tradition-ally by the same craftsmen. The *hun* repertoire consists of stories from the *Ramakien*, and performances take place in front of a painted backdrop, behind which sit the puppeteers, the narrators and the *piphat* orchestra. Among the few surviving sets of *hun* puppets are the magnificent royal puppets some 40cm high (*hun luang* or *hun yai*) in the National Museum in Bangkok, which date from the late 19C and were restored in 1986. The same museum also possesses a set of about a hundred small puppets (*hun lek*), only 25cm high, created by Prince Bowon Wisetchaichan in the 1880s.

Other varieties of *hun* theatre still occasionally found in Thailand are **hun krabek**, which is composed of extremely elaborate rod puppets derived from Chinese originals and used only for the performance of a single 19C story, and a form that makes use of rodless glove puppets in the manner of a Punch and Judy show to perform a repertoire of Thai folk stories.

Dance-drama

The movements of the figures in the Thai puppet theatre are clearly derived from those used in the **khon** masked drama and the classical dance-drama (*lakhon*). There are said to be over a hundred different types of **lakhon** from different parts of the kingdom. In all classical Thai dancing the emphasis is on move-ments of the arms, hands and fingers rather than of the feet, combined with elegant but generally rather static poses. The dancers are barefoot and their costumes are highly elaborate and based for the most part on the court dress of the Ayutthaya period. One distinctive feature of the costume is the tall, tapering, *chedi*-like headdress worn by royal characters. Many of the forms of the dance appear to derive from classical Khmer court dances, which in turn originate from ancient Javanese traditions. In this connection, it is significant that the Thai word *lakhon* is derived from the Javanese *lakon*, meaning the story or plot of a play. The most classical form of *lakhon* is the **lakhon nai** or 'theatre of the inside', which acquired its present form at the courts of the Ayutthaya and Ratanakosin kings. It is so called because it was performed in the Inner Palace, where men were not admitted, and so made use only of female actors, usually ladies of the court. The stories are taken from the *Ramakien*, the story of Krishna and the Javanese tales of Prince Panji, known in Thai as Inao. **Lakhon nok** ('theatre of the outside') is a more popular form of *lakhon*, particularly associated with Buddhist temple fairs. Originally it was only played by male actors, usually professionals, but in modern times women have been permitted to take the female roles. *Lakhon nok* plots are chiefly derived from *jātaka* tales and folk legends and only occasionally from the *Ramakien*. The costumes of the dancers are similar to those of the *lakhon nai*.

In southern Thailand and among the Thai population of the Malaysian state of Kedah an ancient form of dance-drama known as **lakhon manora**, **nora** or **chatri** is still popular. It has a more markedly Indian and Malay-Indonesian character than the *lakhon nai*. The movements of the body are more angular and acrobatic, and the complicated finger movements are emphasised by the wearing of long artificial fingernails. The dancers tend to slide their feet across the floor instead of walking or running. *Lakhon nora* groups formerly consisted only of three male actors, but performances are now usually given by larger groups, with women playing the female roles. The most popular story in the *lakhon nora* repertoire and the one from which it derives its name is the tale of the *kinnari* princess named Manohra. This story was originally a *jātaka* tale, so that some *lakhon nora* performances still have a religious and ritual significance, beginning with the recitation of Buddhist prayers and invocations to Hindu deities, and interspersed with trance sessions.

In the 20C less stylised forms of the *lakhon*, including the **lakhon phut**, in which the performers speak their parts, and various forms of sung or operatic *lakhon* have been developed. Foreign influences have also made themselves felt, as for example in the **lakhon phantang**, which is based on historical themes and includes such imported elements as foreign characters dressed in the costumes of their countries and displays of Chinese martial arts.

Masked drama

In the **khon** or masked drama, which, although not, as is sometimes claimed, invented by Rama II in the early 19C, was encouraged and developed by him, the actors mime their parts, while narrators recount the story and recite the dialogue. The musical accompaniment is provided by a large *piphat* orchestra with singers and a chorus. Originally all the characters wore masks, made, like the *hun krabok* puppets, of papier mâché, but these are now worn only by the actors playing demons and monkeys. Each mask, like each *hun* puppet, has its own distinctive features and colours denoting the identity of the characters and their rank: Rama, for example, always wears a green mask with an immensely tall tapering royal headdress, and the mask of Hanuman, commander of the monkey army, is always white, while the demon-king Ravana, known in Thai as Totsakan, wears a mask with fangs and protruding eyes and carries in his head-dress demonic faces surmounted by the face of a deity. The *khon* was originally performed out of doors without scenery or props, and only male actors took part, but the female roles are now usually played by women, and performances are given in theatres, such as the National Theatre in Bangkok (see p 126), with elaborate sets, modern lighting effects and sometimes as many as a hundred actors taking part. The themes are single episodes of the *Ramakien*, of which some of the texts are thought to have been written by Rama II, and performances last for several hours.

JV

FURTHER READING

General

Bock, Carl, *Temples and Elephants* (London, 1883; reprinted, Singapore, 1986)

Clarac, Achille (trans. and ed. Michael Smithies), *Guide to Thailand* (revised ed., Kuala Lumpur, 1981)

Clarac, Achille and Henri Pagau-Clarac, *Thailande: Guide Touristique* (revised ed., Bangkok, 1985)

Moore, Frank J., *Thailand: Its People, Its Society, Its Culture* (revised ed., New Haven, 1974)

Seidenfaden, Erik, *The Thai Peoples* (Bangkok, 1967)

Sumet Jumsai, *Naga: Cultural Origins in Siam and the West Pacific* (Singapore, 1988)

History

Batson, Benjamin A., *The End of the Absolute Monarchy in Siam* (Singapore, 1984)

Charnvit Kasetsiri, *The Rise of Ayudhya: A History of Siam in the Fourteenth and Fifteenth Centuries* (Kuala Lumpur, 1976)

Chula Chakrabongse, Prince, *Lords of Life: A History of the Kings of Thailand* (revised ed., London 1967)

Collis, Maurice, *Siamese White* (London, 1936; reprinted, 1965)

Gervaise, Nicolas (trans. and ed. John Villiers), *The Natural and Political History of the Kingdom of Siam* (Bangkok, 1989)

Hutchinson, E.W., *Adventurers in Siam in the Seventeenth Century* (London, 1940; reprint, Bangkok, 1985)

Manich Jumsai, *Popular History of Thailand* (Bangkok, 1972)

Tuck, Patrick, *The French Wolf and the Siamese Lamb; The French Threat to Siamese Independence 1858–1907* (Bangkok, 1995)

Vella, Walter F., *Chaiyo! King Vajiravudh and the Development of Thai Nationalism* (Honolulu, 1978)

Vinal Smith, George, *The Dutch in Seventeenth Century Thailand* (De Kalb, Illinois, 1977)

Waugh, Alec, *Bangkok: the Story of a City* (Boston and Toronto, 1971)

Wood, W.A.R. *A History of Siam* (London, 1926; reprinted, Bangkok, 1959)

Wyatt, David K., *Thailand: A Short History* (London and Bangkok, 1984)

Art and Archaeology

Boisselier, Jean, *The Heritage of Thai Sculpture* (Bangkok, 1975, reprinted 1987)

Bowie, Theodore, ed., *The Sculpture of Thailand* (New York, 1972)

Conway Susan, *Thai Textiles* (London, 1992)

Fickle, Dorothy H., *Images of the Buddha in Thailand* (Singapore, 1989)

Ginsburg, Henry, *Thai Manuscript Painting* (London, 1989)

Gosling, Betty, *Sukhothai: Its History, Culture and Art* (Singapore, 1991)

Hoskin, John, *Ten Contemporary Thai Artists* (Bangkok, 1984)

Invernizzi Tettoni, Luca and William Warren, *Thai Style* (Bangkok, 1988)

Labbé, Armand J., *Ban Chiang: Art and Prehistory of Northeast Thailand* (Santa Ana, CA, 1985)

Matics, K.I., *Introduction to the Thai Temple* (Bangkok, 1992)

Moore, Elizabeth, Philip Stott, Suriyavudh Sukhasvasti and Michael Freeman, *Ancient Capitals of Thailand* (Bangkok, 1996)

Naengnoi Punjabhan and Somchai Na Nakhonphanom, *The Art of Thai Wood Carving: Sukhothai, Ayutthaya, Ratanakosin* (Bangkok, 1992)

Piriya Krairiksh, *Art Styles in Thailand* (Bangkok, 1977)

Piriya Krairiksh, *Art in Peninsular Thailand Prior to the Fourteenth Century AD* (Bangkok, 1980)

Ringis, Rita, *Thai Temples and Temple Murals* (Singapore, 1990)

Smithies, Michael, *Old Bangkok* (Singapore, 1986)

Smitthi Siribhadra, Elizabeth Moore and Michael Freeman, *Palaces of the Gods: Khmer Art and Architecture in Thailand* (Bangkok, 1992)

Spinks, C.N., *The Ceramic Wares of Siam* (Bangkok, 1965)

Stratton, Carol and Miriam McNair Scott, *The Art of Sukhothai* (Kuala Lumpur, 1981)

Subhadradis Diskul, M.C., *The Art of Srivijaya* (Kuala Lumpur and Paris, 1980)

Subhadradis Diskul, M.C., *Art in Thailand: A Brief History* (6th ed., Bangkok, 1986)

Van Beek, Steve and Luca Invernizzi Tettoni, *The Arts of Thailand* (Hong Kong, 1985; 2nd ed., 1986)

Warren, William and Luca Invernizzi Tettoni, *Arts and Crafts of Thailand* (London, 1994)

White, Joyce C., *Ban Chiang: Discovery of a Lost Bronze Age* (Philadelphia, 1982)

Wray, E., *Ten Lives of the Buddha: Siamese Temple Paintings and Jataka Tales* (New York and Tokyo, 1979)

Natural history

Boonsong Lekagul and J.A. McNeely. *Mammals of Thailand* (Bangkok, 1977)

Boonsong Lekagul and Philip D. Round, *A Guide to the Birds of Thailand* (Bangkok, 1991)

Gray, Denis, Piprell, Collin, and Mark Graham, *National Parks of Thailand* (Bangkok, 2nd ed. 1995)

Piprell, Collin and Ashley J. Boyd, *Diving in Thailand* (Singapore, 1994)

Cookery books : see under Food and Drink, p27.

Language: see under The Thai Language, p29.

Chao Phraya river, looking upstream from the Oriental Hotel

BANGKOK AND ENVIRONS

1 · Bangkok

Bangkok ('Village of Wild Plums') was originally the name of a village on the east bank of the Chao Phraya River. It was adopted by foreign traders in Siam to denote the port of **Thon Buri** that had been founded on the west bank of the river during the reign of King Chakkraphat (1548–69). Thon Buri had been selected for both strategic and commercial reasons and soon became not only an important trading centre with a substantial Chinese community, but also, in the words of the late 17C French writer Nicolas Gervaise, who called it Bangkok, 'assuredly the most important place in the kingdom of Siam, for it is the only place anywhere on the seacoast that could offer some resistance to enemy attack'. Soon after the city's foundation, a canal (*khlong*) was dug to eliminate some of the bends in the Chao Phraya, the original course of which is today marked by the two largest canals in Thon Buri—Khlong Bangkok Yai and Khlong Bangkok Noi.

After the defeat and sack of Ayutthaya by the Burmese in 1767, the Thai leader, Taksin, established a new capital in Thon Buri. In 1782, Taksin's successor King Rama I moved the court and capital to an area of low-lying marshy land on the other side of the river which he called **Ratanakosin** ('Jewel Abode of the God Indra'). This name is sometimes used and has been adopted in this guide rather than 'Bangkok' to denote the period from 1782 to the present and its art style. Here, in less than five years, Rama I built a fortified city surrounded by massive walls some 7km in length, pierced by 16 large gates and 47 smaller ones and defended by 16 octagonal forts. On the east side two parallel *khlong* were dug, Khlong Banglamphu and Khlong Lot, thus making Ratanakosin into an island and giving the city a double defensive moat. Later a third canal, Khlong Phadung Krung Kasem, was added further to the east. The new city was given the resounding name of Krungthepphramahanakhowonratanakosinmahintarayutthayahadilokphiphopnoppharatratchathaniburiromudomratchaniwetmahasathanamonpimanavatansathirsakkathatityavisnukamprasit, shortened to **Krungthep** ('City of Angels'), the name by which today the whole city, including Thon Buri, is officially known in Thai. Foreign traders in the city, however, continued to call it Bangkok. The Chinese who lived in Ratanakosin were resettled in the Sampeng district to the southeast of the walled city, today's Chinatown.

Partly because of the unhealthiness of the site and the frequent epidemics of cholera, the new capital grew slowly. Houses only began to be built on the banks of the river, chiefly on the Thon Buri side, during the 1820s, and the total population had only reached 200,000 by 1900. In the 20C, and particularly since the Second World War, the population has increased much more rapidly, reaching over 1 million by 1950 and 6 million by 1992. The official estimate of the population of Bangkok today is 6.5 million, which is about 40 times larger than the population of the second city in Thailand, Chiang Mai, but the true figure is thought to be well in excess of that. Of these between 25 and 30 per cent are Chinese. The area covered by Metropolitan Bangkok is more than 1600km.

Transport in the City

Until the mid-19C Bangkok, like Ayutthaya and Thon Buri before it, was a city of canals and all its traffic was water-borne. This earned it, like its predecessors, the title of the Venice of the East. The houses were built of wood on stilts along these canals or *khlong*, from which on either side ran narrow lanes constructed of wooden planks known as *soi*. Most of the *soi* were culs de sac leading to separate groups of houses (*muban*) and did not link one *khlong* with another; and this accounts both for Bangkok's lack of a single centre and also for the inadequacy of the city's present road system, which has been largely created by converting the *khlong* and the *soi* into roads. In central Bangkok roads occupy only 8.1 per cent of the total space, as against 16.6 per cent in London and 23.2 per cent in New York. The severe traffic congestion on the principal thoroughfares which results from this has given Bangkok one of the highest levels of air and noise pollution in the world.

In 1861 King Mongkut ordered the construction of a road running south from the Grand Palace for about 6km along the west bank of the river so as to provide a place where foreign residents could walk and ride in their carriages. It was called **Thanon Charoen Krung** or **New Road** and was opened in 1862. The next year, two more roads were added, Bamrung Muang and Fuang Nakhon, to provide access to temples in the Ratanakosin area. In 1887 the first horse-drawn trams came into operation, and in 1892 electric trams, the first in any Asian city, were introduced. The last tram in Bangkok made its final journey in September 1968.

With the advent of the motor car in the early 20C, further streets and bridges were constructed and the city expanded rapidly. After the Second World War several bridges were built over the Chao Phraya and many canals were filled in to provide more roads. During the wars in Indochina in the 1960s and 70s, Bangkok and the seaside resort of Phatthaya became rest and recreation centres for the American and other armed forces in the region and this further accelerated the expansion of the city. Today, Bangkok is one of the most crowded and congested cities in the world. In 1989 the average speed of vehicles along Bangkok's main streets was less than 10km an hour, and recent research has revealed that over 30 per cent of police officers on regular traffic duty suffer from loss of hearing and 23 per cent from pulmonary disorders. For this reason the *tuk-tuk* or *samlo*, the open-sided three-wheeled motor vehicle that for so long has been one of the easiest, cheapest and quickest ways of getting around in Bangkok, is gradually disappearing from the streets. A number of major projects are now in hand to try to relieve the congestion, including the construction of elevated expressways and the improvement of trunk roads, the building of fly-overs, the construction of an urban railway and the modernisation of the bus system. Unfortunately, progress with these projects has been bedevilled by the multiplicity of government departments and agencies involved and the consequent corruption, inefficiency and lack of co-ordination, and the only one so far completed by the end of 1996 was the 20km long expressway, which cost US$800 million and was opened in 1993. It is feared that, in any case, by the end of the millennium the traffic in Bangkok will have increased so much that the improvements these projects are intended to bring about will be largely nullified.

Flooding and Subsidence

Much of the land on which Bangkok is built is highly unstable and some of it is below sea level, which makes it liable both to flooding and to subsidence. These problems have been exacerbated in recent years by the indiscriminate and largely uncontrolled construction of very large buildings and the boring of artesian wells, which have increased the rate at which the city is sinking. In some areas this is as much as 10cm a year. The most serious flood in recent years was in 1983, when 450 sq km of the city was submerged. The flood problem was first seriously tackled in 1986 by the then governor of Bangkok, the austere Chamlong Srimuang, who was later to lead the riots in May 1992 against the government of General Suchinda (see p 54). Chamlong initiated a programme of clearing the canals of refuse, but this seems to have had little permanent effect.

■ **Information.** The Tourist Authority of Thailand (TAT) is a government-sponsored information and promotion service attached to the Prime Minister's Office. The head office is at 372 T. Bamrung Muang, Bangkok 10100 (☎ (00662) 226-0072/85/98). There is also a TAT desk in the arrivals area at Bangkok Airport and an office at the Chatuchak Weekend Market. One of the most valuable services provided by the TAT is the Tourist Assistance Centre (☎ 281-5051, 282-8129), which offers help to tourists who have been robbed, cheated or suffered other mishaps. The Tourist Police (head office: Unico House, Soi Lang Suan, T. Ploenchit, ☎ 1699 or 6521721) will also assist tourists in difficulties.

There are several English-language magazines that provide information about what is on in Bangkok and give details of shops and restaurants. The best of these is *Metro*, which is published monthly. The *Guide of Bangkok*, which is issued free of charge, also gives some useful information.

Transport

■ **Air.** Don Muang Airport is 25km north of the city. THAI flies from Bangkok to nine destinations in the north (Chiang Mai, Chiang Rai, Lampang, Mae Hong Son, Mae Sot, Nan, Phitsanulok, Phrae), six in the northeast (Khon Kaen, Loei, Nakhon Ratchasima, Sakhon Nakhon, Ubon Ratchathani, Udon Thani) and seven in the south (Hat Yai, Nakhon Si Thammarat, Narathiwat, Pattani, Phuket, Surat Thani, Trang). The head office is at 89 T. Vibhavadi Rangsit.

Bangkok Airways flies from Bangkok to Ko Samui, Hua Hin and Phatthaya, and from Ko Samui to Phuket.

■ **Train.** There are three main stations in Bangkok: **Hualamphong** on T. Rama IV, which takes all the railway services to the north and northeast and most of those to the south; **Wongwian Yai**, for trains to Samut Sakhon and Samut Songkhram; and **Bangkok Noi** (Thon Buri), which handles a few of the southern services. Trains are clean, comfortable but not notably fast. Sleepers can be reserved in advance at Hualamphong, and 20-day rail passes are also available there.

■ **Buses (inter-town).** There are three main public bus terminals. For destinations in the north and northeast and also for Aranyaprathet, the terminal is on T. Phahon Yothin on the way to Don Muang airport near the Chatuchak Weekend Market. For Phatthaya Rayong, Chanthaburi and the east, the terminal is on Soi Ekamai (T. Sukhumvit Soi 40) and for the south in Thon Buri, at the intersection of T. Phra Pinklao and T. Nakhon Chaisi.

Most private buses leave from these three terminals also. They are generally more comfortable than the state-run buses, but tend to be less reliable and to have lower standards of safety.

■ **Buses (local).** Bangkok has a fairly efficient and very cheap, but rather complicated and extremely crowded bus service. Some routes are air-conditioned, others not. There is also a red microbus service on certain routes, which stops taking passengers once every seat is filled and for which a flat fare is charged. Names of destinations are only written in romanised form on air-conditioned buses and microbuses.

It is useful to acquire a bus map before attempting to travel about in Bangkok by bus. There are several good and reasonably accurate bus maps of which the *Bangkok Bus Map (Walking tours)* is probably the best.

■ **Songthaeo** ('two rows'). These are pick-up trucks provided with two benches, which run on set routes like buses and charge fixed fares. Formerly common in Bangkok, as they still are in many Thai towns, they are now found only in the outer suburbs of the capital.

■ **Taxis.** Metered taxis were introduced in Bangkok in 1993 and they now far outnumber non-metered taxis. When taking a taxi without a meter, remember always to agree upon a price by bargaining before setting off. Virtually all taxis, both metered and non-metered, are air-conditioned.

Three-wheeled motor taxis (**samlo** or **tuk-tuk**), which operate on two-stroke engines, are noisy, uncomfortable and entail the risk of inhaling unhealthily large quantities of exhaust fumes. However, owing to their great mobility and the daring of their drivers, they are often quicker than taxis. It is necessary, as with non-metered taxis, to agree a price by bargaining before getting in to a *samlo*. Many *samlo* drivers have only a sketchy knowledge of the geography of Bangkok.

Motorbike taxis are also available throughout Bangkok. The drivers are easily identifiable by their brightly coloured, numbered waistcoats. Some, but by no means all, provide their passengers with crash helmets, which are compulsory in Bangkok.

■ **Boats.** There are still many boats plying for hire on the Chao Phraya River and in the *khlong*. The Chao Phraya River Express (*reua dan*) is a cheap and comfortable way of seeing some of the most interesting sights in Bangkok, as it operates up the river from Wat Ratchasinghon in the south as far as Nonthaburi in the north, stopping at over 40 piers (*tha*) on the way. The whole journey takes between 75 and 115 minutes. Some of the more important piers have excellent riverside restaurants next to them.

There are also many cross-river ferries (*reua kham fak*), which shuttle to and fro across the Chao Phraya and long tailed boats (*reua hang yao*), which either operate somewhat like shared taxis or can be chartered for trips along the *khlong* for a fixed hourly charge.

Transport by boat in Bangkok is only available during the hours of daylight.

■ **Hotels.** The best hotels in Bangkok, such as the *Oriental,* are among the best in the world, and even quite modestly priced hotels in Bangkok, as elsewhere in Thailand, generally have a high standard of service, cleanliness and comfort. Lists of hotels and guest-houses are available from TAT offices. The following is a list of the 21 hotels in Bangkok and environs specially recommended by the Thai Hotels Association (THA). Most of them are either on the Chao Phraya River on in the area around Siam Square and T. Ploenchit in the centre of the city.

Amari Airport Hotel
T. 333 Chert Wudthakas Road
Don Muang, Bangkok 10210
Tel (66-2) 5661020, 5661021
Fax (66-2) 5661941

Amari Watergate Hotel
847 T. Phetchaburi
Bangkok 10400
Tel. (66-2) 6539000
Fax (66-2) 6539045

Central Plaza Hotel
1695 T. Phahon Yothin
Chatuchak,
Bangkok 10900
Tel (66-2) 5411234
Fax (66-2) 5411087

Dusit Thani Hotel
946 T. Rama IV
Bangkok 10500
Tel (66-2) 2360450-9
Fax (66-2) 2366400, 2367238

Felix Arnoma Swissôtel
99 T. Ratchadamri
Pathumwan
Bangkok 10330
Tel (66-2) 2553410
Fax (66-2) 2553456-8

Grand Hyatt Erawan Bangkok
494 T. Ratchadamri
Bangkok 10330
Tel (66-2) 2541234
Fax (66-2) 25446308

Hilton International Bangkok
2 T. Witthayu
Bangkok 10330
Tel (66-2) 2530123
Fax (66-2) 2536509

Holiday Inn Crown Plaza
981 T. Silom
Bangkok 10500
Tel (66-2) 2384300
Fax (66-2) 2385289

Imperial Queen's Park Hotel
199 Sukhumvit Soi 22
Bangkok 10110
Tel (66-2) 2619000, 2619230
Fax (66-2) 2619530-4

Landmark, Bangkok
138 T. Sukhumvit
Bangkok 10110
Tel (66-2) 2540404, 2540424
Fax (66-2) 2534259, 2540439

Mansion Kempinski
75/23 Sukhumvit Soi 11
Prakanong
Bangkok 10110
Tel (66-2) 2557200
Fax (66-2) 2532329-31

Marriott Royal Garden Riverside Hotel
257/1–3 T. Charoen Nakorn
Thon Buri
Bangkok 10600
Tel (66-2) 4760021-2
Fax (66-2) 4601805, 4761120

Monarch Lee Gardens Hotel
188 T. Silom
Bangrak
Bangkok 10500
Tel (66-2) 2381991
Fax (66-2) 2381999

Montien Hotel
54 T. Surawong
Bangkok 10500
Tel (66-2) 2337060, 2348060
Fax (66-2) 2365218-9

Montien Riverside Hotel
372 T. Rama III
Banklo
Bangkok 10120
Tel (66-2) 2922999, 2922888
Fax (66-2) 2922962-4

Oriental Hotel
48 Oriental Avenue
Bangkok 10500
Tel (66-2) 2360400, 2360420
Fax (66-2) 2361937-9

Regent of Bangkok
155 Ratchadamri Road
Bangkok 10330
Tel (66-2) 2516127
Fax (66-2) 2539195

Rembrandt Hotel
Sukhumvit soi 18
Khlong Toey
Bangkok 10110
Tel (66-2) 2617100
Fax (66-2) 2617017

Rose Garden Country Resort, Golf Course and Cultural Centre
Km. 32 Pet Kasem Highway
Sampran
Nakhon Pathom 73110

Sheraton Grande Sukhumvit
250 T. Sukhumvit
Khlong Toey
Bangkok 10110
Tel (66-2) 6530334
Fax (66-2) 6530400

Siam City Hotel
477 T. Si Ayutthaya
Bangkok 10400
Tel (66-2) 2470123
Fax (66-2) 2470175

Sukhothai-Bangkok Hotel
13/3 T. Sathon Tai
Bangkok 10120
Tel (66-2) 287-0222
Fax (66-2) 287-4980

The following list gives the names, telephone numbers and fax numbers of all the other hotels in Bangkok that are members of the Thai Hotels Association:

Hotel	Telephone	Fax
Amari Boulevard Hotel	(02) 255 2930-40	(02) 255 2950
Ambassador Hotel	(02) 254 0444	(02) 254 7506
Ariston Hotel	(02) 259 0960-69	(02) 259 0970

Hotel	Telephone	Fax
Asia Hotel	(02) 215 0808	(02) 215 4360
Best Western Baiyoke Suite Hotel	(02) 255 0330-9	(02) 254 5553
Bangkok Centre Hotel	(02) 238 4848-57	(02) 236 1862
Century Park Hotel	(02) 246 7800-9	(02) 246 7197
Chaleena Hotel	(02) 539 7101-11	(02) 539 7126
Chaophya Park Hotel	(02) 290 0125	(02) 275 8585
Classic Place Hotel	(02) 255 4444-9	(02) 255 4450
Delta Grand Pacific Hotel	(02) 255 4998	(02) 255 2440
De-Ville Palace Hotel	(02) 530 0560-79	(02) 539 2796
Elizabeth Hotel	(02) 279 5342-3	(02) 271 2539
Emerald Hotel	(02) 276 4567	(02) 276 4555
Eurasia Bangkok Hotel	(02) 275 0060-77	(02) 277 7954
First Hotel	(02) 255 0100-20	(02) 255 0121
Florida Hotel	(02) 247 0130-4	(02) 247 0990
Fortune Bluewave Hotel	(02) 641 1500	(02) 641 1551
Four Wings Hotel	(02) 260 2100	(02) 260 2300
Golden Dragon Hotel	(02) 589 0130-41	(02) 589 8305
Golden Horse Hotel	(02) 280 1920-9	(02) 280 3404
Grace Hotel	(02) 253 0651-79	(02) 253 0680
Grand Hyatt Erawan	(02) 254 1234	(02) 253 6308
Hilton International	(02) 253 0123	(02) 253 6509
Holiday Inn Crowne Plaza	(02) 238 4300	(02) 238 5289
Holiday Mansion Hotel	(02) 253 8016-24	(02) 253 0130
Imperial Impala Hotel	(02) 259 0053-4	(02) 258 8747
Indra Regent Hotel	(02) 208 0022-33	(02) 208 0388
Jade Pavilion Hotel	(02) 259 4675-89	(02) 258 2328
Landmark	(02) 254 0404	(02) 253 4259
Majestic Palace Hotel	(02) 280 5610-22	(02) 280 0965
Malaysia Hotel	(02) 679 7127-36	(02) 287 1457
Mandarin Hotel	(02) 238 0230-58	(02) 237 1620
Hotel Manhattan	(02) 255 0166	(02) 255 3481
Manohra Hotel	(02) 234 5070-88	(02) 266 5411
Marriott Royal Garden Riverside Hotel	(02) 476 0021-2	(02) 476 1120
Maruay Garden Hotel	(02) 561 0510-47	(02) 561 0549
Menam Hotel	(02) 289 1148-9	(02) 291 1048
Mercure Hotel	(02) 253 0510	(02) 253 0556
Le Meridien President Hotel	(02) 253 0444	(02) 253 7565
Miami Hotel	(02) 253 5611-3	(02) 253 1266
Morakot Hotel	(02) 319 1461	(02) 319 1465
Nana Hotel	(02) 252 0121	(02) 255 1769
Narai Hotel	(02) 237 0100	(02) 236 7161
New Empire Hotel	(02) 234 6990-6	(02) 234 6997
New Fuji Hotel	(02) 233 8270-2	(02) 233 8247
New Imperial Hotel	(02) 254 0023-49	(02)254 0077
New Peninsula Hotel	(02) 234 3910	(02) 236 5526
New Trocadero Hotel	(02) 234 8920-8	(02) 234 8929
Novotel Bangkok	(02) 255 6888	(02) 255 1824

Hotel	Telephone	Fax
Pan Pacific Hotel	(02) 632 9000	(02) 632 9001
Park Hotel	(02) 255 4300	(02) 255 4309
Plaza Hotel	(02) 235 1760-79	(02) 237 0746
Prince Hotel	(02) 251 6171-6	(02) 251 3318
Rama Gardens Hotel	(02) 561 0022	(02) 561 1025
Regina Hotel	(02) 275 0088	(02) 275 0099
Rex Hotel	(02) 259 0106-15	(02) 258 6635
Rose Hotel	(02) 266 8268-72	(02) 266 8096
Royal Hotel	(02) 222 9111-26	(02) 224 2083
Royal Orchid Sheraton Hotel & Towers	(02) 266 0123	(02) 236 8320
Royal Princess Hotel	(02) 281 3088	(02) 280 1314
Royal River Hotel	(02) 433 0300	(02) 433 5880
S.D.Avenue Hotel	(02) 434 0400	(02) 434 6496
Shangri-La Hotel	(02) 236 7777	(02) 236 8579
Siam Hotel	(02) 252 5081	(02) 252 4973
Siam Intercontinental Hotel	(02) 253 0355-7	(02) 253 2275
Silom Plaza Hotel	(02) 236 8441-84	(02) 236 7566
Sol Twin Towers	(02) 216 9555	(02) 216 9544

The cheapest hotels in Bangkok, as in other Thai cities and towns, are usually Chinese. They are as a rule fairly clean, but austere, and range from dormitory accommodation on a mattress on the floor to private rooms with ceiling fans or even air-conditioning and a bath or shower of sorts. Some have restaurants attached. Many of them, especially those named after their street numbers, are *maisons de passe* and can be easily identified by the car parking bays with curtains round them in front of the ground floor rooms.

The two areas with the largest concentration of cheap hotels and guest houses, much frequented by back packers, are Banglamphu and the area round T. Khao San and the Democracy Monument, and Soi Ngam Duphli near T. Sathon Tai, where Bangkok's most notorious backpackers' hotel, the Malaysia, is situated. The YMCA and the YWCA are also in this area.

■ **Restaurants.** There are said to be over 10,000 restaurants and at least 40,000 food stalls in Bangkok, and the sheer number and variety of places to eat in the city is so enormous that it makes any attempt to give a comprehensive selection both impossible and unnecessary. They range from the very grandest restaurants in the luxury hotels—there are six in the *Oriental Hotel* alone—to food centres in supermarkets and departmental stores and pavement food stalls. Even old-fashioned afternoon tea can be enjoyed at the *Regent*, the *Shangri La* and the *Hilton Hotel*—the last to the accompaniment of a string quartet. It is safe to say that it is extremely difficult to find a restaurant or food stall anywhere in Thailand where the food is poor.

Most of the best Italian, French and German restaurants as well as some of the best known Thai restaurants are in **T. Sukhumvit** or one of the *soi* off it, as this is an area not only frequented by tourists, but also where there are many exclusive residential neighbourhoods. There are also some good cheap foodstalls in T. Sukhumvit. In the area round the Grace Hotel between Soi 3 and Soi 5 Sukhumvit there are many Arabic restaurants and German eating houses and bars. This area was formerly a favourite destination of German tourists and is now patronised chiefly by Arabs,

In **Siam Square** there are several excellent European, Chinese, Japanese and Thai restaurants and also numerous coffee shops, some with live bands.

Patpong and **Silom**, the centre of Bangkok's hectic night life, which has earned the city the reputation of being the sin capital of Asia, has many bars and several first-class hotels, but few good restaurants. The American writer Bernard Trink gives a facetious but informative update on the bar and restaurant scene in Patpong in the *Bangkok Post* every Saturday.

The huge **Pratunam Market** near the Indra Regent Hotel in T. Ratchaprarop has some delicious seafood restaurants, Indian and Pakistani restaurants and innumerable foodstalls, many of them open all night.

In the area round the **Victory Monument** are several foodstalls noted for their noodle dishes, and one of the oldest Thai restaurants in Bangkok is near here, the *Pan Sip* at 140/2 T. Phahon Yothin.

There are numerous cheap restaurants catering for tourists in **T. Nophralan**, near the Tha Chang pier, **T. Maharat** and the area west of Wat Mahathat, and **T. Khao San**. There is a row of good, cheap Thai restaurants, some of them vegetarian, in **T. Dinso**.

The best area for Chinese restaurants in Bangkok is, not surprisingly, **Chinatown**, while in **Pahurat** there are many good north Indian restaurants and Chinese and Thai foodstalls, most of them on the east side of Khlong Ong Ang. In **T. Charoen Krung** there is a large concentration of Indian and Pakistani restaurants, the majority of them rather expensive.

There are several excellent restaurants, some of them open-air, on the west bank of the Chao Phraya in **Thon Buri** and **Bangkok Noi**.

Some restaurants have performances of classical Thai dancing. One of the most popular of these is the *Silom Village* at 268 T. Silom.

■ **Banks and money changers** are to be found all over the city. Many money changers are open at night and over weekends. Credit card facilities are also widely available in hotels, restaurants and shops as well as in money changers. There is no black market exchange rate.

■ **Post and Telecommunications.** The Thai postal services are cheap and efficient. The GPO in Bangkok is in T. Charoen Krung (open Mon–Fri 08.00–20.00, weekends and holidays 08.00–13.00). It operates a reliable poste restante service. In a separate building next to the GPO is a 24-hour international telephone, fax, telex and telegram service.

The American Express office, Suite 414, Siam Centre, T. Rama IV (☎ 251-4862, open Mon–Fri, 08.30–12.00, 13.00–16.30, Sat. 08.30–11.30) operates a poste restante service for Amex-cardholders.

■ **Medical Services.** Most embassies keep up-to-date lists of doctors who can speak English. Among the many hospitals in Bangkok are:
Bangkok Adventist Hospital, 430 T. Phitsanulok (☎ 281 1422)
Bangkok Christian Hospital, 124 T. Silom (☎ 233 6981/9)
Phayathai Hospital, 364/1 T. Si Ayutthaya (☎ 245 2620)

Samitivej Hospital, 133 Soi 49, T. Sukhumvit (☎ 392 0010/9)
Samrong General Hospital, Soi 78, T. Sukhumvit (☎ 393 2131)

Dental Clinics
Dental Polyclinic, 211/3 T. Phetchaburi (☎ 314 5070)
Siam Square, 412/11–2 Soi 6, Siam Square (☎ 251 6315)

■ **Bookshops and Libraries.** English-language bookshops include the numerous branches of Asia Books, three of which are in T. Sukhumvit and two in T. Ratchadamri. DK Book House, which also stocks many books in English, has branches in T, Silom and T. Surawong. The British Council in Siam Square, the American University Alumni (AUA) at 179 T. Ratchadamri and the Neilson-Hayes Library in T. Surawong all have extensive libraries and stock current English-language newspapers and magazines.

■ **Maps.** The best general map of Bangkok is that published by Nelles Verlag. It has Bangkok City (1:15,000) on one side and Greater Bangkok (1:75,000) on the other.
Nancy Chandler's *Map of Bangkok* can also be recommended. It is regularly updated and has plans of Chinatown, the Chatuchak Market and other major places of interest in the city.

The City

There is such an immense variety of places in Bangkok that repay a visit and they are so widely scattered about the city and its environs that it is impossible in this guide to give more than a brief account of some of the most important monuments, together with a small selection of lesser known ones that may be of interest to the discerning traveller with plenty of time and energy to spare. For ease of reference the following section has been divided into seven areas, and a brief description is given of the principal monuments and other attractions in each:

Ratanakosin Island
Pahurat and Chinatown (Sampeng) and the Golden Mount
Dusit and north Bangkok
Nonthaburi
Pathumwan and Sukhumvit
Bangrak, Sathon and Yannawa
The West Bank: Bang Phlat, Bangkok Noi, Bangkok Yai, Thon Buri
   and Khlong San

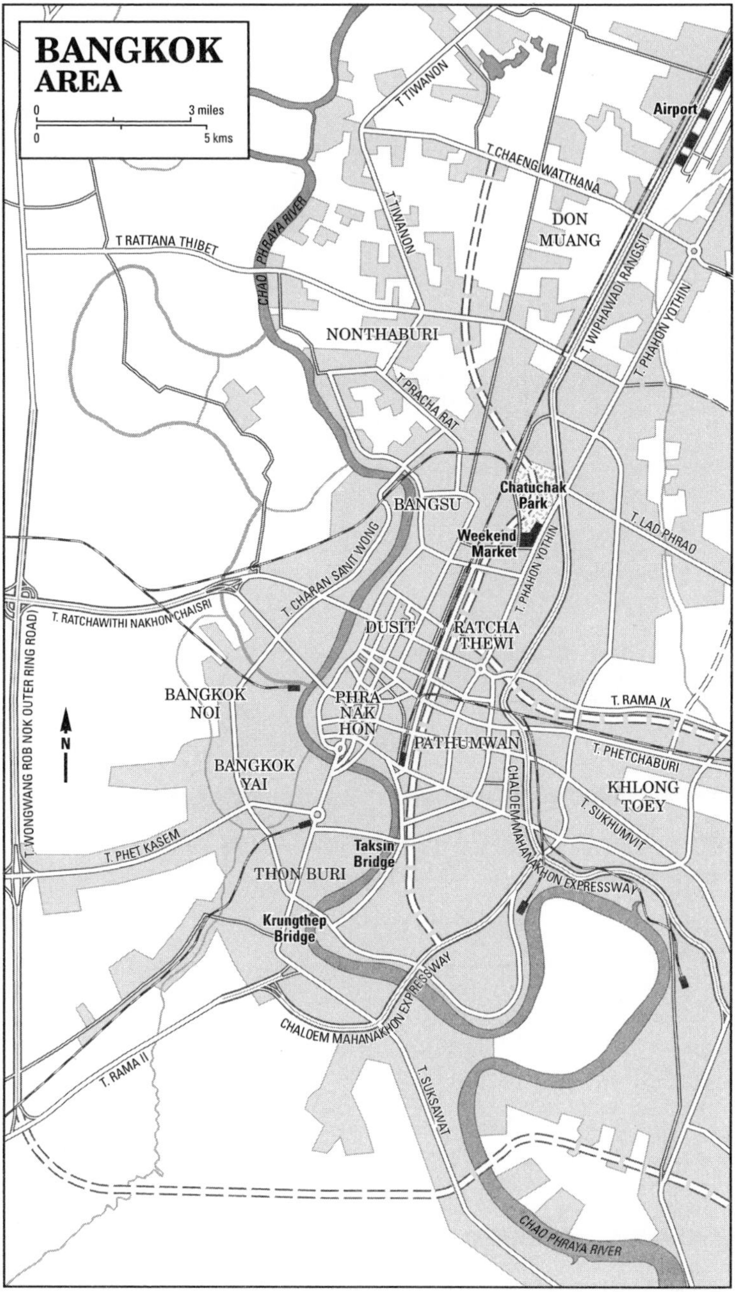

BANGKOK AREA

0 —— 3 miles
0 —— 5 kms

Airport

SAFARI WORLD, MINBURI

T TIWANON

T CHAENG WATTHANA

T RATTANA THIBET

CHAO PHRAYA RIVER

T TIWANON

DON MUANG

T WIPHAVADI RANGSIT

T PHAHON YOTHIN

NONTHABURI

T PRACHA RAT

BANGSU

Chatuchak Park

Weekend Market

T LAD PHRAO

T CHARAN SANIT WONG

T RATCHAWITHI NAKHON CHAISRI

DUSIT

RATCHA THEWI

T PHAHON YOTHIN

T. WONGWANG ROB NOK OUTER RING ROAD

BANGKOK NOI

PHRA NAK HON

PATHUMWAN

T. RAMA IX

T. PHETCHABURI

KHLONG TOEY

T SUKHUMVIT

BANGKOK YAI

CHALOEM MAHANAKHON EXPRESSWAY

N

T. PHET KASEM

Taksin Bridge

THON BURI

Krungthep Bridge

CHALOEM MAHANAKHON EXPRESSWAY

T. RAMA II

T. SUKSAWAT

CHAO PHRAYA RIVER

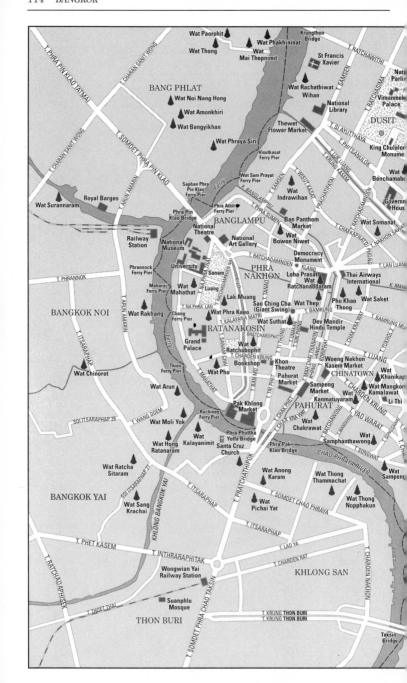

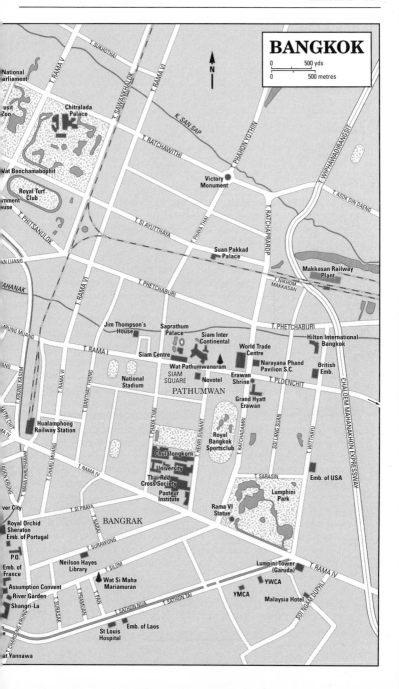

BANGKOK

0   500 yds
0   500 metres

N

National Parliament

usit Zoo

Chitralada Palace

T. RAMA V

T. SUKHOTHAI

T. SAWANKHALOK

T. RAMA VI

T. RATCHAWITHI

K. SAN SAP

PHAHON YOTHIN

T. WIPHAWADIRANGSIT

Wat Benchamabophit

Royal Turf Club

rnment use

T. PHITSANULOK

AN LUANG

AHANAK

T. SI AYUTTHAYA

Victory Monument

T. PHAYA THAI

T. RATCHAPRAROP

T. ASOK DIN DAENG

Suan Pakkad Palace

Makkasan Railway Plant

T. NIKHOM MAKKASAN

T. RAMA VI

T. PHETCHABURI

T. PHETCHABURI

RUNG MUANG

Jim Thompson's House

Saprathum Palace

Siam Inter Continental

World Trade Centre

Hilton International Bangkok

T. RAMA I

Siam Centre

Wat Pathumwanaram

SIAM SQUARE

Novotel

Narayana Phand Pavilion S.C.

British Emb.

T. PLOENCHIT

ANG

KRUNG KASEM

T. RAMA VI

BANTHAT THONG

National Stadium

PATHUMWAN

Erawan Shrine

Grand Hyatt Erawan

T. RATCHADAMRI

SOI LANG SUAN

T. WITHAYU

CHALOEM MAHANAKHON EXPRESSWAY

MAITRI CHI MA IV

CHARU MUANG

Hualamphong Railway Station

T. RAMA IV

PHYA THAI

HENRI DUNANT

Royal Bangkok Sportsclub

MAHA PHRUTHARAM

SUEN KRUNG

ver City

T. SI PRAYA

Chulalongkorn University

Thai Red Cross Society

Pasteur Institute

T. SARASIN

Lumphini Park

Emb. of USA

BANGRAK

NARAI

Rama VI Statue

Royal Orchid Sheraton

Emb. of Portugal

P.O.

Emb. of France

Neilson Hayes Library

T. SURAWONG

T. SILOM

Lumpini Tower (Garuda)

T. RAMA IV

Assumption Convent

River Garden

Shangri-La

PRAMUAN

T. PAN

Wat Si Maha Mariamuran

YWCA

YMCA

Malaysia Hotel

SURASAK

SOI NGAM DUPHI

CHAROEN KRUNG RD

le

T. SATHON NUA

T. SATHON TAI

at Yannawa

St Louis Hospital

Emb. of Laos

Ratanakosin

Sanam Luang

The centre of Rama I's capital was the Grand Palace (Phra Boroma Maharatchawong), and the various buildings of which it is composed are still among the most important and impressive in Bangkok. It stands with the royal temple of Wat Phra Kaeo, which houses the Emerald Buddha, within an enclosure surrounded by a high wall and covering an area of nearly 220,000 sq m. Immediately to the north of the palace enclosure is **Sanam Luang** ('Great' or 'Royal Field'), a huge oval area which once formed part of the Wang Na or Palace of the Front, the home of Rama I's brother, who was second or deputy king. At various times in the past it has been used as a race track and a golf course, but its primary official functions today are as a royal cremation ground and as the site of the annual **Ploughing Ceremony**. This ceremony is an ancient Brahmanic ritual performed in order to ensure a good rice harvest. It was revived by King Mongkut and is now held every year on an auspicious day in May fixed by the royal astrologers. The king generally presides over the ceremony, in which furrows are cut in the ground by a plough drawn by two garlanded oxen, and rice that has been sprinkled with lustral water by *brāhman* priests is scattered. After the ceremony, onlookers take handfuls of the rice to plant in their fields to ensure that their harvests, too, are abundant.

Flying kites (*wao*) and **kite-fighting** has been carried on in Sanam Luang during the months of March and April ever since 1899, when permission was given by King Chulalongkorn, who was himself an enthusiastic kite-fighter. The fights are held between two teams, one with a *chula* or male kite and the other with a *pukpao* or female kite. The two teams stand on either side of a line dividing the field in which the contest takes place, and each tries to bring down the opposing team's kite on its own side of the line. The large star-shaped *chula*, which is nearly two metres high, is armed with bamboo hooks on its long tail with which it attempts to grapple the *pakpao*, while the smaller and more nimble diamond-shaped *pakpao* has a loop with which its tries to lassoo the *chula*. The kite-fighting season reaches its climax at the end of April with the contest for the Royal Cup, which is presented by the king.

Another Thai sport played in Sanam Luang during March and April is **takro**, a game also popular in Malaysia and Indonesia, the object of which is to keep a woven rattan ball (nowadays often made of plastic) about 12cm in diameter in the air, using every part of the body except the hands. The players either stand in a circle and, as in basketball, try to get the ball through a hoop high above the ground in the centre of the circle as many times as possible in a set time, or form teams of three and, as in volleyball, play over a net. The volleyball form is the one that is played internationally, for example in the Asian Games, but the basketball form is more popular in Thailand. It is a game requiring quick reactions and considerable agility, and is fascinating to watch.

■ Saman Luang was formerly the scene of a large Sunday market, which in 1982 was moved to Chatuchak in the north of the city (see p 139).

In the southeast corner of Sanam Luang opposite the Grand Palace is the **Lak Muang** or foundation pillar of the city, and this is as appropriate a place as any from which to begin a tour of Bangkok. The *lak muang*, which is in the form of a wooden *liṅga*, was set up by Rama I in 1782. King Vajiravudh restored it and had the city's horoscope inscribed on it in gold. It is now set below ground level and enshrined in an ornate pavilion with doors inlaid with gold. Next to it is the *lak muang* of Thon Buri, now part of the municipality of Bangkok. As the guardian spirits that dwell within it are believed to be able to grant wishes, it is a scene of constant activity, and many supplicants hire Thai dancers to perform in a small adjoining pavilion in order to please them.

In the southwest corner of Sanam Luang is **Silpakorn University of Fine Arts**, formerly the Institute of Fine Arts, founded by the Italian artist Corrado Feroci, who came to Thailand in the early 1930s, changed his name to Silpa Bhirasri and remained in Thailand for the rest of his life. The university has a hall where special exhibitions are held from time to time (open daily 09.00–19.00).

Wat Phra Kaeo and the Grand Palace

Opposite Silpakorn University on the south side of T. Na Phralan is the Wisetchaisi Gate, which is the principal entrance to the enclosure in which are the Grand Palace and Wat Phra Kaeo (both open daily 08.30–11.30, 13.00–15.30, except Buddhist holidays, when the Grand Palace is closed and entry to Wat Phra Kaeo is free). To reach Wat Phra Kaeo, first cross a large courtyard leaving the *wat* on the left, and then enter a second courtyard. Here tickets can be purchased and there is a small shop. The entrance charge includes an only moderately informative guide book with a plan, a ticket to the Coin Pavilion, which houses a collection of medals and orders presented to the Thai royal family, and a ticket to the Vimanmek Palace (see below). Entry is forbidden to people wearing shorts, singlets and sleeveless shirts.

Wat Phra Kaeo

From the ticket office a narrow alley leads directly to Wat Phra Kaeo, the Temple of the Emerald Buddha.

The **Temple of the Emerald Buddha (Wat Phra Kaeo or Wat Phra Si Ratana Satsadaram)** stands in a precinct bounded by T. Maha Rat, T. Thai Wang, Sanam Luang and T. Na Phralan. It was constructed in the reign of Rama I to house the Emerald Buddha and has been extensively restored and altered several times, most recently in Bangkok's centenary year of 1982.

The **Emerald Buddha** (Phra Kaeo Morokot or Phra Ratana Phimpha), palladium of the Thai kingdom, is a small image, only 75cm high, of the Buddha seated in *dhyāna mudrā*. It is made not of emerald but of green jade, and was first discovered in Chiang Rai in 1434 (see p 293). After many vicissitudes, which took it to Lampang, Chiang Mai, Luang Prabang and Vientiane in Laos, it was finally brought back to Thailand by Rama I in 1778 and installed in the *ubosot* of Wat Arun in Thon Buri, which was the royal chapel of the kings of Thon Buri. In 1784 it was moved to the *ubosot* of Wat Phra Kaeo, which ever since has been the royal chapel of the Chakri kings. Rama I had two sumptuous robes made for the image, one for the dry season and one for the rainy season; to these Rama III added a third costume for the winter. The king changes these robes in an elaborate ceremony three times a year.

The outer entrance to the *wat* is flanked by six gilded *chedi*—two on the right and four on the left—on octagonal bases decorated with a frieze of figures of demons and monkeys. This entrance leads into a gallery roofed with glazed tiles, which contains wall paintings on 178 panels illustrating episodes from the *Ramakien*. The panels date from the reign of Rama III, but were restored in 1882 and again in 1932. In the second restoration some of the panels were completely repainted in a more naturalistic Western style. Parts of the text of the *Ramakien* are inscribed on marble slabs set into the pillars.

The gallery surrounds a huge marble platform on which stand several buildings. The first of these, immediately opposite the entrance, is a pavilion surmounted by a *prang* and flanked by two gilded and redented *chedi*. This is the **Royal Pantheon (Prasat Phra Thep Bidon)**. It was built in 1856 by King Mongkut, reconstructed by King Chulalongkorn and converted by King Vajiravudh into a royal pantheon. It contains statues of previous Chakri kings, the first three in traditional Thai dress, and Mongkut and Chulalongkorn in military uniform. On the terrace there are memorials composed of the emblems of each monarch standing on bases surrounded by bronze figures of the white elephants and other important elephants of his reign. It is only open to the public once a year on Chakri Day, 6 April, the date of the foundation of the Chakri dynasty.

To the west of the Royal Pantheon is a library (*ho trai*) known as **Phra Mondop**. Here Rama I had 12 small open-sided pavilions built, which are now used for the ordination of monks. North of these he constructed a library to house the revised version of the *Tripitaka* which he had commissioned. Unfortunately the library was burnt down during the celebrations for its inauguration. It was replaced by Rama III with the present library (Phra Mondop), in which there is a manuscript cabinet inlaid with mother-of-pearl containing a copy of the *Tripitaka*. Further to the north is another library built for Rama I, known as **Ho Phra Monthien Tham**, where the rest of the *Tripitaka* is housed, in more cabinets inlaid with mother-of-pearl. The double doors of this library are also inlaid with mother-of-pearl and are one of the three pairs of 18C doors that were brought to Bangkok from Wat Borom Phutthabat in Ayutthaya (see p 210). The mural paintings inside, which date from the early Ratanakosin period, have recently been restored.

To the west of Phra Mondop is a replica of the Phra Phutthabat shrine near Saraburi (see p 193) and a gilded *chedi* (Phra Si Ratana Chedi), constructed in 1855 and similar in form to the three *chedi* of Wat Phra Si Sanphet in Ayutthaya (see p 207). To the north is a replica of the Khmer temple of Angkor Wat made in 1882 for the celebrations of the centenary of Bangkok. Here also are large gilded figures of *kinnaris, kinnaras, haṁsas* and other mythical creatures. On the south terrace of Phra Mondop is one of five images of the Buddha obtained by King Chulalongkorn from Java.

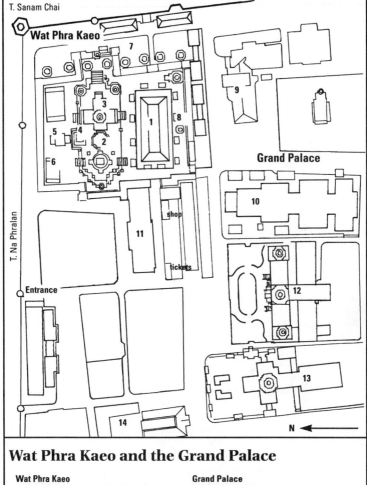

Wat Phra Kaeo and the Grand Palace

Wat Phra Kaeo
1. Temple of the Emerald Buddha (*ubosot*)
2. Phra Mondop
3. Royal Pantheon
4. Model of Angkor Wat
5. Wihan Yot
6. Wihan Phra Nak
7. Cloisters
8. Belfry
9. Boromaphiman Hall

Grand Palace
10. Amarinda Hall
11. Phaisan Hall
12. Chakri Maha Prasat
13. Dusit Hall
14. Museum

The **ubosot** in which the Emerald Buddha is enshrined stands on a marble platform and is surrounded by columns with lotus capitals. The outer walls and the columns are richly decorated with gilded stucco and glass mosaic inlay. The three doors are of mother-of-pearl inlay and date from the reign of Rama I. In front of each of them is a pair of bronze guardian lions in the Khmer style, but probably the work of Thai artists. On the gable above the entrance is a figure of Vishnu mounted on Garuda.

The Emerald Buddha is seated on a high gilded wood throne in a *busabok* shrine with a canopy in the form of a *mondop* above.

In front of the Emerald Buddha's shrine is a small bronze Buddha image called **Phra Samphuttha Panni**, which was commissioned by King Mongkut in 1830 when he was still a monk. The image is seated in *dhyāna mudrā* and is in the new more humanised style of the period, without an *uṣṇīṣa* and wearing a pleated robe. On the base of the throne are ten other gilded bronze Buddha images presented by successive kings of the Chakri dynasty.

On either side of the Emerald Buddha is a bronze image of the **standing crowned Buddha** in the *mudrā* of Calming the Ocean. These statues were set up by Rama III in 1841 in honour of his two predecessors. He dedicated the one on the north side to Rama I and called it Phra Phuttha Yotfa Chulalok, and that on the south to Rama II and called it Phra Phuttha Letla Naphalai. He then declared that henceforth these should be the official names of the two kings.

The *ubosot* also contains some fine wall paintings dating from the reign of Rama I, but entirely repainted during the reign of Rama III. They illustrate the *Traiphum*, the Life of the Buddha and *jātaka* tales.

To the west of the *ubosot* King Mongkut constructed a **pavilion** to house the 34 small bronze Buddha images in various attitudes, representing the 33 kings of Ayutthaya and the single king of Thon Buri, that had been cast for Rama II using copper found at Chantuk in Nakhon Ratchasima province. The **murals** inside this pavilion are the work of Khrua In Khong, one of the first Thai painters to use perspective and other Western techniques, who also worked at Wat Bowon Niwet (see p 130). In the southern of the two buildings, which is called Ho Ratchapongsanuson, are eight small Buddha images representing the kings of the Chakri dynasty, each one protected by a many-tiered parasol. The murals here portray episodes from the life of Rama I.

To the south of the *ubosot* is a belfry in the form of a *mondop*, and to the east are eight *prang* built by Rama I to symbolise the eight major elements of the Buddhist religion: the Buddha, the *Dharma*, the *Sangha*, the order of the Buddhist nuns, *cakravartins*, *bodhisattvas*, Pacceka Buddhas and Maitreya Buddhas.

Rama III laid out the grounds of the enclosure of Wat Phra Kaeo with artificial hills, stone seats and Chinese stone sculptures. He also commissioned the figure of the hermit that sits behind the *ubosot* with a pestle and mortar in front of him, which the people could use to prepare their medicines. There is no *kuti*, as Wat Phra Kaeo has no monastic community attached to it.

The Grand Palace
To reach the Grand Palace leave the precinct of Wat Phra Kaeo by the gate in the southwest corner. Since 1946 the royal family has lived in the Chitlarada Palace (see below), and the Grand Palace is now only used for state receptions and ceremonies. Not all the buildings are open to the public.

On the left side immediately to the south of the temple precinct is the **Boromaphiman Hall**, a handsome building in French style completed by King Vajiravudh. It is used to house visiting foreign royalty and other state guests. To the south of this is the Sala Satathai, which is also a building in Western style,

The Chakri Maha Prasat in the Grand Palace, Bangkok

and is used for royal banquets. To the east of the Boromaphiman Hall is the **Inner Palace**. Here lived the queen and other royal consorts, and the royal children until they reached puberty, when their topknots were cut off in the tonsure ceremony and they moved out. The king was the only man permitted to enter this part of the Grand Palace. In 1900 there were about 3000 women living in the Inner Palace, including servants and the daughters of noble families sent here to learn cookery, embroidery, the making of floral wreaths and other polite accomplishments. The last resident of the Inner Palace died in the 1970s. In its present form the building dates from the reign of King Vajarivudh, who, among other innovations, added a dome over the inner chamber deco-

rated with frescoes depicting the Vedic gods Indra, Yama, Varuna and Agni. Beneath these are inscriptions listing the ten kingly virtues—giving, right conduct, personal sacrifice, honesty, humility, concentration, lack of anger, lack of malice, patience and avoidance of wrongdoing.

Further to the south is a pavilion called **Mahisra Prasat** built by King Mongkut to enshrine the relics of his father Rama II.

On the right to the southwest of the temple precinct is the **Phra Maha Monthien**, which consists of three interconnected buildings. The first of these is the **Phra Thinang Chakrapahat Phiman**, where the first three kings of the Chakri dynasty lived. It contains a royal bedchamber on the east side, a dressing chamber in the centre, and on the west a reception room where now the regalia are kept. The king still spends at least one night in this apartment after his coronation as a mark of having ascended the throne of his ancestors. It is connected by a flight of steps to the hall known as **Phra Thinang Phaisan Taksin** or Phaisan Hall where coronations are held. Here there are two thrones, one on either side of an altar on which is a small figure of a celestial being known as **Phra Siam Thewathirat**, tutelary deity of the Thai nation. One throne is the **coronation chair** itself on which the king sits to receive the regalia of crown, sword, staff, fan, yak's tail fly-whisk, jewelled slippers and parasol; the other is an

The Dusit Maha Prasat throne hall, Grand Palace, Bangkok

octagonal seat where the new king is formally invited to rule by his subjects. In the north wall of the hall is a gate known as **Thewarat Mahesuan**, through which only the king, the queen and the royal children may walk. This leads to the **Phra Thinang Amarin Winitchai**, which was originally the principal audience hall of the Middle Palace and was formerly used for the reception of ministers and officials and foreign ambassadors. In this hall, which is the only one now open to the public, is the **Phra Thinang Busabok Mala**, a pavilion of ornately carved wood with a tiered roof made in the reign of Rama I, standing on a gilded dais of Rama III's reign. It has curtains in front, which were drawn to conceal the king when he entered Phra Thinang Phaisan Taksin and were then parted with a fanfare to reveal him seated in majesty with his regalia about him. The boat-shaped structure behind the throne contains the ashes of previous Chakri rulers. Also in this building is the throne known as **Phra Thaen Sawetachat**, which is used by the king for certain investiture ceremonies and for birthday audiences.

On the southwest side of the palace enclosure is the **Chakri Maha Prasat**, which was built by King Chulalongkorn to designs by the British architect John Chinitz to celebrate the centenary of the foundation of the Chakri dynasty. It is a curious hybrid building in the Italian Renaissance style, but topped with a classical tiered Thai roof surmounted by spires that has led it to be described as a foreigner wearing a Thai dancer's headdress. There is a display of ancient weapons on the ground floor. The only part still in use is the **central throne hall**, where foreign envoys present their credentials to the king and which, appropriately enough, contains four large oil paintings depicting diplomatic receptions. On the right of the entrance is a picture of Queen Victoria receiving an embassy from King Mongkut, and beyond this is a scene of Louis XIV of France receiving the embassy of King Narai in the Galerie des Glaces at Versailles. On the left are pictures of King Mongkut receiving a French embassy and Napoleon III receiving a Thai embassy at Fontainebleau. The chandeliers and other crystal decorations in this hall are mostly presents from foreign monarchs. There is a dining hall by the side of the grand staircase.

To the west of the Chakri Maha Prasat is the **Dusit Maha Prasat**, an audience hall with a four-tiered tiled roof surmounted by a seven-tiered gilded spire. This hall contains Rama I's ebony throne inlaid with mother-of-pearl. The throne is surmounted by a nine-tiered white parasol, symbol of royal legitimacy and authority. Behind this are the former living quarters of the royal family and a museum containing some inscriptions and decorations that were displaced during restorations of the Grand Palace.

A little to the east against the wall surrounding the Dusit Maha Prasat is the **Phra Thinang Aphonphimak Prasat**, a pavilion built by King Mongkut in classical Thai style where the king ceremonially changed his robes before going down the flight of steps to mount the royal palanquin. It was reproduced in the Thai stand at the Brussels exhibition in 1958.

Wat Mahathat and the National Museum

T. Na Phrathat runs north from Silpakorn University past the red stuccoed building of the **Royal Institute**, dating from 1905, to **Wat Mahathat** (open daily 09.00–17.00). In this temple the revision of the *Tripitaka* was carried out in 1786, and in 1803 the examination system for admission to the novitiate and the monkhood was instituted. It is also the temple in which King Mongkut lived for the first few of the 27 years he spent as a monk before succeeding to the throne. It is now an important meditation centre. Much of it was burnt down in 1801 in a fireworks display, and none of the more recent buildings of the *wat* and the meditation centre is of great interest. Attached to Wat Mahathat is a market where amulets, fertility charms, herbal remedies, clothes and food can be bought and which at weekends spills out on to T. Phra Chan and other nearby streets.

Further north along T. Na Phrathat is **Thammasat University**, one of the most important universities in the country and the scene of several student demonstrations in recent years, notably in 1973, 1976 and 1992 (see p 53–4). Beyond that is the **National Museum**. In the reign of Rama I much of the northern half of Sanam Luang was covered by the Wang Na (Palace of the Front), which was the residence of the second or deputy king. In the late 19C the eastern half of the Wang Na was demolished and the western half became the nucleus of the National Museum.

The National Museum is open Wed–Sun, 09.00–12.00, 13.00–16.00; free tours with English speaking guide at 09.30 every Wed.

The first building on the left of the entrance of the museum contains an important collection of prehistoric bronzes and ceramics and other artefacts from Ban Chiang, Ban Kao and other sites. Behind this building is the **Tamnak Daeng** or Red House, which was originally the residence of a sister of Rama I. It is a notable example of an aristocratic house of the early Ratanakosin period and contains some fine pieces of furniture of the same date. A little beyond is the

Samran Mukkhamak Pavilion, an outstanding example of Thai wood-carving in which intricate foliage and vegetal motifs are combined with figures of *nāgas* and other mythical creatures.

Beyond these are two buildings built in 1966 to hold the museum's collection of Hindu and Buddhist sculptures of all periods. The first gallery on the left on the ground floor of the south building contains Japanese, Chinese, Tibetan and other sculptures, including a bronze Roman lamp from Phong Tuk and some statues and relief carvings in the Gandhara style.

In the next two galleries on the **ground floor** is a notable collection of **Khmer and Khmer-influenced sculpture**. Among the most important pieces here are an 8C bronze head of a *bodhisattva*, possibly the Maitreya Buddha, 70cm high, with an elaborate headdress, a beautiful stone standing figure of Uma in the 11C Baphuon style, with lotus-petal decoration on the cylindrical *uṣṇīṣa* and a broad decorated band across the forehead, a 12C stone figure of the crowned Buddha seated in meditation on the the *nāga*, the famous stone statue in the Bayon style of the late 12C from Phimai which is thought to be a portrait of Khmer ruler Jayavarman VII (see p 353), and an extraordinary eight-armed radiating Avalokiteshvara from Muang Sing, exquisitely carved with hundreds of tiny figures of the Buddha on the arms and torso and a seated Amitabha Buddha in the headdress (see p 159), several magnificent lintels, figures of guardian lions, and some small decorative bronzes and ceramics. Here also is a group of unique 8C sandstone figures of Brahmanic deities from Si Thep (see p 80).

On the **first floor** of the south building are two galleries devoted to Mon Dvaravati sculptures. These include a highly important and richly carved Wheel of the Law from Nakhon Pathom dating from the 7C or 8C, which unusually is decorated on both sides of the rim and spokes, and bears a Pali inscription of the Four Noble Truths of Buddhism, a fine and characteristically serene 7C–8C stone image of the Buddha from Wat Na Phra Men, Ayutthaya, a remarkable 8C stone *bodhi* tree, 45cm high, also found at Ayutthaya, and a collection of stucco and terracotta images, which were probably originally pieces of architectural decoration and include figures of the Buddha, *bodhisattvas*, deities and temple guardians, several of them in the *tribhaṅga* pose. Also on the first floor is a group of important early statues from central Java, among them an exceptionally fine Ganesha figure, a collection of *liṅgas* from various sites, and a room devoted to the art of Sri Vijaya. This room contains a four-armed Vishnu from Takua Pa, a 6C *mukhaliṅga* from Chaiya and three figures of *bodhisattvas*, all of them from Chaiya: an elaborately ornamented 8C–9C bronze and silver figure of a *bodhisattva*, thought to be Padmapani, in the *tribhaṅga* pose, which was found in 1905 by Prince Damrong Rajanubhab, a 6C–7C stone figure of Avalokiteshvara, also in the *tribhaṅga* pose, and an ornately jewelled 8C–9C eight-armed bronze Avalokiteshvara from Wat Phra Boromathat (see p 380). The Sri Vijaya collection also contains what is arguably the finest of all the images of the Buddha seated under the *nāga* ever found in Thailand. This is the so-called Buddha of Grahi, from Wat Wieng, Chaiya, Surat Thani, which is described on p 78. Here too is an important collection of Sri Vijaya small bronzes and clay votive tablets.

On the ground and first floors of the building on the north side are ten galleries containing the museum's collection of Lan Na, Sukhothai, Ayutthaya and Ratanakosin sculptures, and of decorative arts, textiles and coins. The collection of **Lan Na sculpture** ranges in date from the late 13C to the 19C. It includes bronze Buddha images and figures of elephants, *haṁsas* and other creatures and a highly important group of votive objects in gilded metal from Hot.

One of the most important objects in the galleries devoted to Sukhothai art is the Ramkhamhaeng stela. This was discovered at Sukhothai in 1833 by the future King Mongkut and is generally accepted to have been composed in part by Ramkhamhaeng himself and to make use of a script invented by him. The Sukhothai collection also contains a fine example of a 15C bronze walking Buddha and two very grand 14C statues of Uma and Vishnu in royal attire with gilded ornaments and attributes.

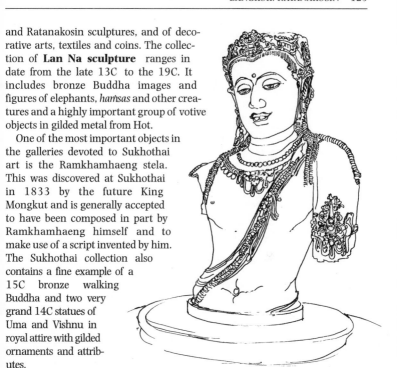

Bodhisattva image from Chaiya, now in the Bangkok National Museum

Perhaps the most important of the large number of objects of the Ayutthaya period are the group of **U Thong** or **early Ayutthaya images of the Buddha**, most of them seated in *bhūmisparśa mudrā*. Downstairs is a colossal Ayutthaya-period head of the Buddha, which in spite of its huge size and the consequent stylisation of the features, has great refinement and spirituality. Several of the Ayutthaya Buddha images are highly ornamented, seated in royal attire with a tapering headdress, pendant earrings hung behind the ears, a jewelled baldric across the chest, and intricate armlets, leg-ornaments and anklets.

The museum's collection of **Ratanakosin sculpture** is more heterogeneous. Some images are in a naturalistic style derived from the Gandhara school in India in the first centuries AD, such as the figure of the standing Buddha Calling down the Rain commissioned by King Chulalongkorn, in which the Buddha is dressed like a Roman senator in a pleated toga-like garment. Others are more stylised, such as a fine standing image of the Buddha made of sandalwood. In this statue, which is c 1.30m high, the Buddha wears a robe with an elaborate gold floral pattern and stands on an ornate five-tiered redented pedestal. Also notable is the group of miniature bronze statues portraying episodes in the Life of the Buddha from his Birth to his *Mahaparinirvāna*, commissioned by Rama III. In the scene of the Victory over Mara, the Buddha image is missing, but the earth goddess Dharani is vividly portrayed, wringing the lustral water from her

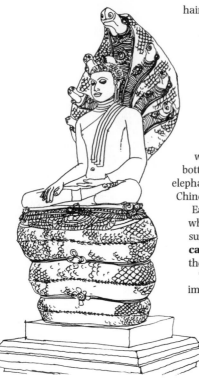

hair to drown Mara's army.

The museum's important collection of **ceramics** contains Ban Chiang and other prehistoric pottery, Si Satchanalai and Sukhothai wares, among which are ceramic finials, tiles, balustrades and other pieces of architectural decoration, northern Thai pottery, brown- and green-glazed Khmer wares, including a remarkable 11C bottle in the form of a monkey and an elephant-shaped 13C to 14C pot, and Chinese and Thai *bencharong* wares.

East of the north building is a hall in which is displayed the museum's superb collection of **royal funerary carriages**, most of them dating from the reign of Rama I.

The museum also contains an important collection of **hun luang puppets** and **khon** masks, and notable examples of the Thai decorative arts, including lacquer, mother-of-pearl, gold, silver and niello, ivory and woodcarving.

The **Phutthaisawan Chapel** is a *wihan* containing a highly revered Sukhothai Buddha image called **Phra Phuttha Sihing**, which is very similar to the

The Buddha of Grahi, dated 1291, from Wat Wieng, Chaiya, Surat Thani, now in the National Museum, Bangkok

images of the same name in Chiang Mai and Nakhon Si Thammarat, and some very fine and exceptionally well preserved **murals** dating from 1795–97. In the lower register these depict 28 scenes from the Life of the Buddha divided from each other in the traditional manner by means of buildings, landscapes or zigzags. The paintings above the windows shows five registers of celestial beings kneeling in homage before the image of Phra Phuttha Sihing in the centre of the hall.

Beyond the National Museum and still on the west side of Sanam Luang, at the corner of T. Na Prathat and T. Saphan Phra Pinklao, is the **National Theatre**, a handsome Thai-style building fronted with lotus columns, where Thai classical dance and drama are performed. Opposite the National Theatre on T. Chao Fa is the **National Art Gallery** (open Tue–Thur, Sat and Sun 09.00–16.00), where work by Thai artists is exhibited.

Wat Pho

Immediately south of the Grand Palace is **Wat Phra Chetuphon Wimonmangkalaram** or **Wat Pho** (open daily 08.00–17.00). The oldest and largest temple in Bangkok, Wat Pho is thought to have been founded in the 16C, although the earliest of the present buildings date from the reign of Rama I. The original temple on this site was known as Wat Photharam or Wat Pho ('Monastery of the Bodhi Tree'), the name by which the present temple is commonly known, and is believed to have been extended during the reign of King Phra Phetratcha (1688–1703), though it does not appear on a Western map of the Thon Buri fortifications made during this reign. It is a large complex of buildings surrounded by a wall with 16 gates, of which only two are open to the public, and containing 91 *prang* and *chedi*. The *wat* proper (*phutthawat*) is on the north side of T. Chetuphon, and the monks' quarters are to the north of the main entrance through the south gate on T. Chetuphon.

The four principal **chedi** were each dedicated by a different king and each is decorated with pieces of porcelain in a different colour. The *chedi* of Rama I is green, and that of Rama II is white, Rama III yellow and Rama IV blue. Its chief attraction is the **colossal reclining Buddha image** made of gilded stucco in a **wihan** built by Rama III in 1832 in the northwest corner of the temple enclosure. This statue, which also dates from the reign of Rama III, measures 46m by 15m and is made of gilded stucco over a brick core. The soles of the feet are inlaid with mother-of-pearl and show the 108 auspicious signs of the Buddha. The **paintings** on the walls of the *wihan* illustrate scenes from the Sri Lankan Buddhist chronicle, the *Mahāvamsa*, and from the lives of disciples of the Buddha. At the bottom of each bay between the windows is a marble slab with an inscription telling the story depicted in the painting above. Some of these slabs are missing. The panels of the doors and window shutters are decorated with gilded lacquer designs of scenes from *jātaka* tales, mythical animals, flowers, constellations and weapons.

Rama I planned to retrieve Buddha images from all over the kingdom and install them in Bangkok. He is reputed to have rescued nearly 1250 bronze, brass and *nak* images in this way; 689 of them are now in Wat Pho. Most of them belong to the Sukhothai and Ayutthaya periods and were placed in four *wihan* built between the inner and the outer gallery, each with a porch at the front and rear. Among the most important of them are a **standing image of the Buddha** with the left hand in *abhaya mudrā* cautioning the Sandalwood Image (*ham phra kaen chan*), 12m high, called **Phra Phuttha Lokanat**, which was brought from Wat Phra Si Sanphet in Ayutthaya and is now in the inner porch of the east *wihan*, and, in the south *wihan*, a Sukhothai-style image called **Phra Phuttha Chinarat**, which has five bronze figures of kneeling disciples in front of it and contains in its base 11 relics from the royal palace of Ayutthaya.

The original **ubosot** of Wat Pho was converted into a *sala kan parian* by Rama I, who built a new ubosot, which was in turn enlarged by Rama III. It contains a late Ayutthaya-style image of the Buddha known as **Phra Phuttha Thewa Pratimakhon** on a three-tiered pedestal. Within this image are buried the ashes of Rama I. In strict accordance with tradition, the image faces west

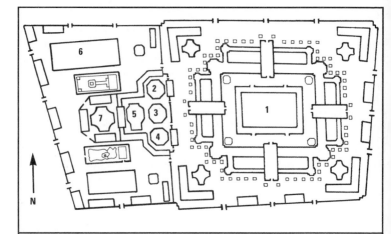

Wat Pho

1. *ubosot*
2. orange *chedi* (King Rama III)
3. green *chedi* for Sri Sanphet image (reign of King Rama I)
4. yellow *chedi* (King Rama II)
5. blue *chedi* (King Mongkut)
6. *wihan* for the reclining Buddha image
7. *ho trai*

towards the Chao Phraya River. On the bottom and middle tiers are a fan, robes, alms bowl, spittoon, betel containers and other monkish paraphernalia. The **mural paintings** illustrate the lives of certain eminent monks and show some fascinating scenes of court and urban life in the early 19C. In one bay is a scene of the king playing polo, in another a nobleman is shown with a gilded caste cord being carried in a palanquin, followed by servants holding a teapot, pipe and betel set, while a third shows the traditional Thai way of delivering babies. Chandeliers hang from the ceiling. Round the base are sandstone panels depicting scenes from the *Ramakien*. The doors also have scenes from the *Ramakien* in mother-of-pearl inlay by Prince Krom Muen Mattayapitak.

Scattered around the temple enclosure are numerous **stone guardian figures** wearing unmistakably Western top hats, stone animals and pagodas. These statues were originally used as ballast for the return voyages of the boats that took Thai rice to China in the 19C.

To the north of the enclosure is a **ho trai**, which was restored in 1956 and again in 1987. The exterior walls are covered with coloured glass mosaic. Inside are wall paintings portraying in a naturalistic manner elephants, horses, cats and mythical animals in the Himavanta Forest, episodes from the *Ramakien*, and scenes of village life, including log-hauling and bricklaying.

Rama III assembled scholars and experts in different arts and sciences to set up an academy at Wat Pho. Their teachings are inscribed on a series of marble slabs, in paintings and drawings, relief carvings and statues, which together form a kind of open-air university.

Seated Buddha images in bhūmisparśa mudrá, *Wat Pho, Bangkok*

Against the east wall of the enclosure is a **massage hall** where the masseurs employ traditional methods. Traditional Thai massage is still widely practised in Thailand, and is considered to be a sovereign remedy for all kinds of disorders. It is also possible to study massage here on brief courses lasting a week or ten days.

Phra Nakhon and Banglamphu

Phra Nakhon lies to the east of Ratanakosin and Sanam Luang and Banglamphu in the area between T. Ratchadomanoen Klang and Khlong Banglamphu.

In the northeast corner of Sanam Luang, opposite the Royal Hotel, is a **fountain** with a statue of the earth goddess **Dharani** (known in Thai as Mae Phra Thorani) wringing the lustral water out of her hair, which was erected by King Chulalongkorn to provide drinking water for the people. From the Royal Hotel T. Ratchadamneon Klang runs east towards the Democracy Monument. The **Democracy Monument** (**Anusawari Prachathipathai**), was built in 1939 to a design by Silpa Bhirasri to commemorate the abolition of the absolute monarchy and the establishment of the constitution of 24 June 1932. It is a curious edifice with four wing-shaped structures each 24 metres high and arranged in a circle with a radius of 24m in reference to the date of the constitution, and 75 cannons buried round the base denoting the year 2475, the equivalent of 1932 in the Buddhist era. It was the rallying point for the anti-government riots of May 1992.

Northwest of the Democracy Monument in Bang Lamphu is **Wat Bowon Niwet** (open daily 08.30–10.00), which stands a the corner of T. Phra Sumen and T. Bowon Niwet, opposite the Ban Phanthom market on the other side of

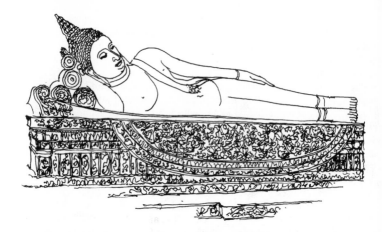

Reclining Buddha image, Sukhothai 14C–15C, Wat Bowon Niwet, Bangkok

Khlong Banglamphu. It was built in 1827 by Rama III. King Mongkut lived here for most of the 27 years he spent as a monk before succeeding to the throne, and became abbot, and it was here that he founded the Thammayutika sect (see p 70). King Bhumipol was ordained as a monk here, and the distinguised Catholic theologian Thomas Merton died here. It is now the seat of the supreme patriarch of Thailand.

The temple is surrounded by a crenellated wall and the entrance doors opposite the *ubosot*, which are only opened at the time of the full moon, are decorated with pieces of ceramic. Within the enclosure is a heavily restored central *chedi* flanked on one side by an **ubosot** and on the other by two *wihan*. The *ubosot* is T-shaped and has a porch supported by two pairs of square pillars. It contains a bronze Buddha image named Phra Phuttha Chinasi, which dates from the Sukhothai period and was brought to Bangkok from Phitsanulok in 1829. The walls are decorated with a series of important **paintings** by **Khrua In Khong**, who was perhaps the most influential of the numerous monk-painters who worked in the temples of Bangkok in the latter half of the 19C, and one of the first to use perspective and other Western techniques (see p 120).

North of Khlong Banglamphu, in the area bounded on the west by T. Samsen, the north by T. Krung Kasem and the south by T. Wisut Kasat, is Wat Indrawihan, which is notable chiefly because it contains a colossal standing Buddha image 32m high.

Wat Suthat Thepwararam

From the Democracy Monument T. Ti Thong runs south to **Wat Suthat Thepwararam** (open daily 09.00–17.00; *wihan* only at weekends and on Buddhist holidays). The principal entrance to Wat Suthat is on the north side on T. Bamrung Muang, but this is only open on Buddhist holidays. At all other times access to the temple enclosure is gained through the entrance on T. Ti Thong. The enclosure is surrounded by a gallery in which there are rows of gilded Buddha images.

The principal building of Wat Suthat is not a *chedi*, but the **Sattamahasathan**, a composite building made up of elements from the seven holiest Buddhist places of worship, including Wat Chet Yot in Chiang Mai. The **wihan**, which is the tallest in Bangkok, was begun during the reign of Rama I and finished in that of Rama III. It is built of brick and is surrounded by low walls adorned with Chinese pagodas. It has a gabled roof and front and rear porches, all of them with pediments of carved and gilded wood decorated with glass mosaic and supported on pillars with lotus capitals. The main pediment shows Indra mounted on the three-headed elephant Airavata (Erawan). It has six pairs of doors each made from a single piece of teak and carved with animals and mythical creatures from the Himavanta Forest. The central doors are said to have been carved and the tree motifs in the niches above the doors to have been designed by Rama II. Inside is an important gilded bronze image of the seated Buddha measuring slightly over 6m from knee to knee. It is named **Phra Phuttha Si Shakayamuni** and was brought in 1808 from Wat Mahathat in Sukhothai, where it had been damaged by fire, and restored. Behind the image is a stone slab with a bas relief carving of the Dvaravati period showing the Miracle at Sravasti and the Buddha Preaching in the Tavatimsa Heaven. In 1950 the ashes of King Ananda were placed under the base of the throne on which the image is seated. The wall paintings depict *jātaka* stories and scenes from the Life of the Buddha and from Buddhist cosmology. They were painted in the reign of Rama III and were extensively restored in the two following reigns. In their present form they are in a naturalistic style, with realistic depictions of water and clouds, buildings in perspective and figures of foreigners.

The **ubosot**, which was completed in 1843, is the longest in Thailand. The roof is supported by a colonnade of square pillars. The carved wooden pediment on the east side shows the sun god Surya seated on a carriage drawn by a lion in a *busabok* with a canopy in the form of a *mondop*, and the west pediment shows the moon god Chandra on a horse-drawn carriage in a similar *busabok*. The great teak doors 5.5m high, 1.5m wide and 15cm thick date from the reign of Rama II. The interior has no columns. On the central altar is a rather crudely restored figure of the Buddha seated in *bhūmisparśa mudrā* with a group of 80 disciples at his feet, known as Phra Phuttha Trai Lokachat. In the 24 spaces between the windows are **paintings** of scenes from the last 24 *jātaka* tales dating from the reign of Rama III. The bays between the windows in the east and west walls contain the only complete depiction in Thai mural painting of Pacceka Buddhas assembled at Mount Gandahmadana in the Himavanta Forest amid many-coloured elephants, *kinnaris*, *nāgas* and *garudas*. Another scene shows the Buddha seated on a crystal throne with Indra in front of him and surrounded by celestial musicians and deities holding parasols, fans and other regalia. The paintings on the window shutters show the celestial city of Indra, king of the gods, and above this scenes from the Life of the Buddha. On the wall facing the altar is a painting of the Buddha subduing Mara and a scene of Shiva's palace in the Khanthamat mountains.

Opposite Wat Suthat on T. Bamrung Muang is the **Giant Swing (Sao Ching Cha)**. This is composed of two upright teak posts painted red and joined by an ornate crosspiece, from which a swing with a wooden seat was formerly suspended. The swing was used for a Shaivite rite that was held every year on the fifth day of the new moon of the second month (i.e. in mid-December or early January) to mark the annual visit of Shiva to earth and to intercede with him to ensure that there would be neither too much nor too little rainfall and therefore a good harvest. Groups of two or four young *brāhmans* would stand together on the wooden seat, and swing up to a height of 25m. The leader of each group would then try to snatch in his teeth one of three bags filled with gold that hung from a bamboo pole, the highest of them 23m above the ground. It is thought that the act of swinging was intended to represent the movement of the sun through the heavens from sunrise to sunset. This exceedingly dangerous ritual caused many fatal accidents, and it was therefore abolished by King Prajadhipok in the 1930s.

To the southeast of Wat Suthat, off T. Siri Phong, is the **Dev Mandir Hindu temple**.

T. Bamrung Muang runs east from the Giant Swing as far as the main railway line and the Kanchanawanit Market, where it becomes T. Rama I. The shops along this street sell monks' robes, Buddha images and image stands, shrines and other religious articles.

Wat Ratchanadda and Wat Thep Thidaram

At the intersection of T. Ratchadamneon Klang and T. Mahachai is **Wat Ratchanadda**, or **Ratchanaddaraman**, which until 1989 was concealed behind the Chaloem Chai cinema. This has now been pulled down and the temple restored. The central *ubosot* is decorated with murals portraying heaven and hell and the angels. It is flanked on either side by a *wihan*. The left hand *wihan* has a large collection of 19C and 20C Buddha images assembled round a standing Buddha image on a high gilded pedestal.

Within the *wat* enclosure and facing Ratchadamneon is the **Loha Prasat** (Metal Tower-Sanctuary), which was begun by Rama III as a memorial to his niece Princess Soamanna Vadhanavadi and only finally completed in the 1980s by the Fine Arts Department. This building, which is more bizarre than beautiful, is modelled on descriptions of the ancient monastery of Sawatti in Sri Lanka and on a metal palace with nine storeys, a golden roof and a thousand cells built later at Anuradhapura, also of Sri Lanka of which only ruins remain. Built in the form of a six-tiered pyramid, the Loha Prasat rises to a height of 33.5m. It is adorned with numerous turrets crowned by iron spires, from which it derives its name. It is not generally open to the public, but it has a central circular stairway leading to the summit, from where there is a fine view of the Golden Mount.

Close by Wat Ratchanadda, is an **amulet market**, where Buddha images and other religious objects are sold.

A little to the south of Wat Ratchanadda on the other side of the *khlong* nearby is **Wat Thep Thidaram**, which also dates from the reign of Rama III. Its three principal buildings stand side by side separated from each other by low walls. In the centre is the *ubosot*, which has a Khmer-style *prang* at each of its four corners. Inside is a small white marble image of the Buddha known as Phra Kaeo Khai, which is about the same height as the Emerald Buddha (75cm), It stands on a gilded boat-shaped pedestal. To the left is a *wihan* containing a seated bronze Buddha on a three-tiered base, at the foot of which are bronze statues of disciples in prayer. On the right is another *wihan* containing an image of the reclining Buddha behind which are two seated Buddha images. In the *kuti* of this temple lived the celebrated Thai poet Sunthorn Phu (1786–1856).

Wat Ratchabophit

Go south from Wat Suthat down T. Ti Thong, turn right down T. Ratchabophit and left down T. Fuang Nakhon to reach **Wat Ratchabophit** (open daily 08.00–20.00). This temple, which was built for King Chulalongkorn between 1869 and 1872, is modelled on Phra Pathom Chedi at Nakhon Pathom (see p 153). It stands in a most unusual circular enclosure, which has *bencharong* ceramic decoration on the outer walls and is entered through doors decorated with relief carvings of soldiers in European uniforms. In the centre is a high *chedi* covered with yellow tiles and standing on a marble-paved platform, with a pavilion decorated with pieces of ceramic at each corner. It enshrines an image of the Buddha seated on the *nāga*. The circular gallery has a double tiered roof supported on marble columns. Built into the north wall is an *ubosot*, which has door and window panels decorated with the insignia of the five royal ranks in gilded black lacquer on the inside and mother-of-pearl inlay on the outside. The interior has a vaulted ceiling in the Gothic style, with gold leaf on the ribbing.

A little to the west of Wat Ratchabophit towards the Grand Palace by Khlong Lot is a **gilded bronze statue of a pig**, erected by King Chulalongkorn in memory of one of his wives, who was born in the Year of the Pig, and a **small cemetery** with tombs of other members of his very large family.

North of Wat Ratchabophit on T. Tanao is **Wat Mahannapharam**, which stands in a large tree-filled compound, and just south of here is **San Chao Pho Sua**, a Chinese Buddhist temple with an elaborate tiled roof surmounted with mythological figures.

Pahurat, Chinatown and the Golden Mount

Prahurat is in the area to the east of Wat Pho and Chinatown is to the east again.

If you are setting off from Wat Suthat or Wat Ratchabophit, follow T. Ti Thong to reach **Pahurat**, the Indian quarter of Bangkok. Here, at the intersection of T. Pahurat and T. Chakraphet, is a huge market of Indian, Chinese and Thai textiles. There are also some good Indian restaurants in this neighbourhood, and an important Sikh temple, the **Siri Guru Sing Sabha**.

A short way further south on T. Tri Phet, at the foot of the Phra Pak Klao Bridge is the **Pak Khlong Market**, an enormous wholesale market for fresh produce.

Immediately to the east of Pahurat is **Chinatown** or **Sampeng**, a colourful and lively quarter bounded by T. Charoen Krung on the north, T. Songwat on the south and T. Krung Kasem and Khlong Phadung Krung Kasem on the east. Formerly a centre of gambling, opium dens and prostitutes, it is now purely commercial. It has some fine early 20C shophouses.

It is virtually impossible to drive through Chinatown, and the best way of seeing it is on foot. A walk through the quarter may begin at **Nakhon Kasem** or the **Thieves' Market**, which is in the warren of little streets between T.

Charoen Krung and T. Yaowarat to the east of Khlong Ong Ang, that runs parallel to T. Mahachai. The boundaries are marked by archways. As the name suggests, it was formerly a centre for stolen goods, but it now chiefly consists of antique dealers and shops selling a wide variety of secondhand merchandise.

To the southeast of Nakhon Kasem are two parallel roads, T. Yaowarat, which is the centre of Thailand's gold trade and where the **Thai Gold Traders' Association** have their headquarters and fix the price of gold, and Soi Sampeng or Soi Wanit, which formerly consisted mainly of brothels, gambling houses and opium dens and is now confined to wholesale trade in various goods.

Go down Soi Wanit towards the old market (**Talat Kao**), to reach on the right **Wat Chakrawat**, an Ayutthaya-period temple chiefly notable for its pond containing several crocodiles and a grotto behind the *wihan* that is reputed to contain a shadow of the Buddha.

Between T. Charoen Krung, T. Yaowarat and T. Traimitr, a little way south of Hualamphong Railway Station is **Wat Traimitr** (open daily 09.00–17.00), a small temple of no architectural distinction, but housing a magnificent Sukhothai-period **seated image of the Buddha** in *bhūmisparśa mudrā* made of solid gold and weighing 5.5 tonnes. It was originally covered in stucco, probably in order to protect it from Burmese looters, and was only discovered to be made of gold in 1957. Twenty years previously, in the course of work by the East Asiatic Company on extending the port of Bangkok, it was moved by crane, together with a bronze Buddha image which is now in Wat Phai Ngoen Chotikam in Thon Buri, from its original site in a small temple near the river to Wat Traimitr. During the time it remained at Wat Traimitr it was exposed to the rain, which softened the stucco, so that when in 1957 it was dropped in the course of again being moved, the stucco cracked to reveal the gold beneath.

There are other temples in Chinatown that repay a visit. The leading Chinese Mahayana Buddhist temple in Bangkok is **Wat Mangkon Kamalawat** in T. Charoen Krung, where enormous candles decorated with Chinese figures are burnt before the altar. Off T. Plap Phlachai is a Chinese temple called **Wat Khanikaphon** or **Wat Mae Lao Fang**, which was founded by a successful brothel keeper. Here it is possible to see worshippers ceremonially burning models of cars, aeroplanes, computers etc. for their deceased relations to use in the after-life. Also on T. Plab Phachai is a Daoist temple known as **Li Thi Mien**. At the south end of T. Songsawat is **Wat Samphanthawong**, also known as **Wat Ko**, a fine temple surrounded by magnificent old teak *kuti*. Further south again on T. Traimitr is **Wat Sampeng**, also known as **Wat Pathum Khongkha**, which dates from the 17C and is one of the oldest temples in Bangkok.

On T. Mangkon, which connects T. Yaowarat and T. Charoen Krung, is **Wat Kanmatuyaram** ('Monastery of the Mother of Kan'). This *wat* was built in the reign of King Mongkut in the gardens of a pious Buddhist lady, whose son Kan had been brought up at Wat Rakhang Khositaram in and later became a court official of King Chulalongkorn. The **ubosot**, which faces north, has some final **mural paintings** in a naturalistic style depicting episodes from the Life of the Buddha and Thai legends. The door and window panels are decorated on the outside with floral motifs in mother-of-pearl inlay, and the inside with highly unusual paintings of the ten kinds of meat that Buddhist monks are forbidden to eat (human, royal lion [*rajasiṁha*], snake, horse, elephant, tiger, yellow tiger, leopard, dog and bear) and the eight kinds of fruit from which they are permitted to make juice (mango, rose-apple, banana, seedless banana, mahua tree, nutmeg, lotus-root, sumac and lychee).

Golden Mount

T. Ratchadamnoen Klang ends at Khlong Banglamphu and divides into three roads running east: T. Ratchadamnoen Nok, T. Nakhon Sawat, and T. Lan Luang. A little to the south of this point at the intersection of T. Boriphat and Khlong Mahanak, and so just outside Phra Makhon and in Pom Prap Sattru Phai is the **Golden Mount (Phu Khao Thong**, open daily 08.00–18.00), one of the most prominent monuments in Bangkok.

> The Golden Mount was begun by Rama III in an attempt to construct an artificial mountain of the same height as the Golden Mount in Ayutthaya (see p 215), but the soil was not firm enough to sustain a building of that height and it collapsed. In the reign of King Chulalongkorn 1000 teak logs were sunk into the ground beneath it, and this made it possible to build the *chedi* up to its present height of 79m. It was restored in 1966.

The *chedi* stands on a high base on which are ornamental stones in bizarre shapes, tombs, funerary urns and frangipani trees. At its foot is **Wat Luang Pho Tho**, a shrine containing an Ayutthaya-style Buddha image and decorated with fine stucco work. At the corners of the platform are four gilded turrets and above it is a circular gallery. The upper part of the monument is surrounded by a spiral staircase. The *chedi* contains relics of the Buddha found at Kapilavastu in Nepal and presented to King Chulalongkorn by Lord Curzon, then viceroy of India.

Today, the Golden Mount is one of the most popular promenades of the people of Bangkok.

At the foot of the Golden Mount and a short distance to the east is **Wat Saket** ('Monastery of the Washing of Hair', open daily 08.00–18.00), so called because Rama I is believed to have stopped and ritually washed his hair here before his coronation in Thon Buri. It is built on the site of a charnel house where victims of the plague were laid out for the vultures to devour. It has no buildings of any architectural distinction except for a remarkable **ho trai** in the late Ayutthaya style with carved wooden doors and window shutters showing everyday life of the period and figures of Persian and French soldiers dressed in the costumes of the early 18C. In the temple enclosure is a *bodhi* tree that is one of several grown from a cutting brought from Sri Lanka in 1818. In the first week in November each year a **temple fair** is held here, during which the Golden Mount is illuminated with coloured lanterns.

Walk south along T. Boriphat to **Soi Ban Bat**, which runs between T. Boriphat and T. Worachak. In this *soi* are the workshops of the few remaining makers of monks' alms bowls (*bat*) in the capital. Increasingly, these bowls are mass-produced in factories, but here they are still made in the traditional manner from eight separate pieces of steel symbolising the Eightfold Path, fused together with copper, heated over a charcoal fire and coated with several layers of lacquer. The average rate of production by a single craftsman is said to be one bowl a day.

Dusit and north Bangkok

Dusit is the name given to the area northeast of Phra Nakhon and Banglamphu that includes the Dusit Park and Zoo and the Chitralada Palace.

The northernmost of the three roads going east from the end of T. Ratchadamnoen Klang is T. Ratchadamneon Nok, which crosses Khlong Padung Krung Kasem and runs into Dusit, a quarter of wide avenues and imposing public buildings. Here it becomes T. U Thong Nai and continues past the National Assembly and the Dusit Zoo up to T. Ratchawithi. The **National Assembly** (The Throne Hall) is a large white marble building of noble proportions in neo-Classical style with a dome built by a group of Italian architects in 1907 as a throne hall for King Chulalongkorn. The vault of the dome is decorated with frescoes of great events in Thai history by Galileo Chini. It was used as the National Assembly until 1974, when Parliament moved to a new building just north of the Vimanmek Palace. In the square in front is an equestrian statue of King Chulalongkorn modelled in Paris and assembled in Bangkok in 1908.

In a large park with a lake opposite the National Assembly is the **Dusit Zoo** (open daily 09.00–18.00), which was originally a botanical garden laid out by King Chulalongkorn and converted into a public zoo in 1938. The entrance is at the U Thong Gate near the equestrian statue of King Chulalongkorn. The zoo contains some interesting rare animals, such as banteng, gaur, serow, rhinoceros, white-handed gibbon, and some Komodo dragons, a giant carnivorous monitor lizard found almost exclusively on the small Indonesian island of Komodo. It has a children's playground and restaurants, and it is possible to hire pedal-boats on the lake. At the weekends there are circus performances.

Just to the north of the National Assembly is the **Vimanmek Palace**, off T. Ratchawithi (open daily 09.30–16.00, last tickets sold 15.00; entrance tickets for the Grand Palace are also valid for Vimanmek). In order to see this palace it is necessary to join a guided tour, which usually takes about one hour. Performances of classical Thai dancing are held here twice a day.

The Vimanmek Palace was built in only seven months for King Chulalongkorn on Ko Si Chang, whence it was moved to its present site in 1901. It is constructed entirely of golden teak decorated with elaborate fretwork and is surrounded on all sides by lakes. Except for the floors, not a single metal nail was used in the construction of any of its 81 rooms. King Chulalongkorn lived here for six years before moving to the Amhonsathan Palace, where he remained until his death in 1910. Vimanmek was abandoned until 1925, when it was occupied for a few months by a consort of King Vajiravudh. In 1982, Queen Sirikit initiated a restoration programme of the palace and it was opened to the public. It contains a fascinating collection of King Chulalongkorn's personal possessions, including some historic photographs, one of them showing the last royal war elephants in Thailand, and one of the first Thai typewriters ever made. In the king's bathroom is a remarkable early shower. There is much hideous 19C furniture, numerous bad portraits of members of the Thai royal family and a small clock museum.

Adjacent to the palace is the **Aphisek Dusit Throne Hall**, a wood, brick and stucco building completed for King Chulalongkorn in 1904 and now housing a fine exhibition of textiles, niello, *yan lipao* baskets and other crafts produced by

Support (Foundation for the Promotion of Supplementary Occupations and Related Techniques), an organisation founded by Queen Sirikit (see p 95). It is open daily 09.00–16.00.

To the east of Dusit Zoo, on the other side of the tree-lined T. Rama V, is another large park full of fine trees and surrounded by avenues and canals with fountains at the intersections. In the centre of this is the **Chitralada Palace**, which was built by King Vajiravudh. The royal family live here when they are in Bangkok. Part of the grounds is devoted to various agricultural research projects in which King Bhumibol is personally interested. It is not open to the public.

To the southwest of the Chitralada Palace is the exclusive **Royal Turf Club** and opposite this at the intersection of T. Rama V and T. Ayutthaya is **Wat Benchamabophit**, commonly known as the Marble Temple (open daily 08.00 –17.00). This magnificent temple was built between 1899 and 1911 to a design by Prince Naris, a half-brother of King Chulalongkorn, and Ercole Manfredi to replace a temple that had been destroyed to make room for the enlargement of the Dusit Palace. The walls are clad in Carrara marble and the three-tiered roof has yellow tiles. In front of the sumptuously decorated porch of the *ubosot* are two marble lions. The windows of the *ubosot* are of stained glass and depict scenes from Thai mythology. The Buddha image here is a copy of Phra Phuttha Chinarat in Wat Phra Si Ratana Mahathat in Phitsanulok (see p 250).

Behind the *ubosot* is a courtyard surrounded by a gallery containing Buddha images, some Thai and others from Burma, Japan, Sri Lanka and elsewhere, some original pieces and others copies. They include two Sukhothai walking Buddha images. Facing the interior of the gallery is a *sala* in which is a fine Khmer-Lopburi bronze image of the Buddha in royal attire. In niches on either side of the south corner of the external wall of the gallery are two Dvaravati standing Buddha images protected by iron grilles.

The temple buildings are surrounded by beautifully kept gardens with lawns, topiary and canals with tiled sides inhabited by turtles. Here also is the *kuti* in which King Chulalongkorn lived while a monk and which has been brought here and reconstructed.

To the south of Wat Benchamabophit on T. Nakhon Pathom near Khlong Phadung Krang Kasem is **Government House**. This mansion, which is in a curious mixture of styles that gives it a vaguely Venetian appearance, was built by King Vajiravudh for one of his male favourites and now contains the offices of the president and vice-president of the Council. It is only open once a year on Children's Day (*Wan Lek*), which takes place on the second Saturday in June.

On the other side of Khlong Phadung Krung Kasem is the **Ratcha-damnoen Boxing Stadium**. Here on Mondays, Wednesdays and Thursdays at 18.00 and on Sundays at 17.00 and 20.00 it is possible to see Thai boxing (*muay thai*), which is Thailand's most popular sport. Muay Thai probably dates back at least to the 15C; in the late 16C King Naresuan made it a compulsory element in the training of his soldiers. Any part of the body may be used to strike an opponent except the head. Originally Thai boxers wrapped their hands in strips of horse or buffalo hide studded with pieces of shell or glass, and this caused so many fatalities that in the 1920s the sport was banned. In the 1930s it was revived and gloves were introduced. Perhaps for this reason, most Thai boxers now prefer to kick with their feet and jab with their elbows than to punch with their hands. Today, most of the best Thai boxers come from the poor northeastern province. They begin their rigorous course of training at the age of six or seven and are often fighting professionally by the age of ten. They seldom continue their boxing careers beyond the age of 25. Some *muay thai* boxers go on to become world champions in international boxing, such as the well-known bantam weight Khaosai Galaxy.

Before each contest the boxers perform a ceremonial dance called *ram muay* to the accompaniment of a Thai oboe (*pi*) in honour of their teachers and of the guardian spirits.

A short way south of the Ratchadamnoen Boxing Stadium and Khlong Phadung Krung Kasem in **Wat Somanat Ratchawora Wihan**, which was built by King Mongkut in 1853 and dedicated to his consort Queen Somanat Watthanawadi, who had died early in his reign.

The *wihan* has a tiled roof supported on round columns and has no *cho fa* or *bai raka* ornaments. The pediment is decorated with stucco and glazed tiles. The door and window frames are lacquered, gilded and inlaid with glass mosaic in floral motifs surmounted by royal crowns. Inside there are two rows of square columns decorated with floral patterns in many colours. The colours in the columns are symbolic, those furthest from the Buddha image being the darkest. The door panels are decorated with *trompe l'oeil* paintings of curtains looped back to show elaborate chandeliers.

The *ubosot* stands behind the *wihan* and is surrounded by low walls in which are niches containing the *bai sema*. It is somewhat smaller than the *wihan* but similar in design, with a roof supported on square columns.

The **murals** in the *ubosot*, which are of exceptionally high quality, are in Western style. They illustrate episodes in the life of Inao (Panji) from the funeral of his grandmother to his wedding. There are numerous depictions of Western buildings among the traditional Thai ones and a remarkable scene of a *nang* performance. The columns inside the *ubosot* have multi-coloured bases, each with a small painting of a *dharma* riddle. The principal Buddha image is seated on a raised platform and surmounted by an elaborate *busabok*.

The *wat* has an unusual drum tower and belfry; both are round with Chinese roofs and round windows.

Near the western end of T. Si Ayutthaya where it crosses T. Samsen are the **Thewet Flower Market**, the new **National Library** building and **Wat Thewarat Kunchon**, a fine temple in the Ratanakosin style. A short way to the north of these buildings are Wat Ratchathiwat Wihan and the Church of St Francis Xavier.

The **Church of St. Francis Xavier** is a building of no great distinction constructed in the late 19C for the Vietnamese Catholic community living in Bangkok.

Wat Ratchathiwat was built in 1909 by Prince Naris, and its *ubosot* has murals painted by the Italian artist Carlo Rigoli working from cartoons by the prince. The *chedi* stands on a square base surrounded by figures of guardian lions and has four niches in which have been placed four Buddha images from the late 8C Buddhist temple of Borobudur in Central Java that were presented to King Chulalongkon when he visited the Netherlands East Indies. To the south are two wooden buildings, one built for King Mongkut when he was a monk at this *wat*, the other moved here from the Grand Palace where it was the residence of a consort of King Chulalongkorn.

To the north of Wat Ratchathiwat on the right of T. Samsen just before it crosses Khlong Samsen is **Wat Bot Samsen**. The front part of the enclosure of this *wat* is occupied by a school, a modern *kuti* and other monastic buildings. Behind these is a fine *ubosot* in Ayutthaya style with a curved base and porches with decorated pediments at each end. The window frames have good stucco decoration. Inside is a large seated Buddha image. The wall paintings, which are in poor condition, depict two rows of praying disciples.

In front of the *ubosot* is a square *chedi* with four niches containing standing Buddha images, and behind the *ubosot* is another smaller *chedi* in a dilapidated state.

Northeast of Dusit, in Chatuchak Park on the corner of T. Phahon Yothin and T. Kamphaeng Phet opposite the Northern bus terminal, is the enormous weekend market which until 1982 was held on Sanam Luang. The **Chatuchak Weekend Market** covers an area of almost 12 hectares (30 acres), in which more than 5000 stallholders sell an immense variety of goods ranging from food and agricultural produce, decorative rocks and bonsai, fighting cocks, flying squirrels and domestic pets, plants, clothes, antiques, hill-tribe products, paintings, *bencharong* and other ceramics, Buddha images and books.

■ Nancy Chandler's map of Bangkok has an inset plan of the market. There is a tourist information centre at the entrance off T. Kamphaeng Phet 2.

In the northern part of Chatuchak Park is a small and interesting **Railway Museum** (open Sun 05.00–12.00). The park also has a 3.1km jogging path.

Beyond Chatuchak, on T. Phahon Yothin, behind Don Muang Airport, is the **Royal Thai Airforce Museum** (open Mon–Fri and first weekend in the month 08.30–16.30), which has an excellent collection of antique military aircraft.

Still further out of the city to the northeast, in the suburb of Minburi, are the **Siam Water Park**, which has a number of pools and slides, and the **Safari World**, a wildlife park covering an area of 68 hectares and containing giraffes, lions, zebras, elephants, orang utans, white pandas and other Asian and African animals.

Nonthaburi

The delightful town of **Nonthaburi** lies on the Chao Phraya River about 20km north of the centre of Bangkok, from where it is easily accessible by the Chao Phraya River Express. It is noted for its traditional wooden houses, its delicious *durian* and its excellent riverside restaurant. It still has tricycle *samlo*, which have been banned in central Bangkok for some years.

There are several attractive *wat* on both sides of the river. Of these the most important is **Wat Chaloen Phra Kiat** on the west bank. This temple was built by Rama III in memory of his parents. It is approached by a causeway flanked with fine trees, and the *wat* enclosure is surrounded by a crenellated wall. Within the enclosure is a tall *chedi* built in the reign of King Vajiravudh, which has recently been restored. The *ubosot*, which has also been restored, and the two *wihan* show a marked Chinese influence in their curved gables decorated with *nāgas* and floral motifs in ceramic, and in the round and square turrets flanking their entrances. The two *wihan*, although ruined, still retain much fine stucco decoration round the windows.

Nonthaburi also possesses a curious museum, the **Museum of the Department of Corrections** (open Mon–Fri 09.00–16.00), which contains a gruesome collection of instruments of torture and execution, including butcher's hooks, axes and a giant wicker *takro* ball with spikes on the inside into which the offender was put before it was given to the elephants for them to play with. (There is still capital punishment in Thailand, now carried out by machine gun.)

Pathumwan and Sukhumvit

Pathumwan is the name given to the area round T. Rama I, Siam Square and Lumphini Park. T. Sukhumvit is the long road that runs southeast and then almost due south from the point where T. Ploenchit joins the Expressway to Chonburi, Phatthaya and the east coast of the Gulf of Thailand.

T. Rama I runs east from the point where T. Bamrung Muang meets Khlong Phadung Krung Kasem, passing on the right the National Stadium and the enormous **Mahboonkrong Shopping Centre**, crosses T. Phaya Thai and reaches **Siam Square**, which is not a square but a rectangular area criss-crossed by a grid of streets. It contains many shops, restaurants and cinemas, the offices of the **British Council** and on the north side of T. Rama I the **Siam Centre**, a large shopping complex with some of the most elegant and expensive shops in Bangkok.

Immediately to the east of the Siam Centre, standing in a large and beautifully maintained garden is the **Siam Inter Continental Hotel**, which is not only one of the most luxurious hotels in the capital, but, with its distinctive sweeping Thai roofs, also architecturally one of the most interesting. A short way further to the east again are the **World Trade Centre**, the **Grand Hyatt Erawan Hotel** and the **Erawan Shrine**, at the corner of T. Ploenchit and T. Ratchadamri.

The **Erawan Shrine** is a Hindu shrine dedicated to Brahma (Phra Phrom) and his elephant mount Airavata (Erawan) that was originally built in 1956 as a spirit house for the local spirits who had been made homeless by the felling of trees in order to construct the first Erawan Hotel on this site and who in consequence caused a number of accidents that had seriously delayed the building works. Once the shrine had been erected there were no further accidents, and the hotel was completed. The shrine itself is of little interest and is in any case almost completely shrouded in garlands, pieces of gold leaf and incense smoke. Dancers and musicians are hired to perform for the spirits, and images of elephants are presented to them. Visitors can also make merit at this shrine by buying caged birds and releasing them into the air.

Opposite the World Trade Centre in T. Ratchadamri are the Novotel and the **Narayana Phand Pavilion**, which is the largest and arguably the best store in Bangkok specialising in Thai arts and crafts.

T. Ploenchit continues eastwards, crosses T. Witthayu (Wireless Road) and then passes under the Expressway, where it becomes T. Sukhumvit. At the intersection of T. Ploenchit and T. Witthayu is the **British Embassy** a handsome building with a spacious formal garden, a statue of Queen Victoria and a memorial to two World Wars in front of it.

To the east of the Inter Continental Hotel, at 969 T. Kwang Pathumwan between T. Rama I and Khlong Saen Saep is the important temple of **Wat Pathumwanaram**, formerly known as Wat Sra Pathum ('Lotus Pool'), which was built by King Monghut in 1857 as a place of relaxation and meditation and presented as a gift to his Queen Thepsirin. At that time this area was outside the city walls and was surrounded by trees and ricefields. The ashes of Prince Mahidol, father of King Bhumipol, are enshrined in a **chedi** in this temple. Most of the monks come from northeast Thailand (Isan) or Laos, and several of the Buddha images in the *wat* are from Lan Xang (Luang Prattang).

In 1972 the **ubosot** was badly damaged by fire, so that the original murals had to be removed and the walls replastered and repainted. The restoration was completed in 1977. The **wihan**, on the other hand, is still more or less as it was in King Mongkut's time. It has a two-tiered roof covered with ceramic tiles and adorned with finials and leaf motifs, and porches at the front and rear. The pediment above the east entrance carries the emblem of King Mongkut, a crown on a pedestal flanked by five-tiered parasols, in carved stucco. Inside the *wihan* are pairs of columns, the bases of which are painted with lotus motifs and figures of holy monks. The colours of the columns are symbolic: those furthest from the principal Buddha are darkest and they become lighter the nearer they are to the image, until those directly in front of it are white.

The upper register of **murals** in the *wihan* shows a procession of royal barges, and the lower register between the windows tells the story of Sri Thanonchai, a court jester who, somewhat in the manner of Til Eulenspiegel, performed various tricks and exploits. In one scene the king orders the ladies of the court to dive in the water for eggs and to make the sound of a hen clucking whenever they bring one up, and then Sri Thanonchai dives, brings up an egg and crows to show he is a cock and not a hen. In another, he is shown winning a wager by dipping his hand in paint and drawing five snakes at the same time. In a third he competes in an underwater basket-weaving contest, which he wins by weaving a basket beforehand and secretly tying it to an upturned boat.

The predominant colours of these wall paintings are blue and orange, and they show evidence of Western influence in their use of perspective and their naturalistic treatment of water and reflections in water. There are scenes with foreigners, especially Americans, horse-drawn carriages, steamships and other Western features.

The doors and window shutters are decorated with charming depictions of mythical creatures, including *nāgas* emerging from lotus pools.

The **ubosot** also has a two-tiered roof covered with ceramic tiles and decorated with *cho fa* finials and leaf-shaped roof ridges. The pediment, as on the *wihan*, displays the emblem of King Mongkut framed by lotus-petals and surmounted by a flame motif. The building is surrounded by a colonnade, and the corners of the bases of the columns are covered with green stone decorated with lotus motifs. The exterior walls are covered in glass mosaic inlay, and the outside of the doors and windows have stucco panels depicting scenes of rural life.

The **paintings** on the interior walls are in two registers: the lower register portrays monks and various merit-making activities, the upper register on the back wall has a series of lotus flowers on each of which seven deities are dancing, and the upper register on the other walls depicts a royal visit to the lotus pool.

The principal **Buddha image** is a very fine 16C seated image from Lan Xang made of gold, silver and bronze alloy and known as Phra Soem. It is seated on a four-tiered lacquered and gilded pedestal.

Behind the *ubosost* is a round *chedi* on a square base embellished at the corners with an ornament of overlapping lotus flowers. The *chedi* contains a Buddha's Footprint on a square base. A staircase leads to the round upper part of the *chedi*, where there is a Sri Lankan marble reclining Buddha image and several other images of the Buddha and of former abbots of Wat Pathumwanaram.

In front of the *wihan* are two *kuti*, each one crowned by a three-storey bell tower. Their roofs have *cho fa* and leaf ornaments and pediments with stucco decoration.

Behind the *wihan* is the **Pariyathitham School** for monks and novices and a *sala* known as Phra Ratchasattha, which is also used for study and meditation.

Follow T. Rama I across T. Phaya Thai; to the right, Soi Kasemsam 2 runs down to Khlong Saen Saep and at the end of the *soi* is **Jim Thompson's House** (open Mon–Sat, 9.00–16.30).

Jim Thompson was an American architect who worked for American intelligence during World II. After the war he settled in Thailand and revived the moribund Thai silk industry (see p 95). In 1959 he bought six traditional teak houses in Ayutthaya, brought them to Bangkok and assembled them on the bank of Khlong Saen Saep. Here also he housed his collection of bronze and stone sculptures, pictures and ceramics, including a large number of *bencharong* pieces. It is a charming and attractive house, even though few of the objects in it are of any great distinction and it retains an obstinately Western atmosphere.

Jim Thompson lived here until his mysterious disappearance and presumed death in 1967 when he was staying with friends in the Cameron Highlands in Malaysia. An interesting biography of Jim Thompson entitled *Jim Thompson : The Legendary American of Thailand* has been written by fellow American and long-time resident of Bangkok, William Warren, who knew him well.

T. Phaya Thai runs north from Siam Square, crosses the main railway and T. Si Ayutthaya and continues to the Victory Monument and T. Ratchawithi. The **Victory Monument** was erected by Marshal Phibun after the Thai War with French Indochina in 1940–41. It consists of a tall stone obelisk at the base of which are a number of bronze statues.

Turn right down T. Si Ayutthaya to reach the **Suan Pakkad Palace** ('Lettuce Garden Palace', open Mon–Sat 09.00–16.00) at 352–4 T. Si Ayutthaya. This palace is situated in a beautiful small garden, inhabited by pelicans, and consists of five houses, which together provide a notable example of traditional Thai wooden domestic architecture. It was formerly the home of the late Prince and Princess Chumbhot of Nagara Svarga and contains their large and varied collection of works of art. These include ceramics, bronze artefacts and beads from Ban Chiang and other Bronze Age sites in northeast Thailand (see p 327), most of which are displayed on the upper floor of House V; some Dvaravati stone and bronze Buddha images, an important 8C–10C Sri Vijaya bronze image of the Buddha with both hands in *abhaya mudrā* several fine Khmer and Khmer-Lopburi stone Brahmanic and Buddhist images dating from the 7C to 14C, among them a notable 7C torso of a female deity, probably Uma, from Aranyaprathet, and a late 10C Khmer head of Shiva; a magnificent 14C gilded bronze Sukhothai walking Buddha image and other important Sukhothai sculptures in bronze, stucco and terracotta; some Sawankhalok ceramics, including several water pots (*kendi*), bronze seated Buddhas from the U Thong and Ayutthaya periods; 18C and 19C *bencharong* wares, woodcarvings and paintings on wood, black and gold lacquered manuscript cabinets, and 18C and 19C mother-of-pearl and niello objects. Two rooms are devoted to an enormous collection of rocks and minerals, crystals and shells.

Perhaps the most important exhibit in the collection is the **Lacquered Pavilion**, which is composed of two superb late Ayutthaya or early Ratanakosin pavilions that were brought here from a site near Ayutthaya. The interior of the pavilion is entirely panelled with scenes from the Life of the Buddha, the *Traiphum* and the *Ramakien* in black and gold lacquer. Some panels show Europeans wearing plumed hats and mounted on prancing horses.

T. Sukhumvit runs southeast from T. Ploenchit to Khlong Toey. Soi 21, better known as Soi Asoke, goes off T. Sukhumvit to the left and runs north to T. Phetchaburi. At 131 Soi Asoke are the offices, lecture hall and library of the **Siam Society** (open Tue–Sat, 09.00–17.00). The Siam Society was founded in 1904, initially solely as an ethnographic museum, and was later extended to embrace the study of natural sciences, archaeology and history. It is now one of the most distinguished learned societies in Asia and enjoys royal patronage. It possesses an excellent library and publishes an important journal (*Journal of the Siam Society*—*JSS*). In the grounds are two traditional Thai houses. One of these, **Ban Kamthieng**, was brought from north Thailand and reassembled here in 1968. On the ground floor it contains a display of farming implements and fish traps and on the first floor some sparsely furnished living quarters. The rectangular lintel above the door to the inner room has a pattern representing testicles, which is intended to ward off evil spirits. Next to it is a rice granary. The other house contains a collection of pottery, basketwork and other artefacts.

Between T. Sukhumvit and T. Phetchaburi is **Khlong Toey**, a largely slum area which is also the port of Bangkok. Because of silting, this port can now only take ships of less than 12,000 tonnes, but it is still extremely overcrowded. A new port has been constructed at Laem Chabang, near Si Racha on the east coast of the Gulf of Thailand, 24km from Chon Buri.

Crocodile Farm and Muang Boran

T. Sukhumvit (Road 3) runs southwest from Bangkok to Samut Prakan (Pak Nam), which is now virtually a suburb of Bangkok, and then to Chon Buri and Phattaya (see p 183).

About 19km out of Bangkok there is a turning to the right which leads to the **Crocodile Farm** (open daily 07.00–18.00). In this farm, which was established in 1950, more than 30,000 crocodiles are kept, chiefly for their highly-prized skin and for their meat, which, particularly among the Chinese, is considered to be a great delicacy. At certain hours of the day performances are arranged in which the crocodiles wrestle with elephants and with their trainers. There is also a small zoo containing elephants, monkeys and snakes.

About 25km from Bangkok a turning to the left leads to the **Ancient City** (**Muang Boran** open daily 08.30–17.00). The Ancient City, which covers an area of some 80 hectares roughly in the shape of the kingdom of Thailand, consists of 89 buildings representing different periods and architectural styles and placed approximately in their correct geographical locations. They include two reception pavilions in Sukhothai style, one of which is situated at the main gate and is used as a ticket office and information centre, while the other contains a statue of Brahma that has been adopted as the official symbol of Muang Boran. There is a city wall and gate modelled on Wat Phra Si Ratana Mahathat at Chaliang and several other imaginative and scholarly reconstructions of buildings that no longer exist or are now in ruins, such as the Sanphet Prasat Palace at Ayutthaya, the audience hall (Thong Phra Rong) of King Taksin at Thon Buri and the Dusit Maha Prasat in Bangkok as it was in Rama I's time. There are several temple buildings copied, some of them on a reduced scale, from famous originals, such as the *sala kan parian* of Wat Yai Sawannaram at Phetchaburi, which houses a museum of Buddhist art, some major Khmer monuments, including Khao Phra Wihan (Preah Vihear) in Cambodia, Prasat Phimai, Sikhoraphum, Phanom Rung and Sdok Kok Thom, the principal *chedi* of Wat Mahathat at Sukhothai, the *prang* of Wat Chulamani at Phitsanulok and of Wat Mahathat at Ratchaburi, Wat Cham Tewi at Lamphun, Wat Chet Yot at Chiang Mai, Prang Sam Yot at Lop Buri and Phra Phutthabat at Saraburi. Some of the buildings are originals that have been brought to Muang Boran and reassembled, notably the *ho trai* and belfry from Wat Bang Yai at Bang Khonthi, Samut Songkhram, and Wat Chong Kham, a wooden Shan temple complex removed from Ngao, a *kuti* from Wat Sitaram in Tak, and the Ho Kham, former residence of the governors of Lampang, which is used to house the Muang Boran art collection. There are typical examples of a Dvaravati house, of a Sukhothai *wihan*, of Ayutthaya and Ratanakosin houses and of central and northern Thai villages. There are several gardens filled with statuary of dubious artistic merit illustrating themes from Thai mythology and folklore. One of the most impressive buildings in Muang Boran is the elaborate Ayutthaya pavilion in the royal garden designed for court performances of *lakhon nai*.

The buildings of Muang Boran are maintained by a team of conservationists and restorers, who thereby contribute to the preservation of traditional Thai arts and crafts.

Between Soi 40 and 42, T. Sukhumvit is the **Museum of Science and Planetarium** (open Wed–Sun, 09.00–16.00).

On Soi 101, T. Sukhumvit is **Wat Tham Mongkhon**, a very large modern temple near which there is a Buddhist Cultural Centre.

Off T. Sukhumvit, Soi 103, is Bangkok's newest park, the **Rama IX Royal Park** (open daily 06.00–18.00), which was inaugurated in 1987 to commemorate the king's 60th birthday.

Bangrak, Sathon and Yannawa

Bangrak is the triangular area bounded on the west by the Chao Phraya River, the north by T. Rama IV and the south by T. Sathon. To the south of T. Sathon is Sathon, and in the area east and south of Sathon is Yannawa.

From the southern end of T. Charoen Krung, T. Rama IV runs southeast towards Lumphini Park. Between T. Rama I and T. Rama IV is **Chulalongkorn University**, which was founded by King Chulalongkorn and is generally considered to be the best university in Thailand. It has several handsome buildings in a hybrid Thai and Western style set in spacious grounds full of fine trees.

On the left hand side of T. Rama IV before it reaches the junction with T. Henri Dunant and T. Surawong is the **Queen Saovabha Memorial Institute** and **Thai Red Cross Society**, where there is a large **snake farm**. Here on every day except Sunday cobras, king cobras, banded kraits, Russell vipers and other poisonous snakes can be seen being milked of their venom.

Immediately to the east of T. Henri Dunant is the **Royal Bangkok Sports Club**, which has a race course, a golf course and a swimming pool. Beyond this, T. Rama IV reaches the junction of T. Ratchadamri and T. Silom at the southwest corner of **Lumphini Park**.

Here stands a statue of King Vajiravudh looking towards Robinson's Department Store and T. Silom. Lumphini Park is Bangkok's largest park and is full of interest. It is frequented by kite-fliers and joggers and by vendors of snake's blood and bile, which are considered to be highly efficacious tonics. There is a weight-lifting area, snack bars and restaurants, and a small lake. From time to time the Bangkok Symphony Orchestra gives Sunday afternoon concerts in the park.

Betweem T. Rama IV and T. Charoen Krung are four parallel streets—T. Si Phraya, Surawong, Silom and Sathon. Of these **T. Silom** has the most interesting buildings, including **Wat Si Maha Mariamman, Wat Khaek** or **Maha Uma Devi**, a Hindu temple founded by the Tamil community in Bangkok. Here is kept a small bronze statue of Uma, which is taken in procession round the quarter at the Mawarathri festival in September or October. At noon on most days a ritual purification ceremony is performed in the temple.

At 193 **T. Surawong**, next to the British Club, is the **Neilson Hayes Library** (open Mon–Sat 09.30–16.00, Sun 09.30–12.30), built in 1921 in neo-Classical style by Dr Hayward Hayes in memory of his wife Jennie Neilson Hayes. This library, which is the oldest English-language library in Thailand, is operated by the Bangkok Library Association and houses a collection of over 20,000 volumes.

T. Sathon, the southernmost of the four streets, is divided by a canal into two—Sathon Tai and Sathon Nua—and has numerous embassies. At the eastern end of Sathon Tai, not far from its junction with T. Rama IV, is Soi Atthakan Prasit, which leads to the **Goethe Institute** and to the **Silpa**

Bhirasri Institute of Modern Art, founded by the Italian artist Silpa Bhirasri (Corrado Feroci). Halfway down Sathon Tai on the left hand side are the Lao Embassy, the Bangrak Hospital and the Saint Louis Hospital. At its western end it is linked by the Taksin Bridge over the Chao Phraya to Thon Buri, where it becomes T. Krung Thon Buri.

At the western end of T. Sathom, T. Charoen Krung crosses the street and continues south to end at the Krung Thep Bridge. A little way south of the Taksin Bridge, between T. Charoen Krung and the river is **Wat Yannawa**, which has a reproduction of the junk that was erected in Sanam Luang to mark the ordination of the future King Chulalongkorn as a monk before his accession to the throne. It represents the vessel of Truth sailing across the ocean of existence to *nirvāna* and instead of a mast it has a seven-tiered parasol, symbol of royalty.

Between T. Charoen Krung and the river there are several luxury hotels, including the *Royal Orchid Sheraton* and the famous **Oriental Hotel**, where once Somerset Maugham stayed and did not find Bangkok greatly to his liking. Immediately upstream (north) of the Royal Orchid Sheraton is the magnificent **River City Shopping Centre**, which has several excellent but expensive boutiques and antique shops.

A short way downstream from the Royal Orchid Sheraton is the **Portuguese Embassy**, the oldest embassy building in Bangkok. It was built on land given to the Portuguese government in 1820 by Rama II in gratitude for services given by the Portuguese to the Thais during the Burmese invasion of Ayutthaya in 1767 and subsequently, and in order to enable them to set up a *feitoria* (trading centre, factory) and consulate. It includes a handsome residence in neo-Classical style and the old *feitoria* building.

Just upstream of the Oriental Hotel is the **French Embassy**, a building in colonial style, and just below that is the **East Asiatic Company** building and the **Convent** and **Church of the Assumption**.

At the southern edge of Sathon near Khlong Chong Nonsi are the elaborately ornamented Chinese temple of **Wat Pho Maen Khunaram** and the important temple of **Wat Chong Nonsi**, which is situated near the Chao Phraya River opposite the mouth of Khlong Tat Bang Kra Chao. This temple was probably built in the mid-Ayutthaya period in the reign of King Narai, and it retains many features characteristic of the temple architecture of that period, notably in the *ubosot*, which stands on a curved boat-shaped base and has a front porch with four brick pillars with slender lotus capitals. The double *bai sema* of sandstone have canopies in the shape of howdahs and carving on them that belongs stylistically to the reign of Prasat Thong in the mid-17C. Inside are the remains of some fine **mural paintings**, in which scenes from *Thotsachat* tales are depicted, separated by hanging garlands of flowers and zigzag motifs.

2 · Bangkok: Thon Buri and the West Bank

The places described in this section are all on the west side of the Chao Phraya River, beginning in the north in Bang Phlat and ending in Khlong San in the south. Thon Buri and the West Bank in general has retained many more of its waterways and traditional wooden Thai houses than the rest of Bangkok, and a cruise through the *khlong* on this side of the Chao Phraya River is a delightful experience.

In **Bang Phlat** in the area between Soi 50/1, T. Charan Sanitwong and the Krungthep Bridge there are several interesting temples, including Wat Paorohit, Wat Thong and Wat Mai Thepnimit.

Wat Mai Thepnimit dates from the late Ayutthaya period and was restored in the reign of Rama III. The **ubosot** stands in an enclosure surrounded by a wall with a redented **chedi** on a decorated, multi-tiered base at each corner. It has doors at the front and rear with porches supported by two pairs of round columns with elongated lotus capitals, and five windows in each side wall. It stands on a low, slightly curved base. The roof brackets are finely carved and the front pediment has exquisitely carved wooden figures of *devas* in adoration amid vegetal motifs. Above the windows are fine framed pediments and niches decorated with stucco and glass mosaic.

On the inner side of the doors of the *ubosot* are figures of Chinese *dvārapālas* holding javelins painted against a red background decorated with peonies. The guardian figures painted on the inside of the window shutters are in Thai style, each one holding a sword and standing on a lion.

The **paintings** on the walls of the *ubosot* depict the *Traiphum*, and episodes from *jātaka* tales and the Life of the Buddha. In the uppermost register are figures of *risis* and *vidhyādharas* separated by zigzags. Some of the paintings are in poor condition, while others have been crudely restored with strident colours.

The entrance to **Wat Paorohit**, which is through a gateway in Western style with a triangular pediment, is on Soi 52, T. Charan Sanitwong. The *ubosot*, which is thought to date from the reign of King Mongkut, has square columns supporting the roof and stucco decoration over the doorways. The *bai sema* are enshrined under canopies in the shape of elephant howdahs.

The **murals** in the *wihan* are of high quality. One painting shows a group of American soldiers, one of whom is chasing a court lady.

Some way downstream of the mouth of Khlong Bangkok Noi, opposite the Tha Chang pier is **Wat Rakhang Khosit Tharam**, built by Rama I and so named after its sonorous bells, which are still rung daily at 08,00 and 18.00. It is easily identifiable by the two plaster figures of sailors standing to attention on either side of the jetty. The *ubosot* was built in the reign of Rama III and was extensively restored in 1995–96. It is surrounded by a gallery. The doors and windows are decorated with fine stucco work. It contains a seated Buddha image of gilded bronze, over which is a nine-tiered parasol used to shelter Rama I's funerary urn. It also contains murals depicting the *Totsachat* by an eminent 19C monk artist called Phra Wannavadvichitre. To the right of the *ubosot* are three bell-shaped *chedi*, and to the left a *prang* dating from the reign of Rama I, which still retains some of its original stucco decoration, and an open-sided cruciform *sala* containing five bronze bells. To the left of the *wihan* is an elegant late 18C wooden *ho trai*, now called the Tripitaka Hall, which contains fine murals dating from 1788 and depicting scenes from the *Ramakien* and the *Traiphum*. It was restored between 1968 and 1983. The original carved wooden pediment and doors made by Rama II have been replaced and are displayed inside the *ho trai*. Nearby are three wooden houses where Rama I lived when he was a monk before becoming king. The beautiful gilded lacquer decoration on the window shutters is also said to be the work of Rama II. Wat Rakhang also possesses an important collection of manuscript chests.

The Royal Barge Museum (open daily 08,00–18.00) is situated on the north bank of Khlong Bangkok Noi, immediately before its confluence with the Chao Phraya River. It houses part of the fleet of 51 royal barges which until recently were used every year to convey the king to Wat Arun for the *kathin* ceremony. These beautiful boats are among the most spectacular examples of the Thai woodcarvers' art.

The barge which carries the king was built for King Vajiravudh and was launched in 1914. It is called **Si Suphannahong** and has a figurehead in the form of a *hamsa* or *hong*, the sacred goose mount of Brahma. At the stern is a *nāga's* tail. The boat is 44.70m long, weighs 15–16 tonnes and has a draft of 41cm. It is paddled by a crew of 50 men, with parasol-bearers, helmsmen, rhythm-keepers and a chanter. The **Ananta Nakharat** was made in the reign of Rama III and rebuilt in Vajiravudh's reign. Its figurehead is in the form of a seven-headed *nāga*. It is nearly 43m long and is used to carry the new yellow robes which the king offers to the monks of Wat Arun. The royal children are carried in a barge named **Anekchatphuchong**, which was built for King Chulalongkorn. It is decorated at the bows and the stern with figures of *nāgas* and *garudas*. It is 45.40m long, weighs 7.70 tonnes and has a draft of 46cm. The most recently built boat on display here is **Khrut Hoenhet**, which was constructed in 1968 to replace a boat damaged in an explosion during World War II. Several of the barges have cannon mounted in the bows.

Wat Suwannaram is to the west beyond the Royal Barge shed on the south side of Khlong Bangkok Noi. The *ubosot* and the *wihan* both date from the reign of Rama I and were restored by Rama III. The *ubosot* has porches at front and rear with roofs supported on six round columns. The pediments have fine stucco and carved wood decoration.

The interior of the *ubosot* is decorated with **wall paintings** by two famous painters of Rama III's reign, Luang Wichit Chetsada and Khru Khong Pae. One of the paintings represents a boat capsizing in a storm and the people in it being eaten by sea monsters, which is thought to represent a group of Muslims returning by sea from the *haj.*

Downstream of Wat Rakhang is the **Temple of the Dawn** or **Wat Arun** (open daily 09.00–17.00), which can be reached by ferry from the Tha Tien pier. Its tall Khmer-style *prang*, which is one of the most familiar landmarks in the city, was originally only 15m high when in 1780 King Taksin brought the Emerald Buddha here, and it did not attain its present height, which with the three-tiered base on which it stands is 104m, until the reign of Rama III. Like all Khmer tower-sanctuaries, it represents the sacred mountain, Mount Meru, and its 33 levels represent the 33 heavens, the topmost one of which is guarded by a ring of demons. Each of the four smaller *prang* at the four corners has a niche containing figures of Phra Phi, god of the wind, on horseback. The upper terraces can be reached by one of four stairways at the four cardinal points. At the bottom of each stairway is a pavilion, one containing an image of the Birth of the Buddha, another of the Buddha in meditation protected by the *nāga*, a third of the First Sermon in the Deer Park at Sarnath, and a fourth the Buddha's

Wat Arun, the Temple of the Dawn, Thon Buri

Mahaparinirvāṇa attended by his disciples. At the top is a niche containing a figure of the god Indra riding his three-headed elephant Airavata (Erewan). The decoration of the *prang* consists of thousands of pieces of broken Chinese ceramics donated by the faithful. The enclosure round this great *prang* is guarded by tall figures of *yakṣas*.

Wat Thong Thammachat Wora Wihan is situated near the Thon Buri Polytechnical School in the area bounded on the west by T. Tha Din Daeng, the east by T. Chiang Mai, the south by T. Somdet Chao Phraya and the north by the Chao Phraya River.

Founded in the Ayutthaya period, this *wat* was restored in the reign of Rama I by his younger sister Princess Ku and her husband. Further restoration was carried out in the reign of Rama III by one of his brothers, Kromkhun Dejadison. In 1915 extensive work was done on the temple, including the almost total rebuilding of the *ubosot* in late Ayutthaya style. This *ubosot* is surrounded by a wall at each corner of which is a redented *chedi*. At the four cardinal points in the wall are gateways surmounted by niches; the east and west gateways are flanked by large stone blocks to warn anyone who is improperly dressed or in the wrong frame of mind not to enter. The *ubosot* itself has a roof decorated conventionally with *cho fa* and *hang hong* ornaments and stands on the boat-shaped curved base commonly found in late Ayutthaya and early Ratanakosin buildings. There are panelled doors at the front and rear beneath porches decorated with wood carvings of worshipping *devas* surrounded by stylised floral designs studded with mosaic glass inlay. On the left and right of the porches are staircases, at the top of which are low balustrades decorated with unusual ring-shaped stucco motifs ornamented with glass mosaic. Each side wall has five windows.

Inside the *ubosot* are some important **murals** depicting scenes from the Life of the Buddha with three registers of *devas*, *ṛṣis* and *vidyādharas* above. Behind the principal Buddha image is an unusual scene showing Thai houses and Chinese shops in a city, as if viewed from above. In one of the shops is a barber, who is portrayed serving his pigtailed customers. The style of the paintings is in general decorative and not naturalistic. Hills and trees are painted in the Chinese manner in pale colours outlined in black, buildings are chiefly red, with details picked out in gold, and figures of divine or royal persons are portrayed making the same highly stylised gestures as in the classical Thai theatre. One scene, indeed, shows a royal *hun luang* performance.

The *wihan* is diagonally opposite the *ubosot* and has a pediment decorated with floral designs in stucco in the Chinese style. Like the *ubosot*, it has doors at front and rear and five windows on either side. Within the *wihan* are many Buddha images in different *mudrās* and *āsanas*. The walls are painted with a pattern of double lotus-buds.

To the north of the *ubosot* is a square *ho trai* on stilts in the middle of a pool.

To the south of Wat Arun on the north side of the mouth of Khlong Bangkok Yai is **Wat Moli Lokayaran**, a small temple in Ayutthaya style. On the south side of Khlong Bangkok Yai are **Wat Kalayanimit**, which dates from the reign of Rama III and is chiefly notable for the immense height of its *ubosot*, built to accommodate a colossal Buddha image of little artistic merit, and **Wat Hong Ratanaram**, a magnificent Ayutthaya-period temple restored by King Taksin, notable not only for the exceptionally **fine stucco decoration of the ubosot** and the wooden **doors** decorated with exquisitely carved figures of *haṃsas* (hong) from which the temples takes its name, but also for the Buddha images it contains, among them a fine Sukhothai image dating from 1422 and known as Phra Trimuk. There is also a beautiful wooden *ho trai*.

Further downstream is the settlement that was formed here after the fall of Ayutthaya in 1767 by a small group of Portuguese, who built the **Santa Cruz Church**, known in Thai as Wat Kuti Chin, in a curious mixture of Western and Chinese styles.

WEST OF BANGKOK

3 · Bangkok to Nakhon Pathom

Roads 4 and 338, c 56km.

Railway from Hua Lamphong station (and less frequently from Thon Buri/Bangkok Noi station), 64km in c 1hr 15mins.

Two main highways, roads 4 and 338, lead west from Bangkok on roughly parallel routes, which merge 16km before Nakhon Pathom. Road 4 (T. Phet Kasem) runs west from the King Taksin monument in Thon Buri; road 338 (a continuation of T. Phra Pinklao) runs northwest from Phra Pinklao Bridge near the Democracy Monument. Both roads can be very congested through Bangkok's suburbs, so an early start is strongly recommended. This route can be done easily as a day-trip from Bangkok.

At the 22km mark on **road 4**, the enormous image of the walking Buddha known as **Phra Phuttha Monthon** can be seen in the grounds of the modern World Centre of Buddhist Culture.

The **Sam Phran Elephant Ground** (open daily), on the left near the 31km mark, has daily shows of performing elephants and crocodile-wrestling. There is also a small collection of other mammals and reptiles. Also on the left, 1500m further, is the **Rose Garden**, a resort on the east bank of the Tha Chin River with fine landscaped gardens, hotel and chalet accommodation, restaurants, an 18-hole golf course, swimming pools and tennis courts. There is also a model Thai village with daily performances of traditional Thai dances, sword fights and Thai boxing.

Visits to the Rose Garden and Elephant Ground are often combined in one-day tours from Bangkok, together with the floating market at Damnoen Saduak (see Rte 7).

▶Travellers taking the alternative route along road 338 will pass the **Thai Human Imagery Museum** (open 09.00–17.30 weekdays; 08.30–18.00 weekends and holidays) on the right near the 31km mark. This museum is a kind of Thai Madame Tussaud's, containing fibreglass sculptures of famous monks and royal personages and tableaux of traditional Thai pastimes. ◀

▶Three km beyond the point where the two highways merge, a short detour to the right can be made on road 3094 to **Wat Klang Bang Kaeo** in **Nakhon Chaisi**, a small town on the west bank of the Tha Chin River founded, according to the *Ayutthaya Chronicles*, in the mid-16C.

Follow road 3094 for 2km and turn right at the intersection in the town centre. The *wat* lies to the left after 1km. Of note are the beautifully restored **murals** inside the *ubosot*, which date originally from the reign of King Chulalongkorn, and the finely gilded decoration on the doors. Close to the river bank is an unusual octagonal wooden *sala*, and nearby a *mondop* intricately decorated with stucco. On the southeast side of the compound is a modern three-storey building housing the **Phra Phuttha Withi Nayok Museum**, which contains a large collection of Buddhist art and religious artefacts. The exhibits include some fine *khoi* manuscripts wrapped in sumptuous fabrics or stored in cabinets, trees of tiny votive tablets, bronze and wooden images of the Buddha, and ceramics from Thailand and abroad. Among the bronze images are several of the compassionate monk, Phra Malai, visiting the unfortunate inhabitants of Hell. ◄

Nakhon Pathom

From Wat Klang Bang Kaeo return to road 4 and continue to the modern town of Nakhon Pathom (pop. 63,000), which is dominated by the great *stūpa* of **Phra Pathom Chedi**.

■ **Hotels and Services**. Comfortable hotels include the *Nakhon (Nakorn) Inn* on T. Ratchawithi, Soi 3, and the *Whale Hotel* further west on T. Ratchawithi, Soi 19. Cheaper and simpler is the *Mit Phaisan* at 120/30 T. Phaya Phan, north of the *stūpa*. The *Thai Farmers Bank* is at 124/8 T. Ratchawithi; the *Bangkok Bank* is on T. Na Phra at the northeast corner of the *stūpa*. The **post office** (international **telecoms** service, 08.00–21.00 daily) is nearby on T. Thesa.

■ **Transport**. Frequent **buses** run to Bangkok and Kanchanaburi, and less frequently to Ratchaburi and surrounding provinces. The **railway station**, north of the *stūpa*, is on the main line between Bangkok and southern Thailand; there are numerous trains daily in both directions. The branch line to Kanchanaburi has only a few services each day: the bus is preferable. **Samlo** and **motorcycle taxis** operate in the town.

Festivals. An annual fruit and food festival is held, usually in September, to celebrate and promote the province's abundant production of fruit. In November there is a seven-day fair round Phra Pathom Chedi, at which, in addition to the numerous food vendors and market stalls, there are performances of Thai classical dancing and shadow plays on the terraces of the *stūpa*.

History

The origins of Nakhon Pathom are shrouded in mystery, but it is certainly one of the most ancient cities in Thailand, and its great monument, Phra Pathom Chedi, is one of the holiest Buddhist monuments in the world. The original *stūpa*, which was 39m high, may have been built as early as the 2C BC and enlarged at some time during the Dvaravati period, when Nakhon Pathom, which was then called Nakhon Chaisi, was an important centre of the Mon Dvaravati kingdom. In the late 11C, possibly as a result of a Burmese invasion, Nakhon Chaisi appears to have been abandoned (some scholars believe that the inhabitants migrated to U Thong, which became the last capital of the Dvaravati kingdom), and the great *stūpa* was allowed to fall into decay. Early in the reign of King Chakkraphat of Ayutthaya in the mid-16C the population returned and a new city was established, possibly on the site of the present town of Nakhon Chaisi. Phra Pathom

Chedi, however, was left to decay further until monks came to live here during the reign of Rama II.

King Mongkut, in the years when he was a monk before becoming king, visited Phra Pathom Chedi on pilgrimage several times. Two years after he succeeded to the throne he initiated the restoration of the monument by the construction of an enormous *chedi* encasing the original *stūpa*. This was completed in 1860. A replica of the original was made at the same time.

King Mongkut also had the *ubosot*, belfries and other monastic buildings restored and built a palace nearby called Pathom Nakhon, of which only one building remains, now used as municipal offices. Mongkut died before the reconstruction was completed, and it was left to his son and successor, King Chulalongkorn, to finish the work, including the construction of the spire of the *chedi* in 1870, and placing the yellow glazed tiles on the dome. When completed, the total height of the *stūpa* from the ground to the top of the parasol (*chat*) surmounting the ringed spire was 120.45m. The spire itself is 41.5m, the *harmikā* 18m, and the bell of the *stūpa* 28m. In 1897 the town of Nakhon Chaisi was moved to the vicinity of Phra Pathom Chedi, which at that time was still surrounded by jungle. In the reign of King Vajiravudh the name of the town was changed to Nakhon Pathom. His brother and successor, King Prajadhipok, constructed other buildings within the precinct of the temple, and between 1975 and 1981 the Fine Arts Department carried out a major restoration of the entire monument.

The principal entrance to **PHRA PATHOM CHEDI** is on the north side and is approached by a broad flight of marble steps edged with a balustrade in the form of a five-headed *nāga*, which leads up to the raised circular terrace surrounding the monument. On both sides there are *sala* in a vaguely Javanese style. At the head of the steps is the *wihan* housing the colossal gilt standing image of the Buddha in *abhaya mudrā*, called Phra Ruang Rochanarit. The original of Phra Ruang Rochanarit was a stone image found in 1909 buried under a ruined *wihan* in Si Satchanalai. Only the head, hands and feet were undamaged. It was brought to Bangkok, where the crown prince, later King Vajiravudh, had a wax model made of it, which was then reshaped and cast in gold. It was installed in Phra Pathom Chedi in November 1915. At King Vajiravudh's request, his ashes were put after his cremation in the pedestal of the image. In the inner chamber of this *wihan* is a statue of the seated Buddha at the end of his 40 days' fast in the wilderness, with two disciples and an elephant and a monkey that are offering him water and honey.

There is a similar *wihan* at each of the three other cardinal points on the terrace. The east *wihan* contains an image of the Buddha seated in *dhyāna mudrā*, the south *wihan* a seated stone image in *bhūmisparśa mudrā* known as Phra Nakprok, and the west *wihan* a reclining image 9m long. At regular intervals all round the terrace are 24 small towers containing bronze bells and at the doorways to the innermost terrace are pairs of the Chinese stone guardian figures that were brought to Thailand in the 19C as ships' ballast. In the alcoves between these doorways are 66 images of the Buddha making different *mudrās*, which are explained in English on plaques behind them. On the lower east terrace is the *ubosot* and the small *wat* **museum** (open Wed–Sun, 09.00–12.00, 13.00–16.00), with a Chinese shrine between them. The *ubosot*, the restoration

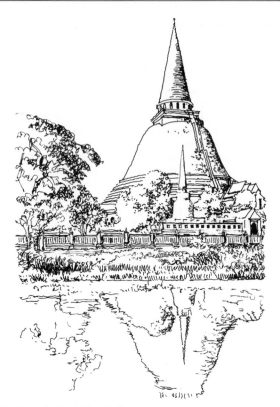

Phra Pathom Chedi, Nakhon Pathom

of which was completed by King Prajadhipok, contains a Dvaravati image of gilded and lacquered quartzite of the Buddha seated in *pralambapādāsana* found at Wat Phra Men (see below). Of note in the museum are some Dvaravati Wheels of the Law, although most are now displayed in the larger Phra Pathom Chedi National Museum (see below). In a corner is the coffin of Ya Lae, King Vajiravudh's dog.

Outside the south *wihan* are two tall Chinese stoves, and on the lower south terrace is an image of the seated Buddha flanked by two white-painted *chedi*. That to the east is a model of the original monument over which the present *stūpa* was erected; to the west is a replica of the *chedi* of Wat Mahathat at Nakhon Si Thammarat (see p 389).

In the **Phra Pathom Chedi National Museum** (open Wed–Sun, 09.00–12.00, 13.00–16.00) on the southeast side of the monument, are some very fine Dvaravati stone Wheels of the Law from Phra Pathom Chedi, and stucco and terracotta relief carvings from Chedi Chula Pathon. Beautifully detailed stucco fragments from Phra Pathom Chedi are also displayed, together with a large fragment of Dvaravati-period carved stone depicting the Buddha preaching his First Sermon. In the museum garden hang some stone gongs.

Round the base of the monument are numerous of food and drink vendors. Parking is allowed.

▶**Phra Prathon Chedi**, on the east edge of the town on road 4, is thought to be the most ancient Buddhist monument in Thailand. It has recently been restored. It consists of a small whitewashed *chedi* on a square base. Traces of the foundations of an early temple and images of the Buddha have been found in the vicinity.

The charming **Sanam Chan Palace (Phra Ratchawang Sanam Chan)**, a 10 minute *samlo* ride to the west of Phra Pathom Chedi, consists of several houses and pavilions in a mixture of Thai and European styles constructed by King Vajiravudh c 1907–11 for the Wild Tiger Corps, the elite paramilitary force that he founded (see p 50). In 1926 King Prajadhipok handed the palace over to the local authorities, and since then it has been used as government offices and residences for government officials. Several of the buildings were made available to Silpakorn University when it established a new campus here in 1967. These include the Tamnak Thap Charoen, which houses the University Institute of Western Thai Culture, the Tamnak Thap Khwan, an exceptionally fine traditional Thai wooden house, and the Tamnak Mari Ratcha Rata Ballang, an orange-painted wooden house in neo-classical style, which is now the King Rama VI museum. A bridge across a canal connects this building to the Tamnak Chali Mongkon At, which is a curious mixture of French Renaissance and English Tudor styles. Painted cream, it has a red tiled roof and round corner turrets. In front is a statue of a dog, believed to be of Ya Lae, King Vajiravudh's dog, which was shot under mysterious circumstances. Most of the buildings are closed to the public, but it is permitted to walk in the grounds.◀

Wat Phra Ngam, c 500m west of the railway station was built during the reign of King Chulalongkorn on foundations dating from the Dvaravati period.

On the main branch of road 4, where it bypasses Nakhon Pathom to the south, are the ruins of **Wat Phra Men**, a brick temple probably of Dvaravati origin. These are of little interest in themselves, but it was here that were found four important stone seated images of the Buddha, one of which is now in Phra Pathom Chedi, one in Wat Phra Men in Ayutthaya, one in the National Museum in Ayutthaya and one in the National Museum in Bangkok.

4 · Nakhon Pathom to Kanchanaburi and Three Pagodas Pass

Roads 4 and 323, 314km. To Kanchanaburi 72km; to Three Pagodas Pass 242km. Private transport is strongly recommended for travel in the vicinity of Kanchanaburi and Three Pagodas Pass. In Bangkok, buses depart from the southern bus terminal in Bangkok Noi.

Railway, 69km (1hr 20mins) to Kanchanaburi. Beyond Kanchanaburi the railway winds for 77km (1hr 50mins) along the Khwae Noi River valley to the railhead at Nam Tok.

From Nakhon Pathom, travel west on road 4 and turn right on to road 323 to follow the course of the Mae Klong River upstream.

In Tha Rua, a short detour to the right off road 323 leads to **Wat Phra Thaen Dong Rang**, a monastery traditionally associated with episodes in the Life of the Buddha and consequently a much frequented pilgrimage site. The *wihan*, which stands on an outcrop of rock, has a carved wooden gable decorated with ceramic mosaics. Inside is a large flat stone slab where, according to local tradition, the Buddha lay at the moment of passing over into *Mahāparinirvāṇa*. According to the same tradition, the Buddha was cremated here. 400m to the west is a small hill at the top of which is a shrine containing a Footprint of the Buddha.

Kanchanaburi

Kanchanaburi (pop. 50,000), situated at the confluence of the Khwae Noi and Khwae Yai rivers, lies in the centre of a fertile plain, where sugar-palm, rice, sugar-cane, tobacco, cotton, maize and cassava all flourish. The province is also one of Thailand's major gem-producing regions and has numerous sapphire and spinel mines. The region's limestone geology has led to the formation of many caverns and waterfalls, some of which are now in the half-dozen national parks in the province. The town is a convenient centre from which to explore the numerous natural and historical sites in the area.

The town's best known attraction is the **railway bridge over the Khwae Yai River**, which achieved notoriety after Pierre Boulle's novel, *The Bridge on the River Kwai*, published in 1954, was made into an immensely popular film by David Lean.

■ **Information**. The TAT office (open daily 08.30–16.30) is on the town's main thoroughfare, T. Saeng Chuto, a short distance from the bus station. It can provide accommodation lists and good maps of the province and town.

■ **Hotels and services**. The wide choice of accommodation ranges from the very comfortable *Felix River Kwai Resort* on the west bank of the Khwae Yai, and the more central *River Kwai Hotel* on T. Saeng Chuto, to the numerous simple riverside guest houses and raft houses found along the east bank, especially on T. Song Khwae and T. Rong Hip Oi. There are several restaurants catering for tourists on the river bank near the bridge. The main **post office** (international **telephone** service, 07.00–22.00 daily) is on T. Saeng Chuto at the south end of the town; a more convenient branch office is beside the city gate. The *Bangkok Bank* is on T. U Thong in the central market area; The *Thai Farmers Bank* is nearby.

■ **Buses**. There are frequent services until early evening between Kanchanaburi and Bangkok, via Nakhon Pathom. Air-conditioned buses for Bangkok leave from beside the Thai Farmers Bank. Less frequent services to Suphan Buri, Sai Yok and Sangkhla Buri leave from the bus terminal on T. Saeng Chuto.

■ **Railway station**. From the station on T. Saeng Chuto two or three trains daily cross the bridge over the Khwae Yai River and follow the route of the old Burma–Siam Railway to the present railhead at Nam Tok. This scenic journey is recommended, at least in one direction. For the best views as the train winds along beside the Khwae Noi River take a seat on the left side of the carriage. It is possible to join the train at the bridge, where it makes a brief stop. In a siding at Kanchanaburi station is what is claimed to be the world's largest, most powerful metre gauge steam locomotive.

■ **Local transport**. *Samlo* and *songthaeo* operate in the town, and it is possible to rent motorcycles and bicycles from some of the restaurants and guesthouses near the river on T. Song Khwae or T. Rong Hip Oi.

History

The area around Kanchanaburi has evidently been a centre of human settlement at least since neolithic times, as is shown by the excavations carried out at Ban Kao. The discovery in 1927 at the village of Phong Tuk, c 16km from Ban Phong on road 323 to Nakhon Pathom, of a Graeco-Roman bronze lamp of the 2C AD in the form of a bird with a mask of Silenus on the cover-flap, suggests that the area may have been on a trade route running through the Three Pagodas Pass, which linked the East Roman Empire via India with Southeast Asia and China. The lamp is now in the National Museum, Bangkok. Later, Kanchanaburi became one of the westernmost outposts of the Khmer empire and the temple of Muang Sing, 32km to the west of Kanchanaburi was part of an important fortified Khmer settlement.

The **JEATH War Museum** (open daily 08.30–16.00) in the grounds of Wat Chai Chumphon beside the river on the south side of the town, consists of three replicas of the atap-roofed bamboo huts which housed POWs in the labour camps during the Japanese occupation. JEATH is an acronym for Japan, England, Australia, America, Thailand and Holland—six of the countries of origin of the men involved in the building of the Burma–Siam Railway. The museum, which was established by the abbot of Wat Chai Chumphon, contains paintings and drawings, photographs, maps, press cuttings and private letters which vividly reveal the atrocious hardships suffered by the POWs under the Japanese and illustrate the construction of the bridge over the Khwae Yai River.

From the museum turn left towards the town centre. On T. Lak Muang, off to the right after a few hundred metres, and near to the pier from where the ferry over the Khwae Yai River leaves, is the **old city gateway**, virtually all that remains of the fortified wall, which dates from the mid-19C. Through the gateway is the shrine containing the town *lak muang*.

Continue north on T. Saeng Chuto to the **Kanchanaburi War Cemetery**, on the left of the road near the railway station. The cemetery, which is maintained by the Commonwealth War Graves Commission, contains the graves of almost 7000 POWs, including 3597 Britons, 1362 Australians and one Canadian, laid amid well-tended lawns.

Bridge over the River Khwae Yai

The bridge over the Khwae Yai River lies a short *samlo* ride away to the north. It was one of more than 680 bridges on the Burma–Siam Railway, the 'Railway of Death', which was built during the Second World War by

Asian conscripts and Allied POWs. The Japanese plan was to create a new supply line connecting their recently conquered territories in Burma and the Malay peninsula by building a railway running from Nong Pladuk, near Nakhon Pathom, to Thanbyuzayat in Burma, a distance of 414km. Work on the railway began in June 1942 at Nong Pladuk, and in September construction of the Khwae Yai bridges commenced. The labour force consisted chiefly of British prisoners brought from camps in Singapore. A temporary wooden bridge, for emergency and light rail use, was built 100m downstream from the main bridge, which was to be nearly 300m long and to be composed of steel spans brought from captured railway stores in Java. By the end of December 1942 the wooden bridge had been completed, and in March 1943 the steel girders were in position.

Work conditions up the line were appalling. Beriberi, dysentery, malaria, typhus and cholera took their toll on the overworked, malnourished POWs and conscripts. The Chungkai cutting, a few kilometres up the line from the bridges, required the excavation of 10,000 cubic metres of rock with only the most rudimentary of tools. By October 1943, when the railway was finally completed, more than 12,000 POWs had died, together with perhaps 80,000 Burmese, Indian, Malay and Indonesian conscripts. The real number of dead will never be known. As recently as 1990 a grave containing the remains of about 700 bodies, probably Indian conscripts recruited in Malaya, was discovered close to Kanchanaburi town hall.

By 1944 the railway had become a regular bombing target of the Allies, and the Khwae Yai bridges were attacked seven times between the end of 1944 and June 1945. The first three raids caused only superficial damage, but the fourth severely damaged the wooden bridge. In the fifth attack in February 1945, USAF B-24s destroyed three of the eleven steel spans and wrecked the wooden bridge. Both bridges were damaged again in April, when the wooden bridge was still being repaired, and in June both were put out of action for the rest of the war by RAF Liberators.

After the war much of the railway was dismantled. The British took up a short section at the Thai–Burmese frontier, and the Thais subsequently dismantled most of the stretch from the border to the present railhead at Nam Tok. The wooden bridge was never replaced, but the three destroyed spans of the steel bridge were replaced by two longer spans from the Japan Bridge Company of Osaka as part of Japanese war reparations, and it is these, together with the eight original curved sections, which can be seen today.

At the small station beside the bridge some steam locomotives from the period are on display and there is a cluster of restaurants and souvenir stalls. A **war memorial** to the dead, erected by the Japanese administration in 1944 after the completion of the railway, lies along the lane a few metres to the south of the bridge, amid frangipani trees.

Much of Kanchanaburi province is extremely beautiful, and several very pleasant excursions can be made into the countryside (see excursions below). Private or chartered transport is highly recommended for these, but not essential.

Muang Sing and the Lower Khwae Noi Valley

Roads 3228, 3229 and 3455 to Chungkai War Cemetery, Wat Tham Khao Pun, Ban Kao Museum and Muang Sing, returning via road 323. Easily done within a day, the route passes through the fertile valley of the Khwae Noi river. The cemetery and Wat Tham Khao Pun are within walking distance of the town, via the ferry from T. Song Khwae. Visitors reliant on public transport will find access to Ban Kao and Muang Sing easiest by **train** *or private charter or rental from the town.*

Across the Khwae Yai River from the ferry pier on T. Song Khwae, a road leads after 2km to the **Chungkai War Cemetery**, on the former site of a base camp and hospital for the prisoners, which now contains 1740 Allied (mostly British) graves. The cemetery is immaculately maintained by the Commonwealth War Graves Commission, but the area's tranquillity is frequently shattered at weekends by the din of barge parties on the river behind. Travellers with their own transport may find it quicker to cross the river on the bridge upstream near T. Angkrit (England Rd) and turn left at the junction 2km beyond; from here it is 4.5km to the cemetery.

1500m further west is **Wat Tham Khao Pun**, where a series of narrow passages descends through a winding cave system lit by coloured strip lights and dotted with images of the Buddha. In the main cavern is a large seated image in *bhūmisparśa mudrā*, and beyond that the route climbs again to emerge up a shaft from where a path leads to a view point over the Khwae Noi; the railway line lies along the river bank below.

Continue west on roads 3228, 3229 and 3455 through the intensively cultivated Khwae Noi valley for 21km to **Ban Kao**. Cyclists on these roads should be wary of the heavily laden sugar-cane trucks, which shed a steady stream of leaves and broken cane in their wake.

Ban Kao is one of several **neolithic sites** on the banks of the Khwae Noi River which were discovered by the distinguished Dutch archaeologist, H.R. van Heekeren, when working as a prisoner on the Burma–Siam railway. In 1961 a Thai–Dutch expedition undertook a systematic excavation of these sites, of which Ban Kao on the left bank of the river proved to be the richest, yielding a large number of human and animal bones, stone beads and stone tools dating from the neolithic period (2500–1350 BC). Most of these finds are displayed in the small but clearly signed **Ban Kao Museum** (open Wed–Sun, 09.00–16.00).

Muang Sing

From the museum continue 7km along road 3455 to the important Khmer site of Muang Sing (open daily 08.00–16.00), on the left bank of the Khwae Noi, 1km from Tha Kilen railway station. This fertile area, which has been populated since neolithic times, is also situated on an ancient trade route that ran up the Mae Klong and Khwae Noi rivers as far as Muang Sing and from there continued overland to the Three Pagodas Pass. The name Muang Sing ('Lion City') is probably a local folk name of relatively recent origin, although attempts have been made to identify it with the city of Singhapura, mentioned as being a dependency of Jayavarman VII, ruler of Angkor, in an inscription on the foundation stela of the temple of Preah Khan at Angkor, which dates from 1191.

Prasat Muang Sing

The **inner wall** of the city ramparts is built of laterite and forms a rough rectangle measuring c 1000m x 800m, with a slight concave bend on the south side where it follows a meander of the Khwae Noi River. Earthen ramparts can still be clearly seen on the east and south sides, and archaeologists have identified seven concentric **ramparts** and **moats** in parts of the perimeter. In addition to their defensive function, the moats may have formed part of a complex system of water management, such as is found in many other early Khmer cities. Towards the south end of the enclosure, opposite today's entrance gate, are the ruins of the Buddhist temple of **Prasat Muang Sing**, built entirely of laterite, standing on a raised laterite platform and surrounded, by an outer laterite wall. Like the majority of Khmer temples, it faces east and has a tall gateway on the east side. The principal **tower-sanctuary** (*prasat*) stands slightly to west of centre in the temple enclosure and houses a sandstone image of Avalokiteshvara; in the southeast corner of the inner courtyard is a small building of the type generally described as a 'library'; in the northwest corner is a jackfruit tree. Immediately to the northwest of the main monument are the remains of a smaller, less complete laterite building with a similar plan, which has yielded some stone bases of statues.

Although Muang Sing is unquestionably Khmer in its style and general plan, it has a number of curious features that are not found in any other monument of comparable size and importance elsewhere in the Khmer empire, such as the incorrect alignment and the varying proportions of the four cellas in the northwest shrine and the differences in the number of redentations in each corner of the same shrine. Furthermore, the stucco decorations, none of which is now in situ, show a marked similarity to Dvaravati stucco work found at sites in Ratchaburi province. It seems probable therefore that Muang Sing was built by local artisans in emulation of Khmer models, but with little or no guidance from Khmer masters. This strengthens the supposition that it was not built in the reign of Jayavarman VII, when the Angkor empire was at its zenith and extended over large areas of northeast and central Thailand, but later, when Khmer power was already beginning to ebb in this region.

Due north of the main *prasat* is a small **museum**, in which are displayed some of the artefacts that have been excavated at the site, including fragments of stucco decoration. However, the most important sculptures, notably two images of the Buddha seated in meditation under the *nāga*, an exceptionally fine 'irradiating Avalokiteshvara' (possibly imported), and several other images of the *bodhisattvas* Avalokiteshvara and Prajnaparamita in the Khmer Bayon style but of inferior workmanship, are now in the Bangkok National Museum or the U Thong National Museum (see p 165). Near the south wall of the city are two further ruins, but so little remains of these that their function cannot be determined. Beside the river bank at the southeast corner of the city is a prehistoric burial site where skeletons and pottery sherds can be seen.

From Muang Sing the most direct route back to Kanchanaburi lies across the railway line on road 3455 to the junction with road 323.

Erawan, Si Nakharin and the Khwae Yai Valley

Roads *323 and 3199, 68km northwest from Kanchanaburi to Erawan National Park. The route follows the Khwae Yai River out of the plain into a more thickly wooded landscape.*

Follow road 323 out of the town and then road 3199 to Ban Lat Ya, 17km from Kanchanaburi. On the left at the 3km stone beyond Ban Lat Ya are the partly rebuilt ruins of **Wat Pa Lelai**, an Ayutthaya-period *wat*, comprising a brick *chedi*, a *wihan* and a *mondop* in which is a large image of the Buddha seated in *pralambapādāsana*, apparently copied from a Dvaravati image that was formerly here. The area immediately to the south was the site of **old Kanchanaburi**.

Road 3199 climbs gently up the valley, passing the **Tha Thung Na Dam** after a further 23km. From here the river is in view for much of the final 20km to where the road forks below the large **Si Nakharin Dam**. The left fork is clearly signed to the dam and to the **Erawan Waterfalls**, which lie beyond the small Si Nakharin market. The beautiful falls, which drop through the forest in a series of cascades and pools, are the main attraction of **Erawan National Park**, which was established in 1975 and is one of Thailand's most popular parks. An uneven path leads from the car park and climbs steeply up beside the water for 2km; suitable walking shoes are recommended, as it is slippery when wet. Although there are tigers and leopards in the park, visitors are more likely to see macaques and bird life. At weekends the area round the lower falls becomes a busy, noisy picnic site; visitors cannot take food and drink above the second tier, nor climb above it after 16.00. Refreshments can be bought from stalls at the car park and beside the falls; there are rudimentary bungalows and dormitories at the park headquarters.

The Erawan Falls are so named because the shape of the limestone formation at the highest level—or perhaps the triple stream of water flowing over the top tier—is rather fancifully considered to be reminiscent of Erawan (Airavata), the three-headed elephant mount of the Hindu god, Indra.

Most of the park's 550 sq km are inaccessible to visitors, but **Phra That Cave**, c 11km along a rough dirt road from Si Nakharin market, has fine stalactites and stalagmites. *Songthaeo* can be chartered from the market.

The dirt road continues up the west side of the Si Nakharin reservoir for c 40km to the **Huai Khamin Falls** in neighbouring **Si Nakharin National Park**, 1km beyond Ban Huai Khamin. An easier way to the falls is to continue north on road 3199 to **Si Sawat**, where there is passenger-ferry access to the west shore of the reservoir. There is basic accommodation at the park head-quarters, but visitors should bring their own food. Being less accessible than the Erawan Falls, the Huai Khamin Falls receive far fewer visitors, but are equally impressive.

Chaloem Ratanakosin National Park

Roads 3398, 3086 and 3306 from Kanchanaburi, 90km. A small, but immensely charming national park with a pair of spectacular caves and delightful forest trails to waterfalls; highly recommended. There are regular bus services from Kanchanaburi to Ban Nong Pru; songthaeo or motorcycle taxis can be hired from there for the final 22km to the park.

Take roads 323 and 3199 towards the Erawan Falls, but turn right 7km north of Kanchanaburi on roads 3398 and 3086 to the gem-mining centre of Bo Phloi. At an intersection 32km beyond Bo Phloi, turn left to **Chaloem Ratanakosin National Park** on road 3306, and follow the road west through Ban Nong Pru for a further 22km to the park.

This beautiful 59 sq km park, established in 1980, is home to c 70 bird species and small numbers of mammals. Beyond the car park and a stretch of food stalls, a charming path forks left to two waterfalls, 2km away. The main path continues straight to the first cave, the 300m-long **Than Lot Noi Cave**, a natural tunnel through which a gentle stream flows. It is only lit for limited periods, when some of the best limestone formations are illuminated and the path is clear; a sign giving the times is posted outside both ends of the cave.

A trail at the far end leads through a lush forested ravine to the bottom of the **Trai Trung Falls**, then climbs steeply beside the water to reach, after 2.5km, the great cavern of **Than Lot Yai Cave**, where there is a Buddhist shrine. The park is best visited in midweek, when there may be no other people in sight. Good walking shoes and plenty of drinking water are recommended. The cave lights are switched off for the day at 16.00; without a powerful torch, there is no means of getting out after that.

The Upper Khwae Noi Valley to Three Pagodas Pass

*Road 323, 223km from Kanchanaburi through beautiful scenery; highly recom-mended. The **train** can be taken as far as Nam Tok, c 1hr 50mins from Kanchanaburi, and buses from Kanchanaburi can be joined here. This journey can be done in one long day, but travellers may prefer to break the journey, perhaps with a stop at Sai Yok National Park, or Thong Pha Phum, where there is simple accommodation.*

Just beyond the 29km stone on the way to Nam Tok, road 3343 turns off left towards Sai Yok and descends to the railway line after 4km. A lane heading south beside the railway leads after 3km to a spectacular wooden trestle viaduct, over which the train crawls on its way to Nam Tok. The trestles, built in 1943 by Asian conscripts and Allied prisoners, have now been strengthened with new steel girders, but many of the original timbers remain. **Krasae Cave**, a small cave containing Buddha images, lies in the cliff wall at the north end of the viaduct. From the restaurant beside the line are fine views over the river.

The railhead at **Nam Tok** is little more than a market surrounded by a cluster of shop-houses. The war-time railway continued from here to Three Pagodas Pass and beyond, but most of the track has long been removed and the course overgrown. Several pleasant boat trips can be made up and down the Khwae Noi River from **Pak Saeng pier** just outside Nam Tok: upstream to the large **Lawa Cave** (c 2hrs return) and the Sai Yok Yai Waterfall (c 6hrs return) near the headquarters of Sai Yok National Park (see below), or downstream to Ban Wang Pho, where it is possible to join the train heading back to Kanchanaburi. These river trips are best made during or soon after the rainy season, when the water level is highest and the boats can avoid the shallows.

1500m north of Nam Tok centre, a rough track to the right leads to the large, spectacular cavern of **Wang Badan Cave**. Just beyond, also on the right, are the pretty **Sai Yok Noi Waterfalls**, a few metres from the main road in a shady bamboo grove; at weekends the area can be very crowded. A Japanese steam locomotive here stands on a section of the old Burma–Siam Railway.

Beyond the 66km stone on road 323, a left turn leads to '**Hellfire Pass**' or the **Konyu Cutting**. Here in early 1943 prisoners laboured round the clock with the simplest of tools to hack out a huge cutting for the railway, which became known as Hellfire Pass because of its appearance when lit at night by torch light. A roughly circular walking trail, taking 40–80 minutes, has been constructed in memory of those who died. It first meanders through a bamboo forest before descending to the north end of the cutting, where an Australian government memorial plaque has been set into the rock wall. Nearby is a plaque in memory of Sir Edward 'Weary' Dunlop, an Australian former POW who died in 1993. The trail continues through the deep cutting itself and back up some steps beyond the south end.

The entrance to the 500 sq km **Sai Yok National Park** and **Sai Yok Yai Waterfall** is clearly signed to the left, 16km further north. Just beyond the ticket office, the park road crosses the course of the old railway: sleepers can be seen leading through the forest. The Sai Yok Yai Waterfall tumbles into the Khwae Noi River and is one of the few that are best seen in the dry season, when the river level is low: at the height of the rains the fall barely exists. On the river near a suspension bridge are rafts where food and lodging can be obtained and boats can be chartered to nearby caves. There are also simple park bungalows for rent.

In 1973 the tiny **Kitti's hog-nosed bat**, barely three centimetres long and weighing up to two grams, was discovered by a Thai naturalist, Kitti Thonglongya, in a cave within the area which subsequently became the national park in 1980. The species, considered to be the world's smallest mammal, has now been found in other caves in the region, but its long term survival remains in doubt because of growing disturbance of its habitat by scientists and tourists.

Beyond Sai Yok National Park, the road passes at the 105km stone a right turn to **Pha Tat Waterfall**, 9km away. Simple accommodation is available at **Thong Pha Phum**, 20km further north, and from there the road skirts the east side of **Khao Laem Reservoir**, where the branches of drowned trees poke above the water. Much of this area has been designated **Khao Laem National Park**, and soon after passing the dam, the road passes through a large reforestation project. Beyond the 34km stone is a left turn to the **Dai Chong Thong Waterfalls**, 900m along a dirt track, which are recommended for a refreshing dip. The road then passes close to the reservoir shore, with fine views of the fishermen's floating raft houses, before winding through hills for the last few kilometres to Sangkhla Buri.

Sangkhla Buri

The old town of Sangkhla Buri was drowned by the rising waters of the reservoir, but the small and very peaceful modern settlement is an interesting enough place, with large Mon and Karen populations and a mosque. In the market can be found Burmese books and food, as well as the usual goods of a Thai market. There are also fine views of the reservoir, itself home to many fishermen.

■ **Hotels and services**. Favoured for their picturesque settings on the water's edge are the very simple, but pleasant *Burmese Inn* and *'P' Guest House*, 600m apart. The English-speaking owners of the former are very helpful; the latter has better lake views. Between the two is the more expensive *Forget-Me-Not Home*. By the central market is the *Phornphailin (Phon Phailin) Hotel* with adequate rooms but no lake view, and there are several other resorts on the edge of town. The *Siam Commercial Bank* and the **post office** are near the central market.

■ **Transport**. Air-conditioned and normal buses depart regularly for Kanchanaburi and towns en route. Bicycles and motorcycles can be rented from some of the guest houses.

Across the Huai Song Ka Lia, a now flooded tributary of the Khwae Noi River, and 6km by road from Sangkhla Buri's market, is **Wat Wang Wiwekaram**, a modern *wat* modelled on the Mahabodhi *stūpa* at Bodh Gaya in India. 100m behind the main monument is an old square-based brick *chedi*, now in total ruin. Beside the *wat* is a long, covered market selling predominantly Burmese goods, or items imported through Burma. 700m from the *stūpa*, in a complex of new buildings, is the *ubosot*, which has unusual stainless steel pillars. Pedestrians and motorcyclists can take a short cut to the *wat* across an impressive wooden bridge spanning the inlet.

The **Three Pagodas Pass**, 22km from Sangkhla Buri, lies a few metres within Thailand and a mere 275m above sea level. The three eponymous whitewashed *chedi*, sitting in the middle of a traffic circle, are small and unimpressive; the significance of the pass lies in the countless Burmese invading armies which have passed through here over the centuries, and the role it has played in the maintenance of trade links between the Indian Ocean and mainland Southeast Asia since prehistoric times. In recent years it has become an important route for both legitimate trade and smuggling. For a while in the 1980s there was fighting round the Burmese border town of Payathonzu between rebel minorities and Burmese government forces. The town is now under government control and visitors are usually permitted to cross the border for a fee on day visits; this cannot be recommended however, as the money goes to the military regime. To the left of the border checkpoint can be seen the course of the Burma–Siam Railway. There are souvenir shops and restaurants beside the pagodas and a few metres away is the under-utilised *Three Pagodas Pass Resort*.

5 · Kanchanaburi to U Thong and Suphan Buri

Roads *324 and 321, 91km via U Thong to Suphan Buri*

Leave Kanchanaburi on road 324 towards U Thong. In the far distance, on a clear day, can be seen the mountains of the **Tenasserim range**, which for c 60km marks the border with Burma.

U Thong

The district centre of U Thong (pop. 16,500) is of little interest except for the U Thong National Museum. It was an important centre of the Mon Dvaravati kingdom from the 6C–11C and subsequently became a centre of Khmer culture. It seems to have been abandoned during the 12C and was resettled in the Ayutthaya period (16C). Nothing remains of the original city except the foundations of some Dvaravati *stūpas* and other monuments scattered about the modern town and the surrounding countryside, some of which can be seen from Wat Si Sanphet, a hilltop monastery on the outskirts of the town.

The 13C and 14C art of the Suphan Buri region, which consists almost entirely of Buddha images in bronze, sandstone or stucco, is generally described as being in the **U Thong style**. This style owes much to Mon and Khmer antecedents and exercised a strong influence on the art of the early Ayutthaya period, so much so that it is often classified as a transitional style between Sukhothai and Ayutthaya (see p 85). The town and the style take their name from the founder of the kingdom of Ayutthaya, a local adventurer known as Prince U Thong ('Golden Cradle'), who reigned at Ayutthaya from 1351 as Ramathibodi and married a daughter of the ruler of Suphan Buri.

The U Thong National Museum (open Wed–Sun, 09.00–16.00), located in two buildings on the left side of the road shortly before the centre of the modern town, was established in 1976 and contains an important collection of Dvaravati sculptures, as well as other artefacts from all periods excavated in the region and elsewhere.

On the **ground floor**, the room on the right of the entrance is devoted to objects of the Dvaravati period (6–9C). There are numerous votive tablets and small decorative objects in stone, lead, terracotta and stucco; bronze images of the Buddha in *vitarka mudrā*; *bodhisattva* images; a fine stone Wheel of the Law from Kamphaeng Saen; a notable 6C or 7C stone statue of the Buddha in meditation, with a Wheel of the Law and crouching deer on the pedestal, from Wat

Khao Phra, U Thong; and a beautiful 8C or 9C bronze demon head from Sala Phraya Chakra, U Thong.

The room on the **left of the entrance** contains two more fine Dvaravati Wheels of the Law from ruined *stūpas* on the site of the old city.

Upstairs, the **room on the left** contains several Khmer-Lop Buri Buddha images from various sources, Lop Buri stucco objects, a beautiful Lan Na image of the Buddha in *bhūmisparśa mudrā* in gilt and painted bronze, and other bronze Buddha images of the Lan Na, Sukhothai and Ayutthaya periods, dark brown glazed ceramic jars from Surin and Buri Ram, and an important Lop Buri bronze pedestal found in Suphan Buri, decorated with a frieze of Buddhist figures with a *garuḍa* at each corner. The **room on the right** upstairs contains bronze Buddha images, bronze vessels, stone and stucco heads, votive tablets and moulds, jewellery, ceramics and roof tiles from various sources and periods. There are also some Hindu and Buddhist stone sculptures from Muang Sing, which although in Khmer style, are probably of local manufacture and date from the 13C. In the **covered courtyard** behind the front rooms is a very fine Wheel of the Law and other finds from *stūpa* No. 11, one of the ruined sites of old U Thong. Beyond the courtyard are several stucco reliefs from Chedi Chula Pathon in Nakhon Pathom.

At a junction 7km before Suphan Buri, road 322 turns left off road 321 towards **Don Chedi** or **Nong Sarai** (24km), the site of a famous **battle** in January 1593 at which the Thais, led by King Naresuan of Ayutthaya and his brother Ekathotsarot, repulsed a Burmese invasion. The site was formerly marked by a brick *chedi* erected by Naresuan after the battle; this has now been covered by a modern white monument built in the 1950s, but the old remains have been preserved inside and can still be seen. In front of the modern *chedi* is a bronze **statue of King Naresuan** mounted on a war elephant by the Italian sculptor Silpa Bhirasri (Corrado Feroci), erected in 1959. Behind Naresuan can be seen his *mahout* signalling the king's orders to the Thai army with both hands raised.

Suphan Buri

On road 321 towards Suphan Buri, the high five-tiered roof of **Wat Pa Lelai** is visible on the right beyond the 160km stone and just before the bridge over the Tha Chin River. Founded during the U Thong period, it was abandoned after the fall of Ayutthaya in 1767, but was subsequently restored by King Mongkut, who added two of the five tiers of the roof. His royal emblem can be seen on the pediment over the principal door of the large plain white stucco *ubosot*, which contains an enormous, much revered Buddha image seated in the *pralambapādāsana*. Fragments of gold leaf have been stuck over the feet and ankles of the image, and coins pressed into holes round the hem of the robe.

On the left side of the road, 400m further east, is a brick *chedi* dating from the early Ayutthaya period which is all that remains of **Wat Chum Num Song**. The road then passes through the reconstructed **city gates** and a **water-filled moat** marking the old city boundary. Soon after this, a road to the left leads to a garish **Chinese pavilion**, which houses the city's *lak muang*.

Just beyond the 163km stone, a lane on the left leads after 200m to **Wat Phra Si Ratana Mahathat**. This *wat* dates from the U Thong period, but was restored in the Ayutthaya period. It has a fine brick *prang* which has been partially rebuilt; steps on the east side climb up to a cella. At one time the *prang* was flanked to north and south by smaller *prang*; these are now in ruin. To the east is a large modern *sala* filled with numerous images of the Buddha, some of which may date from the 14C. To north and south of it are renovated brick *chedi*.

To the north of Wat Phra Si Ratana Mahathat, 3km further along the same lane, is **Wat No Phutthangkun** on the left. Hidden behind modern buildings is a small Ayutthaya-period *ubosot* containing **murals** by the late 19C artist Nai Kham. Once very fine, these are now sadly neglected and deteriorating.

The commercial heart of **Suphan Buri** lies on the east bank of the Suphan Buri River, the upstream part of the Tha Chin River which reaches the sea at Samut Sakhon. It was an important centre during the later period of Khmer rule in the Lop Buri region and in the early Ayutthaya period. Dominating the skyline of the modern town is the slender tower in Chaloem Phatharatchini Park, which has a viewing gallery and restaurant. Suphan Buri today is a lively trading centre, situated in a prosperous rice and sugar-producing area.

■ **Hotels and services**. The better hotels include the *Kalaphruk Hotel* at 135/1 T. Prachathipatai and the *Khum Suphan Hotel* on T. Mun Han. Acceptable cheaper lodgings include the *KAT Hotel* at 533 T. Phra Phanwasa. All major banks are on T. Phra Phanwasa. The **post/telecoms office** is on T. Nang Phim nearby.

■ **Transport**. There are regular **bus** services to Kanchanaburi, Ang Thong, Ayutthaya and Bangkok from the bus terminal on T. Nen Kaeo, on the east side of town. *Samlo* operate in the town. The **railway station**, on the west side of the town near Wat Pa Lelai, is on the northern line, with regular services to the north and stations to Bangkok.

From the centre of the market area, a bridge crosses the river to **Wat Phra Rup** on the west bank. In a *wihan* just inside the entrance is a large image of the reclining Buddha, of which the facial features are in the U Thong style. In a *sala* to the left is a beautiful wooden **Footprint of the Buddha** carved with the 108 auspicious symbols, and possibly dating from the early Ayutthaya period. The eminent Thai art historian, Prince Damrong Rajanubhab, believed it to have been made during the reign of King Luthai (Mahathammaratcha I) in the mid-14C. The reverse side is also carved.

The road heading north from Wat Phra Rup passes **Wat Pratu San**, where the *ubosot* is decorated with 19C **murals** illustrating scenes from the Life of the Buddha, some of them by Nai Nak, a local painter who at the time was apprenticed to a Bangkok muralist and who later painted other murals at Wat Bang Nom Kho in Sena district, Ayutthaya.

Opposite the *Siam Commercial Bank* on T. Phanwasa is the **National Museum of Thai Rice Farmers** (open Wed–Sun, 09.00–16.00), which has a few exhibits of farming equipment, photographs and information on rice cultivation.

6 · Nakhon Pathom to Ratchaburi

Road. *The direct route from Nakhon Pathom lies straight along road 4, a fast and easy journey of 48km. There are frequent bus services. For travellers with their own transport and plenty of time, an alternative route is recommended below. This takes quiet country roads along the west bank of the Mae Klong River to Ratchaburi, passing several notable sites. There are regular buses from Nakhon Pathom to Ban Pong and to Photharam; to reach Wat Muang it is simplest to charter a vehicle in Photharam. There is public transport between Photharam and Khao Ngu, and from there to Ratchaburi.*

Railway, *53km in 55mins (express). There are many trains daily to Ratchaburi, but express services do not stop in Photharam, nor always at Ban Pong.*

From Phra Pathom Chedi, take T. Ratchawithi west to rejoin road 4. Continue west for 9km, then turn right on to road 323 towards Ban Pong and Kanchanaburi. At the intersection on the far side of Ban Pong take road 3089 straight ahead and, 7km further on, turn left into a lane signed to the **Wat Muang Mon Museum**, which is on the left after c 2km. This small museum (open Fri–Sun, 09.00–16.00, and usually by request on other days), established in 1993 with the support of Princess Sirindhorn and help from Silpakorn University, stands on the bank of the Mae Klong River and contains exhibits relating to the Mon people, who, historically, have made up a substantial minority of the area's population. Most important are the fragile *khampi* manuscripts wrapped in hand-woven cloth or stored in wooden cabinets. The earliest date from the reign of Rama I. There are hand-painted wall hangings, pottery recovered from the river bed, an ornate *thammat*, and information about the Mons and their customs.

WAT KHANON lies 5km further south on the same road. In the large, raised wooden *kuti* are kept Buddhist sculptures, Chinese ceramics and objects made by the Chinese craftsmen who built the *wat* and one of the few remaining collections of **nang yai** leather puppets (see pp 96–7). This set, originally made in the late 19C, was restored—and largely replaced—in the early 1990s. There are usually several on display, but performances are rarely given.

Beyond Wat Khanon, the road arrives at a bend of road 3090. Turn left, cross the river bridge, and turn left again immediately before the railway line to reach **WAT KHONG KHARAM**, on the left after 1300m. Inside the *ubosot* are exceptionally fine **murals** which probably date from the reign of Rama III. The land on which the *wat* stands was bestowed on the Mon people by Rama I and became a centre for Mon culture in the Ratchaburi area. The murals, painted in three tiers, are generally in good condition. The lowest tier depicts various *jātaka* tales, which begin sequentially with the *Temi jātaka* in the middle of the north wall, and continue clockwise. Arrayed above are scenes from the Life of the Buddha. The unpainted wooden window shutters are decorated on the inside with intricate carving, some with guardian images; one pair depicts the fruit of the mythical *nariphon* tree, which are in the shape of beautiful women. The doors on the east and north sides are magnificently carved with a predominantly floral motif; the presiding Buddha image is from the Ayutthaya period.

Around the *ubosot* are eight Mon-style *chedi*, and immediately to the west is a large old, teak raised *kuti* with carved shutters and architraves, known as the 'seven-room *kuti*'. Beside it to the left is the 'nine-room *kuti*', an equally fine structure which, alas, is showing signs of severe woodworm infestation. Kept in a glass case inside is the wooden coffin in which the former abbot's body lay during the river procession before its cremation.

Return beside the railway line to road 3090, and continue straight across the road to reach **Wat Sai Arirak**, on the right side. In the *ubosot*, which was restored in the early 1990s, are rather damaged murals, and others only partially completed. They probably date from the same period as those at Wat Khong Kharam, but have been poorly maintained.

It is possible to rejoin road 4 here by returning to road 3090 and turning right across the railway line. The recommended alternative is to turn left and follow road 3090, and then road 3089 towards Khao Ngu. This route passes Wat Chong Phran on the right after c 10km. On the hill on which this *wat* stands is **Tham Khang Khao Cave** ('Bat Cave'), from where, at dusk each evening (around 17.45–18.30), a seemingly endless stream of bats—perhaps millions—emerges to feed.

The road continues south c 17km to the limestone caves of **Khao Ngu** on the right, which contain some of the earliest known examples of **Dvaravati art**. The site is marked by a tall, modern standing image of the Buddha. Be warned that many visitors come here primarily to feed the macaques, which swarm like vermin in the vicinity of the caves, especially Tham Rusi and Tham Fa Tho. The monkeys may seem aggressive, but they are unlikely to attack unless provoked; however, they do defecate and urinate everywhere, and the hillside is strewn with plastic bags in which bananas have been sold to feed them.

The first cave reached on the right, up a flight of steps, is **Tham Rusi** ('Hermit's Cave'), which contains an important gilded bas-relief in Dvaravati style of a Buddha image seated in *pralambapādāsana*, beneath which is a group of stelae recording the name of the hermit who lived in this cave, Si Samadhi Gupta. On the cave wall are several reliefs of smaller images.

Beyond the food stalls, more steps to the right lead up to **Tham Fa Tho** ('Lid of a Cup'), which contains a large stucco relief of the reclining Buddha. On the right wall near the entrance are very faint reliefs of three female deities.

The next flight of steps to the left—more than 450 of them—lead up to a hilltop *sala*, which houses a stone Footprint of the Buddha. This is an arduous, hot climb, and probably not worth the effort: even the view is unremarkable.

Follow the lane round the base of the hill for several hundred metres to the foot of the steps up to two more caves, **Tham Chin** and **Tham Cham**. Both contain stucco fragments of Dvaravati art, but there is very little indeed left in the latter, which is the higher of the two. Tham Chin has reliefs of two Buddha images, originally in the Dvaravati style, but apparently altered in the 16C to that of Ayutthaya.

Back on road 3089, turn left after 700m on to road 3087, which leads directly to Ratchaburi.

Ratchaburi

Ratchaburi (pop. 46,000) was originally a port on the estuary of the Mae Klong River, but over the centuries this has silted up so much that the sea is now 30km away, and the town is surrounded by rice fields.

History

Already during the Dvaravati period it was an important commercial centre, and its position on the Mae Klong River has ensured that it has remained so until today despite the silting. Wat Mahathat, the most important *wat* in Ratchaburi, was founded during the Dvaravati period, and Muang Khu Bua, an important Dvaravati site of the 7C and 8C, lies c 7km to the south of the town. According to the Ramkhamhaeng stela, in the last decade of the 13C Ratchaburi was incorporated by King Ram Khamhaeng into the Sukhothai kingdom. It later came under the rule of Ayutthaya.

■ **Hotels and Services**. The best hotel is the *Golden City Hotel*, isolated 5km north of the town centre on T. Phet Kasem (road 4). More central, simpler hotels include the *Araya* at 187/11–12 T. Kraiphet and the *Nam Sin* at 2/16 T. Kraiphet. The *Thai Farmers Bank* is at 16/1 T. Kraiphet and the *Bangkok Bank* at 131 T. Amarin. The **post office** (international **telephone** service 07.00–22.00 daily) is on the corner of T. Si Suriyawong and T. Samut Sakdarak, and the main market can be found near the clock tower.

■ **Transport**. There are frequent bus and train services to Bangkok and nearby provinces. The terminus for **air-conditioned buses** is on T. Kraiphet. For **ordinary buses** the station is on T. Si Suriyawong. The **railway station** is on the main southern line.

WAT PHRA SI RATANA MAHATHAT lies on T. Khao Ngu, Soi 2, near the Mae Klong River. Coming from the Khao Ngu caves, cross road 4 and turn left after a short distance into Soi 2; the main entrance faces the river. This important monastery, which was founded in the Dvaravati period, altered during the period of Khmer rule and only finished in the 15C, is chiefly notable for its large *prang*, which stands at the centre of a square gallery, the inner wall of which is lined with images of the Buddha. The *prang* still retains some of its original 15C stucco ornamentation, but modern cement additions can be plainly seen. On the east side, a steep flight of steps leads up to the cella, in which can be seen faint traces of 15C **murals** protected by grilles, and two images of the Buddha. Opposite the foot of the steps is a large gilded image behind glass of the reclining Buddha. On the north, west and south faces of the main *prang* are false doorways, which contain partially damaged reliefs of the Buddha. There are three smaller *prang* on the north, west and south sides. Of note are the stone gong at the northeast corner of the main *prang*, and the bronze bell at the southeast corner. The *wat* stands in a large enclosure filled with fine frangipani and other trees and surrounded by a laterite wall with a coping of carved sandstone votive tablets, which date originally from the Khmer-Lop Buri period.

On T. Woradet, which runs beside the river, is the **Ratchaburi National Museum** (open Wed–Sun, 09.00–16.00) housed in the former town hall, which, was built in the 1920s. On display are prehistoric and later artefacts from the area, including stucco fragments from the Dvaravati (6C–8C) site of Muang Khu Bua (see below); the corner of a *stūpa* from the site has also been recreated. Among the Khmer objects is a magnificent 13C sandstone torso of Avalokiteshvara. Other rooms have examples of later art styles, a collection of modern fish traps, basketry and textiles, some of the dragon-motif water-jars for which Ratchaburi is famous, and information on the ethnic minorities who live in the province.

The most important surviving monument of the 7C–8C Dvaravati site of **Muang Khu Bua** is the large raised base of a *wihan* at Wat Khlong Suwan Khiri, 7km south of the town centre along road 3339. A flight of steps at the east end leads up to the platform. Of the other 60 or so monuments found scattered across the 3 sq km site, little remains except *stūpa* bases. The stucco decoration and artefacts from the site are now in the Ratchaburi National Museum.

Chedi Hak is a large, octagonal, U Thong-period brick *chedi* beside road 3291, c 300m west of road 4.

7 · Bangkok to Samut Sakhon and Samut Songkhram

Road 35, 72km. To Samut Sakhon 36km. Samut Sakhon to Samut Songkhram 36km.

Railway, 70km from Wongwian Yai station. In Samut Sakhon it is necessary to alight, cross the Tha Chin River by boat and continue the journey to Samut Songkhram by a connecting train on the west bank.

Boat. Long-tailed boats can be hired in Bangkok for the voyage down the Khlong Mahachai to Samut Sakhon.

SAMUT SAKHON (pop. 40,000) is at the confluence of the Tha Chin River and Khlong Mahachai, and was one of the principal ports for the trade of Ayutthaya, until it was superseded by the port of Bangkok. It is now only a fishing port. In the centre of the town is a clock tower, and next to this is a jetty where fish are unloaded from the boats, packed in ice and despatched to Bangkok and other centres. There is also a lively fish market nearby. All this creates a colourful and animated scene, which in itself makes a visit to Samut Sakhon rewarding. Not surprisingly, there are many excellent fish restaurants in the town.

The royal temple of **Wat Yai Chom Prasat**, in Muang district, a few km north of Samut Sakhon on the right bank of the Tha Chin River, is accessible either by road 35 or by boat. Most of the buildings of this temple date from the Ayutthaya period. The *ubosot* contains a highly venerated seated Buddha image known as Luang Pho Pu. One of the two *wihan* has a finely carved wooden gable; inside, the columns and ceiling are richly painted.

To the northwest of Samut Sakhon at the confluence of Khlong Mahachai and Khlong Kham, a smaller canal dug during the reign of King Naresun, is **Wat Khok Kham**, an Ayutthaya-period temple where there is a shrine commemorating the chief oarsman of King Sua. Nearby is an ancient boat, which the local people adorn with garlands.

Between Samut Sakhon and Samut Songkhram the road and railway pass through a large area of flat marshland, most of which is devoted to salt production and the farming of prawns and other shellfish. To the north of Samut Songkhram is a fertile plain intersected by numerous canals where vegetables and fruit are grown. The **Damnoen Saduak** floating market is in this area, c 5km southeast of Ratchaburi (see Rte 6).

SAMUT SONGKHRAM (pop. 36,000) is near the estuary of the Mae Klong River and owes its prosperity to the production of salt, fish, fruit and vegetables.

■ **Hotels and services**. The best hotel is probably the *Mae Klong Hotel* at 546/10–13 T. Phet Samut. The *Bangkok Bank* is at 125 T. Khao Muang.

The most important temple in Samut Songkhram is **Wat Phet Samut Wora Wihan**. It houses a much revered late Ayutthaya bronze image of the standing Buddha known as Luang Pho Ban Laem, which is traditionally believed to have been found floating in the river.

▶A few km to the northwest of the town along road 325 in Amphawa district is **WAT BANGKAE YAI**. This temple is situated among orchards of orange, guava, coconut and lychee and is surrounded on three sides by canals—Khlong Bangkae to the east, Khlong Meru to the north and Khlong Bangli to the south. The square-based *chedi* and the sandstone *bai sema* surrounding the *ubosot* indicate that the *wat* was founded in the late Ayutthaya period, but an inscription in the *ubosot* states that it was only completed in 1814 by a son of the governor of Ratchaburi, Chao Phraya Wongsasurasak (Sang), who later became minister of war to Rama II.

The gallery surrounding the *wihan* contains some fine sandstone Buddha images of the U Thong and early Ayutthaya periods, but the *wat* is chiefly notable for the superb **mural paintings** in the abbot's residence. This was originally a traditional wooden Thai house built on stilts, but has been reconstructed so that the original house containing the paintings now forms an upper storey above a concrete lower storey. The paintings, which date from the reign of Rama II, were executed in tempera on a partition wall or panel (*prachan*) composed of wooden boards set vertically side by side. They employ a limited palette of ochre, brown, dark red, indigo and black thinly applied on a white foundation. They contain many lively depictions of the traditional village life of the Mons, Karens and other ethnic minorities who live in this part of western Thailand, and illustrate in detail the traditional architecture, much of which betrays Chinese influence, the dress and the agricultural implements of these peoples. Each scene is portrayed with great naturalism and vigour. There is a naval battle between Thais and Mons in which two boats ram each other; a Thai soldier chasing Mon villagers; a European horseman carrying a musket and dressed in the fashion of the 18C; a group of Karen men in their traditional long striped robes fishing on a river bank; another group of Karens surrounded by their baskets fraternising with Thai soldiers; a group of Mon men and women winnowing and pounding rice; a tiger about to pounce on a Thai soldier; and a pair of leaping deer in a mountain landscape. Most of the background details, such as trees and hills, have been inexpertly added or retouched later, using the so-called 'dabbing technique'.◀

Almost due west of Samut Songkhram on the banks of the Mae Klong River where a canal, Khlong Amphawa, leads off the river directly to Samut Songkhram, is the charming small town of **AMPHAWA**, reputed to be the place of origin of the Chakri dynasty. Here is the royal temple of **Wat Amphawan Chetiyaram**, which contains a statue of Rama II. Behind the *wat* is a small park, the **Uthayan Phra Borom Ratchanusorn** dedicated to Rama II and specialising in the cultivation of trees and plants mentioned in Thai literature. Here also is a museum composed of a small group of traditional Thai houses. There are stalls in the enclosure where food and handicrafts are for sale and in front of the temple a floating market. On the other bank of the river opposite Wat Amphawan Chetiyaram is **Wat Phumarin Kuti Thong**, which was founded by King Rama I. Nothing remains of the original buildings of this *wat* except a small *kuti* of gilded lacquer, which is now used as the temple museum.

On the banks of the Mae Klong River between Amphawa and Samut Songkhram are some notable temples. The first of these is **Wat Yai**, on the left bank off road 325, built in the reign of King Mongkut by a rich merchant. The roof of the *wihan* has unusual eaves set on columns. The *ubosot* has gables of carved wood which predate the construction of the temple buildings. On the right bank a short distance further north is **Wat Phuang Malai**, which dates from the reign of King Vajiravudh. The front of the *ubosot* of this *wat* is decorated with pieces of ceramic. On the left bank 4km from Samut Songkhram is **Wat Bang Kaphom**, founded in 1769 and restored in the reign of Rama III.

■ In addition to the Damnoen Saduak and Amphawa markets, there are several other **floating markets** in the area. These include the markets at **Bang Noi** and **Tha Kha**. They can all be reached by boat from Samut Songkhram.

8 · Phetchaburi and environs

Road 35, 120km via Samut Sakhon and Samut Songkhram.

Railway, 167km in c 3hrs by express service from Hua Lamphong station, Bangkok. Slower services from Thon Buri/Bangkok Noi station.

Leave Bangkok on road 35 (T. Phra Ram II), which runs southwest from Thon Buri through a fertile area of orchards and rice fields, and after c 25km bypasses Samut Sakhon (see Rte 7). It continues through a bleak area of marsh and salt pans, where the salt water is pumped up by six-sailed windmills. At the 60 km stone a turning to the right leads to Samut Songkhram. Road 35 continues over the Mae Klong River and joins road 4 at a junction c 30km north of Phetchaburi.

In Khao Yoi district, c 21km north of Phetchaburi, a lane to the left leads after a short distance to **Wat Kuti Bangkhem**. This temple has a remarkable *ubosot*, the exterior walls of which are entirely covered with woodcarvings in relief illustrating scenes from the *jātaka* tales.

▶About 12km north of Phetchaburi and near the coast in the middle of the salt pans is **Wat Khao Takhrao**, on the outskirts of the village of Ban Laem. This Ayutthaya-style temple contains a famous image of the Buddha seated in *bhūmisparśa mudrā* known as Luang Pho Wat Khao, which, like several other revered Buddha images in Thailand, is popularly believed to have been discovered floating in the water.◀

Phetchaburi

Phetchaburi ('Diamond City', pop. 46,000), capital of a province, is situated only 10km from the estuary of the Phetchaburi River and was formerly an important commercial centre with a substantial Chinese merchant community. It has retained considerable charm, with its tree-lined streets, its numerous traditional houses and fine temples.

History

In the 11C and 12C Phetchaburi and Ratchaburi seem to have been the two principal outposts of the Khmer empire of Angkor in the lower Chao Phraya valley. Phetchaburi later became the centre of one of the many small Thai chieftaincies and principalities that emerged in central Thailand as the power of the Khmer empire waned after the death of Jayavarman VII c 1220. By the 1290s it had been conquered by King Ramkhamhaeng of Sukhothai or had acknowledged his suzerainty. It is possible that U Thong, the founder of the kingdom of Ayutthaya in 1351, came from a Chinese merchant family settled in Phetchaburi; certainly, from the outset Phetchaburi was one of the core provinces of the Ayutthaya kingdom. During the 16C, 17C and 18C the city was repeatedly attacked by both Khmers and Burmese.

Phetchaburi is well known for its manufacture of sweets made with palm-sugar. Many of these sweets can be sampled in the town's restaurants, notably the *Ban Khanom Thai* at 130 T. Phetkasem.

■ **Hotels and services**. Unfortunately there are no hotels in Phetchaburi that can be unreservedly recommended, but the town can be easily visited in a day either from Bangkok or from Hua Hin. The newest and the best hotel is the *Regent,* and the *Phetkasem Hotel* at 86/1 T. Phetkasem is just acceptable. The *Bangkok Bank* is at 12 T. Phanit Charoen. The **Post Office** is on T. Rajavithi.

■ **Transport**. The **railway station** is on the northern outskirts of the town. Phetchaburi is on the main line south from Bangkok to Hat Yai. The main bus terminal is on T. Phongsuriya near the Chomrat Bridge. **Air-conditioned bus** services run regularly to and from Bangkok Southern Terminal, Cha-am, Hua Hin and Prachuap Khiri Khan. There is another bus terminal off T. Rot Fai. **Samlo** are readily available in the town and can be engaged for excursions to Khao Luang.

The royal temple of **Wat Yai Suwannaram** is situated on T. Phongsuriya near the east bank of the river. The date of the foundation of this important *wat* is unknown, but it was probably built during the reign of Prasat Thong and is

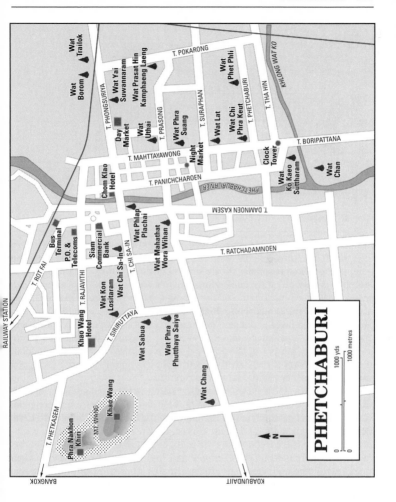

PHETCHABURI

0   1000 yds

0   1000 metres

N

RAILWAY STATION

BANGKOK

KOABUNDAIT

Wat Trailok

Wat Borom

Wat Yai Suwannaram

Wat Prasat Hin Kamphaeng Laeng

T. POKARONG

Wat Phet Phli

KHLONG WAT KO

T. PHONGSURIYA

Day Market

Wat Uthai

T. PRASONG

Wat Phra Suang

T. SURAPHAN

Wat Lat

Wat Chi Phra Keut

T. PHETCHABURI

T. THA HIN

T. BORIPATTANA

T. MAHTTAYAWONG

Night Market

Clock Tower

Wat Ko Kaeo Suttharam

Wat Chan

Chom Klao Hotel

T. PANICHCHAROEN

PHETCHABURI RIVER

T. DAMNOEN KASEM

Bus Terminal

P.O. & Telecoms

Siam Commercial Bank

Wat Phlap Plachai

Wat Chi Sa-In

Wat Mahathat Wora Wihan

T. RATCHADAMNOEN

T. ROT FAI

T. RAJAVITHI

Khao Wang Hotel

Wat Kon Lositaram

Wat Chi Sa-In

T. SIRIRUTTIAYA

Wat Sabua

Wat Phra Phutthaya Saiya

Wat Chang

T. PHETKASEM

Phra Nakhon Khiri

T. NE WANG

Khao Wang

known to have been restored during the reign of King Sua in the early 18C by a patriarch called Chao Taeng Mo. Subsequently it underwent several further restorations. Of these the most extensive was that carried out for the Abbot Phra Kru Maha Wiharaphirak (Phuk) by a monk named Si Wang Yot, who lived in the *wat* during the reign of King Chulalongkorn. His work included the construction or restoration of several buildings, notably the gallery surrounding the *ubosot*.

The **ubosot** is built in the style typical of the later Ayutthaya period. It stands on a high, curved boat-shaped base and is surrounded by double sandstone *bai sema*, each standing in the cup of a lotus-flower on a high redented square base of stuccoed brick. There are three doors at the east end and two at the west end, but, rather unusually, no windows. At both ends are gables which have exceptionally fine stucco decoration in high relief. On the east gable is a *garuḍa* among intertwined tendrils and on the west gable a *deva* standing in triumph above an

Wat Yai Suwannaram, Phetchaburi

asura, surrounded by an intricate pattern of flame and vegetal motifs. Inside, the roof, which has a fine coffered ceiling, is supported by redented square columns terminating in lotus capitals. The decoration of the columns, each of which is different, is also of exceptional refinement. At the west end is the principal image, a stuccoed brick figure of the Buddha, 2.2m wide from knee to knee, seated in *bhūmisparśa mudrā* on a high, intricately carved base. Behind this are two other seated Buddha images, one in stuccoed brick, which may have been the original principal image, and a smaller one, measuring 1.4m from knee to knee, in bronze. In front of the principal image are three more seated Buddha images, and in front of these are two portrait statues, one of Patriarch Taeng Mo and the other of Phra Khru Maha Wiharaphirak.

The chief glory of this *ubosot*, however, is the series of magnificent **mural paintings** that it contains. The earliest of these paintings date from the reign of King Prasat Thong, which makes them among the earliest in Thailand to have survived. The predominant colours are red, brown and gold on a white background. The murals cover not only the walls, but also the wooden panels on the doors. They were most recently restored in 1964. The wall behind the Buddha images at the west end is painted with floral motifs. Above the central door at the west end the earth goddess Dharani is depicted dressed in a long green skirt and wringing out her long black hair. Above her is a painting on glass of a Chinese altar with temple offerings on it, and above this is a representation of the Buddha in *bhūmisparśa mudrā* seated on a lotus throne. To the right of the Buddha is shown the attack of the evil tempter Mara, and to the left, Mara's defeat. On the side walls are almost life-sized depictions of celestial beings arranged in five registers and all turned in homage towards the principal Buddha image. They include representations of the four-faced Brahma and of Indra, and of *garuḍas*, *nāgas*, *riṣis* and *yakṣas*. The costumes and ornaments worn by these figures are rendered with great delicacy, and no two figures are exactly identical. The figures are divided from each other by zigzag lines, and in the triangular space thus created between them are exquisitely painted flame and vegetal motifs. The paintings on the doors are of *dvārapālas*. On the door to the left of the principal Buddha image at the west end are *kinnaris* with *riṣis* and *gandharvas* above them. On the central east door beneath the painting of

Dharani are a pair of magnificent *dvārapālas* standing on lions and surmounted by depictions of a palace building with five spires.

The *ubosot* is surrounded by the gallery built by Si Wang Yot. It has a two-tiered roof and is similar in plan to the galleries that generally surround Khmer *prasat*, with cruciform entrance gates or *gopuras* placed at intervals on each side. It contains rows of identical Buddha images.

To the west of the *ubosot* is a magnificent **sala kan parian**, 10m wide and 30m long, which it is thought was originally the palace of King Sua. It has a four-tiered roof decorated with elaborate roof ridges, finials and acroteria, and brackets ornamented with the so-called 'grasshopper's face motif' characteristic of the later Ayutthaya period. At either end of the roof are protruding eaves set on short columns that rest on a slope of the roof below and form a kind of porch over the wooden pediments, which are carved with floral motifs of exceptional delicacy and have *nāga* heads made of terracotta at each of the bottom corners. There are five doors, three at the front and two at the back, set in elegant carved frames with pointed arches. The central door in the front has panels of carved and gilded wood studded with glass mosaic and frames with pointed arches. The wooden walls of the *sala* were originally decorated on the outside with designs in gilt, but these are now painted red. The roof is supported inside by 22 pairs of lacquered and gilded columns, 11 octagonal and 11 rounded, each pair, as in the *ubosot*, with a different design. At the west end is a superb *thammat* of gilded wood studded with glass mosaic, dating from the reign of King Chulalongkorn.

To the south of the *sala kan parian* are two pavilions, a crematorium and a belfry, which was constructed for Phra Khru Mahawihara Phirak and stands on a high base built in Western style; beyond them are the abbot's and monks' quarters, and the new *ho trai*, a fine two-storeyed wooden building constructed in 1927. To the east of these structures is a large pond in the middle of which is the old wooden **ho trai** standing above the water on three stilts. This beautiful little building was restored in 1975 by the Siam Society but is again deteriorating.

Continue a little way along T. Phongsuriya and turn right to reach **Prasat Kamphaeng Laeng**, a 12C Khmer temple of which the laterite enclosure wall and the central *prang*, with a *gopura* to the east and smaller *prang* on the other three sides, remain in relatively good condition. Traces of stucco decoration are visible on the central *prang*.

Continue on the same road to the south of Prasat Hin Kamphaeng Laeng to reach **Wat Phet Phli**, which has a *chedi* dating from the reign of King Prasat Thong and a small museum containing Buddha images, votive tablets and temple furnishings.

Wat Ko Kaeo Suttharam, which is second only to Wat Yai Suwannaram in importance, is situated on T. Matayawong also on the east bank of the Phetchaburi River, south of Wat Yai Suwannaram. It is bounded on two sides by water, on the west by the Phetchaburi River and on the south by Khlong Wat Ko. Wat Ko means 'island monastery' and it may be that it was originally entirely surrounded by water. It was founded in the early 18C, and most of the buildings belong to this period. The **ubosot**, like that of Wat Yai Suwannaram, is set on a boat-shaped curved base. It has two doors at either end, but no windows. The niches and pediments over the doors contain stucco carving of the highest quality, and there are finely carved wooden brackets supporting the eaves. The eight pairs of sandstone *bai sema* standing on high bases are thought to date from the U Thong period and, if so, are earlier than the *ubosot*. In front of the *ubosot* is a group of small, elegant late Ayutthaya-style *chedi*.

The **wall paintings** in the *ubosot*, which date from 1734, are scarcely less magnificent than those of Wat Yai Suwannaram and bear a close resemblance to them, notably in the range of colours employed and in their use of zigzags to separate scenes. At Wat Ko Kaeo Suttharam, however, the zigzags stretch from floor to ceiling creating large triangular areas in which ornate, elongated *chedi* alternate with scenes from the Life of the Buddha set beneath enormous and richly decorated five-tiered parasols. In one triangle the Buddha is portrayed subduing the Nalagiri Elephant, and beneath this is a group of foreigners, including one dressed as a Buddhist monk and holding a monk's fan, but wearing a European hat. In another a group of turbanned Muslims argue inside and around a pavilion standing on a single column, while the Buddha approaches them standing on a lotus-flower. The triangular spaces on the upper part of the walls contain 27 figures of *vidyādharas* flying through the air, some in attitudes of worship and others holding their attributes, against a back-ground spangled with flowers and little clouds. Most of them wear a lower garment of tiger skin, a form of attire traditionally associated with hermits, but their other garments and adornments and their facial features differ widely and are intended to indicate the various ethnic groups to which they belong, such as Mon, Khmer, Burman, Indian, Chinese, Japanese and European. The murals on the front wall on either side of the doorway depict the sacred cosmic mountain, Mount Meru. The murals behind the principal Buddha image show the seated Buddha in *dhyāna mudrā* vanquishing Mara. This scene is unusual in two respects: in most *wat* it is painted on the wall of the entrance facing the principal Buddha image and it usually shows the Buddha seated in *bhūmisparśa mudrā*. The ceiling of the *ubosot* is decorated with paintings of stars and flowers, and at each corner is a bat, an auspicious creature in Chinese mythology, holding a bunch of flowers in its mouth.

The **wihan** is much plainer in style than the *ubosot*, but it probably belongs to the same period. There are two other buildings in the enclosure that were built in the 1880s by the architect Than Athikarn Chom. These are a *sala kan parian* containing a fine *thammat* of carved wood designed by Si Wang Yot, who also worked at Wat Yai Suwannaram, carved by Athikarn Yit, and painted with scenes from the Life of the Buddha, and the monks' quarters, which also have magnificent roof decorations. There is a small museum established in 1975, which contains numerous Buddha images, ceramics, manuscripts and other Buddhist objects.

Wat Mahathat Wora Wihan is in the centre of the town on T. Damnoen Kasem on the west bank of the river. It was founded in the Ayutthaya period, but was not completed until very much later. The designation of Mahathat ('Great Relic') was added to its name in 1954 when it received a donation from the king of some important relics of the Buddha. It has five white Khmer-style *prang* with some good but much restored stucco decoration, a *wihan*, which also has notable stucco work outside and heavily restored wall paintings within. To the left of the *wihan* is an *ubosot*, which also has exceptionally fine stucco decoration and is surrounded by U Thong-style *bai sema* set in niches. The roofs of both *wihan* and *ubosot* are decorated with figures of *devas* instead of *cho fa* finials. The central *prang* has a *gopura* on the east face and is surrounded by a gallery containing Buddha images. In the enclosure there is also a *mondop* containing a curious statue of Kukrit Pramoj, prime minister of Thailand for a few months in 1975/76 standing in a group of statues of *yakṣas*.

A short way to the north of Wat Mahathat on the right side of T. Damnoen Kasem is **Wat Phlap Plachai**, which has an *ubosot* with richly carved wooden doors set in ornamented stucco frames. It houses a Sukhothai-style seated Buddha image. This *wat* also has an important collection of *nang yai* shadow puppets.

Hat Chao Samran is a popular beach 13km south of Phetchaburi off road 4. There are several small hotels, bungalows and restaurants here. A turning off road 4 at Tha Yang 17km south of Phetchaburi leads through fertile country planted with cotton and sugar-cane to the Kaeng Krachan Reservoir, the construction of which was completed in 1966 and which provides irrigation for the whole of the surrounding plain. On the side of the hill above the reservoir is a comfortable bungalow, where it is possible to spend the night. A further 3km to the south off road 4 is another beach called Hat Puk Tian and 20km beyond this is Cha-am (see Rte 48).

Just before the entrance to Phetchaburi, road 4 turns to the right towards Cha-am and Prachuap Khiri Khan, passes between two hills, called Khao Bandai It and Khao Wang (also known as Khao Maha Sawan) and after about 1.5km reaches a crossing with T. Bandai It. Turn right on to T. Bandai It immediately to the south of Khao Bandai It to reach **Wat Bandai It**, an Ayutthaya-period *wat* with some fine stucco decoration surrounding the doors and on the east wall of the *ubosot*. Nearby is **Tham Rusi**, one of the numerous caves and grottoes in the neighbourhood of Phetchaburi containing stalagmites and stalactites. As its name indicates, this cave was formerly used by hermits.

At the foot of Khao Wang is **Wat Sa Bua**, a notable late Ayutthaya-period temple. Its small *ubosot* has a three-tiered roof and a boat-shaped base. The stucco decoration on the gable above the entrance and on the surrounding *bai sema* is of unusual delicacy and elegance.

Khao Lang Cave

Just before the entrance to the town, turn left on to road 3173. This leads after 3km to **Khao Luang Cave**, which has the most impressive stalactites of all the caves in this area. A staircase bordered by frangipani trees leads to the entrance. The principal chamber, which is reached down a steep flight of steps, is lit in spectacular fashion during the late morning and early afternoon by natural light from a hole in the roof above. It contains several Buddha images and a miniature octagonal *prang* in the U Thong style, which still has traces of stucco decoration.

Khao Klang has two summits, both of which can be reached by a path. Immediately below the northwest summit is the **palace of Phra Nakhon Khiri** (open Wed–Sun 09.00–16.00), begun by King Mongkut in 1859 in the neo-Classical style to designs by Thuam Bunnag. A path with steps at intervals flanked by a *nāga* balustrade leads up the hill through woods full of monkeys to the entrance of the palace. There is also a rack-railway. The palace complex consists of numerous buildings, pavilions and fortifications scattered over the twin summits of the hill at different levels. The main palace building contains a small museum in which a somewhat heterogeneous assortment of objects collected by King Mongkut and King Chulalongkorn is displayed. On the south-east summit is **Wat Phra Kaeo**, a temple closely modelled on the *wat* of the same name in the Grand Palace in Bangkok (see p 117). It has a lavishly deco-rated *ubosot*. A little below the *ubosot* is a red sandstone *prang* and three smaller buildings. A *chedi* in Sri Lankan style c 9m tall known as **Chedi Phra Sutthasela** stands at the highest point. The most prominent among the palace buildings on the northwest summit is the observatory (Chiatchawan Wiangchai) set up by King Mongkut, who was a keen astronomer. Next to the observatory is a building known as **Phra Thinang Wichian Prasat**, in which two sculptures of King Mongkut, one in stone by a French sculptor and the other in bronze by a Thai, are displayed; both are said to have been made from a photograph of the king. The palace complex has recently been restored and is used from time to time by the royal family. The whole area has been made into a historical park, and when no members of the royal family are in residence, it is open to the public. From the terraces there are magnificent views of the surrounding countryside.

EAST OF BANGKOK

9 · The Eastern Seaboard from Bangkok to Rayong

Roads 3 and 34, 179km. To Chon Buri 81km; Chon Buri to Rayong 98km.

Leave Bangkok on road 3 (T. Sukhumvit) to Bang Na, where road 34 goes off to the left through industrial suburbs before rejoining road 3 south of Bang Pakong. A detour to the right off road 34 10km beyond Bang Na, leads to **Bang Phli**, a small town on the banks of a canal called Khlong Samrong, where every year at the end of the Buddhist Lent (*Phansa*) a procession of decorated boats called Ngan Yon Bua and boat races are held. In the principal monastery, Wat Bang Phli Yai, is a much revered image of the Buddha (Luang Pho Bang Phli Yai) said, like the Buddha image of Wat Sothon (see below), to have been found floating in a stream.

Beyond Bang Na road 3 continues to Paknam and from there runs for 30km along the left bank of a canal across flat and monotonous country to the fishing port of Khlong Dan. At Khlong Dan road 304 runs northeast to Chachoengsao on the right bank of the Bang Pakong River.

Chachoengsao is a small but lively town with a substantial Christian community. Traces of the fortifications of the ancient city of Muang Paet Riu, which was on this site, can be seen on the left of the road running along the side of the river. The most important temple in Chachoengsao is Wat Sothon, which contains a statue of the Buddha (Luang Pho Sothon) of Khmer origin that is said to have been found floating in a stream.

From Chachoengsao road 315 goes east and then south to **Phanat Nikhom**. Here in a shrine called Ho Pura Phanatsabodi is a much revered statue of the Buddha standing on a lotus pedestal supported by a *garuḍa*. This is an enlarged copy of an image found in 1931 at Muang Phra Rot by a villager whose descendants still possess it. Phanat Nikhom is also noted for its basket-making.

Just beyond Phanat Nikhom on the left of road 315, a track leads to the important neolithic site of **Khok Phanom Di**, first excavated by the Fine Arts Department in 1978/79 and then in 1985 with the assistance of Charles Higham of the University of Otago.

At the 23km stone beyond Phanat Nikhom another path to the left leads to **Wat Luang Phromawat**. This is also known as Wat Kang Khao ('Monastery of the Bats') on account of the vast number of bats that live in the trees surrounding it and which are protected by the monks of the *wat*.

At the 27km stone, a path to the right leads to the village of **Na Phra That** where traces of the ramparts of a Mon Dvaravati city known as Muang Phra Rot can be discerned. To the west of this site is Noen That, a brick *chedi* of the Dvaravati period which has been restored by the Fine Arts Department.

Chon Buri

Chon Buri (pop. 52,000) was probably founded in the 14C and is now an important commercial centre and fishing port. The chief crops produced in the surrounding area are sugar-cane and tapioca. Buffalo races, which attract thousands of visitors, are held in the streets of the town every October.

The most important monument in Chon Buri is **WAT YAI INTHARAM**. Founded in the late Ayutthaya period and raised to the rank of a royal monastery in 1975, this *wat* is chiefly notable for its **wall paintings**, the earliest of which are thought to date from the late Ayutthaya period.

The **ubosot** is built on a rectangular plan and has the curved boat-shaped base characteristic of the late Ayutthaya period. It has been restored several times, most recently in 1955, and much of the present building dates from the mid-19C or later. The east end has been extended by the addition of an outer wall with three doors and a sloping roof, and the room thus created contains one of the eight *bai sema* that surround the building. These *bai sema* consist of double slabs set on high pedestals and covered with canopies in the form of *chedi*. The window shutters are decorated on the outside with floral patterns in gilt and lacquer and painted on the inside with figures of celestial beings, their hands raised in homage. The gables and the frames of the windows and doors are decorated with ceramic dishes. The roof-ridges are made of plaster carved in the form of celestial figures paying homage. Inside the *ubosot* are 24 Buddha images on a single raised platform. Most of these, including the principal image, which is seated in *bhūmisparśa mudrā*, are made of brick and stucco, lacquered and gilded. There is also a statue of Indra in royal attire. The round pillars, the tie beams and the wooden panels in the ceiling are decorated with gilded vermilion lacquer. The marble floor was laid in 1955. The wall paintings between the windows on the north and south walls illustrate scenes from the last ten *jātakas*. Over the windows are rows of *gandharvas* and *vidyādharas* bearing garlands, above three registers of deities and angels, *garuḍas*, ogres and *nāgas*. On the east wall the Buddha's victory over the tempter Mara is depicted and on the west wall scenes of the three worlds of the Buddhist universe (*Traiphum*) and the life of the Gautama Buddha. These paintings provide much valuable information about architectural styles, costumes and customs in 18C and 19C Thailand.

To the north of the *ubosot* is a **wihan**, which appears also to date from the late Ayutthaya period, but was extensively restored in 1955 and again in 1967. It has a curved base like that of the *ubosot*, with a moulding decorated with lotus motifs. The gables at either end were formerly adorned with ceramic plates, but these were not replaced in the two recent restorations. The outside of the shutters of the window in the west wall have fine paintings of *dvārapālas*, and the east door has similar paintings, which unfortunately have now almost entirely disappeared. The interior is decorated with wall paintings of the Ayutthaya period depicting Buddhist scenes and with much elaborate floral ornament. These are in a very bad condition and in some places are almost completely obliterated.

To the west of the *ubosot* is another, smaller *wihan*. It also has a curved base decorated with lotus motifs and faces east. It has pediments at either end but no gables. Behind this *wihan* is a smaller Khmer-style *prang* with the corn-cob shape, multiple redentations and tall, narrow niches characteristic of the late Ayutthaya period.

Further to the west is a shrine containing a Footprint of the Buddha. The shrine was restored in 1947, and the murals that formerly decorated it were covered with whitewash. Next to this is a *sala kan parian* containing an exceptionally fine pulpit decorated with lacquer, gilding and mirror glass. The steps were formerly decorated with carvings of animals from the Himavanta Forest at the base of the cosmic mountain, Mount Meru, but of these only the elephant remains.

Two other temples in Chon Buri, both Chinese, merit a brief visit. These are **Wat Thep Phuttharam**, a modern temple on the left of the main street of the town, and **Wat Tham Nimit**, which is on the left side of road 315 leading north out of Chon Buri to Phanat Nikhom. Wat Tham Nimit has a colossal Buddha statue that makes up in conspicuousness for what it lacks in artistic merit.

Road 3 runs south out of Chon Buri towards Si Racha and Sattahip through a fertile landscape of palm trees and tapioca, with the sea to the right and rolling green hills to the left. Along this coast are many beaches, of which one of the more agreeable is at **Bang Saen**, 11km from Chon Buri. Here there are several comfortable resort hotels, and a **marine aquarium** (closed Mon) on the campus of Burapha University. To the north of the town is a Chinese temple and monastery called Luk Sam Po, where the monks' quarters and other buildings are in the form of boats and there are two small *chedi* copied from Phra Pathom Chedi at Nakhon Pathom (see p 153).

At the village of Ban Phra a road runs to the left off road 3 to *Bang Phra Golf Club*, which has a good hotel attached, and, after a further 3km, to the reservoir of Bang Phra in **Khao Khieo-Khao Chomphu Wildlife Sanctuary**. This sanctuary, which was established in 1974 and covers an area of 145 sq km, includes the two hills, after which it is named, Khao Khieo and Khao Chomphu, and is home to numerous bird species, protected mammals, including leopards, and many rare butterflies. The adjoining **Khao Khieo Open Zoo** (open daily) has an enormous aviary and many large mammal species on display.

The small picturesque town of **Si Racha**, which lies c 24km down the coast from Chon Buri, has a substantial Catholic community, which has its own church, school and hospital. Off the coast opposite Si Racha is the island of **Ko Sichang**, where the few surviving buildings of a wooden palace called Khao Chula Chom Klao, built by King Chulalongkorn, can still be seen. At the top of the hill behind the palace is a large *chedi* known as Chedi Asadang Nimit. Ferry boats to the island depart from Si Racha.

50km south of Chon Buri a turning to the right leads after 3km to the seaside resort of **PHATTHAYA** (Pattaya). Originally a small fishing village, Phatthaya first began to be developed as a resort during the Vietnam War when Americans based at nearby Sattahip and U Taphao used it for recreational purposes. It quickly became Thailand's principal seaside resort, catering to a mass market, both domestic and international. It is now perhaps better known for its vibrant and garish nightlife than for the beauty of its beaches or its coral reefs, many of which have been destroyed by the depredations of skin divers and motor boats, and it suffers from most of the familiar social and environmental problems that come in the wake of too rapid and inadequately controlled development for tourism. The high season is between November and April. There is a TAT **infor-**

mation office at 382/1 T. Chaihat (Beach Rd), in the middle of the beach strip, and there are dozens of hotels along the coast between Phatthaya and Na Chom Thian (Jomtien) Beach to the south.

Opposite Phatthaya are numerous attractive small islands that can easily be reached by boat. The largest and most beautiful of these is **Ko Lan**, which has several magnificent sandy beaches and can be reached in c 45 mins by fishing boat and 20 mins by outboard motor boat.

Road 3 continues south along the coast of the Gulf of Thailand. 15km south of Phatthaya a turning to the left leads to **Suan Nong Nut**, a landscaped park similar to the Rose Garden near Bangkok (see p 151); it has an artificial lake surrounded by gardens, an orchid house, craft workshops and traditional Thai houses with accommodation for visitors. Displays of Thai dancing and Thai boxing are given here on most afternoons, together with elephant shows.

2km beyond the turning to Suan Nong Nut is the charming little port of **Bang Sare**, which has a good beach, dive operators and chalet accommodation. Here also boats to the nearby island of **Ko Khram** can be hired.

Sattahip (pop. 23,000), formerly an American and now a Thai naval base, is not a town of any architectural distinction, but it is in a delightful natural setting of forest-clad mountains, rocky shores and fine beaches. The former US air base is at U Taphao, c 10km northeast of Sattahip, which now serves as the airport for Phatthaya.

The small fishing port of **Ban Samae San** is situated at the end of a peninsula a few km southeast of Sattahip, immediately opposite the island of the same name. From here boats can be hired to visit the numerous islands and islets off this coast, including Ko Raet, Ko Samae San, Ko Rong Khon, Ko Nang, Ko Chuang, Ko Chan and Ko Kham, where there are beaches, coral reefs and opportunities for diving.

On road 3, 47km east of Sattahip is **RAYONG** (pop. 29,000), which is both a fishing port and a market for the sugar-cane, tapioca and pineapple which is grown in the area. It is also one of the most important centres in Thailand for the manufacture of *nam pla*, the clear brown salty fish sauce used in every Thai kitchen, and of the equally ubiquitous shrimp paste known as *kapi*.

■ **Information**. The TAT office is at 153/4 T. Sukhumvit.

■ **Hotels and services**. There are several acceptable hotels in the town, including the *Burapha Inn* on T. Sukhumvit. However, the best accommodation is along the coast c 30km east of Rayong, between Ban Phe and Laem Mae Phim, where there is a string of expensive but good beach-side hotels. **Banks** and the **post office** can be found in the town centre along T. Sukhumvit.

The island of **KO SAMET**, also known as Ko Kae Phisadan, is situated off the coast 17km east of Rayong. Buses leave from the clock tower in Rayong to Ban Phe, a fishing port 17km to the east on road 3. From here ferries can be hired to the village of Samet on the island. The voyage takes c 45 mins. Largely because it can be reached relatively easily from Bangkok, Ko Samet, which is only 6km long from north to south, is now one of the most popular tourist destinations in Thailand, both for Thais and foreigners, and it has suffered much environmental damage in consequence. It forms part of the **Khao Laem-Ko Samet National Park**, which covers an area of 131 sq km and was established in 1981. The island has numerous sandy beaches, on which bungalow accommodation is available, and some coral reefs off the southern tip. There are also fine coral reefs off **Ko Thalu**, another, smaller island within the park.

10 · Rayong to Chanthaburi and Trat

Road 3, 180km. To Chanthaburi 110km; Chanthaburi to Trat 70km. Boat excursion to Ko Chang from Laem Ngop near Trat.

Road 3 runs east from Rayong through Klaeng (38km), a pleasant little town with many traditional wooden houses and a lively market. A turning to the left at Ban Khao Din on to road 3377, c 7km beyond Klaeng, goes to Ban Nam Sai (16km), where a lane to the right leads after 1km to **Khao Chamao-Khao Wong National Park**.

This 84 sq km park, covering the two hills after which it is named, has a number of waterfalls, caves and short trails, and there are more than 50 bird species in its evergreen forest. Overpriced park bungalows are available, but for travellers with private transport, the hotels of Rayong or Chanthaburi are a better option.

Further east along road 3, a road to the left at the 288km stone leads after c 13km to a series of interconnected caverns known as the **Khao Wong Caves**.

Chanthaburi

Chanthaburi (pop.39,700) is a major gem-trading and fruit-growing centre situated in the fertile plain of the Chanthaburi River between the southeast uplands and the sea. It has a large population of Catholic Vietnamese, most of whom settled here to escape religious persecution in Annam, which after 1802 was ruled by the fanatically Confucian and anti-French emperors of the Nguyen dynasty. More recently Vietnamese and Chinese immigrants have come into the area through Cambodia. The **gem dealers** are clustered around T. Si Chan in the heart of the town, trading in rubies, sapphires, topazes, zircons, spinels and other stones. The nearest mines are at Ban Bang Kacha, c 4km from Chanthaburi.

On the east bank of the Chanthaburi River is the largest Roman Catholic church in Thailand, the **Church of the Immaculate Conception**, also known as the Cathédrale de Notre Dame, built by Vietnamese refugees from 1898 on the site of an earlier mission church.

History

Chanthaburi seems to have been one of the western outposts of the Angkor empire as early as the 10C, and there are several Khmer sites in the vicinity. However, by the end of the 14C it had been incorporated in the kingdom of Ayutthaya. After the fall of Ayutthaya to the Burmese in 1767, the governor of Chanthaburi rebelled against King Taksin, who had established his court in Thon Buri, but was soon defeated and executed. An equestrian statue of Taksin stands in King Taksin Park on the southwest side of the town.

In 1893 after the Pak Nam incident, when French gunboats forced the defences at Pak Nam (Samut Prakan) at the mouth of the Chao Phraya River and sailed up the river to Bangkok, the French occupied the two Siamese seaboard provinces that bordered Cambodia (Trat and Chanthaburi). They did not finally withdraw and abandon their claims of jurisdiction over these territories until the conclusion of the 1907 treaty by which the provinces of Battambang, Siem Reap and Sisophon in western Cambodia were ceded to France. There are some French buildings in the town, including a customs house. On the banks of the river there are some traditional Thai wooden houses.

■ **Hotels and services**. Among the town's better hotels are the inconveniently located *Eastern* at 899 T. Tha Chalaep and the very reasonably priced *Kasem San I*, at 98/1 T. Benchama Rachuthit. The *Bangkok Bank* is at 18 T. Tha Chalaep, and there are other banks nearby.

■ **Transport**. There are frequent services from the **bus station** on T. Saritidet to Rayong and Bangkok, and east to Trat. There are also regular buses north to Nakhon Ratchasima (see Rte 43).

To reach the fortifications of **Khai Noen Wong**, built by Rama III in 1834, take road 3146 southwest for c 4km from the town centre past the King Taksin Park and turn right on to the road to the airport. Shortly after, turn right again. Some of the fort's embrasures contain late 18C and early 19C French and British cannon. On the top of a small hill within the fortified enclosure, on the site of a Khmer temple, is **Wat Yothanimit**, also built by Rama III. The present *wihan* dates from 1977.

Several pleasant **excursions** can be made from Chanthaburi to nearby national parks.

▶Khao Khitchakut National Park
To reach this park, which covers an area of 59 sq km, follow road 316 north out of Chanthaburi, and cross road 3 on to road 3249. From here continue for c 21km to the entrance to the park on the right side, which leads to the **Krathing Falls**. At weekends in the rainy season, the inhabitants of Chanthaburi flock to the falls, but it is usually quiet during the week.

At the summit of **Khao Phra Bat**, the hill down which the Khlong Krathing flows, there is, as the name suggests, a Footprint of the Buddha, which every February is the site of an important pilgrimage. ◀

▶Nam Tok Phliu-Khao Sabap National Park
Take road 3 from Chanthaburi towards Trat for 13km to the turning to the park. There are food stalls near the car park. On the left after entering the park, close to the Phliu Waterfall, is a simple white **chedi** built in 1881 to enshrine the ashes of Queen Sunandakumaritana, wife of King Chulalongkorn, who drowned together with her three children, in the Chao Phraya River near Bang

Pa-in. Her attendants dared not attempt to rescue her for fear of committing the offence of touching a person of royal rank, for which the penalty was death. The bereaved king also had a memorial to her erected in the gardens of the Bang Pa-in Palace (see p 201).

The **Phliu Waterfall** is at the foot of a large jungle-covered hill 250m from the park gate. The top of the falls, which are c 20m high, is reached by a flight of steps next to the *chedi*. From there it is possible for experienced and cautious climbers to hike along the river bed deep into the jungle. It is also possible to climb up to Chedi Olongkon, built by Chulalongkorn to commemorate his visit in 1876, from which there is a fine view of the falls. Another path leads after several kilometres to two other lovely falls—Nam Tok Trok Nong and Nam Tok Klang.◀

▶Khmer ruins at Wat Thong Thua

Turn right off road 3 between the 337 and 338km stones and follow the lane for 1km to **Wat Thong Thua**. The *wihan* here is built on the laterite foundations of an ancient Khmer monument, of which little else remains. Two lintels and other fragments of sandstone with 7C carvings are kept in the *wihan*. To the southeast is a curious structure consisting of two rectangular buildings, 70m x 35m, surrounded by walls 4m high. It is known as the **Phaniat**, as it is believed locally to have been a kraal or *phaniat*, for capturing elephants.◀

▶Khao Soi Dao Cascades

Total distance of return trip, c 130km. This is really only a suitable excursion for travellers continuing north towards Sa Kaeo and Aranyaprathet (see Rte 11).

Take road 3150 over Damrong Bridge out of Chanthaburi, and turn left on reaching road 3. After a short distance turn right on to road 317, passing through low forested hills to Ban Pathong, which is reached after 62km. Turn left on to road 3391 and continue for 6km to the road head, from where it is a 15 minute walk through the forest to the beautiful, secluded Khao Soi Dao Cascades, which tumble down 16 levels. The trail becomes rather obscure above the fourth level.◀

▶Ban Pak Nam and Trat

Continue east from Chanthaburi on road 3 until c 15km from the town, where a turning to the right on to road 3149 leads to the fishing village of **Ban Pak Nam**, on the left bank of the Chanthaburi River estuary. Opposite lies the cape known as Laem Sing ('Cape of the Lion'). On Laem Sing is a small fort, **Pom Phairiphinat**, built during Rama III's reign. In Ban Pak Nam are the remains of fortifications built by the French during their occupation (1893–1906), a small square brick building called **Khuk Khi Kai**, which was used by the French as a prison, and the present municipal library, known as **Tuk Daeng**, which was built as the headquarters of the French garrison.◀

Trat

Trat (pop. 14,000) lies c 70km east of Chanthaburi near the Cambodian frontier at the terminus of road 3. Most travellers only pass through Trat on their way to the beautiful islands of the Ko Chang archipelago that lie to the south of Laem

Ngop. Modern Trat is a somewhat drab town consisting largely of concrete shop-houses. Like Chanthaburi, it is an important centre for the gemstone industry. The older quarters are found along the *khlong* on the south side of the town.

■ **Hotels and services**. The *Thai Rung Rot Hotel* at 296 T. Sukhumvit and the *Sukhumvit Inn* at 234 T. Sukhumvit provide adequate accommodation. There are also several friendly, cheap guest-houses offering rooms at budget prices. Some of these latter rent out bicycles, motorcycles and even canoes for exploring the canal. The *Bangkok Bank* is at 9/7 T. Sukhumvit and the **post office** is on the northeast edge of the town.

■ **Transport**. Daytime and overnight **buses** run regularly to Bangkok. Tickets can be bought from travel agents on T. Sukhumvit. There are frequent bus services and **share-taxis** to Chanthaburi, *songthaeo* to Khlong Yai near the Thai–Cambodian frontier, and to Laem Ngop (for **boats** to Ko Chang).

The most important monastery in Trat, **Wat Buppharam**, 2km southwest of the town centre, is worth a visit for its fine wooden buildings. The *wat* stands on a small hill and is surrounded by trees. Two of the three *wihan* in the grounds are decorated with wall paintings dating from the reign of Rama III.

►Chang Archipelago National Park

This national park on Ko Chang and c 50 neighbouring islands was established in 1982. **Ko Chang**, the largest island, is fringed by magnificent sandy beaches and has a thickly forested and mountainous interior with many rubber and coconut plantations. There are waterfalls in the interior and spectacular coral reefs offshore that are well worth exploring, but there is little bird or mammal life.

■ **Information**. The TAT office is at 100 Mu 1 T. Trat-Laem Ngop in Laem Ngop.

■ **Accommodation**. As on many of Thailand's islands, the development of tourism in the Chang National Park has been rapid and virtually uncontrolled and unplanned. There are bungalow resorts on almost every beach, ranging from the rudimentary to the luxurious. More exclusive accommodation is available on some of the smaller islands, such as **Ko Mak, Ko Lao Ya** and **Ko Kradat**.

■ **Transport**. Several boats sail daily from **Laem Ngop**, 20km from Trat, to both the east and west sides of Ko Chang (c 1hr). *Songthaeo* and motorcycle taxis operate around the island on the ring road, linking the resorts and villages to each other.◄

►From Trat road 318 runs southeast along the narrow coastal strip of Thai territory that separates Cambodia from the sea. The only place of note along here is **Khlong Yai**, a small fishing port that is also a trading and smuggling centre and a transit point for goods entering Cambodia. There are hotels here, including the adequate *Suksamran*, which make an overnight stay feasible.◄

11 · Bangkok to Prachin Buri and Aranyaprathet

Roads *31, 305 and 33, 274km. To Nakhon Nayok 107km; Nakhon Nayok to Prachin Buri 29km; Prachin Buri to Aranyaprathet 138km.*

Railway, *122km in 2hrs 35mins from Hua Lamphong station to Prachin Buri via Chachoengsao. The railway does not pass through Nakhon Nayok. From Prachin Buri to Aranyaprathet, 133km in 2hrs 30mins. Five daily services to Kabin Buri (50min) but only two daily as far as Aranyaprathet.*

Take T. Wiphawadi Rangsit (road 31) north out of Bangkok past Don Muang Airport. This road is frequently very congested in the outskirts of Bangkok. Soon after the intersection linking road 1 with T. Wiphawadi Rangsit, road 305 goes off to the right to Nakhon Nayok.

Another, slightly longer, route is to take road 1 out of Bangkok and at Hin Kong, 93km from Bangkok, turn to the right on to road 33, which leads after 43km to Nakhon Nayok.

Nakhon Nayok (pop. 18,000) is a small town of little interest, but can be used as a base from which to visit the magnificent **Khao Yai National Park** (see p 346).

■ **Information**. The TAT office is on road 305, beside the junction with T. Suwannason (road 33).

■ **Hotels and services**. The *Kobkua Palace* on T. Thongchai Si Muang has reasonably priced, clean rooms. The *Bangkok Bank* and *Thai Farmers Bank* are in the town centre and the **post office** is on the south side of town, off road 33.

To the northeast of the town, road 3049 leads after c 16km to the botanical gardens of **Wang Takhrai**. These gardens, considered to be among the most beautiful in Thailand, were first laid out by Prince Chumphot of Nagara Svarga in 1955 and further developed after his death in 1959 by his widow, who first opened them to the public. There is a statue in the park by Ruansak Arunwedj of the prince in Thai costume seated on a bench. The gardens contain many shrubs and trees brought from outside Thailand, and there are several waterfalls in the vicinity, of which the **Nang Rong Falls**, 5km beyond the gardens, are the most impressive. There is a restaurant and a picnic site in the gardens, and bungalows are available for rent.

At a roundabout 20km east of Nakhon Nayok on road 33, road 3077 turns off north to Khao Yai National Park while road 320 runs 8km south to Prachin Buri.

Prachin Buri (pop. 16,000) is situated on the Prachin River and was an important port and commercial centre at least from the time of the Mons of Dvaravati, and later under Khmer rule. The surrounding area has provided archaeological evidence of settled population since neolithic times. It is now a quiet, small provincial capital in the centre of a rich rice-growing area.

There is little of interest in the town except for the excellent **Prachin Buri National Museum** (open Wed–Sun 09.00–12.00, 13.00–16.00), which is housed in a modern building near the City Hall. On the **ground floor** are displayed objects found at Dong Si Maha Phot and other archaeological sites in the area. These include a superb Dvaravati image of the Buddha seated in meditation, flanked by multi-roofed *stūpas*, several fine Khmer images and relief carvings, including three magnificent figures of Vishnu, two dating from the 7C to 9C from Si Mahasot, and one from the 7C to 8C from Dong Si Maha Phot, several *liṅgas*, Buddhist figures from Ta Phraya, Sa Kaeo, a 10C or early 11C lintel in the Koh Ker style showing Indra mounted on his three-headed elephant Airavata, and a remarkable 11C or early 12C sandstone relief in the Baphuon style found at the *Phaniat*, near Chanthaburi, which illustrates a scene from a *jātaka* tale and shows figures kneeling on low tables against a background of Khmer buildings with pitched roofs and false windows. Among the Khmer bronzes displayed here are palanquin ornaments and a late 12C mirror stand, bowl and tripod, all with inscriptions in Khmer referring to the establishment of two *arogyasālās* in the area. An entire room is devoted to displaying the remarkably fine lintels from Prasat Khao Noi. These are in the style of Sambor Prei Kuk (early 7C) and Prei Kmeng (late 7C to early 8C). The lintel from the east side of the northern *prang*, which is decorated with medallions, flowers and worshipping figures, is particularly notable.

The **upper floor** of the museum is devoted to sculptures of all periods from Dvaravati to Ratanakosin and contains an important display of Sawankhalok ceramics and other pottery found in the sea off the east coast of the Gulf of Thailand.

▶Leave Prachin Buri on road 319, which leads after 19km to Ban Khok Pip. Here road 3070 goes off to the left to Si Maha Phot, where there is a well-preserved Khmer *baray*, known as **Sa Morokot**, dating from the reign of Jayavarman VII. Various blocks of laterite and laterite carvings, including figures of lions and *nāgas*, and a sandstone *liṅga* almost 2m high found in the vicinity have been assembled nearby.

About 1.5km beyond Sa Morokot a path to the left leads off road 3070 to **Wat Ton Maha Si Pho**. This is a modern *wat* containing an exceptionally fine seated Buddha image, which may be of Dvaravati origin. A single round laterite column from an earlier *wihan* stands in front of the door.◀

From Prachin Buri road 33 continues east to Kabin Buri, where road 304 turns off left to Ban Thap Lan, c 32km and **THAP LAN NATIONAL PARK**, Thailand's second largest (2239 sq km) but rarely visited park, established in 1981. The park headquarters are in Thap Lan, to the right of the road. Travel into the park is permitted only in park vehicles from the headquarters. There are two bungalows, each accommodating 20 people, and camping is also allowed. The park is little explored, even by the park rangers, but there is believed to be a wide range of fauna. Forest cover is predominantly tropical evergreen forest, and although heavy deforestation has taken place, there is a healthy core area estimated to cover about 1000 sq km, and this is important for the conservation of many large mammals, including elephants, tigers and bears.

Adjacent to the southern border of Thap Lan National Park is the 845 sq km

Pang Sida National Park, which contains several fine waterfalls, including the Pang Sida Falls. To reach the park headquarters, continue east on road 33 from Kabin Buri and turn left on to road 3462 near Sa Kaeo. The Pang Sida Falls are 1.5km from the park headquarters, and there are trails to other waterfalls in the park. It is possible that the extremely rare kouprey (*Bos sauveli*) still survives here.

Sa Kaeo is the diminutive capital of one of Thailand's newest provinces, created in 1993 out of part of Prachin Buri province. However, the town is of much less interest than Aranyaprathet, the lively border town 52km to the east.

Aranyaprathet (pop. 15,000), a spacious, well-planned town just a few kilometres from the Cambodian frontier, has experienced a modest economic boom since the early 1990s, fuelled by the increase in trade between Thailand and Cambodia. The town provides a convenient centre from which to visit the two important Khmer sites of Prasat Khao Noi and Sdok Kok Thom.

■ **Hotels and services**. There are several hotels, of which the *Inn Pound*, on the edge of the town, is the best. The *Thai Farmers Bank* and the **post office** are in the town centre.

■ **Transport**. There is a regular **bus** service to Bangkok via Sa Kaeo and Nakhon Nayok, and there are two **trains** daily to Bangkok (c 5hrs 15mins).

From Aranyaprathet, take road 348 north through green and fertile country-side towards Ta Phraya, reaching **Ban Khao Noi** after c 15km. Situated on the top of a hill outside this village, and commanding fine panoramic views on all sides, is the Khmer temple of **Prasat Khao Noi**. This temple was founded in the 7C and is therefore one of the earliest Khmer monuments in Thailand.

The first part of the ascent to the temple is by a staircase of c 250 steps flanked by scarlet hibiscus trees. From the top of the staircase a steep path to the right leads up to the site. The temple consists of the ruins of three brick *prang*, of which the central one appears to have been rebuilt in the 11C and has been restored recently by the Fine Arts Department. The entrance door is on the east side; the other three sides have false doors. This *prang* shares a brick platform with the north *prang*, while the south *prang* has its own separate platform. There is some incised decoration on the brickwork. Copies of four of the lintels—the originals of which are now in the Prachin Buri National Museum—have been made for the site; two are leaning on the steps of the north *prang* and two on the south. To the left of the temple on the summit of the hill is a small wooden monastic house and a Footprint of the Buddha in a shrine, also of wood.

Sdok Kok Thom is situated right on the Cambodian frontier down a dirt lane off road 348, c 33km northeast of Aranyaprathet. For a time in the 1980s it was occupied by troops of the Khmer People's National Liberation Front and there-fore could not be visited. Built in the reign of Udayadityavarman II, it is chiefly important for the stela dating from c 1052 that was found on the site and is now in the National Museum in Bangkok. This stela has a long Sanskrit inscription that recounts the history of the priestly family who were endowed with the site by Udayadityavarman II and who had served the Khmer kings ever since the reign of Jayavarman II, founder of the Khmer empire in 802. It is therefore an important source for early Khmer history. The temple itself, which is built of sandstone, is a romantic ruin in a large enclosure surrounded by a laterite wall and a deep moat. All that remains of the central *prang* is the west wall and the false doors on the west and south sides. There are also the ruins of two 'libraries' with unusually large windows and a cruciform *gopura* on the east with a gallery either side of it.

12 · Saraburi and Lop Buri

Roads *31 and 1, 154km. Bangkok to Saraburi 107km; from Saraburi to Lop Buri 47km.*

Railway, *133km in 2hrs 25mins (express) from Hua Lamphong station to Lop Buri on the Northern Line. Trains to Saraburi, 1hr 50mins (express) from Hua Lamphong station on the Northeastern Line. There are no direct rail services between Saraburi and Lop Buri.*

5km south of Saraburi, a right turn off road 1 on to road 3042 leads after c 5km to **Phra Phuttachai** ('Shadow of the Buddha'). If driving from the south, it is necessary to continue past the turning and make a U-turn beyond. Here there is a large sandstone outcrop on which can be seen the faint painted figure of the Buddha, which has become a very popular pilgrimage destination. In the cliff face to the left of the shadowy figure is a shrine with an image of the reclining Buddha. A staircase leads to the cliff top, from where there are excellent views on a clear day.

Further along the right fork on road 3042 is the entrance to **Sam Lan National Park**, Thailand's smallest park (44 sq km), which was established in 1981. There are several small waterfalls here in the rainy season, but in dry periods there is no water at all and there is little to see.

A little further along road 1 towards Saraburi a turning to the left leads to **Wat Nong Yao Sung**, a hilltop temple reached by a flight of steps. It consists of a stuccoed brick *chedi*, a *sala* containing a magnificently decorated throne from the reign of Rama III and a *wihan* with carved wooden gables depicting the sun and moon, and lacquered shutters decorated with figures of animals and scenes from daily life. Inside, there are murals depicting scenes from the *Ramakien* and the Life of the Buddha.

Saraburi (pop. 64,000) is situated on the edge of the Central Plain within sight of the hills that separate the plain from Nakhon Ratchasima and the Khorat Plateau. It is not an attractive town and is chiefly noted for its proximity to two important pilgrimage sites: Wat Phra Phutthachai (see above) and the better known Wat Phra Phutthabat. The latter is not only one of the holiest sites in Thailand and so an important place of pilgrimage, but has recently become a favourite destination for foreign tour groups, with consequent environmental damage.

Near the centre of the town, road 3041 turns off west towards Sao Hai. After c 6km, just before Sao Hai, road 3314 leads north 500m to **Wat Samuha**

Praditaram, on the left bank of the Pasak River. The *ubosot* of this *wat*, which faces north towards the river, has a pair of magnificently gilded doors surmounted by elegant stucco pediments at each end, and contains fine wall paintings in the interior. The *kuti* to the south is entered through unusual Chinese gateways and contains some 19C stone Chinese guardian figures, originally brought to Thailand as ships' ballast.

A short way beyond Sao Hai, a road to the right first passes a series of ditches on the left that mark the fortifications of an ancient and long-disappeared city and then continues for a further 5km before reaching **Wat Chanthaburi**. In the *wihan* of this *wat* are some highly decorative mid-19C wall paintings, possibly by a Chinese artist, depicting scenes from the Life of the Buddha and above them rows of praying disciples beneath floral garlands.

29km north of Saraburi a turning to the left off road 1 leads after 1km to **PHRA PHUTTHABAT** ('Buddha's Footprint'), situtated on the side of a low hill. A hotel has been built here for pilgrims to the shrine, and along the road approaching it are many stalls selling souvenirs and Thai handicrafts.

History

The story goes that King Song Tham or Intharatcha of Ayutthaya sent a group of monks to Sri Lanka to pay homage to the Buddha's Footprint at Sumankut. When the Thai monks arrived there, the Sri Lankans asked them why they had troubled to come so far when, according to the Pali texts, there was another Buddha's Footprint of unimpeachable authenticity in their own country. When Song Tham heard of this, he at once organised a search, and soon after the place was discovered by a hunter, who, following a stag that he had wounded, saw it disappear into the undergrowth and later re-emerge completely unharmed. The hunter cut away the undergrowth and came upon a spring that had formed a pool of clear water in the shape of a foot. He drank from this spring and was cured of a skin disease from which he had suffered for many years. It was here that the king decided to build the temple of Phra Phutthabat.

Nothing remains of the buildings erected in the Ayutthaya period, as these were destroyed by the Burmese in 1765, two years before they invaded the city of Ayutthaya, and all the present buildings belong to the early Ratanakosin period. The most important is the **mondop** that enshrines the **Buddha's Footprint** itself, which is about 1.5m long. It is almost square in plan and stands on a marble platform approached by a triple staircase flanked by a *nāga* balustrade of little artistic merit. It has a seven-tiered roof, richly gilded and covered with glazed tiles, and surmounted by a slender spire. The roof is supported by 20 square columns decorated with gilding and coloured glass mosaics. Bronze bells presented by the faithful are hung round the terrace, and pilgrims make merit by striking these with wooden sticks. The interior of the *mondop* is sumptuously decorated: the coffered ceiling is gilded and lacquered, the floor is covered with a carpet of cloth-of-silver, and the doors are inlaid with mother-of-pearl. Next to the *mondop* is a large *wihan*, the Wihan Luang, which contains a miscellaneous collection of votive offerings. There are also several *chedi* in the temple precincts. From the top of the hill behind the monastery there is a fine view of the glazed tiled roofs and gilded spires of the temple buildings. The temple once possessed a remarkable 17C bronze statue of a humped bull, symbol of one of the four continents of Buddhist cosmology. The legs of this figure, which are 1.24m high, are decorated with floral motifs in low relief. It is now in the National Museum in Bangkok.

Beyond Phra Phutthabat, road 1 continues northwest towards Lop Buri, traversing a fertile area where maize and cotton are extensively cultivated. 46km from Saraburi it reaches a large roundabout in the centre of which is a statue of King Narai, whose summer capital was at Lop Buri and who built many of the temples and palaces in the city. Leave road 1 here and take road 311 towards the town centre. This road crosses a bridge and leads to another roundabout called Sa Kaeo, and then continues straight into the centre of Lop Buri.

Lop Buri
Modern Lop Buri (pop: 46,000) is as unappealing as many provincial Thai towns, but, as its large number of ancient monuments demonstrates, it has played an important part in the history of Thailand for over 1000 years.

History
Already in the 8C and 9C Lop Buri was an important centre of Mon Dvaravati and it evidently had close connections with the northern Mon state of Haripunjaya founded at Lamphun in the early 9C, the first ruler of which, Cham Tewi, was a daughter of the ruler of Lop Buri. By the late 9C it had become a provincial centre of the rapidly expanding Khmer empire of Angkor and, although it enjoyed nominal independence at least until the early 11C and apparently continued to claim it much later (it sent diplomatic missions to China seeking recognition from the emperor in 1001, 1115 and 1155), it was ruled until the mid-13C by Khmer governors, one of whom is known to have been a son of Jayavarman VII. The mid-12C reliefs at Angkor Wat in Cambodia showing the troops of Lop Buri accompanied by 'Syam Kuk' (i.e. Siamese) mercenaries suggest that already by then Lop Buri was the principal city from which the Khmers administered the ethnic Tai population in the region. For these reasons, the Khmer and Khmer-inspired art and architecture produced all over the area covered by modern Thailand and in all periods up to the beginning of the Sukhothai period in the late 13C, is often inaccurately classified as belonging to the Lop Buri school. By the mid-13C Lop Buri had regained its independence of Angkor and had become a Thai principality controlling much of the eastern side of the Chao Phraya valley. The marriage of U Thong, the first ruler of Ayutthaya, with a princess of the ruling house of Lop Buri brought it under the suzerainty of the new Thai kingdom, for which it seems to have provided an administrative model. The city enjoyed a second period of importance in the 17C in the reign of King Narai, who built a palace and established his court here.

■ **Information**. The TAT office is east of the town centre on T. Narai Maharat, almost opposite the *Lop Buri Inn*, and close to the roundabout with the statue of King Narai.

■ **Hotels and services**. There are surprisingly few good hotels in Lop Buri, perhaps because it can be easily visited from Bangkok in a day. Among the best

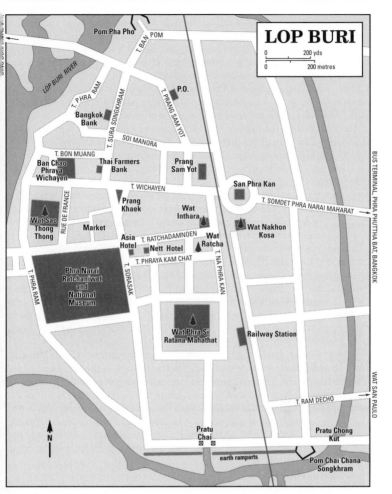

LOP BURI

Pom Pha Pho
T. BAN POM
LOP BURI RIVER
T. PHRA RAM
P.O.
T. PRANG SAM YOT
Bangkok Bank
T. SURA SONGKHRAM
SOI MANORA
T. BON MUANG
Thai Farmers Bank
Prang Sam Yot
San Phra Kan
Ban Chao Phraya Wichayen
T. WICHAYEN
T. SOMDET PHRA NARAI MAHARAT
RUE DE FRANCE
Prang Khaek
Wat Inthara
Wat Nakhon Kosa
Wat Sao Thong Thong
Market
Asia Hotel
T. RATCHADAMNOEN
Wat Ratcha
Nett Hotel
T. PHRAYA KAM CHAT
T. PHRA RAM
Phra Narai Ratchaniwet and National Museum
T. SORASAK
T. NA PHRA KAN
Wat Phra Si Ratana Mahathat
Railway Station
T. RAM DECHO
WAT SAN PAULO
N
Pratu Chai
Pratu Chong Kut
earth ramparts
Pom Chai Chana Songkhram
BUS TERMINAL, PHRA PHUTTHA BAT, BANGKOK

is the *Lopburi Inn*, several kilometres east of the town centre at 3 Soi Suriyathai 2, T. Narai Maharat. More centrally located are the clean, moderately priced and friendly *Asia Hotel* on T. Sorasak, which has a reasonably good restaurant, and the *Nett Hotel* off T. Ratchadamnoen nearby. The *Bangkok Bank* and *Thai Farmers Bank* are on T. Sura Songkhram. The **post office** (international **telephone** service, 07.00–22.00) is west of the Sa Kaeo roundabout on T. Narai Maharat.

■ **Transport**. There are frequent air-conditioned and ordinary **bus** services between Lop Buri and Bangkok (3–4 hrs). The **railway station** is on the Northern Line between Bangkok and Chiang Mai. There are regular services daily in both directions. **Samlo** operate in the town centre.

West of the Sa Kaeo roundabout, on the right of the road is a large park with a gate (**Pratu Phaniat**), which was formerly the entrance to an elephant kraal. The road continues over a bridge and, just before a railway level crossing, reaches **San Phra Khan**, a Khmer temple of which all that remains is the laterite base of what was evidently an important *prang*. Next to it is a modern shrine containing an image of the Hindu deity, Chao Pho San Phra Khan. The site is enclosed by a circular railing, and the ruins have been almost smothered in the roots of a *bodhi* tree in which live scores of monkeys.

The road crosses the railway line and continues into the centre of the town. On the right on a small hill is **Prang Sam Yot** ('Temple with Three Towers'), a fine Khmer temple built originally as a Hindu sanctuary and later converted to Buddhist use. The three *prang* which give the temple its name are built of laterite covered with carved stucco. Much of the stucco is still in good condition, so it is likely that it was restored in the Ayutthaya period. The towers each stand on a separate cruciform base and are linked to each other by corridors. Traces of the original wooden ceilings and fragments of Buddha images can be seen inside. The temple also harbours a large population of monkeys.

A road runs south along the west side of the railway line to two minor temples on the right hand side. These are **Wat Inthara**, which has a ruined Khmer brick *prang* and an Ayutthaya-period *chedi*, and **Wat Ratcha**, which also appears to belong to the Ayutthaya period. Across the railway tracks from here is the more important site of **Wat Nakhon Kosa**, which dates from the reign of King Narai and has a ruined brick *chedi*, a *wihan* and a small stuccoed brick *prang*. In one of the niches on the *prang* is an interesting standing Buddha image in the U Thong style, made of stucco.

A little further to the south opposite the railway station is **Wat Phra Si Ratana Mahathat**, which is the most important temple in the city. It consists of a large and imposing laterite *prang* and an entrance *gopura* in the Khmer-Lop Buri style. Next to it is a large *wihan* still more or less intact, which dates from the reign of King Narai and has windows with the pointed ogival arches character-istic of the architecture of this period. The *prang* and the *wihan* were formerly surrounded by a gallery of which few traces now remain, and between the gallery and the outer wall of the temple enclosure are numerous *chedi* in different styles, dating from the Sukhothai and Ayutthaya periods, many of them with multiple redentations.

A little to the northwest of Wat Phra Si Ratana Mahathat is the palace of King Narai, known as **PHRA NARAI RATCHA NIWET** (open Wed–Sun, 09.00–12.00, 13.00–16.00), which dates from about 1666. Within the palace enclosure is the **Phra Somdet Narai National Museum** (see below). King Narai is thought to have chosen to move his capital to Lop Buri, some 100km north of Ayutthaya, because he feared an invasion from the Dutch, with whom diplomatic and commercial relations were then very bad. He built the palace on an eminence, which enabled him to keep a watch for the approach of enemy forces and which, since it was surrounded by water for six months of the year during the rainy season, provided good natural protection against attack.

The palace enclosure is surrounded by high crenellated walls of stuccoed brick 5m high. At the four corners and at three other points in the walls are seven small triangular bastions with circular openings in their sides through which cannon could be fired. There are eight gateways, and the present entrance to the palace is on the east side through the gate called **Phayakkha** in T. Sorasak. The enclosure is divided into an outer, a central and an inner section or courtyard, and access from one to the other is through a series of gateways with pointed ogival arches. In the walls and doors of the central and inner court-yards are over 2000 small niches in which, according to French accounts of Lop Buri in the time of King Narai, small lamps were placed every evening; on special occasions lights were also lit in the passages and hung in the trees, creating a magical effect.

The first building to which the visitor comes is known as **Phra Khlang Supharat** ('Twelve Halls of Treasures'). It consists of what appear to have been 12 brick buildings, all of them roofless and some with only their foundations remaining, in two rows of six with a wide path between them. The function of these halls is uncertain, but they have small windows set high in the wall, which suggests that they may have been used as warehouses by the many merchants who frequented Lop Buri in the 17C.

To the left of Phra Khlang Supharat is the **Reception Hall for Foreign Envoys**. Only the two end walls of this hall remain. The doors and windows have pointed arches. Further to the left against the south wall of the palace enclosure is a hall known as **Phra Chao Hao**. The meaning of this name is uncertain and the function of the hall is therefore also unknown; it may have been a meeting hall or the royal chapel. The base of a Buddha image can be seen at the east end. For a brief period at the end of his reign King Narai was too ill to rule personally and one of his ministers, Phra Phetratcha, assumed the regency and used this building as his seat of government. From here also Phetratcha made his bid for power after the death of Narai and the disputed succession that followed.

To the right of Phra Khlang Supharat is a water tank built of brick, which, according to the 17C French writer Nicolas Gervaise, was designed by a French and an Italian engineer. Some of the earthenware pipes through which the water from this tank was sent to other buildings in the palace enclosure can still be seen.

The path continues westwards to the centre of the enclosure. On the left against the wall separating the outer from the central courtyard are the elephant stables, consisting of ten buildings, each measuring 10 x 6m and so presumably only providing accommodation for a single elephant, together with some smaller structures which may possibly have been the *mahouts'* quarters.

At the west end of the outer courtyard a gateway leads through into the central courtyard. Immediately in front of the gateway is the **Chanthara Phisan Hall**. This hall, which was built by King Narai in 1665, has balconies high up on the wall at the front and the back; the king would appear on the front balcony to grant audience to his subjects. It was restored in the 1850s by King Mongkut. Near the entrance is a painting of Louis XIV's ambassador, the Chevalier de Chaumont, presenting his credentials to King Narai on 18 October 1685.

To the south of the Chanthara Phisan Hall are the **Phiman Mongkut Pavilions**, a group of adjoining halls erected in 1856 by King Mongkut as part of his plan, which was never fulfilled, to restore the entire palace. Today these contain the collections of the **Phra Somdet Narai National Museum**. On the left is the **hall** known as Phra Thinang Akson Sattrakon, which was the king's

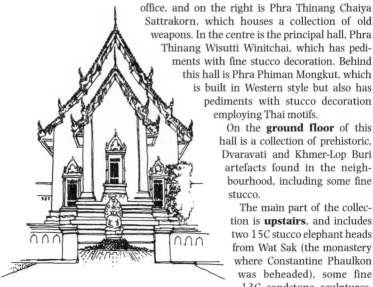

office, and on the right is Phra Thinang Chaiya Sattrakorn, which houses a collection of old weapons. In the centre is the principal hall, Phra Thinang Wisutti Winitchai, which has pediments with fine stucco decoration. Behind this hall is Phra Phiman Mongkut, which is built in Western style but also has pediments with stucco decoration employing Thai motifs.

On the **ground floor** of this hall is a collection of prehistoric, Dvaravati and Khmer-Lop Buri artefacts found in the neighbourhood, including some fine stucco.

The main part of the collection is **upstairs**, and includes two 15C stucco elephant heads from Wat Sak (the monastery where Constantine Phaulkon was beheaded), some fine 13C sandstone sculptures, and an especially notable 11C Baphuon-style lintel of Shiva with Uma from Si Thep

Chanthara Phisan Hall, Phra Narai Ratchaniwet, Lop Buri

(see p 80). There are numerous images of the Buddha from different periods, Ayutthaya-style carved wooden doors, weaponry, ceramics and textiles.

In the far left of the central courtyard is the **Dusit Sawan Thanya Mahaprasat Hall**, which was built by King Narai specially for the reception of foreign ambassadors. The front part has doors and windows with pointed arches, while the back part, the floor of which is raised above that of the front, has more traditional Thai windows and doors. Nicolas Gervaise records that this hall was originally decorated with mirrors brought back from France by the Siamese envoys sent by King Narai to the court of Louis XIV.

To the south of the Dusit Sawan Hall is the inner courtyard containing the **Suttha Sawan Hall**, where King Narai had his private apartments and where he died. Little remains of this part of the palace except its foundations, a part of the south wall and a platform that was used as the royal mounting block.

Behind the Phiman Mongkut Hall are the **Phra Prathiap Buildings**, in a mixed Thai and Western style, where the ladies of King Mongkut's court lived and where no male courtiers were permitted to enter. Some of them now house a display of local folk art and agricultural implements.

In February each year a festival in memory of King Narai (Ngam Phaen Din Samdet Phra Narai) is held in which the participants process in costumes of the period and the palace is illuminated with thousands of oil lamps as it was in Narai's time.

In T. Phetratcha, which runs along the south wall of the king's palace is **Wat Kawisraram**. This fine temple was entirely rebuilt by King Mongkut; it has two *chedi*, the larger of which stands on a square base decorated with nickel.

To the north of King Narai's palace are the ruins of **Ban Chao Phraya Wichayen**, the palace built by King Narai for Constantine Phaulkon, a Greek adventurer who began his career as a servant of the English East India Company in Ayutthaya and rose to become the king's chief minister with the title of Okya Wichayen. This palace contains the ruins of several buildings, including a residence for visiting foreign ambassadors, a church, kitchens and a bathhouse.

To the southwest of Phaulkon's palace is **Wat Sao Thong Thong**, an Ayutthaya-period monastery surrounded by a modern enclosure wall. Here is an elegant *wihan* with a multi-tiered roof called **Phra Wihan**, which was originally built as a Christian church for the Europeans in Lop Buri and was later converted to Buddhist use. A large seated Buddha image on the altar incorporates at shoulder height a cross from the original church. In the nave are niches containing Buddha images.

East of Phaulkon's palace, at the junction with T. Sura Songkhram, is **Prang Khaek**, a 10C or 11C Hindu shrine consisting of three brick towers flanked by a ruined *ubosot* and a *wihan*.

Further out from the town centre are a few other monuments. The road leading north from the Sa Kaeo roundabout reaches a junction with roads 3016 and 3196 after a short way. Turn right along road 3016 and after c 1km, a lane to the north leads to the site of a pavilion named **Phra Thinang Yen Krai Son Siharat**, of which little remains except some terraces and the bases of some of the walls. This is where Narai and a group of Jesuit priests watched a lunar eclipse on 11 December 1685. The site was once surrounded by a water-filled moat; today this lies empty.

Just off T. Ramdecho, to the southeast of the town centre and near the bastion of **Pom Chai Chana Songkhram**, are the ruins of a belfry, all that remains of the church of St Paul built by the Jesuits in the reign of King Narai and now called **Wat San Paulo**.

13 · Pathum Thani, Bang Pa-in and Ayutthaya

Roads *31, 1 and 32, 99km. To Pathum Thani 46km; Pathum Thani to Bang Pa-in 35km; Bang Pa-in to Ayutthaya 18km.*

Railway. *A regular train service runs from Bangkok (Hua Lamphong Station) to Bang Pa-in and Ayutthaya.*

Boats *can be taken from the pier of the Oriental Hotel in Bangkok and from Nonthaburi and Pak Kret up the Chao Phraya River to Pathum Thani, Bang Pa-in and Ayutthaya. Several travel agents in Bangkok organise excursions that go to Bang Pan-in and Ayutthaya by coach and return by boat later the same day, or vice-versa.*

PATHUM THANI (pop. 14,000) was founded by King Taksin, who in 1774 gave permission to a Burmese Mon chief named Phya Jeng to settle with his people at this site. Mon is still widely spoken here. The name Pathum Thani ('Lotus Town') was bestowed on the city in the reign of Rama III by a royal prince as a mark of gratitude to the citizens for offering him a bouquet of lotus-flowers every time he visited it. Today it is a provincial capital in the centre of a rich rice-growing area and is renowned for the making of rice noodles. It is also at the centre of a network of canals, and many interesting places in the vicinity can be easily reached by water.

About 20 minutes upstream from Pathum Thani on the left bank of the Chao Phraya River is **Wat Phailom**. This temple is chiefly remarkable for the thousands of white-billed storks (*Anastomus oscitans*) that come each year in November to build their nests and remain here until the following July. The storks have stripped the trees surrounding the *wat* of their leaves and whitened them with their droppings. They feed on snails, which they find in the irrigated rice fields surrounding Pathum Thani. They now enjoy government protection, and it is forbidden to hunt or shoot them. Bamboo hides are available for their observation. As a result of the high density of the population, some of these naturally monogamous birds have become polygamous and sometimes several families share a single nest. There is also a large colony of lizards, which eat the eggs if, as not infrequently happens, they fall from the nest.

Bang Pa-in

To reach the royal palace and pleasure gardens on the island of Bang Pa-in in the middle of the Chao Phraya River, either continue north from Pathum Thani on road 1 and turn off to the left 52km from Bangkok on to a road which passes under road 32 and leads after 8km to the palace, or take the quieter and longer route by road 3309, which runs along the east bank of the Chao Phraya River. Bang Pa-in can be reached also by boat from Pathum Thani, or directly from Bangkok. The palace grounds are open to the public daily 08.30–15.30.

History

According to a chronicle of the Ayutthaya period, the first palace on the island of Bang Pa-in was built by the usurper King Prasat Thong. The 17C Dutch commentator Jeremias van Vliet relates how, as a young man, King Ekathotsarot was shipwrecked on the island and was rescued by a woman by whom he fathered the child who later became King Prasat Thong. In 1632 Prasat Thong founded the monastery of Wat Chumphon Nikayaram on his mother's land on the island and to the south of the monastery built a palace. The only building in this palace specifically mentioned by the Ayutthaya chronicle is the Aisawan Thipya-at, which was constructed in 1632, possibly to mark the birth of the king's son, the future King Narai. It is not known whether it ceased to be used as a royal residence before or after the fall of Ayutthaya in 1767, but when the poet Sunthon Phu visited Bang Pa-in in 1807 he found it overgrown and deserted. King Mongkut returned to Bang Pa-in and built a temporary residence here; after him his son Chulalongkorn became a regular visitor and eventually built the present palace and the monastery of Wat Niwet Thamprawat. Bang Pa-in is still occasionally used by the royal family as a residence, for state banquets and other ceremonial occasions, and for accommodating important foreign guests.

As is usual with Thai palaces, the enclosure of Bang Pa-in is divided into an Outer and an Inner Palace. The former is used for public functions, while the latter is reserved for the royal family and household, and entry to it was formerly forbidden to male courtiers.

The principal entrance to the palace enclosure, which is surrounded by a wall with fortified towers at intervals, leads through to a long path running along the side of a canal. At the end on the right is a pool, in the centre of which, standing on a stone platform surrounded by a balustrade, is a Thai **pavilion** with four porches named Phra Thinang Aisawan Thipya-at ('Divine Seat of Personal Freedom') after the original pavilion built by Prasat Thong. This was constructed by King Chulalongkorn in 1876 and is a copy of the Phra Thinang Aphonphimok Prasat in the Grand Palace in Bangkok, built by his father, King Mongkut, as a pavilion in which to change his ceremonial robes before entering the royal palanquin (see p 123). It was originally built entirely of wood, but the wooden floor and the main supports were replaced by concrete in the 1920s. It contains a bronze statue of King Chulalongkorn in the uniform of a field marshal erected by his son and successor, King Vajiravudh.

In the same pool are two more pavilions. On the left is the **Phra Thinang Warophat Phiman** ('Excellent and Shining Abode'), a single-storeyed building in neo-Classical style built by Chulalongkorn in 1876 on the site of a two-storeyed wooden pavilion erected by King Mongkut for use partly as a throne hall and audience chamber and partly as a private residence. The present king and queen use the private apartments in this pavilion when they visit Bang Pa-in. The state rooms are decorated with paintings depicting scenes from Thai history and literature, commissioned by Chulalongkorn in 1888. A covered bridge with a louvred wall, from which the ladies of the court could look out without being seen, leads from the Warophat Phiman to the gate called Therawat Khanlai ('The King of the Gods Goes Forth'), which is the principal entrance to the Inner Palace.

The **Inner Palace** contains several buildings. One of these, **Phra Thinang Uthayan Phumisathian** ('Garden of the Secure Land'), built in 1877 in the style of a Swiss chalet, was King Chulalongkorn's favourite residence. It burnt down in 1938, leaving only the terrace and the water tank, which is in the form of a hexagonal, crenellated tower made of brick. A replica of the building was constructed on the site in 1989.

To the north is **Phra Thinang Wehat Chamrun** ('Heavenly Light'), a large two-storeyed house in the Chinese style, with an elaborately decorated tiled roof and glazed windows, built by an association of Chinese merchants and presented to King Chulalongkorn in 1889. Inside, it is furnished in Chinese style with fretwork decoration on the columns and windows, and Chinese furniture, including an ornately carved ebony bed and a lacquered writing table used by King Vajiravudh, who liked to stay here when he visited Bang Pa-in.

▶Other monuments include the ornate marble **obelisk** set up by King Chulalongkorn in memory of his wife, Queen Sunandakumariratana, who in 1881 when on her way by boat up the Chao Phraya River to Bang Pa-in fell into the water and was drowned. She drowned because it was considered sacrilegious to touch a royal person and so none of her attendants dared attempt to rescue her. The memorial bears an inscription in Thai and English composed by the bereaved king himself. Nearby is a marble cenotaph erected by King Chulalongkorn in 1887 in memory of one of his consorts, Princess Saovabhark

Nariratana, and three of his children, who all died in that year. On a small island between the Outer and Inner Palace is a **tower** built as an observatory by King Mongkut, who was an enthusiastic amateur astronomer and indeed died in 1868 as a result of malaria contracted when watching an eclipse of the sun. ◄

On the island separating the Chao Phraya River from the canal to the south of the palace is **Wat Niwet Tham Prawat**, a Buddhist *wat* built by King Chulalongkorn in 1878 in the style of a Gothic church. The *ubosot* contains a highly revered image of the Buddha by Chulalongkorn's court sculptor, Prince Praditvorakan.

Wat Chumphon Naikayaram, founded by King Prasat Thong, lies to the north of the palace. It has been much restored and altered by later kings, but it still has two polygonal *chedi* that date from Prasat Thong's reign. The pediment and lintel above the entrance porch have fine stucco decoration. Some of the interior walls of the *ubosot* have murals dating from the time of King Mongkut, which were renovated during Chulalongkorn's reign.

Ayutthaya

History
Ayutthaya (pop: 63,000) was capital of the Siamese Thai kingdom from its foundation in 1351 until it was sacked by the Burmese in 1767 and at the height of its power was one of the richest and most magnificent cities in Asia. After the death of Ramkhamhaeng of Sukhothai in 1298, a period of confusion ensued, during which a number of principalities vied with each other for mastery of the Chao Phraya plain. This was brought to an end and the supremacy of the Siamese Thais in the region assured by an adventurer of obscure origins known as U Thong, who was born in 1314, according to some scholars into a family of Chinese merchants in Phetchaburi, and who married a princess of the ruling house of Suphan Buri. In 1351 he founded the city and kingdom of Ayutthaya at a strategic site on a peninsula at the confluence of the Chao Phraya, Pasak and Lop Buri Rivers. A canal was later dug between the Chao Phraya and the Lop Buri to make the peninsula into an island. The name Ayutthaya is derived from the Sanskrit Ayodhya, the legendary city of Rama, hero of the *Rāmāyaṇa*. U Thong adopted the regnal name of Ramathibodi and sent his brother-in-law to govern Suphan Buri on his behalf, and his eldest son, Ramesuan, to 'mount the royal throne of Lop Buri', the ancient centre of Angkorian Khmer power in the region.

Ayutthaya soon established itself as the successor of Sukhothai, which it finally annexed in 1438. During the 15C it extended its power over most of central Thailand and into Laos, Cambodia and the Malay Peninsula to become one of the richest and most powerful states in Southeast Asia. Its great capital city, with its hundreds of temples and palaces, its canals and rivers, and its port frequented by merchants of many nations soon became known in Europe as the Venice of the East. Ayutthaya remained the capital of the Thai kingdom until 1767, when the Burmese in the last of their many invasions overthrew and sacked it so thoroughly that it had to be abandoned and the capital moved south down the Chao Phraya River, first to Thon Buri and then in 1782 to Bangkok.

■ The temples and other monuments of Ayutthaya are too widely scattered to be visited on foot, and a **car** or **bicycle** is therefore essential. Since they are also very numerous, only the most important can be described here. It is possible to see many of the temples on the water's edge by taking a **boat trip** part of the way round the island. Boats can be hired at several points, including the landing stage in front of the Chantharakasem Palace (popularly known as Wang Na or Front Palace) in the northeast corner of the island near the Pom Mahachai fort, and also from some of the riverside restaurants. The trip takes c 1 hr.

■ The modern city of Ayutthaya contains several good **hotels** including the U Thong Inn, 210 T. Rojana, the *Ayutthaya Grand Hotel*, 55/5 T. Rojana and the *Krung Sri River Hotel*. There are numerous excellent riverside **restaurants**.

51km from Bangkok turn to the left off road 1 on to road 32 and left again at the crossing with road 309. Before arriving at the eastern edge of the old city, road 309 crosses another road running north to south from a point marked by a fine brick *chedi*, which is all that remains of a temple named **Wat Sam Pleum**. The road to the left leads to **Wat Chedi Sam Ong** and **Wat Chai Yai Mongkon**. The imposing bell-shaped brick *chedi* of the latter *wat* was built by King Naresuan to commemorate his victory against the Burmese in 1592. In its present form, it is about 60m high. It has an octagonal *harmikā* and stands on a high rectangular base surrounded by a gallery, of which only a few columns remain. Rows of modern Buddha images have been placed in this gallery, and on the north and south side of the base of the *chedi* are two other large Buddha images. On the east side of the *chedi* is a staircase giving access to an inner cella, and on either side of the staircase are the ruins of two other buildings which once contained Buddha images. To the left of the entrance to the temple complex is a large reclining Buddha image of stuccoed brick taken from an earlier temple on this site. This image dates from the Ayutthaya period but has been heavily restored. Most unusually for a reclining Buddha image, the eyes are open.

The road going to the right off road 309 at Wat Sam Pleum leads north to two interesting groups of smaller temples that were restored in the early 1990s. On the left of the road is a group of three temples, including **Wat Somanakot Tharam**, of which little remains but the high square brick base of its *chedi*, and **Wat Kuti Dao**, an early Ayutthaya-period *wat* which was largely rebuilt in the early 18C. It stands in a spacious enclosure surrounded by a wall pierced by doorways with pointed arches. Its fine bell-shaped *chedi* is surrounded by four smaller *chedi* of which only the bases survive, and is flanked on either side by a *wihan* that has doors and windows with similar pointed arches and columns with lotus capitals. Some of the original wooden beams in the window frames are still in place. Immediately opposite on the right of the road is the other group of temples, of which the most important is **Wat Maheyong**. This *wat*, which was built c 1438, has a large and magnificent brick *ubosot* with nine windows with pointed arches, surrounded by a low double wall, on each corner of which is a round *chedi*. Next to the *ubosot* is a round *chedi* in Sri Lankan style with niches at the cardinal points. It is the only *chedi* in Ayutthaya that is set on a hexagonal base above a square platform surrounded by the foreparts of elephants in the Sukhothai manner. Immediately to the north of Wat Kuti Dao is **Wat Pradu Songtham**. This late Ayutthaya-period temple has a tall and elegant *ubosot* containing three notable Buddha images seated in *bhūmisparśa mudrā*, a *wihan* decorated with some remarkably fine late 18C wall paintings illustrating scenes from *jātaka* tales and a curious two-storeyed square belfry surmounted by a miniature redented *chedi*.

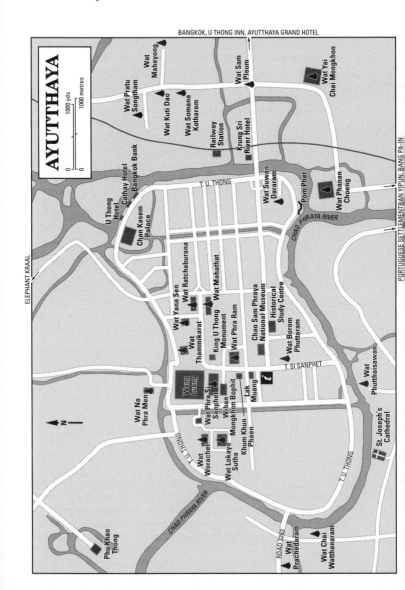

Road 309 continues into Ayutthaya over the Pridi Thamrong bridge and immediately beyond crosses T. U Thong, which circles the island. To the left T. U Thong runs south to **Pom Phet**, the only one of the several forts and bastions built in the late 16C by King Maha Thammaratcha and King Naresuan at strategic points round the city, to have survived more or less intact, and **Wat Suwan Dararam** ('Monastery of the Golden Star'), a late Ayutthaya-period *wat* which still houses a community of monks. It was totally destroyed in 1767, rebuilt by Rama I and completely restored in 1968. The *ubosot* is set on a platform with an unusually pronounced boat-shaped curvature and has a deep porch with four square columns at either end. Inside there is a fine coffered ceiling and wall paintings dating from the reign of Rama II and restored in 1968. The paintings on the side walls depict rows of praying disciples and scenes from the *jātaka* tales, while those on either side of the entrance show the Buddha's victory over Mara. At the west end is a seated Buddha image of the Ayutthaya period. Next to the *ubosot* is a later *wihan* containing some rather crude but attractive wall paintings illustrating the life and deeds of King Naresuan, which were commissioned by King Prajadhipok and completed in 1931.

The main prang of Wat Ratchaburana, Ayutthaya

Turn right immediately over the Pridi Thamrong bridge into T. U Thong, which leads north to the modern town of Ayutthaya, where the banks, shops and public buildings are to be found. In the centre of the modern quarter is the **Wang Na** (Front Palace), which was originally built by King Ramesuan before his accession to the throne in 1590 and later became the residence of successive crown princes. It was totally destroyed in 1767 and partly rebuilt by King Mongkut.

T. U Thong curves round the northeastern corner of the island and runs west along the Lopburi River. On the right is the bastion of **Pom Pratu Khao Pluak**, and a little beyond this a turning to the left leads south directly to two of the most important temples in Ayutthaya, **Wat Ratchaburana** and **Wat Mahathat**, both of which are on the right-hand side of the road.

Wat Ratchaburana was long thought to have been founded in 1424 by King Borommaratcha II in memory of his two elder brothers Ai and Yi at the place where they were cremated after being killed in a duel fought on elephant back to decide which of them should succeed to the throne, but it is now believed that this was another *wat* called Wat Ratchabun, the location of which is unknown, and that Wat Ratchaburana was founded by King Ekathotsarot. It seems also that the present buildings of Wat Ratchaburana for the most part date from no earlier than the reign of King Borommakot in the mid-18C.

The temple is surrounded by an enclosure wall pierced by great gateways with pointed arches. It consists of a large and monumental *prang* with a porch on the east side set on a square platform with a circular *chedi* at each corner. This *prang* is thought to be the prototype for all later Thai *prang* derived from the Khmer *prasat*. Traces of the original stucco decoration can still be seen on the outside, and in the crypt are early 15C wall paintings, some of them betraying Khmer-Lop Buri and Burmese influence and some in the Chinese style, confirming the presence of a Chinese merchant community in Ayutthaya during this period. To the east and west are two *wihan*; in the former the remains of a seated Buddha image can be seen. In the temple enclosure are several other, smaller *chedi* and *prang*. In 1957 a magnificent gold treasure consisting of more than 2000 objects, most of them dating from the late 17C, was found in the crypt of the main *prang* of Wat Ratchaburana, together with a smaller quantity at Wat Mahathat. The **Chao Sam Phraya National Museum** (see below) was constructed specially to house this treasure and objects found in other temples were subsequently added to the collection.

The date of **Wat Mahathat** is also uncertain. Although there is some evidence to suggest that it was founded in the late 14C, most of the existing buildings are thought to date from the 18C. The general plan and the architectural style of Wat Mahathat is similar to that of Wat Ratchaburana. The central laterite *prang* has collapsed, but was once almost 50m high. The terrace on which it stood and the staircases that led up to it have been restored. To the east and west of the *prang* are the remains of two symmetrical *ubosot*, with porches in front and galleries at the sides with columns with lotus capitals. Within the enclosure are numerous other *chedi* and *prang*, among them one highly unusual *chedi* in the form of a truncated cone. Also in the enclosure is the head of a Buddha image, embedded in the roots of a *bodhi* tree, which is the object of much veneration.

Wat San Si Sanphet, Ayutthaya

Continue west on T. U Thong, passing the elegantly proportioned *chedi* of **Wat Yana Sen** on the left of the road, to **Wat Thammikarat**, where next to a modern *wat* are the ruins of a large temple of the late Ayutthaya period that have recently been cleared of undergrowth and reinstated. The *wat* has a large and imposing *ubosot* with two rows of ten tall brick columns and behind it an unusual *chedi* with stuccoed brick figures of guardian lions surrounding the base and four staircases flanked by *nāgas* and lions. The lions have a somewhat Khmer appearance, and in Khmer art lions were frequently placed in front of temples as guardians, so these figures may date from the period immediately following the Thai conquest of Angkor in 1431. There are two *wihan*, one of which formerly contained the important U Thong or early Ayutthaya-style bronze Buddha head which is now in the Chao Sam Phraya National Museum (see below). The other enshrines a large brick reclining Buddha image 12m in length in Ayutthaya style, with soles ornamented with gilding and coloured glass mosaic.

A short way beyond Wat Thammikarat, T. Si Sanphet goes to the left off T. U Thong towards the **old royal palace** (Wang Luang) and **Wat Phra Si Sanphet**. There is little to be seen of the palace apart from a few foundations of some of the buildings in the palace enclosure, which was laid out by King Borommatrailokanat (Trailok).

Immediately to the south of Wang Luang and still within the original palace enclosure is **Wat Phra Si Sanphet**. This *wat* was built by King Trailok as his state temple and c 1500 was extended by Ramathibodi II to house an important gilded bronze Buddha image called Phra Si Sanphet, from which the temple derives its name. Phra Si Sanphet was stripped of its gilding and badly damaged by the Burmese in 1767, and King Rama I later had it removed to Bangkok and installed in Wat Pho (see p 127), along with Phra Lokanat, another image of the

Buddha from Wat Phra Si Sanphet. A third image from here, Phra Phuttha Sihing, was taken to the Phutthaisawan Chapel in Bangkok, which now forms part of the National Museum (see p 126).

The principal entrance to the temple complex is on the east side, though visitors are generally obliged to enter from the south where there is a ticket office and an entrance fee is charged. Immediately in front of the east entrance is a large *wihan*, which once contained Phra Si Sanphet, and on either side are two smaller *ubosot*. The south *ubosot* is surrounded by double *bai sema*, denoting that it was a royal foundation. All these buildings are of brick. Beyond them is a ruined gallery surrounding a row of three elegant bell-shaped *chedi* in classical Ayutthaya style. The east and central *chedi* were built by Ramathibodi II in 1492 to enshrine the ashes of his father, King Trailok, and his elder brother, Borommaratcha III, and the west *chedi* was added c 1540 by his son, Borommaratcha IV for the ashes of Ramathibodi II himself. They have been rather clumsily restored and covered with greyish-white cement. The east *chedi* was found to contain numerous Buddha images in gold, silver, lead, bronze and crystal, and these are now in the National Museums in Ayutthaya and Bangkok. The other two principal *chedi* have long since been broken into and looted. Between each *chedi* is a smaller building of which only the base remains. Within the *wat* enclosure are numerous smaller *chedi* and other buildings, several of them leaning at crazy angles as a result of subsidence.

Opposite Wat Phra Si Sanphet is a **statue of King U Thong** on a high plinth approached by a flight of marble steps. A wide avenue runs along the south side of Wat Phra Si Sanphet and leads to **Phra Mongkhon Bophit**, a *wihan* reconstructed in 1956–58 to house a colossal brick and bronze image of the seated Buddha. This statue, which is one of the largest bronze images of the Buddha in Thailand, is thought to date from the reign of King Trailok. It was moved to its present site in 1603. It is known to have been repaired and restored several times, most recently after the Burmese invasion of 1767, when the roof of the *wihan* in which it was then housed fell on top of it, breaking the *uṣṇīṣa* and the right arm. It is now difficult to see the statue clearly because the present *wihan* has been built round it so that it fits exactly into the space provided for it. On the south side of the avenue leading up to Wihan Phra Mongkhon Bophit are many stalls selling souvenirs and Thai handicrafts.

Turn to the left at the beginning of the avenue leading to Wihan Phra Mongkhon Bophit to reach **Wat Phra Ram**, which stands in a public garden established by Marshal P. Phibun Songkhram, prime minister of Thailand from 1948–57. The garden has been landscaped round a large natural pool known as Bung Phra Ram and contains a floral clock and a pavilion in which local handicrafts are displayed. Wat Phra Ram was probably founded or completely rebuilt by King Trailok, and, like Wat Ratchaburana, was again reconstructed by King Borommakot in 1741–42. The enclosure wall has several gates with pointed arches. The central *prang* stands on a high stepped platform ornamented with small *chedi* on square bases. Access to the shrine is gained by two staircases on the east and west sides. Much of the stucco decoration of the *prang* has survived and includes figures of the walking and standing Buddha, *nāgas* and *garuḍas*. There are several *wihan* surrounding the *prang* and to the north an *ubosot*, of which only one wall and some columns remain.

Wat Pho

Wat Phra Chetuphon Vimol Mangklaram Rajwora Mahaviharn.

Wat Phra Chetuphon or Wat Pho was built during Ayutthaya period in 1688–1706 to house the Buddha Saiyat or the Reclining Buddha, the most beautiful and second biggest Buddha in Thailand. The most outstanding feature is a great ornamented foot in 108 pictures. In this temple there are also Yoga postures of a hermit number 80 around its wall very beautiful.

DATE 1 1 ก.ค. 2544

Wat Phra Chetuphon

№ 643489 ...Mangklaram Rajwora Mahaviharn

20 Baht

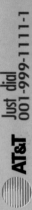

Immediately opposite Wat Phra Ram is a traditional wooden Thai house standing on stilts and with a roof of palm thatch. It was constructed in 1940 and is known as **Khum Khun Paen**.

Immediately to the south of Wat Phra Ram is the **CHAO SAM PHRAYA NATIONAL MUSEUM**, which was opened in 1961 and is housed in a handsome white building on the edge of a lake. It was constructed with money raised from the sale of votive tablets found in the ruins of Wat Ratchaburana, and it is therefore named after the supposed founder of that temple, Prince (Chao) Sam Phraya, later King Borommaratcha II. It contains a fine collection, consisting mainly of objects found in the ruins of Ayutthaya.

On the ground floor near the entrance is a colossal 14C bronze Buddha head 1.8m high from Wat Thammikarat in Ayutthaya. It is remarkable for the extremely fine treatment of the curls of the hair.

The chief glory of the museum is the **gold treasure** found in the crypt of Wat Ratchaburana in 1957 and treasures from other temples, including Wat Mahathat, Wat Phra Ram and Wat Chai Watthanaram. These treasures are exhibited in two rooms at either end of the upstairs gallery on the first floor. Most of the objects are thought to have belonged to the two elder brothers of Borommaratcha II, Prince Ai and Prince Yi (see Wat Ratchaburana above). Together they give a vivid idea of the splendours of religious and court life in Ayutthaya at the height of its wealth and power.

Among the most important of the objects are seven articles of royal regalia: the **Victory Sword**, which is 1.15m long and has a double-edged iron blade and an ornately decorated gold scabbard studded with precious stones, a miniature gold shoe, two fans, two fly-whisks and a parasol. There are **gold headdresses**, including a small crown encrusted with gems and an exquisite hairnet woven

The magnificent gold kneeling elephant in the Chao Sam Phraya National Museum, Ayutthaya

out of gold wire, neck and chest ornaments, many of them adorned with precious stones, pearls, beads and small bells, and armlets, bracelets, bangles and rings. There are round, oval and octagonal boxes for cosmetics, betel sets, water flasks and ceremonial vessels, one of the finest of which is in the form of a gourd decorated with *nāgas* and floral motifs and has a four-faced head of Brahma on the lid. There are numerous **gold and silver Buddha images**, some cut out of sheets of metal, and some beaten out in repoussé work on plaques. There are Buddhist and Hindu images, some in high relief and others free-standing. There is a variety of votive offerings, some in the form of miniature *chedi, prang, bodhi* trees and leaves, and others of animals and mythical creatures such as *garuḍas, haṁsas* and winged elephants. Of these the most magnificent is the figure of a **kneeling elephant** with a howdah on its back and holding a jewelled leaf in its trunk. There are several inscriptions, chiefly in Pali, written on gold and silver plates and on terracotta votive tablets; some of the latter are in Chinese. Finally, there are the **reliquaries and the relics** they contain. The most important of these is from Wat Mahathat. The relic, which is the size of one third of a grain of rice and is preserved in sandalwood oil, has been placed in a gold casket, which has then been encased in a series of seven miniature *chedi*, one on top of the other, made respectively of tin, silver, *nak* (a gold and copper alloy), ebony, rosewood, glass, and gold and precious stones.

Among the important Ayutthaya-period woodcarvings preserved in the museum are a notable tympanum from Wat Mae Nang Pleum showing Vishnu mounted on Garuda surrounded by *yakṣas*, a ship's figurehead in the form of a *garuḍa*, and several door panels. The museum also houses some human skele-tons, pieces of ceramics and other artefacts excavated from the Portuguese settlement in Ayutthaya, which was first established in 1518 and remained in existence until the Burmese invasion of 1767.

The road south from Wat Phra Ram continues past the National Museum to **Wat Borom Phuttharam**, which is situated between the road and Khlong Chakrai Noi. This temple, of which the walls are still largely intact, was founded by King Phra Phetratcha in 1683 and is chiefly notable for its magnificent doors deco-rated with mother-of-pearl inlay, which were commissioned by King Borommakot. Three pairs survived the sack of 1767 and are all now in Bangkok, one pair in Wat Phra Kaeo, another in Wat Benchamabophit, and a third, which was cut down to make a manuscript cupboard, in the National Museum in Bangkok. The temple is also known as Wat Krabueng Kluep ('Ceramic Monastery') on account of the yellow roof-tiles which once adorned the *ubosot*, the *wihan* and the *sala kan parian*.

Beyond the turning to Wat Ratchaburana and Wat Mahathat, T. U Thong continues west along the north side of the island to the point where the road to Wang Luang and Wat Phra Si Sanphet leads off to the left. Here on the right side of the road is a bridge over the Lop Buri River which leads to **Wat Na Phra Men**. The date of the foundation of Wat Na Phra Men is uncertain, but it was restored by King Borommakot and then again in the 19C. It is one of the few temples in Ayutthaya to have escaped destruction by the Burmese, and its *ubosot*, which was probably built in the reign of King Prasat Thong, may have provided a model both in form and decoration for *ubosot* of the Ratanakosin period. It is built on a north–south axis and stands on a stepped platform surrounded by a low wall. There are double *bai sema* at the cardinal and sub-cardinal points. The roof has three tiers and is covered with glazed tiles. The eaves of the roof are supported on the east and west sides by round columns with lotus capitals, and the walls beneath are pierced by narrow slits, which provide the only light and ventilation in the interior. At the north and south ends is a large window ornamented with gilt and coloured glass mosaic and covered by a porch with a carved pediment supported by columns with lotus capitals. On either side of the window is a smaller door under a similar porch, with gables added during the reign of Rama III. The sumptuously carved and gilded pediment over the south porch depicts Vishnu mounted on Garuda with a rather unusual figure of a *kāla* head and arms beneath.

The interior of the *ubosot*, which has recently been restored, is notable for its ceiling decorated with carved floral and lozenge motifs and supported by two rows of eight octagonal columns with lotus capitals. At the west end is a large Ayutthaya-period crowned and jewelled **Buddha image** of gilded bronze, which is believed to have been originally unadorned and later embellished by King Prasat Thong to make it the largest extant Buddha image of its kind in Thailand. The iconography of Buddha images crowned and in royal attire such as this is thought to be derived from Khmer models.

To the right of the *ubosot* is a small **wihan** built in 1838, which now houses an important Dvaravati limestone image of the Buddha seated on a throne in *pralambapādāsana*, with legs apart, hands on knees and feet placed on a lotus pedestal, that was discovered by King Mongkut and is known as Phra Kanthararat. It is believed to have been originally in Wat Na Phra Men in Nakhon Pathom and to have then been moved in the mid-16C to Wat Mahathat in Ayutthaya. This *wihan* also contains wall paintings depicting *jātaka* tales, of which only a few traces now remain.

T. U Thong continues west and crosses road 32 before reaching the Hua Laem food market and turning south along the Chao Phraya River. A road to the left leads to **Wat Lokaya Sutha**, of which little remains except for a ruined *prang*, a heavily restored reclining Buddha image 42m long in a *wihan* of which only the bases of 24 octagonal pillars have survived, the ruins of an *ubosot* with a porch at each end and two *chedi* that still retain some of their stucco decoration. A little way beyond Wat Lokaya Sutha are **Wang Lang** ('Palace Behind') and **Wat Suan Luang Sop Sawan**, of which all that remains is the elegant *chedi* of Queen Si Suryothai. Beyond this a road to the right leads over the Chao Phraya River to Wat Prachedaram.

On the south bank of the Pasak River near its confluence with the Chao Phraya and immediately opposite Wat Suwan Dararam in the village of Khlong Suan Plu is **Wat Phra Chao Phanan Choeng** ('Monastery of the Great Seated Buddha'), which was founded in 1344 before U Thong established his capital in Ayutthaya. This temple has a *wihan* of unusually tall and narrow proportions, built to accommodate the colossal **Buddha image** 19m high from which it takes its name, but which is popularly known as Luang Poh Toe and is greatly venerated, especially by the Chinese. Both *wihan* and Buddha image were restored in the reign of King Mongkut.

Further west along the south bank of the Chao Phraya River is **Wat**

Phutthaisawan, built in 1354 by U Thong on the site of the palace that he occupied before becoming king of Ayutthaya. This temple, which has recently been restored, contains two fine modern buildings near the landing stage—a *sala* and, behind it, the patriarch's house, which contains fragments of some 17C wall paintings. To the east of these buildings is an *ubosot* and a large Khmer-style *prang* on an exceptionally high base with an entrance porch on the east side. On either side is a *mondop* containing a seated Buddha image. The *prang* was restored in the reign of King Chulalongkorn and the two *mondop* more recently. The enclosure is surrounded by a gallery containing rows of seated Buddha images.

Wat Som is an early Ayutthaya temple located in the southwest corner of the island almost opposite Wat Phutthaisawan. It has a small Khmer-style prang and fine stucco decoration, which has recently been skilfully restored.

Further again to the west on the south bank of the Chao Phraya is the **Cathedral of St Joseph**, which was originally built by the leader of the French mission in Ayutthaya, Mgr de Bérythe of the Société des Missions Etrangères between 1685 and 1695 for the Catholic population of the city. It was heavily restored during the 19C and is now of little architectural interest.

Beyond St Joseph's Cathedral and the entrance to Khlong Khun Lakhon Chai the Chao Phraya bends round to the north. Just before Khlong Klaep on the west bank of the river and easily accessible both from the water and from the land is Wat Chai Watthanaram.

WAT CHAI WATTHANARAM is one of the grandest, and certainly the most extraordinary of all the surviving temples of Ayutthaya. It was founded c 1630 by the usurper King Prasat Thong, who is thought to have built it on the site of the palace where his mother, or perhaps his foster-mother (see Bang Pa-in above), lived before his accession to the throne, in memory of her and as a symbolic act to establish the legitimacy of his rule. It was sympathetically restored by the Fine Arts Department in the early 1990s.

Like most of Ayutthaya's temples, Wat Chai Watthanaram is built of stuccoed brick, though little of the original stucco now remains. Approaching from the river, the visitor first comes to the east side of the temple enclosure. This was originally surrounded by a high wall, of which only the base and two of the eight gateways—one on the west and one on the south side—still remain. Both gateways have triple-tiered roofs and are decorated with vertical ribs of stucco in imitation of tiles. At the northeast and southeast corners of the enclosing wall is a large **chedi**, bell-shaped but narrower and squarer than earlier Sri Lankan-style Ayutthaya *chedi*, and set on a high square base with two redentations at the corners and a staircase on the east side giving access to the circumambulatory path round the top. Between these two *chedi* a brick path leads to a platform 1.5m high, that was also once surrounded by a wall. On this stands a long, rectangular **ubosot**, of which only the base and traces of the porch that once ran round it remain. The *bai sema* have also disappeared, but their foundations have been rebuilt in brick and placed in the appropriate positions. At the west end of the *ubosot* are three stone seated Buddha images; of these the central and right hand images have no heads, while only the base remains of the image on the left. Some 13m beyond the *ubosot* is a **square gallery** c 55m in length. It is pierced by gateways on the east and west sides. A moulding runs along the base of the outer wall and in the upper part is a series of bays decorated with five vertical stepped mullions of stuccoed brick and divided by engaged pilasters. These stepped mullions are a characteristic feature of the architecture of the later Ayutthaya period and appear to be derived from the round balusters that often decorate the windows of Khmer temples.

At the cardinal and sub-cardinal points of the gallery are **eight conical towers** called **men**, each c 25.5m high. These appear to be unique to this temple and are thought to be copied from the so-called 'golden *meru*', the tall, multi-tiered wooden structures used as funeral pyres in royal cremations. These wooden towers, which in the 17C were often extremely elaborate and reached enormous heights of over 100m, are, as the name suggests, in turn representations of the cosmic mountain, Mount Meru. The *men* have a square plan with several redentations at the corners, which give them an octagonal profile, and consist of seven tiers of diminishing size surmounted by a finial in the form of a miniature *prang*. Of these finials only fragments remain.

It is possible to walk through each *men* round the gallery. Traces of the wooden beams that supported the gabled roofs attached to each of the four sides of the *men* can still be seen. On the outside wall of each *men* in the small chamber formed by the porch is a stucco relief panel illustrating a scene from the Life of the Buddha. All the reliefs are poorly preserved and some have disappeared altogether. One of the few in relatively good condition is on the north side of the northeast corner *men*. This shows the Buddha standing under a pavilion with a multi-tiered roof with rows of kneeling figures below him, which may be a depiction of the Buddha's visit either to the Tavatimsa Heaven, or more probably, to his former wife and son in their palace. There are two more or less identical crowned and jewelled Buddha images seated in *bhūmisparśa mudrā* on ornately decorated thrones in each of the corner *men* and one in each of the midpoint *men*, making a total of twelve. These images are almost 4m high and can only be seen from inside the *men*. The coffered wooden ceilings of the *men* have survived and appear to have been richly decorated with gilding, mother-of-pearl and glass inlay. Against each of the four outside walls of the gallery is a row of 26 identical stuccoed brick images of the Buddha seated in *bhūmisparśa mudrā*. All of them have lost their heads and many have been almost totally destroyed.

In the centre of the enclosure formed by the gallery is a square platform more than 1m high on which is a large **prang**, 35m high, and at each corner, forming a quincunx, four smaller *prang*, less than one-third of the height of the central *prang*. All five *prang* stand on a high square base with multiple redentations at the corners and decorated with mouldings. On each side of the four smaller *prang* is a shallow niche, which probably originally contained a standing Buddha image, surmounted by a double pediment. The central *prang* has a cella—which once contained a Buddha image—on the east side, and on the other three sides more deeply recessed niches for Buddha images with triple pediments. The cella and the niches are approached by a steep staircase. The sides of the central *prang* are decorated with antefixes and horseshoe-shaped ornaments. There are numerous holes in the stucco covering all five *prang* and these are thought to indicate that sheets of gold-plated tin were originally pinned to the surface.

To the north of Wat Chai Watthanaram and Khlong Klaep on the west bank of the Chao Phraya are several more temples of only minor interest. These include **Wat Ratcha Phili**, which is largely modern, **Wat Kasatra Thirat**, which has an ornately decorated Ayutthaya-style *ubosot* and two *wihan*, and the partly ruined **Wat Thammaram**, which has a tall and imposing *chedi*, but no other buildings of importance.

Beyond Wat Thammaram is the confluence of the Chao Phraya, which here turns to the northwest, and the Lop Buri River. Here there are more temples on the river bank and inland, as well as many charming individual wooden houses. The most beautiful of the temples on this stretch of the river is **Wat Sala Pun** ('Monastery of the Stucco Pavilion'), which has a small Khmer-style *prang* of stuccoed brick on an octagonal base and an exceptionally elegant *ubosot* dating from the Ayutthaya period and beautifully restored in the 19C, with elaborately carved roofs and porches at front and back supported by octagonal pillars. Inside are some attractive wall paintings showing marked Western influence and dating from the reign of King Chulalongkorn. Beyond Wat Sala Pun is the important temple of **Wat Choeng Tha**, which is opposite the mouth of Khlong Tao near the bridge that carries road 309 from Ang Thong into the city. The fine *prang* of this temple, which dates from the mid-17C or earlier, still retains much of its stucco decoration and has niches on the north, east and west sides. The niche on the north contains a 2m high image of a walking Buddha in red sandstone, and those on the east and west contain stucco images of the Buddha in *abhaya mudrā*. All three images are badly damaged. Inside the *ubosot*, which is now roofless, is a brick image of the Buddha in *bhūmisparśa mudrā*, 1.4m high and covered in gold leaf and black lacquer. The *sala kan parian*, which was built in the reign of King Mongkut, has a roof covered with ceramic tiles and carved wooden gables that were brought here from Wat Phra Si Sanphet and date from the reign of King Borommakot. The door panels are painted with figures of *dvārapālas* holding spears. Inside the *sala* are two Ratanakosin-period *sangket* of carved wood decorated with gilding and glass mosaic. On the interior walls are paintings of the life of the Buddha, and the ceiling is painted red and gold.

In addition to the Chao Sam Phraya National Museum, Ayutthaya has two other museums of note. The **Chantharakasem Palace Museum** (open Wed–Sun, 08.00–12.00 and 13.00–16.00) is housed in a building on T. U Thong in the northeast corner of the island a short way to the east of the Pom Mahachai fort. It was constructed by King Mongkut on the site of the original Wang Na (Palace of the Front), which was first built by King Naresuan when he was heir to the throne and became the residence of all subsequent heirs to the throne until it was destroyed by the Burmese in 1767. The palace enclosure is surrounded by a crenellated wall. The museum's collection is housed in the Chaturamuk Pavilion, a wooden building on a stone platform to the left of the entrace of the enclosure and in the Piman Rataya Hall, another building facing the entrance. It consists of a miscellany of objects, none of outstanding importance, including some of the regalia of King Mongkut, numerous Sukhothai- and Ayutthaya-period Buddha images in stone and bronze, and some ceramics. At the western end of the enclosure is the Pisai Sayalak Tower, a four-storey building in European style which was used by King Mongkut as an observatory.

The **Ayutthaya Historical Study Centre** (open Mon–Fri, 09.30–15.30, Sat and Sun 09.30–16.30) is housed in two well-appointed modern buildings in T. Rojana near the Chao Sam Phraya National Museum, on a site that was formerly part of the Japanese settlement in Ayutthaya. It was established following an agreement between the Thai and Japanese governements signed in September 1987 and was opened by Princess Sirindhom on 22 August 1990. It contains on the first floor of the main building a fascinating display of models based on early foreign accounts and maps of the city of Ayutthaya and of individual monuments such as Wat Mahathat and Wat Chai Watthanaram as they were in the 17C, models of junks and other craft, including a French three-masted galleon, and examples of some of the many products that were exchanged at Ayutthaya, ranging from coral and camphor to sealing wax and edible bird's nests. There are also numerous video presentations and models portraying scenes of village life, festivals and ceremonies in the Ayutthaya period, supported by explanatory texts and sound commentaries, a display of traditional utensils and implements and a reconstruction of a complete traditional Thai house on stilts.

Road 32 leads out of Ayutthaya towards Ang Thong. After 2km turn left at a crossroads to reach **Phu Khao Thong** ('Golden Mount'), an enormous *chedi* with multiple redentations built by the Burmese after the capture of Ayutthaya by King Bayinnaung in 1569 next to an older temple, founded by King Ramesuan in 1387, of which only a few scattered ruins remain. It was renovated and enlarged by King Borommakot in 1744. More recently, it has been rather clumsily restored and painted white, but it is still impressive.

The turning to the right at the crossroads leads after 3km to the *Phaniat* or **Elephant Kraal** which was first built in the reign of King Yot Fa, but has been restored several times since. It consists of a rectangular sunken enclosure into which the elephants were driven one at a time down channels constructed from large wooden stakes. After selection, the elephants were put in a pen also composed of wooden stakes in the middle of the enclosure. This is the last such kraal still in existence in Thailand. One of the last great elephant round-ups to be held here was that arranged in 1890 for the Tsarevitch, later Tsar Nicholas II, then on a state visit to Siam.

On the north bank of the Lop Buri River, almost opposite Pom Mahachai is **Wat Mae Nang Pleum**, which is one of the earliest temples in Ayutthaya and may even predate the foundation of the city. In 1767 the invading Burmese armies set up their camp here, and traces of their fortifications can be seen near the *ubosot*. The square base of the *chedi* is surrounded by lions similar to those at Wat Thammikarat. The *sala kan parian* formerly contained wall paintings illustrating the Life of the Buddha, painted by Kru Kae during the King Mongkut's reign, but these have unfortunately been recently painted over and obliterated.

Many trips by boat can be made from Ayutthaya. One of the most interesting of these is north up the Pasak River about 18km to Nakhon Luang, where can be seen the ruins of several temples of the Ayutthaya period, including **Prasat Nakhon Luang**, built by King Prasat Thong in 1631 in imitation of the great Cambodian temple of Angkor Wat to commemorate the Thai conquest of Angkor 200 years before in 1431.

THE CENTRAL PLAIN

14 · Ayutthaya to Ang Thong and Sing Buri

Road 309, 74km. To Ang Thong 32km; Ang Thong to Sing Buri 42km.

Take road 309 north from Ayutthaya through flat and fertile country towards Ang Thong, and after c 15km turn left on to a road signed to **Wat Tha Sutthawat** (1500m). The modern *ubosot* of this *wat* has exceptionally fine murals on its interior walls, and magnificent lacquered, gilded window shutters. This is a rarity in Thailand: a newly built monastic building which shows the very best of contemporary Thai craftsmanship.

4km further north, but on the right bank of the Chao Phraya, is the important monastery of **Wat Pa Mok** (Wat Phra Phuttha Saiyat Pa Mok), which is reached by small ferry boat from the enclosure of **Wat Phinit Thammasan** on the left side of road 309. (An alternative, if this ferry is not running, is to take the larger public ferry c 650m further north, which crosses to the centre of Pa Mok on the west bank.)

Within the enclosure of Wat Pa Mok is a large *sala* with a triple-tiered roof and a gable decorated with coloured glass mosaic, a *wihan* containing traces of painting on the walls and another *wihan* approached by a pillared arcade and containing a colossal reclining Buddha image (Phra Phuttha Saiyat) dating from the 15C. Local tradition has it that this statue was transported in 1726 from a riverside chapel that had been destroyed by flooding. A boat race festival is held each year to commemorate this event. In front of the *wihan* is a *mondop* containing a Footprint of the Buddha.

13km north of Wat Pa Mok on road 309 is the small provincial capital of **Ang Thong** (pop. 12,000). The town, which lies in the centre of a rich rice-producing area on the Chao Phraya River, is modern and of no particular interest, but there are several important monasteries in the vicinity.

At **Wat Khian**, c 9km west of Ang Thong, the *ubosot* contains rather damaged murals depicting scenes of late 18C battles against the Burmese. In an attempt to protect the murals, new walls have been built round the outside of the old walls. To reach this *wat*, take road 3064 from Ang Thong towards Pho Thong and then turn off west along road 3195 towards Suphan Buri. Soon after passing the 26km stone, turn north on to road 3454 and continue 700m to the *wat*.

Return eastward to the junction with road 3064 and turn north towards Pho Thong once more. After c 5km, turn right and continue 2km to **Wat Khun In Pramun**. Here, in the open air, there is an enormous Ayutthaya-period reclining Buddha, 50m in length, which has been rather carelessly restored. In front is a statue of Khun In Pramun, a revenue official who is said to have pilfered government taxes in order to pay for the extension of the original 40m image by a further 10m. When the king of Ayutthaya heard this, the official was executed, but nevertheless the *wat* was named after him.

Leave Ang Thong on road 309, and head north along the west bank of the Chao Phraya River. Near the 72km stone is **Wat Chaiyo Wora Wihan**. The *wihan* of this 19C *wat* contains a colossal seated image of the Buddha in *dhyāna mudrā*, known as Phra Maha Phuttha Phim, dating from the reign of King Mongkut. Unusually, the *ubosot* is connected to the *wihan* by a transverse room, the two thus forming a single building with a series of triple-tiered roofs, their gables adorned with carved wooden scrolls. The interior walls of the *ubosot* are decorated with wall paintings by a local artist.

2km before Sing Buri, turn left on to road 3032 and go 3km to reach **Wat Phra Non Chak Si**, on the left of the road. Here there is yet another enormous reclining Buddha image, 46m in length. Immediately to the west of the *wat* is a lane which leads through a small hamlet to the ruins of **Wat Na Phra That** 400m away. This has a restored brick central *prang*, in the Ayutthaya style, which has retained much of its original stucco decoration. It is surrounded by several ruined brick buildings, partially overgrown by vegetation.

Almost 8km further west, on the left side of road 3032 are replicas of the wooden ramparts of **Bang Rachan**, a fortified town where for five months in 1765 the Thais successfully resisted the invading Burmese armies led by Thihapatei.

Sing Buri (pop. 21,500) has little of interest for the visitor except **Wat Sawang Arom**, which has one of Thailand's largest collections of **nang yai puppets**. This *wat* is on the east side of road 309, on the bank of the Chao Phraya River, just south of the junction with road 3032. Performances are only given very rarely, but the monks are usually willing to show the puppets to visitors.

■ **Hotels and services**. Of Sing Buri's few hotels, the *Sing Buri Hotel* on T. Khun San and the *City Hotel* at the north end of the town offer adequate, cheap rooms. All the main banks have branches in the town centre, and the **post** and **telecoms office** is near the City Hotel.

■ **Transport**. There are regular **buses** north to In Buri, Chai Nat and beyond, southwest to Lop Buri and south to Ayutthaya and Bangkok. The nearest **railway station** is at Lop Buri.

▶ A short excursion can be made from Sing Buri to **Wat Lai**, c 15km east of Sing Buri along road 311. To reach the *wat*, turn north just east of the 178km stone on to road 3028 and continue c 5km. Shortly before reaching Ban Tha Khlong, take a left fork; the *wat* lies 400m further, on the left. This Ayutthaya-period monastery has exceptionally fine stucco reliefs dating from the reign of King Borommakot on the end walls of the unusual, double *ubosot*. Although they have been severely damaged and crudely restored in places, these reliefs remain among the finest surviving examples of stucco decoration of the Ayutthaya period. There is more stucco carving on the wall separating the two parts of the double *ubosot* which contains a seated Buddha image of the Ayutthaya period. Behind it is a *wihan* with an ornately decorated façade, where another highly venerated Buddha image known as Phra Si-an was formerly enshrined. This image is now housed near the gateway of the temple enclosure in a *mondop* with four richly carved doors. ◀

15 · Sing Buri to Chai Nat and Uthai Thani

Roads *311 and 3183, 95km. To Chai Nat 53km; Chai Nat to Uthai Thani 42km.*

From Sing Buri, road 311 runs north beside an irrigation channel to **In Buri** (15km), a small market town spread along both banks of the Chao Phraya River. The two banks are joined by a bridge.

On the west bank, to the south of the town centre, is the **In Buri National Museum** in the grounds of Wat Bot. The museum houses a small collection of religious images and local archaeological finds. The first room upstairs beyond the ticket desk contains some 7C–8C Mon heads of Buddha images and other artefacts, many of them from Muang Ku Muang and Huai Chan, two Mon Dvaravati sites in the vicinity. Among the more notable of these are an 8C–9C Mon Dvaravati stone image of the standing Buddha with characteristic frontality and elongated arms; a gaunt 19C image of a *bodhisattva* surrounded by five disciples; and some fine 15C and 16C Ayutthaya-style standing Buddha images in *abhaya mudrā*.

The second room upstairs contains a large collection of monks' fans and more images, including a notable small 17C–18C Ayutthaya Buddha image seated in *pralambapādāsana*.

On the ground floor there is some pottery from the 16C River Noi kilns at Chonnasut, excavated by the Fine Arts Department in 1988.

From In Buri, road 311 continues north towards Chai Nat. After 18km, road 3010 turns off left to **Sankhaburi** (Sanburi), which was known as Muang Phraek in the Sukhothai period and became capital of one of the most important provinces of the early Ayutthaya kingdom. Today it is a small market town with some minor 14C–16C ruins.

To reach the town and ruins, turn left off road 3010 after 12km, just beyond the bridge over the River Noi. After 800m, T. Na Phra Lan, Soi 7 turns off right to the ruins of **Wat Song Phi Nong**. An U Thong-style brick *prang*, built without mortar, and a smaller *chedi* are all that remain of this 14C temple. A niche on the west side of the 12m *prang* holds a stucco U Thong-style standing image of the Buddha, the head of which was stolen c 1980. The adjacent *chedi* was completely rebuilt by the Fine Arts Department in 1992-93, thereby losing much of its charm.

400m further along the road towards the town centre on the left side is **Wat Mahathat**. The large *chedi* of this *wat* (**Phra Boromathat Chedi**), which appears from the form of its base to belong to the Ayutthaya period, has been almost completely destroyed. Beside the adjacent *ubosot* are the stuccoed brick columns of a ruined *wihan*, enclosing a large seated U Thong Buddha image. On the north side of the *wihan* is a restored *prang* with niches containing four stucco Buddha images, all partially damaged. Wat Mahathat formerly overlooked the San River to the east, but is now separated from it by a road and a row of pleasant wooden houses.

The road leading off to the right from the small roundabout with the clock in the town centre leads after 350m to a crossroads beside an irrigation canal. Turn left here and go 2km to reach **Wat Phra Kaeo**, which has a tall, brick, U Thong-style *chedi*, visible across the irrigation channel. This *chedi*, which is in a style reminiscent of the *stūpas* of the Pala period in northeast India, once held a stucco image on each of its four sides, but of these two are now missing and the others are damaged. Much of the original architectural detail was lost in the course of a rather careless renovation by the Fine Arts Department in 1983.

Return to the crossroads beside the irrigation canal and turn left over the canal to reach road 340. From here **Chai Nat** is 17km to the right, on the far bank of the Chao Phraya River. Just before the bridge over the Chao Phraya, a right turn along road 3183 leads after 600m to the **Chainatmuni National Museum**, visible to the left of the road. This museum contains a notable collection of Buddha images in various styles found in the area, including an important seated Buddha image in the U Thong style.

Chai Nat (pop. 28,000) has little of interest for visitors, although the *Nam Chai Hotel* offers clean and comfortable accommodation, and the usual bank and postal services are available. To the south of the town is a dam across the Chao Phraya, which provides irrigation for a large part of the rice-growing area of the central plain.

3km southeast of Chai Nat along road 1 is **Chai Nat Bird Park**, a popular recreation park with aviaries and a swimming pool. Each February, the bird park is the focus for a Straw Bird Fair, when enormous straw birds are constructed out of stubble left over from the rice harvest.

Uthai Thani

Road 3183 continues north for 36km to **Uthai Thani**, a bustling, pleasant market town on the west bank of the Sakae Krang River, a tributary of the Chao Phraya.

- **Hotels and services**. The *Phibunsuk Hotel* on T. Si Uthai offers clean, comfortable accommodation and secure parking. **Banks** are located in the streets near the municipal market, and the **post office** is on T. Si Uthai, south of the Phibunsuk Hotel.

- **Transport**. Regular **bus** services run to Chai Nat, Nakhon Sawan, Bangkok and elsewhere. **Samlo** operate in the town and can always be found near the market.

The present town of Uthai Thani only dates from the mid-19C. It is situated c 30km east of an earlier settlement on the site of the village of Ban Uthai Kao, which was a moderately important centre of trade and communications during the Ayutthaya period.

Uthai Thani is flanked to the west by the long narrow hill of Sakae Krang. At the south end of the hill is **Wat Sangkat Ratanakhiri**, from where a long flight of steps leads to the summit. In a shrine opposite the foot of the steps is the greatly revered **Phra Mongkhon Saksit**, a bronze Buddha image seated in *bhūmisparśa mudrā*, dating from the Sukhothai period.

On the hilltop, which those disinclined to climb the steps can reach from the northern end by road, are several monastic buildings and a *mondop* sheltering a Footprint of the Buddha. The summit, from which there are fine views over the town, is a popular leisure spot for the local inhabitants; food is available from vendors in the car park at the north end.

On T. Si Uthai, just north of the post office, is **Wat Phichai Puranaram**, probably the oldest surviving *wat* in the province. Its well-preserved 13C *wihan* faces the river in accordance with the requirements of Buddhist cosmology and has an unusual short extension at the back built to house the principal image. The low-sweeping roof, supported by squat columns on each side, is characteristic of the Sukhothai and U Thong periods.

To reach **Wat Ubosatharam** head back towards the town centre and turn right towards the river at a small roundabout decorated with imitation elephant tusks. A busy **food market** is held here in the early morning. A footbridge across the Sakae Krang River leads to Wat Ubosatharam, which has some fine but badly damaged murals of the Ratanakosin period.

The banks of the river here are lined with dozens of houseboats, and the river is a scene of continual activity. The esplanade between the market and the river is filled with food hawkers from late afternoon till after dark.

▶Excursion to Plara Hill

An interesting but arduous excursion, necessitating a tough climb of up to two hours with a guide, can be made from Uthai Thani to **PLARA HILL** (Khao Plara, c 50km) where, in a rock shelter near the summit, some of Thailand's most important **prehistoric rock paintings** can be seen. It is advisable to take refreshments—especially plenty of water—and to start early so as to avoid the hottest hours of the day.

Leave Uthai Thani on road 333 towards Nong Chang (21km) and turn left at the junction beyond the 23km stone, just before Nong Chang itself. After 2km, turn right on to road 3438 towards Lansak and continue for 21km to a point just beyond the 21km stone, where there is a turning to the left on to a dirt road. Follow the track south along the eastern side of the 8km-long limestone massif. The paintings are on the southwest side, at a height of 480m, but the best path starts from the east side and climbs steeply over the top to the site.

The paintings, which were discovered in the 1970s by a local hunter seeking shelter from the rain under the rock overhang, consist of about 30 human and animal figures in four groups. Some are only outline drawings, others are coloured black, red or ochre. There are fine views

Examples of the prehistoric rock paintings at Plara Hill, near Uthai Thani

from the hill, and the area is rich in bird life. There are also numerous other caves in the area, some of them containing stalactites and stalagmites.◄

Further west is **Huai Kha Khaeng Wildlife Sanctuary**, accessible from Ban Rai or Lan Sang districts. This magnificent reserve, covering 2574 sq km, is one of Thailand's most important sanctuaries and has for many years been at the forefront of the Royal Forestry Department's struggle against poaching and deforestation. Four park rangers who have died attempting to defend Thailand's flora and fauna are commemorated by memorial stones in the sanctuary. It remains one of the country's prime areas for birds, especially lowland deciduous forest species, and for many rare carnivores, including Malayan sun bears, tigers, leopards, and clouded leopards. Huai Kha Khaeng, together with the adjacent Thung Yai Naresuan Wildlife Sanctuary, is a UNESCO World Heritage Site. Permission to visit the sanctuary may be obtained from the Royal Forestry Department offices on T. Phahon Yothin in Bangkok. Food and simple accommodation are available, and there is a nature trail.

16 · Uthai Thani to Nakhon Sawan and Kamphaeng Phet

Roads *333 and 1, c 200km. To Nakhon Sawan, 40km; a choice of routes from Nakhon Sawan to Kamphaeng Phet: (a) direct route on road 1, c 117km; (b) extended route via Khlong Lan, c 160km.*

From Uthai Thani, road 333 runs northeast to join road 1 on the east side of the Chao Phraya River. From here **Nakhon Sawan** is c 28km. For travellers with their own transport who would prefer not to drive on one of Thailand's busiest highways, there is a less hectic and slower route through rice fields via Krok Phra along road 3220 on the west side of the river.

Nakhon Sawan
Nakhon Sawan (pop. 107,000) is a large, modern and singularly charmless town, capital of a province which produces more rice and freshwater fish than any other in the country. Maize, jute and peanuts are also grown in the area. Situated at the junction of northern Thailand's two major river systems, the Ping and the Nan, which converge here to form the Chao Phraya, the town has been an important entrepôt since the 11C, and today has become one of the world's busiest rice-trading centres as well as an important centre for the timber trade. Barges carrying hundreds of tonnes of rice depart daily for Bangkok's Khlong Toey port. This trade has led many Chinese to settle in Nakhon Sawan, which is thought now to have the largest Chinese community in Thailand outside Bangkok.

■ **Hotels and restaurants**. There are several clean and comfortable hotels in the city, although many appear to be permanently fully booked, chiefly by commercial travellers, and it is advisable to make advance reservations if possible. There are also some excellent Chinese and Thai restaurants. Nakhon Sawan is at its most festive during Chinese New Year in late January or early February, when Chinese arrive from all over Thailand to visit their families, and hotel rooms become even scarcer.

■ **Transport**. Nakhon Sawan lies beside the main highway linking Bangkok to the north, and is therefore well served by **buses** departing each day in both directions. Less frequent services operate along the scenic road 225 to Chaiyaphum and the northeast (Isan). The **railway station** is rather inconveniently located c 6km southeast of the town in Ban Nong Pling, but a regular bus service operates to and from the centre. Within the town, **songthaeo** and **samlo** can be hired.

■ **Festival**. The 10-day Chinese New Year festival in late January or early February is the most important event of the year for the large Chinese community of Nakhon Sawan. Offerings are made to the goddess of prosperity (Chao Mae Thap Thim), the god of safety (Chao Pho Theparak) and the goddess of mercy (Chao Mae Kuan Im), and the festival celebrations include a spectacular dragon dance.

On **Chom Khiri Hill**, 600m south of Dechatiwong Bridge over the Chao Phraya River, is **Wat Chom Khiri Nak Phrot**, from where there is a good view of Nakhon Sawan. At the north end of the summit, reached either by road or by a long staircase, is a Sukhothai-period (late 13C) *ubosot*, surrounded by a double row of *bai sema* and housing a large seated image of the Buddha in *bhūmisparśa mudrā*. On the reverse side of this image is a bas-relief carving of a walking Buddha, probably dating from the mid-13C. Behind and to the left of the *ubosot* is a huge and magnificent bronze bell cast c 1870. In the *wihan* at the south end is a large collection of Ayutthaya-style images.

In the northeastern corner of the town, on Kop hill (Khao Kop), is **Wat Woranat Banphot** or **Wat Khao Kop**, where a stone Sukhothai-period Footprint of the Buddha, thought to date from the reign of King Mahathammaratcha I (Luthai), is housed in a cruciform *mondop*. A lane climbs past the TV5 relay station to the summit, from where the vast Boraphet swamp can be seen to the east of the town.

Near the foot of the hill is a large Sukhothai-period brick **chedi**; Sukhothai Inscription 11, which recounts part of the history of Sukhothai, was found nearby. A Buddha image with both hands raised in *abhaya mudrā*, in a manner characteristic of Mon Dvaravati images, stands on the south side of the *chedi*.

To the east of the town is the immense marsh of **Bung Boraphet**, which is of interest to naturalists as the only known habitat of the endemic and extremely rare **white-eyed river martin**, discovered only in 1968. Freshwater crocodiles, found here until the mid-1970s, have been exterminated by hunting and the diversion of water for irrigation purposes. Bung Boraphet is best visited between October and February, when the rains have replenished the lake's water and when bird activity and plant life are at their most abundant; visitors in May or June will be disappointed. Simple chalet accommodation is available, and boats may be rented for excursions into the swamp from a designated waterfowl park on the lake's southern shore.

To reach the waterfowl park, head south from Nakhon Sawan for 3km over Dechatiwong Bridge. Turn left on to road 3001 towards the railway station and continue past the station for 9km. The park is signed to the left shortly after the 9km stone on road 3004.

Mae Wong and Khlong Lan National Parks

From Nakhon Sawan, road 1 heads northwest to **Kamphaeng Phet**. Travellers with their own transport can make an interesting detour to the two national parks of Mae Wong and Khlong Lan, both of which are in the hills c 50km west of road 1.

The 900 sq km **Mae Wong National Park** has some spectacular mountain scenery and waterfalls, and a fine trail into its still densely forested heart. There is rudimentary bungalow accommodation, and the park rangers will act as guides. There are thought to be still c 100 tigers in the park, which borders the huge Huai Kha Khaeng Wildlife Sanctuary, but hunting by the local Hmong people has taken its toll of these and of most of the other large mammals.

The nearby **Khlong Lan National Park** has a number of impressive waterfalls, two of which, Nam Tok Khlong Lan and Nam Tok Khlong Nam Lai, can be easily reached by road.

To reach the parks, turn left on to road 1242, 73km north of Nakhon Sawan. This road passes through delightful scenery and villages. After 36km, turn right at a T-junction on to road 1072, which after 12km reaches a crossroads in the centre of the village of Ban Khlong Lan. The road to the left leads to Mae Wong National Park; the road straight ahead climbs up to the lovely 90m-high **Khlong Lan Waterfall**, a very pleasant picnic spot, where drinks, snacks and delicious *kai yang* are available. Visitors can stay overnight near the falls in simple bungalows. As with waterfalls everywhere in Thailand, it is better to come after the rains for the best display, and to avoid the crowds at weekends and holidays.

Until these areas were declared national parks in the 1980s, both were inhabited by Hmong and other minority peoples. Since then, these people have been resettled outside the park boundaries and have been aided and encouraged by the Interior Ministry's public welfare department to sell their handicrafts from shops on the road to Khlong Lan Waterfall.

Khlong Nam Lai Waterfall can be found by taking road 1117 towards Kamphaeng Phet from the crossroads and then turning left in Khlong Lan district centre.

Wat Wang Phra That and Wat Chet Yot

Continue north along road 1117 for 36km to rejoin road 1, from where Kamphaeng Phet is 12km to the north. However, a short detour to the south along road 1 passes a popular **roadside market**, where fruit and other produce are on sale. An earth road to the left, just south of the 339km stone, leads to **Wat Wang Phra That**, a very large Sukhothai-period stuccoed brick *chedi* visible from the main road. This *chedi*, which has been clumsily restored, and its associated *wihan*, of which only the terrace and the bases of the columns remain, were evidently part of the old settlement of **Muang Trai Trung**, one of the earliest cities of the Sukhothai kingdom, on the west bank of the Ping River. The *wihan* once housed an enormous Buddha image, of which only the head remains, cemented to the ground beside the *chedi*.

Muang Trai Trung was rectangular in shape with rounded corners, measuring 480 x 730m and surrounded by a rampart and a moat. An excavation by the Fine Arts Department has produced evidence of settlements dating from the Dvaravati, Sukhothai and Ayutthaya periods.

A track north along the river bank from Wat Wang Phra That leads after a short distance to some other ruins. The *chedi* of **Wat Chet Yot** has been renovated, but the niche on its eastern side, which once held a Buddha image, is now empty. To the west is another ruined *chedi* surrounded by dense vegetation. From Wat Chet Yot, a track runs west back to road 1, passing through the ramparts and moat of the old settlement, which are here clearly discernible.

Kamphaeng Phet lies to the north, back along road 1. Turn off right to the town centre on road 101, which passes through the site of another ancient Thai city, **Nakhon Chum**, of which little remains except the ruins of one of the forts of the city, **Pom Thung Setthi**, and beyond this on the same side of the road are six *chedi* dating from the early Ayutthaya period. Road 101 then crosses the Ping River into the town centre.

17 · Kamphaeng Phet

Kamphaeng Phet ('Diamond Ramparts') (pop: 32,000) is situated on the Ping River, on the edge of one of the great teak forests that formerly covered wide areas of central and northern Thailand, and until 1988, when in a belated attempt to preserve what is left of Thailand's forests the government instituted severe restrictions on the felling and sale of timber, was one of the principal points from which teak was floated down the Ping River to Bangkok.

History
According to one of the chronicles, in 1017 a Mon invasion of the area round Chiang Saen compelled the Thais of a principality named Wiang Chai Prakan to emigrate south and found a new city, which they called Muang Chakang Rao, on the left bank of the Ping River in the vicinity of modern Kamphaeng Phet. In the 13C the king of Sukhothai founded Kamphaeng Phet on the site of Muang Chakang Rao, and this city became, with Si Satchanalai and Sukhothai itself, one of the three capitals of the Sukhothai kingdom. By 1378, however, King Borommaratcha I of Ayutthaya had captured Kamphaeng Phet, Nakhon Sawan and Phitsanulok and annexed them to his kingdom.

■ **Hotels and services**. The best hotels in the town are the *Chakrangrao Hotel* at 123/1 T. Thesa, the *Nawarat* at 2 Soi Prapan, T. Thesa and the *Phet Hotel* at 99 T. Wichit. A cheaper but still acceptable hotel is the *Ratchadamnoen* at 114 T. Ratchadamnoen The **post office** is on T. Thesa and there are banks on T. Ratchadamnoen and T. Charoensuk.

■ **Transport**. The **bus station** is on the west side of the Ping River. There are several services daily south to Bangkok, north to Sukhothai, Tak and beyond, and east to Phichit and Phitsanulok. The nearest **railway station** is at Phitsanulok.

According to the inscriptions, the laterite walls of Kamphaeng Phet date from 1403, but the forts outside the gate were probably not built until the 16C. A good point from which to begin a tour of the **old city** is at the old fort called **Pom Chao Chan**, just outside the gate known as **Pratu Dun**. A modern road now runs through the ramparts to the two principal monasteries of the Sukhothai city of Kamphaeng Phet: on the right, Wat Phra That and on the left, Wat Phra Kaeo. Both are entered from the east end of Wat Phra That.

Wat Phra That consists only of the foundations of a laterite *wihan* flanked by two small *chedi* and a third, much larger *chedi* of brick with an octagonal base standing on a laterite platform. On the ringed spire of this *chedi* are traces of the original stucco.

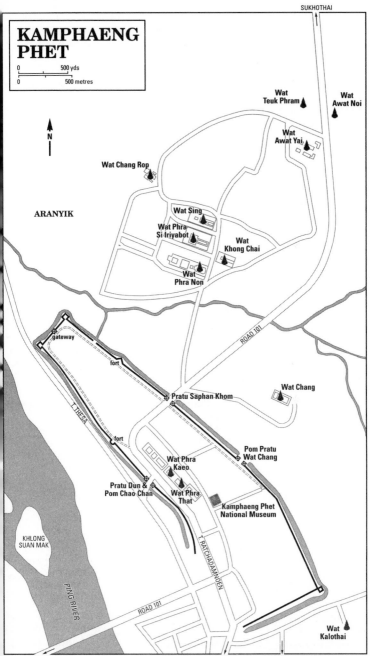

KAMPHAENG PHET

0   500 yds
0   500 metres

N

ARANYIK

SUKHOTHAI

Wat Teuk Phram

Wat Awat Noi

Wat Awat Yai

Wat Chang Rop

Wat Sing

Wat Phra Si Iriyabot

Wat Khong Chai

Wat Phra Non

ROAD 101

gateway

fort

T. THESA

fort

Pratu Saphan Khom

Wat Chang

Pom Pratu Wat Chang

Wat Phra Kaeo

Pratu Dun & Pom Chao Chan

Wat Phra That

Kamphaeng Phet National Museum

KHLONG SUAN MAK

PING RIVER

T. RATCHADAMNOEN

ROAD 101

Wat Kalothai

ROAD 1, TAK, NAKHON SAWAN, BUS STATION

MODERN TOWN, NAWARAT HOTEL   CHAKRUNGRAO HOTEL

Immediately beyond Wat Phra That is **Wat Phra Kaeo**. This consists of an *ubosot* in which the laterite core of a seated Buddha image and some columns can still be seen. Beyond this is a laterite *mondop*, which has been restored, a *wihan* and beyond this again the central *chedi* of the temple complex, which is also built of laterite and still has traces of its original stucco decoration. Round the octagonal base of the *chedi* are 16 niches, which formerly contained Buddha images. The high square platform on which the *chedi* stands was flanked by stuccoed figures of lions, of which fragments are still visible. Behind the *chedi* are two seated Buddha images of laterite and another *wihan* with square columns, which contains a reclining Buddha and two more seated Buddha images. Many of the images have been much weathered and eroded, some so much so that they have been reduced to vestigial forms. They are thought to date from the late Sukhothai or early Ayutthaya period.

A little way to the west beyond Wat Phra Kaeo are some more ruined *chedi* and the *lak muang* of the city.

The **Kamphaeng Phet National Museum** (open Wed–Sun 09.00–16.00) is situated within the ramparts of the old city near the **San Phra Isuan**. It houses a small but interesting collection of objects, most of them found in the vicinity of Kamphaeng Phet. In the entrance is a fine bronze statue of Shiva 2.1m high, which, according to the inscription on its base, was cast in 1510 by a sculptor of the Sukhothai school on the orders of the governor of the city and dedicated to King Ramathibodi II of Ayutthaya. The image was found in the San Phra Isuan, where a replica now stands, and suffered various vicissitudes before being placed in this museum, including the theft of its head and hands by a German visitor in 1886. The hieratic posture and the treatment of the elaborately decorated short garment with its frontal flap at the waist, the pendants on the belt, the diadem and the Brahmanic thread tied into a *nāga* head over the left shoulder suggest that it is the work of a sculptor of the later Sukhothai school inspired by a Khmer model of the 13C Bayon style. Also on the ground floor are some important bronze and stone Buddha images, including an exceptionally fine bronze seated Buddha of the U Thong period.

On the **first floor** are other important sculptures, including a colossal stuccoed head of the Buddha from Wat Chang, and two 15C–16C bronze torsos, one of Vishnu and one of a female deity, perhaps Lakshmi, that are no less remarkable than the Shiva figure of about the same period on the ground floor, though of less obviously Khmer inspiration. Also on this floor are some Sawankhalok ceramics, votive tablets and stucco and terracotta pieces, and some 15C and 16C bronze cannon.

Some of the most beautiful *wat* in the vicinity of Kamphaeng Phet are in **Aranyik**, a densely wooded area to the northwest of the old city. Most of them were built in the Sukhothai period or later by communities of devout Buddhist monks anxious to pursue their religious vocation in tranquil surroundings away from the city. A major programme of restoration of the Aranyik temples has been undertaken in recent years, which has made them more accessible, but at the same time has somewhat lessened the romantic charm of the ruins and of their surroundings.

Access to Aranyik is best gained by taking road 101 to the northeast through one of the gates in the north wall of the ramparts, **Pratu Saphan Khom**. A

Jewelled elephants surrounding Wat Chang Rop, Aranyik, Kamphaeng Phet

short way beyond this, a lane forks left to the Aranyik area.

On the left just before the ticket office is **Wat Pa Mut Nok**, of which only the base of the *wihan* and some laterite columns still remain. **Wat Phra Non** ('Monastery of the Reclining Buddha'), a few metres further on, has a large *ubosot* with fine laterite columns. Behind this is the *wihan* of the reclining Buddha, which is divided into two rooms, both with massive square laterite columns. The image of the Buddha is no longer recognisable. Beyond the *wihan* is a *chedi* in Sri Lankan style on an octagonal base and the ruins of a *mondop* and another small *wihan* containing the remnants of a laterite brick seated Buddha image.

Across the road is **Wat Khong Chai**, where there is an octagonal *chedi* on a square base, the base of a *wihan*, and several other minor structures, including a well.

A few metres further, to the left, is **Wat Phra Si Iriyabot**, which contains images of the Buddha in all four of the postures—sitting, standing, walking and reclining. The remains of the columns of the *wihan* of this *wat* and the base on which the principal Buddha image was once placed stand on a large, high laterite platform surrounded by a balustrade and approached by a staircase. In front stood four stuccoed figures of lions, of which only the pedestals and a few fragments remain. Behind the *wihan* is a *mondop* where stuccoed laterite figures of the Buddha in the four postures are placed back to back in four niches. The best preserved of the four is the standing Buddha on the west side; of the walking Buddha on the east side much of the body remains; little is discernible of the seated Buddha on the south side, or of the reclining Buddha on the north.

Wat Sing, the next monument on the left side, has an *ubosot* containing a laterite brick, seated image of the Buddha, which has been restored. Beyond Wat

Sing the road bends left round the north side of the *wat* enclosure to **Wat Chang Rop** ('Monastery Surrounded by Elephants'), the finest of the monasteries of Aranyik. This stands on an eminence and has a small *ubosot*, a somewhat larger *wihan*, and behind these a monumental *chedi*. The superstructure of the *chedi* has disappeared, leaving only the circular base, which still retains some of its stucco decoration. This stands on a high square platform, which has a staircase with figures of guardian lions at each of the four cardinal points and is surrounded by the foreparts of 68 elephants of stuccoed laterite with stucco panels depicting demons and *bodhi* trees between them. The elephants are elaborately adorned with anklets, necklaces and other jewellery. Some of them are still in good condition; one has been reconstructed and removed to the garden of the Kamphaeng Phet National Museum.

Beyond Wat Chang Rop the road curves sharply towards the north to reach **Wat Awat Yai**, which lies on the edge of the Aranyik perimeter, close to road 101. Just outside the perimeter fence is a deep, rectangular pit known as **Bo Sam Saen**, which may have been the quarry from which the laterite used in the construction of the monastery was extracted.

There are more than a dozen other, minor sites scattered throughout the Aranyik area, many of them still unexcavated and covered by thick vegetation. Several more can be found in different parts of the town.

Near Pratu Saphan Khom, and directly opposite the road leading to the Aranyik ruins, is a lane leading to **Wat Chang** ('Monastery of Elephants'), a modern *wat* behind which are the partially restored remains of an octagonal brick *chedi* surrounded by a water-filled moat. The square base of the *chedi* was once surrounded by stuccoed foreparts of elephants, but most are in ruins or have been completely reconstructed.

The renovated *chedi* of **Wat Kalothai** can be found on T. Ratchadamnoen, Soi 1, just east of the east ramparts of old Kamphaeng Phet and on the edge of the modern town. An earth track to the right after 700m leads to the *chedi*, which has a lotus-bud finial in the Sukhothai style on a high square base.

Across the Ping River on the south bank is the old city of **Nakhon Chum**, of which little evidence remains except several fine brick *chedi* scattered among the rice fields. This is a tranquil spot, however, and a pleasant circular walk can be made, starting opposite the bus station. 100m south of the bus station is **Wat Sum Ko** to the east of the road. Directly opposite the bus station, a track runs 400m east to the *mondop* of **Wat Nong Phikun** on the right and to **Wat Mong Ka Le**, 250m further. A path to the left before Wat Mong Ka Le leads to **Wat Nong Langka**, and onward through the fields to **Wat Nong Yai Chuai** and **Wat Chedi Klang Thung**, returning to road 101 beside the Ping River bridges. Although restored, these *chedi* are rarely visited and the vegetation is once more taking hold.

On the south bank of the Ping River, 700m west of the bridges, is the large white *chedi* of **Wat Phra Boromathat**, constructed in the early Ratanakosin period to replace three earlier *chedi* which according to tradition were built by King Si Intharathit of Sukhothai in the 13C to house relics of the Buddha.

From Kamphaeng Phet, road 101 leads northeast to Sukhothai (see Rte 18), while road 1 continues northwest 65km to Tak (see Rte 20).

18 · Sukhothai

Road 101, 80km from Kamphaeng Phet.

From Kamphaeng Phet, road 101 passes through the old Saphan Khom Gate in the city ramparts and, following for part of the way the course of the ancient road or canal built in the 12C to link Kamphaeng Phet to Sukhothai and Si Satchanalai, runs northeast across a flat plain towards the east side of the Khao Luang hills and thence to Sukhothai. In 1980 the **Ramkhamhaeng National Park** was established on the slopes of Khao Luang. The park covers an area of 342 sq km and is home to numerous bird species and small mammals. It is well served by trails that climb through the open savanna to a height of 1200m, from where excellent views may be obtained, especially between October and February when the air is usually cooler and cleaner. There are standard park bungalows for rent, although travellers with their own transport can easily visit the park from Sukhothai or Kamphaeng Phet and return the same day. The park headquarters and car park lie 16km from road 101, off to the west side c 21km south of Sukhothai.

Road 101 continues through **Khiri Mat**, a village noted for its manufacture of pottery, and joins road 12 near the site of the ancient capital of the kingdom of Sukhothai.

Sukhothai

The modern town of **Sukhothai** (pop. 26,000) is situated on the banks of the Yom River 13km to the east of the ancient city. Most of its traditional wooden houses were burned in a fire in 1968 and it is now singularly lacking in buildings of architectural interest.

■ **Hotels and services**. A wide variety of accommodation is available, including the large and well-appointed *Pailyn Sukhothai Hotel*, which is conveniently located near the ancient city, the *Northern Palace Hotel* (Thai: *Wang Nua*) at 43 T. Singhawat and the *River View Hotel* at 92 T. Nikon Kasem. The older *Ratchathani Hotel* at 229 T. Charot Withithong has an excellent restaurant attached. There are also numerous cheap guest-houses, such as *No.4 Guest House* close to the river, and several standard Chinese hotels, such as the *Chinnawat* at 1–3 T. Nikon Kasem. The unusual *Dream Café* opposite the *Bangkok Bank* on T. Singhawat offers good food in pleasant surroundings, and is renowned for its wide variety of coffees and health tonics. The *Thai Farmers Bank* is beside the river on T. Charot Withithong, and the **post office** (telecoms office upstairs) is on T. Nikon Kasem.

■ **Transport**. **Buses** run frequently to Bangkok, north to Chiang Mai, Uttaradit, Lampang and Phrae, east to Phitsanulok and west to Tak. The central bus station is on T. Nikon Kasem, but some services operate from different locations near the town centre. Services to Sawankhalok and Si Satchanalai leave regularly from beside Phra Ruang Bridge. The nearest **railway station** is at Phitsanulok, c 58km away. *Bangkok Airways* has several **flights** each week from Sukhothai to Chiang Mai (30 mins) and Bangkok (70 mins). **Bicycles**, sometimes in rather poor condition, can be rented at the

Kamphaeng Hak Gate in the ancient city and provide a practical means of transport round the ruins. Even cycling is hot work, so it is worth starting early in the day. Take the bicycle for a test ride before renting: some are in rather poor condition.

History

Sukhothai ('Dawn of Happiness'), capital of the Thai kingdom of the same name, was founded in the mid-13C by a Thai chief named Pha Muang, ruler of a small principality called Muang Rat, which seems to have been in the Uttaradit area and was tributary to the Khmer rulers of Angkor. At some time in the 1230s, Pha Muang, in alliance with another Thai prince called Bang Klang Hao, attacked and conquered a Khmer outpost in the vicinity of Sukhothai. Here, probably c 1240, he installed Bang Klang Hao as the first king of Sukhothai with the Khmer title of Sri Indraditya that he had himself borne. Sri Indraditya is thought to have ruled until the 1270s. At first the new state was small and insignificant, and was probably confined to the area round the city of Sukhothai and its sister city of Si Satchanalai (see Rte 19), 55km to the north, to which it was linked by a road or canal known as the Phra Ruang Highway. It was Sri Indraditya's second son, Ramkhamhaeng, who transformed it by a mixture of warfare and skilful diplomacy into the first powerful Thai kingdom. He is credited with having made Theravada Buddhism the official religion of the kingdom and having devised the script of the Thai language. During its short existence of less than 200 years, Sukhothai, which was finally annexed by Ayutthaya in 1438, was the centre of a school of Buddhist and Brahmanic architecture and sculpture of great distinction and originality, and the Sukhothai period is generally considered to have been a golden age of Thai art. The Sukhothai artists were responsible for two entirely new forms—in architecture, the so-called lotus-bud tower finial (although it is not certain that it was in fact intended to represent a lotus-bud), and, in sculpture, the image of the walking Buddha.

The Thai city of Sukhothai was built immediately to the south of an earlier Khmer city, which may have been located in the area round Wat Phra Phai Luang, where there are three Khmer *prang* and a *wihan* built in the 12C or 13C (see below). Both Sukhothai and Si Satchanalai were built on a rectangular plan, surrounded by three concentric earth ramparts. Parts of the ramparts of Sukhothai are still visible today.

Sukhothai Historical Park

Road 12 runs west c 12km from modern Sukhothai across the Yom River to the fortified city of old Sukhothai, which, together with peripheral sites, has been partially renovated and developed by the Fine Arts Department to form the Sukhothai Historical Park. The road passes through the old gateway known as Pratu Kamphaeng Hak, near which are several shops with bicycles for rent. The first site reached beyond the gate is **Wat Traphang Thong** ('Monastery of the Golden Lake'), on an island to the left, surrounded by a pond filled with lotus-flowers. Here there is a restored Sri Lankan-style brick *chedi* with a laterite base, and on the east side, a small pavilion containing a stone Footprint of the Buddha, which is believed to date from the 14C and was brought here in recent times from Khao Phra Bat Yai, a hilltop site to the west of the ancient city.

West of the *wat* is the **Ramkhamhaeng National Museum** (open Wed–Sun, 09.00–16.00), which was inaugurated in 1964 by King Bhumipol and Queen Sirikit and consists of two main exhibition halls. The first contains old photographs of the Sukhothai ruins before restoration and rebuilding; the second contains an interesting collection of sculptures, ceramics, votive tablets and other artefacts of all periods and styles found in old Sukhothai, Kamphaeng Phet and Si Satchanalai. Of note are a magnificent carved wooden ceiling panel from Wat Phra Si Ratana Mahathat at Chaliang, Si Satchanalai, and some 12C–13C stone torsos from San Ta Pha Daeng. Here also is a copy of the famous

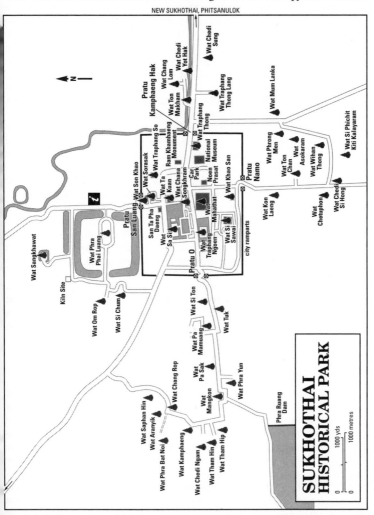

Ramkhamhaeng stela of 1292, the original of which is in the National Museum in Bangkok. In this stela, the authenticity of which has recently been questioned by some scholars, Sukhothai is described as powerful and prosperous and its ruler as just, wise and beneficent. It is c 1m high and 45cm square and is written in Thai in the script which Ramkhamhaeng is believed to have invented. In the grounds of the museum is a Dvaravati Wheel of the Law from Si Thep (see p 344–5) and a replica of a Sukhothai-period cross-draft kiln.

Just beyond the museum, and close to the centre of the walled city, is **WAT MAHATHAT**, the most important monastery in the city and the state temple of the kings of Sukhothai, the foundations of whose palace can be seen immediately opposite it to the east. Wat Mahathat was probably founded by Sri Indraditya and reconstructed in the 1340s by King Lo Thai to house two sacred relics, a hair and a neck bone of the Buddha, brought from Sri Lanka by a Thai monk named Sisatta, who had gone there for re-ordination. On the east side of the temple enclosure is a *wihan* with circular columns placed on a high brick platform. Beyond this is the central **chedi**, terminating in a lotus-bud finial with an elegantly tapering spire. The *chedi* has a redented shaft similar in form to a Khmer-style *prang* and may therefore originally have had niches for images on each face. On either side is a double staircase leading up to a platform that enables pilgrims to circumambulate the *chedi*. It stands on a high two-tiered base decorated with a bas-relief frieze of walking monks with their hands joined in worship. Unfortunately, this has been insensitively restored by the Fine Arts Department. The tower of the central *chedi* is surrounded by eight smaller towers. Of these the four at the cardinal points are conventional Khmer tower-sanctuaries built of laterite, with niches for Buddha images and pediments decorated with stucco reliefs depicting scenes from the Life of the Buddha. Of these only two, illustrating the Buddha's Birth and his passing into *Mahāparinirvāṇa* survive. The pediments are surmounted by *kāla* heads disgorging arched garlands that terminate either in *makaras* turning inwards or in *kinnaras*. On the tympana are more stucco reliefs depicting scenes from the Life of the Buddha. The three-tiered superstructures of the towers were originally adorned with antefixes of mythical animals, but few of these now remain. The stucco decoration, which was probably added by Lo Thai, shows clear signs of Sri Lankan influence, no doubt introduced by the artisans who accompanied Sisatta and the relics from Sri Lanka (see p 45). By contrast, the four corner towers are of brick and are in the form of a bell-shaped *chedi* with a high square cella on an octagonal base. On each side of the base is a niche with no pediment, but surmounted by a *makara* disgorging a many-headed *nāga*.

On either side of this central group of shrines is a colossal image of a standing Buddha of the type known as the Eighteen-Cubit Buddha, or Phra Attharot, enclosed in half-walls of brick. Within the enclosure are numerous *chedi*, *wihan* and other structures in different styles.

A little way to the south of the lotus-bud *chedi* is a *stūpa* in the form of a stepped pyramid. It is popularly known as **Ha Yot** ('Five Spires'), which suggests that it may originally have been surmounted by five spires representing the five peaks of Mount Meru. It is surrounded by a low wall covered with stucco decoration portraying mythical creatures, three-headed elephants, acrobats, dwarfs, lions and horses. Alone of the five pyramid-*stūpas* in Sukhothai (see Wat Wihan Thong and Wat Asokaram below), Ha Yot has an opening at the fourth level that gives access to a deep shaft within the *stūpa*; the other four are virtually solid monuments. Here, perhaps, were placed the ashes of Mahathammaratcha I, the king who built it.

To the southwest of Wat Mahathat is **Wat Si Sawai**, a Khmer-style temple which is thought by some scholars to have been founded in the 12C as a Shaivite temple by the Khmers and converted in the 14C into a Buddhist monastery. However, it is more likely to have been from the first a Thai Buddhist foundation dating from the 14C, when there was a revival of Khmer architectural forms. It consists of a *wihan* with columns on either side on the south and a row of three Khmer-style *prang* instead of a *chedi* on the north. These *prang*, which are all more or less intact, still have some of their stucco decoration. The restoration of the temple leaves much to be desired; many of the original carved antefixes have been replaced by crude concrete copies.

North of Wat Si Sawai is a large rectangular pool, in the middle of which is the small *ubosot* of **Wat Traphang Ngoen** ('Monastery of the Silver Lake'), approached by a narrow causeway from the north. On the west shore, and also surrounded by water, is the base of a very small *wihan* containing a seated Buddha image, and an elegant brick *chedi* with a renovated lotus-bud finial standing on a high laterite base.

A short distance further north is **Wat Sa Si**, also on an island, in a large artificial lake known as Trakuan Traphang. This exquisite monastery has the base of a *wihan* and two brick *chedi*, the larger of which is in pure Sri Lankan style with a bell-shaped relic chamber on a square base. A footbridge east of the *wihan* leads to a separate island on which stands the remains of a tiny *ubosot*.

At the southeast corner of Trakuan Traphang is **Wat Chana Songkhram**, which consists of a round bell-shaped *chedi* of Sri Lankan type on a square base, flanked by a *wihan* to the east and an *ubosot* to the west. On the east side of Trakuan Traphang is a **statue of Ramkhamhaeng** seated on a throne. Close by is the site of **Wat Mai**, which has a very large *ubosot* on a high platform and retains some of its stucco decoration. This *wat* was probably built in the 15C, after the conquest and annexation of Sukhothai by Ayutthaya.

Near the northeast corner of Trakuan Traphang is **Wat Ta Kuan**, another monument with a 14C *chedi* of Sri Lankan type with a ringed spire.

Beyond the ticket barrier and across the main road, is **San Ta Pha Daeng**, a small Khmer shrine of which only the lower part of a laterite *prang* with a porch survives. Apart from the *prasat* of Wat Phra Phai Luang, this is the only building in Sukhothai that certainly dates from the Khmer period. Sandstone figures dating from c 1200, now in the Ramkhamhaeng Museum, were found here during restoration of the temple c 1960.

Road 113 runs north from beside San Ta Pha Daeng and passes through the gateway known as Pratu San Luang. On the right before the gateway is the charming **Wat Sorasak**, which was founded in 1412 and is the last *wat* in Sukhothai that has a dated inscription. It has a Sri Lankan bell-shaped *chedi* on a square base surrounded with the foreparts of elephants. Immediately to the north are the *chedi* and the four rows of columns of the *wihan* of **Wat Son Khao**. To the east, and at present inaccessible, is another island temple called Wat Traphang So.

North of Pratu San Luang, the road passes minor ruins before reaching **WAT PHRA PHAI LUANG** on the left. The three 12C–13C laterite *prasat* here, of which only the northern one is intact, constitute the most important of the surviving monuments of the Khmer city of Sukhothai. A fragment of a statue which is thought to be one of the 23 portrait statues of Jayavarman VII that were distributed throughout the Khmer empire has been found at Wat Phra Phai Luang and is now in the Ramkhamhaeng National Museum. The three multi-tiered tower-sanctuaries are embellished with stucco decoration. Some of this decoration is Khmer, notably the antefixes in the shape of *nāga* heads that adorn each tier and the tympana of the pediments above the doorways, which contain depictions of Buddhist scenes, one of them a seated Buddha in *bhūmisparśa mudrā*; some of it is Thai, dating from the 14C.

Immediately behind the towers to the east is a *wihan* with laterite pillars and base, which is probably also Khmer and dates from the late 13C. Along the south side of the *wihan* are rows of small laterite *stūpas* of Mon type, with rings instead of a box-shaped *harmikā* between the bell-shaped relic chamber and the spire.

East of the *wihan* is a *chedi*, which appears to have been built in different stages, probably between the late 13C and the 15C. A renovation by the Fine Arts Department on the west side has revealed evidence of some of these stages. An early design incorporated small niches containing Buddha images, which were later partially hidden by the placing of large Buddha images at the cardinal points. Later, these niches were completely bricked up.

A *mondop* to the southeast of the *chedi* contains relief sculptures of the Buddha in the four postures—standing, sitting, reclining and walking. Of these only the standing image on the north side is more or less intact, although the walking image on the east has been partially reconstructed. West of the *prasat* is an *ubosot*, of which only the base remains. It was probably built a little later than the towers and the *wihan* and indicates that this was a Theravada Buddhist temple.

On the northwest corner of the road which encircles the moat of Wat Phra Phai Luang are the remains of several kilns known as **Tao Thuriang**, where Sukhothai ceramics were formerly made. More than 50 kilns have been found here and elsewhere in Sukhothai, only 11 of them of the cross-draft type, which could have fired stoneware. It is probable that production in Sukhothai started around the mid-14C and may have continued until the mid-16C. It seems likely that the Sukhothai potters brought their techniques from Si Satchanalai, where production was already well established by the mid-14C (see Rte 19). It is not clear, however, whether they were Chinese immigrants, ethnic Tai who had migrated from southern China over a long period, or possibly entrepreneurs from Angkor or Vietnam, where local ceramic industries had operated since the 1C and 9C respectively.

What is rather more certain is that ceramic production spread from Si Satchanalai to Sukhothai partly in response to an edict of 1371 issued by the xenophobic Ming emperor, Zhu Yuanzhang, who had banned private Chinese overseas trade. The consequent shortage of Chinese ceramics in the export market led to a steep increase in ceramic production outside China and intense competition among other producers.

A lane running north from a point just east of the kilns leads through thick undergrowth to the unrestored site of **Wat Sangkhawat**, where there is a large, damaged, head-less Buddha image.

To the west of Wat Phra Phai Luang, the road passes through old earthen ramparts and turns south towards Wat Si Chum. From this corner, a track continues west for 300m to the *chedi* of **Wat Om Rop**, which has a fine lotus-bud finial.

WAT SI CHUM, immediately to the south of Wat Om Rop, consists of the foundations and some of the columns of a *wihan* in front of a tall cube-shaped *mondop*, now roofless, that houses a colossal stucco brick image of a seated Buddha almost 15m high, called Phra Achana. Access is gained through a narrow opening running almost the full height of the front wall of the shrine. A narrow stair, now closed to the public, runs inside the thickness

The huge image of a seated Buddha can be seen through the columns of the wihan *at Wat Si Chum, Sukhothai*

of the wall on the left side of the Buddha image up to the top of the wall. About 50 slate slabs engraved with scenes from the *jātaka* tales cover the ceiling of this stair. One of them is preserved in the Ramkhamhaeng National Museum.

South of Wat Si Chum, the lane returns to road 12. To visit the numerous ruins scattered to the west of the old city, turn northwest along road 12 for c 1500m to a lane on the left which leads south along the foot of low hills before eventually heading east back to the west gate of the old city.

The first monument reached is **Wat Saphan Hin** ('Monastery of the Stone Bridge'), which stands on the summit of a hill to the west of the lane and is reached by a very ruined flight of steps. This *wat* is chiefly notable for an **Eighteen-Cubit Buddha image** or Phra Attharot, made of stuccoed laterite, standing with the right hand raised in *abhaya mudrā*, at the end of a small *wihan* with laterite columns. This statue, which is one of the best known of the numerous Eighteen-Cubit Buddha images in Thailand, dates from the late 13C. It has been restored many times, most recently in the 20C.

The lane continues south, past **Wat Aranyik**, which is probably the earliest of this group of temples. There is little to be seen here except the base and columns of a small *wihan*. **Wat Chang Rop**, which has a fine Sri Lankan-style *chedi* and a *wihan* built on a single platform surrounded by 24 niches containing the foreparts of elephants, lies on the left side of the lane; opposite, a path climbs to **Wat Khao Phra Bat Noi** ('Monastery of the Hill of the Lesser Buddha Footprint'), which consists of a group of shrines and *kuti* and a highly unusual

The giant standing Buddha at Wat Saphan Hin, Sukhothai

chedi with a slender redented bell standing on a square base with a niche on each side. Four Footprints of the Buddha have been found here and are now in the Ramkhamhang Museum in Sukhothai.

The lane continues past Wat Kamphaeng Hin, **Wat Chedi Ngam**, which has a large Sri Lankan-style *chedi* on a round multi-tiered base, and the hilltop sites of Wat Tham Hin and Wat Tham Hip, both of which are very ruined, to **Wat Mangkon**, where the ruins of a large *wihan* and a *chedi* in Sri Lankan style on a high brick platform, and parts of a late 14C ceramic balustrade can be seen. Other fragments of ceramic decoration from this temple are now in the Ramkhamhaeng National Museum.

The track to the south from here leads after c 1km to a small **reservoir** known as Sarit Phong or Thamnop Phra Ruang, which is believed to have provided the water supply for old Sukhothai.

East from Wat Mangkon the road passes **Wat Phra Yun** on the south side, which contains a *mondop* with a fine and well-preserved standing Buddha image of stuccoed brick, and then Wat Pa Sak on the north side. A short distance to the east, near to **Wat Pa Mamuang** ('Monastery of the Mango Grove'), where four inscriptions written in Thai, Khmer and Pali in honour of King Mahatham-maratcha I, who entered the monkhood here in 1361, have been discovered, is a Hindu shrine, of which eight high brick pillars on a square base remain and which is known as **Ho Thewalai Maha Kaset Phiman**. Before reaching the west gateway of the old city, known as Pratu O, the lane passes several more minor sites. These include **Wat Tuk**, which has the remnants of a fine square *mondop* with fragments of stucco decoration, including a scene of the Buddha descending from the Tavatimsa Heaven, and contains a seated Buddha image, and **Wat Si Ton**, of which little except four square pillars of stuccoed brick remains.

The road south out of old Sukhothai leads from the gateway known as Pratu Namo through rice fields. After 350m it passes on the right **Wat Kon Laeng**, which has a laterite *chedi* and the brick base of a *wihan*, and then **Wat Ton Chan**, ('Monastery of the Sandalwood Tree'), which probably dates from the late 14C and has a fine Sri Lankan-style *chedi* and a brick *wihan* containing a large seated Buddha image of stuccoed brick, now headless. At a road junction 500m further south is **Wat Chetuphon**, which consists of a small *wihan* and a brick *chedi* surrounded by a low wall, constructed most unusually of grey slate and pierced by windows of which only the bases of the frames remain, and a *mondop* with figures in relief of the Buddha in the four postures. Of these only the walking figure is relatively well preserved.

Turn left at Wat Chetuphon and continue east for 50m to reach **Wat Chedi Si Hong** on the right. This temple still retains most of the laterite columns of its small *wihan* and the remains of a seated Buddha image, and round the base of the *chedi* some fragments of charming stucco decorations of *garuḍas* mounted on elephants and deities carrying vases of flowers.

About 350m further east a turning to the right leads after 300m to **Wat Si Phichit Kirati Kalayaram**, which has a nobly proportioned Sri Lankan-style brick *chedi* on a high redented square base, built, according to a Pali inscription found nearby, in 1404.

380m further east the road turns due north and passes Wat Wihan Thong, Wat Asokaram, Wat Phrong Men and Wat Mum Lanka. Built of laterite, **Wat Wihan Thong**, which probably dates from the first half of the 14C, is one of the earliest of the five extant stepped pyramid *stūpas* erected in Sukhothai to house Buddhist relics. With a base measuring 4.8 sq m, it is also one of the largest. **Wat Asokaram** is also a stepped pyramid *stūpa*, but built of brick. It was constructed in 1399 to house two important relics of the Buddha brought from Sri Lanka, and the monastery that was attached to it early in the 15C was donated by Queen Chulalakasana, wife of Mahathammaratcha III. Both these stepped pyramid *stūpas* are similar to the Ha Yot pyramid at Wat Mahathat (see above).

About 1km after Wat Mum Lanka, the road joins road 12 a little to the east of Pratu Kamphaeng Hak. 400m east of the gate, a lane off the north side of road 12 leads after 450m to **Wat Chang Lom**, a beautiful large brick *chedi* surrounded by the foreparts of elephants, some of them clumsily restored. Further east on road 12, on the south side, is **Wat Traphang Thong Lang** ('Monastery of the Coral Tree Pond'). On the south wall of the *mondop* in this temple is one of the finest and best preserved stucco reliefs in Sukhothai. It shows the Buddha descending from the Tavatimsa Heaven, flanked by Brahma and Indra, and other deities carrying conical ringed parasols. There is also some fine stucco decoration with *makara* and *kinnari* motifs above the arches of the *mondop*. Traces of red pigment can still be seen on the stucco.

19 · Sawankhalok and Si Satchanalai

Road *101 or roads 1195 and 1201 from Sukhothai, 53km. To Sawankhalok 36km; from Sawankhalok to Si Satchanalai Historical Park 17km.*

Railway. *There are regular train services from Bangkok to Sawankhalok.*

The ruins of the ancient city of Si Satchanalai, one of the capitals of the Sukhothai kingdom, are best visited on a day trip from Sukhothai, although they can also be conveniently visited on the way to Uttaradit, which is c 36km east of Si Satchanalai on road 102. Neither the modern town of Si Satchanalai, c 11km from the ruins, nor Sawankhalok, c 18km distant, has any hotels that can be recommended, but simple, clean accommodation is available at the Si Satchanalai Cultural Centre outside the Si Satchanalai Historical Park, and there is an excellent restaurant, the *Kang Sak*, on the banks of the Yom River nearby.

To reach **Sawankhalok** take road 101 north from Sukhothai for 36km. A less frequented but more scenic route is by road 1195, which runs roughly parallel to road 101 along the west bank of the Yom River. Sawankhalok, which was founded in the 19C, is a pleasant but not very interesting market town. At the south end of the town, however, on the west bank of the Yom River, is the **Sawankha Woranayok National Museum** (open Wed–Sun, 09.00–12.00, 13.00–16.00), which houses an excellent collection of 14C–19C ceramics from the Sawankhalok kilns and elsewhere, and some fine images of the Buddha from different periods, many of them collected by the former abbot of nearby Wat Sawankharam.

The most important exhibit in the museum is a large assembly of wares recovered from 15C and 16C shipwrecks in the Gulf of Thailand. It was the discovery in 1975 of a mixed cargo of Sawankhalok-Si Satchanalai and Sukhothai wares in one such wreck site that revealed that both centres were producing ceramics in the early 15C. Subsequent research in the 1980s has indicated that production spread from Si Satchanalai to Sukhothai in the late 14C and not the other way about as had previously been supposed. Though the ceramics of Sukhothai and Si Satchanalai are often both loosely classified as Sawankhalok (or commonly, Sangkhalok), they are in fact easily distinguished from one another. Sukhothai designs are simpler and sketchier than those of Si Satchanalai wares and are generally confined to fishes, chrysanthemums and wheel motifs.

Also on display are some wasters (ceramics damaged during firing) and upstairs some Buddha images from different periods, including a very fine sandstone Khmer image of the Buddha sheltered by the *nāga* king, Mucalinda. In the museum garden are two 16C–17C cannon salvaged from a shipwreck in the Gulf of Thailand.

From Sawankhalok, road 101 continues north for 17km to **SI SATCHANALAI HISTORICAL PARK**, which lies to the left across the Yom River. Just before the river bridge is a restaurant advertising bicycle rentals. A bicycle is recommended for visitors without their own transport, as the ruins are spread over an extensive area. At the intersection just beyond the bridge, the lane to the left leads to Chaliang; to the right is **Si Satchanalai Historical Park**.

Chaliang

Along the lane which leads east towards Chaliang, the first ruins to be reached are those of **Wat Noi Champi**, to the right after 140m. This temple consists of a laterite *stūpa* and the remains of a *wihan*, its wall showing the characteristic slit windows of the period. 260m further east is **Wat Chao Chan**, a Khmer temple dating from the late 12C or early 13C that appears to have been one of Jayavarman VII's resthouses (*dharmasālā*), the northernmost of any yet found, and to have been later converted into a Buddhist *wat*. It consists of a beautifully proportioned laterite *prang* decorated with niches and antefixes and a lotus finial; traces of stucco are visible. On the north side of the *prang* there is a *mondop*, now roofless, containing the laterite core of a tall standing Buddha image, unusually facing north.

To the right after a further 100m is **Wat Chom Chun**. This consists of a *wihan*, *mondop* and a damaged bell-shaped *stūpa*; part of the spire is lying on the ground on the south side. The niches on each side of the *stūpa* base once contained images of the Buddha. The *mondop* at the west end of the *wihan* houses the remains of a stuccoed, seated image.

Wat Chao Chan, Chaliang

WAT PHRA SI RATANA MAHATHAT, the most important of the Chaliang monuments, lies 500m further east on a narrow peninsula created by a sharp bend in the river. It was probably built in the late Sukhothai period on the site of a Khmer *prasat* and was restored in the mid-18C in the reign of King Borommakot. Parts of a wall composed of large blocks of laterite still surround the enclosure. The entrance is through a gateway in the east wall which is surmounted by a curious cylindrical ornament composed of four human faces facing the four cardinal directions in a manner reminiscent of the face-towers of the Bayon at Angkor. This leads through to a *wihan* with laterite columns and narrow slit windows, at the west end of which is a large seated Buddha image in the Sukhothai style in stuccoed brick. Flanking this are the remains of two standing Buddha images, sunk low in the ground; beside the standing image on the south side is a remarkable relief carving in stuccoed laterite of a walking Buddha, which has been attributed by some art historians to the end of the 13C. If this is correct, it is one of the earliest representations of the walking Buddha in Thailand. However, it is more likely that it was much restored or even first made at a later date, as it has all the features characteristic of walking Buddha images of the classic Sukhothai style of the late 14C—a long oval face with downcast eyes and arched eyebrows joined above an aquiline nose, abnormally broad shoulders and long arms like the trunk of an elephant, undulating torso and legs and others of the 32 marks of the superman (*lakṣaṇa*) described in the Pali texts.

Immediately behind the images, narrow steps lead up to the cella of the tall Khmer-style *prang*. It is surmounted by a five-pointed *vajra*, which is both the weapon of Indra and a Tantric Buddhist symbol. Beyond the *prang* is a very large laterite *stūpa* with steps on the east side leading up to a narrow circular terrace with four entrances into the relic chamber. Further west is a *mondop* containing a large stuccoed image of the standing Buddha in *abhaya mudrā*, facing north, and beyond that lies another *wihan* in which are two stuccoed images of the seated Buddha, one behind the other, both flanked by smaller images. In the northeast corner of the enclosure is a small niche containing a fine Khmer image of the Buddha sheltered by Mucalinda.

Along the river bank beside the *wat* is a row of stalls, where on most days fake antique ceramics and other souvenirs, drinks and snacks are for sale.

Return to the intersection near the river bridge, follow the lane across the bridge and continue west through a village, past the diminutive ruin of **Wat Noi** and several shops selling 'antiques', to reach **Wat Khok Sing Kharam** on the left side after 500m. The main feature of this temple, which has been partially restored by the Fine Arts Department, is the row of three laterite *chedi* on a single base at the west end. Of note also is the small *ubosot* close to the road, which unusually contains a small bell-shaped *chedi* on a laterite base surrounded by octagonal columns. 600m further west, the road passes through the old gateway called **Pratu Don Laem** and into the walled city.

Si Satchanalai Historical Park

The ruins of Si Satchanalai are picturesquely situated in park-like surroundings, with the Yom River to the northeast and hills to the west and north. The city was built on a roughly rectangular plan similar to that of its sister city, Sukhothai, to which it was linked by a highway or canal called **Phra Ruang**, (research in the mid-1990s indicates that it was probably a canal), and was surrounded by a wall pierced with seven gates and up to three concentric earth ramparts, parts of which can still be seen.

At the first T-junction beyond the ticket barrier, the road to the right runs to the foot of a long flight of laterite steps leading to the summit of a low hill, on which stands **Wat Khao Phanom Phloeng** ('Monastery of the Fire Mountain'). This *wat* has a large bell-shaped *chedi* and, at the east end, the remains of an *ubosot* with an image of the seated Buddha in *bhūmisparśa mudrā*.

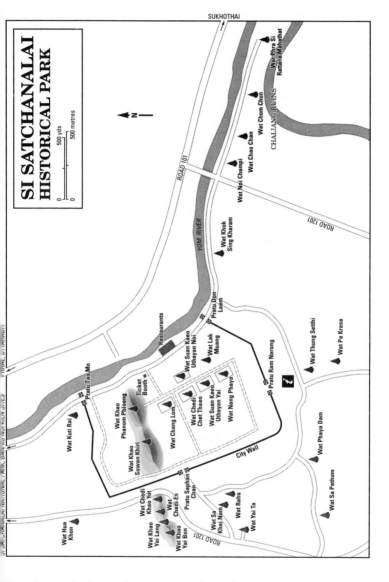

SUKHOTHAI

SI SATCHANALAI HISTORICAL PARK

0   500 yds
0   500 metres

N

Wat Phra Si Rattana Mahathat

CHALIANG RUINS

Wat Chom Chun

Wat Chao Chan

Wat Noi Champi

ROAD 101

YOM RIVER

ROAD 1201

Wat Khok Sing Kharam

Pratu Don Laem

Restaurants

Wat Thung Setthi

Wat Pa Krasa

Pratu Tao Mo

Ticket Booth

Wat Suan Kaeo Uthayan Noi

Wat Lak Muang

Pratu Ram Narong

Wat Khao Phanom Phloeng

Wat Kuti Rai

Wat Chedi Chet Thaeo

Wat Suan Kaeo Uthayan Yai

Wat Nang Phaya

Wat Chang Lom

Wat Khao Suwan Khiri

City Wall

Wat Phaya Dam

Wat Hua Khon

Wat Chedi Khao Yot

Wat Chedi- Et

Pratu Saphan Chan

Wat Rahu

Wat Sa Pathum

Wat Khao Yai Lang

Wat Khao Yai Bon

ROAD 1201

Wat Sa Khai Nam

Wat Yai Ta

It is believed to be the site of a very ancient shrine dedicated to a fire or solar cult. From here a path leads southwest across a saddle to a slightly higher hill, where stands **Wat Khao Suwan Khiri** ('Monastery of the Golden Hill'). Behind the *wihan* is a very large *chedi* on an unusually broad and high, multi-tiered, laterite base. A smaller *chedi* of similar type lies beyond.

To the southeast of the laterite steps, lying close to the centre of the royal city, is **WAT CHANG LOM** ('Monastery Surrounded by Elephants'). Some scholars believe this temple was built in the 1290s for Ramkhamhaeng; others date it to as late as the end of the 15C. If the former date is correct, this *wat* has the earliest known bell-shaped *chedi* of Sri Lankan type in Thailand and may be considered as a prototype for all other such *chedi* built during the Sukhothai period. The *chedi* stands on a square, two-storeyed base round which are 39 stuccoed laterite elephants, separated by tall pillars from which lanterns were hung. Most of the elephants' heads and trunks have been lost, as well as much of their stucco; a few have been reconstructed by the Fine Arts Department. They also are derived from Sri Lankan prototypes and represent the celestial elephants that in Hindu mythology supported the dome of the universe on their backs. In Thai *wat* usually only the foreparts of the elephants are represented, emerging from the walls of the base, so that they look as though their hind parts are supporting the weight of the *chedi* above them. The elephants of Wat Chang Lom are unusual in that they are free-standing on the platform in front of the base.

A staircase climbs to the second storey of the base, where 20 niches contain seated Buddha images in *bhūmisparśa mudrā*. Like the walking Buddha of Chaliang, with which they share certain features, these Buddha images have also been ascribed by some scholars to the reign of Ramkhamhaeng. Above the base is a shallow octagonal plinth, and above this are four circular mouldings of which the uppermost is decorated with a lotus motif. These support the bell-shaped relic chamber, which has almost vertical sides. Above it is a square *harmikā*, separating the bell from the tapering ringed spire. On the shaft at the base of the spire is a frieze of images of the walking Buddha. Southeast of the *chedi* is the *wihan*; a small *ubosot* lies in the east corner of the site.

Immediately southeast of Wat Chang Lom is **Wat Chedi Chet Thaeo** ('Monastery of the Seven Rows of Chedi'), which probably dates from the mid-14C. The central *chedi* and *wihan* are surrounded by 33 smaller *chedi* of different types in nine, not seven, rows, some of them showing south Indian influence. They are thought to have been built to contain the ashes of members of the ruling dynasty of Sukhothai. At the northwest end, directly behind the central *chedi* is a *mondop* which contains, in a thin corbelled archway now locked by a gate, a fine stuccoed image of the Buddha, its head, hands and feet missing. In a niche in one of the smaller *chedi* is an exceptionally fine stuccoed image, probably dating from the late Sukhothai period, of the Buddha in meditation protected by the *nāga* Mucalinda, which most unusually has seven coils and nine heads. The head of this beautiful statue was cut off by thieves and has been replaced by a copy. Another *chedi* base nearby is surrounded by the remains of small stucco elephants. A double flight of steps climbs up the base of the central *chedi*, which has a fine lotus-bud finial, and is traditionally believed to have been built for King Mahathammaratcha I when he was deputy king (*uparaja*) in Si Satchanalai. Wat Chedi Chet Thaeo was the site of the only known fragment of painting to survive from the Sukhothai period; it showed a series of Buddha figures in horizontal rows, but is no longer visible.

Across the road is **Wat Suan Kaeo Uthayan Noi**, which dates from the mid-14C. The *chedi* has a fine lotus-bud finial above a redented tower on a multi-tiered square base. Like the *chedi* of Wat Chedi Chet Thaeo, it has a double flight of steps leading up to the top of the base. In the *mondop* at the northwest end of the *wihan* are the remains of a laterite Buddha image.

Southeast of Wat Chedi Chet Thaeo is **Wat Suan Kaeo Uthayan Yai**, which comprises the remains of a laterite *wihan* and a *chedi*. On the other side of the road is the charming Khmer-style **Wat Lak Muang**. The area to the northwest of here, now planted with trees, was the site of the **royal palace** which covered an area of 3.5 hectares between here and the river.

The *wihan* of **Wat Nang Phaya**, southeast of Wat Suan Kaeo Uthayan Yai, contains some magnificent **stucco decoration** on its southwest wall, thought to date from the early Ayutthaya period. On the *chedi* to the northwest, steps climb up to the relic chamber, which has now been partially destroyed.

Scattered within the walled city are many other minor ruins. Outside the gate known as **Pratu Ram Narong** in the southeast wall is an **information centre**, where there are photographs and displays illustrating the city's history. Immediately across the road from this are the base of a *wihan* and a small *chedi*, all that remains of **Wat Thung Setthi**. Behind that is another minor site, **Wat Pa Krasa**. The road past the information centre continues round the south corner of the city wall, with a branch to the left leading to **Wat Phaya Dam**, and then to **Wat Sa Pathum**. In the *mondop* of the former is the laterite core of a very tall standing relief image of the Buddha. **Wat Rahu** lies to the left further along the road by the southwest wall; its *chedi* once had a lotus-bud finial, but the top section has broken off. A right turn at the next junction leads past **Wat Sa Khai Nam** to join road 1201. On the left at the junction is **Wat Yai Ta**, a minor ruin.

Road 1201 runs north from here through a gap in the ridge of low hills. Aligned up the ridge to the left is a series of four *chedi* linked by an easy path. Closest to the road is **Wat Chedi Khao Yot**; a few metres further is **Wat Chedi En**, which has a large Sri Lankan-style *chedi* and a stuccoed laterite *mondop* containing a seated Buddha image flanked by figures of disciples and retaining traces of painted red and black foliate decoration and inscriptions on the walls. Higher up are **Wat Khao Yai Lang** and **Wat Khao Yai Bon**, both of which contain large *chedi*.

Just beyond the hills, road 1201 passes **Wat Hua Khon** on the left. Of the seven large standing images which the *mondop* here once contained, only three remain.

Ban Ko Noi kiln sites

To the north of the old city are three groups of early **kiln sites**, which have been discovered and excavated since the early 1980s by a team of archaeologists led by Don Hein. More than 200 kilns have so far been discovered, and Hein has estimated there may be at least 600 more. They certainly date back to the 13C and some may be as early as the 10C.

The oldest kilns of the Sukhothai kingdom have been found in the group at **Ban Ko Noi**, c 5km north of the city walls. This was by far the most productive of the sites and the source of a great variety of wares. Two excavated kiln sites, numbered 42 and 123, have been left open, and it is possible to see within the site of kiln 42 a mound of many cross-draft kilns built on top of one another. They display a gradual evolution in structure from a bank type to an in-ground type to an above-ground type.

The Ban Ko Noi site can be reached either via road 1201, or by leaving the old city through the gate known as **Pratu Tao Mo** and continuing northwest past **Wat Kuti Rai**. This *wat* consists of two *mondop*, of which the one further from the road contains the damaged torso and legs of a seated Buddha image. The lane continues north for c 4km, passing the **Ban Pa Yang** kiln site to reach the **Centre for the Study and Preservation of Sangkhalok Kilns**, where there is a small **museum** of ceramics and another excavated site showing a collapsed in-ground kiln still containing its last load of storage jars. The major site of Ban Ko Noi is c 1km further on.

Most scholars agree that the technology for these kilns, which was relatively crude, was introduced from outside, perhaps from China or Vietnam. The latest evidence suggests that the kilns continued in existence at least until the mid-16C, when they may have ceased production as a result of Burmese invasions. Many imitations of these Si Satchanalai wares are now manufactured and fired locally and sold in shops nearby and at the ruins of Sukhothai.

▶Si Satchanalai National Park

To reach the isolated, but delightful **Si Satchanalai National Park**, take road 1201 north from the Ban Ko Noi kiln site and turn left after c 2km on to road 1305, from where the park is signed 51km. Turn right at the next intersection, and continue to the park headquarters at the roadhead, where there are pleasant bungalows, a good campsite and a restaurant which can provide simple meals and drinks. Trails of several kilometres lead to waterfalls and a cave, and there appears to be a wealth of bird life. Infrequent buses run along the park road from Si Satchanalai. ◀

Road 101 continues north along the east bank of the Yom River and road 1201 along the west bank to modern Si Satchanalai, which, like Sawankhalok, was founded during the 19C. The adjoining small village of **Ban Hat Sieo** is inhabited by Lao Phuan, who came from Laos to settle here in the late 18C and early 19C, and is noted for its textile weaving. On the west bank opposite Ban Hat Sieo is another weaving village, **Ban Hat Sung**. At the north end of Si Satchanalai is **Wat Hat Sieo**, which has a fine mid-19C wood-panelled *ho trai* with a tiled roof, built on stilts over a circular pool. On the main road nearby are workshops selling Lao Phuan textiles, for which demand has greatly increased in recent years.

On the northern outskirts of Si Satchanalai, road 102 turns off right to Uttaradit (c 36km), while road 101 continues north towards Phrae (c 76km; see Rte 22).

20 · Kamphaeng Phet to Tak and Mae Sot

Roads 1 *and* 105, *150km. To Tak 68km; Tak to Mae Sot 82km.*

Leave Kamphaeng Phet (see Rte 17) over the Ping River bridge and turn north on road 1. After 34km, a **detour** to the left on road 1109 leads to **KHLONG WANG CHAO NATIONAL PARK**, one of Thailand's largest (748 sq km) and remotest parks. The 29km road to the park headquarters is poorly maintained in parts, but the hill scenery is magnificent, with striking limestone cliffs, caverns and high waterfalls. Simple bungalow accommodation is available and camping is possible, but visitors need to bring all provisions with them.

Tak

Continue north on road 1 for c 33km (or take the quieter road 104, which goes to the right off road 1 beside the 390km stone in the centre of Ban Wang Chao) to the provincial capital of Tak (pop. 21,000). In a picturesque location on the east bank of the Ping River, Tak makes a convenient overnight stop on the way to the western border town of Mae Sot. The town's narrow streets have retained many of their older buildings, including a number of beautiful teak houses, and, especially in the evenings, there are fine views across the river to the hills beyond.

Tak is chiefly notable as the birthplace of **King Taksin** or **Phya Tak**, the Siamese general who, after the sack of Ayutthaya by the Burmese in 1767, escaped with a small band of followers by sailing down the Chao Phraya River to Thon Buri, where in 1770 he re-established the Ayutthaya monarchy with himself as king. Later he became insane and in 1781 was deposed by his chief general, Chaophraya Chakri, founder of the present reigning dynasty (see p 46). Taksin is commemorated by a monument containing a bronze statue of him, known as **Sala Somdet Phra Chao Taksin Maharat**, which stands in the centre of a small park on T. Chotwithithong, close to Wat Bot Mani Sibunruang.

■ **Information**. The TAT office (open daily, 08.30–16.30) is just north of the King Taksin monument dedicated to on T. Chotwithithong.

■ **Hotels and services**. Tak has several acceptable hotels, including the *Wiang Tak 2* on T. Chomphon overlooking the river, the comfortable *Wiang Tak* at 25/3 T. Mahat Thai Bamrung, and the cheaper, friendly *Tak Hotel* on the same street. The *Bangkok Bank* is at 683 T. Taksin, and the **post office** is off T. Mahat Thai Bamrung near the government offices.

■ **Transport**. The **bus station** is beside the junction of roads 1 and 12. There are regular services to Lampang, Chiang Mai, Sukhothai and other northern towns, and overnight services to Bangkok. Fast **minibuses** operate on the steep and winding route to Mae Sot. *THAI* has a booking office at 485 T. Taksin, but the nearest **airport** with scheduled flights is at Mae Sot. **Samlo** operate around the town.

The most interesting monument in Tak is **Wat Bot Mani Sibunruang**, at the northern end of the town between T. Mahat Thai Bamrung and T. Taksin. The entrance to the *wat* enclosure is from the lane on the south side. Beneath a modern corrugated iron porch, two crudely painted lions guard the simple wood-panelled doors of the beautiful Lan Na-style *ubosot*. Although the doors are usually locked, the monks are generally willing to open them on request. The exterior is decorated with wooden *khan tuai* and a fine front gable of stuccoed wood. The interior contains round wooden pillars and charming wooden panels painted in a very simple style. Attached to the large white *chedi* nearby is a small *sala*, which has a standing figure of a *dvārapāla* on each side of the entrance, and houses the fine Sukhothai-period Buddha image known as **Luang Pho Phutthamon**.

For the 82km journey to **Mae Sot**, travellers with their own transport should head south from Tak on road 1 and turn right on to road 105 c 2km after crossing the Ping River. Road 105 climbs steadily through magnificent deciduous forest scenery, and after 12km passes a turning to the left to **Lan Sang National Park**, a popular and attractive area with hiking trails and waterfalls. Simple but adequate bungalow accommodation is available near the visitor centre.

Continue along road 105, which eventually emerges from the forest to provide fine views on both sides. Just before the 26km stone, a steep lane on the right leads to the headquarters of **Taksin Maharat National Park**, where there is a huge *krabak* tree reached down a steep, slippery path. Attractive bungalow-style accommodation is available, but visitors should bring all their own provisions. There are several waterfalls in the vicinity, but they are difficult to reach.

Beyond the park entrance, road 105 descends gradually. After 3km, there is a **roadside market** where fresh produce, snacks and small souvenirs are for sale. This is a pleasant resting place and provides an opportunity to see some of the local minority peoples from surrounding villages.

Mae Sot

30km before Mae Sot, the road ascends once more, to a col between limestone cliffs where there is a shrine to the greatly revered spirit of the mountain, Pha Wo. From this point road 105 descends to Mae Sot in the valley of the Moei River, which here runs along the Thai–Burmese frontier. Mae Sot is a small but lively town, and, owing to its proximity to Burma, has sizeable populations of Burmese (ethnic Burmans and Karens). There are also numerous Chinese traders in the town, and one of Thailand's most picturesque and interesting **street markets**, where Karens, Thais, Burmans and Chinese, Christians, Buddhists and Muslims rub shoulders, and buckets of giant frogs, haunches of beef, piles of sarongs and a thousand other goods are displayed for sale. There are Burmese Muslim cafés selling delicious samosas and sweet tea, and fabric shops full of Thai, Burman and Karen materials. Mae Sot is also a centre for the gem trade, notably rubies and jade. The large Burmese population of Mae Sot accounts for the numerous *wat* in Burmese style in the town; the Karens are mostly Christian, but there are also some *wat* in Karen (Thai: *karieng*) style.

■ **Hotels and services**. Accommodation in Mae Sot ranges from the expensive, comfortable and often rather empty *Central Mae Sod Hill Hotel*, located on the town's northern bypass, to simple teak guest-houses such as the very cheap, rudimentary *Number Four Guest House* at the west end of town and the *Mae Sot Guest House and Travel Centre* also on the northern bypass. The latter can arrange tours to Umphang (see below). In between are several centrally located, medium-priced hotels, such as the *Siam* on T. Prasat Withi. **Banks**, the **post office** and most shops are along two parallel, one-way streets called T. Prasat Withi and T. Inthakhiri. The **telecoms** office (open 07.00–22.00) is c 1km west of the town centre

■ **Transport**. Frequent **bus** services operate to Tak and Sukhothai, and there is a direct overnight service to Bangkok. The main bus station is on the north side of town, but buses on certain routes depart from different locations. Ask at the hotel. **Songthaeo** depart frequently throughout the day to the Moei River border to the west of the town. A few *songthaeo* go to Umphang, c 160km south along a steep, but spectacularly beautiful route, while others run north along the border to Mae Ramat and Tha Song Yang. *THAI* operates direct **flights** to Chiang Mai (45mins) and Phitsanulok (40mins). The booking office is at 76/1 T. Prasat Withi. **Samlo** provide transport in the town; **motorcycles** can be rented from a number of shops on T. Prasat Withi, including *Tit Motor Co.* at No. 127.

A good place to start a tour of Mae Sot is the **morning market** in the lane to the west of the Siam Hotel, off T. Prasat Withi. The narrow street is crowded with women selling fresh vegetables and fruit, cuts of meat, freshly caught fish and much else. The adjacent covered municipal market sells more of the same. A short way east of the Siam Hotel, a turning to the right leads to the Nurul Islam mosque and the Burmese Muslim quarter.

From the morning market, a street leads due north directly to **Wat Don Chai** (Wat Chumphon Khiri) on T. Inthakhiri. Its tall, slender *chedi*, covered with yellow tiles and standing on a redented octagonal base, betrays Ayutthaya as well as Burmese influences.

To the west along T. Inthakhiri, at the junction with T. Prasat Withi, is **Wat Aran**, where there is a small gold-painted Burmese *chedi* on a square base in front of the *ubosot*. The niches on each side contain Burmese-style Buddha images, some in postures rarely seen in Thai Buddhist art, and the bell-shaped relic chamber is decorated with stucco dieties.

In the grounds of **Wat Thai Wattanaram**, 4km west of Mae Sot on the road to the border, is an enormous brick and cement Burmese-style reclining Buddha image, built in 1993. Along the back wall of the enclosure is a gallery filled with images of *arhats*. In a building to the right of the main courtyard there is a curious but amusing mechanical alms-giving device: while music plays, a model boat circles a small pond and deposits the donor's coins into an alms bowl held by a Buddha image. The room is usually kept locked, but the monks are willing to open it up for visitors in return for a donation of a few *baht*.

At the bridge over the Moei River, 1km further west, is a large **market**, which is very popular with Thai visitors. When relations between Thailand and Burma are peaceful, there is a steady flow of people and goods across the river to and from the Burmese border town of **Myawaddy**. Several times in the past few years, however, this stretch of the border has been the scene of shelling and incursions by Burmese soldiers. Thousands of Karens and Mons live in refugee camps just inside the Thai frontier, and occasionally these have been the target of Burmese raids. It is wise to be aware of the current situation along this border.

▶**Excursion to Umphang**

Travellers with plenty of time available can make a very pleasurable excursion to **Umphang**, 164km south along the border, where one of Thailand's loveliest **waterfalls** is located. For much of the way, the mountainous road snakes through magnificent forest scenery. At the 84km stone, very basic, limited accommodation and food and drinks are available in the Hmong settlement of **Ban Rom Kao 4**.

Umphang is a charming, friendly village with several simple guest-houses. In the surrounding hills are Hmong and Karen villages and numerous hiking trails. A rafting trip along the Mae Klong River and a visit to the magnificent **Thi Lo Su Waterfalls** are most worthwhile after the rains, from October to January. For bird-watchers and travellers seeking solitude and beautiful scenery, the forest around Umphang is a delight.◀

To Ban Tak

From Mae Sot road 105 runs north 35km to Mae Ramat, then onwards along the border to Tha Song Yang and eventually to Mae Sariang (see Rte 33). An alternative route is on road 1175, which winds east through thickly forested hills from just beyond Mae Ramat to **Ban Tak**. Shortly before this market town on the banks of the Ping River, a sign to the left indicates a track to **Chedi Yuttha Hat**, an early Sukhothai-period *chedi* in stuccoed brick standing on a square base and surmounted by a lotus-bud spire. It is thought to have been built by King Ramkhamhaeng of Sukhothai to commemorate a victory over the Burmese in which he defeated the Burmese leader in a duel on elephant-back. It was restored in 1970.

Across the road from the *chedi* is **Wat Phra Boromathat**, an important walled monastery with a fine gilded *chedi* on an octagonal base, similar to the Shwe Dagon in Rangoon, surrounded by smaller *chedi* and shrines and hung with bells that sound in the breeze. To the north of the *chedi* is an *ubosot* with beautiful carved wooden doors and gable, and a wooden *wihan* nearby, which has a fine wooden ceiling, lacquered gold and black, and the original wooden roof supports. Unfortunately, an ugly modern concrete wall has been built on the site.

Turn right at the junction beyond the *wat* and after 4km cross the bridge over the Ping River to the centre of Ban Tak. From here, visitors can travel south back to Tak or north towards Lampang (see Rte 23).

21 · Sukhothai to Phitsanulok and Phichit

Roads *12, 117 and 115, 123km. To Phitsanulok 59km; Phitsanulok to Phichit 64km.*

Railway. *Frequent trains cover the 42km from Phitsanulok to Phichit in 45 mins. There are no trains from Sukhothai.*

Phitsanulok

Road 12 runs east from Sukhothai through a flat and monotonous landscape of rice fields to Phitsanulok (pop. 80,000), which is on the banks of the Nan River.

To reach the city follow road 12 through the old ramparts to the bridge over the river. A turning to the left along T. Theparuk, c 200m before the bridge, leads in 400m to the recently renovated ruins of **Wat Wihan Thong**, which once housed a bronze Sukhothai-style standing image of the Eighteen-Cubit Buddha, Phra Attharot. Rama III took this image to Bangkok, where it is now in Wat Saket (see p 135). The town centre lies to the right on the east bank, along which are moored many houseboats and floating restaurants.

History

From at least the 12C Phitsanulok was an important provincial centre of the Khmer empire of Angkor. The Khmers were succeeded in the area in the 13C by the Thais, and Phitsanulok became a provincial capital of the Sukhothai kingdom. It was captured by Borommaratcha I of Ayutthaya in the 1370s and thereafter became the centre of one of the core provinces of the kingdom. From 1463 King Borommatrailokanat (Trailok) used it as his capital in order better to conduct his military campaigns in the north, and he died here in 1488. After Trailok's death it retained its importance, and more than one king of Ayutthaya appointed his heir as governor of Phitsanulok. The Burmese conquered the city in 1765 and after their invasion and sack of Ayutthaya in 1767, Phitsanulok briefly became an independent state, before being reconquered in 1770 by King Taksin and incorporated into the new Siamese kingdom. In 1955 most of the city was destroyed by fire and today it is sadly lacking in buildings of any architectural merit other than its principal monument, Wat Phra Si Ratana Mahathat, which was unscathed in the fire.

■ **Information**. The TAT office is at Surasi Trade Center, 209/7–8 T. Borommatrailokanat.

■ **Hotels and services**. There are several good **hotels**, including the *Phitsanulok Thani Hotel* at 39 T. Sanambin, which opened in 1996 and is probably the best hotel in town. Others include the *Amarin Nakhon* at 3/1 T. Chao Phraya and the *Pailyn (Phailin) Hotel* at 38 T. Borommatrailokanat. A less expensive alternative is the *Inthra Hotel* at 103/8 T. Sithama Traipidok. Best of the cheap lodgings is *Phitsanulok Youth Hostel*, at 38 T. Sanambin. The adjoining restaurant is very popular with locals. Other excellent restaurants include the *Phun Si* on T. Phaya Lithai, the *Song Anong* on T. Sanambin, and the *Pastime Riverside* at 66 T. Phuttha Bucha. The *Bangkok Bank* and other **banks** are on T. Naresuan. The **post office** is beside the river and next door to the international **telecoms office**.

■ **Transport**. Regular **bus services** run north to Uttaradit, Phrae, Lampang etc, east to Lom Sak, Khon Kaen, Loei etc, and to Sukhothai, Phichit and Bangkok. The **railway station** is on T. Ekathotsarot. Several trains run daily north to Uttaradit, Lampang and Chiang Mai, and south to Phichit, Lop Buri, Bangkok etc. *THAI* has several **flights** daily to Bangkok and less frequent services to Lampang, Chiang Mai, Mae Sot and Nan. The booking office is at 209/26–8 T. Borommatrailokanat, near the TAT office. **Samlo** and **city buses** are readily available for transport in the town.

To reach **WAT PHRA SI RATANA MAHATHAT** turn left off road 12 immediately after crossing the bridge over the Nan River. The monastery is situated near the east bank of the river a few metres from the bridge. In the centre of the complex is a great Khmer-style tower-sanctuary or *prang* 36m high. The antefixes of this *prang* are covered with golden mosaic tiles and at the top is a metal finial with six prongs representing the *vajra* of Indra. The *prang*, which stands on a redented square base containing the relic chamber, is thought to be one of the earliest examples in Thailand of this architectural form derived from the Khmer *prasat* or tower-sanctuary representing the sacred mountain, Mount Meru. One of the lintels, which was taken from a nearby shrine, is in fact Khmer work of the late 11C or early 12C, but the rest of the *prang* is late 13C or early 14C. It is surrounded by a gallery on all four sides containing a miscellaneous collection of Buddha images, temple furniture, ceramics and other objects. The *prang* is somewhat obscured by the gallery and the other ancillary buildings surrounding it, and it is therefore best viewed from the open space outside the temple enclosure to the north, where the ruins of the *wihan* of an earlier temple complex with laterite columns and a heavily restored standing Buddha image can be seen.

The principal *wihan*, which was rebuilt in its present form in the mid-18C by King Borommakot of Ayutthaya, has a low-sweeping triple-tiered roof and a deep porch supported on tall columns painted white and gold. On either side is a gallery containing rows of seated Buddha images in the Sukhothai and Lan Na styles. The magnificent late 18C double doors leading into the *wihan* are of ebony inlaid with mother-of-pearl. Inside is one of the most celebrated and revered Buddha images in Thailand, known as **Phra Phuttha Chinarat**, a gilded bronze statue c 3m high of the Buddha in *bhūmisparśa mudrā* seated on a round lotus base. It was probably cast in the 1420s for the last king of Sukhothai, Mahathammaratcha IV. Numerous copies have been made of it, of which the best known is in Wat Benchamabophit in Bangkok. It has several stylistic features that are absent from Buddha images of the early Sukhothai period and therefore indicate that it belongs to the later period, notably the serene and remote expression of the rather broad face, the relatively slight arch of the eyebrows and the equal length of the four fingers. On either side is a figure of a praying disciple. The image is framed in a superb decorative aureole of gilded wood, in which flame and lotus motifs predominate, and is set against a blue-black background ornamented with gold painted fleurettes and two figures of celestial beings. According to local tradition, Phra Phuttha Chinarat wept when the troops of Ayutthaya entered Phitsanulok in 1438. The columns supporting the roof are painted black and gold and have gilded lotus capitals, and the west wall is decorated with paintings illustrating the Life of the Buddha.

Phra Phuttha Chinarat in Wat Phra Si Ratana Mahathat, Phitsanulok

Wat Ratchaburana, on the south side of road 12 opposite Wat Phra Si Ratana Mahathat, is another of the small number of old temples in Phitsanulok to have survived the fire of 1955. The *ubosot*, which is next to the road, is notable for its double *bai sema*, its finely carved doors and its wall paintings, which date from the reign of Rama III and illustrate episodes from the *Ramakien*, the Thai version of the *Rāmāyaṇa*. The other buildings in the complex are modern.

A little to the north of Wat Phra Si Ratana Mahathat, T. Phaya Sua turns right off T. Ekathotsarot and leads across the railway line to **Wat Chedi Yot Thong**, which has a fine 15C brick *chedi* on a square base. It has niches at the four cardinal points containing badly damaged stucco standing or walking Buddha images. The road continues a little further east to the enclosure of **Wat Aranyik**, of which only the central section of a brick *chedi* in Sri Lankan style on a square base still remains.

To reach **Wat Chulamani** leave Phitsanulok on road 1063 (T. Borommatrailokanat) running south towards Bang Krathum. 1300m south of the junction with road 1058, and 5km south of the town centre, Wat Chulamani can be seen on the right. This important *wat* was probably restored and embellished by King Trailok when his capital was at Phitsanulok. It has a laterite *prang* in Khmer style standing on a square base. The lintels over the main entrance, which has a porch, and over the two side entrances have retained some of their exquisite original stucco decoration. Round the base of the walls of the *prang* is a stucco frieze composed of running *haṁsas* and floral motifs. This stucco work probably belongs to the early Ayutthaya period.

Also well worth a visit is the **Sergeant-Major Thawee Folk Museum** on T. Wisut Kaset (open Tues–Sun 08.30–16.30), which contains a large and fascinating collection of rural craft work, including animal traps, farming implements, traditional games and wooden bells. Many of the rarer tools used in rural daily life are a real delight. Across the street is an interesting bronze Buddha image foundry, owned by the same family that owns the museum.

There are two main routes between Phitsanulok and Phichit. The first is by road 12 from Phitsanulok 18km to Wang Thong, where a turning to the right on road 11 leads after 38km to Ban Sak Lek. Here another turning to the right on to road 111 leads after 18km to Phichit. The other route, which is slightly shorter, leaves Phitsanulok by road 12, heading west over the Nan River before turning south on road 117 towards Kamphaeng Phet. After 38km, a left turn on to road 115 leads after a further 24km to Phichit.

The small town of **Phichit**, capital of a province, is situated on the bank of the Nan River. A popular **boat race** is held here every September. The town contains no important monuments or works of art except for a notable Lan Na Buddha image known as Luang Pho Phet in the *ubosot* of **Wat Tha Luang** situated beside the river. However, there are several sites in the neighbourhood worth visiting, of which Wat Rong Chang and Wat Pho Prathap Chang are the most remarkable.

To reach **Wat Rong Chang** go out of Phichit to the west on road 115 and after 3km turn left on to road 1068 towards Ban Wang Chik. Wat Rong Chang is clearly visible from the road on the left side after c 5km. It has a beautiful *ubosot* with a triple-tiered roof and painted stucco decoration round the windows. It stands in a garden full of statues, including numerous Buddha images and a life-size figure of an elephant. There is also a curious painted *chedi* with a covered gallery round its base containing numerous inscribed votive tablets, some set into the walls of the *chedi* and others stacked in groups of 48 to form a cube, each cube standing on four short legs and surmounted by a crude miniature *chedi* with four pediments and painted red or blue.

A gateway on the left of the road c 1km beyond Wat Rong Chang marks the entrance to an avenue which leads through a wood to the site of the ancient city of **Muang Kao Phichit**. This site contains the ruins of a number of buildings of the late Sukhothai and early Ayutthaya period standing among the trees. The most complete of these is **Wat Mahathat**, which has a fine Sri Lankan-style bell-shaped brick *chedi* on a square base, and a *wihan* and *ubosot*, of which only the foundations remain. Nearby is a small tank full of young crocodiles. There is also an inexpertly restored *lak muang* in a *sala*.

To reach **Wat Pho Prathap Chang**, continue c 8km south on road 1068 and just before the village of Ban Wang Chik turn left and go 7km towards the village of Pho Prathap Chang. 1km before the village turn left again on to road 1300 and go a further 4km to reach the temple, which is on the left of the road. This magnificent ruined *wat* was built between 1699 and 1701 by King Phra Phetratcha of Ayutthaya for his son and successor Suriyentharathibodi (Sua), who was born here. It is entirely built of brick and is picturesquely situated in a walled enclosure, round which are numerous fine old trees. In front of the principal entrance is a large Ayutthaya-period seated Buddha image incongruously housed in a wooden shed painted blue. The temple has an exceptionally large *ubosot*, now roofless, with redented square columns standing on a brick platform, 14 window embrasures, on some of which traces of stucco decoration still remain, and doors with finely decorated porches and redented jambs. The *bai sema* surrounding it are still in situ. There are also several subsidiary *chedi* and the ruins of other monastic buildings in the temple complex.

▶Road 1300 continues east to join road 113, where a left turn leads south towards Taphan Hin. The road soon passes a hill called **Khao Rup Chang**, on the slopes of which is a temple with a stuccoed brick *chedi* where an important festival takes place in March each year. 28km from Phichit, a little to the east of Taphan Hin, is **Wat Thewa Prasat**, which contains in the grounds an enormous seated Buddha image, clearly visible from the road, known as Phra Phuttha Ket Mongkon.

23km further south, a turning to the right at Ban Mun Nak on to road 1067 leads after 18km to the village of **Pho Thale** on the bank of the Yom River. A small road running south of Pho Thale leads after 8km to **Wat Bang Khlan**, where there is a small museum of Sawankhalok and *bencharong* ceramics (open daily, 09.00–12.00, 13.00–16.00), assembled by an abbot of the *wat*.◀

▶Road 111 to the east out of Phichit crosses road 11 at Ban Sak Lek and becomes road 1115, which ends after 26km at the village of Ban Mung on the western boundary of Thung Salaeng Luang National Park (see p 318). Near here is a limestone outcrop called **Khao Pha Thaphon**, where there are numerous caves with impressive formations of stalactites and stalagmites. To view these caves a powerful torch is necessary.◀

THE NORTHERN HIGHLANDS

22 · Phitsanulok to Uttaradit and Phrae

Roads 11 and 101, 192km. To Uttaradit 118km; from Uttaradit to Phrae 74km.

Railway, 96km in 1hr (express) from Phitsanulok to Uttaradit. No rail service to Phrae; nearest station is Den Chai, c 1hr from Uttaradit.

From Phitsanulok take road 12 c 6km east and turn north on road 11 towards Uttaradit. The country is flat and the route fast. After 76km road 1246 goes off to the right and leads to the remote and rarely visited **Chat Trakan National Park**, which has outstanding waterfalls and beautiful mountain scenery.

The centre of **UTTARADIT** (pop. 32,000), on the west bank of the Nan River, was almost completely razed by fire in 1967 and it is now a town singularly lacking in buildings of any architectural merit, consisting chiefly of rectangular blocks of unimaginative and strictly functional concrete shop-houses. However, it provides a convenient base from which to explore the magnificent countryside to the east. The construction of the Sirikit Dam and Reservoir 60km northeast of Uttaradit has greatly increased the agricultural production of the area and brought considerable prosperity to the town.

■ **Hotels and services**. The *Siharat* at 163 T. Boromat is probably the town's best hotel, but it cannot be recommended with any confidence. Good value is the cheaper *Pho Wanit 2* at 1-3 T. Si Utra, near the river. **Banks** and the **post office** are in the central market district.

■ **Transport**. Regular **bus** services run north to Phrae, Nan, Lampang and Chiang Mai, and south to Sukhothai, Phitsanulok and Bangkok. The main bus station is on the south side of the town. **Songthaeo** to the Sirikit Dam leave from the esplanade on the west bank of the Nan River. **Train** services to Chiang Mai and Bangkok run from the railway station on T. Samran Ruen.

Near the railway station is **Wat Tha Thanon**, which houses a greatly revered early Lan Na-style Buddha image, Luang Pho Phet. Upstairs in the *wihan* of **Wat Thammathipatai**, just north of the town centre on T. Samran Ruen, is a pair of immense and beautifully **carved wooden doors** taken from the ruins of Wat Phra Fang outside the town. These doors, decorated with intricate floral motifs and inlaid with glass, are among the finest surviving examples of Ayutthaya-period woodcarving.

Wat Phra Fang itself lies 11km along road 1213 to the east of the town. To get there, return to road 11, and where it crosses the Nan River, turn east to follow the river's south bank upstream to the village of Ban Phra Fang. The ruins of this *wat* lie in a delightful spot shaded with great trees. The huge **Wihan Luang**, from which the doors at Wat Thammathipatai were taken, dates from the late Ayutthaya period and is being gradually restored as funds become available. To

Wat Phra Yun Phutthabat Yukhon, near Uttaradit

the west is a weed-covered *chedi*, restored during the reign of King Mongkut, but still displaying early Ayutthaya-period characteristics. Beyond lies a charming Sukhothai-period *ubosot* with a magnificent coffered wood ceiling. It was completely restored in the Ayutthaya period, perhaps in the reign of King Narai, when the fine stucco decoration round the windows was probably added.

▶To Nam Pat and Fak Tha

Travellers with a serious interest in **textiles** should make an excursion to Nam Pat and Fak Tha districts in the remote hills to the northeast of Uttaradit, where there are Lao (Thai Phuan) communities with a well deserved reputation as silk and cotton weavers. Also in this region stands what is claimed to be the world's largest **teak tree**. Teak trees do not grow to be as large as the great sequoias of California, but this 1500 year-old tree was once 47m high with a girth of 10m. It lost 10m of its height in a storm in 1977. To find it, take road 1045 northeast from Uttaradit, past the Sirikit Dam to the junction with road 1047. Turn left on to road 1047 to Nam Pat and Fak Tha, and, just beyond the 57km stone, a track to the right leads to the teak tree. ◀

▶A more accessible weaving centre is **Lap Lae**, 8km northwest of Uttaradit on road 1041, where small communities of Thai Phuan have settled in some of the surrounding villages. ◀

▶To the southwest of Uttaradit, c 4km along road 102 towards Si Satchanalai (see Rte 19) is **Wat Phra Boromathat Thung Yang**. This *wat* has a remarkable *wihan* with a triple roof in Lao style sweeping down almost to the ground and porches at either end with exceptionally fine wooden gables painted gold and inlaid with blue glass mosaics. It has been restored several times, most recently in 1984. The principal *chedi* dates from the Sukhothai period and was restored in the Ayutthaya period. It is in Sri Lankan style, hemispherical in form, with a lotus ornament in stucco round the foot, and stands on a redented square base with a miniature *chedi* at each corner. Nearby are the sites of the ancient cities of Wiang Chao Ngo and Muang Thung Yang Kao, of which nothing remains except some vestiges of dikes and ramparts.

1km further west are **Wat Phra Yeun Phutthabat Yukhon** and **Wat Phra Taen Sila** At, two *wat* on the left-hand side on top of a small hill. The former contains an unusual *mondop* with a multi-tiered roof and peristyle. The latter, a popular pilgrimage site, houses a stone Footprint of the Buddha.◄

Phrae

From Uttaradit go north on road 11 towards Den Chai. After c 25km the road climbs up to a pass which marks the border between the provinces of Uttaradit and Phrae and from where there are excellent views to the right. The road descends on the north side and after 20km reaches the junction with road 101. Phrae lies to the right, Lampang (see Rte 23) to the left.

A brief stop can be made on the Phrae road in Sung Men, where a lane to the left, 750m north of the 124km stone, leads to **Wat Phra Luang**, rebuilt in the late 18C after three centuries of neglect. As well as a dramatically leaning *chedi* tucked away behind the main *wihan*, this *wat* has a beautiful little library on the right, with a pair of picturesquely dilapidated porches over the steps.

The old town of **PHRAE** (pop. 24,000) lies 72km north of Uttaradit, on the east bank of the Yom River. It was formerly part of the Mon kingdom of Haripunjaya and its ancient town wall has been preserved largely intact. In more recent times it has become an important centre for timber, especially teak. The older part of the town, which still has many traditional teak houses, is bounded by ancient earth ramparts and a water-filled moat. Recent expansion has been to the north and east, where the commercial district is now located. Several *wat* show clear signs of Burmese influence, which is partly the result of the sizeable population of Burmese who have been settled in Phrae since the late 19C, when they were attracted here by the lucrative timber industry.

■ **Hotels and services**. The *Mae Yom Palace* and the *Pharadon Hotel*, both on T. Yantarakit Koson, are two of the best hotels in Phrae. A comfortable alternative is the *Nakhon Phrae* on T. Ratchadamnoen nearer the old ramparts. There are cheaper hotels near the junction of T. Charoen Muang and T. Yantarakit Koson. The **banks** are on T. Charoen Muang and the **post office** is opposite Wat Phra Bat Ming Muang in the centre of the old town.

■ **Transport**. The main **bus station** lies off T. Yantarakit Koson near the Mae Yom Palace Hotel. There are daily buses to Bangkok and frequent services to Nan, Uttaradit, Lampang and Chiang Mai. The nearest **railway station** is in Den Chai (c 20km). *THAI* has daily **flights** from Phrae to Bangkok (1hr 20mins) and Nan (30mins). The booking office is at 42 T. Ratchadamnoen. **Samlo** operate in the town.

A good place to start a tour of Phrae is **Wat Chom Sawan**, a delightful Burmese-style *wat* on the northern edge of the town, built in the early years of the 20C with money provided by local Burmese timber traders. Two flights of steps covered with a tall five-tiered roof lead up to the *wihan*, which is divided into two main rooms. The first has a magnificent **coffered wooden ceiling** decorated with coloured glass inlay and stucco. Gilded wooden pillars support

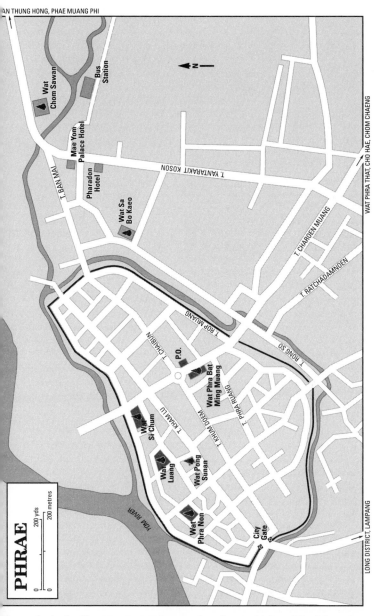

the roof, which still retains many of its wooden tiles. To the front left of the *wihan* is a stuccoed brick *chedi* with four niches containing standing Buddha images and surrounded by smaller *chedi*.

Wat Sa Bo Kaeo, a Burmese-style wat at Phrae

Most of Phrae's other important buildings lie within the ramparts of the old town, which can be approached from Wat Chom Sawan along T. Ban Mai. Just before crossing the old moat, turn left to **Wat Sa Bo Kaeo**. This Burmese-style *wat* has a large white principal *chedi* and numerous minor *chedi*, all with elaborate stucco decorations, and a *mondop* in the form of a stepped pyramid with four storeys, each surrounded by a gallery with intricate *kranok* ornamentation. Back on T. Ban Mai, go through the old gateway on the northeastern side of the ramparts and continue past the prison to the roundabout at the centre of the old town. Along the quiet, narrow lanes within the ramparts are many beautiful teak houses, both old and new.

At the roundabout turn right to reach **Wat Si Chum**, where a large square-based 16C brick *chedi*, somewhat overgrown, stands behind a row of three *wihan*. The left-hand *wihan* houses a notable standing image of the Buddha, his hands held close to his sides in the local Phrae style. Behind this *wihan* is a small *ho trai*, its exterior walls decorated with faded murals. The central *wihan*, which is approached by three staircases, contains a seated Buddha image similar to the famous statue known as Phra Phuttha Chinarat in Wat Phra Si Ratana Mahathat in Phitsanulok (see p 250). The right-hand *wihan* is used as living quarters for the monks.

Turn left beside Wat Si Chum to the gateway of **WAT LUANG**. The original porch of the *wihan* of this *wat*, which dates from 1514, has been closed up with laterite blocks and the recently made wooden doors are beautifully carved with animals, birds and plants. Inside is a greatly revered seated Buddha image in *bhūmisparśa mudrā*, called **Phra Chao Saen Luang**. Behind the *wihan* is a fine early Lan Na-style *chedi*, Phra That Luang Chai Chang Kham, which has an octagonal base with four niches containing standing Buddha images and four foreparts of elephants. Four parasols of gilded bronze stand at the corners of the terrace on which the *chedi* and its base stand. In the *wat* enclosure is a **museum**, housed in several buildings, that contains a collection of religious and historical artefacts. A restored *ho trai* with a wooden-tiled roof houses a small collection of cooking utensils and basketry, while next to the main museum building is an old wooden house where the first ruler of Phrae is said to have lived.

From the back gate of Wat Luang, turn left along Soi Kham Lu 1, passing **Wat Pong Sunan**, which has a beautiful carved wooden gable. Turn left on to T. Kham Lu and then left again to **Wat Phra Non**. The Lao-style *ubosot* here also has a superbly **carved wooden gable** and porch painted red and gold, with prominent *hang hong* and *bai raka* decorations. Beside the *ubosot* is an old library with wooden shutters painted black and gold. To the left of the *ubosot* is a *wihan* housing an 18C reclining image of the Buddha, restored in 1980, from which the *wat* takes its name.

A short way beyond the old city's southwest gate, signed to the right, is **Ban Pratap Chai**, a huge house built of golden teak, which is open to the public.

At the junction of T. Rop Muang and T. Charoen Muang beside the municipal market, a lively night market operates from early evening till after dark, offering a wide range of cooked dishes.

▶To Wat Phra That Cho Hae

An easy excursion from Phrae can be made to **Wat Phra That Cho Hae** by taking road 1022 to the east. This *wat* is located in a grove of teak trees on a low hill 9km from the town and is approached by flights of steps. In a shrine outside the covered gallery surrounding the *wat* is a seated Buddha image, the much revered **Phra Chao Than Chai**, which is reputed to induce fertility in women. Inside the enclosure is a 33m-high octagonal *chedi* clad in gilded copper plates. It is said to contain a hair of the Buddha, traditionally believed to have been brought here by the first Buddhist missionaries sent from India to Southeast Asia in the 3C BC by the great Maurya emperor, Ashoka. The *chedi* was enlarged and the adjacent *wihan* rebuilt in 1924 by Phra Khru Ba Siwichai. The *wihan* is garishly decorated inside with neon lights and coloured glass mosaic, but despite this retains a certain attraction. During the fourth lunar month (usually March or April) a festival is held at the *wat* in the course of which the local population wrap the *chedi* in the yellow satin cloth called *cho hae* after which the *wat* is named.

In front of Wat Phra That Cho Hae, near a small zoo, a road to the right leads after 2km to **Wat Phra That Chom Chaeng**, which has an octagonal *chedi* similar to that at Wat Phra That Cho Hae, and is thought to be the oldest monastery in Phrae. Beside the *chedi* is a tall Burmese-style standing Buddha image of little merit. The *wat* was extensively restored in 1992. On the western side of the enclosure is a small museum containing old wooden buffalo carts, looms, bells etc.◀

▶To Phae Muang Phi Forest Park and Mae Yom National Park

Another excursion from Phrae can be made by going north on road 101 beyond Wat Chom Sawan, passing through the village of Thung Hong, where the traditional indigo-dyed Thai peasant shirts are made. A turning to the right 10km north of Phrae leads to a forest park called **Phae Muang Phi** ('City of Ghosts'), where sandstone outcrops have been weathered into strange shapes.

Further north, a turning to the left on to road 103 at the intersection in Ban Rong Khem leads to **Mae Yom National Park**, which has one of the few remaining mature **teak forests** in Thailand and offers some attractive walks. To reach the park centre, turn right on to road 1154 c 14km after joining road 103, and continue beyond the small town of **Song**, from where the park is signed. A full day is needed for this trip to make it worthwhile, and the park is difficult to reach by public transport.◀

From Phrae, travellers can continue c 120km north on road 101 to Nan (see Rte 31). This route passes through beautiful forested hills as it crosses the watershed between the Yom and Nan river valleys, before descending to the Nan valley floor.

23 · Phrae to Lampang

Roads *1023 and 11, 90km.*

Railway, *108km in 2hrs 10mins (express) from Den Chai to Lampang.*

Travellers with their own transport are recommended to leave Phrae on road 1023, a pleasant minor road which climbs out of the town through teak plantations before descending to the rice fields in the plain beyond. A turning to the right shortly before the 41km stone leads through a village and after c 2km reaches **Wat Salaeng**, located on the edge of rice fields. A beautiful open-sided wooden *wihan*, typical of the Lan Na architecture which is slowly disappearing throughout the north, has been preserved by the conscientious abbot. Behind it stands a brick *chedi*, **Phra That Kha-um Kham,** of uncertain date, which is traditionally believed to contain a relic of the Buddha brought here by Phra Nang Cham Thewi, daughter of the Mon ruler of Lop Buri while on her way to found the kingdom of Haripunjaya at Lamphun in the 7C. There is an elegant modern *ubosot* on the right side of the compound, its interior simply but meticulously decorated with delicate lacquer work. Behind a large modern *wihan* at the centre of the compound, is a *kuti* containing a number of artefacts found within the *wat* enclosure, including prehistoric stone beads and axe heads, textiles, old Lan Na manuscripts and several stone Buddha images and fragments. Especially notable are two magnificent Footprints of the Buddha, made from wood inlaid with intricately etched glass, brought from Burma in 1991.

In **Long** district, in which Wat Salaeng lies, are several villages populated by **Thai Yuan**, who are renowned for their hand-loom weaving skills. Beautiful *phasin* can be seen in several of these villages.

From Wat Salaeng, continue for 14km along road 1023 to the intersection with road 11. Lampang lies 48km to the right, but a brief **detour** straight ahead leads after 15km to **Wiang Kosai National Park**. On the way, c 8km beyond the intersection, the road passes the rather neglected **Wat Chayasit**, which has amusing *khan tuai* supporting the roof in the form of human figures and carved in a rustic style. Within the park, which is mountainous and thickly wooded, are attractive waterfalls and hot springs.

Back at the intersection, road 11 snakes to the northwest through forested hills before finally descending to the Wang River valley and the prosperous town of Lampang.

Lampang

Lampang (pop. 52,000) can be roughly divided into two sections: a peaceful residential neighbourhood of winding narrow lanes to the north of the river, and a bustling commercial district on the south bank. Within the town are numerous excellent examples of Burmese temple architecture, streets of old Chinese shop-

houses and warehouses, remains of ancient fortifications, beautiful teak houses
in large gardens and fine river scenery. Nearby is the district of **Ko Kha**, which
has some magnificent Lan Na-style *wat*.

■ **Hotels and services**. Lampang has several good hotels, including the
comfortable *Thipchang Lampang Hotel* on T. Takhrao Noi and the more luxurious, but rather inconveniently located *Lampang Wiengthong Hotel* off T.
Phahonyothin. Other, cheaper hotels are more centrally located along T.
Boonyawat, including the *Asia Lampang* and the *Si Sanga*, both recommended
for visitors on a small budget. **Banks** can be found throughout the commercial district. The **post office** is on T. Thip Chang near Ratchada Phisek Bridge.
The delightful *Riverside Restaurant* is highly recommended for its ambience , its
eclectic decor and excellent food, although in the evenings it can be very busy.

■ **Bus services**. The bus station is on the southwest side of the town, off the
main highway. There are frequent services to Chiang Mai, Phrae and other
northern towns, and more than a dozen buses depart for Bangkok daily,
including several overnight services.

■ The **railway station** on T. Prasan Maitri lies on the main line between
Bangkok (c 10hrs) and Chiang Mai (c 2hrs).

■ There are daily **flights** by *THAI* to Bangkok (2hrs) via Phitsanulok (35mins).
The booking office is at 314 T. Sanambin.

■ **Samlo** and the **pony carts** characteristic of Lampang are the best means of
transport within the town; carriage rides are most agreeable in the evening
when the streets are quieter and the air is cooler.

History
Lampang was originally part of the Mon kingdom of Haripunjaya, founded
at Lamphun in the late 8C or early 9C (see p 297), and was called Muang
Khalang Nakhon. In the 11C it was brought under the control of the
Khmers of Angkor. From the 13C it formed part of the Lan Na kingdom,
which fell under Burmese suzerainty in the second half of the 16C.
Burmese influence remains strong to this day. Lampang has long been a
centre of trade in various commodities, notably teak, tobacco, textiles and
opium. Its commercial importance was greatly enhanced by the extension
of the northern railway line from Bangkok between Den Chai and Lampang
in 1916. Its present prosperity is based chiefly on the production of rice,
maize and cotton in the fertile plain of the Wang River.

A good place to start a tour of Lampang is on the north side of the river at **WAT
PHRA KAEO DON TAO** and its neighbour **WAT SUCHADARAM**, two of
Lampang's most important *wat*. For 32 years (1436–68) the former housed the
image of the Emerald Buddha, Phra Kaeo Morokot or Phra Ratana Phimpha,
now kept at Wat Phra Kaeo in Bangkok (see p 117). Within the compound,
which is entered from T. Phra Kaeo, **Wat Phra Kaeo Don Tao** lies up a few steps
to the left, while the elegant buildings of Wat Suchadaram are to the right. At
the foot of the steps is a shrine to Chao Mae Suchada, a woman in a local legend
according to which about the year 500, when a famine struck Lampang, a monk
came down from heaven to be reborn in human form. Chao Mae Suchada

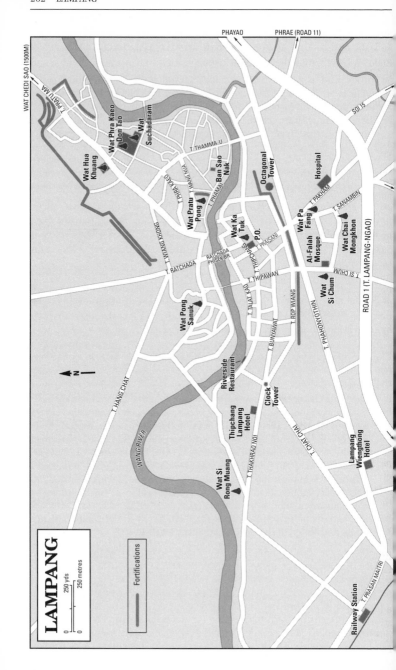

offered him a water-melon, in which, when he cut it open, he found a huge emerald. Together they then tried to fashion the emerald into an image of the Buddha. This they finally succeeded in doing with the help of the god Indra, and the monastery in which the monk lived thus acquired the name Wat Phra Kaeo. However, the story does not end happily. The king accused Suchada and the monk of sexual misbehaviour; Suchada was put to death, the monk fled, and a second famine struck Lampang.

Dominating Wat Phra Kaeo Don Tao is a magnificent **mondop** in the style of a Burmese *pyathat*, with its characteristic multi-tiered roof, and behind it the 50m high **Phra Boromathat Chedi**, its round relic chamber sheathed in very thin gilded copper sheets and standing on a square base. The *mondop* was built in 1909 by the governor of Lampang, Bunwat Wongmanit, and his wife, probably using Burmese immigrant labourers who were working for British teak companies in Lampang. It has an elaborately coffered wooden ceiling ornamented with mother-of-pearl, coloured glass and enamel inlay and small figures in high relief. On the ceiling of the porch is a relief, perhaps depicting Sut Sakhon, a character from Central Thai literature, riding a *makara*. On the main ceiling is the figure of a young boy, perhaps representing Cupid, and, if so, reflecting the spread of European influence through the British in Burma, which had already by 1909 been a British possession for 50 years. British influence can also be seen in the intricate fretwork borders around the porch. Against the northern wall of the *mondop* is a Burmese seated bronze Buddha image, flanked by smaller images also Burmese in style.

The *chedi* is all that remains of the original 14C–15C *wat*, although even this has been renovated several times. To the left is a small *wihan*, **Wihan Phra Non**, housing an unremarkable reclining image of the Buddha made in 1926. To the right is the main *wihan* (**Wihan Luang**), built in 1924, which houses the *wat's* principal image, cast in 1957. Behind that is another smaller, sadly neglected *wihan*.

On the south side of Wihan Luang is an open-sided *sala* housing some Burmese drums—a heavy wooden *klong yao* on a wagon and several *klong bucha* —and some lacquered manuscript cabinets. Other artefacts, including some fine pieces of woodcarving, can be seen in a small museum in the southwest corner of the compound.

Wat Suchadaram on the south side of the central parking area was built in the late 18C by migrants from Chiang Saen. It comprises two Lan Na-style *wihan*, with tiered roofs sweeping almost to the ground, and a finely carved wooden gable. The columns on either side of the entrance are surmounted by figures of lions, and the *khan tuai* supporting the roof are of unusual intricacy. Inside is a large seated Buddha image in stuccoed brick, heavily restored, in the Lan Na style. The *chedi* of Wat Suchadaram is similar in form to that of Wat Phra Kaeo.

On the other side of T. Phra Kaeo, opposite the entrance to Wat Phra Kaeo, is a lane leading after 130m to **Wat Hua Khuang**, which has another Lan Na-style *wihan*, with a wooden gable painted red, built by the same group of migrants from Chiang Saen who built Wat Suchadaram. Inside are some fine Lan Na Buddha images.

Turn northeast from Wat Hua Kuang along T. Wiang Khong to the old city ramparts and pass through the former **Pratu Ma** ('Horse Gate'), part of which has been very crudely and carelessly rebuilt in recent years. Continue for c 1500m to a turning to the left signed to **Wat Chedi Sao**, so named after the 20 whitewashed *chedi* in the enclosure. Of little artistic interest, the modern buildings do, however, house a number of well crafted Buddha images and a small museum containing musical instruments, stuffed animals, votive tablets and weapons, and some ceramics from a late 14C or early 15C kiln site a short distance northwest of the *wat*. Here also is a small golden image of the Buddha behind an iron grille, which was discovered—and decapitated—by a farmer ploughing a rice field nearby.

Return to the Pratu Ma, where a lane to the left just inside the gateway follows the ramparts past other ancient gateways to emerge once more near Wat Phra Kaeo Don Tao. To the southeast of Wat Phra Kaeo Don Tao, a maze of narrow lanes leads down to the river. Here there are numerous beautiful **teak houses** hidden away in unkempt gardens. A wander here is most rewarding in the cool of the morning. On T. Ratwattana is the lovely teak house of *Ban Sao Nak*, ('House of Many Pillars'), so called because it stands on 116 teak pillars. Built in 1895 in a blend of Burmese and Lan Na styles, it was restored by its owner in 1964 and is now occasionally open to the public. It contains collections of ceramics, silverware and traditional agricultural and cooking utensils.

On the north side of T. Wang Nua the **old entrance gate** of a now ruined *wat*, c 200m from the junction with T. Thamma-u, displays intricate stucco work dating from the late 15C or early 16C. Continue from here towards T. Ratchada, past the rear entrance to Wat Pratu Pong. A section of the old city wall runs on a north–south axis beside this *wat*, between T. Wang Nua and T. Phamai.

Continue a short distance west from T. Ratchada to **WAT PONG SANUK TAI**. Raised on a man-made, brick-lined mound representing Mount Meru, is the open-sided *mondop* of Wat Pong Sanuk Tai, which is unusual in being approached by flights of steps on all four sides. The main staircase, on the southeast side, climbs up to an arched gatehouse decorated with stucco. To the left of the *mondop* is a Lan Na *chedi* sheathed in thin copper plates. Inside the *mondop* behind an iron grille are four seated Buddha images facing the four directions and with their backs to a painted metal model of a *bodhi* tree. The beautifully decorated gables on the false upper storeys and the multi-tiered roof of the *mondop* make this one of Lampang's most charming *wat*, a characteristic Lampang blend of Thai and Burmese styles. Also noteworthy are the elaborate decorations on the roof ridge of the *wihan* behind the *mondop*, where there is a reclining Buddha image, 11m in length.

Return to Ratchada Phisek Bridge and cross to the commercial district on the south side of the Wang River. Directly opposite the bridge, at the junction with T. Thip Chang, stands **Wat Ka Tuk**, where an open-sided wooden *wihan* in the Lan Na style lies somewhat hidden behind another *wihan* of more recent date.

In the heart of this quarter, in front of the government offices on T. Praisani, is a small *sala* containing the *lak muang* of the town in the form of three tall gold-painted posts.

Running west along the south bank from T. Ratchada is **T. Talat Kao** ('Street of the Old Market') in the 19C commercial heart of Lampang, where there are a number of fine old **wooden shop-houses and warehouses** which have escaped the modernisation of the rest of the quarter and have retained their ornate gingerbread woodcarving. These houses give an idea of how the town looked in the late 19C and early 20C, with its mixture of European, Burmese and Chinese architectural styles.

On the west side of the town, beyond the Thipchang Lampang Hotel on T. Takhrao Noi, is **Wat Si Rong Muang**, a Burmese *wat* painted yellow and red, which has a magnificent *wihan* with wooden columns and a ceiling decorated with gilded stucco and coloured glass inlay. It contains some fine wooden furniture and several notable Buddha images, one of them in an intricately decorated *ku*.

From T. Talat Kao turn south along T. Thipawan, at the northern end of which are more old wooden buildings. Continue south across the parallel streets of T. Thip Chang and T. Boonyawat, which today form the busy centre of Lampang's market district, and cross T. Rop Wiang, at the east end of which is an **octagonal tower** that once formed part of the town's fortified wall, to reach the sad remains of **WAT SI CHUM**, most of which was tragically razed by fire in January 1992. Once one of Thailand's finest examples of Burmese temple architecture, little remains of the *wihan* except blackened porches over the two flights of steps which led up to the building. Rumour has it that the fire was started by a monk accidentally setting his blanket alight by sleeping too close to an electric fire. The local Burmese community is trying to raise funds to rebuild it, but it will be difficult to restore to its former magnificence. To the left of the compound stands the *ubosot*, which was built in 1900 at the same time as the *wihan* and survived the fire. It has a similar, elaborately carved, multi-tiered wooden roof and magnificent wooden doors, which give some idea of the exquisite craftsmanship of the *wihan*. The construction of the adjacent *chedi* was paid for by a local Burmese benefactor in 1949.

Opposite Wat Si Chum lies the **Al-Falah Mosque**, which serves the small Burmese Muslim community. It is of no architectural distinction.

Wat Pa Fang, another Burmese *wat*, is located on nearby T. Sanambin, almost opposite the THAI booking office. The buildings were thoroughly renovated in the mid-1980s and today are well maintained. The Burmese *chedi* is surrounded by eight small shrines, each containing a gilded alabaster Buddha image in the Mandalay style. The *ubosot* to the right of the *chedi* houses beneath a green corrugated zinc roof a beautiful Burmese seated Buddha image, its pedestal richly decorated with sculpted scenes from the *jātaka* tales.

A few metres further south along T. Sanambin, on the right-hand side, is **Wat Chai Mongkhon**. The covered staircase leading to the platform of the *wihan* of this *wat* has finely carved fretwork beneath the eaves, and the roof supports are beautifully decorated with glass inlay. Inside is a gilded Ayutthaya-style seated Buddha image with a broad double baldric crossed over the chest and clasped by a diamond-shaped plaque, a characteristic feature from the 17C of images of the Buddha in royal attire.

On the edge of the town, across the southern bypass, are two hilltop *wat* that can be reached along T. Pakham. Turn left at the fork just south of Lampang hospital, and cross the bypass to the lane opposite T. Lampang-Ngao, Soi 15. A short way up this lane is a track on the left which climbs to **Wat Mon Puyak**, where there is a large whitewashed *ubosot* containing several seated Burmese Buddha images. The wooden *kuti* nearby, which has a Burmese multi-tiered roof, is rather dilapidated. Within the walled enclosure of the *ubosot* is a Burmese-style *chedi*, while on the hilltop behind are the three large whitewashed Burmese *chedi* of **Wat Mon Chamsin**.

To the northeast of Lampang, c 16km along road 1, is **Wat Phra That Sadet**, an ancient *wat* which lies near the remains of an old city (*wiang*). Turn left just north of the 617km stone to reach the *wat*, c 1500m from the highway. It has undergone so many restorations over the years that nothing remains of the original buildings, which it is alleged date from the mid 7C when Phra Nang Cham Thewi is traditionally believed to have been on her way to Lamphun from Lop Buri to become the first ruler of the kingdom of Haripunjaya.

The principal *wihan* is a modern, open-sided building, housing a Sukhothai-style walking Buddha image, 4.5m high, in a tall *ku*. The image was apparently found in pieces in a ruined *wat* near Chiang Kham in Phayao province, was taken from there to Nan c 1880, and then in 1934 to Lampang, where it was reconstructed. Behind the *wihan* is a bell-shaped *chedi* on a redented square base, clad in thin sheets of gilded copper, which was built in 1449 over an earlier *chedi* said to contain a relic of the Buddha. Beside the *chedi* is a renovated Lan Na-style *wihan* with a low-sweeping porch and wooden *khan tuai* painted red and gold. Inside is a seated Buddha image behind an iron grille. Flanking the compound wall is a small museum containing votive tablets, wooden *wat* furniture and lacquerware.

Beyond the lane to Wat Sadet, road 1 continues north for c 115km to Phayao (see Rte 30).

24 · Environs of Lampang: Ko Kha district and Chaeson National Park

Two very pleasant half-day excursions can be made from Lampang: one to the southwest, downstream along the Wang valley to Ko Kha district, where there are several magnificent examples of Lan Na architecture, notably the majestic Wat Phra That Lampang Luang; and the other upriver along the Wang valley through pleasant scenery to the waterfalls and hot springs of Chaeson National Park, passing along the way some unusual Lan Na buildings and the weaving villages of Chae Hom. The national park makes a fine picnic place for travellers heading north to Phayao (see Rte 30) or Chiang Rai (see Rte 28).

Ko Kha District

To the southwest of Lampang, on the west bank of the Wang River, lie three of the finest monasteries in northern Thailand. Although it can be time-consuming to reach them all by public transport, they are well worth the effort. As far as Ko Kha, at least, there is frequent transport.

Travellers with their own vehicles should head south from Lampang on road 1 and turn right to **Ko Kha** after c 15km. In Ko Kha, just beyond the bridge over the Wang River, the road divides. To the right along road 1034 are three major *wat*: **Wat Phra That Lampang Luang**, **Wat Lai Hin** and **Wat Pong Yang Khok**. A detour of c 12km to the left leads to **Wat Phra That Chom Ping**, of little interest except for the amusing *camera obscura* effect found in the *ubosot*. The caretaker will happily show visitors how a hole in the window shutter can be made to project the image of the *chedi* outside on to a piece of white cloth inside the darkened *ubosot*.

Return to the junction in Ko Kha and continue north for c 1500m. Here a turning to the left, initially along a brick road, leads after c 6km to the old walled enclosure of **Wat Lai Hin**, which is on the left beyond a school, amid newer buildings. If requested, the monks will unlock the door of the elaborately stuccoed gate tower. The charming open-sided *wihan* has undergone many renovations inside, particularly noticeable in the concrete pillars which have replaced the old timber columns. However, the wooden gable has retained its superb stucco decoration, and there is fine lacquer work within. Behind the *wihan* is a small *chedi*, while to the right is a smaller chapel, also with beautiful wood carving.

In a modern building in front of the enclosure is a small museum where pieces of wooden architectural sculpture, ceramics, seashells and currency are displayed.

From Wat Lai Hin return to road 1034 and turn left to reach the imposing fortified enclosure of **WAT PHRA THAT LAMPANG LUANG**, a further 1500m on the left. The enclosure is surrounded by a high brick wall that made it possible to use the *wat* as a fortress in time of war. On the south side it abuts the ancient fortified city of Muang Lampha Kampa, or Lampha Kampa Nakhon, which was one of the citadels of the kingdom of Haripunjaya. The legend that the Gautama Buddha himself visited this spot in his lifetime led many successive rulers of Lan Na and governors of Lampang to perform acts of merit-making at the monastery. The *bodhi* tree immediately to the south of the main enclosure is considered to be exceptionally holy. Offerings are made at a shrine in its shade to the spirits who are believed to inhabit it, and carved and painted poles are put to support its branches as a merit-making act by the faithful.

A flight of steps flanked by a *nāga* balustrade leads up from the road to the principal **entrance** in the east wall, which is richly decorated with intricate stucco work. However, this is usually closed and visitors enter the precincts of the *wat* through a door in the south wall where the great *bodhi* tree stands. On the inside above the east entrance is a round lintel on which is carved in gilded stucco a Wheel of the Law. The principal *wihan* (**Wihan Luang**), originally built by a governor of Lampang in 1486, is directly ahead. It has a beautiful wooden pediment and a fine triple-tiered roof supported by 46 columns. Beneath the eaves are some faded mid-19C murals on wooden panels. The interior was clumsily restored in 1830, the original teak columns replaced by cement painted black and gold and the floor covered with ceramic tiles. At the west end is an exceptionally fine gilded and stuccoed brick *ku* reaching to the ceiling, housing the principal Buddha image, **Phra Chao Lan Thong**, cast in 1563. To the left of the *ku* is an ornate, beautifully painted *thammat*, while behind the *ku* is an

The ku *at Wat Phra That Lampang Luang, near Lampang*

altar on which are five seated Buddha images backed by engraved stelae.

Immediately to the west of Wihan Luang is the principal **chedi**. An imposing brick monument with an elegant tapering spire, a bell-shaped relic-chamber and a redented base, its lower part is clad in copper plates and its upper part is gilded. It is said to contain neck bones and a hair of the Buddha. To the left of the *chedi* is **Wihan Phra Phut**, which dates from 1802, and has a magnificent gable of wood inlaid with glass mosaic. The entrance is flanked by tall parasols painted red. Inside is a gilded brick seated Buddha image in *bhūmisparśa mudrā*, 5.25m high, with several smaller images. To the west of the *chedi* is a small building known as **Ho Phra Phutthabat**, which, as the name indicates, contains a Footprint of the Buddha.

On the north side of Wihan Luang is the smaller Wihan Ton Kaeo, which was extensively restored in the late 1960s. Behind this is **Wihan Nam Taem**, a wooden building which the evidence of the chronicles suggests may have been built in the mid 15C. Inside faint traces of mural paintings, possibly dating from the late 18C, are visible. Wihan Nam Taem enshrines a wooden Footprint of the Buddha and a bronze Buddha image of uncertain date.

In the west wall of the enclosure is a small hole through which Thip Chang, a local hero in one of many wars fought against the Burmese in the 16C and 17C is supposed to have climbed, and in one of the copper plates on the base of the *chedi* is a hole made by the bullet with which Thip Chang killed the commander of the Burmese troops who were billeted in the *wat*.

Behind the great *bodhi* tree a path leads to a small and dingy museum of poorly displayed exhibits, including a number of lacquered manuscript cabinets, gongs and Buddha images. Beyond is a **ho trai**, and next to it is a building containing the Buddha image called Phra Kaeo Don Tao, formerly at Wat Phra Kaeo Don Tao in Lampang (see p 261). This image, which is of jadeite or green jasper, is said to have been carved from the same block of stone as the Emerald Buddha in Bangkok.

From Wat Phra That Lampang Luang, continue north on road 1034 for c 7km where a turning to the right is signed to **Wat Pong Yang Khok**. This *wat*, which was founded in 1253, has a modern *wihan* and *chedi*. Behind these is an earlier Lan Na-style, open-sided *wihan* with carved roof brackets, but a plain wooden gable. It houses a Buddha image, barely visible within a stuccoed *ku* flanked by three-headed *nāgas*. The interior woodwork of the *wihan* is decorated with 17C gilded stencils of flowers in vases; this motif, which in Sanskrit is called *pūraṇa kalaśa*, signifies growth, prosperity, happiness and sufficiency. In the enclosure is a drum of the type known as *klong bucha*, made from a hollowed tree trunk.

Road 1034 continues north from Wat Pong Yang Khok to the junction with road 11, from where Lampang lies c 16km to the right.

Sopli and Chaeson National Park

Leave Lampang on road 1035, past Wat Chedi Sao. After a few kilometres, the road leaves the Wang River valley and starts to wind through young teak plantations and thick forest before emerging after c 20km on to an open plain. Turn left on to road 1287 c 7km beyond the weaving centre of Chae Hom and follow the signs to Chaeson National Park, which is situated off to the right along road 1252. However, first make a brief **detour** by continuing straight on at the intersection of roads 1287 and 1252. After 500m this road reaches a very sharp bend to the left, where a turning to the right leads into Ban Sopli and, after 1200m, to the carefully restored Lan Na-style **Wat Sopli** on the right.

A Lampang-based conservation group carried out the restoration of this *wat* in 1986. Much of the woodwork has been renewed, but the *wat* has retained its original character, and the villagers are justifiably proud of it. On the simple but colourful altar is a crude but attractive image of the Buddha, probably of local craftsmanship. Faded paintings are discernible on wood panels on the interior walls.

Back on the road to Chaeson National Park, a turning to the left at an intersection just beyond the 56km stone leads in c 2km to **Wat Chaeson Luang**, on the right side. This rather dilapidated *wat* is chiefly noteworthy for the curious collection of mythical creatures and human images seated on the staircase in the porch.

Back on road 1252, continue north to the signed turning to the left towards the 593 sq km **Chaeson National Park**, which covers a large hilly area between the densely populated Wang valley and the main Chiang Mai–Chiang Rai highway. There are waterfalls and hot springs, which are easily accessible from the car-park and make this an attractive picnic spot, although it can become very crowded and noisy at weekends. Cold drinks, grilled chicken, sticky rice and other snacks can be bought from stalls near the waterfalls, and there is adequate bungalow accommodation available.

Road 1252 continues north along the Wang River valley to Wang Nua, from where a good road cuts east through the hills of Doi Bussaracum to Phayao (see Rte 30), offering magnificent views along the way. To the west, travellers can join the main road between Chiang Mai and Chiang Rai (see Rte 28).

25 · Lampang to Chiang Mai

Road 11, 92km.

Railway, 109km in 2hrs (express).

Road 11 runs northwest from Lampang and after c 30km passes on the right the **Thai Elephant Conservation Centre**, which is run by the government's Forest Industry Organisation. Here elephants have traditionally been trained for work in the timber industry. However, in recent years a ban on logging in Thailand imposed by the government after several ecological disasters has put many trained elephants out of work, and increasing numbers of abandoned animals are being brought to the centre to be cared for. Visitors can feed them and watch their training classes, which are usually held several times daily.

Beyond the elephant-training centre, the road climbs steadily for c 10km to a pass that marks the Lampang–Lamphun provincial boundary before descending to the broad Ping River valley. A turning to the right 9km beyond the pass leads to the 255 sq km **Doi Khuntan National Park**, a delightful park with hiking trails to the 1373m summit of Doi Khuntan. Khuntan station is on the Bangkok–Chiang Mai line, so the park is most easily reached by train, but road access has recently been improved and need only be avoided after heavy rains when the last few kilometres along an earth track can be difficult.

Chiang Mai

Road 11 bypasses the town of Lamphun (see Rte 27) and continues to **Chiang Mai** (pop. 160,000), which, although its population is less than one thirtieth of that of Bangkok, is Thailand's second largest city and is generally considered the most beautiful, being often described as the 'Rose of the North', the 'Pearl of the North', the 'City of Golden Temples' and similar extravagant epithets. Its name simply means 'New City'.

From the year of its foundation in 1296 until the death in 1939 of the last ruler nominated by the Bangkok government, Chiang Mai was the capital of the northern Thai kingdom of Lan Na. Its golden age was in the 15C, when Lan Na was at the height of its power and prosperity and before internal strife, dynastic disputes and Burmese attacks had brought about a decline, which led eventually to surrender to the Burmese in 1558 and the subsequent fragmentation of the kingdom. In recent years it has become so overwhelmed with tourists that it is beginning to lose its Thai character and cultural identity, but it is still a charming and attractive city and an excellent centre from which to explore northern Thailand.

■ **Information**. The TAT office at 105/1 T. Chiang Mai-Lamphun, just east of Nawarat Bridge, can provide city maps and information about hotels, restaurants, shops, tourist attractions and transport. In the same building is the office of the Tourist Police (open 06.00–24.00). An excellent, though highly idiosyncratic guide to the city is the regularly updated *Nancy Chandler's Map of Chiang Mai*, which has a wealth of detail about markets, sightseeing, shopping, sports facilities, public transport and much more. The *Suriwong Book*

Centre (open Mon–Sat, 08.00–19.30; Sun, 08.00–12.00) on T. Si Donchai and *DK Book House* (open daily 09.00–20.00) on T. Tha Phae are the best bookshops for English language publications.

■ **Hotels**. There is a vast choice of accommodation in Chiang Mai, from five-star luxury hotels to comfortable guest-houses in traditional teak buildings. Among the best hotels are the *Chiang Mai Orchid* at 100–102 T. Huai Kaeo, the *Chiang Mai Plaza* on T. Si Donchai and the *Royal Princess* (*Dusit Inn*) on T. Chang Klan. Good value for money are some of the cheaper guest-houses on the river bank such as the *Galare* at 7/1 T. Charoen Prathet near Nawarat Bridge. Convenient for its very central location is the mid-priced *Montri Hotel* adjacent to the Tha Phae Gate on T. Mun Muang. In the peak tourism months (November–February and July–September) the most popular places are often full.

■ **Eating Out**. Chiang Mai has an equally large range of restaurants, cafés, coffee shops and market stalls. Northern Thai food is on the whole less spicy than in other regions of Thailand and includes several dishes of Lao, Shan, Burmese and Chinese origin. Specialities include *khao soi* (curried noodle soup with chicken, beef or pork) and *gaeng hang le* (pork curry made with ginger, tamarind and turmeric). The staple is *khao niao* (sticky rice) which is generally preferred to the plain boiled rice eaten in central Thailand. Some northern Thai dishes contain ingredients not used elsewhere in the kingdom, such as buffalo meat and giant beetles (*maeng da*).

■ **Banks, Post Office and Telephones**. Banks and money-changers can be found at many locations throughout the city, including T. Tha Phae, T. Chang Klan and beside the east moat. The main branch of the *Thai Farmers Bank* is at 169–171 T. Tha Phae, and the *Bangkok Bank* has branches at 53–9 T. Tha Phae and 164/14 T. Chang Klan. The main post office is on T. Charoen Muang, near the railway station, and smaller branches are located on T. Praisani near Nawarat Bridge, on T. Phra Pokklao within the old city moat, and on T. Chotana to the north. International telephone calls can be made from the main post office (daily, 24hrs). Hotels usually add a substantial surcharge for telephone calls.

■ **Consulates**. USA at 387 T. Wichayanon (Tel. 053-252 629). UK at 54 Mu 2, Tambon Suthep (Tel. 053-222 571).

■ **Inter-provincial buses**. Most of these leave from the Arcade bus station, on the ring road in the northeast of the city. Services operate to most major towns in north and central Thailand, and to some destinations in the northeast, including Khon Kaen, Udon Thani, Nakhon Ratchasima and Ubon Ratchathani. On the Bangkok route, the so-called 'VIP' and 'super-VIP' services usually provide drinks and meals and offer more spacious seating. Slow buses to Lamphun and Lampang leave from opposite the TAT office on T. Chiang Mai-Lamphun, while direct buses to Lampang leave from the Arcade bus station.

■ **Provincial buses**. These depart from several different points in the city. The Chang Phuak bus station on T. Chang Phuak just north of the moat serves the towns in the northern part of Chiang Mai province, including Chiang Dao, Fang and Tha Ton. Minibuses to Doi Suthep also depart from here.

■ **City transport**. There are five **city bus** routes in the city. Most useful are No. 3, which serves Arcade bus station; No. 5, which does a circuit around the city moat; and No. 6, which runs from the airport to the railway station. **Songthaeo** do not operate fixed routes; tell the driver your destination and he may or may not agree to go there. Be prepared to bargain hard if taking a **samlo**, as drivers often demand very high prices. It is essential to agree on the price before getting in.

■ **Railway station**. The terminus for southbound trains lies to the east of the river on T. Charoen Muang; most services depart in the morning or evening. Travellers requiring sleeping berths are advised to book several days in advance, especially during public and school holidays and at the height of the tourist season. The computerised booking system is fast and efficient.

■ **Domestic flights**. *THAI* operates direct flights to Bangkok, Chiang Rai, Mae Hong Son and Phuket. There are also flights to Phitsanulok via Mae Sot or Nan. The booking office (open 07.30–17.00) is at 240 T. Phra Pokklao within the city moat. Taxis and *songthaeo* operate to and from the airport on the southwest side of the city, and *THAI* provides a shuttle bus service between the airport and the main hotels. *Bangkok Airways* has several flights a week to Sukhothai.

■ **International flights**. From Chiang Mai *THAI* flies to Kunming in China. *SilkAir* has non-stop flights to Singapore three times a week. *Air Mandalay* has several weekly flights to Yangon (Rangoon) and *Lao Aviation* flies to Vientiane. *THAI* and *Malaysia Airlines* share two weekly direct flights to Kuala Lumpur.

■ **Car, motorcycle and bicycle rentals**. There are numerous local rental companies, especially near Tha Phae Gate on the east moat, with motorcycles, jeeps and sometimes saloon cars for rent. *Avis* and *Hertz* have desks at several hotels. The *Hertz* main office is at 90 T. Si Donchai. Several of the cheap guest houses rent bicycles for a few baht per day.

■ **Shopping**. Chiang Mai has long been a major centre of arts and crafts, including pottery, silk-weaving, jewellery, gold- and silversmithing, bronze-casting, lacquer-making and the manufacture of teak and other hardwood furniture. Many of these crafts were until recently chiefly confined to a single area or street: the silversmiths, for example, were found mostly in T. Chom Thong to the south of the city; the principal centre for the production of lacquer was the Ban Khoen neighbourhood; the potters' village was near the Chang Phuak gate in the north; the woodcarvers' workshops were chiefly in T. Wualai and T. Ratchanasang; some of the finest silk and cotton textiles were woven in the village of San Kamphaeng, east of the city; and the nearby village of Bo Sang was almost entirely devoted to the production of varnished paper umbrellas. Increasingly, however, both the manufacture of all these goods and their sale is becoming concentrated in the San Kamphaeng/Bo Sang area, and there are wide variations in standards of craftsmanship. Furthermore, many so-called 'antiques' are artificially distressed modern products, although they are often most attractive.

There is a **hill-tribe products promotion centre** (Patron: HM the King) on T. Suthep, and another branch on T. Huai Kaeo, opposite the university.

Profits go towards hill-tribe welfare programmes. There is a self-help agency owned by the hill-tribes and called *Thai Tribal Crafts* at 208 T. Bamrung Rat.

A lively **night market** is held every evening along T. Chang Klan between T. Tha Phae and T. Si Donchai. Not all goods sold in this market are of local manufacture.

The Old City of Chiang Mai

Much of central Chiang Mai can be explored on foot or by bicycle, and a wander along the narrow lanes of the old city within the rectangular area bounded by the moat can be very rewarding. This enclosure, surrounded by the remains of brick-faced earthen ramparts, is pierced by five gates, four of them dating from the last years of the 13C when the city was founded. These four are Chang Phuak (formerly Hua Wiang) on the north, Tha Phae (formerly Chiang Ruak) on the east, Chiang Mai on the south, and Suan Dok on the west. King Pha Yu reinforced the earth walls with brick c 1341, and at the beginning of the 15C King Sam Fang Kaen built a gate named Suan Rae, which is generally identified with the present Suan Prung on the south wall. A sixth gate known as Si Phum was apparently built at the northeast corner by King Tiloka in 1465 at the entrance to his palace. King Muang Kaeo rebuilt the walls with brick in 1517. He also left King Tiloka's palace and moved his residence to Wat Pa Daeng; at the same time Si Phum Gate, presumably because it no longer served any purpose, was walled up. Water from the Huai Kaeo stream was originally channelled along an aqueduct into the moat at the northwest corner (Hua Rin) and flowed in both directions round the moat to exit at the southeast corner, known as Katam, where the water collected in a pond well stocked with fish. The traps (*katam*) used to catch the fish gave this corner its name.

In addition, an outer wall originally extended from Ku Ruang corner in the southwest to Si Phum corner in the northeast, thus forming a rough semicircle pierced by five outer gates round the east and south sides of the inner enclosure.

Chiang Mai was devastated and depopulated by the almost continuous warfare between the Thais and the Burmese in the late 18C, and Kavila, a prince of Lampang who in 1781 became ruler (*chao*) of Chiang Mai under Siamese suzerainty and reigned until 1813, devoted 15 years from 1796 to 1811 to repairing its fortifications. In 1873, Chao Inthanon carried out further major repairs.

Tha Phae Gate, one of the original 13C gates, was formerly known as Chiang Ruak Gate after a nearby village. At that time, Tha Phae ('Raft Landing') referred to the gate in the outer earthen rampart near Wat Saen Fang. In the early 20C, when the outer gate was dismantled, the inner gate became known as Tha Phae Gate. This was rebuilt in 1986 after a photograph of an unidentified gate taken in 1891, and the adjacent paved area is now frequently the scene of festivals, business promotions and *takro* tournaments.

Chiang Mai Gate, another of the original gates, formerly gave on to the road to Lamphun on the south side. In the 1960s the wall was reconstructed for a few metres on either side of the gate, and now T. Phra Pokklao runs through it. **Suan Prung Gate** on the south wall was traditionally the gate through which the dead were taken for cremation outside the city. Like Chiang Mai Gate, it was rebuilt in the 1960s with a section of wall c 30m in length on either side. T. Samlan now runs through it. In the southwest corner (Ku Ruang), a small

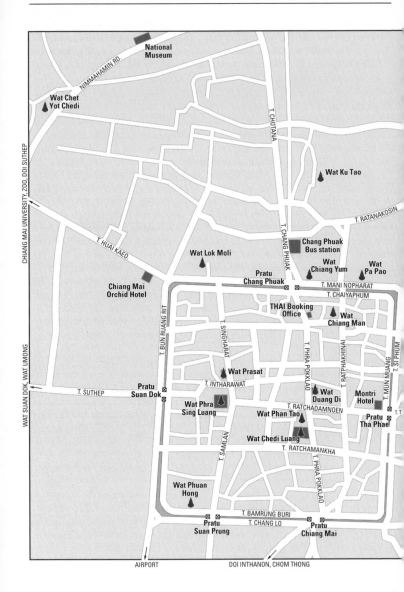

section of the old fortified wall remains. Prince Khrua, son of King Mangrai, was kept prisoner here from 1321 to 1325.

Suan Dok Gate on the west moat was also completely rebuilt in the 1960s. Outside this gate was the flower garden (*suan dok*) where King Ku Na founded Wat Suan Dok in 1371.

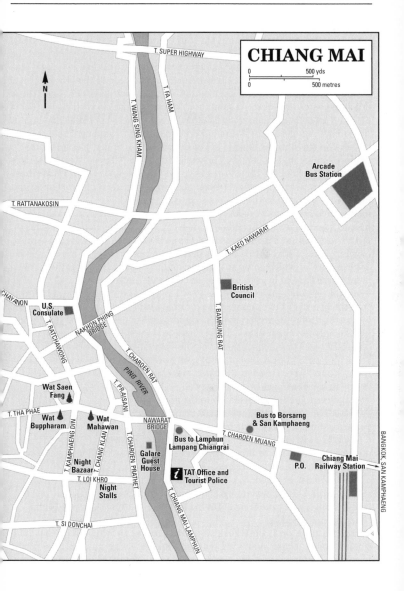

The fourth of the original city gates is **Chang Phuak Gate** on the north moat. This gate was also rebuilt in the 1960s. Beyond it on T. Chotana is a group of shrines containing statues of sacred white elephants (*chang phuak*). The inner gates have been reconstructed, but virtually nothing remains of the outer ramparts.

Tour of the Old City

A tour of the old city of Chiang Mai can conveniently begin at **WAT CHEDI LUANG**, which is situated on T. Phra Pokklao near the centre of the walled and moated enclosure and is the largest and most important temple in Chiang Mai. By the side of a *bodhi* tree, just inside the main entrance to the *wat*, is a small shrine containing the *lak muang* of the city, restored in 1993. The temple building nearest the road is a sumptuously decorated *wihan* with a triple-tiered roof and an entrance flanked by *nāga* balustrades covered in gaudy glazed tiles. The *wihan* contains a large and much venerated bronze standing Eighteen-Cubit Buddha image (Phra Attharot) flanked by two figures of disciples and some 30 or more smaller Buddha images. The vaulted ceiling is painted red and decorated with gold stars. Behind the *wihan* stands the colossal brick *chedi*, **Phra Chedi Luang**, from which the whole temple takes its name. The construction of this monument was begun in the late 14C by King Saen Muang Ma of Lan Na as a memorial to his father, King Ku Na. The work was completed during the reign of his successor, Sam Fang Kaen. In the mid-15C King Tiloka increased the height of the *chedi* to 86m. The main body of the *chedi* was originally covered with gilt copper sheets, of which a few remain *in situ*. The base was surrounded by figures of elephants, of which only one remains, and the four staircases at the cardinal points were flanked by *nāga* balustrades. In 1458 the Emerald Buddha, now in Bangkok, was brought from Lampang and installed in the east niche of the *chedi*.

In the late 15C, King Muang Kaeo restored Chedi Luang again, but in 1545, in the reign of Queen Chiraprapha, an earthquake destroyed the upper part, leaving only the north side of the structure and the base intact. It was partially and rather controversially restored by the Thai Fine Arts Department between 1990 and 1992. During restoration, numerous small Buddha images, some of them bronze, were found in the *chedi*, and these are now displayed inside the *wihan*, in a cabinet against the north wall.

Wat Phan Tao lies immediately to the north of Wat Chedi Luang on T. Phra Pokklao. The *wihan* has panelled teak walls and its gable is set on tall teak red painted columns. Over the door is an ornately carved pediment decorated with a peacock, *nāga*, and other creatures, and, at the base, a carved wooden pelmet in the form of a double arch, the so-called 'eyebrow motif', characteristic of much Lan Na temple architecture.

Just beyond Wat Phan Tao, further north on T. Phra Pokklao at the intersection with T. Ratchadamnoen, is a monument marking the spot where a thunderbolt is said to have struck at the moment that King Mangrai, founder of Chiang Mai, passed by.

Further north on T. Phra Pokklao is **Wat Duang Di**, which has a beautiful small wooden *ubosot*, now used by the monks as living quarters. Beside the *ubosot* is a larger *wihan* with an exceptionally fine decorated wooden pediment, and at the west end of the *wihan* is a *chedi* in Sri Lankan style, with a figure of an elephant at each of the four corners of the base. Access to this *wat* is easiest from the eastern side of T. Phra Pokklao, just south of the junction with T. Intharawat.

From Wat Duang Di turn west along T. Intharawot to reach the royal monastery of **WAT PHRA SING**. The entrance to this *wat*, which is one of Chiang Mai's finest temple complexes, is on the west side of T. Singharat, directly opposite the end of T. Ratchadamnoen. It was founded by King Pha Yu, who in

The ho trai of Wat Phra Sing, Chiang Mai

1345 had a *chedi* constructed here to enshrine the ashes of his father, King Kham Fu, and two years later built a *wihan* and other monastic buildings around it. At the end of the 14C, King Saen Muang Ma had the famous Buddha image known as Phra Phuttha Sihing, from which the monastery takes its name, brought from Chiang Rai and placed here. The monastery was extensively restored in the reign of Muang Kaeo and again in 1924 by Khruba Siwichai (see p 284) for the last ruler of Chiang Mai, Chao In Kaeo.

Immediately to the right inside the main entrance of the monastery enclosure is a **ho trai** said to have been built by King Tiloka in 1477 and restored in 1867 by Chao Kavilorot of Chiang Mai and again in 1927 by King Prajadhipok. The upper section is of carved wood with panels studded with glass mosaic and stands on a high stuccoed brick base. The base has four windows in the north and south walls, between which are figures of celestial beings in various attitudes of adoration carved in stucco in high relief. Above and below these figures is a frieze of stucco medallions depicting elephant-lions and other mythical creatures against a background of foliage. The carving of this stucco decoration is of the greatest refinement and elegance.

In front of the entrance to the enclosure is a large modern **wihan** (Wihan Luang) with a three-tiered roof and *nāga* balustrades flanking the steps of the main entrance. Behind this is an **ubosot**, which, unusually, is built on a north–south axis. It has a three-tiered roof and porches over both north and south entrances. The porches have pediments of intricately carved, lacquered and gilded wood and stucco, with the 'eyebrow motif' at the base. The doors also have magnificent pediments of gilded wood in the form of Wheels of the Law in a frame composed of entwined *nāga* and *haṃsa* motifs, and superb stucco decoration on the jambs, which are flanked by stucco figures of celestial beings similar to those on the walls of the *ho trai*.

Behind the *ubosot* is a square-based **chedi** with a figure of an elephant on each side. To the south of the *chedi* is an exquisite small *wihan* known as **Wihan Lai Kham**, which contains an image of the Buddha that is widely believed locally to be the original Phra Phuttha Sihing. The front part of the roof of this beautifully proportioned building has three tiers; the back part has two. As in the *ho trai* and the *ubosot*, the pediment over the entrance is of gilded wood and stucco, intricately carved, lacquered and gilded; the wooden roof brackets are also finely carved with floral motifs. The steps of the entrance are flanked by *nāga* balustrades. **Phra Phuttha Sihing**, a 15C gilded bronze image in Lan Na style of the Buddha seated in *bhūmisparśa mudrā*, is flanked by two smaller but iconographically identical gilded bronze Buddha images. As is frequently the case with Lan Na Buddha images of this period, the flap of the *sanghati* over the left shoulder reaches only as far as the chest. Each of the three images has a separate base and is placed on a single redented platform. The wall behind is decorated in gold paint with elaborate arches framing each image and a background of dragons and vegetal motifs. The other interior walls of the *wihan* are decorated with exceptionally fine early 19C murals, some in Lan Na style and some in central Thai style. In the upper register are depicted celestial beings in flight, some holding five lotus flowers in one hand and a triangular flag in the other, and others with sprays of flowers in both hands. Beneath them are scenes from two uncanonical *jātaka* tales—to the left of the Buddha image the tale of Sang Thong ('Golden Prince of the Conch Shell') is depicted, and to the right is the tale of Phra Suwannahong ('Golden Goose'). Many of the paintings vividly illustrate 19C Burmese and Lan Na architecture, customs and costumes. They include scenes of women smoking cigars, men with elaborately tattooed legs, soldiers wearing Western hats and shirts with stiff collars, figures of princes and courtiers of Lan Na, and Shan, Kha and other neighbouring peoples. The paintings use a wide range of colours, including ochre and dark green, and are informal and naturalistic in style, which distinguishes them from the more hieratic, stylised and sumptuously gilded temple paintings of central Thailand.

Across T. Intharawot from Wat Phra Sing, a few metres to the north, is **Wat Prasat**, which contains a fine wooden *wihan* with a pediment decorated with gilded stucco and mirror glass, connected by a tunnel to a square *chedi* with three niches.

In the northeastern sector of the old city's walled enclosure, on T. Ratphakinai, is **Wat Chiang Man**, which was founded by King Mangrai soon after the building of Chiang Mai began in 1296. It is considered to be the oldest monastery in the city. It has a modern *wihan* containing two famous Buddha images: on the right is the image known as **Phra Sila**, a relief carving which is thought to date from the 8C–10C and to be of Indian origin, and which depicts the Buddha subduing the Nalagiri Elephant. According to an 18C chronicle, this image came from Bihar in India, via Sri Lanka, Burma and Si Satchanalai. On the left is **Phra Sak Tang Khamani**, a tiny image made of rock crystal seated on a hollow gold base, probably dating from the late 19C, which is believed to have miraculous powers of bringing rain and dispelling evil spirits and consequently is carried ceremonially round Chiang Mai once every year. Both images are kept behind bars in a glazed *ku*.

To the left of this modern *wihan* is another of little interest. Behind this is a *chedi* with gilded copper plates covering the upper part, and figures of the foreparts of elephants round the lower portion of the two-storeyed, redented square base. Further to the left is a *ho trai* that has been extensively renovated, but still retains some charm, and to the left again is a fine *ubosot*, with a superb lacquered and gilded wooden pediment above the porch. On the right of the porch of the *ubosot* is a stela with an inscription in archaic Thai that has not yet been deciphered. Inside are several bronze Buddha images. The roof is supported by teak pillars.

Wat Suan Dok, Chiang Mai

Outside the north moat of the old city, towards the west end of T. Mani Nopharat, in Soi 2, which goes off the north side, is **Wat Lok Moli**, which was founded in the second half of the 14C in the reign of Ku Na. Little of this *wat* remains except the very large *chedi*, built 200 years later in the reign of King Ket Chettharat, which still has some stucco figures of deities remaining near the top. The *chedi* consists of a small bell-shaped relic chamber, surmounted by a slender spire above a redented square section, with a niche on each side, and standing on a square base.

Further to the north, on T. Chang Phuak (T. Chotana), is **Wat Ku Tao**, a temple in the Burmese style with a modern *wihan* and a highly unusual *chedi* that is more curious than beautiful, made of stuccoed brick in the form of five bowls of diminishing size placed one upon the other, standing on a redented square base and decorated with ceramic tiles in the shape of petals. To find this *wat*, turn east off T. Chang Phuak on to Soi 6, to the north of the Chang Phuak bus station.

Outside the moat of the old city on the west side, T. Suthep leads from Suan

One of the superb stucco carvings of a deity at Wat Chet Yot, Chiang Mai

Dok Gate to **Wat Suan Dok**. The *chedi* of this temple was built by King Ku Na in the flower garden of his palace for the Sukhothai monk Phra Sumana (see p 283–4). It has been restored many times, most recently in 1932 by Khruba Siwichai (see p 284). The enormous and profusely decorated *sala kan parian*, which was built in 1932, contains two images of the Buddha back to back, one seated and one standing. In the *ubosot*, which has been most insensitively restored, is a fine seated Buddha image in the Lan Na style dating from 1504. Behind the principal *chedi* are numerous smaller *chedi*, all dazzlingly white-washed, in which the ashes of various members of the royal family of Chiang Mai are enshrined.

To reach the subterranean **Wat Umong Thera Chan**, continue west beyond Wat Suan Dok along T. Suthep for c 1200m to a lane off to the left, signed 1km to the *wat*. Wat Umong is one of the earliest foundations of King Mangrai and was restored in 1371 by King Ku Na for the monk Maha Thera Chan. Little remains of the original monastery except for a ruined *chedi* on a brick base on which a few fragments of stucco can be seen. Next to the *chedi* are several subter-ranean galleries where Buddha images have been placed. These were formerly used by hermits for meditation. Recently Wat Umong has again become an active meditation centre for people of all nationalities interested in Buddhism.

Nearby is **Wat Pa Daeng Luang**, which was built in the early Chiang Mai period and has an unusual *chedi* displaying a mixture of Haripunjaya and Sri Lankan styles.

Wat Chet Yot is situated on the ring road to the northwest of the old city. This important *wat* was built c 1455 for King Tiloka as his funerary temple and to commemorate the 2000th anniversary of the foundation of Buddhism. In 1477 the Eighth World Buddhist Council was held here. The principal *chedi*, like the *chedi* of Wat Phra That Nongbua at Ubon Ratchathani (see Rte 47), is copied from the Mahabodhi temple at Bodh Gaya in Bihar, where the Buddha achieved

Enlightenment. The temple takes its name from the seven spires of the *chedi*, which are thought to symbolise the places where the Buddha stayed in the seven weeks after his Enlightenment. The spires are made of laterite and stand on a high brick base decorated with superb stucco carvings in high relief of more than 70 figures, all slightly larger than life-size, of male deities, seated or standing in various attitudes of adoration, richly bejewelled and wearing intricately patterned garments. To the right of the main *chedi* is another of about the same date made of brick. This is decorated with an image of the Buddha in stucco and was probably built to enshrine the ashes of King Tiloka.

A short distance further north round the ring road from Wat Chet Yot is the excellent **CHIANG MAI NATIONAL MUSEUM** (open Wed–Sun, 09.00–16.00), which was first opened in 1973. Displayed in the grounds are two kilns. One, excavated in 1973 near Ban Pong Daeng, in Phan district, Chiang Rai province, was probably constructed in the 15C. The other, brought from Wang Nua district, Lampang province, is one of about a dozen excavated at that site, and is thought to date from the late 14C or early 15C.

On the **ground floor**, the first case to the right of the entrance contains prehistoric artefacts from San Kamphaeng district, just east of Chiang Mai and from Ban Chiang (see p 327), including axe and spear heads, bronze bracelets, cord-marked pottery and baked clay rollers for decorating textiles.

The next few cases contain examples of Dvaravati, Sri Vijaya, Lop Buri and Lan Na art, followed by further displays of pieces from the Sukhothai, U Thong and Ayutthaya periods, and a case containing bronze tableaux of Phra Malai's visit to Hell. Beyond is a case full of Lan Na wooden Buddha images of the 14C and 15C.

Round the corner on the end wall is a magnificent Footprint of the Buddha made of wood inlaid with exquisite mother-of-pearl and glass mosaic decoration from Wihan Lai Kham in Wat Phra Sing. The central motif depicts the sacred mountain, Mount Meru.

In the middle of this wall is a large gilded bronze Buddha image, also from Wat Phra Sing. Along the next wall are cases displaying Lan Na Buddha images and ceramics from several northern Thai kiln sites. On the far side of the staircase are four more display cabinets. The first contains some votive tablets from Wat Pratu Li, Lamphun and the next a 12C terracotta figure of a disciple in adoration, a superb example of Mon Haripunjaya art. Dominating the end wall is the enormous head of a 15C Lan Na bronze Buddha image.

Along the last wall before the entrance is reached again are a remarkable 16C–17C cylindrical sandstone base for a Buddha image, decorated with a lotus surround at the top and supported on the foreparts of four elephants, and two important 16C painted cloth banners from Hot, both damaged, depicting Buddhist subjects.

In the centre of the long gallery downstairs are four beautifully lacquered manuscript cabinets. Opposite the foot of the stairs are cabinets of Sawankhalok ceramics.

Upstairs is a display of northern Thai and hill-tribe clothing and textiles, jewellery, lacquerware, kitchen and agricultural utensils, musical instruments, regalia and weaponry, coins and rattan. Among the more spectacular of the objects in this display is a very large rice container, made of woven rattan, c 2.5m in diameter. Directly at the top of the stairs is a fine early 19C Mandalay-style standing Buddha image in *abhaya mudrā*.

In the middle of the upstairs hall are three intricately decorated howdahs, a late 19C bed which formerly belonged to the ruler of Chiang Mai, a wooden loom, and at the far end, two large Burmese drums (*klong yao*) on carts.

In the grounds of Chiang Mai University on T. Huai Kaeo is the **Tribal Research Institute**, which has a small ethnographic museum (open Mon–Fri 08.30–16.30) containing displays of clothing, textiles and everyday utensils of the highland region's ethnic minorities. There is also a small library here.

Further along T. Huai Kaeo is **Chiang Mai Zoo** (open 08.00–17.00), which is notable for the large open area it contains in which numerous rare species of deer and other animals live in their natural habitat. Nearby is the Chiang Mai Arboretum and Huai Kaeo Waterfall.

To the east of the old moated city, along T. Tha Phae, are three *wat* that repay a visit. **Wat Buppharam** is on the south side of the street, just to the west of T. Kamphaeng Din. The original *wat* was built in 1497, but all the present build-ings date from the Ratanakosin period. There are two *wihan*, of which the larger is notable for the fine woodcarving on the gable, the arches over the doors and the window shutters. Behind this *wihan* is a Burmese-style *chedi* of no great distinction. To the left is another, much smaller *wihan* of great charm; its pedi-ment has a large 'eyebrow motif' at the base and is decorated with stucco relief carving inlaid with coloured glass. The entrance steps are flanked by balustrades in the form of sea monsters.

Wat Saen Fang is c 50m east of Wat Buppharam, on the north side of T. Tha Phae, at the corner with T. Kamphaeng Din near DK Book House. It is approached by a path bordered with *nāga* balustrades and has a fine *chedi* and other buildings in Burmese style, with gilded woodcarving of high quality and exceptional elaboration.

Wat Mahawan is on the southwest corner of T. Tha Phae and Tha Phae Soi 4. It has a *wihan* with stucco decoration of unusual richness on the wooden pedi-ment and modern doors of intricately carved wood. To the west of the *wihan* is a whitewashed *chedi* in Burmese style, surmounted by a gilded parasol and with niches on each side, those to the north and south containing Buddha images. The small *ubosot* also has some fine woodcarving, chiefly of floral motifs. The monks' *kuti* has a remarkable multi-tiered roof.

To the east of the city, across the ring road on road 1006 to Bo Sang and San Kamphaeng (the east extension of T. Tha Phae), is **Wat Buak Khrok Luang**, which has a beautiful Lan Na *wihan* with late 19C murals on the interior walls. To reach this *wat*, turn right off road 1006, c 1300m east of the intersection with the ring road.

26 · Environs of Chiang Mai

Several pleasant day and half-day excursions can be made from Chiang Mai. The three described below offer the chance to see some of the beautiful scenery of the area as well as some of the most important historical sites. It is possible, with a little persistence and plenty of time, to get almost everywhere on public transport, but if time is limited, it is better to rent a vehicle from one of the numerous rental outlets in Chiang Mai. Although driving in the city's busy streets may seem somewhat daunting at first, it looks far worse than it is, while away from the city, even the major roads are generally not crowded, and with the help of a good road map, it is possible to reach many destinations using quiet minor roads.

Doi Suthep-Doi Pui

Road, *total distance c 20km to the top. Return the same way.*

This is a short excursion, but provides a pleasant break from the bustle of Chiang Mai. It can be cool enough at the 1685m summit, especially in the morning, to warrant wearing a jacket. *Songthaeo* depart frequently from near the junction of T. Mani Nopharat and T. Chang Phuak and go as far as Wat Phra Boromathat Doi Suthep.

Leave the city along T. Huai Kaeo, past the zoo and the arboretum. The road starts climbing almost at once, and 1km beyond the zoo it passes into **Doi Suthep-Doi Pui National Park**. This park, which covers an area of 261 sq km, lies so close to the city that it is one of the most frequently visited parks in Thailand and consequently has suffered considerable degradation. Nevertheless, the winding route up the mountain to Wat Phra Boromathat Doi Suthep passes through some magnificent forest scenery and provides fine views over the city and the flat valley of the Ping River.

A turning to the right after a few kilometres leads to the pretty **Monthathan Waterfall**, while **WAT PHRA BOROMATHAT DOI SUTHEP** lies 8km further on.

History

The story of the foundation of this important monastery is closely linked to that of Wat Suan Dok. King Ku Na of Lan Na, having invited the holy monk Phra Sumana to come from Sukhothai to Chiang Mai, was anxious to find a place to enshrine a sacred relic of the Buddha he had brought with him. He chose a garden (Suan Dok) in the royal park and it was there that Wat Suan Dok was founded (see p 280). At the moment when the relic was to be placed in the *chedi*, it divided into two pieces and the king now had to find another place for the second piece. On Sumana's advice, he put it in a shrine on the back of a white elephant, which was then allowed to wander at will. The elephant walked towards Doi Suthep and, after stopping on one small hill now called Doi Chang Non ('Mountain of the Resting Elephant') and then on another, finally climbed up to a hermitage called Wasuthep, near the summit of Doi Suthep, where it trumpeted three times, turned round three times, knelt down and died. The king and Phra Sumana interpreted this as a clear indication that this was where the second relic should be enshrined, and so built there the *chedi* which stands at the centre of Wat Phra Boromathat Doi Suthep today. The road leading up to the temple was constructed in 1935 through the efforts of Khruba Siwichai (Srivijaya) (1877–1938), a monk who was responsible for the restoration of many temples throughout northern Thailand and who organised the building of this road entirely by voluntary labour and with materials bought with the donations of the faithful. The monastery is now one of the most visited in Thailand, both by Buddhist pilgrims and by tourists. Candlelit processions are held here on the anniversary of the Buddha's Birth, Enlightenment and Death, and other important days in the Buddhist calendar.

The temple can be reached from the road either on foot up a **staircase** with 306 steps flanked by *nāga* balustrades covered in green and brown tiles and by plaques inscribed with the names of donors and benefactors, or by funicular railway. The **octagonal chedi**, which in its present form dates from the reign of Muang Kaeo, is 22m high and stands on a deeply redented square base. The entire monument is covered in finely ornamented sheets of gilded copper. Its tapering spire is surmounted by a five-tiered parasol of gilded copper filigree and at each of the four corners is a single parasol of the same gilded copper filigree. There are **two wihan** standing opposite each other with ornately carved wooden gables and steep double-tiered roofs, and several smaller shrines. The enclosure of the *wat* is surrounded by a **gallery** containing numerous Buddha images belonging to different periods and styles, and some modern wall paintings depicting scenes from the Life of the Buddha. On the terrace outside the principal entrance to the enclosure are four magnificent temple bells of bronze with fine incised decoration. From the terrace there are spectacular views over the plain of the Ping valley and the eastern spur of Doi Suthep.

The road continues upward from the food stalls at the foot of the *wat*, passing the national park headquarters after 600m. Bungalow accommodation is available and there are easy hiking trails from the headquarters through the cool of the forest.

Climbing further, the road passes the **Phu Phing Palace**, summer residence of the royal family. The palace gardens, which are in the English style, are open to the public (Fri–Sun and public holidays). Beyond, the road reaches the pine forest at the summit. From here a steep track descends to the Hmong village of **Doi Pui**, a popular stop for tourists.

Doi Inthanon National Park

A visit to Thailand's highest mountain, **Doi Inthanon** (2565m) can be combined with a journey onward to Mae Chaem and Mae Sariang (see Rte 33) but its easy access from Chiang Mai and the number of fine waterfalls and hiking trails in the vicinity make it a pleasant day excursion. An early start is advisable in order to reach the summit before the clouds roll in. Public *songthaeo* from Chom Thong usually run up the mountain road only as far as the turning to Mae Chaem, c 9km below the summit, so it is preferable either to rent a vehicle in Chiang Mai, or to charter a *songthaeo* privately in Chom Thong. Buses from Chiang Mai to Chom Thong depart from near the Chiang Mai Gate on the south moat.

Leave Chiang Mai on road 108, heading southwest. This busy highway passes several villages where highly developed cottage industries produce large quantities of woodwork and pottery for the tourist trade. **Ban Muang Kung**, on the right of the road, specialises in pottery; **Ban Tawai**, off to the left in Hang Dong, produces vast quantities of woodcarvings. Visitors are welcome in both villages.

Road 1009 turns off right to Doi Inthanon c 1km before Chom Thong. Recommended after the rains is a **detour** to the beautiful **Mae Ya Cascades**, which are signed to the left off road 1009 just after it leaves road 108. Snacks and drinks are available at the falls, which are the most impressive in the park.

Back on road 1009, a left-hand fork just before the park gate leads to the **Mae Klang Waterfall**. A nominal entrance fee is charged at the park gate, beyond which is an information centre offering maps and an audio-visual show.

The road climbs steadily beside the Mae Klang River, past the pretty **Wachirathan Waterfall** and terraced rice fields. Once completely forest-covered, **DOI INTHANON NATIONAL PARK** today is occupied by several thousand Karens and Hmongs, who have felled parts of the forest for agriculture.

■ The park headquarters, near the 30km stone and close to the Hmong village of Khun Klang, offers bungalow accommodation and camping facilities, snack stalls and a small café, which, however, is often closed. Visitors staying overnight are advised to bring their own food and cooking equipment.

Much of the area around the headquarters has been severely deforested, but as the road climbs further, dense vegetation once more occurs on either side. Road 1192 turns off left to Mae Chaem (see Rte 33) after the 37km stone, from where the mountain road begins to climb very steeply to the summit.

Near the 42km stone, two modern *chedi* stand to the left of the road, commemorating the 60th birthdays of King Bhumibol and Queen Sirikit, in 1987 and 1992 respectively. The queen's *chedi*, **Chedi Naphaphon Phumisiri**, to the right, has interior walls of granite, covered with fine modern bas-reliefs and coloured ceramic mosaics.

At the summit, there is a rather dull **chedi** built to hold the ashes of Prince Intawitchayanon, after whom the mountain is named. A short walk from the summit car park there is a sphagnum bog, which is a popular **bird-watching area**. Ornithologists have reported more than 380 bird species on Doi Inthanon. January to April is the best time for bird-watching. A pocket-sized checklist entitled *Birds of Doi Inthanon National Park* is published by Mahidol University in Bangkok, and is sometimes available in bookshops in Chiang Mai. The bog at the summit is the only habitat of the **green-tailed sunbird**, endemic to Doi Inthanon (another race is endemic to highlands in the peninsula). **Gould's sunbird** can usually be spotted along the board walk, especially between December and June, when the rhododendrons are in full bloom. Near the summit, too, is a proliferation of **orchids**. The park is also home to the slow loris and numerous bat species, but few large mammals remain in significant numbers. Although casual visitors are unlikely to see many animals, there are numerous rewarding hiking trails through magnificent scenery, some of them starting near the park headquarters.

There are several more waterfalls and a pleasant hiking trail 7km along road 1192 towards Mae Chaem. It is rare to see other visitors here, although there is a ranger station, and camping is allowed.

From here it is possible to continue along the narrow road to the Mae Chaem valley (see Rte 33), a charming area noted for its numerous attractive northern Thai temples and its thriving cotton-weaving tradition.

Mae Rim-Samoeng circuit

Road, total distance 96km on roads 107, 1096, 1269 and 108. The route can be covered with equal ease in a clockwise or anti-clockwise direction and provides a pleasant half-day excursion into the hills to the west of Chiang Mai. However, most of the sights are along road 1096, so it is preferable to follow the route anti-clockwise, as below, allowing time for stops.

Leave Chiang Mai on road 107 to the north, towards Mae Rim (13km) where road 1096 turns off left to Samoeng up the **Mae Sa valley**. The lower section of this beautiful valley has become popular with tourists, attracted by the orchid and butterfly farms, antique dealers, snake farms and elephant camps which have been set up along the way in recent years. After the first few kilometres, the scenery is delightful and there are wonderful views.

After climbing steadily for 10km, the road descends gradually to **Samoeng**, off to the right at the junction. Road 1269 to the left heads southeast to road 108, on the south side of Chiang Mai. In a grove of sugar palms on the right side, shortly before the junction of road 1269 with road 108, is **Wat Ton Kuen**, a renovated Lan Na *wat* of considerable charm, with a multi-tiered roof sweeping almost to the ground and richly carved wooden gables.

27 · Lamphun and Wiang Kum Kam

Roads 106 and 1008, 29km. To Lamphun 23km. Detour to Wiang Kum Kam, c 3km each way.

Railway, 22km in 25mins. Services are at awkward times, either very early in the morning, or late in the afternoon.

■ There is no decent accommodation in Lamphun, so this route is best covered in a day trip from Chiang Mai.

Travellers without their own transport can hire a *tuk-tuk* or even cycle to the ruins of the ancient city of Wiang Kum Kam, one of several early Mon sites near Lamphun. Public buses to Lamphun depart frequently from near the TAT office on T. Chiang Mai-Lamphun, and stop near the Hariphunchai National Museum and Wat Phra That Hariphunchai in Lamphun. The train station in Lamphun is on the north side of town, an easy *samlo* ride from the town centre.

From the Nawarat Bridge in Chiang Mai, head south past the TAT office on T. Chiang Mai-Lamphun and take the right fork in Ban Nong Hoi, c 3km from the

Nawarat Bridge. Cross the ring road and continue along road 1008 for c 400m as far as a turning to the left, clearly signed to the ancient city of **WIANG KUM KAM**, which was one of several early Mon cities in the area surrounding Lamphun and may have been associated with the Mon kingdom of Haripunjaya. The site, which covers an area of c 3 sq km, contains the ruins of numerous monuments, some of which are thought to date back to the 8C. Follow the signs from here for c 1km. The first evidence of Wiang Kum Kam is the remains of a *chedi* and *wihan* that once formed part of **Wat Noi**, beside a sharp bend to the left c 100m before **Wat Chang Kham**.

To the south of the modern *wihan* of Wat Chang Kham are the ruins of a much older *wat*, excavated in the 1970s and dating from the reign of Mangrai. Between the two is an attractive Lan Na *wihan*. On the west side of the buildings is a *chedi*, which is believed to contain relics of the Buddha enshrined here in 1291 by Mangrai after a victory over the Burmese. Beside the *chedi* is a spirit house where it is believed Mangrai's spirit still dwells.

Return c 250m towards road 1008 and take a turning to the left to reach other ruins of Wiang Kum Kam, now hidden away in the quiet countryside. The first, **Wat Ikang**, has a large brick *chedi* on a square base, with the remains of a *wihan* beside it. Part of the *chedi* is still covered with stucco. A few metres further along the road on the left are the remains of **Wat Pupia**. Turn right at the junction just beyond Wat Pupia and go 120m to reach the ruins of **Wat Phra That Khao**, which lie to the left. The foundations of the *wihan* have been largely rebuilt up to floor level, but there is little left of the *chedi* above its square base. There are more ruins 150m further along the road on the right. The Fine Arts Department is gradually excavating more sites. Continue along the lane, which eventually rejoins road 1008 beside **Wat Chedi Liam**. This *wat* has a *chedi* similar in style to Chedi Suwan Chang Kot at Wat Cham Tewi, Lamphun (see p 289), consisting of a five-storeyed brick pyramid with niches containing seated Buddha images. It was restored in 1908.

Lamphun

From Wiang Kum Kam, return to T. Chiang Mai-Lamphun (road 106) and continue south for c 22km to Lamphun (pop. 14,750). The road can be horribly slow and congested, and travellers in a hurry should take the main Chiang Mai-Lampang highway (road 11), which runs further east.

According to the chronicles, Lamphun was founded in the late 7C by Phra Nang Cham Thewi, a Mon princess from Lop Buri who was invited there to become the first ruler of the kingdom of Haripunjaya (Hariphunchai). The actual foundation was probably in the late 8C or early 9C. In the 11C it fell under Khmer hegemony and in 1292 it was conquered by the Thais of Lan Na. Most of the temple architecture, with the notable exception of the two *chedi* at Wat Cham Tewi, dates from the 15C or later. Today it is a quiet provincial town of considerable charm, noted for the production of fine silk cloth, which can be purchased directly from the workshops where it is made, and of a lychee-like fruit called *lam yai*, which provides the occasion for a festival known as *Ngan Lam Yai* held every year in August and lasting for several days.

The **Hariphunchai National Museum** (open Wed–Sun, 09.00–16.00) on T. Inthayongyot in the centre of the town houses a small and rather haphazard collection of Haripunjaya and Lan Na art, including some fine terracotta pieces, bronzes, woodcarving, silverware and ceramics.

Straight ahead inside the entrance are a beautiful gilded wooden candle-holder dated 1927, composed of writhing *nāgas* and inlaid with glass mosaic, and a wooden pediment from Wat Phra That Hariphunchai, similarly inlaid with glass mosaic and painted red and gold.

Along the left-hand wall early ceramics and other Lan Na objects are displayed. Among the ceramics is an important early Haripunjaya-period anvil used for shaping jars, and a fine burial urn decorated with incised patterns. Production of pottery made from coarse clays began in Haripunjaya in the 10C–11C, but had ceased by the time of the Thai conquest at the end of the 13C. By contrast, late Haripunjaya wares, such as the red water bottle with white clay patterns displayed here, were often made from exceptionally fine clays. Sherds found in the old walls of Chiang Mai indicate that these later unglazed wares were in turn largely superseded by glazed wares. Also on display are examples from the Kalong and San Kamphaeng kiln sites in Chiang Rai and Chiang Mai.

Other notable exhibits include a magnificent silver statue, dated 1924, of a caparisoned elephant bearing three seated Buddha images in an elaborately ornamented howdah beneath a five-tiered parasol; a superb bronze Lan Na head of a Buddha image, similar to the immense Phra San Saeo image in the Chiang Mai Museum; and, near the back wall, some fine Haripunjaya terracotta statues, including a 12C or 13C smiling head of a crowned divinity from Wat Pratu Li, Lamphun, and a late 12C head of a Buddha image.

Buddha images of different periods are displayed along the right-hand wall. Of particular note is the group of three large bronze 15C–16C statues from Wat Phra That Hariphunchai, and the fragmentary remains of a fine 12C bronze Buddha image.

In the centre of the room is an early 16C bronze lantern from Wat Phra That Hariphunchai and, nearby, a glazed ceramic *cho fa* with a *nāga* head finial from Wat Phra That Sadet in Lampang, dated 1646.

Beneath the main exhibition hall are nearly 40 inscribed stelae dating from the 12C–16C.

Directly across the street from the museum is the back entrance to **WAT PHRA THAT HARIPHUNCHAI**. This is the usual way in to the *wat*, as the main entrance gives directly on to the river. As its name suggests, Wat Phra That Hariphunchai was a royal monastery of the Haripunjaya kingdom and may therefore have been founded as early as the 9C.

Inside the back entrance, in the right-hand corner of the enclosure, is a **museum**, housed in a modern building. It has a notable collection of Lan Na Buddha images, including one, in a cabinet to the left of the entrance, that has an inscription saying it was cast in 1489 by the metal workers of the village of Sop Li at the confluence of the Ping and Li Rivers.

The most important building of Wat Phra That Hariphunchai is the great *chedi* in the centre of the enclosure known as the **Golden Relic Chedi**. The first *chedi* on this site probably dates back to the foundation of the temple in the 9C and was built to house a relic of the Buddha (possibly a hair or skull fragment). The present *chedi*, which is 59m high, dates from the 15C, but has been much altered since. In the northwest corner of the enclosure is **Chedi Suwanan**. This

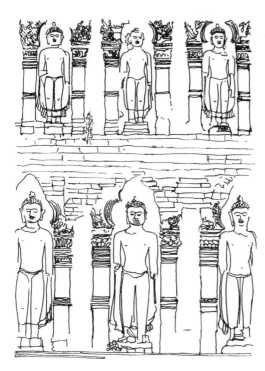

Standing Buddha images on Chedi Suwan Chang Kot, Wat Cham Thewi, Lamphun

is a square stepped brick pyramid similar in form to Wat Cham Tewi, dating from the early 15C. It still retains some of its original stucco decoration. In front of the Golden Relic Chedi is the principal *wihan*, **Wihan Luang**. This is a modern building constructed in the 1920s. The interior is embellished with some indifferent murals depicting scenes from the *jātaka* tales.

On the right of the *wihan* is a **bronze gong**, cast in 1860 at Wat Phra Sing and said to be one of the largest in the world, and on the left is a **ho trai**. This elegant building dates from the early 19C and has some fine woodcarving on its upper storey. **Chedi Mae Krua** is situated in the outer enclosure to the north of Chedi Suwanan. This is a fine example of late or post-Hariphunchai architecture. It was restored at some time not long after the founding of Chiang Mai.

On the left of road 1015, c 1km from the town moat, is **WAT CHAM THEWI**, also known as Wat Ku Kut, which contains two chedi of exceptional interest and importance. On the right inside the entrance is **Chedi Suwan Chang Kot**. This is a notable example of Mon Haripunjaya religious architecture and dates from between the 8C and the 10C. It is built of laterite and is in the form of a square five-storeyed stepped pyramid. On each side of each storey is a row of three niches decorated with stucco containing standing Buddha images. On the left is

Chedi Ratana, a small octagonal brick structure only 11.5m high, decorated with eight niches containing standing Buddha images in stucco. These sculptures date from the 12C, but the *chedi* itself is probably considerably earlier. The modern *wihan* beside the two *chedi* is garishly decorated with coloured glass and is of little interest.

Wat Phra Yun is c 1km from the front entrance of Wat Phra That Hariphunchai and is reached across a footbridge over the Kuang River. Motorcycles can cross on the bridge; cars must take a more circuitous route. This *wat* was built c 1370 by King Ku Na of Lan Na, ninth king of the Mangrai dynasty, for the scholar monk Phra Sumana whom he had invited to come to Lamphun from Sukhothai with an assistant (see pp 280 and 283). A sandstone inscription in Thai and Pali in the enclosure records this event. The present *chedi* was erected in the early 20C on the site of the original *mondop* built for Sumana. It stands on a terrace which has four smaller *chedi* at the corners.

From Lamphun, road 106 continues southwest for c 10km to Pa Sang, once an important cotton-weaving centre, and then a further 8km to **Wat Phra Bat Tak Pha**, a large temple complex on a hillside. Several Footprints of the Buddha have been found here and it is consequently an important place of pilgrimage. It is best seen in the late afternoon when there are few visitors. The modern cruciform *wihan* beside the car park contains two unremarkable Footprints of the Buddha beneath a square altar on which are four bronze seated Buddha images facing the four directions. The building is garishly decorated with coloured glass mosaic and murals.

Within the enclosure are two large Burmese *klong yao* drums, an enormous gong and a large bronze bell. Nearby is a small museum. Climb to the summit for fine views across the plain.

28 · Chiang Mai to Chiang Rai

Road 118, 182km on the direct route to Chiang Rai. The alternative route on roads 107, 1089 and 110, 239km via Fang and Tha Ton is preferable.

Boat, c 3–5hrs from Tha Ton to Chiang Rai. Boats depart from Tha Ton around noon.

There is a choice of two main routes to Chiang Rai. The eastern route, along road 118, is the faster and more direct, and runs through pleasant scenery for much of the way. The buses go this way, and it is recommended for those with limited time.

The longer, more interesting route, detailed below, is along road 107, past the Doi Chiang Dao massif and caves to Tha Ton, from where travellers can take an exhilarating boat ride along the Kok River to Chiang Rai. Beyond Tha Ton, the road deteriorates somewhat, but continues to the mountain-top Kuomintang (KMT), village of Mae Salong and thence to Chiang Rai.

Leave Chiang Mai by the old Chang Phuak Gate along T. Chotana. On the northern edge of the town, a right turn along Chotana, Soi 28 leads to **Wat**

Phra Non Khon Muang, which has a reclining Buddha image of great anti-quity that has, however, been repeatedly restored.

Beside the market in Mae Malai, c 36km from Chiang Mai, road 1095 turns off left to Pai and Mae Hong Son (see Rte 32) Beyond the town of Mae Taeng traffic is lighter and the scenery becomes wilder. The road winds through a narrow gorge beside the Ping River, passing the **Chiang Dao elephant training centre** just beyond the 56km stone, which is a popular stop for tour coaches.

To the west, Doi Chiang Dao looms into view. In the small market town of **Chiang Dao**, a turning to the left leads to a cave-shrine, **Tham Chiang Dao**, composed of a group of caverns containing Burmese-style Buddha images built so that they follow the natural contours of the cave walls.

Beyond Chiang Dao the route winds through densely wooded hills towards Fang. Before reaching Fang itself, an extremely steep road off to the left climbs up Doi Ang Khang to the KMT village of **Ban Tam Ngop**, the former base of General Lee Wen-huan's 3rd Army HQ. It can be chilly up here, but the views across the Ping valley are magnificent.

The town of **Fang** (pop. 12,000) is situated on either side of the main road c 14km further on. Fang was an important trading centre of the Lan Na kingdom and is thought to have been founded in the late 13C by Mangrai. Almost nothing remains of the original fortified town, and Fang's chief importance today lies in its location near the notorious Golden Triangle. It also provides an outlet for the produce of the Akhas, Lisus, Hmongs and other hill peoples in the region.

The accommodation available in Fang is generally poor, and travellers are advised to continue 24km further to Tha Ton, where there are better hotels.

▶From Fang, however, an easy **detour** is possible to the hot springs in **Mae Fang National Park**, c 9km from the town. Turn left off the main street and follow the signs to the park, where there are several hot pools, a small geyser, food stalls and a sauna.◀

The village of **Tha Ton**, on the banks of the Kok River, offers pleasant accom-modation and charming scenery. Recommended is the comfortable *Mae Kok River Lodge* on the left bank upstream of the bridge.

■ **Boats to Chiang Rai** depart daily at about midday from near the bridge, and the trip takes between three and five hours, with one or two stops en route. The ride is noisy and can be uncomfortably cramped, but it is also a refreshing change from the road. More persevering travellers can hire a bamboo raft and float gently downstream for three days. For those who have plenty of time and are prepared to get wet, this can be a delightfully exhilarating journey.

The road beyond Tha Ton is rough in places, although it is being steadily improved. Public *songthaeo* depart in the morning for Mae Salong (c 50km to the northeast) and Mae Chan (65km), from where there are regular services to Chiang Rai.

Chiang Rai

The provincial capital of Chiang Rai (pop. 36,500), situated on the right bank of the Kok River, is notable more for the exceptional beauty of its surroundings than for the splendour of its monuments. It is increasingly being visited by tourists as a quieter and cheaper alternative to Chiang Mai.

■ **Information**. The TAT office and Tourist Police are at 448/16 T. Singkhlai and produce a good map of the town. Staff can provide information on hotels and restaurants, sights, trekking and vehicle rentals. An excellent map of Chiang Rai province is V. Hongsombud's *Guide Map of Chiang Rai*, usually available in newsagents in the town. Less reliable is the *Map of Chiang Rai* published by Prannok Witthaya Maps Center.

■ **Hotels and Services**. There is a large choice of accommodation, ranging from the expensive *Dusit Island Resort* on an island in the Kok River to the many simple guest-houses scattered round the north side of the town. The *Wang Kham* (Wang Come) on T. Premawiphat and the *Wiang Inn* at 893 T. Phahon Yothin are both very comfortable and central. Cheap and acceptable guest-houses include *Chat House*, close to Wat Phra Kaeo, and the *Mae Hong Son Guest House* off T. Singkhlai. The *Bangkok Bank* is at 517 T. Suksathit, and there are numerous **money changers** near the town centre. The **post office** is on the corner of T. Utarakit and T. Tha Luang.

■ **Transport**. The **bus station** is off T. Phahon Yothin to the south of the town centre. Regular bus services operate to Chiang Saen, Chiang Mai, Mae Sai, Chiang Khong, Phayao, Nan and further afield. *THAI* has direct **flights** to Chiang Mai (40 mins) and Bangkok (1hr 15 mins). The booking office is at 870 T. Phahon Yothin, near the bus station.

History

According to both the *Chiang Mai Chronicle* and the *Chinakalamali Chronicle*, Chiang Rai was founded in 1262 by Mangrai as capital of the Lan Na kingdom. Mangrai's ashes are preserved in a brick *chedi* in Wat Ngam Muang (see below), and a statue of the king surrounded by elephants stands near the entrance to the town on the road from Mae Chan. In 1296 Mangrai moved his court to Chiang Mai ('New City'), but during the early 14C the Lan Na rulers had their court in Chiang Rai or Chiang Saen as well as in Chiang Mai. After 1339 Chiang Mai became the permanent capital of the kingdom, and the importance of Chiang Rai consequently diminished. In 1558 the Burmese captured Chiang Mai, and Lan Na came under Burmese suzerainty, although the descendants of Mangrai continued to reign in Chiang Mai until the dynasty became extinct in 1578. In 1775 Chiang Mai was retaken from the Burmese by the joint forces of Lan Na and Siam, to whom the rulers of Lan Na had declared their vassalage. Chiang Rai was recaptured in 1786, and Chiang Saen, the last Burmese stronghold in Lan Na, in 1804. During this period of reconquest and subsequently, Chiang Rai declined still further, and by 1844 its population had become so depleted that it had to be re-founded. Settlers were brought in from Chiang Mai, Lamphun and Lampang, and the size of the walled town was approximately doubled.

On the corner of T. Trairat and T. Singkhlai is the old **Overbrook Hospital**, founded in 1911 by an American missionary, Dr Briggs. At that time Chiang Rai was surrounded by snake-infested swamps and consequently suffered frequent outbreaks of typhoid and cholera. Briggs proposed that the city walls be pulled down in an attempt to improve drainage and sanitation, and this was finally done c 1920. Part of the wall on the eastern side of the city, opposite the end of T. Nong Si Chang, was reconstructed in 1988 following a sketch made by a French physician, Dr P. Neis, in 1884.

Near the hospital on T. Trairat, is **Wat Phra Kaeo**, one of several temples that have successively housed the famous **Emerald Buddha**, Phra Kaeo Morokot, a small jadeite or green jasper image which is variously alleged to have come originally from Burma, from Sri Lanka and from Angkor, and is now the palladium of the Thai kingdom, enshrined in Wat Phra Kaeo in Bangkok. It was first revealed in Chiang Rai in 1434 in a *chedi* that had been split open by lightning. The ruler of Lan Na wished to take it to his capital in Chiang Mai, but the elephant that was carrying it refused to go in that direction and the king, interpreting this as a sign from heaven, had it carried to Lampang, where it was enshrined in Wat Phra Kaeo Don Tao. In 1468 King Tilok removed it to Chiang Mai, where he installed it in Wat Chedi Luang. In 1546 the son of King Phothisarat of the Lao kingdom of Lan Xang (Luang Prabang) was enthroned as king Setthathirat of Lan Na. Less than two years after this he succeeded his father as king of Lan Xang and in 1552 took the Emerald Buddha to Luang Prabang. There it remained until 1564, when it was taken to Vientiane. In 1778 General Taksin conquered Vientiane and carried the image off to Bangkok, where it was first housed in Wat Arun and since 1784 in Wat Phra Kaeo in the Grand Palace (see p 117).

A new and almost identical image named Phra Yok Chiang Rai, made from Canadian jade by a Chinese craftsman, was consecrated on 20 September 1991 by King Bhumibol and installed in the *ubosot* of this *wat*. The *ubosot* has a lovely wooden gable, painted red and gold. On the altar behind the jade Buddha image is a fine bronze Lan Na-style seated representation of the Buddha in *bhūmisparśa mudrā*. Flanking it are six other bronzes, including figures of two disciples, Sariputta on the left, and Moggallana on the right, both, according to inscriptions on their bases, cast in 1727 by the ruler of Chiang Rai, Mang Phara Saphaek, his wife and his son. The pair was brought sometime before 1957 from the ruins of Wat Ngam Muang nearby.

Wat Phra Sing, entered from T. Tha Luang, a short distance east of the hospital was built c 1385 during the rule of Maha Prom, younger brother of King Ku Na of Lan Na. The *ubosot* has some finely carved wooden doors, and inside contains octagonal wooden pillars and some rather gaudy murals. On a glass and gilt throne to the left of the altar is one of the four almost identical Sukhothai-period bronze images of the Buddha known as Phra Phuttha Sihing. The other three are in Wat Phra Sing in Chiang Mai, Wat Phutthaisawan in the National Museum in Bangkok and Ho Phra Phuttha Sihing in Nakhon Si Thammarat. Each of these is claimed by some to be the original.

Behind the *ubosot* is a white square-based *chedi* surmounted by a gilded seven-tiered parasol.

To reach **Wat Ngam Muang**, which was founded in the early 14C, turn left off T. Trairat to the north of Wat Phra Kaeo, along T. Sangkaeo. The *wat* is at the end of this narrow street up a flight of steps. The brick *chedi* (Ku Phra Chao Mangrai), which was built much later, is believed to contain Mangrai's remains. It stands on a square base of laterite blocks.

Wat Phra That Doi Thong, on the summit of Doi Chom Thong nearby, marks the centre of the original *wiang* of Chiang Rai. There is little to see here now, except the modern *lak muang*, completed in January 1988, which stands at the centre of a model of the universe laid out according to Buddhist cosmology, with Mount Meru in the centre.

Wat Chet Yot, on the south side of the town, owes its name to the form of its *chedi*, which consists of a central spire and relic chamber surmounted by six smaller spires, all set on a high rectangular base. Each of the seven spires is surmounted by a gilt parasol. The whole edifice is whitewashed. Inside the *chedi*, which has an opening on the east side opposite the *ubosot*, is a small shrine with a reclining Buddha image of no great merit. The modern *ubosot* has a porch with a painted wood ceiling, predominantly blue, depicting astrological motifs. Within is a huge gilded, seated Buddha image in *bhūmisparśa mudrā*.

29 · Chiang Rai to Chiang Saen

Roads *110 and 1016, 60km on the direct route via Mae Chan. The preferred alternative route on roads 110 and 1290 includes detours to Mae Salong (81km) on roads 1089, 1234 and 1130, and to Doi Thung (36km) on road 1149.*

From Chiang Rai road 110 runs north towards Mae Sai and Chiang Saen. In the small market town of Mae Chan (29km), road 1016 turns off right to Chiang Saen. This is the way for those in a hurry, but an enjoyable **detour** can be made to the Kuomintang (KMT) village of Mae Salong, now officially known as Santikhiri.

Mae Salong
Set high in the hills near the Burmese border, **Mae Salong** is one of a number of predominantly Chinese villages in northern Thailand settled by members of the defeated KMT forces in the early 1960s. It retains a clearly definable Yunnanese atmosphere: many of the older houses are built in traditional Yunnanese style, and there are restaurants offering Yunnanese dishes, and market vendors selling Chinese foodstuffs. Until the early 1980s Mae Salong was an isolated and virtually autonomous community. Before the tarmac road was completed in 1986, pack-horses were used to transport goods to and from the village, and the area was a transit point for opium smugglers. It now appears peaceful and prosperous.

There are two roads to Mae Salong from Mae Chan, and travellers are recommended to go out on one and return on the other. Turn left off road 110 on to road 1089, on the south side of Mae Chan. This delightful road follows the Chan River valley west for c 30km, past a number of Akha, Lisu and Lahu villages, before turning right and climbing through the hills to Mae Salong.

■ **Hotels**. Mae Salong has several simple guest-houses, and there is also the smart, comfortable *Mae Salong Villa* on the eastern approach, which has a good restaurant and pleasant views. It can be chilly in the village, so visitors should bring warm clothes.

History

When the main KMT forces of Chiang Kaishek retreated to Taiwan in 1949 after their defeat by Mao Zedong's communist forces, fighting continued in Yunnan and other remote parts of China. Mao proclaimed victory on 1 October 1949 in Beijing, but Kunming, the provincial capital of Yunnan, did not fall until December. The surviving KMT stragglers fled south towards Burma and French Indochina in order to establish a base area in the isolated valleys of southern Yunnan near the Lao border, from which to launch a reoccupation of China. However, the communists got there first, and the KMT were forced instead to flee into Burma. In an attempt to avoid the Burmese authorities, they settled near the junction of the Lao and Thai borders, but the Burmese soon discovered this foreign army on their soil and launched an offensive against it. The KMT retreated westwards along the Thai–Burmese frontier and took over a small town called Mong Hsat on the Burmese side of the border, just north of Fang and Tha Ton in Thailand.

This event coincided with the outbreak of the Korean war. Syngman Rhee's anti-communist regime established friendly relations with Taiwan, and a plan to establish a second front in Yunnan against China was discussed. General Douglas MacArthur, commander of the UN forces in Korea, was agreeable to the idea, and in 1951 US army engineers were sent to upgrade the tiny airstrip in Mong Hsat. By the end of the year the secret KMT army, which was commanded by General Li Mi, had grown to 6000 men. The KMT's numbers were supplemented by brigands and local warlords, and by opium traders who, in exchange for the drug, sold arms to the various ethnic minorities waging war against the Burmese government. By selling arms instead of the traditional rice, the traders were able to increase their opium purchases as much as thirtyfold, and consequently looked to the KMT for protection. They were also fearful of a communist victory, which would have put their lucrative trade at risk, and this prompted a further increase in the KMT forces, which soon rose to c 12,000.

Between 1951 and 1953 the KMT forces made seven unsuccessful attempts to invade Yunnan. The Burmese complained to the UN General Assembly, and UN resolutions were passed demanding that the KMT leave Burma. By May 1954 the US and Taiwan had airlifted more than 6000 troops out through northern Thailand. However, thousands were left behind, so the Burmese turned to Beijing for help. In 1961 20,000 Chinese swept down on the remaining KMT, whose defeated remnants fled into Thailand, where they still are to this day. The KMT were initially used by the Thais to patrol the border and in return were given unofficial permission to trade across it in any goods they chose, including opium.

Mae Salong is a good base from which to walk to surrounding Akha, Lahu and Lisu villages, but visitors are strongly advised to take a guide, as it is easy to get lost.

From Mae Salong, return to Mae Chan past Mae Salong Villa on road 1234, a winding road which descends through magnificent scenery for c 36km, past Mien and Akha villages to the cultivated fields in the valley below.

Back on road 110, travellers heading directly for Chiang Saen should return to Mae Chan and turn left on to road 1016. The alternative and more interesting route, which is described here, is via Mae Sai to the north.

Continue north along road 110. A turning to the left c 11km north of the Mae Salong junction leads past the residence of the late Princess Mother, mother of King Bhumibol, who died in 1995, and through several Lahu villages, and continues for 18km through mountain scenery to **WAT PHRA THAT DOI TUNG**, which is in a charming location, surrounded by woodland just below the summit of Doi Tung (1330m). It has twin golden *chedi* in Burmese style, which are said to date from AD 911, and were extensively restored in the 1960s. The *wat* is much visited by pilgrims, who ring the bronze bells lining the terrace. Every March there is an important pilgrimage here.

Road 110 continues north for 18km to the border town of **Mae Sai**, a dusty, unattractive place which nevertheless attracts local tourists in great numbers because of its location on the river bank opposite the Burmese town of Takhilek. The steady flow of traders and local tourists over the bridge provides the main interest. There are banks, hotels and restaurants here, but there is more agreeable accommodation in Sop Ruak or Chiang Saen to the east.

A turning to the right off the main street leads southeast to **Sop Ruak**, a village on the Mekong River at the heart of the so-called Golden Triangle. The frontiers of Thailand, Laos and Burma meet here, and during the day it is a cluster of souvenir stalls, cafés and tour buses. The luxurious *Baan Boran Hotel* 1km north of Sop Ruak offers excellent but expensive accommodation, and there are also a few simple guest-houses in the town.

On the hill behind the main road is **Wat Phra That Pu Khao**, which has an attractive brick *wihan* and a ruined *chedi* built on the site of a monastery originally established in AD 759. This is the best place from which to view the river and surrounding countryside.

Chiang Saen

Chiang Saen (pop. 16,000), 8km downstream, is a delightful little town spread over the ruins of a considerably larger, fortified *wiang*, first capital of the Lan Na kingdom, most of which is now hidden beneath trees and thick vegetation. Most visitors come here on day trips from Chiang Rai, but a longer stay provides a peaceful change from the busy towns of Chiang Rai and Chiang Mai.

■ **Hotels**. The choice of accommodation is restricted to a few rudimentary guest-houses along the river bank.

History

Stone tools excavated at sites along the Mekong River and around the town provide evidence of prehistoric human settlement in the area. There is also some evidence to suggest that in the 9C the Khmers exercised influence in the Chiang Saen area (Yonok), but little is known of the course of events in this area before the 14C. The chronicles of Chiang Mai trace the origins of the ruling dynasty of the northern Thai kingdom of Lan Na to Chiang Saen in the mid-12C, and it was the birthplace in 1239 of Mangrai, who moved the capital of Lan Na from Chiang Saen to Chiang Rai in 1262 and to Chiang Mai in 1292. In 1281 Mangrai conquered Haripunjaya. One of the Chiang Mai chronicles states that in 1327 King Saen Phu, grandson of Mangrai, founded a new city at Chiang Saen and established it as the centre of one of the major principalities of the Lan Na kingdom. In 1558 Chiang Mai was conquered by the Burmese, and from then until the late 18C Chiang Saen and most of Lan Na remained under Burmese suzerainty, albeit sometimes only nominally. In 1775 the Thais recaptured Chiang Mai from the Burmese and during the next 30 years brought the whole of Lan Na under their control. Chiang Saen was the last Burmese stronghold in Lan Na and was not retaken until 1804, when Rama I, first ruler of the Chakri dynasty in Bangkok, in an attempt to deter the Burmese from further attacks, razed the city to the ground, leaving only the monasteries standing. Chiang Saen remained virtually deserted until 1881, when King Chulalongkorn, following the example of Chiang Rai, which had been resettled in the 1840s, ordered a prince of Lamphun to bring people from Lamphun, Chiang Mai and Lampang to repopulate the town. The modern settlement covers only a small part of the area of the old city, which was originally surrounded by a wall 8km long.

Chiang Saen is small and quiet enough to make it possible and pleasant to see the main sights on foot. Visitors are recommended to start their tour at the **Chiang Saen National Museum** (open Wed–Sun, 09.00–16.00), which lies a short walk from the old Chiang Saen Gate and contains a small collection of local artefacts. In the front room on the ground floor is an aerial photograph clearly showing the old city fortifications, those of Wiang Pruksa further downstream, and those of a fortified town opposite Wiang Pruksa on the Lao side of the Mekong. Straight ahead inside the entrance are four magnificent 15C Lan Na bronze seated images of the Buddha in *bhūmisparśa mudrā*. A fifth, standing image, cast in 1577, once held an alms bowl. To the left in the front room are a number of c 15C stone inscriptions and stone heads in the Phayao style. To the right are mid-14C stucco fragments from Wat Pa Sak, including a ferocious *kīrttimukha* baring its teeth by stretching its mouth with its hands. Nearby is a collection of prehistoric tools found in the area.

Upstairs are several display cases containing stucco ornaments from Wat Chedi Luang, votive tablets, pottery from the San Kamphaeng and Wiang Kalong kilns, some beautiful **silver objects** excavated at Wat Ngam Muang in Chiang Rai in 1967, and a fine clay torso of a 16C–17C Buddha image found at Wat Song Phi Nong.

The back rooms downstairs contain a variety of folk art and crafts, including textiles, looms, traps, swords, guns and pipes, some small 15C Chinese bronze cannon and two bronze Dong Son drums. There are also some fine **Mien ceremonial paintings** depicting the Taoist pantheon, unfortunately rather poorly displayed.

Beside the museum is the *chedi* of **Wat Phra That Chedi Luang**, built in the 13C. A short distance to the west is the ancient, but recently restored, Chiang Saen city gate. On the right just before the gate are the ruins of **Wat Mahathat**,

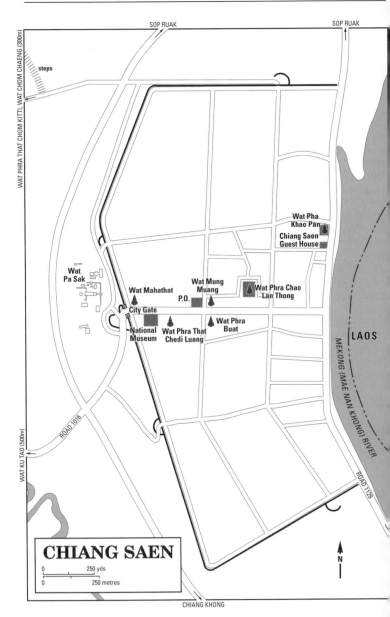

CHIANG SAEN

much of which is now covered in vegetation. Outside the Chiang Saen gate are the ruins of **WAT PA SAK** ('Monastery of a Thousand Teak Trees') in a glade of teak trees. This temple, founded by Saen Phu, probably in 1319, to enshrine relics of the Buddha brought from Sri Lanka, is one of the most important

The chedi of Wat Pa Sak, Chiang Saen

monuments in Chiang Saen. Little remains of it now except a single *chedi* in the form of a square stepped brick pyramid with images of the standing Buddha in stuccoed terracotta set in niches on each level. The form of the *chedi* is similar to that of the late Dvaravati square chedi of Wat Cham Thewi (Wat Ku Kut) in Lamphun (see p 289). The stucco decoration has elements showing Burmese, Sri Vijaya and Sukhothai influences.

Directly in front of the *chedi* are the foundations of two ancillary buildings aligned on an east–west axis, and a few metres north of the *chedi* are more restored foundations. One more site, to the south of the main *chedi*, contains the bases of a *wihan* and a *chedi*. A small fee is charged to enter the grounds.

Return past the museum along the main street towards the river. On the left beyond the post office is the square-based *chedi* of **Wat Mung Muang**, opposite the smaller *chedi* of **Wat Phra Buat**. A short distance further east along the road, turn left just before reaching the river bank to **Wat Phra Chao Lan Thong**, which is said to have been founded by a son of King Tilok of Lan Na. It was restored in 1967. In the modern *wihan* is a large bronze image of the Buddha called Phra Chao Lan Thong, flanked by smaller ones. To the right is an image cast in 1726 and known as Phra Chao Saen Swae ('The Buddha with

100,000 Pins'), so named because it was cast in several parts and then joined together with pins. Behind the *wihan* are the remains of a *chedi*, the base of which appears to have been constructed at a different time to the octagonal upper section, since the latter is disproportionately small.

Continue to the river front and turn left. Beyond the Chiang Saen Guest House are the ruins of **Wat Pha Khao Pan**, which appears stylistically to date from the 16C. The *chedi* has niches containing walking images of the Buddha in *abhaya mudrā*.

To the northwest of the old fortifications are **Wat Chom Chaeng** and **Wat Phra That Chom Kitti**, two monasteries that stand together on the summit of a tree-covered hill and can be reached either by a steep flight of steps or by road. Wat Phra That Chom Kitti has a fine round *chedi* with a crooked spire and is covered with gilded bronze plates. Each of the four niches in the *chedi* contains a standing image of the Buddha; these were retouched sometime between the mid-16C and the 18C. Immediately opposite is the smaller brick *chedi* of Wat Chom Chaeng. Although both are surrounded by trees, they command a fine view of the Mekong plain and the distant mountains.

On the western edge of the town across the bypass are the ruins of **Wat Ku Tao**, lying amid rice fields. To find them, leave the town on road 1016 towards Chiang Rai, and turn left just beyond the 29km stone, c 2km from the town centre. The large circular *chedi*, renovated in 1993, leans dramatically; it has some fine stucco decoration round the top. Beside the *chedi* are the ruins of other monastic buildings.

Take road 1129 c 4km south from the town along the river bank to **Wat Phra That Pha Ngao**, on the right side by the 49km stone. The enclosure is entered through an ornate gateway. On the right is a renovated *wihan* containing the stuccoed brick torso of a colossal image of the Buddha. In front of it is a partially buried stuccoed brick image called Luang Pho Pha Ngao, discovered in the 1970s when the building was renovated. Behind the *wihan* is Phra That Pha Ngao, an octagonal brick *chedi* perched on a large rounded boulder. The road continues up the hill behind the *wat* to a concrete *chedi* covered in white tiles, known as **Phra Boromathat Phuttha Nimit Chedi**. It was built in the 1980s and encloses a much earlier brick *chedi*.

Further to the southwest, a turning to the left just beyond the 48km stone leads to **Wat Song Phi Nong**, where the ruins of two *chedi* and two *wihan* can be seen. One *chedi* and one *wihan* have been partially restored; the others remain totally untouched.

A further 48km to the east on road 1129 is the quiet riverside market town of **Chiang Khong**, where the annual hunt for the giant Mekong catfish begins each April. The route passes through hills and cultivated fields. A large Hmong village at the top of a pass, 19km before Chiang Khong, has a rudimentary guest-house in a picturesque setting. Beyond the village the road descends to the Mekong again, and finally to Chiang Khong. Accommodation is available either at the *Chiang Khong Hotel* at the north end of the town, or at the more agreeable *Tammila Guest House* on Soi 1. The most comfortable place, however, is the *Pla Buk Resort* at the south end of the town.

The quickest route from Chiang Khong back to Chiang Rai is along roads 1174, 1098 and 1173 via Wiang Chai, c 103km.

30 · Chiang Mai to Phayao

Roads 118 *and* 120, 142km. *Phayao can also be easily reached from Chiang Rai on road* 1, 94km.

From Chiang Mai head north on road 118 towards Chiang Rai, and just before the 79km stone, turn right on to road 120 to Wang Nua. After c 2km this road passes a track off to the left, leading up to the old hilltop fortifications of **Wiang Kalong**. There is little to be seen of this site today, except some earth ramparts and an imaginative model of how the settlement may have once looked. There is no documentary evidence for the history of Wiang Kalong, but a large number of ceramic kilns, probably dating from the late 13C to the mid-16C, have been discovered nearby.

Road 120 continues c 15km east to Wang Nua, where a road to the left by the small clock tower leads after c 24km to Wang Kaeo Waterfall in **Doi Luang National Park**. The road runs through a string of villages, past tobacco and rice fields, gradually narrowing as it approaches the falls. The area round the falls makes a delightful picnic spot, with trees providing shade and food stalls offering snacks and drinks.

Beyond Wang Nua, road 120 winds through the forest-covered Doi Bussaracum range, with splendid views on all sides. Beyond the watershed, the lake on which Phayao is built comes into view far below. The road descends to the valley floor, where it joins road 1 on the south side of the town.

Travellers coming from Chiang Rai should head south on road 1 past **Phan**, where an extensive 15C kiln complex was excavated by the Fine Arts Department in 1973. The ceramics from here are very similar to those from the Sukhothai and Sawankhalok sites, and it is highly probable that these kilns were established by Sawankhalok potters. The highway is fast and direct to Phayao.

Phayao

Phayao (pop. 26,000) is picturesquely situated on the eastern shore of a large lake, Kwan Phayao, c 6km long and 4km wide. It is surrounded by high mountains. Much of the lake is clogged with water-hyacinth.

■ **Hotels and services**. The *Than Thong* at 55 T. Don Sanam and the *Wattana* at 69 T. Don Sanam offer clean rooms and secure parking near the town centre. More comfortable but inconveniently located on the town's bypass is the *Phayao Hotel*. The *Bangkok Bank*, *Thai Farmers Bank* and the **post office** are also on T. Don Sanam.

■ **Transport**. From the **bus station** off T. Rop Wiang, outside the old city moat, there are frequent services to most towns in the north and to Bangkok. **Samlo** operate around the town centre and from the bus station. The nearest **airport** is in Chiang Rai.

History

Phayao was formerly the capital of an independent kingdom that was absorbed by Lan Na in 1338, and the sites of several early fortified cities have been found in the vicinity. Among these is Wiang Phra That Chom Thong on the hill to the north of the town centre. All are probably contemporaneous and date from the 15C–16C. Nothing is left of the old city ramparts of Phayao except a drainage canal which follows the course of the old moat along the north side of T. Rop Wiang.

From T. Don Sanam, turn south opposite the sprawling and rather gloomy market to reach **Wat Ratchasanthan**. This 12C monastery was almost entirely destroyed during a storm in 1988, and little now remains of the original building, which was chiefly constructed of teak, except for the finials of the two *nāga* balustrades that formerly flanked the steps leading to the entrance. The fine teak columns and teak roof tiles in the new *wihan* were taken from the old building. There are traces of paintings on the interior walls of the *wihan*, which also contains an important Sukhothai bronze Buddha image.

To the southeast of the *wat* is a large grassy square, in the centre of which is the city's *lak muang*. Between this square and the lake is a pleasant residential neighbourhood with some fine **teak houses** in large spacious gardens. Two of these are especially notable: one near the junction of T. Prasat and T. Prasat, Soi 1, and the other on the shore of the lake to the west.

Along the shore are numerous **fish restaurants** serving excellent, although sometimes rather overpriced dishes and, in the late afternoon, stalls selling grilled and fried food.

To the north of the town centre on the lake shore is **Wat Si Khom Kham**. The *wihan* of this *wat* is in an enclosure surrounded by a gallery containing a collection of Lan Na Buddha images and heads. In the *wihan* is a huge stuccoed and gilded brick image of the Buddha, **Phra Chao Ton Luang**. In a small open pavilion in front of the *wihan* are a pair of Footprints of the Buddha dating from c 14C, and to the south is a modern *ubosot* built on concrete piles over the lake, its interior walls decorated with magnificent **murals** by one of Thailand's best known modern artists, Angkarn Kalyanapongsa. In the garden beyond the *wihan* are some grotesque modern painted cement sculptures representing the visit of the legendary monk Phra Malai to Hell.

To the north of Wat Si Khom Kham a turning to the right leads up a hill to **Wat Phra That Chom Thong**. This, like the centre of Phayao itself, was once also the site of a fortified *wiang*, but few traces of it remain.

To the east of the town, across a busy bypass, is a large bell-shaped brick *chedi* of somewhat Sri Lankan appearance standing on a high brick base, which is all that remains of **Wat Bunnak**. It is surrounded by the foundations of other, earlier buildings. To reach it, head north from the town on Pratu Khlong, Soi 1 and continue c 700m across the bypass.

Return to the bypass and turn south towards Wat Si Chom Ruang. Before reaching the *wat*, turn right along Soi Wat Li to reach **Wat Li** after a few hundred metres. The monastery itself is of little interest, but beside the abbot's house is a small **museum** on two floors which he is willing to show to visitors. The display cases are crammed with flints, Lan Na-style Buddha images, ceramics, animal figurines, coins, lacquer bowls, pipes, votive tablets and other oddments that he has collected. Outside is a large collection of Buddha heads.

Visitors with their own transport can make a circular tour around Kwan Phayao, stopping on the west side of the lake at **Wat Analayo**, a very popular pilgrimage spot, which can also be reached by *songthaeo* from Phayao.

31 · Phayao to Nan

Roads *1021, 1091 and 1120, 181km. To Chun, 48km; from Chun to Pong, 31km; Pong to Chiang Muan, 35km; Chiang Muan to Nan, 67km.*

*This is a delightful route on quiet roads through sparsely populated hill scenery; the public **bus** from Phayao to Nan follows this route.*

Head south from Phayao on road 1 and take road 1021 to the left after c 5km. The route runs along the Ing River valley to **Chun**, from where a **detour** can be made to the Thai Lu villages of **Chiang Kham** district, c 30km to the north. The **Thai Lu**, originally from southern Yunnan in China, were forcibly resettled in the provinces of Phayao, Nan and Chiang Rai during the 18C and 19C as a result of warfare between the states of Nan and Sip Song Panna (Xishuangbanna) in Yunnan. Many Thai Lu in Chiang Kham still weave their traditional textiles.

From Chun, road 1091 runs southeast through undulating hills to **Pong**, which has some fine wooden houses, where it joins the upper reaches of the Yom River. After c 20km more it reaches the Thai Lu village of **Ban Tha Fa Thai**. The village **wat** on the left side is worth a look. Its roof is one of a diminishing number in Thailand still clad with shingles, and although the well-maintained *ubosot* has been renovated, it still has its original wooden pillars. Note also the embroidered *thong* hangings, woven by the women of the village.

Beyond Ban Tha Fa Thai the road continues along the valley for c 15km to an intersection at Chiang Muan. This charming village lies c 2km to the left, while the road to the right goes to Nan. 2km beyond the intersection, the Nan road turns left and starts winding very steeply upwards through **magnificent forest scenery,** with spectacular views to the watershed which marks the provincial boundary. In contrast to Phayao, the Nan side has suffered severe deforestation. The road passes a number of Mien and Hmong villages as it descends to the Nan valley, reaching the town centre near the Nan National Museum.

Nan

Nan (pop. 22,000) is in an area of outstanding natural beauty, but after the journey from Phayao, the visitor may feel somewhat disappointed to find that the town has the same concrete shop-houses and dusty streets that are a feature of so many Thai towns. Looks can deceive, however, for Nan is a friendly and pleasant place with a number of beautiful *wat*, one of Thailand's best provincial museums, and plenty to explore in the surrounding countryside.

■ **Hotels and services**. The best hotels are the *Thewarat* and the *Nan Fa*, close together on T. Sumon Thewarat. Recommended for travellers on small budgets is the simple, friendly *Nan Guest House*, close to the THAI office off T. Maha Phrom. The *Bangkok Bank* and *Thai Farmers Bank* are near the Thewarat Hotel. The **post office** is on T. Mahawong.

■ **Transport**. Nan has two main **bus** stations. Buses to the north and west, i.e. Chiang Mai, Chiang Rai and Phayao, leave from near the west end of T. Ananta Woraritthidet, opposite the restored city wall. Buses to Phrae,

Uttaradit, Phitsanulok and other destinations to the south, including Bangkok, depart from the bus station on T. Kha Luang. *THAI* has daily **flights** to Bangkok (2hrs 10 mins) via Phrae (25 mins), and direct flights to Chiang Mai (40 mins) and Phitsanulok (50 mins). The booking office is at 34 T. Maha Phrom.

Samlo operate around the town centre, and travel agents near the Thewarat Hotel can arrange car, motorcycle and bicycle **rentals**, and organise **treks** into Nan's magnificent mountains.

■ **Boat races** are held on the river during Thot Kathin, usually in October.

History

Nan, isolated and protected by the mountains, remained the centre of a small independent Thai kingdom from the foundation of the city of Muang Pua (Varanagara) near Tambon Silaphet in the late 13C until the early 20C. In 1359 the city was relocated on the eastern bank of the Nan River at the site of the present Wat Phra That Chae Haeng and renamed Phu Phiang Chae Haeng; it was moved again in 1368 to its present site on the western bank.

As a small city-state, Nan was frequently at the mercy of its more powerful neighbours. Already in the late 13C and early 14C it seems to have been a dependency of Sukhothai, and in the mid-15C it became a tributary of Chiang Mai after a battle in which, according to the chronicles, cannon were used—an early reference to the use of firearms in Southeast Asian warfare. When Chiang Mai was invaded by the Burmese in the mid-16C, Nan too came under Burmese suzerainty. During the 17C successive governors took advantage of Nan's geographical isolation to revolt against their feudal overlords, but in 1703 the Burmese sacked Nan and tore down the city walls, and in 1726 appointed a local prince, Luang Tin Mahawong as vassal ruler. A period of turmoil ensued, which was only ended in 1788 when the ruler, Chao Atthawon Pannyo (r. 1786–1811) went to Bangkok and appealed successfully to King Rama I to place Nan under Siamese suzerainty. One result of this was that, although Nan was given greater security, throughout the 19C it repeatedly had to raise armies to fight wars for Bangkok against unruly neighbours in the north and east. In 1931, with the death of the last descendant of Luang Tin Mahawong, Nan was formally incorporated into the kingdom of Siam.

Nan's relative isolation once again encouraged rebellion when, from 1968 to 1982, much of this mountainous province was controlled by the Communist Party of Thailand. The CPT's 'Nan Revolutionary Base', set up in parts of Pua and Thung Chang districts inhabited by the Thai Lu, was not taken by government forces until 1983.

The building at the corner of T. Maha Phom and T. Phakwang housing the **NAN NATIONAL MUSEUM** (open Wed–Sun, 09.00–12.00, 13.00–16.00) was constructed in 1903 for Phra Chao Suriyaphong Phritadet, governor of Nan (r. 1893–1918), whose statue is outside the front entrance.

The rooms on the **ground floor** are chiefly devoted to local cultures and crafts, and contain reconstructions of a kitchen and a bedroom, various utensils, including tobacco boxes and betel sets, hunting and fishing equipment, nets

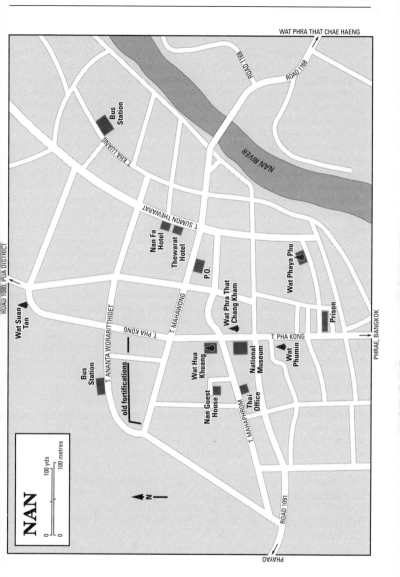

and traps, and agricultural implements, such as rice baskets, ploughs and water-buffalo yokes. In the third room is a display of local textiles, and the fifth room contains costumes and photographs of some of Nan's ethnic minorities, including the Thai Lu, Hmong, Mien, Phi Tong Luang and Htin peoples.

The main hall **upstairs** contains exhibits illustrating Nan's history. Inside the doorway are two fine manuscript cabinets, one made in the late 18C, the other in the mid-19C. In the same room is a rather damaged stone inscription

(Inscription 64) found at Wat Chang Kham, which is believed to date from the late 14C. This is related to Sukhothai Inscription 45, dated 1392, and refers to an oath of fealty made by Chao Kham Tam, ruler of Nan, to Mahathammaratcha III (Sai Luthai) of Sukhothai.

On the back wall above two 19C howdahs are portraits of the last two rulers of the Luang Tin Mahawong dynasty. On the left is Phra Chao Suriyaphong Phritadet and on the right is his brother and successor, Chao Maha Phrom Surathada (r. 1918–31). In the centre of the wall is an elaborate late 18C standing image of the Buddha from Wat Bun Yun in Wiang Sa district.

To the left is a smaller room containing a general survey of Thai art and beyond this is a strong-room housing an impressive 18kg **elephant tusk**, an object of great local pride and reputed to date from the late 17C. It is held aloft by a brightly painted wooden figure of a *garuḍa*.

The next room contains artefacts excavated during the construction of the Sirikit Dam in **Tha Pla district**, Uttaradit province. Most were found inside old *chedi* and date from the late 18C, when the court of the ruler of Nan, Chao Mongkon Worayot was at Tha Pla. They include small Buddha images, coins, silver ornaments and utensils, and ceramics from a late 15C kiln site in Muang district, Nan. From a *wat* in Tha Pla is a badly damaged 16C Ayutthaya-style wooden standing Buddha image, which once held an alms bowl.

In the room beyond are numerous **Buddha images**. Most of these are wooden and date from the 19C, and many display local stylistic influences. Here also are the bases and feet of two 19C jewelled images of the Buddha stolen in 1981 from Wat Phra That Chae Haeng, and two wooden 19C votive tablet racks decorated with finely carved *nāgas*. There are several charming late 19C standing and seated images of the Buddha displaying a clear Burmese influence, and an unusual, rather crudely carved early 19C wooden image of the Buddha seated under a two-headed *nāga*.

The next two rooms contain more Buddha images in various styles, and beyond are photographs of some of Nan's most important images. The final room has a display of prehistoric tools found in the area of Sao Din, together with a diorama of Stone Age life in Nan province. These indicate that this area was inhabited at least as early as the mesolithic period.

Directly across the street from the museum is **Wat Phra That Chang Kham Wora Wihan** ('Monastery Supported by Elephants'). This temple, which was founded in the early 15C and has been rebuilt and restored many times since, is where the stone inscriptions in the museum were found. It has two adjacent *wihan* built on a north–south axis. The east *wihan* is largely derelict. In the **west wihan** is a fine Buddha image of gilded stuccoed brick, flanked by several smaller ones. Among these are two of five famous images commissioned in 1426–27 by Chao Ngua Pha Sum. On the left is a walking Buddha performing the *abhaya mudrā* with the left hand; on the right is a standing image performing the same *mudrā* with both hands. The *wihan* has a fine wooden ceiling and traces of painting on the walls.

To the north of the *wihan* is the c 15C **chedi** from which the monastery derives its name. It stands on a square base decorated with the foreparts of 24 elephants in a manner reminiscent of Wat Chang Rop in Kamphaeng Phet (see p 227). Behind is a smaller *chedi* said to contain the remains of Chao Ananta

Woraritthidet (r. 1852–91), and nearby is an old brick *ku* elaborately decorated with stucco. At the north end of the compound is a simple Lan Na-style *ubosot*, built in 1857 and renovated in 1993, with finely carved wooden doors.

Housed in a glass case in the modern residence of the abbot, is a gleaming golden, walking Buddha known as **Phra Phuttha Nanthaburi Si Sakayamuni**, the third of Chao Ngua Pha Sum's five images cast in 1426–27.

Wat Phumin, Nan

Turn south along the street to the beautiful cruciform structure of **Wat Phumin**, which unusually combines both *wihan* and *ubosot* in a single building. Built in the 1590s by the ruler of Nan, Chao Chetabut Prohmin, it was completely renovated c 1867 by Chao Ananta Woraritthidet. There are four entrances, each approached by a staircase. The north and south staircases are flanked by *nāgas*, their heads to the north, their coiled tails to the south. The magnificently carved wooden doors date from Chao Ananta's renovation. Those on the east side depict figures of door guardians in the Chinese style; those on the north side have floral motifs; the west and south doors show birds and forest creatures amongst elaborate foliage.

Inside is a central square altar on which are four large gilded brick and stucco Buddha images with the right hand in *bhūmisparśa mudrā*, placed back to back and facing the four directions. The stuccoed pillars are decorated with stencilled gilt motifs and inlaid glass; the ceiling is lacquered and gilded. The finely carved wooden *thammat* is also lacquered and gilded, with *nāgas* decorating the steps.

The interior walls of the *wat* are covered with magnificent **murals** depicting scenes from two of the *jātaka* tales, the *Khatthana Kumara* and the *Nimi Jātaka*, and the Life of the Buddha. They were probably painted in the 1880s or 1890s by the same artist—possibly a Thai Lu—who painted those at Wat Nong Bua (see below).

Return past the museum to **Wat Hua Khuang**, which is on the next corner. According to the *Nan Chronicle*, the *wihan*, now used as an *ubosot*, was built by Chao Ananta Worarittthidet sometime between 1857 and 1877. It has a beautiful pediment of carved wood over the entrance. Inside are several bronze Buddha images and a gilded, carved wooden pulpit decorated with inlaid glass, made in 1915. Against the back wall is a tall rack containing dozens of tiny votive tablets. Beside the *ubosot* is a late 19C *ho trai* now used as monks' living quarters, with a wood-panelled upper storey. Behind this is a 16C *chedi* with a four-tiered spire and a square base, on each side of which is a niche decorated with elaborately carved stucco *nāgas* and figures of deities.

Continue past Wat Hua Khuang to the intersection of T. Pha Kong with T. Mahawong, leaving the petrol station on the left. To the right, T. Mahawong passes through the town centre and continues over the bridge to the southeast. At the next intersection on T. Ananta Worarittthidet, the city ramparts can be seen to the left. These were built in 1857, the old fortified walls having been destroyed by a series of floods of the Nan River in the early 19C. The present walls were renovated in 1993. Continue straight ahead for 400m on T. Pha Kong to Wat Suan Tan on the left of the road. The original 14C *chedi* of this *wat* was of the so-called 'lotus-bud' type, characteristic of Sukhothai temple architecture (see p 73). It was entirely rebuilt in its present form in 1914 by Chao Suriyaphong Phritadet. In the *wihan* is a large bronze seated Buddha image in *bhūmisparśa mudrā*, known as Phra Chao Thong Thip, which is said to have been commissioned in 1449–50 by King Tilok of Lan Na after his conquest of Nan. Further north on T. Sitthisan is the high-sided chedi of **Wat Satharot**, built by Chao Mahawong in 1838, the year of his accession.

One other *wat* in the town centre worth a visit is **Wat Phaya Phu**, which, although architecturally unexciting, contains in the *wihan* two more of the five bronze walking Buddha images commissioned by Chao Ngua Pha Sum in 1426–27. Both are placed in front of a much larger gilded stucco image and are surrounded by many others. The image on the left performs the *abhaya mudrā* with the left hand and that on the right with the right hand. There is also a large gong and a *thammat* reaching almost to the ceiling. Figures of *dvārapālas* are carved on the main doors. Behind is a white *chedi* constructed in 1857.

Wat Phra That Chae Haeng is reached by crossing the bridge over the Nan River in the town centre. Continue c 2km beyond the bridge along road 1168 to the *wat*, which stands on top of a small hill on the site of Phu Phiang Chae Haeng, capital of the Nan kingdom from 1359–66. According to the *Nan Chronicle*, this temple was founded in 1354–58 by Chao Phraya Kan Muang, who had gone to Sukhothai to get help in the construction of a *wat*. On completion of the Sukhothai monastery, he was presented with 20 gold and 20 silver votive tablets, and seven relics of the Buddha, 'two the size of mustard seed, which looked like crystal, three which looked like pearl, and two the size of sesame seed, which looked like gold'. On his return to Nan, Kan Muang had a bronze urn cast, in which he put the relics and the votive tablets. The urn was buried at Phu Phiang Chae Haeng and over it he built a *chedi*. In 1359 he moved the city to be near the *chedi*, but in 1366 his successor, Chao Pha Kong, moved the city again to the west bank of the Nan River, and the *chedi* of Wat Chae Haeng was abandoned. In 1474, a new ruler set about restoring the *chedi*, which had been reduced to an anthill. Digging down into the anthill, he discovered a large round rock, which he broke open to reveal the urn containing the relics. Subsequently, the *wat* was repeatedly restored and added to by merit-making rulers. In 1806, Chao Atthawon Pannyo had two large *nāga* balustrades constructed to line the approach to the *wat*. A rebuilt version of these can be seen today.

The enclosure of the *wat* is surrounded by a covered gallery and contains a beautiful Lao-style **wihan** with a triple-tiered roof and finely carved *khan tuai*, as well as a *chedi* containing the relics. Inside the *wihan* is a large seated Buddha image of gilded stucco, flanked by two kneeling disciples and surrounded by numerous bronze images. To the left of the altar is a fine wooden *thammat*. The *chedi* stands on an octagonal base and is more than 50m high. It is clad in copper sheets, regilded in 1994.

In front of the enclosure stands a large *bodhi* tree and three smaller *chedi* built in the early 20C, one of them heavily overgrown. To the left is a *wihan* known as **Wihan Phra Non**, which contains a 15m reclining Buddha image, and behind this is a small zoo with a rather pitiable collection of animals.

On the far side of Nan, take road 101 south towards Phrae, passing Wat Ming Muang on T. Suriyaphong, which contains the city *lak muang*. After c 500m turn right to **Wat Phaya Wat**, which has a distinctive square brick **chedi**, strongly resembling Chedi Suwan Chang Kot at Wat Cham Tewi in Lamphun and other northern Thai square *chedi*. Some scholars believe this *chedi* may date from the 13C–14C, but it is more likely to be 17C–18C. The Buddha images now standing in the niches, as well as the remaining stucco decoration, are certainly 17C–18C.

Beyond Wat Phaya Wat the lane continues for 1500m to the hilltop site of **Wat Phra That Khao Noi**, of little architectural interest, but worth a visit for the fine **views** it commands over the rice fields of the Nan valley.

Several excellent **excursions** can be made into the countryside around Nan. However, public services are limited, so travellers are strongly recommended to organise their own transport if possible.

Tha Wang Pha and Pua

The districts of Tha Wang Pha and Pua, north of Nan, with a return journey over the mountains of Doi Phukha make a good excursion. Allow at least a full day, or be prepared to spend a night in Doi Phukha National Park.

Total distance, *including recommended detours, c 230km.*

Road, *from Nan to Pua, c 59km on road 1080. Pua to Chiang Klang, 15km on road 1080. Pua to Doi Phukha, 25km on road 1256. Doi Phukha to Nan via Bo Klua, c 105km on roads 1256, 1081 and 1169.*

Leave Nan on road 1080 northward towards Tha Wang Pha and Pua. On the left beyond the 9km stone is **Tham Pha Tup Forest Park**, where there are more than a dozen caves in two sheer limestone outcrops. In a pleasant shady grove at the foot of the cliffs are picnic tables and a rough map showing the locations of the caves.

Continue up the valley and near the 39km stone, turn left on to road 1082, just beyond a small bridge, to the village of Tha Wang Pha. Cross the Nan River on the west side of Tha Wang Pha, and on the far bank turn left to the charming Lan Na-style **Wat Nong Bua**, 2km away.

Built c 1862, the *wihan* of this *wat* has an extended porch with low-sweeping roofs, a beautiful wooden gable inlaid with glass mosaic, and *nāga* and *makara* figures on the roof-ridges. On either side of the entrance are stucco figures of lions. The interior walls are covered with murals illustrating the *Chanthakhat Jātaka*, painted by a Thai Lu artist soon after the *wat* was constructed. Unfortunately those on the lateral walls have been severely damaged by humidity. The principal Buddha image, a seated figure in *bhūmisparśa mudrā*, has lost much of its gilt, especially on the hands and legs, and the ceiling is badly in need of a coat of paint. Despite this air of slight decay, or perhaps because of it, this is one of Lan Na's most delightful *wat*. Donations from visitors are much appreciated. On the south side of the *wihan* is a tiny *ubosot*.

In the village behind the *wat* live several **Thai Lu weavers**. One household in the village has a good selection for sale, and visitors are welcome to watch the women at work.

Return through Tha Wang Pha to road 1080 and continue northeast through rice fields and past bamboo and eucalyptus groves to **Pua**, from where a short **detour** can be made to **Wat Ton Laeng**, a monastery built in characteristic Thai Lu style. To find it, turn left at the Pua market and then right at a mini-roundabout after c 600m. After a further c 300m a turning to the left leads in 1km to the *wat*.

The renovated *wihan* has a triple-tiered roof with traditional wooden shingles, unusual triple acroteria in the form of *nāga* heads at the ends of the edging of the lower two of the tiers, and gables decorated with highly coloured geometric designs. Lions guard the east entrance. Inside, the principal Buddha image is decorated with coloured glass inlay lappets. To the front left of the altar is a very tall *thammat*, decorated with gilt stencilled motifs and coloured glass.

Further north towards Chiang Klang on road 1080 is **Wat Nong Daeng**, another excellent example of Thai Lu architecture. Turn left off road 1080 near the 71km stone on to the road signed to Tat Man Waterfall. This leads to the central intersection beside the market in Chiang Klang. From here, continue straight ahead for 1900m, then take a turning to the left signed to Ban Nong Daeng. After 500m turn left again down a lane to the *wat*.

The simple rectangular *wihan* has a shingled roof, badly in need of repair, and a porch across the front wall. In the austere interior note the *nāgas* intertwined around the image of the Buddha, and the Thai Lu woven *thong* hangings, similar to those of Wat Ton Laeng and Wat Nong Bua.

Doi Phukha National Park

Return south to the main road in Pua and turn left on to road 1081. Turn left again after 300m on to road 1256, signed clearly to Doi Phukha National Park (25km), a mountainous region inhabited by Akha, Hmong, Mien and Htin hill peoples. On the left 200m after this turning are the *chedi* and sadly neglected *wihan* of **Wat Phra That Bengsakat**, built in 1857.

After c 6km, road 1256 crosses a narrow tributary of the Nan River that becomes a raging torrent after heavy rain, and immediately starts climbing steeply. The views are magnificent, although severe deforestation has occurred on many of the mountain slopes. The national park headquarters, perched on a hilltop up a steep track to the left, has rudimentary accommodation amid splendid scenery. An overnight stop here is highly recommended, although visitors should bring their own food. Several pleasant walks can be made to nearby villages and caverns.

The road climbs on up the side of the valley through thick vegetation, which provides a refreshing contrast to the almost total denudation of the lower slopes. Of note are the giant palms growing on the slopes above the road.

The 1684m pass is reached beyond the 33km stone, where a vast panoramic view opens up to the right. From here the road descends c 12km to join road 1081 beside the village of **Bo Luang**, where two salt-water wells produce high quality salt. In the past, salt from here and the surrounding district of Bo Klua was traded throughout northern Thailand. In the 15C–16C production reached c 850 tonnes yearly, and during the reign of King Tilok salt from here was used as tribute.

Turn right at the junction on to the road that heads southwest to Nan. The scenery is still glorious, but the road surface is poor in places and somewhat overgrown, so progress can be slow. Traffic is extremely light, and travellers using public transport will find it far quicker to return to Nan via Pua. After c 48km, road 1169 turns off left to Nan along a winding switchback, before descending through a string of villages back to the town.

32 · Chiang Mai to Pai and Mae Hong Son

Roads 107 and 1095, 237km. To Mae Malai, 33km; Mae Malai to Pai, 97km; Pai to Mae Hong Son, 107km.

Leave Chiang Mai on road 107 towards Fang. After c 33km turn left beside the market in Mae Malai on to road 1095 to Pai and Mae Hong Son.

Shortly before the 10km stone, a turning to the left leads after 1km to the charming Lan Na-style **Wat Tha Kham**, which has a finely carved wooden pediment. The interior walls are covered in fine, though rather faded murals.

The route ahead continues past **Pong Duet Forest Park**, where there are some hot springs, and a turning to the right which leads to **Huai Nam Dang National Park**. Beyond this, the road descends gradually to the lovely Pai River valley and the small settlement of **Pai**. Within easy hiking distance of several Lahu and Lisu villages, Pai has become a popular **trekking centre**, and there are numerous agencies that organise walking, rafting and elephant-riding expeditions. There are also plenty of guest-houses, some clean and friendly, others somewhat shabby.

Opposite the 98km stone on the main road, which bypasses the heart of the village, is **Wat Luang**. This *wat* has a large white *chedi* surrounded by 12 smaller ones, and a wooden *kuti* containing several fine Buddha images. A few metres north of Wat Luang a lane to the left leads past the hospital to **Wat Hua Na**, which has a *chedi* similar to that at Wat Luang. Further along the lane is **Wat Nam Hu**, which has a modern *wihan* in traditional northern Thai style and an old wooden *kuti* on the right, and is set picturesquely just above a small pond and terraced rice fields.

Beyond Pai the road climbs once again, eventually reaching a 1480m pass, which marks the boundary between Pai and Pangmapha districts. On a clear day the panoramic **view** is magnificent. The road descends to the small settlement of **Soppong**, which is a centre for **hill trekking** and **caving expeditions**. Soppong has become a popular stopping point for travellers in recent years, and there are now several simple guest-houses in the area. Speleologists are advised to stay at the isolated *Cave Lodge* in **Ban Tham**, along a rough track c 8km northeast of Soppong. The owners know an immense amount about the extensive cave systems and the minority peoples of the area.

Mae Hong Son

After passing another fine viewing point 14km beyond Soppong, the road descends again past the pretty village of **Huai Pha**, set among rice fields on the narrow valley floor. For the final few kilometres to **MAE HONG SON** (pop. 15,000) the road winds through thick forest. This once isolated town is now capital of a province and a popular tourist destination, easily reached by air (40 mins) from Chiang Mai. It has many fine old wooden houses and several notable *wat*.

■ **Hotels and services**. There are several good hotels, including the *Holiday Inn*, *Baiyok Chalet* and *Mae Hong Son Mountain Inn Hotel*, all on T. Khunlum Praphat. An adequate medium-price alternative is the *Siam Hotel* at 23 T. Khunlum Praphat, near the bus station. There are several cheap simple guest-houses near Chong Kham Lake. **Banks** and the **post office** are further south on T. Khunlum Praphat. **Travel agents** on T. Khunlum Praphat can organise treks and rafting trips in the surrounding countryside.

■ **Transport**. The **bus station** on T. Khunlum Praphat has services to Pai, Chiang Mai, Khun Yuam, Mae Sariang and Bangkok. *THAI* Airways has several daily **flights** to Chiang Mai (35 mins). The booking office is at 71 T. Singhanat Bamrung near the airport.

History

Before the conquest of Lan Na and its reduction to vassalage by the Siamese at the end of the 18C, Mae Hong Son was a small and insignificant outpost of the kingdom of Lan Na, and most of its inhabitants were engaged in the felling of the teak trees that abounded in the dense forests surrounding the town. After 1830 the vassal princes of Chiang Mai made use of it as a centre for the capture and training of elephants, and it grew in size and importance until King Mongkut made it capital of a new province. Most of the population of the province are now either Thai Yai (Shan) or members of one of the hill tribes (Hmong, Karen etc), and strong Burmese influence is evident in the monastery architecture. In April each year the Poi Sang Lang festival, in which Thai Yai boys are ordained as monks, is held in Mae Hong Son. The boys are dressed as Thai Yai princes and carried round the town in a procession with drummers and musicians, a caparisoned horse and people bearing temple offerings.

Next to the lively **morning market** on T. Phanit Wattana is **Wat Hua Wiang**, which has a beautiful Burmese-style **wihan**, rebuilt in 1993, with an elaborate multi-tiered roof. It houses Phra Chao Phala Lakhaeng, a bronze Buddha image brought from Mandalay in the 1930s. Beside the *wihan* there is an *ubosot* and behind these a simple wooden *kuti* containing several fine Buddha images.

At the south end of the town beside the tranquil Chong Kham Lake are two attractive Burmese *wat*. **Wat Chong Klang**, to the west, was built in the 1860s. In the elaborately roofed *wihan* are several gilded Burmese images of the Buddha

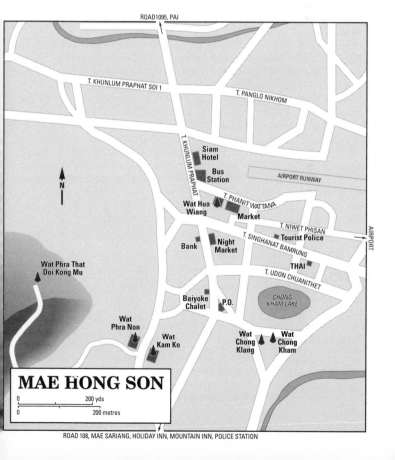

ROAD1095, PAI

T. KHUNLUM PRAPHAT SOI 1

T. PANGLO NIKHOM

T. KHUNLUM PRAPHAT

N

Siam Hotel

Bus Station

AIRPORT RUNWAY

Wat Hua Wiang

T. PHANIT WATTANA

Market

T. NIWET PHISAN

Tourist Police

AIRPORT

Bank

Night Market

T. SINGHANAT BAMRUNG

Wat Phra That Doi Kong Mu

THAI

T. UDON CHUANITHET

Baiyoke Chalet

P.O.

CHONG KHAM LAKE

Wat Phra Non

Wat Kam Ko

Wat Chong Klang

Wat Chong Kham

MAE HONG SON

0   200 yds

0   200 metres

ROAD 108, MAE SARIANG, HOLIDAY INN, MOUNTAIN INN, POLICE STATION on intricately decorated thrones, and on the left-hand wall nearly 200 painted glass panels set in lacquered wood illustrating scenes from the *jātaka* tales. In a room at the back left of the *wihan* is a collection of wooden statues representing figures from the *Vessantara Jātaka*, which were brought from Burma in 1857. In front is a white and gold *chedi* with small niches containing Buddha images on three sides and on the fourth side a small chapel with a dazzlingly elaborate seven-tiered roof.

Wat Chong Kham, on the east side, commissioned by the ruler of Mae Hong Son in the 1820s, was rebuilt after a fire in the early 1970s. On the right is the *ubosot*, a squat rectangular building guarded by a pair of lions. On the roof is a small ornamental *chedi*. The *wihan* to the left is of little interest, apart from its elegant roof. Further to the left is a rather dilapidated pink building, which houses a large Burmese-style seated Buddha image known as Luang Pho To.

To the west of the town centre, a narrow lane climbs up to **Wat Phra That Doi Kong Mu** on a hill overlooking the town. The larger of the two white-washed *chedi* in this *wat* was built in 1860 over the ashes of a venerated Burmese monk; the smaller was built in 1874. Further up the hill behind the two *chedi* is a very tall, rather inelegant standing image of the Buddha with the left hand in *abhaya mudrā*.

At the foot of the lane leading up the hill is **Wat Phra Non**, which houses a large reclining Buddha image dating from 1875. The badly decayed *ubosot* is now used as a monks' *kuti*. Behind it are two figures of lions, flanking the now overgrown stairway that formerly led up to Wat Phra That Doi Kong Mu.

Directly across the road is **Wat Kam Ko**, which, unusually, is entered along a covered corridor leading to an ornate multi-tiered porch. The 19C *wihan* has a finely crafted wooden ceiling and houses several notable Buddha images.

At Nai Soi 25km northwest of Mae Hong Son is the original village of 'long-neck' women, members of the Padaung tribe who have come into Thailand as refugees from Burma. These women wear brass rings round their necks, beginning with the first ring about the age of six and having one or two added each year until the age of fifteen or sixteen. The origin of this curious custom, which seriously incapacitates the women, is unknown and, if it were not for its commercial value as a tourist attraction it would probably have already disappeared. As it is, there are now fewer than twenty long-neck Padaung women in Nai Soi.

▶ A pleasant **excursion** can be made from Mae Hong Son to the pretty **Pha Sua Waterfall** and an isolated **Kuomintang settlement** in the hills close to the Burmese border, called Ban Mae O. Take road 1095 north c 16km from the town and turn left along a clearly signed lane. The waterfall, reached after 11km, is suitable for swimming. Beyond, the road climbs steeply for 10km to the Hmong village of Ban Na Pa Paek, from where the left fork of the road continues a further 7km to **Ban Mae O**. There are several other Hmong villages in the vicinity◀.

33 · Mae Hong Son to Mae Sariang and Mae Chaem

Roads *108, 1088 and 1192, 412km. To Mae Sariang 168km; Mae Sariang to Op Luang 82km; Op Luang to Mae Chaem 50km; Mae Chaem to Chom Thong 57km; Chom Thong to Chiang Mai 55km.*

Two days at least should be allowed for this route, which runs for much of the way through pleasant wooded scenery. Adequate accommodation is available at Khun Yuam, Mae Sariang and Chom Thong.

From Mae Hong Son, road 108 winds south through forest for 68km to **Khun Yuam**, a small town stretching for 2 or 3km along either side of the main road. Simple but pleasant accommodation is available at *Ban Farang*, a small guest-house at the north end of the town near the bus station.

▶From Khun Yuam an **excursion** can be made to the magnificent Mae Surin Waterfall in **Nam Tok Mae Surin National Park**, 38km to the northeast. Take road 1263 to the east on the north side of Khun Yuam to reach the park, passing several Hmong villages on the way. This road is sometimes impassable in the rainy season. Simple accommodation is available at the park, and camping is permitted.◀

Continuing south, road 108 winds through hills to the Karen settlement of Mae La Noi, beyond which it runs across flat countryside for the final 31km to **Mae Sariang**. This small market town has several Burmese-style *wat* and can offer adequate lodging for travellers wishing to break their journey here.

■ In the town itself the rudimentary but charmingly situated *Riverside Guest House* is recommended. On the road c 2km towards Hot is the *Mae Sariang Resort*. From the **bus station** there are several services daily to Mae Hong Son or back towards Chiang Mai, and there is an overnight service to Bangkok.

The *wihan* of **Wat Suphan Rangsi**, on the southwest side of the town near the bridge over the Yuam River, is worth a quick look, if only for its flamboyant multi-tiered roof. It was extensively rebuilt in 1993.

Also worth a brief visit are **Wat Chong Sung** and **Wat Si Bun Ruang**, two adjacent Burmese-style *wat* on the road to the bus station.

▶Several interesting **excursions** can be made from Mae Sariang into the surrounding countryside. Road 1194 runs west over the bridge from Mae Sariang for 49km to Ban Mae Sam Laep on the bank of the Salween River, from where **boat rides** can be made upstream and downstream along the Thai–Burmese frontier through magnificent scenery. Public *songthaeo* leave Mae Sariang in the morning for Mae Sam Laep.

To the south, road 1085 climbs out of the Yuam valley and descends to Tha Song Yang, from where it runs close to the border all the way to Mae Sot (see p 246).◀

Mae Sariang to Mae Chaem and Chom Thong

From Mae Sariang, road 108 heads east through forested hills as far as Kong Loi (47km), where the landscape opens out. Just beyond the 22km stone, road 1088 turns off left to Mae Chaem. The traveller here has a choice between two routes. The recommended one, detailed below, follows road 1088 to Mae Chaem and then goes east to rejoin road 108 at Chom Thong, 55km before Chiang Mai. The alternative route, which is taken by most buses, remains on road 108 all the way through Hot to Chom Thong.

Before turning north on road 1088 towards Mae Chaem, continue east 5km to **Op Luang National Park**, where a tributary of the Ping River has cut a narrow but impressive gorge along the north side of the road. Up the slope on the north bank is a gneiss overhang where red and white mesolithic rock paintings of elephants, humans and other animals were discovered in 1984. Lower down the slope a Bronze Age burial site was found.

Return to road 1088 and follow this road north to Mae Chaem, passing through the riverside village of **Om Khut**, a popular rafting spot for trekking tours from Chiang Mai. Beyond is a string of Hmong villages and intensively cultivated fields.

On the edge of the tiny village of **Ban Pa Daet**, a few kilometres before Mae Chaem itself, is a lane down a slope to the left leading through rice fields to **Wat Pa Daet**. The Lan Na-style *wihan* has an elaborately decorated wooden gable inlaid with glass. Inside, are teak columns and wall paintings, some in good condition, others severely damaged. The principal Buddha image in the *wihan* is seated and the pleat of the *sanghāṭī* draped over the left shoulder is inlaid with white glass. Note the very narrow doorway to the left side of the image for the use of the monks. A family living in one of the houses beside the *wat* organises a local **weaving co-operative**, which as far as possible uses only natural dyes from locally collected plants. Visitors are welcome.

Ban Pa Daet is one of several predominantly Thai Yuan villages in the Mae Chaem valley where, during the quiet months of the rice farmers' year, the women weave traditional cotton textiles to sell in the markets of Chiang Mai.

■ Simple accommodation is available in **Mae Chaem** at the *Mae Chaem Hotel* and the *Mae Chaem Guest House*.

From Mae Chaem road 1192 runs east on a twisting route to join the main Doi Inthanon road (24km). At the junction turn left up the hill to the summit, and right to Chom Thong and Chiang Mai. A brief stop can be made in **Chom Thong** to visit **Wat Phra That Si Chom Thong**, on the south side of the road in the town centre. The beautiful square-based copper-plated *chedi* of this *wat* is in the Burmese style and was built in 1451, while the cruciform *wihan* behind, which has exceptionally fine carved wooden gables, was rebuilt in the early 19C on the site of the original structure, erected in 1516 by King Muang Kaeo of Lan Na. It contains a Footprint of the Buddha in a *ku*, sumptuously decorated with gilded stucco, and several fine Buddha images in gold, silver and wood. This *wat* is also believed to contain a fragment of the skull of the Buddha. The door now used as the entrance was formerly the back door of the *wat*, which originally faced the canal behind.

From Chom Thong, road 108 runs northeast to Chiang Mai (55km; see Rte 25).

THE UPPER KHORAT PLATEAU

34 · Phitsanulok to Phetchabun and Lom Sak

Road 12, 133km on the direct route to Lom Sak. Recommended **detours** *(a) from Ban Yaeng to Lom Sak via Phu Hin Rong Kla on roads 2013 and 2331, c 120km; (b) to Khao Kho and Phetchabun on roads 2196, 2258 and 21, 74km.*

Road 12 runs east from Phitsanulok, climbing gradually upstream along the north bank of the Khek River. To the right of the road at the 33km stone is the shady **Sakunothayan Arboretum**, in which the first of the many waterfalls along this road can be found. Near the 45km stone are the **Kaeng Song Cascades**, which can be viewed from a number of riverside cafés serving locally grown coffee. More impressive, especially when in full spate after heavy rain, is **Poi Waterfall**, 2km along a rough road to the right near the 60km stone.

▶From Ban Yaeng, 9km further east, a **detour** can be made to the 300 sq km **Phu Hin Rong Kla National Park** (55km). Turn to the left on to road 2013, follow it for 24km towards Nakhon Thai, and then turn right on to road 2331.

History
From the mid-1960s to the early 1980s, Phu Hin Rong Kla was at the centre of a struggle between government forces and a loose coalition comprising disaffected Hmong farmers, members of the Communist Party of Thailand (CPT) and anti-government students and intellectuals. The Hmong people had migrated here from northern Thailand in the 1940s, bringing with them their traditional skills at cultivating opium. They were opposed by the government, and their cause was taken up by the CPT, which established a command base at Phu Hin Rong Kla in 1967. This base was in remote and rugged terrain and for five years remained impregnable, until in 1972 the military mounted a campaign to take the area. After the student protests of October 1976 in Bangkok, which led to the military resuming political power, the Hmong farmers and the CPT were joined by students and intellectuals, and by the late 1970s there were as many as 4000 people living in the area. Gradually, however, the rebels' position was weakened as the government built roads in the area and cut off their supplies of weapons, until by the end of 1982, government forces had finally regained control.

It is possible to hike through the area and to see some of the former CPT camp buildings and equipment. Road 2331 continues east to join road 203 a short distance north of **Lom Sak**, from where Phetchabun lies c 60km to the south. ◀

▶Another **detour** can be made by returning to road 12 and continuing east. Back on road 12, a turning to the right beside the 71km stone leads to **Kaeng Sopha Waterfall**, one of the most spectacular of the many along the highway. 9km further along road 12, are the headquarters of **Thung Salaeng Luang**

National Park, where visitors can rent simple park bungalows. The 1262 sq km park was established in 1972 and offers good walking. It consists mostly of mixed deciduous forest, interspersed with tropical evergreen, pine savanna and grassy meadows. Wildlife includes elephants, palm-banded civets and yellow-throated martens. At least **200 species of bird** have been recorded here, including the beautiful **Siamese fireback**. The park was a major stronghold of the CPT from the late 1960s until 1982. During that time there was extensive clearing of forested land by resident hill-tribes. Today the pine savanna and meadows offer excellent hiking, especially between September and November when there are many wild flowers in bloom.

Beyond the park, the road passes through a landscape that has been severely deforested, as a result partly of intensive fighting in the 1970s and early 1980s, and partly of the subsequent excessive logging of newly accessible land. ◄

► From a point just beyond the 100km stone on road 12, a further **detour** is possible to the right on road 2196 to **Khao Kho**, another area fiercely contested between the government and the CPT from 1968 to 1982, by which time more than 1200 government troops and an unknown number of the CPT had been killed. Today efforts are being made to rehabilitate Khao Kho. New settlements have been built, the royal family has a palace in the area, and there is a hilltop memorial to the government troops who died. However, the overwhelming impression remains one of desolation; there is scarcely a tree in sight.

Road 2196 twists and turns for 17km to the T-junction with road 2325. A turning to the right here leads after 6km to **Khao Kho Open Zoo** on the left. The beautiful **Si Dit Waterfall** is 3km further, on the right. Here, a broad curtain of water tumbles over a 10m rock ledge into a pool below. 9km beyond the waterfall, the road reaches the junction with road 2258. A turning to the right here leads to a back gate of Thung Salaeng Luang National Park; 11km to the left is the **Khao Kho Palace** (Phra Tamnak Khao Kho). This palace, which was completed for the royal family in 1985 at a cost of US$1 million, stands high on the hillside.

Beyond the palace, turn off left on road 2196 (Phetchabun is straight ahead along road 2258), and after a further 700m turn left again on to road 2323, which climbs steeply to **Itthi Fire Base**, the former government stronghold in its war against the CPT. Today there is a small collection of war memorabilia here, including vehicles and guns. At the summit beyond is a **war memorial** commemorating the government soldiers who died.

In **Phetchabun**, is the comfortable *Burapha Hotel*. **Lom Sak**, 31km to the north, is more conveniently located for travellers continuing further east or northeast, but has only rudimentary accommodation. Both towns have **banks** and a **post office**. ◄

Further east from Lom Sak, road 12 crosses the flat Pasak River valley before entering **Nam Nao National Park**. The park's rolling sandstone hills, covered with mostly dry evergreen forest and beautiful dipterocarp forest, is an excellent area for **bird-watching**. Two main trails lead through different habitat types, and there are more than 200 confirmed species, including three pitta species and three hornbills. Mammals include gaur, banteng, sambar and barking deer, tiger, white-handed gibbon and slow loris. In the park is Nam Nao Yai Cave, which is reportedly home to many thousands of bats in the rainy season (although their population drops considerably in the dry season). Bungalow accommodation is available and camping is permitted.

Beyond the 95km stone, road 201 turns left off road 12 to **Phu Pha Man National Park** and **Phu Kradung National Park** (37km). Phu Kradung, which covers an area of 349 sq km, was the second national park to be established in Thailand and is now one of the most visited in the kingdom. Much of this area consists of the roughly circular mountain of Phu Kradung, so the vegetation is chiefly submontane evergreen forest, but it also includes 60 sq km of flat land covered with pine forest and grass meadows. The park is noted for its wide variety of **wild flowers**, and especially its numerous species of **orchids** and **rhododendrons**, which flower from February to April, and its maple stands, which bloom in December. There are only six confirmed species of mammal, and these include elephants and gibbons. The bird life is more prolific, with 130 recorded species, including hornbills and snowy-browed and pale blue flycatchers. There are several excellent walking trails up to the summit, which is a plateau at a height of 1300m. The park is closed during the rainy season from June to August to protect the slippery trails from erosion.

Road 12 continues east through **Chum Phae**, passing through flat, rather featureless scrub, typical of the Khorat Plateau, which covers much of northeast Thailand. Shortly before the 79km stone, in the village of **Ban Non Sa-at**, an unsigned turn to the left marks the start of a steep trail up to a large whitewashed, reclining **Dvaravati Buddha** image carved into the rock face on the southwest slope of **Phu Wiang**, an old volcanic crater. Khon Kaen lies 78km ahead (see Rte 39).

35 · Lom Sak to Dan Sai and Chiang Khan

*Roads 203, 2014, 2113 and 2195, 227km. To Dan Sai 63km; Dan Sai to Na Haeo 36km; Na Haeo to Chiang Khan 227km. An **alternative route** from Dan Sai to Loei 82km on roads 2013 and 203; Loei to Chiang Khan 48km on road 201. Both routes are extremely beautiful in parts.*

Take road 203 north from Lom Sak for 52km and turn left just beyond the 91km stone on to road 2014 to Dan Sai. This road climbs steeply over a low ridge before descending in a series of sharp bends to **DAN SAI** (11km).

On the left side shortly before the centre of this lively market town is the Lao-style *chedi* of **Phra That Si Song Rak**.

History

A stela on the north side states that it was built between 1560 and 1563 to mark the friendship between King Maha Chakkraphat of Ayutthaya and King Setthathirat of the Lao kingdom of Lan Xang (r. 1548–71). In 1546, Setthathirat, the son of King Phothisarat of Lan Xang (r. 1520–48), was installed as king of Lan Na. On the death of his father 13 months later, he returned to Luang Prabang to rule as king there, and the Lan Na kingdom fell into anarchy. Later, he and Chakkraphat concluded a treaty of alliance which delineated the frontiers between Lan Xang and Ayutthaya along the watershed between the Chao Phraya and the Mekong basins.

By the early 20C little remained of the original *chedi* except the base, but a subsequent renovation has attempted to combine Ayutthaya and Lan Xang (Lao) styles. A modern shrine immediately adjacent to the *chedi* has somewhat spoiled the ensemble. In late June or early July a colourful masked festival called **Ngan Prapheni Hae Phi Ta Khon** takes place in the town.

From Dan Sai there is a choice of routes to Chiang Khan. The first runs north through sparsely populated but outstandingly beautiful hill country to Na Haeo, and thence follows a small tributary of the Mekong River east through a series of small hamlets.

The alternative route is along the main road past Phu Rua National Park to the provincial capital, Loei. As far as Loei this is also a very scenic road, while for the final 48km to Chiang Khan it runs along a flat and intensively cultivated river valley.

To Chiang Khan via Na Haeo

Take road 2113 northwest from Dan Sai. Regular, but infrequent *songthaeo* ply along the beautiful, twisting road that climbs up to **Na Haeo** (36km). Shortly before Na Haeo, on the right side of the road in the village of **Ban Na Phung** is the old *wihan* of **Wat Pho Chai Na Phung**. The interior walls of this lovely but rather dilapidated building are covered with detailed but crudely painted murals. On the simple altar are some attractive Lao images of the Buddha. The monks here seldom receive visitors, but are happy to show the *wat* to guests.

From Na Haeo turn right on to road 2195, which immediately starts climbing through thickly wooded country, before opening out into a broad fertile valley. There are fine views along this road, which for much of the way winds beside the narrow stream marking the Thai–Lao frontier. Simple guest-house accommodation is available in several of the villages, including **Pak Huai** and **Tha Li**. Travellers using public transport should be prepared for long waits, as services are infrequent.

For the last few kilometres to Chiang Khan there are fine views of the Mekong River, a magnificent sight, especially in the late afternoon sun.

To Chiang Khan via Phu Rua and Loei

Road 2013 leads from Dan Sai back to road 203, the main Lom Sak–Loei road. Turn left and continue towards Loei, until the village of Ban Phu Rua, where, shortly before the 49km stone, **Phu Rua National Park** is signed to the left.

The climb up this 1365m mountain is easy, and on a clear day there are spectacular views of the Mekong River to the north and of limestone escarpments to the south. However, it is necessary to start very early to beat the clouds.

There are bungalows and food stalls in the park, and camping is allowed. During school holidays the camp site is sometimes full with students on vacation.

Beyond the park, road 203 winds through thick forest before descending to the plain. To the left shortly before Loei is the highly recommended *Dap Lek Restaurant*, which offers delicious fish dishes in a pleasant outdoor setting. Continue 3km to **Loei** (pop. 18,000) which, although of no great architectural interest, offers adequate accommodation, good food and all the services of a provincial capital. It is also a suitable base for **excursions** to Phu Rua and to the **wildlife sanctuary of Phu Luang** to the south. This sanctuary, which covers an area of 848 sq km at the north end of the Phetchabun range, contains important **elephant populations** and is the most important protected area for **orchids** in Thailand. More than **200 bird species** have been recorded here, including many montane species usually found only in northern Thailand. Its central feature is a sandstone plateau covered in pine savanna and montane forests, reaching 1500m in elevation. The provincial authority organises three-day visits, but the ascent to the plateau is a strenuous five-hour hike and is not suitable for the unfit. Visits can be arranged from *Nong Sam Guest House* in Chiang Khan (see below).

Chiang Khan

From Loei road 201 runs north through densely populated countryside to the quiet and charming market town of **Chiang Khan**, which lies along the south bank of the Mekong River. In the narrow street beside the river there are still many old wooden houses, and the town has several Lao-style *wat*.

■ **Hotels and services**. The best place to stay is *Nong Sam Guest House* (Tel. 042 821457), 1km west of the main intersection, which has simple wooden and brick bungalows in a charming riverside garden of tamarind, papaya, banana, longan and young teak trees. The English-speaking family who own it know the district well and will lend bicycles to guests to explore the countryside. They can also arrange three-day visits to Phu Luang Wildlife Sanctuary to the southwest of Loei. The *Thai Farmers Bank* is to the right at the main T-junction in the centre of the town. The **post office** is near the river on the east edge of the town.

■ **Transport**. Regular **buses** run to Loei and Nong Khai. *Bangkok Airways* has a daily **flight** to Bangkok from Loei.

Walk east along the street by the river to reach **Wat Si Khun Muang**, between Soi 6 and Soi 7. The *sim* of this monastery, completely renovated in 1992–93, is thought to date from the reign of Rama III. The original murals on the front wall were unfortunately lost in the renovation and have been replaced by rather inferior work by a local Lao artist. Inside, there is a long wooden *hong hot* with a *nāga*'s head, used for the ceremonial anointing of the monks' heads with water.

At the east end of the enclosure is a tiny museum containing a few noteworthy exhibits, including a beautifully carved and gilded wooden *thammat*, believed to date from the reign of Rama III, and a gilded wooden standing image in the Lao style of the Buddha with both hands in *abhaya mudrā*. There are also numerous votive tablets, small Buddha images and manuscript cabinets, including a good example of a *sum khong*, a small wooden box with shutters, used to house a Buddha image (in this case missing).

Further east along the street, between Soi 20 and Soi 21, is **Wat Tha Khok**, which has an unusually deep, west-facing porch and decorative painted stucco relief carving on the exterior walls.

Go down Soi 20 away from the river to the main road, and turn west (right), back towards the main T-junction. Between Soi 14 and Soi 15 is **Wat Mahathat**. Of the two *sim* in the enclosure of this *wat*, the southern one is believed to date originally from the mid-17C, but has a more recent gable of wooden fretwork decorated with motifs of vine leaves and intertwined *nāgas*.

The chapel behind, which has been rather awkwardly extended, has some indistinct murals on the exterior west wall. The upper part is decorated with *nāgas* and a small seated image of the Buddha, while the base depicts a figure thought to be Rahu, the demon responsible for eclipses of the sun and moon, surrounded by a flaming aureole. Inside is a superbly carved, gilded candelabrum inlaid with coloured glass.

3km downstream from Chiang Khan are the **Khut Khu Rapids** (Kaeng Khut Khu), which make a pleasant place for a picnic, although the site can be very crowded on weekends and holidays. They are best visited in the dry season, when the low water level reveals the rocks; after the rains there is little to see, although the vegetation is much more lush. There are numerous food and drink stalls and small bamboo shelters to provide shade. To get to the rapids take road 211 east from the town and after 3km turn left.

36 · Chiang Khan to Nong Khai

Road 211, 201km.

Take road 211 out of Chiang Khan, past the Khut Khu Rapids and follow the Mekong River downstream towards Pak Chom (41km) and Sang Khom (103km). A short distance beyond the lane to the rapids, a road to the right leads after c 6km to Phu Thok, a hill with a telecommunications mast on the summit, from where there are panoramic views. In the village of **Ban Pha Baen**, c 10km from Chiang Khan, a dirt road to the right leads after 2.5km to **Wat Loi Phra Phutthabat Phu Khwai Ngoen**, a hilltop monastery also offering good views.

On the right side of the road in the village of **Ban Khok Lao Nua**, c 19km from Chiang Khan and shortly before the 168km stone, is **Wat Si Som Sanuk**, which has a corrugated iron roof and roughly carved wooden doors. Simple paintings cover the interior walls. Outside, on the front left side of the building is a painting of Rahu, the demon responsible for eclipses of the sun and moon, seen here swallowing the moon.

Continue east through Pak Chom and Sang Khom. For short stretches the road runs along the river bank, offering magnificent views across the water to Laos. Two small waterfalls can be visited along the way. The first, **Than Tip Waterfall** is shortly before Sang Khom, up a track to the right, just beyond the 98km stone, whilst the other, **Than Thong Waterfall**, is beyond Sang Khom, to the left by the 73km stone. Simple lodgings are available in **Pak Chom** and **Sang Khom**, and in **Si Chiang Mai**, a busy market town 50km before Nong Khai, where a flourishing cottage industry has developed for the manufacture of the translucent discs of rice flour used to wrap spring rolls.

Beyond Si Chiang Mai, a turning to the right beside the 31km stone leads after 2km to **Wat Si Chompu Ong Tu** (Wat Nam Mong) in Ban Nam Mong. This *wat* is architecturally uninteresting, but it houses a beautiful and greatly revered bronze **image of the Buddha**, Phra Chao Ong To, cast in 1562.

Further along road 211, a turning to the left shortly before the 11km stone leads north to **Ban Wiang Khuk**, on the site of the capital of a 12C kingdom, Muang Wiang Khuk, which flourished at least until the 16C. The 6km road to Ban Wiang Khuk is in poor condition and there is now little to see there apart from two 16C Ayutthaya-style brick **chedi** in the grounds of a monastery called **Wat Thephon Pradit Tharam**. To reach this *wat*, turn right at the junction in the village, and then right again after 450m. Both *chedi* have been restored, but fragments of the original stucco decoration remain.

Back on road 211, turn left just before the 10km stone into the enclosure of **Wat Phra That Bang Phuan**, which is thought to have been founded to enshrine 29 relics of the Buddha by King Setthathirat of Lan Xang between 1559 and 1562, when he extended his capital at Viang Chan (Vientiane) across the Mekong. The main Lao-style *that*, 34m high, collapsed during heavy rain in 1970, but was rebuilt in 1977. Beneath a modern shelter to the south of the *that* are the brick walls and columns of an old *wihan*, housing a seated stone image of the Buddha in *bhūmisparśa mudrā*. To the west of this *wihan* is the massive round base of a *chedi*, made of laterite and clay bricks. Several other ruins are scattered about the *wat* enclosure.

Nong Khai

The thriving border town and regional centre of Nong Khai (pop. 27,000) lies on the south bank of the Mekong River, over which it commands long, open views, 14km north of the junction of road 211 and road 2. This formerly rather somnolent town is now a booming commercial centre and the major transit point for trade with Laos. Its central streets are already far too narrow for the heavy volume of traffic that passes through them, but it remains a pleasant town in which to spend a day or two. Since the opening in 1995 of the Australian-financed Friendship Bridge across the Mekong between Nong Khai and Vientiane its importance has still further increased. A regular shuttle service of buses operates across the bridge in both directions.

■ **Hotels and services**. A wide range of accommodations is available, from the *Mekong Royal Holiday Inn* near the bridge to simple **guest-houses** such as the *Mutmee Guest House* on the river bank. There are some good restaurants on the river bank near the pier on T. Kinkhong. Most **banks** and the **post office** are on T. Meechai in the town centre. The immigration office is on the pier.

■ **Transport**. Frequent **buses** leave from the bus terminal on T. Prachak, including overnight services to Bangkok and Chiang Mai. Several **trains** run south towards Bangkok daily from the railway station, 2km west of the town centre, near the bridge. *THAI* has two daily **flights** to Bangkok from Udon Thani, 53km south of Nong Khai. Tickets and an airport bus are available from the booking office (open Mon–Fri 08.00–17.00) at 453 T. Prachak. Travellers with the required visas may either cross the Friendship Bridge into

Laos or use the regular **ferries** which operate from the main pier, Tha Sadet, to cross to the Lao side. All arrangements for travel in Laos must be made in Bangkok through one of the agencies recognised by the Lao authorities, and independent travel is not permitted. Particulars of these agencies are available from the Lao Embassy in Bangkok. **Samlo** operate all over the town and **bicycles** can be rented from some of the cheaper guest houses.

The heart of the town is the vibrant network of narrow streets near the main **pier**, which are filled with market traders and small shops offering a wide variety of goods from Indonesian batik to plastic toys. From the pier turn east along T. Meechai. This street was once lined for much of the way with attractive Chinese shop-houses with overhanging first floor balconies. Most of these have now vanished and been replaced by featureless concrete buildings, but a few may still be seen on the north side of T. Meechai beside the entrance to **Wat Si Muang**. This *wat* was completely refurbished in 1992–93 and is now a typical example of a modernised late 20C Thai monastery. The exterior walls are adorned with a dazzling array of coloured glass, while the interior is covered with garish paintings of little artistic merit. Within the *ubosot*, however, are two important 16C **images of the Buddha**—a standing image on the right named Luang Pho Phra Chai Chetta, and a seated image to the left called Luang Pho Si Muang. The latter has a beautiful lustre as a result of its having been cast in an unusual alloy of gold, silver and copper.

Continue east along T. Meechai past more old shop houses and turn right along T. Pho Chai to reach **Wat Pho Chai**. In the cruciform *ubosot* of this temple are three 16C seated images of the Buddha. The central one, named Luang Pho Phra Sai, is held in great esteem and is carried in procession through the town during the Songkran festival at the beginning of the Buddhist year. Murals on the east wall of the *ubosot* narrate the story of the image's journey from Lan Xang, its sinking in the river during a storm, and its subsequent recovery. Other murals on the walls show scenes of everyday life in Thailand, including a rocket festival, water-throwing during Songkran and people watching a film at the cinema. The **window shutters** and **doors** of the *ubosot* are superbly carved.

To the east of the town, road 212 leads to the very unusual **Sala Kaeo Ku** (Wat Khaek), which is situated on the right soon after the 4km stone. This has a garden full of extraordinary concrete statues, established in the 1970s by a monk of eccentric tastes, who assembled an eclectic assortment of Hindu, Buddhist and purely fantastical sculptures, including a large meditating Buddha image, a statue of the elephant-headed Hindu god of wisdom, Ganesha, mounted on a rat, and a group of skeletons sitting with clasped hands, apparently symbolising the finite nature of love. Unfortunately some of the statues are starting to crumble away.

▶Phu Phra Bat Historical Park

An excursion can be made from Nong Khai to Phu Phra Bat Historical Park, to the southwest, a 500 sq km site on the top of a wooded hill, notable for its strangely shaped rocks, cave paintings and pleasant trails for hiking. Travellers with their own vehicles can reach it easily, but it is more difficult to get there by public transport. A full exploration can take several hours, so an early start is strongly recommended. Alternatively, it is possible to stay a night in one of Ban Phu's rudimentary lodgings.

Head south from Nong Khai and turn right after 14km towards Chiang Khan. In Tha Bo, turn left on to road 2020 at the 29km stone. The road runs south for 24km to the pleasant little market town of **Ban Phu**, which has some attractive wooden shop-houses. Turn right at the far end of the main street and follow the signs for the remaining 12km to Phu Phra Bat Historical Park.

The entrance road divides before reaching the park information centre; the left fork leads to **Wat Phra Phutthabat Bua Bok**, a *chedi* built between 1917 and 1927 in the Lao style to house a Footprint of the Buddha. According to local folklore, the Buddha left the print for a *nāga* to worship. The *nāga* duly did so and then asked to be ordained as a monk. When the Buddha refused, the *nāga* disappeared into a nearby fissure.

Near the white-painted *chedi*, which is a copy of the *chedi* of That Phanom (see p 338), is a smaller stone *chedi* with painted carvings of elephants, and a much newer one of little interest.

The right fork of the road leads to an excellent **information centre**, opened in 1992. It contains replicas of some of the prehistoric rock paintings found within the park, illustrations of some of the rock shelters and formations, and historical details of the site.

At various sites in the park examples of **rock art**, all of them now very damaged, have been found. These suggest that there was human settlement here from an early date, possibly as long ago as 3000 BC. It is thought that some of the prehistoric rock shelters were later transformed into sites for Buddhist ceremonies. The best examples are the huge slab called **Ho Nang Usa** (Usa's Tower), and the shelters known as **Wat Pho Ta** ('Father-in-law's Monastery') and **Wat Luk Khoei** ('Son-in-law's Monastery'). The discovery at Wat Pho Ta of Dvaravati-style sandstone carvings in bas-relief of standing and seated images of the Buddha indicates that between the 6C and the 8C Dvaravati influence spread to the northeast of Thailand from the Chao Phraya valley. There is also evidence of Hindu-Khmer influence in the area during the 10C or 11C.

At **Wat Luk Khoei** there are some 16C Ayutthaya-style images of the Buddha.

The park is spread over a wide area, and footpaths link the various sites. A visit that includes most of the sites and the best views takes between one-and-a-half and three hours. English-speaking guides can usually be found at the information centre. ◄

It is possible to follow the course of the Mekong River to the east of Nong Khai downstream to Nakhon Phanom (see Rte 40) along road 212. The river itself is rarely in sight on this route, but the scenery is very pleasant.

In **Bung Khan** (c 140km), a road runs south to **Ban Si Wilai** and the huge sandstone outcrop of **Phu Thok**, which is honeycombed with small caves and is used as a retreat by the monks of **Wat Phu Thok**. A detour to this most unusual *wat* is highly recommended for anyone taking the route between Nong Khai and Nakhon Phanom. The views across the plain from the upper levels are excellent.

37 · Nong Khai to Ban Chiang and Khon Kaen

Roads 2 and 22, 272km. To Udon Thani 53km; Udon Thani to Ban Chiang 51km; Ban Chiang to Khon Kaen 168km. The roads are flat, straight and fast for much of the way, although traffic can be heavy.

Railway, 174km in 2hrs 30mins (express) from Nong Khai to Khon Kaen via Udon Thani (50mins).

Road 2, the Friendship Highway, which was built with funding from the USA in the 1960s and 1970s, runs south from Nong Khai through undulating, rather dull scenery.

Udon Thani

Udon Thani (pop. 85,000), on the flood plain of the Luang River, is a busy commercial town and communications centre, frequently choked with traffic, but offering excellent food and accommodation. It developed rapidly during the Vietnam War, when it was both a major American air base and an intelligence-gathering post. Numerous American servicemen settled here after the war.

- **Information**. The TAT office is temporarily on T. Pho Si near the Provincial Education Office, but may move in the near future.

- **Hotels and services**. There are numerous **hotels**, catering to all pockets. Among the better ones is the *Charoen* at 549 T. Pho Si on the east side of the town and the *Udon Hotel* at 81–89 T. Mak Khaeng. There are **banks** on T. Pho Si and T. Prachak Silpakhom, and the **post office** is on T. Watana. Delicious *kai yang* and *som tam* are served in three adjacent, rather grubby **restaurants** at the west end of T. Prachak Silpakhom, near the corner of T. Phan Phrao. There is a **US consulate** at 35/6 T. Suphakit Chanya, on the north side of Prachak Silpakhom Lake.

- **Transport**. There are frequent **buses** to many destinations, but rather confusingly there are three bus terminals and numerous other possible boarding points in the town. Ask for advice at your hotel or the TAT office. Udon is on the main Bangkok–Nong Khai **railway** line, with regular services in both directions. *THAI* has three daily **flights** to Bangkok (1hr). The booking office is at 60 T. Mak Khaeng, opposite the Udon Hotel. **Cars** can be rented from agencies nearby.

Udon Thani has almost no ancient monuments or buildings of historical interest, but the important prehistoric site of Ban Chiang is c 50km to the east and can be visited either on an excursion from Udon Thani, or as a detour on the way to Khon Kaen.

To Ban Chiang

Head east from Udon Thani on road 22, which runs across a dry plateau towards Sakon Nakhon. Just before the 35km stone, a left turn towards the centre of

Nong Han leads after 200m to **Wat Samakkhi Si Bamphen Phon**, which has a plastered brick *ubosot* with arched windows beneath an ill-fitting corrugated iron roof and a broad wooden verandah. On the verandah are two large wooden drums. Behind the *ubosot* are the heavily overgrown remains of a brick *chedi* on a laterite base, probably dating back to the 10C–13C and modified during the Ayutthaya period. Lying in the undergrowth nearby is a headless sandstone image of the Buddha, possibly of Khmer origin.

The modern market town of **Nong Han** is on the site of a fortified 10C–13C Khmer settlement. It is virtually impossible to see the remains of the ramparts and moats from the ground, as they are now covered by rice fields, but their position can be seen clearly in an aerial photograph in the museum at Ban Chiang (see below).

Back on road 22 continue east for 13km to **Ban Kham O**, near the 48km stone, where a cottage industry has developed for the manufacture of copies of both the blackware pottery and the later and better known red-on-buff painted wares excavated at Ban Chiang.

A short distance further on, road 2225 turns off left to Ban Chiang (c 5km), running through rice fields and past Ban Pulu, where more imitation Ban Chiang pottery is made. The area surrounding the village of **BAN CHIANG** is only one, and arguably not the most important, of several prehistoric occupation sites excavated on the Khorat Plateau since 1963 (e.g., Non Nok Tha, Ban Na Di, Ban Chiang Hian, Ban Kho Noi) that have revealed the existence in the area of the advanced **Bronze and Iron Age culture** to which the village has given its name. The Ban Chiang culture appears to have flourished from c 3600 BC to c AD 200 in the area now covered by the four provinces of Udon Thani, Sakon Nakhon, Nakhon Phanom and Khon Kaen, and it shares a number of features with cultures that developed later in the same period elsewhere in Southeast Asia. In its earliest phase it lacked metallurgy, but was already characterised by the manufacture of highly distinctive **ceramics**. About 1000 BC bronze-working by the *cire perdue* (lost wax) process was first introduced. During the 1C AD major cultural and social changes occurred and iron-working was developed. At some sites on the Khorat Plateau (e.g., Khao Chan Ngam) cave paintings have been found, but their dating is not yet certain.

The chronology of **Ban Chiang ceramics** has been established by thermoluminescence dating carried out at the University of Pennsylvania, and may be divided into three main periods: an early period from c 3600 to 1000 BC, characterised by black, footed, cord-marked wares, sometimes with incised designs and appliqué coils of clay, but without painted decoration; a middle period from c 1000 to 300 BC, in which carinated pots, some with incised and painted designs and thick red rims, were made; and a late period from c 300 BC to AD 200, which saw the appearance of the elaborately painted red-on-buff wares for which Ban Chiang is chiefly noted.

Between 1967 and 1975 the Fine Arts Department, working with archaeologists from Silpakorn and Thammasat Universities in Bangkok, and from 1974 with the Museum of the University of Pennsylvania, carried out a series of excavations near Ban Chiang, which yielded thousands of bronze artefacts, including socketed adzes, spearheads and other tools, bracelets and bells, glass beads (associated chiefly with late period burials), carnelian, agate and other stone beads, and a very wide variety of ceramics, painted and unpainted, cord-marked and incised, ranging in date from early black wares with incised or cord-marked designs, to red-on-buff wares painted with spirals, swirls, whorls and other curvilinear motifs. In addition to cups, bowls and pedestalled jars, these ceramics include ladles, rollers, spindle whorls, design stamps, clay anvils and a few figurines. The artefacts excavated at Ban Chiang and related sites have yielded an immense amount of information about early metallurgy, agriculture, burial practices and art in northeast Thailand in the late prehistoric and early historic periods.

The **Ban Chiang National Museum** (open Wed–Sat, 09.00–16.00), on the northwest edge of the village, has excellent displays of some of the many arte-facts excavated in the area. The main building, on the left, has the most impor-tant exhibits. In the first room on the left there are general explanations of the site's history, maps and aerial photographs of the village, pots, Bronze Age tools and ornaments, and glass beads dating from c 700 BC to AD 200.

The right-hand room downstairs contains a large variety of ceramics. One case shows pottery from sites other than Ban Chiang, including Khok Khon in Sakon Nakhon, and Ban Prasat in Khorat.

Upstairs is a display of objects that formed part of an exhibition entitled 'Ban Chiang: Discovery of a Lost Bronze Age' which toured the USA from 1982–86. There is also a display of artefacts from Non Nok Tha, a more modest site west of Khon Kaen, excavated in 1966–68 by the Fine Arts Department and the University of Hawaii, which yielded some very early bronze tools and bracelets.

In the other museum building is a display providing information on exca-vating techniques. This includes an aerial photograph of Nong Han, clearly showing the site's rectangular moats.

In the grounds of Wat Pho Si Nai on the northeast side of Ban Chiang, one of the first excavations, carried out in 1972, has been preserved under a shelter. It contains pots, sherds and human skeletons.

From Ban Chiang, return to Udon Thani and turn south on road 2 again, towards Khon Kaen (117km).

38 · Khon Kaen and environs

Khon Kaen (pop. 130,300) is the second most important centre in northeast Thailand after Nakhon Ratchasima and is the seat of the only university in the northeast. It is a modern city and, like Nakhon Ratchasima, it has undergone rapid development since the construction of the Friendship Highway (road 2) with American funding. Khon Kaen is now a major transport hub with good connections to all parts of the region. However, apart from the excellent museum, it has little of interest for the visitor. Most of the important sites are in the surrounding countryside, and are best visited in a series of excursions using Khon Kaen as a base.

■ **Information**. The TAT office is at 15/5 T. Prachasamoson (road 209), between the junctions with T. Klang Muang and T. Lang Muang.

■ **Hotels and services**. Among the best hotels are the well appointed *Sofitel Khon Kaen* and the *Charoen Thani Princess*. Slightly cheaper are the *Kosa* at

250–2 T. Si Chan and the *Kaen Inn* at 56 T. Klang Muang. A medium-priced alternative is the pleasant *Roma* at 50/2 T. Klang Muang. The *Bangkok Bank* is at 254 T. Si Chan and the *Thai Farmers Bank* is on T. Na Muang. The **post office** and **telecoms office** are on T. Klang Muang.

■ **Transport**. Frequent services run from the main **bus station** on T. Prachasamoson to all neighbouring provinces and to Bangkok, Chiang Mai and other regional centres. The terminal for **air-conditioned buses** is just off T. Klang Muang.

The **railway station** is on T. Darun Samran, on the southwest side of town. There are several trains daily south to Bangkok and north through Udon Thani to Nong Khai.

THAI has several daily **flights** to Bangkok. The booking office is at 183/6 T. Maliwan (road 12).

Public **songthaeo** follow fixed routes around the town and out to the huge university campus on the northwest side of the town; **samlo** also operate in the town centre.

Car rentals are available from *Avis* at the airport and from local rental agencies in the town.

KHON KAEN NATIONAL MUSEUM (open Tues–Sun 09.00–12.00, 13.00–16.00) is in the north of the city just off T. Langsun Ratchakan. The **ground floor** contains a fine collection of 7C–11C Dvaravati terracotta heads of deities and architectural decorations, and a remarkable assembly of Dvaravati sandstone and laterite *bai sema*, most of them from Muang Fa Daet Sung Yang in Maha Sarakham province. The finest of these *bai sema*, which dates from the 9C, stands at the east end of the front hall and shows a group of deities in front of a temple building. The lively and rhythmic treatment of the figures is especially notable.

The west end of the room contains several cabinets of Ban Chiang pottery and bronzes, and a prehistoric human skeleton excavated in Sakon Nakhon province. Other displays include prehistoric tools and jewellery, a tiny Dong Son frog and small pots from excavations at Ban Na Di near Phu Wiang.

Behind the front hall is a pleasant **courtyard**, its walls lined with several engraved sandstone *bai sema*, some of them in excellent condition, portraying scenes from the life of the Buddha.

The rooms leading off the courtyard contain a collection of rural folk crafts, including metal tools, animal and fish traps, wooden betel trays, elephant and ox bells, drums, cymbals, xylophones and other musical instruments, old wooden *wat* decorations and modern examples of local crafts, including bamboo wickerwork and hand-woven fabrics.

The **upper floor** exhibits some magnificent sandstone images, including, at the top of the stairs, a c 11C lintel from Ku Suan Taeng depicting Indra on his three-headed elephant mount, Airavata (Erawan). In a cabinet to the left is a delicate late 18C or 19C gilded wood image of the Buddha protected by the seven-headed *nāga* Mucalinda.

At the east end upstairs are several cabinets of Dvaravati votive tablets and Lop Buri-style heads dating from the 13C–14C, and a few stucco heads from Muang Fa Daet. Here also are some Khmer bronze ornaments and examples of 12C–13C Khmer pottery from Ban Kruat district, Buri Ram province, where c 100 kilns have been discovered and which, since only one kiln has so far been found in Cambodia itself (at Phnom Kulen), it is thought may have been the chief kiln site for the whole Angkor empire.

Standing near the stairs is a superb 12C–13C 2m-high sandstone figure of a guardian *dvārapāla* with a third vertical eye in his forehead, from Ku Noi, one of the sanctuaries of the ruined city of Muang Nakhon Champasi in Maha Sarakham province. The image is clad in *sampot* and belt, a cylindrical mitre, earrings and necklace, the details of which are exceptionally finely executed. Of note also are two 12C–13C images of the Buddha protected by the *nāga* Mucalinda, each of a different type, but both from Ku Santarat, Muang Nakhon Champasi.

On the west side of the room, of special note is the c 60cm Khmer sandstone four-armed torso found at Ku Noi, dating from the late 10C or early 11C, which may be a figure of Vishnu or of another deity.

In the middle of the floor on the west side are four 13C figures from Ku Kaeo, Khon Kaen, including a badly damaged figure of Shiva mounted on the bull Nandi. Nearby is a stone inscription in Sanskrit language and Khmer script dating from Jayavarman VII's reign, found at Ku Kaeo.

The museum also contains numerous Buddha images in bronze, silver and gold, stone, crystal and stucco, terracotta votive tablets and other sculptures of the Sri Vijaya, Lop Buri, Chiang Saen, Sukhothai, U Thong, Ayutthaya and Ratanakosin periods, some of them transferred from the Bangkok National Museum.

In the grounds outside the museum building are further *bai sema* stones from several sites in the northeast, some of them with four faces and decorated with vegetal motifs.

■ Some of the most important sites in the countryside surrounding Khon Kaen can only be reached with difficulty by public transport. However, it is possible to rent cars in Khon Kaen, and the TAT office may occasionally be able to offer assistance. Private charters of *songthaeo* or motorbike taxis can easily be arranged.

The following are some of the possible excursions from Khon Kaen. At least half a day should be allowed for each.

Ku Puai Noi and Chonnabot

From Khon Kaen head south on road 2 for 44km to Ban Phai and turn right to Ban Hua Nong (signed in Thai only) just north of the 398km stone. Turn left at the crossroads in the village centre after 1.5km to reach **Wat Sanuanwari Phathanaram**. Both the interior and exterior walls of the charming little *sim* of this monastery were painted in the 1930s. The interior walls depict scenes from the *jātaka* tales, predominantly blue and yellow in colour, with delightful depictions of soldiers, elephants, traditional houses, wildlife etc. The exterior walls are decorated between and above the arched windows with floral motifs and village scenes. The principal Buddha image is of extreme simplicity, typical of rural *wat* in Isan.

Return to the main road and turn east from Ban Phai on road 23. After 8km turn right on to road 2301, which runs south towards Nong Song Hong. Just beyond the 4km stone on the right is the *sim* of **Wat Chim**, its exterior walls covered with murals. These are worth a quick look, but the *wat* has been renovated rather insensitively.

Continue south and turn left just before the 8km stone on road 2297 to Puai Noi (15km). The road runs through flat country to the important Khmer site of **Ku Puai Noi**, which is in the grounds of Wat Ku Thong, on the right side of the road, 1km before the centre of Puai Noi itself.

This late 11C site, which was largely rebuilt between 1991 and 1994, consists of a central brick *prang* on a cruciform laterite platform, two cruciform *gopuras* and other subsidiary buildings in sandstone and laterite. The site is surrounded by a rectangular moat, which can be crossed at the centre of the east and west sides. Several carved lintels and pediments remain in place, including a fine portrayal of Shiva mounted on the bull Nandi, which is on the pediment of the east façade of the small building in the southeast corner. Laid out on the ground to the east of the complex are several lintels, colonnettes and carved sandstone blocks from the original structure.

Return to road 2301 and turn left towards Nong Song Hong. At the junction with road 207 turn right towards Phon and take a left turn in Ban Wang Khun, just beyond the 27km stone, to **Wat Sa Bua Kaeo**. Beneath a scruffy corrugated iron roof, the exterior walls of the *sim*, which are of stuccoed brick, are decorated with colourful murals painted in 1932. There are rather fantastical lions guarding the entrance behind seated human figures. Above the doorway is a painting of the Hindu deity Rahu swallowing the moon. The murals are painted in a vigorous and naive style, using a restricted palette of indigo, yellow ochre, brown, black, turquoise and green. They vividly portray scenes of daily life in Isan and provide valuable details of the costumes and textiles of the region.

Continue west on road 207 to rejoin road 2 about 30km south of Ban Phai. Back in Ban Phai, a short detour can be made to **Chonnabot**, a few kilometres to the west along road 229 from where it crosses the main road. This is an important silk-weaving centre, where the various stages of silk production can be observed and there are several shops selling a wide selection of both silk and cotton fabrics. From here Khon Kaen lies 44km back to the north.

Phu Wiang National Park

Take road 12 west from Khon Kaen and turn right at the intersection just before the 14km stone. After 3km, fork right on to an earth road and continue for 4km through rice fields to **Wat Chai Si** in **Ban Sawathi**.

The walls of the recently renovated *sim* of this *wat* are painted inside and out with simple but lively murals. Most have been carefully preserved, and the old leaking corrugated iron roof has been replaced with tiles. Note the beautifully carved wooden door, which retains traces of its original gilt decoration, and the very simple triple *bai sema*, emerging just a few centimetres above the ground. Inside is an extremely crude image of the Buddha.

Back on road 12, continue west to the junction with road 2038, just beyond the 48km stone. Turn off here to **Phu Wiang National Park**, the wooded rim of an ancient volcanic crater where numerous dinosaur footprints have been discovered, together with fossilised bones and teeth, dating back an estimated

160 million years. One trail leads past several sites containing examples of prehistoric rock art to Tat Fa Waterfall. Another leads to some of the dinosaur excavation sites.

To reach the park, head north along road 2038 for c 20km to Phu Wiang market, where a left fork leads after c 18km to the park's visitor centre.

Continue west along road 12 to Ban Talat 52, where a turning to the right just east of the 53km stone leads to **Wat Sawang Arom**. This rather curious *wat* lies surrounded by trees on the edge of Ban Non Tun, 1200m from the highway. Built during the 1920s, the building has suffered from neglect in recent years, and funds are now being sought to repair the corrugated iron roof and renew the flaking blue paint on the walls. The *wat* has some unusual features, including two false upper storeys, the lower one of painted zinc sheeting, the upper of wood, and, round the lower exterior walls, niches which once contained small images of the Buddha. Some of these small wooden images, together with several larger ones, have been placed inside the *wat*.

Ubon Rat Reservoir and Phu Khao-Phu Phan Kham National Park

To the northwest of Khon Kaen is the large **Ubon Rat Reservoir**, named after the eldest daughter of King Bhumibol, a beautifully landscaped stretch of water 80km long that forms a key component in a massive irrigation scheme carried out in the 1960s in an attempt to improve Isan's water supply. The dam itself is a popular recreation place for Khon Kaen's population. The 323 sq km **Phu Khao-Phu Phan Kham National Park**, in which part of the reservoir is situated, offers lakeside accommodation in simple bungalows and boat trips on the lake.

To reach the reservoir, take road 2 north from Khon Kaen and turn left on to road 2109 just south of the 27km stone. Shortly before reaching the dam wall (24km), turn left along a lane which climbs up to a colossal white seated Buddha image, from where there is a fine view over the lake. When the water level is low, dozens of small flat grass-covered islands are revealed, dotting the lake.

Road 2109 joins road 2146 just beyond the dam, and the headquarters of the national park lies 3km beyond this junction, in a pleasant setting on the lake shore.

39 · Khon Kaen to Kalasin and Sakon Nakhon

Roads 209 and 213, 205km. To Kalasin 77km; Kalasin to Sakon Nakhon 128km.

Leave Khon Kaen on road 209 towards Kalasin. Just beyond the 12km stone, a turning to the left leads in c 14km to **Wat Chedi Phum**. This *wat*, which is an important place of pilgrimage for the people of Khon Kaen province, has an exceptionally elegant, white-painted Lao-style *chedi* with a deeply redented bulbous relic-chamber surmounted by a slender spire and a seven-tiered parasol. Adjacent to the *chedi* is a little chapel with two humorous paintings of guardian soldiers on either side of the doorway.

Return to road 209 and continue east through Chiang Yun. The road runs very straight through dry, sparsely vegetated countryside to the intersection of roads 209, 213 and 2116. The most direct way to Kalasin from here is to the left on road 213. However, a more interesting route is straight ahead on road 2116. This leads to the site of the fortified Mon Dvaravati city of **Muang Fa Daet Sung Yang**, which flourished from the 9C to the 11C. Almost nothing remains of the city except the ruins of a group of *chedi* and the ramparts and moat between them, which have been excavated by the Fine Arts Department. To reach Muang Fa Daet Sung Yang, turn left off road 2116 just before the 19km stone and travel for c 3km along a new road which passes through the ramparts to the village of **Ban Sema**. Here, in the grounds of **Wat Po Chai Semaram** is a collection of sandstone and laterite *bai sema* and stelae found in and around the former settlement. Some are housed in a simple shed beside the *wat*. Many of them are decorated with bas-relief carving of high quality. Some of the finest are now in the Khon Kaen National Museum or the National Museum in Bangkok, along with other Dvaravati artefacts from Muang Fa Daet Sung Yang, including terracotta heads, pieces of decorative stucco carving and small bronzes.

Almost directly opposite Wat Po Chai Semaram, a track to the left leads in 400m to a group of four Dvaravati brick *chedi*, which stand in a row among trees in an open field. The largest, **Phra That Ya Khu**, has been rebuilt, but excavations have revealed traces of the original square brick base. Fragments of the original stucco relief carving are now in Khon Kaen National Museum. The other three *chedi* stand along a north–south axis to the south of Phra That Ya Khu.

To reach Kalasin, continue past Wat Po Chai Semaram through Muang Fa Daet Sung Yang and out through the ramparts on the northeast side to Kamalasai, where the route joins road 214. Kalasin lies c 13km to the left.

Kalasin (pop. 24,000) offers adequate accommodation for travellers wishing to break their journey here, but otherwise has little of interest. The *Suphak Hotel* at 81/7 T. Saneha is comfortable and inexpensive.

Sakon Nakhon

From Kalasin, road 213 runs northeast across flat country before climbing through the forested Phu Phan range and **Phu Phan National Park**, a 666 sq km park where there are standard bungalows for rent. Several trails lead from the park headquarters to caves and waterfalls. The most spectacular of the waterfalls is **Nam Tok Kham Hom**. From the forested hills, the road descends in sweeping curves past a palace used by the royal family to **SAKON NAKHON** (pop. 30,000), a quiet, rather dreary town on the western shore of Lake Han. This is the largest natural lake in Thailand and marks the western edge of a broad, fertile plain that stretches east as far as the Mekong River.

■ **Hotels and services**. Among the better hotels is the *Imperial* at 1892 T. Suk Kasem. An alternative is the *Dusit* at 1782 T. Yuwa Phatana. The *Bangkok Bank* is at 1324/2 T. Suk Kasem and the **post office** is at the east end of T. Sai Sawang.

■ **Transport**. There are regular **bus** services to Nakhon Phanom, Kalasin, Udon Thani and Bangkok. *THAI* has daily **flights** to Bangkok (2hrs 15mins) via Nakhon Phanom (25mins). The booking office is at 1446/73 T. Yuwa Phatana.

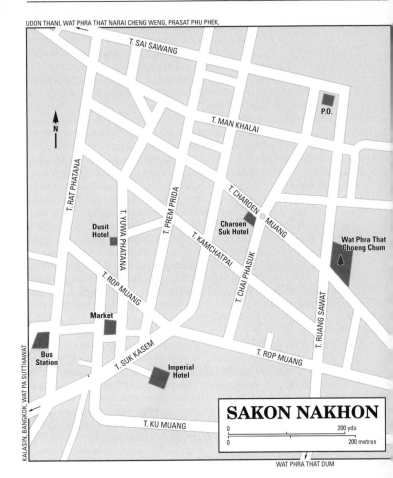

The most important *wat* in Sakon Nakhon is **Wat Phra That Choeng Chum**, at the junction of T. Charoen Muang and T. Ruang Sawat. This has a fine white stuccoed, lotus-shaped *chedi* in Lao style enclosing an earlier (probably 11C) Khmer *prang* on a laterite base, which can be glimpsed through the partly opened doors of the *chedi* and seen more clearly through a doorway behind the two large seated Buddha images in the adjoining *wihan*; this, however, is seldom opened. On the ground within the *wat* enclosure is a row of *luk nimit*, the stone balls that are buried at the four cardinal and four sub-cardinal points round the *ubosot* to demarcate the consecrated precinct, and over which the *bai sema* are set as markers.

In Sakon Nakhon are two other Khmer monuments. The more important of these is **Wat Phra That Dum**, which is in the southeast corner of the town. To reach it turn south from Wat Choeng Chum along T. Ruang Sawat and continue for c 3km. The temple consists of a heavily restored brick *prang* on a laterite base.

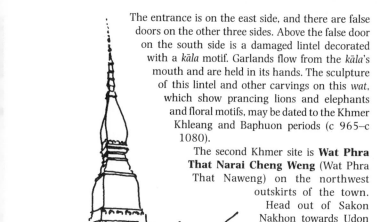

The entrance is on the east side, and there are false doors on the other three sides. Above the false door on the south side is a damaged lintel decorated with a *kāla* motif. Garlands flow from the *kāla's* mouth and are held in its hands. The sculpture of this lintel and other carvings on this *wat*, which show prancing lions and elephants and floral motifs, may be dated to the Khmer Khleang and Baphuon periods (c 965–c 1080).

The second Khmer site is **Wat Phra That Narai Cheng Weng** (Wat Phra That Naweng) on the northwest outskirts of the town. Head out of Sakon Nakhon towards Udon Thani for c 4km, and turn left up a narrow lane in Ban That Naweng, just before the intersection of roads 22 and 223. The temple lies 400m ahead.

This beautiful and well preserved monument consists of a single 11C *prang* built of sandstone on a laterite base, with its entrance on the east and false doors on the other three sides. It has especially fine lintels of pinkish sandstone. The lintel over the east entrance depicts the

Chedi of Wat Phra That Choeng Chum, Sakhon Nakon

twelve-armed dancing Shiva, while that over the north false door shows Krishna in combat with the lion-king, and above him Vishnu slumbering on the cosmic serpent Ananta. To the north is a small pavilion containing a Footprint of the Buddha.

Signed to the south off T. Suk Kasem on the southwest side of the town is **Wat Pa Sutthawat**, where there is a small **museum** dedicated to the memory of Phra Achan Man Phurithatta, one of Thailand's most revered monks and masters of meditation of recent times, whose preserved relics are on display in front of his statue. Exhibited in cases around the room are his possessions, including robes, sandals, books, wooden spittoon, toothbrushes and thermos flask.

▶Prasat Phu Phek

A pleasant **excursion** can be made from Sakon Nakhon to Prasat Phu Phek, which lies to the northwest of the town. Phu Phek is a remote site and is more easily reached by car than by public transport. Take road 22 from Sakon Nakhon towards Udon Thani and turn left after 21km, just beyond the 139km stone, on to a road that winds through wooded hills for 12km to Prasat Phu Phek. From the roadhead there is a steep flight of nearly 500 steps to the summit of Phu Phek (Doi Thaen). This is an exhausting climb in the heat of the day, so a visit early in the morning or in the evening is recommended. At the foot of the steps is a **shrine** containing Buddha images and a curious statue of a seated sage wearing a leopard skin and a round leopard-skin hat. A path flanked by wild lilies leads from the top of the steps to the centre of the flat top of the hill, on which the temple and monastic buildings stand among frangipani and other trees. The sandstone tower-sanctuary stands on a double square laterite base and opens to the east. It has no decorations and appears to be unfinished. In front of the east entrance is the lower part of a large sandstone *liṅga* and a sandstone slab that may have been a roof beam.

History

According to local folklore, Prasat Phu Phek was built in a single day to enshrine a breastbone relic of the Buddha. One version of the story goes that the rulers of two nearby city-states, Nong Han Luang and Nong Han Noi, ordered their subjects to build a stone monument on top of Phu Phek, where the Buddha had once stopped. It was decided that the men of Nong Han Luang would build a temple on top of the mountain, while the women of both states would unite to compete with the men and build one nearby at Ban Naweng (see above, Wat Phra That Narai Cheng Weng). Both sides agreed to start at dawn, at the ring of a bell, and stop when Venus (Dao Phek) had risen in the evening. The temple that was nearer completion would be the repository for the relic. The men of Nong Han Luang, confident of their greater strength, boasted that they would not only complete the temple in a single day, but would also build a causeway to the foot of the hill and a stairway to the summit.

When the women saw that the men would finish first, they dressed in their best clothes and set out to seduce a group of the men who were carrying stone blocks to the building site. On seeing them, the men abandoned their work, hung a lantern in the branches of a tree, proclaimed that Venus had risen, and set off after the women. The relic was subsequently brought up to the hilltop, but the ruler of Nong Han Luang, when he saw the monument was not completed and heard the reason, was angry, especially with the women. Accordingly, the senior monk accompanying the ruler declared that the relic should instead be enshrined at Phu Kamphra (the site of That Phanom, see p 338), since this was what the Buddha himself had commanded. As a punishment, the women were forbidden to go to Phu Kamphra, and instead, the senior monk gave them three scoops of the Buddha's ashes to enshrine in Wat Phra That Narai Cheng Weng.

Descend a few metres through the trees on the north side for an excellent view across the flat plain. The hill itself is thickly wooded and home to many birds. ◄

▶Another pleasant **excursion** can be made from Sakon Nakhon south to the 830 sq km **Huai Huat National Park**. Take road 223 towards That Phanom and turn right towards Tao Ngoi soon after joining the main Sakon Nakhon bypass. Park bungalows are available near Huai Huat Reservoir.◄

40 · Sakon Nakhon to Nakhon Phanom and That Phanom

Roads 22 and 212, 145km. To Nakhon Phanom 88km; Nakhon Phanom to That Phanom 57km. Excursion from That Phanom to Mukdahan 52km on road 212.

Leave Sakon Nakhon on road 22, skirting the north side of Han Lake across the flat, wide flood-plain. After c 15km the road passes **Ban Tha Rae**, which is the seat of a Roman Catholic bishop and has a modern cathedral near the lake shore to serve the large Vietnamese Catholic community.

Nakhon Phanom

Nakhon Phanom (pop. 34,000) lies on the west bank of the Mekong River opposite the town of Muang Khammouan (Tha Khaek) in Laos, which is clearly visible across the water. Behind it, beautiful limestone hills stretch away into the distance. A ferry service carries commercial traffic between the two towns. Nakhon Phanom is a pleasant modern town and, partly as a result of its use as an American base during the Vietnam War, it has the best hotels along this stretch of the Mekong. It provides a suitable base from which to explore the northeast corner of Thailand.

■ **Information**. The TAT office is on T. Sunthon Wichit, on the north side of the town just beyond the post office.

■ **Hotels and services**. The *Mae Nam Khong Grand View Hotel* to the south of the town is the best hotel and has a magnificent location on the river bank. Cheaper, more central hotels include the *Nakhon Phanom* at 403 T. Aphiban Bancha and the *Si Thep* at 197 T. Si Thep. There are several pleasant riverside restaurants near the clock tower. The *Thai Farmers Bank* is on T. Aphiban Bancha, and the *Bangkok Bank* is at 137 T. Si Thep. The **post office** is c 400m north of the clock tower on T. Sunthon Wichit.

■ **Transport**. **Buses** operate to most of the northeastern provinces and to Bangkok. The *THAI* agent is on T. Ruamchit Thawai, off T. Si Thep. There are daily **flights** to Bangkok (1hr 10mins).

Nakhon Phanom has been an important commercial city, trading with the ports on the Vietnamese coast to the east and Cambodia to the south, at least since the 16C when, according to tradition, King Phothisarath of Lan Xang (r. 1520–47) made the great reliquary of That Phanom, 76km south of Nakhon Phanom, a religious centre for the whole of the Mekong area to the south of Vientiane.

A **detour** can be made c 30km northwest of the town along road 212 to the small market centre of **Tha Uthen**, where the Lao-style *that* of **Wat Phra That Tha Uthen** stands beside the river.

That Phanom

The road south from Nakhon Phanom along the river bank to That Phanom passes through well irrigated rice fields, offering occasional glimpses of the Mekong River. After 45km road 2031 branches right to the village of **Renu**

Nakhon (6km), where the brightly decorated Lao-style **Phra That Renu** is worth a visit. This village is also a centre for handloom weaving. Fine cotton textiles can be found at the weekly market—usually held on Wednesdays—near the *that*, especially during the months of November to January, when the rice planting has been completed and the women have more time for weaving.

That Phanom lies 7km further south on road 212. It is a quiet market town on the river bank and offers the visitor a peaceful place to rest after the bustle of Nakhon Phanom. There are a few simple hotels and guest-houses, and a market for Lao traders is held twice a week on Mondays and Thursdays on the river bank.

Dominating the town is the *that* of **WAT PHRA THAT PHANOM**, across the main road which bypasses the town. Wat Phra That Phanom consists of a central *chedi* or *that* surrounded by a covered gallery and numerous modern monastic buildings set in a large enclosure. The *that* stands on a high, square brick base of Khmer type, which suggests that the original temple on this site may have been a Khmer *prasat*. The four sides of the base are decorated with bas-relief carvings in the style of Kulen (c 825– c 875), but also showing evidence of Dvaravati and Cham influences. The *that* was restored several times between the 15C and the 17C, and the present building dates largely from the 17C. According to an inscription in Thai Noi script on a stela which was discovered buried in the foundations in the 1940s, and which stands today on the east side, the *that* was restored in 1614. In the late 17C, the ruler of Vientiane increased its height to 47m.

Partly as a result of endemic warfare in the area, the temple was largely abandoned during the 18C and 19C, and by 1901, when Phra Khru Wirocana, a monk from Ubon Ratchathani, visited the *that*, it was in ruins, and there were banyan trees the size of a human arm poking through crevices in the brick. The two inscriptions left by Phra Khru Wirocana can be seen today beside the *that*.

In the 1940s, the Fine Arts Department renovated the temple again, rather insensitively, and in 1954 a new seven-tiered golden parasol was put on top of the spire to replace the previous five-tiered one, which was made in c 1692 and can now to be seen in the *wat* museum. Disaster struck on 11 August 1975, when, after several days of heavy rain, the entire *that* collapsed. The present structure was completed in March 1979 and the relic re-interred in it in a ceremony conducted by the king and the supreme patriarch.

In the *wat* **museum** is a photograph of the collapsed *that* in 1975, and a collection consisting largely of objects found during the subsequent rebuilding.

Upstairs are other artefacts, including Buddha images, votive tablets, Lan Xang pottery, cow bells, a bronze drum and a collection of gongs.

In **Ban Nam Kham**, 3km south of That Phanom along the river bank, is **Wat Pho Kham**, which has a *sim* with interior murals, painted in the 1930s, depicting scenes from the *Ramakien*, the *Vessantara Jātaka* and the story of Suriwong, a local folk-tale. Along the back wall are three rather simple Lao-style seated Buddha images.

▶To Mukdahan

An **excursion** can be made to Mukdahan, 58km to the south on road 212. Travellers with their own transport can make an easy **detour** (c 2km) to **Wat Phutthasima** in **Ban Fang Daeng**, another village *wat* with colourful murals.

To find this *wat*, leave That Phanom on road 212 towards Mukdahan and after 6km turn right on to road 223 towards Na Kae and Sakon Nakhon. The *wat* is along a dirt lane to the right, 1km from the junction. The murals on the exterior walls are of little interest, but all four walls inside are covered in delightful **paintings**, including scenes from the *Totsachat Jātakas*, armies fighting, monkeys in trees, Chinese soldiers on horses, people hunting and daily life in the northeast.

Return to road 212 and continue south towards Mukdahan. A turning to the left south of the 188km stone leads to **Wan Yai**, a pretty little village on the west bank of the Mekong River. Turn right at the river bank to **Wat Phra Si Mahapho**, where a charming little west-facing *sim* lies beside the river. Built in 1916, the interior walls are covered with simple murals depicting scenes from the *Vessantara Jātaka*. The old roof shingles have unfortunately been replaced by corrugated iron, but the beautifully carved wooden supporting beams have survived.

Continue south along the river past **Wat Manophirom** in Ban Chanot. The large, heavily built *wihan* of this *wat* has enormous painted *khan tuai* and an elaborately decorated gable. The road beyond leads south to the riverine town of **Mukdahan**, which has a popular market along the embankment. On the opposite bank is the Lao town of Sawannakhet, with which there is a flourishing trade. Probably the best of Mukdahan's few adequate hotels is *Saensuk Bungalow* at 2 T. Phitak Santirat. Turn right off T. Samlan Chai Khong south of the pier to find the excellent *Mukdarat Restaurant*.

Apart from the busy market and several *wat* built by Vietnamese migrants, there is little to see in Mukdahan. However, a pleasant **excursion** can be made to **Mukdahan National Park**, 15km south of the town on road 2034. Here are magnificent views from the clifftop trails, which lead past sandstone outcrops that have been weathered into unusual shapes. Food stalls in the car park provide drinks and snacks.◄

41 · Maha Sarakham, Roi Et and Yasothon

__Roads__ 2, 208 and 23, 184km. From Khon Kaen to Maha Sarakham 73km; Maha Sarakham to Roi Et 33km (or an alternative detour via Wapi Pathum on roads 2040 and 2045, 105km); Roi Et to Yasothon 69km on road 23 (or an alternative detour via Suwannaphum on roads 215 and 202). The route runs east across the flat Khorat Plateau, through extensive areas of rice cultivation.

From Khon Kaen travel south on road 2 for 12km and turn left to **Maha Sarakham** on road 208. Behind the central market area in the town centre is **Wat Maha Chai**, which has a small museum housing a fine collection of religious woodcarvings and folk art. It is usually kept locked, but the monks can sometimes be persuaded to open it.

There are few inducements to stay overnight in Maha Sarakham but the *Wasu Hotel* provides adequate accommodation. The *Marina Restaurant* is recommended.

From Maha Sarakham to Roi Et the traveller has a choice of two routes. The most direct goes southeast for 33km along road 23. 12km from Maha Sarakham turn left just east of the 93km stone to reach the Khmer site of **Ku Khu Mahathat**, also known as Prang Ku, which is on the left side after 1200m. Ku Khu Mahathat consists of a simple laterite *prang* surrounded by a well-preserved laterite wall. The foundations of a *gopura* are still visible. Return to road 23 and continue southeast to Roi Et.

The more circuitous alternative route (c 105km) goes south from Roi Et to the remains of the 10C–12C settlement of **Muang Nakhon Champasi** before turning northeast to Roi Et.

Take road 2040 south from Maha Sarakham for 37km to Wapi Pathum. Turn left here on to road 2045 which leads in 6km to **Ku Ban Daeng**. This temple, which is a simple, very ruined *prang* in a field on the north side of the road at the 42km stone, may have marked the entrance to the ancient Khmer city of Muang Nakhon Champasi. Beyond Ku Ban Daeng, a turning to the right towards Na Dun leads in 700m to **Ku Santarat**, a laterite tower-sanctuary with a porch, surrounded by laterite walls and shaded by great trees. In a field c 500m to the east is **Ku Noi**, of which little remains except parts of the laterite enclosure wall and a ruined sandstone tower-sanctuary on a laterite base. Both Ku Noi and Ku Santarat have yielded some important sculptures, which are now in the National Museum in Khon Kaen.

Return on road 2045 through Wapi Pathum to **ROI ET** (pop. 34,000), a well planned, spacious town built around an artificial lake, Bung Phlan Chai. On a small island in the lake is a shrine containing the *lak muang* of the city.

■ **Hotels and services**. The *Mai Thai Hotel* at 99 T. Hai Sok, and the nearby *Phetcharat* at 66–104 T. Hai Sok are two of Roi Et's better hotels. The *Bangkok Bank* is at 23 T. Suriyadet Bamrung. The **post office** is on the southeast side of the lake. There are several busy **markets** on the north side of the lake.

■ **Transport**. Frequent **buses** run to neighbouring provinces, and there are regular services to Bangkok.

The charming monastery of **Wat Klang Ming Muang**, on the north side of the town has an *ubosot* with some highly decorative murals on the upper part of the outside walls showing scenes of the *Vessantara Jātaka*.

In the grounds of **Wat Burapha Phiram** off T. Ploenchit on the northeast side of the town is an immensely tall and hideous modern image of the Buddha, Phra Phuttha Ratana Mongkhon Mahamuni. It stands nearly 70m high and is covered with mosaic tiles the colour of milk chocolate for the flesh and of dark chocolate for the robe. The buildings of Wat Burapha Phiram are of unparalleled gaudiness.

Take the road east from Wat Burapha Phiram and turn right at the 8km stone. After 1km a signpost marked 'Hue Prang' indicates the way to **Prang Ku**, also known as Prasat Hin Nong Ku, a notable example of a Jayavarman VII *arogyaśālā* (see Prasat Ta Muen Tot, p 365), situated in the vicinity of a modern *wat*. It is surrounded by a laterite enclosure wall with a large ruined *gopura* on the east side. In the centre of the enclosure is a laterite *prang* with a porch and a door on the east side and three false doors, all devoid of ornamentation except for some rather rudimentary carving on the lintel and colonnettes of the east door. This *prang* now contains a Buddha image. To the south are the remains of another building, which may have been a 'library'. Some badly eroded carved colonnettes and lintels and a *linga* from the temple have been collected together and placed on a pile of stones in the northeast corner of the enclosure. Outside the enclosure to the northeast is a *baray* with laterite sides and steps. To the southwest is a large platform with three plinths, on each of which is a *yoni* and which may originally have formed the bases of three *prang*.

Roi Et to Yasothon

There is a choice of routes from Roi Et to Yasothon. Most direct (69km) is road 23, which runs southeast across the flat plateau. 5km from Roi Et, a turning to the left 300m east of the 26km stone leads to **Wat Pratu Chai** in Ban Pratu Chai. The once charming *sim* of this *wat* is now crumbling and neglected, and the murals which formerly covered the exterior walls have almost disappeared.

The longer route via **Suwannaphum** follows road 215 almost due south through Muang Suang. In Suwannaphum turn right opposite the police station and then turn left at a T-junction to reach **Wat Klang** on the right side of the road. This ancient monastery has a reconstructed brick *wihan* and behind it two unrestored brick *chedi* partially covered in grey cement.

6km south of Suwannaphum along road 214 towards Tha Tum and Surin, turn left in the village of Ban Ku into a grove of trees where there are many monkeys. Here is the important temple complex of **Wat Ku Phra Ko Na**. The enclosure is surrounded by a laterite wall and within are three Khmer *prang* of brick and pink sandstone on a single laterite base. Unfortunately these are now partly obscured by a clutter of later buildings, and the central *prang* has been entirely covered by a Lao-style *chedi* of grey stucco decorated with pieces of ceramic and coloured glass. Little can be seen of the north *prang,* because it has been encased in another building under a corrugated iron roof. The entrance to the south *prang,* which is still largely intact, is to the east, and there are false doors on the other three sides. Buddha images have been placed directly in front under a flimsy shelter of wood and corrugated iron. There is a fine lintel over the north door.

►A detour to the west of Suwannaphum

Back in Suwannaphum, a detour west towards Kaset Wisai leads to the important 11C Khmer Hindu temple of Prasat Ku Ka Sing. Follow road 214 northwest from Suwannaphum c 11km to a left turn which leads down an avenue of eucalyptus trees. The road, which is only metalled in parts, crosses a river and then passes through more groves of eucalyptus. The site is on the left after c 10km, in the precinct of a large and hideous modern wat by a lake. Within a rectangular enclosure surrounded by a laterite wall with laterite structures built on top of it is a group of sandstone platforms set on high laterite bases on which the lower parts of the brick walls of the principal temple buildings have been reconstructed. There are several pink sandstone door and window frames in situ, some of the former with finely carved thresholds, and seven lintels in the 11C

Baphuon style carved in unusually high relief. In the central shrine is a sandstone statue of the bull Nandi, the mount of Shiva. There are also several ancillary buildings of laterite, some with small balustered windows. ◀

From Suwannaphum, road 202 runs northeast to Phutthaisong and Phisai. The road leads through a flat, monotonous landscape. Just after the 16km stone and before a turning to the right to Nung Hong Song, turn left again and after 500m the mid-12C temple of **Ku Suan Taeng** comes into view. This consists of three brick *prang* on a low laterite base built on a north–south axis. No pediments or lintels survive and only the frame of the false door on the west side of the central *prang* is still *in situ*. The interior of this *prang* has a finely corbelled brick vault. Traces of a surrounding laterite wall can be discerned, and on the ground there are a broken antefix in the form of a five-headed *nāga*, the circular base of a *kalaśa* finial and some laterite blocks.

Continue northeast on road 202 to the provincial capital of **YASOTHON** (pop. 29,800), which is chiefly notable for its popular rocket festival (Ngan Bun Bang Fai), held every year at the end of the dry season in May. This was originally an animist rain-making ceremony and involves the making of a great number of bamboo rockets, which are carried through the town in procession on decorated floats to the accompaniment of dancing and music and are then fired up at the sky to remind the rain god of the need for rain.

There are several interesting monasteries in the town. These include **Wat Si Traiphum**, which has a large, imposing and extremely elaborate *ubosot* with a triple-tiered roof and is the place where the procession of floats at the rocket festival ends and the prizes for the best floats are awarded; **Wat Mahathat**, which has an ancient *chedi* or *that*, very inexpertly restored, and a beautiful, ornately decorated *ho trai* built over a pool; and **Wat Thung Sawang**, which has a curious *that* on a high square base covered with stucco and surrounded by numerous smaller white *chedi*.

■ **Accommodation** in Yasothon is rudimentary. The best hotel is the *Yot Nakhon* on T. Uthai Ramrit, which, together with all others in the town, is fully booked during the rocket festival. There is a better selection of hotels in Roi Et or in Ubon Ratchathani c 100km southeast along road 23, where there is an even wider choice.

7km from Yasothon on road 23 towards Ubon Ratchathani, turn left in the attractive village of **Ban Kong Khao Noi**, which has many fine old wooden houses, and then right to a grove of trees in which is the fine Lao *that* of **That Khong Khao Noi**, also known as That Luk Kha Mae. The stucco decoration of this tall and elegant brick *that* dates from the Ayutthaya period and was restored by the Fine Arts Department in 1980. Numerous sandstone *bai sema* are scattered around the *that*.

To Ubon Ratchathani

Road 23 runs southeast directly to Ubon Ratchathani (see Rte 47), a fast and easy journey of c 100km. A longer but more interesting route, which passes a couple of interesting *wat*, is through **Amnat Charoen**, 56km east of Yasothon along road 202. Although it was upgraded to provincial capital status in 1993,

Wat Mahathat at Yasothon

Amnat Charoen is little more than a busy junction. Turn right here on to road 212 and after c 20km turn left in Ban Amnat on to road 2134. After 700m, a lane on the left leads after 1km to **Wat Ban Yang Cha**. Of interest is the old *sim*, now very neglected, with a rusty corrugated iron roof. The interior walls are painted in a characteristically naive Isan style with scenes from the *Vessantara Jātaka*.

Continue east to **Phana** on road 2134. At the main junction in the centre of Phana, turn left along a narrow lane, past one *wat* of no interest to **Wat Phra Lao Thep Nimit**. In the *sim* of this monastery is a magnificent and much revered seated image of the Buddha in *bhūmisparśa mudrā*, cast in 1693. Behind this image to the right is a fine old wooden rack for votive tablets. The *sim* has been repeatedly renovated and now has several additional windows as well as a rather garish new roof of glazed ceramic tiles. The window shutters and doors have stencilled gilt decoration. In the centre of the pediment above the entrance, which is of carved wood painted red and gold, is a depiction of Rahu devouring the moon. The *sim* is surrounded by a heterogeneous collection of *bai sema*, some double, some triple, some quadruple and, at the front, even quintuple.

From Phana, Ubon Ratchathani lies 58km to the south on roads 2049 and 212.

THE LOWER KHORAT PLATEAU

42· Lop Buri to Si Thep and Chaiyaphum

Roads 1, 205, 21 and 225, 232km. To Si Thep 113km. From Si Thep to Chaiyaphum 119km.

Si Thep Historical Park

Leave Lop Buri on road 1, which runs from the roundabout with the statue of King Narai on the east side of the town, and head north for 40km to the intersection with road 205. Turn right here and continue east along road 205 for 29km to the intersection with road 21. Turn north on road 21, and after c 40km, Si Thep Historical Park (open daily, 08.30–16.30) is signed to the right along road 2211. Follow the road for c 9km to reach the park, which is near the village of Ban Bung.

The ancient city of Si Thep owed its importance to its strategic location on a major route connecting the Khorat Plateau through the valley of the Pa Sak River with the basin of the Chao Phraya. The site is therefore of considerable historical significance. It was first excavated by H.G. Quaritch Wales in 1935, and further excavations and restoration of the principal monuments have been carried out subsequently by the Fine Arts Department. The site has been cleared and is now maintained as a park full of fine trees, which provides a magnificent setting for the reconstructed monuments. It covers an area of c 4.7 sq km and is divided into two parts known as the Inner City and the Outer City. In the 6C Si Thep appears to have been ruled by the Mons, who built the Inner City. By the 9C it had fallen under the rule of the Khmers, who constructed the Outer City and remained at Si Thep until the 12C, when the city was abandoned.

The **Outer City** is roughly elliptical in shape and measures 4 x 1.5km; it was surrounded by a wall and moat and had seven entrances.

The most important sites are all in the **Inner City**: Khao Klang Nai, a *stūpa* belonging to the period of Mon rule, and two largely brick Khmer monuments, Prang Si Thep and Prang Song Phi Nong. All three were sensitively restored in the early 1990s. **Khao Klang Nai** is the southernmost of the three and consists of a brick *stūpa* on a rectangular laterite base about 12m high facing east. It was evidently once covered with stucco, and parts of a frieze of stucco figures in relief still surround the base. The style of these suggests that it was a Dvaravati Mon *stūpa* built in the 7C or 8C.

A little to the northwest of Khao Klang Nai is **Prang Si Thep**, which consists of a single brick tower-sanctuary on a laterite base. It was formerly surmounted by a lotus finial, which is now exhibited in the site museum. The two decorated lintels found here reveal that it was a Hindu Khmer monument built in the late Baphuon or early Angkor Wat style (mid-11C–mid-12C).

To the northeast of Khao Klang Nai is **Prang Song Phi Nong**, which consists of two brick *prang* on a single laterite base. At the entrance of the larger *prang* is a stone slab, which suggests that the monument was built with material taken from an earlier building on the same site. The temple is approached by a long raised laterite causeway.

The religious sculpture of Si Thep chiefly consists of a number of exceptionally fine **statues of Hindu deities** carved in an elegant and naturalistic style. They include a superb 8C mitred figure of Vishnu (or possibly Krishna), 1.19m high, in the *tribhaṅga* pose and another badly damaged, but equally graceful figure of Krishna, 1.04m high, holding the Govardhana Mountain aloft to protect his disciples. Some Buddhist images, both Mahayana and Theravada, have also been found at Si Thep. These include a severely damaged image of the Buddha in *samādhi*, with an inscription in Pali, and three images of the standing Buddha in *vitarka mudrā*, which show similarities in style and in the details of their dress with Khmer bronze images of the 8C and 9C found in the Buri Ram area. All these Hindu and Buddhist sculptures are now in the National Museum, Bangkok (see p 124).

Chaiyaphum

From Si Thep, continue north on road 21 to the intersection with road 225, which leads east directly to Chaiyaphum. The road crosses the wide valley floor before climbing steeply through the Phang Hoei hills. This part of the route offers excellent views, before the road descends to the upper Chi River valley and thence to Chaiyaphum (pop. 26,000).

Chaiyaphum was evidently an important provincial centre of the Khmer empire, when it was known as Jayabhumi, and seems to have been a staging-post on the road from Angkor to Si Thep. Today the town itself is of no great interest, although it is a pleasant place to stay and has a lively night market. It is also a convenient point from which to visit the silk-weaving centre of Ban Khwao, which is on road 225 15km west of Chaiyaphum and easily reached by *songthaeo*.

■ **Hotels and services**. The *Loet Nimit Hotel* at 1/447 T. Niwet Rat is quite acceptable; the *Sirichai* at 565 T. Non Muang, however, is dirty and should be avoided. The **post office** is on T. Bannakan, to the west of the roundabout, and there are **banks** in the vicinity of T. Ratchathan.

■ **Transport**. Regular **bus** services run to Khon Kaen, Khorat and Bangkok.

From the roundabout in the town centre take T. Bannakan to the east, past the hospital to the neighbourhood of Muang Kao, where the foundations of an ancient city are still discernible. To the right, in the grounds of **Wat Klang Muang** are some sandstone *bai sema* and other stones from earlier buildings on the site. 300m ahead is the Khmer site of **Prang Ku**, which dates from the reign of Jayavarman VII. Prang Ku is attractively situated in a grove of frangipani trees and consists of a well preserved tower-sanctuary and a ruined *gopura*. It has some fine but badly effaced carved lintels and pediments, particularly the lintel resting on laterite blocks on the north side of the *gopura*, which portrays the Churning of the Sea of Milk surmounted by a *kāla* head. There is a Dvaravati seated image of the Buddha (the head is a modern replica of the stolen original) in a cella on the north front of the sanctuary and an Ayutthaya-period standing Buddha image on the west front. The enclosure is surrounded by the remains of a laterite wall.

To the north of Chaiyaphum, 16km along road 2051, is the 218 sq km **Tat Ton National Park**. This park, which covers an area of 218 sq km, has some cascades that are impressive late in the rainy season, but at other times can be disappointing. Near the 12km stone, before the falls, a dirt road to the east leads after 7km to a small tree-covered hill, **Phu Phra**, where eight U Thong or early Ayutthaya images of the Buddha have been carved into two small sandstone outcrops in the grounds of **Wat Sila At**. The largest image, Phra Chao Ong Tu, is 2m high and is especially revered. Unfortunately, the natural shelter provided by the large overhanging sandstone boulders has been enveloped by an ugly man-made structure, which detracts somewhat from the beauty of the site.

Stretching across the northern end of Chaiyaphum province is the 1560 sq km **Phu Khieo Wildlife Sanctuary**, which occupies the southern end of the Phetchabun range. This sanctuary contains important **elephant** and **gaur populations**, and possibly also the last **Sumatran rhinos** in Thailand. Both the Eld's deer and the sarus crane have been reintroduced to the wild here. Accommodation can be arranged through the office of the Royal Forestry Department in Bangkok. Food is available, and there is a recently completed nature trail.

43 · Nakhon Ratchasima and environs

Roads 1 *and* 2, *255km from Bangkok. Both these highways are good, but they carry a great deal of traffic at least as far as Saraburi (107km). Travellers starting from Bangkok are therefore strongly advised to set out early. On the outskirts of Saraburi turn right off road* 1 *on to road* 2, *which runs northeast for 148km through a flat and fertile rice-growing area to Nakhon Ratchasima. Road* 1 *continues north to Lop Buri. From Nakhon Ratchasima the important Khmer sites of Phanom Wan and Phimai can be visited.*

Railway, 264km in 4hrs (express) from Hua Lamphong station in Bangkok.

▶To reach **KHAO YAI NATIONAL PARK** turn right on to road 2090 a few kilometres before Pak Chong. Thailand's first national park, established in 1962, Khao Yai is also the third largest and has been declared an ASEAN National Heritage Site. It covers an area of 2172 sq km and contains a variety of habitats, including dense tropical evergreen forest, submontane evergreen forest and meadows. The highest mountain peak in the park is Khao Rom (1351m). Wildlife is abundant and includes many endangered species, among them elephants, gibbons, tigers, leopards, Asiatic black bears and Malayan sun bears. More than **300 bird species** have been recorded, including four hornbill species, the Siamese fireback and the silver pheasant. The highest waterfall, Heo Narok, is a magnificent sight in the rainy season. There are numerous hiking trails, and for these it is advisable to hire a guide.

■ **Hotels and Tours**. Only **camping** is currently permitted in the park, but there are plenty of **hotels** nearby, both in Pak Chong and along road 2090 on the approach to the park gate. In Pak Chong, the comfortable *Rim Than Inn* at the south end and the *Phu Phaya* at the north end can be recommended. Travellers on a low budget might try the simple *Jungle Adventure Guest House* off T. Kongwaksin, Soi 3 in the town centre, but you will be expected to take the organised tour to the park. Along road 2090 are numerous, rather over-priced resorts catering mainly to Thai visitors. One that can be recommended is *Khao Yai Garden Lodge* near the 7km stone, where staff speak English and can arrange tours of the national park.

National Park staff at the entrance gate can also arrange **wildlife-watching tours** in the park, including night drives, when there is more chance of finding elephants at salt licks etc. ◄

20km east of Pak Chong, road 2 runs along the shore of a pleasant **reservoir** created by the building of the Lam Takhong dam and then goes straight across the plain towards Nakhon Ratchasima. On the right of the road shortly before the junction with road 201 at Sikhiu is a hill called **Khao Chan Ngam** ('Hill of the Beautiful Moon'). Here at the village of **Ban Loet Sawan** a path to the right leads after 6km to a monastery at the foot of the hill, from where it is possible to climb up to see a remarkable series of **prehistoric rock paintings** of unknown date showing a group of human figures, one of them carrying a bow.

Also near **Sikhiu**, on the south side of road 2 near the 207km stone is an important **Khmer sandstone quarry**. Part of it was unfortunately destroyed when the Friendship Highway (road 2) was built in the 1950s, but it is still possible to see some of the places where the sandstone was removed or cut in preparation for moving. It is not known for which buildings the stones from Sikuiu were quarried, but it seems likely that they were used at Muang Khorakhapura, which is only c 20km to the east (see below).

32km from Nakhon Ratchasima, between the 222 and 223km stones in the village of Ban Bu Yai, turn off road 2 on to road 2161, which leads after 2.5km across open heath country to the village of **Ban Sung Noen**. Turn right in the village. After 2km, the road curves left and crosses the railway line. 800m beyond the railway on the left are the ruins of the ancient Khmer city of **Muang Khorakhapura**, founded in the early 10C and first excavated in 1959 by the Department of Fine Arts. There are two principal sites: **Prasat Non Ku**, and 500m beyond it, **Prasat Muang Khaek**.

Prasat Non Ku consists of the sandstone base of a *prang* and, at the front of the temple complex, two brick structures on sandstone bases, one to the north and one to the south. These have entrances on the west, which suggests that they may have been 'libraries' and not shrines.

Prasat Muang Khaek dates from the late Koh Ker period (c 940). The temple complex was originally surrounded by two concentric walls with a moat between them. All that remains of the buildings are the undecorated sandstone door frames of the central sanctuary and of a *gopura* to the north, which, unusually, was the main entrance to the temple, and the high sandstone base of the main *prang*, which probably had brick walls and a corbelled brick roof. To the east of the main *prang* is a long chamber with brick walls, which was probably roofed with wood and tiles. Atypically for a Khmer building of this early date, it is walled on both sides and at the south end, instead of having columns on one side. Several fine relief carvings, including antefixes with figures of *garuḍas*, deities, praying *riṣis* and *dvārapālas*, have been found both here and at Prasat Non Ku and are now in the Somdet Maha Wirawong National Museum in Nakhon Ratchasima.

3km beyond Muang Khorakhapura, in the precincts of a hideous modern *wat* called Wat Prang Muang Kao, is a well-preserved **arogyasālā** of Jayavarman VII (see Prasat Ta Muen Tot, p 365). This consists of a laterite central *prang* with entrance doors on each of the four sides, surrounded by a low sandstone wall. The doors still retain their sandstone frames. Inside the *prang* is a Footprint of the Buddha. The east entrance has a *gopura* built of sandstone on a laterite base with a vaulted roof. To the northeast outside the enclosure is a square pond with sandstone sides.

5km to the northwest of Sung Noen is the site of the Mon Dvaravati city of **Muang Sema**, which dates from the 9C and is thus earlier than Muang Khorakhapura. Very little of this city remains except for parts of the ramparts and ditches which surrounded the oval enclosure, some ponds and a few piles of stone and brick.

The road from Muang Sema leads through Ban Hin Tang to **Wat Thammachak Semaram** in **Ban Khlong Kuang**, where there is a colossal reclining Buddha image of pink sandstone. Here also are numerous sandstone *bai sema*, colonnettes and other stone relics lying scattered under the trees. At the back of a dark shed in the temple enclosure is an exceptionally fine Mon Dvaravati Wheel of the Law, which was discovered in Ban Hin Tang and is the object of great veneration, as is shown by the many pieces of gold leaf placed on it by the faithful.

Nakhon Ratchasima

The city of Nakhon Ratchasima (pop. 203,000), also known as **Khorat**, is situated on the southwest edge of the great Khorat Plateau which covers most of the northeast region of Thailand (Isan) and is watered by the Mun and Chi rivers.

History
The city is believed to have been founded by the Thais when they first penetrated into this area in the second half of the 13C as a stronghold against the Khmers. It remained a semi-independent outpost of the Thai kingdom for most of the Ayutthaya period and was frequently in revolt against the rule of Ayutthaya. It was fortified in the 17C by King Narai. Its role as gateway to the northeast was greatly strengthened by the arrival of the railway here in 1900, and it has remained an important industrial and communications centre ever since.

■ **Information**. The TAT office (open daily, 08.30–16.30) and Tourist Police are at 2102–4 T. Mittaphap. The TAT can provide lists of hotels and city maps etc. The *DK Book House* on T. Chomphon has maps and books in English.

■ **Hotels and services**. Among the best is the *Sima Thani Hotel*, near to the TAT office on T. Mittaphap. The recently renovated *Chomsurang Hotel* at 2701/2 T. Mahat Thai is clean, comfortable and moderately priced. Cheap, clean rooms can be found at the *Siri Hotel* at 688–90 T. Pho Klang. The *Bangkok Bank* and *Thai Farmers Bank* both have branches on T. Chomphon and T. Mittaphap. The **post office** is on T. Asadang. There is a lively **night market** in T. Chomphon.

■ **Transport**. **Buses** depart from several points in the city, according to their destination. Ask at your hotel or TAT. There are frequent services to Bangkok, Buri Ram, Phimai, and other towns throughout Isan.

The **railway station** is on T. Mukhamontri. The northeast line from Bangkok divides at Nakhon Ratchasima, and one branch runs north to Nong Khai, the other east to Buri Ram, Surin and Ubon Ratchathani. Computerised advanced booking is available at the station.

There are daily **flights** to Bangkok (40 mins). The *THAI* booking office is at 14 T. Manat.

Nakhon Ratchasima still retains some of the fortifications built by King Narai. One of the fortified gateways, Pratu Chumphon, on the west side of the old city on T. Ratchadamnoen, has been reconstructed to form the base for a terrace on which there is a statue of Thao Suranari or Khunying Mo, wife of the governor of Nakhon Ratchasima, who in 1827 repelled a Lao invasion led by King Anuvong of Vientiane by going outside the city with a group of women and making the Lao soldiers so drunk that they were easily overpowered. A festival in her honour is held every year at the end of March. It lasts for a week and is marked by parades, processions, and displays of local dances and costumes.

The *lak muang* of the city is at the entrance to T. Chomphon, almost opposite the Chomsurang Hotel.

Apart from the Thao Suranari statue, Nakhon Ratchasima has few monuments of interest. In the southwest of the city near the Thao Suranari statue and the railway line is **Wat Bung**, an Ayutthaya-period temple with an attractive small *ubosot* with a curved base and a four-tiered low-sweeping roof adorned with richly carved wooden pediments and *khan tuai*.

Wat Phra Narai Mahathat, also known as **Wat Klang**, is situated on T. Prajak in the centre of the city near the *lak muang*. The large *wihan* of this monastery has a bare whitewashed interior with plain square columns and contains an ancient stone image of Vishnu. In the enclosure are several pieces of carved sandstone from Khmer temples in the vicinity.

Wat Phayap, on T. Chomphon in the northwest corner of the old city, has an imposing modern *ubosot* built in 1992 in the Ayutthaya style. It is raised on a curved boat-shaped platform, the walls are clad in grey marble tiles and the roof with pink marble.

Another notable temple is **Wat Sala Loi**, which is situated in the northeast corner of the city outside the walls about 400m off the ring road. It was built in 1973 to the designs of the Thai architect Wirot Sisuro and is one of the very few Buddhist temples in Thailand built in a modern idiom and not in a slavishly traditional style. It has a large *ubosot* with inward-sloping walls, deep box-like window embrasures and steeply pitched interlocking asymmetrical tiled roofs, the irregular curving lines of which recall the Sydney Opera House. Its tall double doors have bronze panels depicting scenes from the *Vessantara Jātaka*. The *bai sema* are in the form of lotus buds with *nāgas* at their base. Inside, the walls are decorated with terracotta panels made specially for the *wat* in Ban Dan Kwian (see below), depicting scenes from the Life of the Buddha. A tall standing image of the Buddha is at the east end. The whole building is surrounded by a low balustrade made of terracotta. Next to it is an ornamental pool, in the

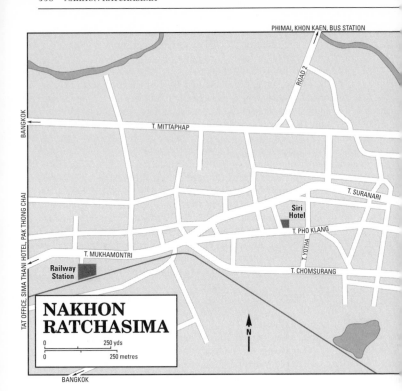

middle of which is a *mondop* containing a monument to Phra Mahami, the abbot of the monastery who commissioned the building of the *wat*.

A short way to the south of Pratu Chumphon on T. Ratchadamnoen is **Wat Sutthachinda**, situated in an attractive garden just outside the walls. In the precinct of this *wat* is the **Somdet Maha Wirawong National Museum** (open Wed–Sun, 09.00–16.00), which consists of a single room containing a small but interesting and well-displayed collection of sculptures of all periods found at sites in the region. Outside the entrance are several fragments of Khmer lintels and other decorative sculptures carved in pink sandstone. Inside, among the most notable objects are a lovely Ayutthaya wooden pediment with a figure of Erawan, the three-headed elephant, from Wat Sa Kaeo, Nakhon Ratchasima, and a remarkable Khmer-Lop Buri frieze of figures of crowned deities on their mounts.

Nakhon Ratchasima is a suitable base from which to visit the magnificent Khmer sites of Phanom Wan and Phimai, although these can be visited just as easily en route to Khon Kaen (see Rte 39). Also near the city is the important silk-weaving centre of Pak Thong Chai.

▶To reach **Pak Thong Chai**, take road 2 southwest from Nakhon Ratchasima and after 5km turn left on to road 304. Shortly before Pak Thong Chai on the left

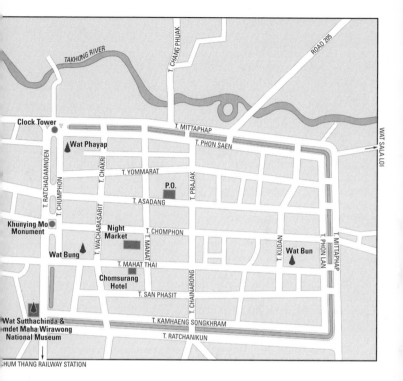

Map labels:
TAKHONG RIVER
T. CHANG PHUAK
ROAD 205
Clock Tower
T. MITTAPHAP
Wat Phayap
T. PHON SAEN
WAT SALA LOI
T. RATCHADAMNOEN
T. CHUMPHON
T. CHAKRI
T. YOMMARAT
T. PRAJAK
P.O.
T. ASADANG
T. WACHARASARIT
Khunying Mo Monument
Night Market
T. CHOMPHON
T. MANAT
T. KUDAN
Wat Bun
T. PHON LAN
T. MITTAPHAP
Wat Bung
T. MAHAT THAI
Chomsurang Hotel
T. SAN PHASIT
T. CHAINARONG
Wat Sutthachinda & Somdet Maha Wirawong National Museum
T. KAMHAENG SONGKHRAM
T. RATCHANIKUN
CHUM THANG RAILWAY STATION

of the road is the entrance to the **Silk Culture Centre**, flanked by colossal figures of silkworms. The centre consists of a single street of shops and silk factories. There is also a building containing a photographic exhibition illustrating the silk-weaving process. At the end of the street is the very pleasant *Nopparat Hotel*, set in beautiful gardens on the edge of a small lake.

In Pak Thong Chai turn west off road 304 on to road 2238, which leads after 4.5km to **Wat Na Phra That**, an attractive small 19C monastery chiefly notable for its *ubosot* surrounded by pink sandstone *bai sema*, which contains late 19C murals. Beside the *ubosot* is an unusual Lao-style *chedi*, and behind that a charming wooden *ho trai* built on stilts in the middle of a pool. ◄

From Nakhon Ratchasima, road 2 heads northeast towards Khon Kaen. A turning to the right at the 15km stone leads to **PRASAT PHANOM WAN**, one of the most important Khmer monuments in this region. Stylistic and epigraphic evidence indicates that Phanom Wan was founded as early as the mid-9C and was altered and enlarged at various times between the late 9C and the end of the 11C. An inscription in Sanskrit dated AD 891 refers to two late 9C Khmer rulers, Indravarman I and Yasovarman I, and one of the lintels, which is decorated with a *kala* head disgorging garlands terminating in five-headed *nāgas* and is now in the National Museum in Bangkok, is in the Preah Ko style of this period. Other lintels date from the early 10C (Bakheng style) and 11C (Baphuon style). The predominant building materials are white and pink sandstone. Two other inscriptions found here, one dated 1055 and the other 1082, and the discovery of two stone carvings—a *linga* and a hand holding a lotus that has been identified as part of an image of Uma—show that Phanom Wan, like many other Khmer temples, was originally a Hindu (Shaivite) foundation and was later converted to Buddhist use, probably in the 13C. Its relationship with Phimai (see below) has not yet been firmly established. Although still used as a Buddhist shrine, Phanom Wan had become a picturesque ruin before it was extensively restored in the early 1990s.

The plan of the temple is similar to that of Phimai and Phanom Rung. It was originally surrounded by a moat, but little of this is now visible. To the east is a large *baray* c 500m in length. A rectangular gallery concentric with the moat surrounds the central sanctuary, which consists of a *prang* with porches on all four sides and an *antarāla* and *maṇḍapa* to the east. Numerous Buddha images of all periods, some as early as the 12C , have been placed in the *maṇḍapa*, where they are the objects of much veneration.

In the southwest corner of the enclosure are the ruins of a small undecorated sandstone *prang* that is thought to date, like the principal *prang*, from the 11C.

Some of the lintels, the earliest of which date from the first half of the 10C (Bakheng style), have been put back in their original places, while others are in the National Museum in Phimai and other museums. Several important stone statues found in the vicinity, including images of the Buddha and of Hindu deities, are also in the Phimai museum.

Continue on road 2 towards Khon Kaen. At the 27km stone turn left on to road 2067 to **Non Sung**. The road passes a reservoir with earth ramparts and fringed with tall palm trees and after 9km reaches the pleasant little town of Non Sung, which has many attractive whitewashed houses.

Beyond the turning to Non Sung, a turning to the left off road 2 at the 44km stone, signposted to **Ban Prasat** leads after 500m to **Wat Ku Prasat**, a modern temple painted bright yellow on the edge of Ban Prasat, an attractive village with many traditional houses. Just beyond Ban Prasat is an important **archaeological excavation** on a site that was occupied from the neolithic period up to the 10C. There are three excavation pits containing skeletons and pottery sherds. In the village is an excellent small museum where some of the excavated artefacts are displayed. These include Bronze and Iron Age tools and ornaments, crucibles and moulds for bronze socketed axes, stone beads and both black pottery and the red slipped and painted wares that succeeded it, Mon Dvaravati objects and 10C Khmer sandstone carvings, and brownish-green glazed Khmer pottery.

Phimai

Further north on road 2, turn off right on to road 206, which leads after 10km to Phimai. Modern Phimai is a small market town dominated by the great Khmer temple of Prasat Phimai, which, together with Phanom Rung in Buri Ram province, is the most important Khmer monument in the kingdom. Boat races are held on the river here each November.

■ **Hotels and services**. There is only simple accommodation in Phimai, which is usually visited from Nakhon Ratchasima. Recommended is the relaxed *Old*

Phimai Guest House near the Phimai Historical Park or the more formal *Phimai Hotel* near the bus station. Both places have bicycles for rent. The *Bai Toei* is a pleasant restaurant in the main street. The *Bangkok Bank* and *Thai Farmers Bank* are both in the town centre.

■ **Transport**. The **bus station** is at the south end of the main street; there are frequent services to Nakhon Ratchasima. The nearest **railway station** is at Hin Dat, c 30km south of Phimai on the Nakhon Ratchasima–Ubon Ratchathani line.

History

In the 11C Phimai seems to have been the seat of a Khmer viceroy or perhaps the northern capital of the Khmer rulers of Angkor. An inscription in Sanskrit and Khmer dated 1082 found at Phanom Wan refers to **Vimayapura**, the city of Vimaya or Phimai, which some scholars have suggested is derived from Bhimapura ('City of Bhima'). It also mentions Jayavarman VI (r. 1080–1107), who appears to have been the founder of Prasat Phimai as well as of Preah Vihear (Khao Phra Wihan; see p 369) in northern Cambodia and Wat Phu in Laos. Inscriptions of his elder brother and successor, Dharanindravarman I (r. 1107–13), have also been found in the vicinity. It is not certain that Jayavarman VI ever ruled in Angkor itself and it is possible therefore that his succession, which was before his elder brother's, was irregular and that Phimai was his capital, while a successor of Harshavarman III ruled in Angkor. The entire complex of Prasat Phimai and the old city wall were restored in two phases between 1954 and 1969 and between 1981 and 1989 by the Fine Arts Department in collaboration with the French government and UNESCO. It now forms the Phimai Historical Park, established in 1989.

PRASAT PHIMAI stands on a site bounded on three sides by the Mun River, which turns south at this point, and on the fourth by an old bed of the river, which during the wet season is covered with water and thus makes the site into an island. The abundance of waterways has created a fertile alluvial plain in the area, and Phimai has consequently been a centre of human habitation since neolithic times.

The old city of Vimayapura is surrounded by a wall c 500m in length from east to west and 1km from north to south, which was built in the reign of Jayavarman VII (1181–c 1220). On the south side is the **Pratu Chai** (Gate of Victory), the main city gate, which leads through to the south entrance of the temple. It is built of sandstone and laterite and is wide enough to allow an elephant to pass through. There are also subsidiary gates in the north and west walls of the city.

Like many Khmer monuments in Thailand, Prasat Phimai was originally built as a Hindu temple and was later converted for use as a Mahayana Buddhist sanctuary, probably by Jayavarman VII. Whereas most Khmer temples, whether Hindu or Buddhist, face east towards the rising sun, Phimai faces almost due south towards the Khmer capital of Angkor (Yasodhapura), to which it was linked by a great road that ran northwest to Lop Buri via Nakhon Ratchasima. It has been suggested that Jayavarman VI may have founded Prasat Phimai in honour of his ancestors and may therefore have chosen to orientate the temple towards the south, as this is the direction associated with worship of the ancestors.

The outer wall of the temple is pierced by **four sandstone gopuras**, of which that on the south side is the largest and forms the main entrance to the temple precinct. Just inside the entrance on the right is a bookshop where several photographs are displayed showing the temple before reconstruction. In front of the south *gopura* is a **cruciform terrace** with balustrades terminating in seven-headed *nāgas*. To the left of this terrace is a rectangular building dating from the reign of Jayavarman VII and known as the **Khleang Ngoen** ('Golden Treasury or Storehouse'), which was probably built as a place for important visitors and pilgrims to rest.

A causeway leads through the south *gopura* into the outer enclosure. To the left, near the west *gopura*, are two square stone **pavilions**, the function of which is not known. A **rectangular gallery** built of pink sandstone runs concentrically within the wall round the inner enclosure, in the centre of which is the principal sanctuary of the temple. This gallery, which is raised almost 1m above the ground, is walled on both sides and has a curved and corbelled roof, much of which has collapsed. It is pierced by four further *gopuras* aligned with the entrances to the central *prang*.

On the west side of this inner enclosure are two buildings dating from the reign of Jayavarman VII: **Prang Phromathat** and **Prang Hin Daeng**. Prang Phromathat is a square laterite building, which appears to have been left unfinished. Three stone statues were found in it, one of which is a statue presumed to be a portrait of Jayavarman VII. According to an inscription of 1191 found at Preah Khan of Angkor, Jayavarman VII, at the time he consecrated the temple, caused 23 statues of the Buddha, or rather of himself as a Buddhist monk in meditation, to be carved and placed in temples throughout the Khmer realm. The Phimai statue, which is now in the National Museum in Bangkok, bears a close resemblance to several others of these presumed portrait statues.

Prang Hin Daeng is also a square building, but is built of pink sandstone. Behind it is another small building constructed of laterite dating to the late 12C. As several small *lingas* were found here, the building is known as the **Ho Phram** ('Hindu Shrine').

The principal sanctuary at the centre of the temple enclosure is built of white sandstone and consists of a *prang* with a long narrow *antarāla* and *maṇḍapa*. The tower of the *prang* is constructed in tiers that gradually narrow to a lotus-bud finial at the top and has multiple redentations with elaborately carved, inward-sloping antefixes at the corners. These features give the tower a curved profile quite distinct from the stepped profile of earlier Khmer towers, and this has led some scholars to suggest that Phimai may have provided the model for the towers of Angkor Wat and also for later Thai *prang* inspired by Khmer models.

Prasat Phimai has a great number and variety of 11C and 12C carved lintels, pediments, antefixes, pilasters and colonnettes, some of them of superb quality. They portray not only stories from the Hindu epics and such Hindu deities as Shiva, Vishnu, Krishna and Rama, but also depictions of the Buddha and other Buddhist subjects. Many of these carvings are *in situ*, while others are in the National Museum in Phimai. The temple has also yielded numerous free-standing Buddha images, a Footprint of the Buddha and several important inscriptions.

1500m south of Pratu Chai, the road crosses the Mun River. On the left in the middle of a vast rectangular enclosure is **Kuti Rishi** ('Hermit's Cell'), which is a chapel of one of the numerous hospitals (*arogyasālā*) established by Jayavarman VII throughout the Khmer empire. It is made of laterite, except for the superstructure of the principal sanctuary, which is of sandstone.

The **PHIMAI NATIONAL MUSEUM** (open Wed–Sun 08.30–16.30) contains a notable collection of Khmer art from all over northeast Thailand and beyond, together with a few Dvaravati objects found in the region, beautifully displayed in a handsome new building specially constructed on the site of the earlier museum and opened in 1994. It is situated just inside the old city walls to the northeast of Prasat Phimai and on the east side of the road.

The Dvaravati objects include a fine 8C or 9C standing **Buddha image** and a seated Buddha image in *bhūmiśparsa mudrā* dating from the same period. Both are headless.

At the entrance to the museum is an exceptionally fine bronze figure in the 11C Baphuon style of Shiva's assistant, the guardian doorkeeper Nandikeshvara, 126cm high. This statue, which was found at Prasat Kamphaeng Yai, is one of the most important Khmer bronzes to have been discovered in recent years. The right arm is missing from above the elbow, the left hand is on the hip. The short pleated *sampot*, the belt, necklaces, bracelets and anklets are finely rendered. The figure still retains traces of the gilding with which originally it was probably entirely covered.

The bulk of the collection consists of **lintels and pediments** from temples in the region, many of them displayed in association with door frames and colonnettes as if *in situ*. The earliest of these is a lintel in the Prei Kmeng style of the 7C–8C from Prasat Phumphon, the oldest Khmer sanctuary in Thailand, which is displayed in association with some fragments of stone pillars. There is also a fine sandstone Ganesha image of about the same date from Phanom Rung. A century later is a lintel in the late 9C Preah Kho style from Sathan Phra Narai decorated with a *kīrttimukha* holding a garland terminating at each end in a *makara*. There is an important group of lintels and pediments from Prasat Muang Khaek in the Koh Ker and Pre Rup styles of the mid-10C. One of these shows Durga, Shiva's consort in her terrifying aspect, slaying the buffalo demon Mahisa. Another shows Vishnu as the dwarf Vamana striding across the ocean, which is represented by swimming fish, with a garland ending in an elephant-headed *gaṇa* mounted on its own trunk, figures of *haṁsas* behind and a row of six *riṣis* above. A third, in high relief, shows Indra mounted on Airavata, with a garland on either side decorated with triangular leaves containing figures of *haṁsas* and also terminating in a *gaṇa*, with, at the top, a row of *riṣis* in meditation. A fine pediment from Prasat Muang Khaek shows Shiva and his consort Uma mounted on the bull Nandi. From Phanom Wan comes a lintel in the early 10C Bakheng style showing Vishnu mounted on Garuda, who is holding the tails of two *nāgas* in his hands. A remarkable 11C rectangular stone from Sathan Phra Narai shows the deities of the nine planets or *navagraha*.

From Prasat Phimai itself comes a group of lintels in the 12C Angkor Wat and 13C Bayon styles. Some of these portray Buddhist scenes, such as the fine carving in the Angkor Wat style of a row of figures of the Buddha standing with both hands in *vitarka mudrā*, and another in the Bayon style showing a row of figures of the Buddha seated in *dhyāna mudrā*, and a third in the Angkor Wat style of the Buddha under the *bodhi* tree subduing Mara, his daughters and their attendant evil spirits. One beautiful 12C lintel from Phimai shows a row of standing Buddha images with both hands in *vitarka mudrā* and clad in a robe with a U-shaped frontal flap, both features characteristic of Dvaravati Buddha images. Others show Hindu deities, especially Vishnu and his incarnations Rama and Krishna, and Shiva, who is portrayed in a fine 12C lintel seated in a niche with Ganesha on his right and Skanda, the god of war, mounted on a peacock on his left. Others show scenes from the Hindu epics, such as that portraying soldiers of the monkey army in the *Rāmāyaṇa* carrying Laksamana, Rama's younger brother, and Sugriva, the king of the monkeys, on litters with *nāga* finials, accompanied by monkey musicians with drums. Also in the Angkor Wat style are the lintels from Ku Saen Tang, Buri Ram. One of these, in high relief, shows the Churning of the Sea of Milk to create the magic elixir or *amṛta*, with Vishnu in his incarnation as the cosmic turtle at the base and numerous lively figures of celestial beings, birds and animals.

There are numerous important freestanding **sandstone sculptures** in the museum, including a superb female torso from Prasat Phimai, which is thought to be of Jayarajadevi, the first wife of Jayavarman VII. There are several statues in stone and bronze of the Buddha sheltered by Mucalinda, of the *bodhisattvas* Avalokiteshvara, Vajrasattva and Prajnaparamita, and of Bhaisajyaguru, the Buddha of healing. From Phanom Rung come two fine 10C figures, one of Brahma with four faces, and the other of Brahmi kneeling in worship on a lotus pedestal, and an interesting group of figures in the Angkor Wat style of the mounts of the guardians of the four quarters of heaven—the rhinoceros of Agni, guardian of the southeast, the *haṁsa* of Varana, guardian of the west, and the buffalo of Yama, guardian of the south. There is also a collection of ante-fixes, *liṅgas*, pedestals, stelae, *bai sema* and other stone carvings, and a selection of objects excavated at Ban Prasat (see above), including pottery, stone and glass beads, shell disc ornaments, bead necklaces, bangles, clay pellets, bronze ornaments and iron tools. There are also numerous votive tablets and bronze moulds for tablets, jewellery, engraved gold sheets and various small bronze artefacts.

To the northeast of the town, a lane leads east off road 206 to **Sai Ngam** ('Beautiful Banyan Tree'), an enormous banyan tree covering an area of almost 5000 sq m. Under its shade is a shrine dedicated to the animist spirits of the place, and round about are many popular open-air restaurants and food stalls.

44 · Phanom Rung, Muang Tam and Buri Ram

Roads *224, 24 and 219, 174km from Nakhon Ratchasima. To Chok Chai 28km; Chok Chai to Prakhon Chai 102km; Prakhon Chai to Buri Ram 44km. There is a direct but uninteresting route from Nakhon Ratchasima to Buri Ram on road 226 (c 120km).*

Railway, *110km in 1hr 30mins (express) direct service from Nakhon Ratchasima to Buri Ram.*

Road 224 runs south out of Nakhon Ratchasima from the southeast corner of the moat of the old city, and after c 15km passes through the small village of **Ban Dan Kwian**, where brown and black glazed and incised pottery inspired by ancient Khmer ceramics can be purchased direct from the potteries on either side of the road.

Turn left in Chok Chai c 13km further south on to road 24, which runs east c 70km to **Nang Rong**.

▶From Nang Rong, a **detour** to the south on road 348 leads to the remote Khmer temple site of Prasat Nong Hong. Follow this road to Pa Kham (c 21km), where there is a small *arogyasāla* of Jayavarman VII known as **Prasat Ban Khok Ngiu** or **Prasat Khok Prasat**.

Continue south on road 348 towards Ta Phraya. After c 18km the road passes the north end of the Lam Nam Rong reservoir and then bears left down a hill. A left turn at the bottom of the hill leads after a short distance to **Prasat Nong Hong**, on the right of the road in a large sunken enclosure surrounded by a laterite wall, parts of which are well preserved. The temple consists of three very ruined brick *prang* with corbelled vaults standing on a single high base. Each *prang* has an entrance to the east and three false doors with sandstone frames. The sandstone lintel above the door of the south *prang* is still in place. ◀

Road 24 continues east from Nang Rong to Ban Tako (c 14km). Turn right here on to road 2117, which leads after 6km to Ban Tapek, where road 2221 goes off right and climbs steeply up past a Thai Air Force radar station to **PRASAT PHANOM RUNG** ('Temple of the Broad Mountain'). This temple, one of the most important Khmer sanctuaries in Thailand and one of the few to have retained its original Khmer name, stands on the summit of an extinct volcano 383m above sea level. The site commands extensive views over a vast and fertile plain bordered to the south by the Dangrek Mountains. On two neighbouring hills, Khao Plai Bat and Khao Phra Angkhan, which are also extinct volcanoes, there are ruined sanctuaries.

▶**Prasat Khao Plai Bat** is on the summit of Khao Plai Bat. As there is no path through the woods up to this temple, a guide is necessary, and these can be hired on payment of 100 baht at Wat Wiwet Asom at the foot of the hill. It takes c 25 minutes walking over stony terrain and through dense undergrowth to reach the temple, which consists of the remains of a small *prang* built of brick and sandstone standing on a sandstone base and an even smaller laterite building to the northeast. Neither building has any carved decoration. To the west can be seen Khao Phra Angkhan and the outline of what little remains of the brick *prang* on the summit.◄

The ruins on of **Prasat Khao Phra Angkhan** date to the 8C. They are therefore more than 100 years earlier than the earliest extant buildings at Phanom Rung, which are the bases of two **brick sanctuaries** dating to the early 10C. The earliest of the 11 Sanskrit and Khmer inscriptions from Phanom Rung is also thought to be 8C or even earlier, and one of the Khmer Ganesha images that was found here has been ascribed to the 7C Prei Kmeng style. The foundation of Phanom Rung may therefore predate the present buildings by more than a century. The entire temple complex was meticulously restored between 1971 and 1988, and it is now unquestionably one of the most magnificent Khmer monuments in Thailand.

This group of mountain sites of which Phanom Rung is the most important had probably been considered sacred since the earliest times and, with the arrival of the Khmers in the region, became associated with Shaivite cults. In addition to being the centre of a religious cult and a place of pilgrimage, Phanom Rung was also strategically important, as whoever controlled it could dominate the whole of the plain to the south as far as the Dangrek Mountains. Moreover, it was situated on the great road that ran from Angkor to Phimai and on to Lop Buri.

Like Prasat Phimai, Phanom Rung was originally a Hindu monument, dedicated to Shiva Mahayogi (Shiva in his aspect as the Great Hermit or Ascetic), and was later converted to Mahayana Buddhist use, probably at the end of the 12C in the reign of Jayavarman VII. There was evidently a community of ascetics (*riṣi*) here, as is indicated by the large number of relief carvings on lintels, pediments and the bases of pilasters of *riṣis*, with pointed beards and tangled locks tied in a chignon, seated in positions of meditation. Phanom Rung may also have been a Tantric Buddhist centre; one of the Khmer inscriptions mentions offerings of rice spirit to the gods. This spirit could have been used in Tantric ceremonies, in many of which drinking was an important element.

The **temple enclosure** is approached by a flight of steps, which is still partly overgrown and begins about 500m down the east side of the hill. The steps lead to a large cruciform platform, measuring 40 x 30m, immediately to the north of which is a sandstone and laterite building with a gallery and porch. This building is known as the **Rong Chang Phuak** ('White Elephant Stable'), but was more probably a resthouse for visiting dignitaries. It is thought to date from the late 10C and to have been restored in the late 12C. Some of the tiles that once covered the roof have been found nearby.

Beyond the cruciform platform is a broad processional causeway, 200m long and 12m wide, paved with laterite and flanked at intervals of about 4m by short sandstone posts with lotus-bud finials (*sao tien*). This causeway was constructed in the first half of the 12C in the reign of Suryavarman II, who is mentioned in an inscription in Sanskrit language and Khmer script found in the vicinity, and was renovated during Jayavarman VII's reign. It leads to a second cruciform

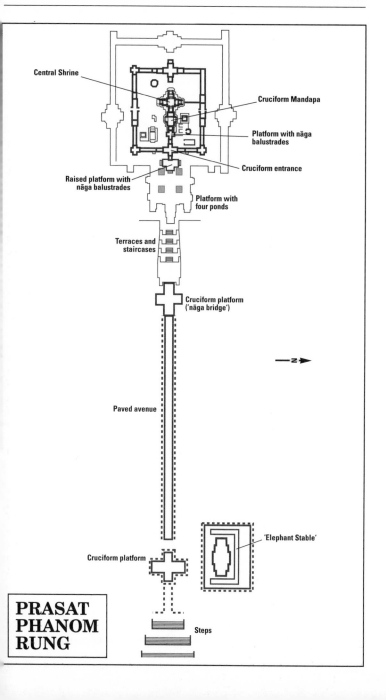

Central Shrine

Cruciform Mandapa

Platform with nāga balustrades

Cruciform entrance

Raised platform with nāga balustrades

Platform with four ponds

Terraces and staircases

Cruciform platform ('nāga bridge')

Paved avenue

'Elephant Stable'

Cruciform platform

PRASAT PHANOM RUNG

Steps

platform built of sandstone, supported on short, elegantly carved sandstone pillars and accessible by means of staircases on the north and south sides as well as on the east. The balustrades of this terrace are in the form of five-headed *nāgas* with elaborately carved diadems and with scales and other details minutely rendered. Beyond the platform rises a series of five staircases. At the top of these is a terrace built of sandstone and laterite with four square pools and, on the terrace, immediately in front of the principal sanctuary, is a third cruciform platform raised on short sandstone pillars and flanked by balustrades, this time in the form of *makaras* from whose mouths five-headed *nāgas* emerge.

The principal sanctuary is surrounded by **walled galleries** about 5.50m wide. These have stepped roofs and are divided into cells, which may have been used for meditation. The north gallery is built of laterite and appears to be later than the other three, which are of sandstone. The stones covering the roofs are carved to look like tiles, and the peaks and ridges have ornamental finials. The entire area enclosed by the galleries measures c 66 x 88m. At each of the four cardinal points is a *gopura*. There are four more steps in front of the east *gopura*, which is also built on a cruciform plan and has windows both in the central porch and in the chambers on either side. The entrance is surmounted by a richly carved lintel and a double pediment and flanked by beautiful octagonal colonnettes. The carving on the front pediment portrays Shiva the ascetic seated in the *lalitāsana* position, surrounded by female deities.

The main **prang** stands on a redented raised platform in the centre of the inner enclosure. In front of the east entrance is a cruciform *maṇḍapa* with carved pediments of exceptional quality. The north pediment shows an episode in the *Rāmāyaṇa* in which the monkey army swoops down on the demons (*asuras*) from the sky, accompanied by a flock of birds. On the south pediment is a relief of Shiva seated on the bull Nandi with his consort Uma on his knee; above this relief are two tiers of exquisitely carved flame motifs. On the east pediment is another figure of Shiva—this time as lord of the dance—with ten arms, his hair arranged in two pigtails. Below this figure are figures of Ganesha and two unidentified female figures. On the lintel beneath the pediment is a magnificent carving of Vishnu asleep on Ananta in the Ocean of Milk. From his navel comes the golden lotus from which Brahma was born. On the right side of the lintel are the figures of two parrots beneath a *kāla* head. This lintel, which dates from the 12C, was missing for many years, having been illegally exported to America, where it was acquired by the Art Institute of Chicago. In 1988, after prolonged negotiations between the Thai and American authorities, it was returned and placed in its original position.

Connecting the *maṇḍapa* with the central *prang* is an *antarāla* with entrances on the north and south. Above the north entrance is a fine but badly eroded pediment on which the episode in the *Rāmāyana* of Sita's abduction by the demon Ravana is portrayed. Over the door leading from the *antarāla* to the *prang* is a lintel showing a row of five *riṣis* with palms joined in salutation seated under decorated arches.

The *prang* itself is a characteristic Khmer tower-sanctuary, with multiple lintels and pediments on the axial faces and inward-sloping antefixes that emphasise the gradual diminution of the tiers rising to the *kalaśa* finial at the top. The **antefixes**, **pediments** and other elements are richly decorated. Particularly notable are the figures of the gods of the four directions—Indra,

Yama, Varuna and Kubera—on the antefixes of the cornice on the east, south, west and north sides respectively, the scenes from the *Rāmāyana* and the story of Krishna on the pediments, and the magnificent crowned *nāga* heads that spring from the corners of the pediment frames.

On either side of the entrance to the enclosure is a rectangular laterite building of the type generally known in Khmer monuments as a 'library', dating from the late 12C or early 13C. In the northeast corner, near the right hand 'library', are the remains of **two brick buildings**, one facing east and one south, that date from the 10C and are therefore the oldest surviving structures in the temple complex. One still has a door frame and a decorated octagonal colonnette in place. It is thought there may have been a third brick sanctuary here, as early Khmer temples often consisted of a row of three brick sanctuaries on a single platform. In the southwest corner is a small building of pink sandstone known as **Prasat Noi** ('Little Tower'), which either originally had a superstructure, perhaps of brick, or was left unfinished. It faces east and has false doors on the other three sides. It stands on a laterite base and, unusually, is lined with laterite blocks. The decorated lintels on the east and south sides have been dated on stylistic grounds to the late 10C and early 11C (Khleang and Baphuon styles).

Immediately under the ridge on which Phanom Rung stands, on the left side of the road to Muang Tam, is **Prasat Nong Buarai** in the village of the same name. This temple is a typical chapel of a Jayavarman VII *arogyasālā*, built of laterite with sandstone door frames and lintels and an entrance *gopura* with a small porch on the east. It is surrounded by a low laterite wall. To the north of the temple is a large *baray*.

On the right of the main road opposite Ban Nong Buarai in an idyllic rustic setting near a lily pool in the middle of a large field is **Kuti Rishi** ('Hermit's Cell'), which is the chapel of yet another Jayavaraman VII *arogyasālā*, consisting of a laterite *prang* with an entrance *gopura*. The door frame has finials with carved *nāga* heads and there are other stone pieces on the building decorated with foliate motifs.

5km southeast of Phanom Rung on the road leading from Ban Tapek to Lahan Sai is **PRASAT MUANG TAM** ('Temple of the City Below'). It is not certain exactly when this monument, which appears to have been originally a royal palace, was founded, as no inscriptions have yet been found, but it was probably built after the first phase of building of Phanom Rung in the late 10C or early 11C. The general plan of the monument and much of the decoration of the lintels and colonnettes, the floral motifs on the pilasters and *nāgas* spewing garlands at the corners of the pediments suggest a date in the Baphuon period (c 1010–c 1080), but the style of some of the *kāla* heads above the doors, notably that on the inner lintel of the south door of the eastern *gopura*, seems to belong to the earlier Khleang period (c 965–c 1010). The decoration of several pilasters and lintels in the western outer *gopura* and of the pediment of the northern *prang* in the front row was left unfinished. Formerly an exceptionally picturesque ruin, Muang Tam was extensively restored during the early 1990s and has consequently lost some of its charm.

The temple is surrounded by two concentric enclosures paved with laterite. The walls of the outer enclosure, also of laterite, are c 2.75m high and have

A view of Prasat Muang Tam before restoration

retained much of their finely carved coping. The entrance is through the eastern *gopura* in the outer enclosure wall. Within the enclosure are four L-shaped ponds surrounded by five-headed *nāgas*, their tails terminating in stone gateways from which steps lead down into the water. This arrangement, which is presumably a representation of the four oceans surrounding the cosmic mountain, Mount Meru, is unique to Muang Tam. The gallery surrounding the inner enclosure has rows of small rectangular windows, like those at Sdok Kok Thom (see p 191), both on the outer and the inner wall, and a *gopura* at each of the cardinal points. The east, south and north *gopuras* are cruciform in plan and built of sandstone; the west *gopura*, which has collapsed, was rectangular and built of brick, as probably were the roofs of all four *gopuras*.

In the centre of the temple complex is a row of three brick **prang** with two further *prang* behind them to the west. The five towers, four of which have been reconstructed, all stand on a single laterite platform. Although they are not disposed in the quincunx pattern that is characteristic of many Khmer temples in Cambodia and is found also at Prasat Sikhoraphum (see p 367), it is probable that, as in these temples, they symbolise the five peaks of Mount Meru. In front of the row of three *prang* are the brick bases of two 'libraries'. This arrangement of *prang* and libraries is similar to that found at Prasat Sa Kamphaeng Yai (see p 368). The northwest *prang* has an important lintel showing Shiva seated on the bull Nandi with his consort Uma on his knee. Nandi is standing on a pedestal above the face and hands of a *kāla* grasping the leg of a rampant lion holding a garland in its mouth. On the upper register is a row of *riṣis* seated cross-legged in meditation. Similar figures of *riṣis* occur at the bases of the colonnettes flanking the entrances to some of the gopuras.

In addition to the four L-shaped pools in the temple enclosure, Muang Tam has two **baray**. The smaller of these, which has not yet been excavated, is situated behind a modern *wat* immediately opposite the entrance and is aligned with the outer *gopura*. The other, called Fai Nam Lon, is very large, measuring 1150 x 400m, and was probably built later. It is situated immediately north of the temple enclosure. Nearby is a ruined sanctuary known as Kuti Rishi (see p 361).

Return to road 24 and continue east to **Prakhon Chai**. Here, road 219 runs north 51km to Buri Ram, the provincial capital.

▶From Prakhon Chai, a **detour** to the south on road 2075 leads to some minor Khmer sites. After 3km a turning to the right along a dirt road leads after 8km to **Prasat Thamo**, a *dharmasālā* of Jayavarman VII. According to the inscriptions, these resthouses, of which 15 have so far been located, were all built during the reign of Jayavarman VII along the roads leading from Angkor to the great shrines of the Khmer empire, such as Phanom Rung and Phimai. All that remains of this is a south wall with square windows and a windowless north wall, both leaning dangerously outwards.

Continue south on road 2075 for a further 8km to reach **Ban Kruat** and the Ban Kruat **stone quarries**, the entrance to which is marked by two sandstone megaliths. These quarries, which cover an area of more than 1 sq km contain some impressive sandstone outcrops scattered over the site, but there is less visible evidence of past quarrying activities here than at Sikhiu (see Rte 43). Ban Kruat probably provided the stone for the building of Phanom Rung, which is only 20km away, as well as of other Khmer temples in the area.◀

From Prakhon Chai follow road 219 north towards Buri Ram. A road to the right c 15km before the town winds up a steep hill on the summit of which is **Prasat Khao Kradong**. Here there is a colossal white seated Buddha image known as Phra Suphat Bophit and the remains of a Khmer sanctuary consisting of an assembly of sandstone and laterite blocks arranged in a square up to a height of c 3km and somewhat incongruously surmounted by a three-tiered roof painted white. The whole edifice forms a kind of *mondop*, in which a gilded bronze Footprint of the Buddha of is enshrined.

Buri Ram (pop. 30,000) is a pleasant small town with all the services of a provincial capital, but little of specific interest to the casual visitor.

■ **Hotels and services**. There are several reasonably good hotels, including the comfortable *Thep Nakhon*, the *Thai Hotel* on T. Rom Buri, and the *Grand* and *Buri Ram Hotel* on T. Niwat. The **banks** are clustered near the junction of T. Thani and T. Sunthon Thep. The **post office** is nearby on T. Niwat.

■ **Transport**. There are regular **bus** services to Nakhon Ratchasima and Surin, and several **trains** daily both east to Surin and Ubon Ratchathani and west to Nakhon Ratchasima and Bangkok. The railway station is on T. Niwat.

45 · Surin and environs

The provincial capital of **Surin** (pop. 40,000) is an important silk-weaving centre c 50km east of Buri Ram. It is best known for its **elephant rally**, which is held every year in early November and attracts visitors from all over the world. During the rally, the elephants process, fight mock battles, play football and perform various tasks to demonstrate their intelligence and the skill of their *mahouts*. Between each appearance of the elephants there is a performance of local dances.

■ **Hotels and services**. The *Tharin Hotel* at 60 T. Sirirat, and the older *Phet Kasem* at 104 T. Chit Bamrung are the best hotels in the town. A friendly low-budget guest-house is *Pirom's Guest House* at 242 T. Krung Si Nai. All hotels in Surin are fully booked up many months in advance for the elephant rally. The *Bangkok Bank* is at 222 T. Thonasan and the **post office** is nearby.

■ **Transport**. Regular **bus** services run east to Si Sa Ket and Ubon Ratchathani and west to Nakhon Ratchasima and Bangkok. There are several **train** services along the same route every day from the station on the north side of the town.

Surin is a convenient centre from which to visit some of the numerous Khmer sites in the area. Several one-day or half-day excursions are possible, of which the most interesting are detailed below.

Prasat Ban Phluang, Prasat Ta Muen and Prasat Ta Muen Thom

Take road 214 to the south out of Surin towards Prasat. After 10km turn to the left down an earth road and after 2km turn right. The road crosses an open area of marsh and lakes. Turn left and after 500m is **Prasat Chenieng**, which is in the precincts of a modern *wat*. All that remains of this Khmer temple are a laterite platform and a well-preserved small square pond with eight steps. The *ubosot* of the nearby *wat* has a garishly painted *nāga* balustrade flanking the steps up to the entrance and contains a fine Ayutthaya-period Buddha image.

7km before Prasat turn right on to the road to Ban Phlai. After 3km **Prasat Ban Phlai** can be seen in the middle of a large field to the right of the road. This temple consists of three small brick *prang* on a laterite base. All three are very ruined and are devoid of decoration; of one only the base remains.

The Khmer temple of **Prasat Ban Phluang** lies to the right side of road 214, c 4km south of the intersection with road 24 at Prasat. This beautiful small temple was built in the second half of the 11C in the Baphuon style. It was meticulously restored in the 1970s. It was apparently never completed: during the work of restoration two unfinished cornices and some of the iron chisels and mallets used to dress and carve the stone were excavated, and one of the figures of a *dvārapāla* on the southwest corner of the building is unfinished. The temple consists of the lower part of a single *prang* built of sandstone, standing on a high laterite platform. It is likely that the upper part of the *prang* was of brick and was left unfinished. During the restoration, great quantities of bricks were unearthed around the temple. The laterite platform is surrounded by a moat, which is traversed by a causeway leading up to the entrance on the east side. The doors on the other three sides are false. The large size of the platform in relation to the *prang* suggests that the original intention was to construct other buildings on it, perhaps two flanking *prang*. The sandstone carving, which, in the absence of any inscriptions found in association with the site, provides the only means of dating Prasat Ban Phluang, is of the highest quality. The lintel over the east door shows Indra on his elephant mount Airavata, here shown with only one head instead of the more usual three, and the east pediment above depicts Krishna lifting Mount Govardhana to protect the herdsmen and their cattle from Indra's rain.

Continue on road 214 southeast from Prasat. After c 20km turn right on to road 2121, which leads through flat, wooded country towards Lahan Sai. After 38km turn left at **Ban Tamiang** on to a dirt road, which leads after 4km to **Prasat Ta Muen**. This beautiful and relatively well preserved temple, sometimes known by its Khmer name of Prasat Bay Kream ('Laterite Sanctuary'), is a chapel attached to a *dharmasāla* (see Prasat Thamo on p 363). It has a long entrance hall with small square windows on the south side. The door frames, lintels and roof decorations are of sandstone, while the rest of the building is of laterite.

100m to the south of Prasat Ta Muen is **Prasat Ta Muen Tot**. This temple is a chapel of one of the 102 hospitals or *arogyasālās* dedicated to Bhaishajyaguru, god of healing, many of which were established throughout the Khmer empire by Jayavarman VII. An inscription found here states that Jayavarman VII built this *arogyasālā* and lists the doctors and nurses attached to it, and the medicines that it supplied. It consists of a central *prang*, unusually constructed entirely of sandstone, standing on a laterite base and surrounded by a laterite wall.

500m beyond Prasat Ta Muen Tot is **Prasat Ta Muen Thom**, the most important of this group of temples. It was occupied for a time by the Khmer Rouge and has suffered severe damage in consequence. Since then almost all the relief carvings, which are in the late Baphuon style of the end of the 11C, have been removed by looters. A programme of reconstruction has recently been undertaken. The temple buildings are surrounded by a gallery with four *gopuras*, of which the south one provides the principal entrance to the temple. Inside there is a central sandstone *prang*, which is constructed on a natural rock platform running from the east to the west *gopura* and contains a natural stone *linga* on a circular pedestal, discovered in 1992. There is a fissure in the rock running out from the central sanctuary to the northeast corner of the enclosure, which was used to create the conduit (*somasutra*) for the lustral water poured over the *linga*. These natural features probably determined the choice of site for this temple.

To the north there are two subsidiary sandstone *prang*, of which the northwest one is the more complete. The upper parts of the inner walls of this *prang* are of brick and laterite. The three false doors are, most unusually, hewn from a single block of stone. There are also two complete laterite buildings, one near the east wall of the enclosure and one near the west, and the foundations of two others.

Although it is usually safe to visit these sites, it is advisable not to wander outside the temple enclosures, as the Cambodian frontier runs immediately to the south of Ta Muen Thom, and the whole area round the temples is heavily mined.

Prasat Phumphon and Prasat Yai Ngao

Leave Surin on road 2077 running southeast to Lamduan and Sangkha. After c 34km turn left down an earth road, passing a lake and then a eucalyptus plantation on the right. After 7km a turning to the right leads after a few metres to **Prasat Tapriang Tia**, a Khmer temple consisting of a single small brick *prang* on a brick base in the grounds of an unusually garish modern *wat*. The *prang* has an entrance door only about 1m high on the east side and false doors on the other three sides.

Continue on road 2077 to **Sangkha**, at the junction with road 24, and from there head south on road 2124 towards Buachet. 6km south of Sangkha and just before the village of Ban Dom is **Prasat Tamoi**, a Khmer temple consisting of a small single brick sanctuary of interest only to specialists. In **Ban Dom**, 2km further, is **Prasat Phumphon** (also known as Prasat Phumipon), on the left of the road, surrounded by tall palm trees. This temple, which was built in the Prei Kmeng style in the 7C, is one of the earliest surviving Khmer monuments in Thailand. Of the four buildings of which traces remain only the central *prang* is more or less intact. It is built of brick with sandstone steps and window frames and decorated pilasters at the corners. The three false doors are surmounted by a replica of a building instead of the more usual portico. There are a few pieces of carved stone in the wall above the east door. Inside are a finely corbelled brick vault, and traces of the red paint that must once have covered the whole interior. The *prang* shares its brick base with another building to the north. Of this all that remains is the east door, which, unusually in a building of this date, has colonnettes and jambs carved from a single piece of sandstone. To the south is a laterite platform with a pit in the middle where Buddhist relics have been found. This platform probably originally formed the base of an open-sided wooden pavilion. A fine lintel in the Prei Kmeng style, now in the National Museum in Bangkok, has been found at Prasat Phumphon.

Return north to road 24 and turn east a short distance towards Det Udom to reach the notable 12C Khmer temple of **Prasat Yai Ngao**. This temple consists of two brick *prang*, both facing east, on a low laterite base. The north *prang* is the smaller of the two and is badly ruined. *Kāla-makara* ornaments carved in very shallow relief decorate the brickwork of the north, south and west pediments of the south *prang*, which is the principal sanctuary of the temple. Today it is used by Buddhist monks and contains an image of the Buddha reclining on a low couch. There are no traces of a third *prang* flanking the principal *prang* on the other side, but it is likely that one was planned and for some reason never built. Recent excavations by the Fine Arts Department have revealed a number of sandstone relief carvings of *nāgas*, *dvārapālas* etc, which are displayed in front of the temple.

Prasat Chom Phra

Leave Surin on road 214 to the north. After c 28km, in the town of **Chom Phra**, a turning to the right just before the police station leads to **Prasat Chom Phra**, which is in the grounds of a modern *wat*. This Khmer temple is a typical Jayavarman VII *arogyasālā*, built entirely of laterite and devoid of decoration. In the northeast corner of the enclosure is a *baray* which is full of water and still in use.

46 · Surin to Si Sa Ket and environs

Road *226, c 105km from Surin to Si Sa Ket.*

Railway, *95km in c 80 mins.*

Take road 226 east from Surin towards Si Sa Ket and after c 15km turn right on to a secondary road to **Prasat Muang Thi**. This Khmer temple consists of three very small square brick towers, all that remain of what was probably a larger complex of five towers in quincunx. The date of the foundation is unknown, but the stucco decoration belongs to the Ayutthaya period.

Continue further northeast and take a road to the left leading after a short distance to **PRASAT SIKHORAPHUM**. This beautiful temple, which consists of five brick *prang* on a laterite platform surrounded by a moat, dates from the early 12C, but the superstructure of the towers was evidently added subsequently by Lao builders. It was formerly surrounded by fine trees, but these have almost all been removed in the course of the restoration by the Department of Fine Arts. The lintels and door jambs of pink sandstone are finely carved with figures of Hindu deities, *apsarasas* and *yaksas*. The capitals of the pilasters are decorated with foliage and figures of *garudas*. Traces of stucco have been found on the brick, which suggests that all the towers may originally have been stuccoed and painted.

Continue on road 226 from Sikhoraphum towards Si Sa Ket and, c 50km from Surin, turn right on to road 2234. After 5km turn left on to road 2167, which after 20km reaches the village of **Prang Ku**. Turn right in the centre of the village and travel a further 6km to a large lake at the west end of which is the important 12C Khmer temple of **Prasat Ban Ku**. This temple consists of three *prang*, one of laterite and two of brick, on a laterite base. Most of the carved sandstone lintels and other stone carvings have been removed by looters, but some, which are of the highest quality, are now in the Phimai National Museum. The north *prang* still has some

The beautiful small temple of Prasat Ban Prasat, near Si Sa Ket

carved colonnettes *in situ*. The site is surrounded by great trees and at each corner is a pond full of water lilies.

Continue on road 226 towards Si Sa Ket and turn left on to a dirt road in the village of Ban Huai Thap Than. This leads after c 10km to **Prasat Ban Prasat** (Prasat Ban Non That). This exquisite small, almost miniature temple is situated in a glade near a small village and consists of three prang of rose-coloured brick, each one only some 15m high and surmounted by lotus-bud finials, but all different in form and the details of their ornamentation. The monument is surrounded by a low laterite wall. There are traces of stone carving on some of the lintels.

A turning to the left at Uthumphon Phisai, 20km further towards Si Sa Ket on road 226, leads to **PRASAT SA KAMPHAENG YAI** ('Temple of the Great Rampart'). This important Hindu Khmer temple complex, which underwent major restoration in the early 1990s, is situated next to a highly decorated modern wat with an ornate entrance gate of black basalt. It consists of the lower part of five brick *prang* on laterite foundations surrounded by a sandstone and laterite gallery with small balustered windows and a *gopura* at each of the four cardinal points. The *gopura* on the east side is on a cruciform plan with three porches, the central one of which is flanked by a small antechamber. The central prang is partly of sandstone and partly of brick and has a porch with a pediment, a lintel and pilasters. The north and south *prang* on either side are wholly of brick with sandstone door frames, colonnettes and lintels. To the southwest is another smaller *prang*, and in front of the three central *prang* in the east of the enclosure are two other brick buildings which may have been 'libraries'. The lintels, of which some are still in place and others have been left lying on the ground, portray scenes of Hindu mythology; one that is exceptionally fine represents Shiva and Uma mounted on the bull Nandi. They range in date from the late 10C (Banteay Srei style) to the early 11C (style of the Khleangs). There is an inscription in Khmer dated 1043 on the left of the entrance to the east *gopura*. In the *wihan* of the *wat* nearby is an important *Dvaravati* seated image of the Buddha protected by the *nāga*, and other sculptures that have been found on the site. Also found here was a magnificent 11C bronze statue 1.26m high of a *dvārapāla* wearing a short pleated *sampot*, a belt hung with small pendants and a triple necklace. The eyebrows, mouth, moustache and beard are deeply incised and were probably originally inlaid with gold. This statue is now in the National Museum, Bangkok.

Return to road 226 and continue northeast to **Ban Sompoi Noi**, where road 2083 turns off to the north.

▶Follow road 2083 north to Hua Chang, and turn left here on to road 2349. After 7km a turning to the right on to an earth road is signed 'Hue Somboon'. Here is **Prasat Ku Sombun**, also known as **Prasat Nong Ku**. This temple consists of three *prang* of which only the lower portions remain, standing on a laterite base. The central *prang* has a laterite core with brick cladding, and the two flanking *prang* are entirely laterite. Over the east door of the central *prang* is a sandstone lintel with badly eroded carving; the other three doors are false. In the south *prang* is a *yoni* pedestal. ◀

East of Ban Sompoi Noi on road 226, on the left side is **Prasat Sa Kamphaeng Noi** ('Temple of the Small Rampart'), a small temple in a grove of trees surrounded by a modern concrete wall. This is another example of a chapel of one of the *arogyasālās* established by Jayavarman VII throughout the Khmer empire. The temple enclosure is surrounded by a laterite wall, which is pierced on the east by a laterite and sandstone *gopura*. Within the enclosure is a single laterite *prang* with a porch facing east. The other three sides have false doors. The *prang* is devoid of ornament, although a few lintels and other pieces of sculpted stone can be seen lying on the ground nearby.

Si Sa Ket

The provincial capital of Si Sa Ket c 8km further east, makes a suitable overnight resting place, although the town is rather dull.

■ **Hotels and services**. One of the better hotels here is the *Phrom Phiman* at 849/1 T. Lak Muang, on the south side of the railway line. The *Bangkok Bank* and *Thai Farmers Bank* are on T. Khukhan. The **post office** is on T. Thepha.

■ **Transport**. Regular **buses** run from the bus station on T. Kuang Heng. Several **trains** run daily east and west from the railway station. The *THAI* agent is *Northeastern Travel Co* at 998/43-45 T. Kuang Heng, but the nearest **airport** is Ubon Ratchathani.

Preah Vihear (Khao Phra Wihan)

Leave Si Sa Ket on road 221 to the southeast to **Kantharalak**, 62km from Si Sa Ket, and then for a further 47km through verdant and well-wooded country to reach a point on the Thai side of the Thai-Cambodian frontier near the great Khmer Hindu temple of **Preah Vihear** (known in Thai as **Khao Phra Wihan**).

This magnificent temple appears to have been founded at the end of the 9C, though almost all the buildings belong to later periods up to and including the reign of Suryavarman II in the early 12C. It is spectacularly situated in the Dangrek mountains on an upward-sloping, triangular escarpment projecting 600m above the densely forested Cambodian plain. It consists, not, as is more usual in Khmer temple complexes, of a tower-sanctuary (*brasat*) surrounded by concentric enclosures, but of a series of three courts and two cruciform *gopuras* built on different levels along the escarpment and linked by causeways flanked by *nāga* balustrades and staircases guarded by lions. The main *Prasat*, of which only the antechamber survives intact, stood at the end of the escarpment almost on the edge of the sheer cliff, and is thought to have been c 20m high. The temple contains numerous carved sandstone lintels and pediments depicting scenes from Hindu mythology and other architectural sculptures of the very highest quality.

For many years Preah Vihear's possession was a cause for dispute between Thailand and Cambodia. This was eventually decided by the International Court in the Hague in Cambodia's favour, and the temple is now in Cambodia. A detailed description of it is therefore not included in this guide. At the time of writing, the temple is only accessible very intermittently, as much of the surrounding country is still controlled by the Khmer Rouge. However, on the infrequent occasions when the political situation permits, it is best approached from the Thai side. On the cliff face a little to the east of the escarpment and still on the Thai side of the frontier are some remarkable **relief carvings** of unknown date of three crowned deities and incised drawings of a rhinoceros, a pig, a rabbit and other animals.

A little way off road 221, 10km north of Preah Vihear on the Thai side of the frontier is the Khmer temple of **Prasat Don Ton**. This picturesquely sited 10C Shaivite temple, which may have been associated with Preah Vihear, has recently been restored and the site cleared. It consists of a brick and laterite tower on a laterite base facing east, with a *mandapa* in front with sandstone columns. To the southeast is the sandstone base of another building and to the west the base of a *linga* shrine. A *linga* image, remnants of pilasters and an inscription in Old Khmer have been found near the site.

47 · Ubon Ratchathani and environs

Road 226 from Nakhon Ratchasima, 391km and from Si Sa Ket, 63km; road 23 from Yasothon, 100km.

Ubon Ratchathani (pop. 60,000) is situated on the Mun River 75km from the Lao frontier. It is capital of one of the poorest provinces in Thailand and has only begun to develop in the last 30 years, as Thai government programmes to develop Isan have begun to yield results. Every year on Khao Phansa Day, which marks the beginning of the Buddhist Lent in late June or early July, a colourful candle festival (*Ngan Hae Thian Phansa*) is held, and giant carved wax candles are carried in procession through the streets of the city accompanied by music and dancing.

■ **Information**. The TAT office is at 264/1 T. Khuan Thani.

■ **Hotels and services**. There is a wide range of hotels in the town. Among the best are the *Regent Palace* at 256–271 T. Chayangkun and the *Pathumrat* at 337 T. Chayangkun. Cheaper, efficient alternatives include the *Tokyo* at 360 T. Uparat and the *Krung Thong* at 24 T. Si Narong. *Bangkok Bank* is at 13 T. Ratchabut near the river. The *Thai Farmers Bank* is on T. Phromthep near the bridge. The **post office** is near the intersection of T. Si Narong and T. Luang. The **Tourist Police** are at the corner of T. Si Narong and T. Uparat.

■ **Transport**. **Buses** depart from several points in the town, depending on the destination; hotel staff or the TAT can advise. From the **railway station** in Warin Chamrap, on the south side of the Mun River, there are several daily services to Bangkok (c 10hrs), via Surin, Buri Ram and Khorat. Computerised advanced booking is available at the station. *THAI* operates two daily **flights** to Bangkok (1hr). The booking office is at 364 T. Chayangkun. **Car** and **motorcycle rentals** are available from several local companies; the TAT can provide current information.

A short walk from the TAT office is the **Ubon Ratchathani National Museum** (open Wed–Sun, 09.00–16.00) which contains a heterogeneous collection of local artefacts, ranging from prehistoric polished stone axe heads and 9C Khmer statues to modern textiles. The museum building, built in the early 20C as the governor's office, is arranged around two attractive small courtyards. Of partic-

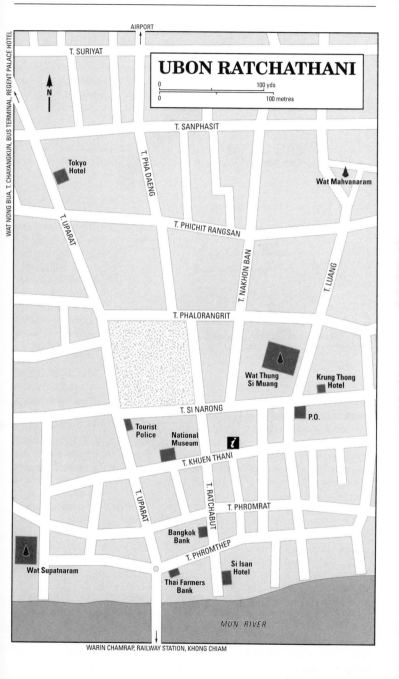

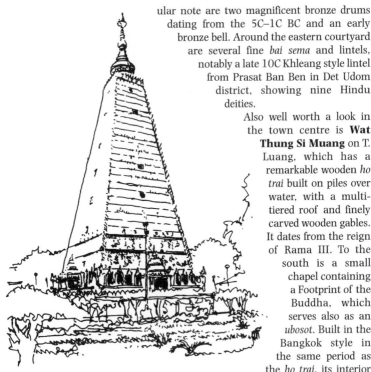

The white stuccoed pyramid of Wat Nong Bua,
Ubon Ratchathani

ular note are two magnificent bronze drums dating from the 5C–1C BC and an early bronze bell. Around the eastern courtyard are several fine *bai sema* and lintels, notably a late 10C Khleang style lintel from Prasat Ban Ben in Det Udom district, showing nine Hindu deities.

Also well worth a look in the town centre is **Wat Thung Si Muang** on T. Luang, which has a remarkable wooden *ho trai* built on piles over water, with a multi-tiered roof and finely carved wooden gables. It dates from the reign of Rama III. To the south is a small chapel containing a Footprint of the Buddha, which serves also as an *ubosot*. Built in the Bangkok style in the same period as the *ho trai*, its interior walls are decorated with some fine murals.

On the north side of the town is **Wat Nong Bua**, which was built in the 1950s. Like many temples in Thailand, it is modelled on the great Mahabodhi Temple at Bodh Gaya in northeast India and is in the form of a tall white stuccoed pyramid surmounted by a bulbous ringed spire with a lotus finial and a parasol on top. At the base is a double frieze of stone relief carvings made to commemorate the 2500th anniversary of the foundation of Buddhism in 1957, and beneath them a row of Buddha images in gilded niches. At the four cardinal points are four ornately decorated entrances with tiered pyramidal roofs in the form of a *mondop* and at the corners gilded seven-headed *nāgas*.

To reach this *wat*, take T. Chayangkun (road 212) north from the town centre and turn left along an indistinctly signed lane after c 3km. The *wat* is on the right side after 500m.

Two interesting **excursions** can be made to the east and south of Ubon Ratchathani, to see some of Thailand's best-preserved **prehistoric rock art**, some rarely visited **Khmer monuments** and one of the country's remotest **national parks**.

►Khong Chiam and Pha Taem

Cross to the south bank of the Mun River and take road 217 east from Warin Chamrap to Phibun Mangsahan, c 43km downstream. Here a turning to the left through the town centre leads over the bridge and on to road 2222 on the north bank. Immediately downstream of the bridge are the **Saphu Rapids** (Kaeng Saphu), which are very scenic in the dry season and are a popular picnic spot with rows of food stalls along the south bank.

Road 2222 continues east along the north bank to **Khong Chiam**, a charming little village on the peninsula formed by the junction of the Mun and the Mekong rivers. Just upstream from the village is the controversial Pak Mun Dam on the Mun River, which was completed in 1994 despite heavy criticism from local and international conservation and human rights organisations. Built to produce hydro-electric power, the dam has been blamed for damaging the livelihoods of local fishermen, and causing the displacement of villagers, who were not adequately compensated.

Simple guest-house accommodation is available in Khong Chiam for visitors wishing to stay overnight. Recommended is *Apple Guest House* near the post office.

Above the village is **Wat Tham Khuha Sawan**, built into a rock overhang in the side of a cliff. Most easily approached from the terrace above, steps lead down to the cavern, where there are seven identical, rather inelegant seated images of the Buddha, together with others of different sizes and postures. At the far end, there is an inner room containing a glass coffin high up on an altar, which holds the remains of a venerated abbot. There is little of artistic merit here, but the *wat* is rather unusual.

From Khong Chiam, take road 2134 north towards Trakan Phutphon and turn right on to road 2112 towards Khemarat beyond the 57km stone. Turn right again on to road 2368 beyond the 8km stone, to the summit plateau above the sandstone cliffs of **Pha Taem**, **Pha Kham** and **Pha Mon**, overlooking the Mekong River. The whole of this area lies within the 340 sq km **Pha Taem National Park**.

The prehistoric rock art on these cliffs is thought to date from c 1000 BC and is some of the finest in Thailand. The Pha Taem group of paintings, especially, is one of the best known in the country. From the cliff top there are spectacular views across the Mekong River to Laos. A footpath leads down from the cliff edge and skirts the cliff foot, passing the three groups of paintings. The clearest are those of Pha Taem, and include human and animal figures. The path continues through woodland to emerge back on the clifftop further to the north, from where it is an easy walk back along the crest of the cliff to the car park. ◄

The return journey to Ubon can be varied by taking the small vehicle ferry across the Mun River from Khong Chiam. On the south bank, the road leads after c 6km to a T-junction. To the right are the **Tana Rapids** (Kaeng Tana) and the headquarters of the 80 sq km **Kaeng Tana National Park**. To the left the road comes to a T-junction with road 217. Here, a turning to the right leads straight back to Warin Chamrap and Ubon Ratchathani. To the left, the road skirts the reservoir created by the Sirindhorn Dam to reach the border market of **Chong Mek**, which is of little interest except for travellers on their way to Laos.

▶Det Udom and Phu Chong Nayoi National Park

Take road 24 south from Ubon, through Warin Chamrap and on to Det Udom district, where there are two minor Khmer monuments of some interest: the 11C **Prasat Nong Thong Lang** at Ban Pho Si, and **Prasat Ban Ben**, which probably dates from the second half of the 10C, at Ban Ben.

From Det Udom, continue south on road 2171 to Nam Yun. Turn left here towards Na Chaluai to reach the beautiful, but rarely visited 687 sq km **Phu Chong Nayoi National Park**, close to the Thai-Cambodian border. The park is home to the very rare **white-winged duck**, several **hornbill** species and the endangered **pileated gibbon**, and contains some of Isan's last surviving ever-green forest. In the park are some fine waterfalls, including **Huai Luang Waterfall**.

> **A note of warning**. In 1993 there were problems in the park involving poaching and illegal timber cutting, which led to a park ranger being killed by a land mine. This border area is also subject to occasional raids by bandits crossing the border from Cambodia. It is highly advisable to check the current situation with the National Parks Office in Bangkok and with local police.

From the park, continue north on road 2248 to Bun Tharik, from where road 2182 heads west back to Det Udom.◀

THE EAST PENINSULAR COAST

48 · Phetchaburi to Hua Hin and Chumphon

Road 4, *341km. To Hua Hin 68km; Hua Hin to Prachuap Khiri Khan 90km; Prachuap Khiri Khan to Chumphon 183km.*

Railway, 318km in c 4hrs 40mins (express). To Hua Hin, 62km in 1hr; Hua Hin to Prachuap Khiri Khan, 89km in c 1hr 20mins. Prachuap Khiri Khan to Chumphon, 167km in c 2hrs 30mins.

This is a very long journey to do in one day and travellers are advised to stop for at least one night either in Cha-am, Hua Hin, Prachuap Khiri Khan, or one of the other beach resorts, or in a national park along the way. The beach resorts on this route are becoming increasingly popular with both Thai and foreign tourists, and as a result they are often crowded, especially at weekends.

Between Hua Hin and Prachuap Khiri Khan the road passes through many sugar and pineapple plantations. Beyond Prachuap Khiri Khan these give way to banana, coconut and rubber plantations.

Kaeng Krachan National Park

From Phetchaburi, road 4 runs south for c 18km to the nondescript market town of **Tha Yang**, on the south side of which a signed road to the right leads to **KAENG KRACHAN NATIONAL PARK**, Thailand's largest (3083 sq km) and undoubtedly one of its finest national parks. From the turning it is 48km to the park headquarters, which can be reached by *songthaeo* from Tha Yang.

Established as a national park in 1981 on the initiative of King Bhumibol, Kaeng Krachan protects a vital part of the Tenasserim hills watershed. More than **310 bird species** can be found in the park's tropical evergreen forest, together with some **40 mammal species**, including leopard, tiger, elephant, banteng, white-handed gibbon and possibly the Sumatran rhinoceros. The thickly forested hills, rising higher than 1000m in the west, are the source of the Phetchaburi and Pran Buri rivers, both of which have been dammed in an attempt to provide a regular water supply for agriculture downstream. There are extensive hiking trails, although to get deep into the park a vehicle must be chartered from the park headquarters, where bungalow accommodation and food are also available. Boats can be chartered for trips on the reservoir, except sometimes towards the end of the dry season when the water level may fall too low.

Adventurous travellers with their own transport may drive southeast from Kaeng Krachan directly to Hua Hin (see below), but the roads are poor in places and there are few signposts. It is simpler to return to road 4 and continue south to **CHA-AM**, a beach resort 38km south of Phetchaburi, where the road reaches the coast.

■ **Information**. The TAT office is at 500/51 T. Phet Kasem (road 4) on the south side of Cha-am.

■ **Hotels and services**. Among the best resort hotels are the luxurious *Dusit Resort and Polo Club* and the *Regent Cha-am Beach Resort*, both on the seashore between Cha-am and Hua Hin. Cheaper hotels are available in the centre of Cha-am.

■ **Transport**. Frequent **buses** run north to Phetchaburi and Bangkok, and south to Hua Hin and beyond. The **railway station** is to the west of road 4 at the main intersection in the town centre. *Avis* **car rentals** are available from the Dusit Resort and Polo Club, and the Regent Cha-am Beach Resort.

Near the beach at **Ban Huai Sai Nua**, c 12km south of Cha-am, is **Phra Ratcha Niwet Marukha Thai Wan**, a palace built in 1923 for King Vajiravudh, consisting of a group of teak buildings on stilts surrounded by balconies and linked to each other by raised, covered walkways. Parts of the structure were transferred from an earlier palace which Vajiravudh had had constructed in 1918 on the beach of Hat Chao Samran near Phetchaburi. Most of the teak buildings have now been restored and are open to the public.

Hua Hin

The town of Hua Hin (pop. 57,000), c 30km south of Cha-am, has a magnificent beach of fine white sand c 3km long, and has long been a fashionable resort favoured by Thai royalty and the wealthy classes of Bangkok. Today it has several hotels, but has retained its peaceful atmosphere and air of exclusivity. King Mongkut and his son Chulalongkorn came here in 1868 to watch an eclipse of the sun on 18 August. Both caught malaria, and Mongkut died of the fever on 1 October, soon after returning to Bangkok.

The development of Hua Hin as a resort began after the First World War with the construction of the railway linking Bangkok with peninsular Thailand. A summer palace, **Phra Ratchawang Klai Kangwon**, built by Chulalongkorn's son, King Prajadhipok, was completed in 1926 on the north side of the town, and is still used by the royal family. Hua Hin is also an important fishing port, and there is a large and busy fish market on the north side of the town. There is also an 18-hole golf course.

■ **Hotels and services**. One of the most agreeable hotels in Hua Hin is the *Sofitel Central Hua Hin* on the edge of the town near the beach. Built originally in 1923 as living quarters for the staff of the Royal Thai Railway, which had reached the town one year earlier, this charming two-storey, French colonial-style building was for many years known as the Railway Hotel. After a period of neglect and gradual decay, it was modernised in the mid-1980s, with many of its original features, including the rich wooden panelling and high ceilings, carefully retained. Another excellent hotel is the *Sailom*, which has its own private beach.

The *Bangkok Bank* is on T. Phet Kasem. The **post office** is further east along T. Damnoen Kasem. There is a lively **night market**, with many restaurants and food stalls, on T. Dechanuchit.

■ **Transport**. Frequent **bus services** run to north and south along road 4. The **railway station** is at the west end of T. Damnoen Kasem. Express trains run from here to Bangkok (3hrs 50mins). On the platform there is a royal waiting room built in traditional Thai style with multi-tiered roofs. *Bangkok Airways* has two daily **flights** to Bangkok. *Avis* **car rentals** are available at the Hotel Sofitel Central Hua Hin.

From Hua Hin, road 4 and the railway continue south for c 25km to **Pran Buri**, where a turning to the left at the main intersection leads after c 30km to **KHAO SAM ROI YOT NATIONAL PARK**. This park, established in 1966, covers an area of 98 sq km, some of it consisting of coastline and some of limestone hills. The hills are chiefly covered with mixed deciduous and dwarfed evergreen trees. The park has suffered severe degradation as a result of commercial shrimp and prawn farming, for which part of the ecologically important and fragile marshland, which once covered 30 per cent of the park, has been drained. Both local and international conservation organisations are fighting to save these wetlands, which provide a resting and breeding ground for many migratory birds. The park is home to more than 275 bird species, including numerous large waterfowl and birds of prey such as the **greater spotted eagle** and the rarer **imperial eagle**. Crab-eating macaques can be observed in the vicinity of the park headquarters. There are good **hiking paths** through the park, which also contains some remarkable caves, including the magnificent **Phraya Nakhon Cave**, where there is a pavilion built in the 1890s for a visit by King Chulalongkorn, and Tham Sai and Tham Kaeo, which have fine limestone formations. A torch is recommended. Bungalows are available at the park headquarters and near Phraya Nakhon Cave, and camping is permitted.

Road 4 continues south from Khao Sam Roi Yot for c 55km to the pleasant fishing port of **PRACHUAP KHIRI KHAN** (pop. 18,000). This is the narrowest part of Thailand, wedged between the mountains along the Burmese border to the west and the sandy beaches along the coast. A force of 2000 Japanese soldiers landed here on 8 December 1941, the day after the attack on Pearl Harbor, and took over the police station and the railway station before they were repulsed by the Thais. The TAT organises a *son et lumière* every year on 8 December to commemorate this event. On the north side of Prachuap Khiri Khan is the steep limestone hill of **Khao Chong Krachok** ('Mirror Mountain'). The hill, which is home to many wild monkeys, takes its name from a natural arch at its centre, through which the sky on the other side can be seen so that it looks from a distance like a piece of mirror glass. At the summit is **Wat Thammikaram**, which is reached by a flight of nearly 400 steps. From here there is a good view over the coast.

■ **Hotels and services**. The *Hat Thong Hotel* at 7 T. Susuk is one of the town's better hotels. Simpler lodgings are available nearby. The *Bangkok Bank* is at 168/1 T. Salachip. The **post office** is near the Hat Thong Hotel. The tourist information office is on T. Salachip. Excellent **seafood** is served at numerous restaurants and food stalls in the town.

■ **Transport**. Frequent **buses** run to towns north as far as Bangkok and south to Chumphon and beyond. The **railway station**, on the west side of the town, is on the main southern line.

To the north of the town is the bay of **Ao Bang Nang Lom**, where traditional fishing boats are made. Beyond is **Ao Noi**, where there is a picturesque fishing village at the foot of a hill called Khao Mong Rai. Further north still is Ao Khan Kradai, where, on the slopes of Khao Khan Kradai, is **Wat Tham Khao Khan Kradai**, a cave monastery composed of several chambers containing a number of seated and reclining Buddha images. The view from here is spectacular.

Along the coast to the south of Prachuap Khiri Khan there are a number of pleasant, little-frequented beaches. 19km before reaching Thap Sakae, a turning to the left leads to the beach of **Hat Wanakon National Park**, where there are bungalows.

At an intersection 13km north of Thap Sakae a turning to the right leads to the Huai Yang Falls in the low forest-covered hills near the border. Along the sandy coast between Thap Sakae itself and Bang Saphan are several **quiet resorts**, which travellers may find preferable to the rather unappealing town of Chumphon, 80km further south.

The main highway to the south divides near Chumphon. Road 4 turns due west towards Kra Buri on the far side of the isthmus, while Road 41 continues due south, parallel with the railway, towards Surat Thani. Several **small islands** off the coast near Chumphon have fine coral reefs and have become quite popular with scuba divers. Many of them have caves inhabited by the swiftlets that build the nests from which bird's-nest soup is made.

Bird's-nest soup

The nests are built by two species of swiftlet, the edible-nest swiftlet (*Aerodramus fuciphagus*) and the black-nest swiftlet (*A. maximus*). These birds inhabit the caves, navigating in the darkness by echolocation and laying their fragile nests made of dried saliva high on the cave walls and ceilings. Rickety bamboo poles tied with vines are used by the nest gatherers—mostly Muslim Malays—to reach the nests. This highly dangerous work is made worthwhile by the huge prices paid for the nests. Most valuable are the pure white nests built by the edible-nest swiftlets. The black-nest swiftlet produces a darker nest, which contains feathers mixed with the saliva. The tiny translucent nests, just five or six cm in diameter and rubbery to the touch, have been a prized delicacy among the Chinese at least since the early Ming period (14C–15C). The greatest demand for bird's nests today comes from Hong Kong and Chinese communities in the USA. Nest-gathering takes place in February and March, and again in May, and at these times the caves are closed to visitors.

Chumphon Cabana on Thung Wua Laen beach, 15km north of Chumphon, is a resort and diving centre where equipment can be hired.

Chumphon (pop. 17,000), which is named after Prince Chumphon, founder of the Thai Navy, lies on the east coast of the Kra Isthmus, the narrowest part of the peninsula, and only c 40km from the Indian Ocean on the west side of the isthmus. To the southeast of the town, road 4001 heads to Pak Nam, the port of Chumphon. Here is the pier from which boats leave to **Ko Tao**, the northernmost island in the beautiful Samui archipelago (see Rte 50).

■ **Hotels and services**. There are several good hotels in Chumphon, including the *Jansom Chumphon* at 188/65–6 T. Sala Daeng and the *Pharadon Inn* at

180/12 T. Pharadon. There are also some good hotels on nearby beaches, including *Phornsawan House* on Sai Ri Beach to the southeast of Pak Nam, and the *Chumphon Cabana*.

The *Bangkok Bank* and *Thai Farmers Bank* are on T. Saladaeng. *Chumphon Travel Service* on T. Tha Taphao can help with travel arrangements to Ko Tao and other islands.

■ **Transport**. Frequent **buses** run to the north and south, and to the west on road 4 to Kra Buri and Ranong. Chumphon **railway station** is on the main southern line and has several daily services in both directions. **Boats** bound for Ko Tao depart most nights from the pier to the southeast of the town.

49 · Chumphon to Chaiya and Surat Thani

Roads 41 and 401, 193km. To Chaiya 144km; Chaiya to Surat Thani 49km.

Railway, 166km in 3hrs from Chumphon to Phun Phin (Surat Thani).

Buses run regularly along road 41 between Chumphon and Surat Thani, passing the turning to Chaiya, which lies only 3km from the main road.

Take road 327 west from Chumphon for 6km to rejoin road 41, which runs south through flat countryside straight to Chaiya. There are several attractive small fishing ports and many beaches off to the left along the way and also a number of caves and waterfalls, including the cavern of **Tham Khao Kriap**, to the south of Lang Suan. Boat races are held at Lang Suan during the *kathin* festival in October or November.

Chaiya

The important historical site of Chaiya in the small town of the same name lies 141km south of Chumphon, to the left on road 4011, 3km to the left off road 41 and a few km from the coast.

History
Archaeological evidence suggests that from at least the Gupta period in India (4C–6C), Chaiya was an important port frequented by traders from the Bay of Bengal, and that it became one of the principal commercial cities of the Sri Vijaya maritime empire, which flourished from the 8C to the 13C. Some scholars have even suggested it may have been the capital of Sri Vijaya, and not, as is more generally thought, Palembang or Jambi in southeast Sumatra. Little is known of the history of Chaiya after the fall of Sri Vijaya, and few relics of its former grandeur now remain apart from Wat Kaeo, which is one of the few Sri Vijaya buildings still in its original form, and Wat Phra Boromathat, perhaps the best known and most important surviving monument of the Sri Vijaya period, which has also retained its original form, although it has been restored and altered many times, most recently in 1930.

Chaiya National Museum and **Wat Phra Boromathat** are on the south side of road 4011, 1700m east of the junction with road 41. The exhibits in the main building of the National Museum (open Wed–Sun 08.00–16.00), are arranged around a tiny central garden and are best viewed in an anti-clockwise direction. Displays in the first room include prehistoric stone tools, some small Khmer-Lop Buri Buddha heads, and two fine bronze Dong Son drums. The magnificent larger drum was discovered on the island of Samui; the smaller was found locally. In the same room is a replica of the famous head and torso of the *bodhisattva* Padmapani ('The One who Carries a Lotus'). The original statue of bronze inlaid with silver, discovered at Wat Wiang in Chaiya and dated AD 775, is now in the National Museum, Bangkok.

A display cabinet in the room beyond contains a c 8C stone head of a Buddha image discovered at a *wat* in Tha Chang, to the south of Chaiya. In the same case is a small 8C stone standing image of the Buddha, its head missing, from Tha Uthen near Kanchanadit, to the east of Surat Thani. Also of note in this cabinet is a tiny, but superbly carved 7C fragment of a stone Wheel of the Law, found near Chaiya.

Further along the same wall are several notable sculptures, including a beautiful 6C stone figure of the Buddha in *dhyāna mudrā*, one of the earliest and finest stone images of the Buddha found in Thailand. Stylistically related to South Indian Buddha images, its somewhat enigmatic smile and downcast eyes convey a marvellous impression of serenity. Nearby is a 7C stone standing Buddha image, its head and forearms missing and feet damaged, found at Wat Kaeo (see below). The style of this statue, with its somewhat stiff formality and the rigid symmetry of the robe, is very similar to that of Mon Dvaravati sculptures of the same period.

Against the rear wall of the museum is a tall, 14C gilded red sandstone standing image of the Buddha, with the left hand in *abhaya mudrā*. In the rear part of the building is a simplified model of the *chedi* of Wat Kaeo, together with some of the objects found at the site, including a 10C stone statue of Akshobhya, the transcendental Buddha of the eastern quarter. There are also some photographs of Wat Kaeo taken before its renovation, which convey something of the romantic appeal of the ruin that is lacking in the rebuilt monument.

Other items of interest in the museum include some enormous leather *nang yai* puppets, and an 18C–19C wooden panel from Wat Chaiya.

From the museum it is only a step across the driveway to **Wat Phra Boromathat**, an 8C monument which, although it was extensively restored in 1901 and subsequently,

Wat Phra Boromathat, Chaiya

has largely retained its original form. In the centre of the complex of buildings, which is surrounded by walls and a moat, is a brick shrine similar in plan and elevation to those represented on the reliefs of early 9C temples in central Java, standing on a high, richly decorated base. On each side of the base is a projecting false door, one of which has a niche in it, and at each corner is a small *chedi*. In front of the east door the eminent Thai archaeologist Prince Damrong found the famous 9C bronze figure of the *bodhisattva* Avalokiteshvara which is now in the National Museum in Bangkok.

Turn right out of Wat Phra Boromathat and continue east along road 4011 for c 750m to a lane on the right, which leads to **Wat Long** and **Wat Kaeo**. The former is on the left side after c 400m. Both are brick monuments that appear to belong to the early Sri Vijaya period (8C–9C). Little remains of Wat Long except the rebuilt cruciform base of the *chedi*. Continue c 450m to the entrance to Wat Ratanaram, also on the left side. Here is the restored brick *chedi* of Wat Kaeo, which also has a cruciform plan, with a central cella surrounded by four small shrines similar to Candi Kalasan and other 9C central Javanese monuments. However, the decorative elements of Wat Kaeo—pilasters, arches, colonnettes and mouldings—seem to be derived from Cham models. The bricks of the original structure were bonded together with a vegetal glue, the secret of which has been lost. Traces of the original stucco decoration remain. The *wat* was restored in the Ayutthaya period and again in the 1980s.

Return to road 4011 and continue east into the centre of **modern Chaiya**. The road crosses the railway line and runs east to Phum Riang, a rather grubby fishing port with a sizeable Muslim population, which has a well-deserved reputation for weaving beautiful silk brocade. Some historians believe the Muslims in Chaiya may be descended from prisoners seized in Kedah in the early 19C, when the ruler of Nakhon Si Thammarat quashed a rebellion there. Although most of the captives were taken to Nakhon Si Thammarat, it is conceivable that some found their way here.

From Chaiya, travellers can return to road 4 and continue south along the main highway to Phun Phin and thence to Surat Thani. An alternative, more interesting route runs through a string of villages and the small district centre of Tha Chang. To follow this route, take road 4011 east from Chaiya towards Phum Riang, and turn right just beyond the 4km stone on to road 4112, which leads south, repeatedly crossing the railway line, to Phun Phin (38km) and road 4. Regular buses run along this route.

Surat Thani

Surat Thani (pop. 46,000) is a busy, traffic-snarled port, situated on the estuary of the Ta Pi River. This area has been continuously inhabited since neolithic times, and in the early centuries AD Surat Thani was an eastern terminus of the overland trade route across the Kra Isthmus from Takua Pa. It is now an important centre of shipbuilding, fishing and mining.

There are many beautiful islands off the coast, and Surat Thani consequently receives a steady flow of visitors bound for the islands of **Samui**, **Phangan**, and **Tao**, and the outstandingly beautiful **Ang Thong Marine National Park** (see

Rte 50). The port is called Ban Don, which until 1905 was the name of the whole town.

In September or October every year, the Chak Pura Festival is held in Surat Thani to mark the end of the Buddhist Lent. The principal Buddha image of the town is taken down the Ta Pi River on a raft adorned with *nāgas*, and other images are carried on floats through the streets, boat races are held, and citizens place branches in front of their houses on which they hang offerings for the monks.

■ **Information**. TAT and Tourist Police at 5 T. Talat Mai (open daily 08.30–16.30; tel. 077/288818–9).

■ **Hotels and services**. Near the town centre are the *Siam Thara* at 1/44 T. Don Nok and the cheaper *Thai Thani* at 442/367–369 T. Talat Mai near the bus stations. The best hotel is the *Wang Tai*, rather inconveniently located on the southwest edge of the town, at 1 T. Talat Mai. Excellent food is served at *Kampen* on T. Pakdi Anuson; and superb northeastern specialities at *Suan Isan*, a restaurant in a pleasant teak house on T. Rat Uthit. 6km west of Surat Thani is **Ban Pak Nam Tapi**, which has some good **seafood restaurants**.

The *Thai Farmers Bank*, *Bangkok Bank* and the **post office** are on T. Na Muang. The **Telecoms Centre** for international phone/fax is on T. Don Nok.

■ **Transport. Buses**. There are two **bus stations** on T. Talat Mai—Talat Kaset I on the north side for local buses and services to neighbouring provinces (Chumphon, Chaiya, Nakhon Si Thammarat etc); and Talat Kaset II on the south side for long-distance buses to Bangkok, Songkhla, Phuket etc.

Share-taxis to Chumphon, Songkhla, Nakhon Si Thammarat, etc, run from the taxi station beside Talat Kaset II bus station.

The **railway station** at Phun Phin, on the Southern Line, can be reached by public bus shuttle service from Talat Kaset I bus station. Train bookings can be made in Surat Thani at approved agents or at the station's computerised booking office.

THAI has three daily **flights** from Surat Thani to Bangkok (1hr 10mins) and less frequent flights to Nakhon Si Thammarat (35mins), Phuket (35mins) and Ranong (25mins). The booking office at 3/27–28 T. Karunrat has a minibus service to the airport.

Car rentals are available from local rental companies.

Surat Thani is a dull town, but there are several pleasant **excursions** that can be made into the surrounding countryside, particularly to the waterfalls of **Tai Rom Yen National Park**, which lies to the south of Surat Thani, along road 4009. From 1967 to 1983 the Southern Zone of the Communist Party of Thailand (CPT) had bases in the hills in the park and the surrounding area. In the early 1970s there was intense fighting in the districts of Ban Na San, Khian Sa, Phrasaeng and Wiang Sa, where local rubber smallholders, finding themselves excessively taxed by corrupt local officials, turned to the CPT in desperation. In 1981 the Thai military introduced a largely successful Tai Rom Yen ('southern peace and security') pacification programme, from which the 213 sq km park gets its name.

Turn left near the 33km stone for **Dat Fa Waterfall**, or continue south past the beautiful karst scenery near Ban Na San and turn off left just beyond the 53km stone to **Muang Tuat Waterfall** and the park headquarters.

▶Khao Sok National Park

A longer excursion, requiring an overnight stay to make it worthwhile, is possible to the magnificent limestone hills of Khao Sok National Park, to the west of Surat Thani on road 401.

Take the road towards Phun Phin and turn left on to road 401, which crosses road 41 after a few kilometres. Just beyond the 35km stone, a road to the right leads after c 3km to **Wat Tham Singkhon**. This cave monastery in the side of a limestone cliff is reached across a covered wooden bridge on the right of the road. The principal Buddha image within the cave dates from the reign of Rama III and is seated in *pralambapādāsana*, with both hands in *varada mudrā*. Around it are numerous smaller images, and to the left, figures of stuccoed elephants. A flight of steps behind leads up to a second chamber containing large stalactites, lit by a natural opening in the roof. A third, darker chamber lies beyond.

Back on road 401, continue west to **Khao Sok National Park**, on the right side by the 109km stone. The park, which was established in 1980, covers an area of 650 sq km and adjoins the much larger **Khlong Saeng Wildlife Sanctuary**. Several hiking trails lead through the landscape of towering limestone cliffs and lush vegetation to waterfalls, caves and swimming holes. More than **170 bird species** have been recorded, including the beautiful **great argus**, and tigers and elephants are known to inhabit the park. It is also home to one of the strangest flowers in the world, *Rafflesia kerrii*, a huge parasitic plant which can reach 70cm in diameter. Its buds, which sometimes grow to the size of a football, develop within the root of its host plant—often a liana—and eventually burst out to produce a foul-smelling flower, which shrivels away again after a few days. To the northeast is the large reservoir created by the Chieo Lan Dam, where boats can be chartered.

■ There is a good choice of **accommodation**—a rarity in most of Thailand's national parks—ranging from the simple and friendly *Bamboo House*, to the rather more sophisticated *Our Jungle House* and *Art's Riverview Lodge* nearby.

50 · Ko Samui, Ko Phangan, Ko Tao and Ang Thong National Park

The Ang Thong archipelago lying off the coast to the northeast of Surat Thani, of which **Ko Samui**, **Ko Phangan** and **Ko Tao** are the most important islands, is one of Thailand's most popular tourist destinations, with a wide choice of attractive accommodation and numerous restaurants, bars and nightclubs. The islands are extremely beautiful, with rolling green hills, fine sandy beaches and warm seas, and the inhabitants, the Chao Samui, are on the whole friendly, although increasingly jaded by the waves of tourism which have engulfed their islands, especially Ko Samui. Many have become rich from tourism, but others have found themselves pushed aside by investors and land speculators from Bangkok.

■ **Information**. The TAT office in Surat Thani can provide details of accommodation and transport on Ko Samui and Ko Phangan. For visitors planning to explore the islands, the *Guide Map of Koh Samui, Koh Phangan & Koh Tao* published by V Hongsombud is highly recommended.

■ **Accommodation**. There are scores of hotels and bungalow- chalets on Ko Samui and Ko Phangan, ranging in price from Ko Samui's expensive and luxurious *Imperial Thong Sai Bay* to the cheap bamboo and wood bungalows on Lamai beach.

■ **Services. Ko Samui:** The *Bangkok Bank* and *Thai Farmers Bank* both have branches in Na Thon on Ko Samui, and there are many currency exchanges in Na Thon and on Lamai and Chaweng beaches. Travel agents in Na Thon can arrange onward travel, including bus and train tickets for mainland destinations. On Lamai and Chaweng beaches international telephone services are available, and there are second-hand book shops, mini-marts selling everything needed for the beach, and scores of eating and drinking establishments. **Ko Phangan**: currency exchanges, post office, international telephone service and travel agents can all be found in Thong Sala.

■ **Passenger ferries**. **Express boats** operate two or three times daily to Ko Samui from Tha Thong, 6km east of Surat Thani. Timetables and information can be obtained from *Songserm Travel* at 295 T. Talat Mai in Surat Thani. Slow overnight boats to both Ko Samui and Ko Phangan leave Surat Thani late in the evening from the quay on T. Ban Don, arriving at the islands early the next morning. Accommodation aboard is very rudimentary. The *Jumbo Ferry Company* in Bangkok operates a ferry between Bangkok and Songkhla via Ko Samui, which sails twice a week in each direction. The voyage from Bangkok to Ko Samui takes 16 hours, from Songkhla 10 hours.

　Inter-island ferries operate between Ko Samui and Ko Phangan and between Ko Phangan and Ko Tao. The islands constituting **Ang Thong National Park** can be reached from either Ko Samui or Ko Phangan.

■ **Vehicle ferries** operate to Ko Samui and Ko Phangan from **Don Sak**, 70km east of Surat Thani. Take road 401 (T. Talat Mai) from the centre of Surat Thani and turn left after c 39km on to road 4142. The ferry terminal is on a pretty bay to the left shortly before the 28km stone. There are usually five services daily to Ko Samui (1hr 30mins).

■ **Air services**. *Bangkok Airways* has many daily direct services from Ko Samui to Bangkok (80 mins), although flights are often cancelled when weather conditions are bad; two daily flights to Phuket (50mins); and daily direct services to both Hua Hin (1hr) and Patthaya's nearest airport at U Taphao (1hr).

■ **Transport on Ko Samui and Ko Phangan**. Frequent *songthaeo* operate from Na Thon, the main town on the west coast of Ko Samui, and go round the ring road to the major beaches. Flag them down at the roadside and let the driver know when you want to get out. **Jeep** and **motorcycle rentals** provide the easiest way to get around the island, but beware of occasional dangerous driving, usually by inexperienced, macho or drunk tourists. Rental outlets can be found in Na Thon and along Lamai and Chaweng beaches.

On Ko Phangan, *songthaeo* operate to most beaches from near the jetty in Thong Sala where the ferries dock. **Rentals** can be arranged in Thong Sala.

Ko Samui

Ko Samui, the largest island (230 sq km), attracts the vast majority of the tourists who throng the pleasant beaches of this archipelago from November till August. Until the start of the tourism boom in the 1970s, the inhabitants were predominantly fishermen and coconut gatherers. The hilly interior of Ko Samui is still covered with thousands of coconut palms, but tourism has firmly established itself as the island's main source of income.

Apart from some waterfalls, there are few specific sites to visit; it is the natural beauty of the area as a whole which makes it so attractive.

Ko Phangan

Quieter than Ko Samui and wilder, with a smaller population (c 8000), Ko Phangan has a less developed transport network, which means access to some beaches is by foot or boat only—an attraction for many visitors wanting to find greater peace and solitude.

The range of accommodation on Ko Phangan is not quite as wide as that on Ko Samui, but there are still nearly 200 places to choose from.

Ko Tao and Ang Thong National Park

Ko Tao is the least visited and the smallest (barely 2.5 x 6km) of the three islands. Very pleasant hiking trails cross the island from the port on the west side to some charming little bays on the east coast. Accommodation is scattered mainly around the south and west coasts, and there are some fine coral reefs on the west coast, especially near the northwest corner around Ko Nang Yuan, a delightful islet joined by sand bars to two other little specks of land.

Ang Thong National Park became Thailand's second marine national park in 1980 and covers 102 sq km. The 40-odd islands of Ang Thong are made of limestone, flooded by the rising post-glacial sea level. The corals are less spectacular than those in the Andaman Sea, but there are some good reefs on the west side of Ko Sam Sao and the north side of Ko Thai Phlao. As the soils are thin and the limestone is porous, the lush forests of the lower areas are typically deciduous and shed their leaves in the cool season. The jagged upper ridges are sparsely covered with scrub forest.

Dolphins and sea otters can be found in the coastal waters. Ashore, there are long-tailed macaques, leopard cats, dusky langurs, monitor lizards and pythons. There are 40 recorded bird species, including little herons and brahminy kites. Two features of particular interest are the beautiful **emerald saltwater lake** on Ko Mae Ko, and the fine view to be had from the 400m summit on Ko Wua Talap. Bungalow accommodation is available at the park headquarters on Ko Wua Talap.

Transport to the park is most easily arranged in Na Thon on Ko Samui; a trip is very highly recommended.

51 · Surat Thani to Nakhon Si Thammarat

Road *401, 139km.*

Railway, *181km in 4hrs from Phun Phin to Nakhon Si Thammarat.*

Road 401 runs east from Surat Thani towards the coast. There is often heavy traffic on the outskirts of the town. After 58km, a turning to the left on to road 4014 leads to **Khanom** and a string of beach resort hotels, the best of which is *Khanap Nam Diamond Cliff Resort* on Nai Phlao beach. However, they cannot compare in quality and variety with the numerous hotels and bungalows on the nearby islands of Ko Samui and Ko Phangan (see Rte 50).

Further south, near the fishing port of Tha Sala, 28km north of Nakhon Si Thammarat, road 4140 turns off right towards the hills of Khao Luang. This scenic detour is recommended for travellers with their own transport, who should take this route to the 17km stone, where road 4016 leads off left towards Phrommakhiri, running for the first few kilometres through rubber plantations, and flanked on the right by the Khao Luang range of hills. Just before the 24km stone, a lane to the right leads after 5km to the **Ai Khieo Falls**. From the car park a path climbs up beside a boulder-strewn watercourse through lush vegetation to the main falls.

Continue south on road 4016 for 3km to Phrommakhiri, where road 4132 turns off right to a second series of cascades, **Nam Tok Phrommalok** c 5km up a winding, thickly wooded road. 21km further south, road 4016 reaches Nakhon Si Thammarat.

Nakhon Si Thammarat

Nakhon Si Thammarat (pop. 82,000) is the second largest town in southern Thailand and a major religious centre, with the most important Buddhist monastery in the southern peninsula. The town is also one of the few places in Thailand where the *nang thalung* shadow play is still performed and where the puppets are manufactured. **Bull fights** in which bulls fight each other are held on Saturdays a short distance west of the town on road 4016.

■ Information. The TAT office is on the west side of Sanam Na Muang, backing on to T. Tha Chang.

■ **Hotels and services**. Among the better hotels are the *Thai Hotel* on T. Ratchadamnoen, the *Bua Luang* at 1487/19 Soi Luang Muang, T. Chamroen Withi, and the *Nakhon Garden Inn* at 1/4 T. Pak Nakhon. Low budget travellers are well served by the excellent value *Thai Li Hotel*, entered through a hardware shop at 1130 T. Ratchadamnoen. Nakhon Si Thammarat is famed for its food and there are many good Thai and Muslim **restaurants** in the town. *Khanom Chin Muang Khon* on T. Phan Yom is one of the best known and most popular. There is a lively **night market** on T. Chamroen Withi with stalls selling local dishes. **Banks** and the **post office** are on T. Ratchadamnoen.

■ **Transport**. The main **bus** terminal is on road 4016 on the west edge of the town, but for many destinations buses can be picked up nearer the town centre. Ask at your hotel or the TAT office. There are **share-taxi** services to Phatthalung, Trang, Surat Thani and other southern towns. Most leave from T. Yomarat. From the **railway station** on T. Yomarat there are a few daily services to Bangkok (c 15hrs), but for routes to the south, passengers must change trains at Thung Song. *THAI* has **flights** from Nakhon Si Thammarat to Bangkok, and to Phuket (1hr 35mins) via Surat Thani (35mins). The booking office is at 1612 T. Ratchadamnoen. In the town, frequent **songthaeo** run back and forth along the main thoroughfares, T. Ratchadamnoen and T. Si Thammasok. There are several **car** and **motor-cycle rental** companies in the town.

■ **Festivals**. There are two important Buddhist festivals: *Ngan Prapheni Sat Duan Sip* ('Festival of the 10th Month'), held in the 10th month of the Thai lunar year (September or October), in which offerings are made in the monasteries to the dead who are in Hell to relieve their sufferings, accompanied by processions, performances of shadow puppet plays and a great fair on Sanam Na Muang in the centre of the town; and the *Ngan Hae Pha Khun That*, in which homage is paid to the relics of the Buddha in **Wat Phra Maha That Wora Maha Wihan** (see below).

History

Nakhon Si Thammarat, formerly known as Ligor, is one of the most ancient cities in Thailand, having been a capital of Tambralinga, one of the Indianised states in the peninsula over which Sri Vijaya gained a measure of control, perhaps as early as the 8C. It seems to have become at least nominally subject to Sukhothai in the 1290s and to have become part of the Ayutthaya kingdom by the early 16C.

Most of the sights in Nakhon Si Thammarat lie close to T. Ratchadamnoen, the city's main north–south artery, which runs for 6km through the heart of the town from the National Museum at the south end to Wat Chaeng in the north. Distances are too great to walk in comfort, so the use of a *samlo* or *songthaeo* is advised.

The **NAKHON SI THAMMARAT NATIONAL MUSEUM** (open Wed–Sun, 09.00–16.00), opposite Wat Suan Luang on T. Ratchadamnoen, is one of the best museums in southern Thailand. On the ground floor, in a room to the right of the entrance hall, is a small display of prehistoric exhibits, including beads and stone tools. Here also are two bronze Dong Son drums, dating from c 500 BC. In the room on the left of the entrance hall is a damaged Dvaravati (6C–11C) sandstone image, missing head, hands and feet, and votive tablets, small bronzes from various periods, bronze and stucco heads and complete images of the Buddha from the Sukhothai, Lan Na, U Thong and Ayutthaya periods. Some Sawankhalok ceramics are displayed in the middle of the room, and against the south wall is a magnificent, if somewhat damaged, late 19C wooden gable from Wat Sa Riang.

In the room behind are several early stone images of Vishnu, one of them, to

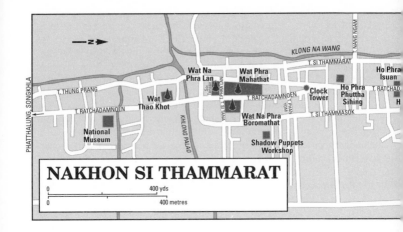

NAKHON SI THAMMARAT

Map labels: KLONG NA WANG, NANG NGAM, T. SI THAMMARAT, Ho Phra Isuan, Wat Na Phra Lan, Wat Phra Mahathat, Clock Tower, Ho Phra Phuttha Sihing, T. RATCHADA, H, T. THUNG PRANG, T. RATCHADAMNOEN, Wat Thao Khot, T. SI TAKA, T. RATCHADAMNOEN, T. SI THAMMASOK, PHATTHALUNG, SONGKHLA, National Museum, KHLONG PALAO, Wat Na Phra Boromathat, Shadow Puppets Workshop

0   400 yds
0   400 metres

the left of the doorway, dating from the 5C. A group to the right of the doorway, all found in Tha Sala district on the coast to the north of the town, includes a fine 6C–8C torso of Vishnu, clad in a knee-length Indian-style loincloth, and another torso of a four-armed Vishnu dating from the early 7C from Wat Phra Narai. There is also a third Vishnu image, of which only the lower half remains.

In the case beyond the 5C Vishnu, there is a fine, but damaged 14C U Thong-style Buddha image from Wat Yai in Phrommalok district. Further along are some beautiful wooden Buddha images found at Wat Chaeng, and several more Vishnu images and torsos from the 5C–9C.

In the northwest corner are several *lingas*, some of which date from the 7C. In the centre of the north wall is a replica of an image of Vishnu now on display in the Thalang National Museum in Phuket. This is one of a group of three sandstone statues, thought to date from the 9C, found on the bank of the Takua Pa River in Phangnga province partially embedded in the trunks of a large tree which had grown round them. On the museum wall are some photographs of the site as it was until the 1960s when the statues were moved. The face of one of them, an image of a kneeling *rişi*, Markandeya, was stolen in 1966, together with the face of the third statue, which is of the goddess Bhudevi. This last was recovered from a London art dealer and returned to Thailand in 1973. The face of the *rişi* has never been recovered. In the northeast corner of the room is a stone inscription in Tamil, found at the same site as the three statues and probably dating from the same period. It seems likely that both the inscription, which refers to the building of a water tank, and the images, which display Pallava influences in their dress, were the work of a southern Indian merchant guild at Takua Pa, which at that time was an important trade entrepôt.

A cabinet near the east wall contains numerous bronze Hindu images, including Ganesha, the elephant-headed son of Shiva; Uma, Shiva's consort; a largely intact four-armed 17C image of Shiva himself, still retaining most of his attributes, and a *haṁsa*, the goose mount of Brahma.

Halfway up the stairs are some huge *nang yai* and smaller *nang thalung* shadow

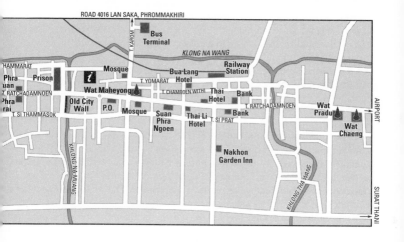

puppets. The display on the first floor includes farming implements, fish and animal traps, baskets, weapons, ceramics and textiles.

From the museum turn right along T. Ratchadamnoen to **Wat Thao Khot**, on the west side of the street. On the left inside the compound is the *ubosot*, which is surrounded by whitewashed stone *bai sema*. It has been completely renovated in recent years, and its side walls have been extended to the east in a curious fashion, beyond the span of the roof. Within is a large gold-painted stucco image of the Buddha. Along the top of the interior walls are wooden panels painted with scenes of the life of the Buddha. Behind this *ubosot* is another newer one, beside which stands a large, clumsily restored brick *chedi* in the Sri Vijayan style.

Continue north along T. Ratchadamnoen and cross a small stream, Khlong Palao, to reach the intersection with T. Chonwitti. This is the south edge of the old fortified city, but there is nothing to see here today. A short distance further north, turn left along T. Phra Lan to **Wat Na Phra Lan**. On the east side of the enclosure is a well in a simple brick enclosure, one of the original city's four sources of drinking water, which determined the settlement's linear growth. The *ubosot*, which was completely renovated in 1994, contains a fine Ayutthaya-style image of the Buddha.

One block further north is **WAT PHRA MAHATHAT WORA MAHA WIHAN** (Wat Mahathat), one of the most important *wat* in southern Thailand. Archaeological evidence has confirmed the tradition that it was built during the Sri Vijaya period (7C–12C). Every year it is visited by many pilgrims, chiefly in September or October for the festival of *Ngan Prapheni Sat Duan Sip*, when a strip of yellow cloth several hundred metres in length is ceremonially wound round the *chedi*.

The outer enclosure of the *chedi* is a gallery containing 170 images of the Buddha. On the east side of the gallery is a small shrine containing a tall stucco standing image of the Buddha in *abhaya mudrā*. Within the courtyard formed by the outer gallery are scores of small *chedi*, grouped densely around the great whitewashed central monument, Phra Boromathat, which consists of a monumental *chedi* 77m high with a bell-shaped relic chamber in the Sri Lankan style and an elegant spire covered with gold leaf and precious stones. To the north of the *chedi* is a staircase enclosed in a *wihan* (Wihan Phra Ma) which gives access to the high platform on which the *chedi* stands. On either side of the staircase is a small shrine decorated with fine bas-reliefs. Facing the staircase is a very tall standing Buddha image in gilded stucco, flanked by a pair of disciples. Round the foot of the *chedi* and entered from the northeast is a charming inner gallery with a roof of coloured tiles, containing numerous Buddha images and relief carvings of elephants in niches.

To the north of the Wihan Phra Ma is the **wat museum**, built round a courtyard containing a *bodhi* tree, one of 16 brought by King Chulalongkorn from Sri Lanka. The museum contains numerous Buddha images of all shapes and sizes, votive tablets, little silver and gold tribute trees (known in Malay as *bunga mas* and *bunga perak*) offered by the rulers of states under Thai suzerainty, jewellery, ceramics, weapons, silver betel boxes and much else.

At the south end of the complex, outside the main enclosure, is the principal *wihan*, Phra Wihan Luang, which contains a fine late U Thong-style image of the Buddha seated in *bhūmisparśa mudrā*. The building has been heavily restored, but originally dates from the Ayutthaya period. It is chiefly remarkable for the unusual extent to which the columns supporting both the roof outside and the elaborately ornamented coffered ceiling inside lean inwards, thus giving the whole edifice a somewhat bizarre appearance.

Opposite Wat Mahathat, on the other side of T. Ratchadamnoen is Wat Na Phra Boromathat, which contains the living quarters of the monks at Wat Mahathat. Further north along T. Ratchadamnoen, just beyond the clock tower on the left is a small modern shrine, **Ho Phra Phuttha Sihing**, squeezed between two government offices. This modest shrine houses the small but greatly venerated **Phra Phuttha Sihing**, one of four very similar but not identical bronze images of the seated Buddha in *bhūmisparśa mudrā*, traditionally believed to have been made in Sri Lanka and brought to Thailand during the Sukhothai period. The other three versions of this statue are in Wat Phutthaisawan in Bangkok, Wat Phra Sing Luang in Chiang Mai, and Wat Phra Sing in Chiang Rai. Each of the four is claimed by some to be the original from which the other three were copied. In front of the image is a replica on which the faithful can place their offerings of gold leaf. Beside the Phra Phuttha Sihing are two fine standing images of the Buddha that once held alms bowls—the one on the right covered in silver and the one on the left in gold.

Ho Phra Isuan ('Hall of Shiva') is a rather dull little shrine further north on the left side of T. Ratchadamnoen. It houses a sandstone *linga* and a small statue of Shiva. Outside is the wooden frame of an old swing, used at least until the early 20C for an annual Brahmanic ceremony in honour of Shiva like that which was formerly held at the Giant Swing at Wat Suthat in Bangkok (see p 131). Directly opposite on the other side of T. Ratchadamnoen is **Ho Phra Narai**, a similar shrine containing an extremely poor replica of the famous Vishnu image in Thalang National Museum in Phuket.

Further north, the road passes the prison on the left and crosses Khlong Na Muang. To the right of the road at this point is a restored part of the old city wall which formed the city's fortifications on the northern side.

On the east side of T. Ratchadamnoen, directly opposite Wat Maheyong, is a mosque which, together with the rather more elegantly proportioned mosque on the corner of T. Karom and T. Yomarat nearby, serves the sizeable Muslim community that has been established here at least since the 16C.

Further north beyond the mosques is **Suan Phra Ngoen**, a small garden, containing a revered gilded image of the Buddha seated in *bhūmisparśa mudrā*, known as Phra Ngoen. Behind the shrine is **Chedi Yak**, a large brick *chedi* thought to have been founded in the 15C and restored during the later Ayutthaya and early Ratanakosin periods, most recently in 1967.

At the north end of the commercial centre, in T. Ratchadamnoen just before the bridge over Khlong Tha Wang, can be seen some of the very few remaining old Chinese shop houses in Nakhon Si Thammarat.

Wat Pradu Phathanaram lies on the east side of T. Ratchadamnoen, c 600m north of the bridge. Here, inside a small Chinese-style shrine beside the road, is a *chedi* said to contain the ashes of Chao Phraya Nakhon Noi, son of King Taksin.

In the grounds of nearby **Wat Chaeng** shaded by great trees is a more substantial shrine, also in the Chinese style, but with a small walled enclosure entered through ornate stuccoed gateways. Inside are two small *chedi* said to contain the ashes of an 18C ruler of the town, Phra Chao Khattiya Ratcha Nikhom, and his wife.

Visitors interested in **puppetry** should visit the workshop of Suchat Sapsin, a master craftsman of *nang thalung* and *nang yai* shadow puppets made from buffalo hide. Examples of his work are on sale at the workshop, at 110/18 T. Si Thammasok Soi 3, a few metres off T. Si Thammasok on the south side of the town.

▶Travellers wishing to explore further the hills of the Khao Luang range to the west of the town can make a pleasant **excursion** to the Karom Waterfalls and Kaeo Surakan Cave in **Khao Luang National Park**. This park covers an area of 570 sq km and is named after southern Thailand's highest point, Khao Luang (1835m).

Take road 4016 (T. Karom) west from the town centre and turn left on to road 4015 after 9km. The road skirts the southern edge of the hills, passing beautiful limestone cliffs and occasional rubber plantations. Continue beyond Lan Saka until, shortly before the 15km stone, the entrance to **Kaeo Surakan Cave** can be seen on the right side of the road at the foot of a cliff. A good torch is needed to explore this 560m tunnel-like cavern. Visitors are required to sign in at the office beside the entrance.

Continue 5km further to a right turn to the **Karom Waterfalls**. The cascades are visible high up on the hillside to the right. The lane climbs up past the visitor centre to the falls, which are well worth a visit after the rainy season. Easy paths link the various pools and levels.◀

52 · Nakhon Si Thammarat to Phatthalung and Hat Yai

Roads *403 and 41, 189km. To Phatthalung 99km; Phatthalung to Hat Yai 90km.*

Railway, *83km in 1hr 20mins from Phatthalung to Hat Yai. There is no direct rail service from Nakhon Si Thammarat to Phatthalung.*

Leave Nakhon Si Thammarat along T. Ratchadamnoen, heading south past the National Museum, and then turn right on to road 403 towards Ron Phibun. Turn left at the T-junction with road 41 and continue south through rolling countryside to the small provincial capital of **PHATTHALUNG** (pop. 24,000).

The town lies at the foot of rugged limestone cliffs, 9km to the west of the shore of Thale Luang, an inland sea of brackish water. Phatthalung has few sites of special note, except for some interesting cave temples and a delightful market, but in the surrounding countryside are several natural attractions, which make it a worthwhile overnight stop on the route southwards.

■ **Hotels and services**. The *Thai Hotel* at 14 T. Disara Sakharin and the *Ho Fa Hotel* at 28–30 T. Khuha Sawan can be recommended. **Banks** are on T. Ramet and the **post office** is near the railway station. There is a busy and colourful **morning market** along T. Pho Sa-at to the north of the Ho Fa Hotel.

■ **Transport**. There are frequent **buses** south to Hat Yai, west to Trang and north to Nakhon Si Thammarat. The **railway station** is on the southern line between Bangkok and Malaysia, with regular daily services.

On T. Khuha Sawan, to the west of the Ho Fa Hotel, is **Wat Tham Khuha Sawan**, a temple with several caves in the surroundings. In the hill behind the *ubosot* is the cavern of **Tham Phra**, containing a large reclining image of the Buddha and a score of smaller images set amid stalactites and stalagmites. At the rear of the cave is a flight of steps leading a few metres to a lower chamber, while to the right of the cave entrance are more steps going up to a craggy outcrop with fine views over the town and Thale Luang. The smaller **Tham Nang Khlot**, a cleft at the foot of the hill near the monks' living quarters, is filled with naive concrete statues of religious and secular figures.

Road 4047 runs east from Phatthalung, across the railway line towards **Ban Lam Pam**, a small fishing port and market on the shore of Thale Luang. On the right side of the road, 7km from Phatthalung, is **Wat Wang** ('Monastery of the Palace'), which has a fine late 18C *chedi* in front of the enclosure. The *ubosot* behind can be entered through a doorway in the rear wall of the surrounding gallery. The interior walls are covered with magnificent murals, painted in the late 18C or early 19C and still in remarkably good condition. Note also the simple, faded paintings on some of the window shutters. The murals in the architecturally similar *ubosot* of **Wat Wihan Buk**, across the road from Wat Wang, are by the same artist. These are now in extremely poor condition.

Two old palaces belonging to former governors of Phatthalung lie 150m east of Wat Wang. **Wang Kao** ('Old Palace') and **Wang Mai** ('New Palace') are good examples of late 19C secular architecture. Wang Kao, which is entirely of wood, was built in 1866–68 for the governor of Phatthalung, and Wang Mai in 1889 for his son and successor. Both palaces were restored by the Fine Arts Department in 1988 and are now open to the public.

Road 4047 ends at **Lam Pam**, on the lake shore, where visitors can enjoy excellent fish dishes at tables overlooking the lake.

▶Two enjoyable **excursions** can be made in the vicinity of Phatthalung. Of special interest to bird watchers is the waterfowl sanctuary of **Thale Noi** (Uthayan Nok Nam Thale Noi), a freshwater lake and marsh to the northeast of Phatthalung. This is an important nesting site, with more than 180 recorded species. It is best visited at dawn, when the birds are at their most active and the temperature is still cool. Boats can be hired from the park office on the lake shore. To reach the park, head north to Khuan Khanun along road 4048, and there turn east to Ban Thale Noi. There are buses from Phatthalung to Ban Thale Noi, but visitors using these will find it difficult to arrive early enough to see the waterfowl at their best. Another possibility is to stay overnight at *Thale Noi Villa*, which provides adequate accommodation in lakeside bungalows.

A visit to Thale Noi can be combined with a trip to **Khao Pu-Khao Ya National Park**. There is some delightful woodland near the park headquarters, which makes an excellent picnic site, and there are easy trails of several kilometres to waterfalls and to a beautiful cave, **Tham Matcha**. Visitors should bring their own refreshments. To reach the park from Thale Noi, take road 4048 back through Khuan Khanun and continue west across road 41 on road 4164. The park is signed to the left along a lane which cuts through a rubber plantation to the park headquarters. Attractive simple wooden bungalows can be rented in the park.◀

From Phatthalung, return to road 4 and turn south towards Hat Yai. Near the 46km stone, a turning to the left on to road 4081 leads to **Wat Khian Bang Kaeo**, which has an important *chedi*. Turn left off road 4081 just beyond the 14km stone and continue for 3km to the *wat*, which is visible from the road on the right side. The *chedi* is of Sri Lankan type and stands on a round base. It is surrounded on three sides by a gallery. The *harmikā* is decorated with pieces of ceramic.

Hat Yai

Continue south on road 4 and then on road 43 to Hat Yai (pop. 120,000), a brash and rather soulless modern commercial centre situated on the main trade route between Thailand and Malaysia and Singapore, and an important road and rail junction. It is also noted for its textile production, particularly batik. Travellers bound for Songkhla (see Rte 53) can avoid Hat Yai altogether by turning right off road 43 on to road 414.

The markets and lively nightlife of Hat Yai attract a constant stream of visitors, and this accounts for the wide choice of hotels and good food available here.

An enormous reclining Buddha image, c 35m in length, of little artistic merit, can be seen at **Wat Hat Yai Nai**, 4km west of the town on road 4 (T. Phet Kasem). As in Nakhon Si Thammarat, bull fights are held regularly in Hat Yai, on the first Saturday of each month.

■ **Information**. The TAT (open daily, 08.30–16.30) and Tourist Police are at 1/1 Soi 2, T. Niphat Uthit 3.

■ **Hotels and services**. There are hotels catering to every taste and budget. Among the best is the *Regency* at 23 T. Prachathipat. There are numerous **banks** and **money changers** in the town centre and the **post office** is on T. Ratakan near the railway station.

■ **Transport**. Regular **bus** services run from Hat Yai to towns all over southern Thailand and to Bangkok. Different bus routes start from different points in the town; ask for the required route at your hotel or the TAT office. **Share-taxis** go to several southern towns, including Songkhla, Phatthalung, Yala and Pattani. Two **railway** lines run south from Hat Yai. Most services are via Yala to Sungai Kolok on the Malaysian frontier. There is one international service a day to Butterworth in Malaysia, which crosses the border at Padang Besar. *THAI* has several daily **flights** to Bangkok (1hr 25mins), and two daily flights to Phuket (c 55mins). The booking office is at 166/4 T. Niphat Uthit 2. *SilkAir* has a daily direct **international flight** to Singapore (1hr 25mins). *THAI* flies several times weekly to Singapore and shares five direct weekly flights to Kuala Lumpur (1hr) with *Malaysia Airlines*. There is a *Hertz* **car rental** office at the airport.

53 · Songkhla and Sathing Phra

Road 407, 30km from Hat Yai to Songkhla.

Songkhla

Songkhla (pop. 182,000) occupies a narrow peninsula separating the inland sea of Thale Sap Songkhla from the South China Sea. With its well-protected natural harbour, it has long been an important fishing port, but the lake has suffered recently from over-fishing. Despite being the provincial capital, Songkhla has little of the brashness of Hat Yai and remains a quiet and leisurely seaside town.

■ **Hotels and services**. Among the better hotels are the *Pavilion Songkhla Thani* at 17 T. Platha, the *Queen* at 20 T. Sai Buri and the *Royal Crown Songkhla* at 38 T. Sai Ngam. Cheap and cheerful is the *Narai* at 12/2 T. Chai Khao, which has bicycles for rent.

The *Bangkok Bank* is at 28–32 T. Nakhon Nai, and a branch of *Thai Farmers Bank* is near the Queen Hotel. The **post office** is close to the Songkhla National Museum,

■ **Transport**. **Buses** depart from several different places, depending on their destination. Ask at the hotel. *THAI* has a booking office at 2 Soi 4, T. Sai Buri, directly opposite a branch of Thai Farmers Bank, but the nearest airport is at Hat Yai.

FERRY TO SATHING PHRA

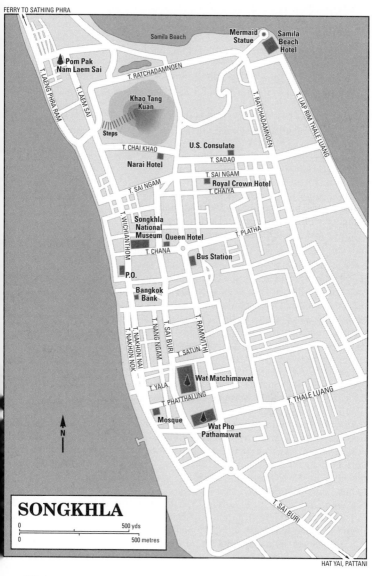

Samila Beach

Mermaid Statue

Samila Beach Hotel

Pom Pak Nam Laem Sai

T. RATCHADAMNOEN

T. LAENG PHRA RAM

T. LAEM SAI

Khao Tang Kuan

Steps

T. RATCHADAMNOEN

T. LIAP RIM THALE LUANG

T. CHAI KHAO

U.S. Consulate

Narai Hotel

T. SADAO

T. SAI NGAM

Royal Crown Hotel

T. CHAIYA

T. SAI NGAM

Songkhla National Museum

Queen Hotel

T. PLATHA

T. WICHIANTHOM

T. CHANA

Bus Station

P.O.

Bangkok Bank

T. NAKHON NAI

T. NAKHON NOK

T. NANG NGAM

T. SAI BURI

T. RAMWITHI

T. SATUN

T. YALA

Wat Matchimawat

T. PHATTHALUNG

T. THALE LUANG

Mosque

Wat Pho Pathamawat

T. SAI BURI

N

SONGKHLA

| 0 | 500 yds |
| 0 | 500 metres |

HAT YAI, PATTANI

History

Songkhla seems to have been an important centre in the maritime empire of Sri Vijaya, which flourished in Sumatra, the Malay peninsula and the Gulf of Thailand at least as far north as Nakhon Si Thammarat from the 8C to the 13C. It was still an important trading centre in the 16C when the first Europeans, who called it by its Malay name of Singora, arrived in the Gulf of Thailand. Little remains of the architecture of the Sri Vijaya period in southern Thailand or elsewhere, but a large number of important stone and bronze sculptures have been found at several sites in the area, including Sathing Phra, c 30km north of Songkhla between the east shore of the Thale Sap and the sea.

At the beginning of the 19C the city was moved from its original site on the north side of the narrows of the harbour to a more protected position to the south of the lake and further from the sea. The ruins of the old city, notably the fortifications of Khao Hua Daeng, can still be seen.

Today, Songkhla, although still the provincial capital, has been overtaken by Hat Yai and has become an economic backwater, relatively unscathed by modern development and retaining much of its traditional charm. It has substantial Malay and Chinese populations.

The collection of the **SONGKHLA NATIONAL MUSEUM** (open Wed–Sun, 09.00–16.00), is housed in the former town hall, a two-storey house in the southern Chinese style, with fine woodcarving. The entrance is opposite the remains of the old city wall on T. Chana, which was built during the reign of Rama III. The house was built in 1878 for the deputy governor of Songkhla, but became the governor's residence in 1894. The governorship of Songkhla had by then become hereditary in the Na Songkhla family, descendants of a Chinese marshal who in 1769 had been given a monopoly by King Taksin of the collection of edible birds' nests on the offshore islands of Songkhla and in 1775 had been appointed governor of the province. Subsequently the house became the town hall and then fell into neglect in the 1950s, until it was restored by the Fine Arts Department for use as the Songkhla National Museum.

Beyond the ticket desk at the west end is a central courtyard, off which are the display rooms. In the **courtyard** are old black and white photographs of the house and of old Songkhla, including the old city gate, which was demolished early in the 20C to make way for road improvements, and the *chedi* of Wat Chathing Phra, covered with thick vegetation.

The most important room on the **ground floor** is to the left of the ticket desk. Exhibits here include two from Sathing Phra: a 7C stone image of the Buddha in *dhyāna mudrā*, possibly from Funan, and the torso of a long-robed Vishnu image attributed to the 7C–8C. Also of note are a number of fine small bronzes, including an 8C–9C bronze figure of the *bodhisattva* Padmapani, backed by a flaming aureole and seated on a lotus throne in the *lalitāasana* posture, which was found at a village near Sathing Phra, but may have been made at Nalanda in India; a standing 9C–10C image of Shiva with a flaming aureole round his head; and an elaborate standing four-armed image of the *bodhisattva* Avalokiteshvara dating from the 10C or 11C.

There are three small rooms on the south side of the courtyard. The first has prehistoric exhibits, including Ban Chiang pottery, clay rollers, bracelets and beads. The second room is devoted to Dvaravati art, and the third contains a variety of artefacts found locally, including Northern Song (10C–12C) and Ming (14C–17C) ceramics. Along the north side of the courtyard are more displays of ceramics.

On the **upper floor** can be seen examples of the magnificent carved wooden panels in the Chinese style that were made in the 19C for the houses of Chinese merchants in Songkhla. Exhibits in the room of Sri Vijaya art include a late 6C stone *linga* from old Yarang in Pattani province; an 8C–9C bronze dancing *yoginī* from Sathing Phra; a beautiful 7C–9C bronze image of Avalokiteshvara holding a rosary in his right hand (the left arm is missing); a 9C–10C bronze image of the Tantric goddess Shyamtara seated in *lalitāsana*, the right hand in *varada mudrā* and the left holding a blue lotus; wooden Buddha images, some of them gilded and lacquered; and votive tablets.

Other rooms contain furniture, including a finely carved bed used by King Mongkut when he visited Songkhla in 1859; an unusual teapot made from an ostrich egg; and examples of different Thai art styles. Of note among the latter is a late 12C sandstone image of Vishnu.

In the **outer courtyard** are some wooden gables removed from Wat Wang in Phatthalung, and another from Wat Matchimawat in Songkhla.

To the north of the museum along T. Laem Sai is a small hill known as **Khao Tang Kuan**. A flight of steps leads up from T. Ratchadamnoen past a red brick pavilion built for a visit by King Mongkut to the summit, where there is a small **lighthouse** and a rather dull *chedi*. The views over the town and coast are good.

At the north end of T. Laem Sai are the crenellated walls of **Pom Pak Nam Laem Sai**, a fort built during the reign of King Mongkut. Apart from a number of cannon, there is now little to see here. Beyond the fort a road runs north to the northern tip of the peninsula, past the ferry station, which operates a regular shuttle service across the strait. Amid the pine trees on the cape are several excellent **seafood restaurants**. **Samila beach**, which runs along the coast from the *Samila Hotel*, becomes quite lively at weekends.

A block east from the National Museum is a small building dedicated to the life and career of Prem Tinsulanonda, a native of Songkhla who was prime minister from 1980–88. It is of interest chiefly to specialists.

To the south of the National Museum are the main shopping district and markets of Songkhla. Further south on T. Sai Buri is **WAT MATCHIMAWAT**, one of the town's most important monuments. It was founded in the late Ayutthaya period by the citizens of Songkhla and elevated to the status of a royal monastery by King Vajiravudh in 1917. The entrance is through a gate on T. Sai Buri, opposite the junction with T. Yala. On the front left is the Sala Rusi ('Hermit's Pavilion') built during King Mongkut's reign. The walls of this curious building are pierced on all sides by entrances with rounded arches. Also of note are the murals on the inner cornices, painted in 1902 and restored in 1967, which show different yogic positions of the ascetic, with explanatory captions in verse. On the inner side of the gables are inscribed recipes for certain illnesses. The texts are now very faded, but the paintings can still be clearly seen.

Beyond the Sala Rusi are the three main buildings of the *wat*: the museum on the left, the *ubosot* in the centre, and the *wihan* on the right. The **ubosot**, which is built of stuccoed brick and is surrounded by a low wall of glazed ceramic tiles, dates from between 1851 and 1865, although the pairs of *bai sema* placed on elaborate pedestals were probably removed from the original late 18C *ubosot*. At each end are two pairs of carved wooden doors flanked by the Chinese stone statues which were widely used in the 19C as ballast on Chinese merchant ships and frequently then served as *dvārapālas* to ward off evil spirits. Those at the west

end hold a miniature pagoda, a stringed instrument, a parasol and a serpent; those at the east end carry a stick, a perforated disc, and a short sword.

The interior walls are entirely covered with **magnificent murals** painted in 1863, depicting episodes from the ten last *jātaka* tales, especially the *Vessantara Jātaka* and the life of the historical Buddha. Many of them are painted in a realistic style showing Western influence and portray scenes from daily life, houses in Chinese or

Mural painting in Wat Matchimawat, Songkhla.
A detail from an episode of the Mahajanaka Jātaka

Western style and figures of Chinese and Westerners. They were extensively restored when the *wat* was renovated by the Fine Arts Department in 1971. The principal Buddha image in the *ubosot* is carved from alabaster and is seated in *dhyāna mudrā*. To the south of the *ubosot* is the **wihan**, a plain rectangular building of stuccoed brick, which was the *ubosot* of the original 18C temple. On the gable above the entrance is a woodcarving portraying the five first disciples of the Buddha.

In the **museum**, which is housed in the *sala kan parian* next to the *ubosot*, is a greatly venerated late 6C stone image of Ganesha. This image, which is covered with gold leaf, has four arms and is seated in the posture of royal ease (*mahārāja lalitāsana*).

The museum also contains a miscellany of other objects, ranging from bronze heads of Buddha images to stuffed animals and antique typewriters, most of little importance. Near the far end is a glass cabinet in which are several fine, small bronzes, including a 9C–10C image found near Sathing Phra of the bearded, pot-bellied Agastya, one of the Vedic seers and considered to be a manifestation of Shiva as the divine teacher. In the same case is a 13C image of the Tantric Buddhist tutelary deity Hevajra or Heruka, only 14cm high; and a 9C–10C image 16cm high of the plump Jambhala, the Buddhist god of wealth, seated in *lalitāsana* on a circular cushion, with a lemon in his right hand, his left hand round the neck of a mongoose disgorging a garland of jewels, and a row of money bags at his feet.

Wat Pho Pathamawat, further south on T. Ramwithi, has murals in the renovated *ubosot*, which was built during Mongkut's reign. The murals on the lower parts of the interior walls are older than those in Wat Matchimawat and rather damaged. There are painted imitation bamboo columns between the windows, and above each window is a niche containing a seated Buddha image. The principal Buddha image at the east end is flanked by two standing images in high relief in niches behind.

The oldest part of Songkhla is in the narrow streets to the west of Wat Matchimawat and Wat Pho Pathamawat. Here a number of late 19C houses can be seen, especially on T. Nakhon Nai and T. Nakhon Nok. This is also the Muslim quarter, with a mosque and small cafés serving halal food.

Ko Yo

A very pleasant day-long **excursion** can be made to the small island of Ko Yo in the Thale Sap Songkhla, and along the coast to Sathing Phra.

Ko Yo is joined to the mainland by two long bridges to north and south. Take road 407 towards Hat Yai and turn right to the island at the intersection with road 408. Pass through Ban Suan Thurian, the southernmost village on the island, and continue across the island to a turning to the left which runs along the west side of the island before rejoining the main road near the north bridge. This delightful detour passes many charming old wooden houses roofed with Songkhla's distinctive clay tiles and runs through several picturesque fishing villages before reaching **Wat Thai Yo**, which is set in a pretty lakeside location amid coconut palms. Of note is the rickety *kuti* consisting of a central arched gateway flanked by raised timber buildings. On the hill behind is an old *chedi*, damaged by lightning, but still with its original stucco decoration on the east side. Ko Yo can also be reached by long-tailed boat from Songkhla.

The road rejoins road 408 near the foot of the driveway leading to the **Institute for Southern Thai Studies**, built in the late 1980s. This has an interesting **museum** with displays illustrating southern Thai culture, crafts and traditions. The museum buildings stand on a steep hillside overlooking the sea, some of them with wooden panelling in the southern Thai style. Only a few of the huge number of exhibits are labelled in English, although a pamphlet in English and a rough plan are available from the ticket desk.

Included in the displays are collections of prehistoric artefacts, ceramics, shadow puppets, basketry and woven mats, traditional musical instruments and hand-woven textiles. There are some delightful painted wooden partitions from Wat Thale Noi in Phatthalung province.

From the museum, continue north on road 408 across the second bridge towards Sathing Phra. On the right 2.5km beyond the bridge is **Pom Khao Noi**, a small crenellated fort, now rather overgrown. 200m further, a turning to the right leads to **Wat Khao Noi** (500m). On the hilltop behind this monastery is the partially repaired ruin of a very large brick *chedi* on a square base. Scattered around the low hills to the east are several more ruins of buildings that formed part of the 18C settlement of Songkhla.

Further north on road 408, a turning to the left beyond the 126km stone leads through rice fields dotted with sugar-palms to **Khu Khut Waterfowl Sanctuary** (3km) on the east shore of the Thale Sap, where boats may be chartered. This important sanctuary, which has more than 220 resident and visitor species, is best visited between November and January, early in the morning when the birds are most active.

1km further north, in the middle of **Sathing Phra**, is **Wat Chathing Phra**, which has a fine *chedi* (Phra Chedi Prathan), 20m high, in pure Sri Vijaya style, but in its present form probably dating only from the 17C. The *wihan* has fine stucco decoration, which may date from the Ayutthaya period, on the gable and round the doors. It contains a reclining image of the Buddha, above which on the east wall is a very faded mural.

Sathing Phra was probably founded in the 11C and flourished during the late Sri Vijaya period until the end of the 13C. The sites that have been excavated in the area have yielded many sculptures, but few architectural remains of this period.

Continue north on road 408 to the 110km stone, where a turning to the left leads to **Wat Pha Kho**, which stands on the top of a low hill. The base of the *chedi*, founded in 1514 during the reign of King Ramathibodi II of Ayutthaya, is surrounded by a portico with a tiled roof. The bell-shaped relic chamber is similar in shape to that at Wat Chathing Phra. In one of the buildings of the *wat* is a statue of the greatly venerated monk, Phra Luang Pho Thuat, who resided here in the 17C. A local legend tells how he was kidnapped by pirates, who took him off in their ship. When they were becalmed and ran out of drinking-water, their lives were saved by the monk, who miraculously changed salt water into fresh water and was then freed by his grateful captors. Behind the *chedi* is a large reclining Buddha image.

On the return journey to Songkhla, an alternative to crossing to the mainland by the bridges and Ko Yo is to take the vehicle ferry across the mouth of the Thale Sap Songkhla.

54 · Songkhla to Pattani

Roads *408, 43 and 42, 101km. The route runs close to the sea for part of the way. Detour c 50km to Sai Khao Falls National Park and Wat Chang Hai on road 409.*

Leave Songkhla on T. Ramwithi (road 408) to the south and after 27km turn right on to road 43, the main Hat Yai–Pattani highway. The small market town of **Chana**, 11km further south, is an important **dove breeding centre**. Barred ground doves are highly prized by local Muslims, who breed them for singing competitions. Winning birds can be worth several thousand dollars and bring considerable prestige to their owners. During competitions, which can attract several hundred entrants, the birds are raised in cages on five-metre poles placed in a field about four metres apart. The judges select the winning birds according to standard rules relating to the tone and clarity of their song. Shops in Chana sell delicate wooden cages for the birds.

Beyond Chana the road runs towards the coast. In the small fishing village of **Ban Pak Bang** soon after the 12km stone, a turning to the left leads over a small wooden bridge to the edge of the estuary where a number of the beautifully painted traditional Malay fishing boats known as *kolae* can often be found drawn up on the beach. These distinctive fishing craft are a common sight along the coast of Pattani and Narathiwat.

Road 43 runs along the coast for c 15km beyond Ban Pak Bang, separated from the beach by pine trees and coconut palms. There are quiet resorts and cafés at regular intervals along the coast.

At the junction of roads 42 and 43, Pattani lies 16km to the left, but a 50km detour can be made to the right to the delightful **Nam Tok Sai Khao National Park** and Wat Chang Hai. To reach the park, take road 42 to the south and after 7km turn on to road 409. After a further 7.5km, turn right in Ban Na Pradu to the park headquarters and car park on road 4072. The cascades are situated a short walk from the car park, buried in a deep gully and flanked by thick vegetation. A charming path climbs through the narrow gorge beside the torrent to the main falls. Food stalls near the car park offer snacks and drinks.

A further 2.5km south on road 409, a right turn leads to **Wat Chang Hai**, which is in an enclosure beside the railway line. This *wat* is dominated by a huge modern *chedi* and the mausoleum of a revered monk, Phra Luang Pho Thuat, who lived at Wat Pha Kho in Sathing Phra district (see p 400). The principal image of the monk is behind glass, but a smaller replica has been placed within reach of pilgrims to enable them to make their offerings of gold leaf.

Pattani

Return north to road 42 and continue through Nong Chik to Pattani (pop. 36,000).

The modern part of Pattani, containing the government offices and schools, is on the west side of the town along road 42, but the older and more interesting heart of the town lies on the east bank of the Pattani River. Pattani is the capital of one of Thailand's four predominantly Muslim provinces, and there is a large Muslim Malay quarter on the south side of the town, centred round the former ruler's palace of Chabang Tigo. Here goats and sheep wander in the streets, and there are small Muslim cafés serving delicious mutton samosa. The town centre is dominated by Chinese, who have been trading in Pattani since at least the 15C. There is also a large fishing fleet, which, since only the smaller *kolae* can pass beneath the bridge, uses moorings on the river bank downstream of it.

■ **Hotels and services**. The *Chong Ah* at 190–4 T. Prida and the adjacent *Palace Hotel* round the corner have adequate, clean rooms. Most comfortable is the inconveniently located *My Gardens*, in the western suburbs at 8/28 T. Charoen Pradit. Cheap rooms are available at the riverside *Thai Ann* and *Thai Wah* hotels, on the east bank.

The *Thai Farmers Bank* is on T. Yarang on the east side of the town; the *Bangkok Bank* is at 26 T. Udomwithi. The **post office** is on the corner of T. Phiphit and T. Pattani Phirom, near the bridge.

A lively **night market** selling food and drinks fills the lane between T. Phiphit, Soi Talat Tet Niwet 2 and T. Udomwithi, near the Palace Hotel. A **municipal market** is held during the day on the corner of T. Rudi and T. Naklua. The *DK Book House* on T. Nong Chik near the clock tower has a good selection of English-language publications.

■ **Transport.** There are regular express **bus** services to Narathiwat, Yala and Hat Yai, and slower services stopping at Chana, Sai Buri etc. **Share-taxis** to Hat Yai and Songkhla can be hired from termini on T. Prida and T. Pattani Phirom.

History

The area around modern Pattani (Malay: Patani) and Sai Buri most probably formed the nucleus of Langkasuka, one of several small Indianised harbour kingdoms that first emerged in the Malay peninsula and the Gulf of Thailand in the early centuries AD. Langkasuka is mentioned in Chinese sources of the early 2C and in Arab and Chinese sources of the 7C, and is listed among the dependencies of the east Javanese maritime power of Majapahit in the 14C. During the 15C control over Pattani was disputed between the Muslim rulers of Malacca and the kings of Ayutthaya, but by the time of the Portuguese conquest of Malacca in 1511, it was firmly under Thai suzerainty. By that time also the ruler of Pattani had been converted to Islam, probably in the 1470s. The exodus of Chinese merchants from Malacca to Pattani after 1511 led to the development of strong trading links between Brunei and Pattani. The Pattani Chinese brought pepper to Brunei in exchange for camphor, benzoin, sago, wax and slaves, and by the early 17C Pattani had become the leading entrepôt outside China for the buying and selling of Chinese goods, notably silk and porcelain, as well as an important trading centre for a wide variety of other Indian and Indonesian goods. The Portuguese acquired a share in this trade after their conquest of Malacca by gaining permission under the terms of their commercial treaties with Ayutthaya to trade at Pattani, Nakhon Si Thammarat and other Thai ports on both sides of the peninsula, as well as at Ayutthaya itself, but by 1630 they had been ousted from their position in these places by the Dutch East India Company, which established its first factory at Pattani in 1602. In 1611 the English East India Company sent two Dutchmen, known in the English records as Peter Floris and Luca Antheunis, in the *Globe* to trade in the Bay of Bengal and the Gulf of Thailand, and the following year English factories were established at Pattani and Ayutthaya. After the fall of Ayutthaya to the Burmese in 1767, Pattani attempted to reassert its independence. However, the Thais retaliated and in 1786 destroyed the city. A new city was founded on the present site, and since that time Pattani has been a fully integrated province of the Thai kingdom, although the relations between the predominantly Muslim Malay population and the authorities in Bangkok are often uneasy.

A pleasant exploration of central Pattani lasting about an hour can be made by *samlo* or on foot. Follow the east bank of the river north from the bridge along T. Pattani Phirom, past some rather rickety hotels on the river bank and a simple concrete mosque. Between T. Rudi and T. Aneru are several lovely **traditional Thai buildings** with ornate wooden panelling, and in the same area a few large late 19C and early 20C brick houses built in southern Chinese style with tiled roofs.

Turn right along T. Aneru to the Chinese temple of **Ling Che Kong** (San Chao Leng Chu Kiang), on the left side. The original temple was built in 1547 and today houses a statue of Lim Kun Yew (Lim Ko Nieo), a character from a local legend of the 17C.

The story goes that a Chinese Muslim craftsman called Tok Kayan, or Lim Toh Kiam before he embraced Islam, had come from China to make his fortune in Pattani. During the reign of Queen Raja Biru (1616–24), he worked at the harbour as a supervisor of exports and imports and also cast cannon for the queen, who needed them for the defence of the kingdom. At this time his younger sister, Lim Kun Yew, arrived in Pattani to try to persuade her brother to return to China. When she learned he had adopted Islam, thereby dishonouring his religion, and did not want to return, she hanged herself from a cashew tree. The Chinese in Pattani saw her death as a heroic sacrifice, took the cashew tree, made an image of her and worshipped it. The image was called Tok Pe Kong Mek and was kept in the Tok Pe Kong temple in the old harbour until the destruction of Pattani in 1786, when it was moved to its present site at the Ling Che Kong temple. Lim Toh Khiam may perhaps have been an historical figure, Lin Tao-ch'ien, an infamous Teochiu pirate active off the Chinese coast in the South China Sea in the 1560s and 1570s, who settled in Pattani after 1578. Each February or March, four statues of Lim Kun Yew are carried in procession through the streets.

At the south end of the town, on T. Yarang, is Pattani's principal **mosque** (**Masayit Klang**). It has conspicuous green domes and is surrounded by gardens.

Further south is the Muslim quarter of Chabang Tigo (Malay: Cabang Tiga). The former governor's residence, **Wang Chabang Tigo**, is hidden away in an area of quiet shady lanes near the river. The house was built in 1847 for the governor of Pattani and remained his official residence until the early 20C. Subsequently, the last raja of Pattani, Tengku Abdul Kadir bin Tengku Kamaruddin, lived here till his abdication in 1921. He died in Kota Baharu, Kelantan in 1931.

The rather dilapidated house, in a simple blend of Thai and Chinese styles, is closed to visitors, but can be seen through the Chinese-style gateway in the east wall. William Cameron, an English visitor writing in 1883, describes the palace as:

> 'a rather handsome one-storeyed building situated about a furlong from the river, it is built of brick plastered, and the roof, which is tiled, is decorated in the Siamese fashion, which much resembles that of the Chinese, if indeed it is not altogether borrowed there from; it has an extensive court and very wide double verandahs at front and sides, the floor of the inner one being raised a step above that of the outer; both floors are handsomely laid with large squares of polished tiles, and the roof is supported by numerous massive pillars, which give to the whole a rather imposing effect. Here the Râja holds court, receives visitors, and deals out judgement; the dwelling rooms are partitioned off by tall wood screens extending from floor to roof...and elaborately carved, coloured and gilt.'

Over the bridge on the west bank on the corner of T. Sai Buri, is the shrine containing the town's *lak muang*. When the fishing fleet is in port, the river bank is busy with fishermen repairing nets and unloading their catches.

55 · Pattani to Narathiwat

Road 42, 53km from Pattani to Sai Buri. Detour via Yaring (8km) and coastal route via Panare on roads 4061 and 4157. From Sai Buri to Narathiwat, 50km on road 42. Alternative coastal route via roads 4155 and 4136 from Bacho.

Leave Pattani on road 42 and head east towards Sai Buri. On the left side after 5km, just before the 11km stone, is the restored ruin of the 19C brick **Kru Se Mosque** (Masayit Kru Se) beside a large Chinese tomb. The mosque was built by Tuan Sulong (1817), possibly on the site of an earlier mosque thought to have been built by Chinese Muslims during the reign of Mudhaffar Syah (d. 1564), ruler of the Malay kingdom of Patani. Local folklore tells of a Muslim Chinese community, perhaps of Yunnanese origin, which once lived in Pattani and may have played a significant role in Pattani's conversion to Islam.

Local histories and archaeological evidence indicate that the area round the mosque was the site of the old capital of Pattani. Aerial photographs have revealed the outline of a 10ha rectangular area surrounded by moats, just east of the present village of **Ban Kru Se**. It is likely that this rectangle contained a fortified citadel in which was the royal residence. Nothing of the fortifications remains today, but Ayutthaya-style ceramics have been found in considerable quantities in the area, together with Chinese porcelain of the Ming (1368–1644) and Qing (1644–1911) dynasties, indicating that Pattani was an important centre of international trade at the time. Like Sathing Phra, old Pattani was built on sand ridges, allowing close access to the sea without the danger of flooding.

A short distance beyond the mosque a turning to the left leads to **Yaring**, a predominantly Muslim market town on the bank of the Yaring River. In the town centre is the former governor's residence. There are still many traditional wooden houses in this pleasant little town.

Beyond Yaring the road rejoins the main highway, which continues southeast to **Palat**. Turn left in Palat on to road 4061 to **Wat Khuan Nai**, which is on the right side after 1km. The adjacent Wat Khuan Nok is of little interest, except for a reclining image of the Buddha on the hill behind. Wat Khuan Nai, however, has a charming raised wooden *kuti* with painted interior wall panels and ceilings. A small concrete terrace reached up two flights of steps has been added to the front. On the hilltop behind the *kuti* is an *ubosot*, its interior walls painted with amusing murals depicting scenes of daily life—people fighting, policemen, bicycles and carriages. The predominant colours are blue and yellow. Some parts have been rather carelessly repainted. On a large altar are three images of the Buddha seated in *bhūmisparśa mudrā*.

Continue along road 4061 for 12km to the coastal fishing village of Panare, from where road 4157 runs southeast for 26km along the coast to **Sai Buri**, a small port near the mouth of the Sai Buri River. In the town is the ruin of a 19C brick mosque with a clay tiled roof. Nearby is the former governor's residence, Wang Kao Sai Buri, and several other beautiful old wooden houses.

From Sai Buri road 42 continues inland, south to Narathiwat. Just beyond Bacho, a road to the right between the 71km and 72km stones runs through rice fields for 4km towards the hills of **Budo-Sungai Padi National Park** and the **Bacho Waterfalls**. Food stalls and a small café near the car park offer cheap snacks.

Taloh Mano Mosque, Pattani

Just north of **Ban Lubosawo**, between the 75km and 76km stones, is a concrete road on the right leading to the charming **Taloh Mano Mosque** (Masayit Wadin Husen). This distinctive building is one of Pattani's oldest mosques, probably dating from the mid-19C, although there has been a mosque on this site since 1624. It once had a thatched roof, but now has the characteristic orange-brown terracotta tiles found commonly in Pattani and Songkhla. Although renovated several times, it is one of the few surviving examples of a mosque in a style which was probably indigenous to southern Thailand and northern Malaysia. Behind the more recent *balai* or entrance hall and separated from it by a decorated wooden partition is the main prayer hall. The ventilation panels above the windows are of finely carved wood. At the far end of the prayer hall is the *mihrab*, a later addition.

Road 42 continues south directly to Narathiwat, but travellers with their own vehicles should consider returning north to Bacho, where a turning to the right on to road 4155 leads to the more interesting coast road.

NARATHIWAT (pop. 33,000), at the mouth of the Bang Nara River, only 67km from the Malaysian frontier, is a small and friendly town, inhabited mainly by ethnic Malays and Chinese. It is the most southerly settlement of any significance on Thailand's east coast, and is pleasant enough to merit an overnight stop.

■ **Hotels and services**. The *Tan Yong* at 16/1 T. Sopha Phisai is one of Narathiwat's best hotels. The friendly and simple *Narathiwat* at 341 T. Phupha Phakdi is a good choice for low budget travellers, with fine river views.

The *Bangkok Bank* is at 311 T. Phupha Phakdi and the *Thai Farmers Bank* is nearby. The **post office** and international telephone is on T. Phichit Bamrung.

■ **Transport**. There are frequent **buses** to Tak Bai, Sungai Kolok, Pattani and Yala etc from different termini in the town. Ask at the hotel. **Share-taxis** and **air-conditioned minibuses** run to Sungai Kolok and Ban Taba. The nearest **railway station** is at Tan Yong Mat, 18km southwest of Narathiwat, with several services daily to Sungai Kolok and two trains daily to Bangkok. *THAI* has **flights** thrice weekly to Phuket. The booking office is at 322–4 T. Phupha Phakdi.

■ **Festival**. *Kolae* races are held on the Bang Nara River in September.

Most of the hotels, markets and banks can be found along T. Phupha Phakdi, the town's commercial heart. At the north end of the town, along T. Phichit Bamrung, is the Muslim fishing village of Bang Nara, where dozens of small boats, including the distinctive *kolae*, can usually be seen. On the left side shortly before the village is the modern **provincial mosque**. Over the bridge near the fishing village is **Narathat Beach**, where there are several cafés beneath the casuarina trees. However, this beach is dangerous for swimming and bathers are recommended to go to the beach at **Ao Manao**, 3km south of Narathiwat.

A couple of pleasant short **excursions** can be made from Narathiwat, either as day trips or en route to Malaysia.

▶Road 4084 runs southeast from Narathiwat over the Bang Nara River and after 7km passes on the left side the palace of **Phra Tamnak Thaksin Ratcha Niwet** where the king stays every year in August and September for the *kolae* races. When the royal family is not in residence, this modern palace is open (09.00–16.00) to the public. The *Panan Resort*, 2km further south, has adequate rooms near the sea.

Stop in the small market square of **Tak Bai**, and walk the few hundred metres to **Wat Chonthara Singhe** on the river bank. This monastery has a beautiful wooden raised *wihan*, painted pale blue, red and gold, with terracotta roof tiles. In the nearby *ubosot*, built in 1873 and thoroughly renovated in 1985, are some magnificent murals painted during the reign of King Chulalongkorn. The *ubosot* is usually kept locked, but the monks are happy to show it to visitors.

From the market square in Tak Bai a sturdy wooden footbridge crosses the Tak Bai River to the narrow island of **Ko Yao**, where there is a fishing community, and *kolae* can usually be seen drawn up on the eastern shore.

The frontier village and market of **Taba** lies a few kilometres south of Tak Bai. A regular ferry service operates across the Kolok River to the Malaysian frontier checkpoint of Pengkalan Kubor, from where there are frequent taxis and buses to Kota Baharu.◀

▶Leave Narathiwat on road 4055 towards Tan Yong Mat. After 7km a huge image of the Buddha seated in *vajrāsana*, known as **Phra Phuttha Thaksin Ming Mongkhon**, can be seen on a small hill to the right of the road. This 23m concrete image, built in the 1960s, has on several occasions been the target of sabotage attempts by radical Muslim groups.

Continue to Manang Tayo and turn right on to road 4056 towards **Sungai Kolok**, the border town and railhead of the southern line. For travellers arriving from Malaysia there is a TAT **information** office near the frontier, but there is little to do in the town, which has acquired a somewhat unsavoury reputation as a weekend entertainment centre for Malaysian men. Note that the frontier checkpoint (open 05.00–18.00) may sometimes close early.◀

56 · Pattani to Yala and Betong

Road *410, 174km. To Yala 39km via Yarang. Yala to Betong 135km.*

Take T. Yarang south from Pattani town centre and turn left at the end on to road 410. At the intersection in the centre of the small market town of **Yarang** (15km) the turning to the left leads to the archaeological sites of the so-called Yarang complex, which some scholars have suggested may have been the location of the early Indianised kingdom of Langkasuka (p 402). The excavations have concentrated on three moated sites to the east of modern Yarang.

The earliest evidence has come from the sites at **Ban Wat**, to the south of road 4061, and **Ban Chalae**, to the north, where Dvaravati Wheels of the Law and Buddha images (6C–8C), and some stucco and terracotta objects which show influence of Indian Gupta art (4C–5C) have been found, indicating that this area was already by this early date established as a centre of Mahayana Buddhism. At the Ban Chalae site are the ruins of two large brick *chedi* inside the old east moat.

Ban Prawae, to the north of Ban Chalae, is the site of the 12C or 13C city of **Muang Prawae**. Some traces of ramparts and dikes and the bases of several brick *chedi* are all that remain of the original city, but the site is surrounded by a rectangular wall and moat with bastions at each corner, which appear to date from the 17C–18C. Local accounts record that the governor of the vassal Malay state of Patani moved his capital to Prawae after the Thais destroyed the port in 1786. In 1790, as he was preparing to reassert Patani's independence, he received word that the Thais were planning an attack. He fortified Prawae accordingly, but was defeated and killed in 1791.

From Yarang road 410 continues south for 24km through Malay villages and occasional bamboo groves to **YALA** (pop. 52,000), capital of Thailand's southernmost province. The town itself has few sites of interest, but it is a convenient base from which to explore the surrounding area. The commercial centre containing the hotels and markets lies on the south side of the railway line, while to the north is the largely residential Muslim quarter, where goats wander in the weed-covered lanes and where the principal mosque in the province is located.

■ **Hotels and services**. Best is the comfortable *Yala Rama* at 21 T. Si Bamrung. Cheaper and good value for money is the *Thep Wiman* at 31–37 T. Si Bamrung.
The *Bangkok Bank* is at 112–8 T. Phiphit Phakdi and the *Thai Farmers Bank* is on T. Phrachin. The **post office** and international telephone are on T. Sirorot.

■ **Transport**. **Buses** leave from different points, depending on their destination. **Share-taxis** to Hat Yai, Songkhla and Betong are available from T. Phiphit Phakdi. The **railway station** has several services daily to Sungai Kolok, and there are two trains daily to Bangkok.

■ **Festivals** Yala hosts the annual ASEAN Barred Ground Dove Festival, usually in May, when dove lovers from all over Southeast Asia converge on Suan Khuan Muang, a large park on the south side of the town.

Go 8km west of Yala along road 409 to reach **Wat Khuha Phimuk** (Wat Na Tham, open 08.30–17.00). This important place of pilgrimage is an impressive cave temple in the side of a limestone cliff on the left of the road. The modern temple in front of the caverns is of little merit. A figure of a humorously fearsome *yakṣa* guards the entrance to the most important cavern (Tham Phra Non), inside which is a large image of the reclining Buddha sheltered by two entwined seven-headed *nāgas*. This statue, known as Phra Phuttha Saiyat, is nearly 25m in length. It is thought to date back to the Dvaravati period and to have been restored in the U Thong period. The airy cavern, lit by natural openings to the sky, contains numerous other statues, including images of Chinese deities.

A British traveller, William Cameron, writing in 1882 described it thus:

> 'On entering I found, after penetrating a small cavern, a couple of large doors closing up the approach to what was apparently the cave we were seeking. On opening these doors, I was startled at the sight of what appeared, in the dim light, to be a row of giant men guarding the entrance; a closer investigation proved them to be statues, and, as I afterwards found, Siamese idols. Passing this guard, we made our way along a lofty natural corridor or vestibule, and found ourselves in an immense cavern about 60 feet in height, 200 feet wide, and about 500 feet long. From its roof hung masses of stalactites resembling the groins of an arched roof, and stretched in a recumbent position, and facing a large opening in the cliff, which let in a flood of light, lay a figure, about 100 feet long, of what I took to represent Bhudda [sic]. The head reclined upon the right arm, whilst the left arm lay by the side of the figure, the face was tolerably well painted, and the robe was coloured green and its edges gilt.'

Continue several hundred metres along the road which passes in front of Wat Na Tham, and then turn left to reach another cave temple, **Wat Tham Silpa**, which is in a cliff on the left side after c 1km. This rarely visited cave contains fragments of murals in poor condition dating from the Sri Vijaya period. A good torch is essential, and visitors must beware of the snakes which dwell within.

From Yala, road 410 heads south through thickly forested countryside towards Betong, the last town before the Malaysian frontier. Beyond Bannang Sata the road starts climbing gently into the border hills. Turn right along a rough track after the 56km stone to reach **Bang Lang National Park** and the beautiful **Than To Waterfalls**. The charming scenery of this park provides a fine setting for a picnic, but visitors should bring their own food.

The border town of **Betong** can be quite damp and chilly in the early morning and, despite the large number of hotels, there is little to detain the visitor. At weekends the town fills up with Malaysians seeking shopping bargains and enjoying the raucous nightlife.

■ **Hotels and services**. Among the better hotels are the expensive *Betong Merlin*, and the more moderately priced *Cathay*. The **tourist information** office is at 2/1 T. Amontit. The *Bangkok Bank* is at 11/2 T. Saritdet.

■ **Transport**. **Buses**, **share-taxis** and **air-conditioned minibuses** operate from Betong to Yala. **Songthaeo** run a shuttle service to the border.

In **Ban Piyamit**, 9km from Betong, there is a network of tunnels built by Malaysian communist guerrillas in the 1970s and used by them as a camp. The camp was one of several close to the Thai-Malaysian border from which the Communist Party of Malaya launched hit-and-run attacks into Malaysia. Some stretches of tunnels have been preserved, and artefacts from the camp are on display. To explore the tunnels, a torch is needed.

THE WEST PENINSULAR COAST

57 · Chumphon, Ranong and environs

Roads 327 and 4, 117km. The route runs west to the Burmese border before turning south to run parallel to the Kra River estuary. This route has many natural beauties, including waterfalls, caverns, beaches, coral reefs and islands. Especially recommended are excursions to the Surin Islands and the magnificent Similan archipelago.

Leave Chumphon on road 327, crossing the Tha Taphao River on the south side of the town, and after c 6km join road 4, which runs west across the isthmus to Kra Buri, passing along the way several waterfalls and the Phra Khayang Cave. The road follows the Kra River estuary south to the small provincial capital of **RANONG** (pop. 22,000), from where it is possible to arrange excursions to the beautiful Surin Archipelago National Park in the Andaman Sea, or the nearer islands of the Phayam Archipelago National Park. Ranong is a pleasant town and, like Phuket and Songkhla, has some good examples of late 19C Chinese architecture. It is well known for its hot springs, c 1500m east of the town centre.

■ **Hotels and services.** The *Jansom Thara* at 2/10 T. Phetkasem is the best hotel, but it is outside the town centre next to the thermal springs. More central are the *Sin Thawi Hotel* and the *Asia Hotel*, both on T. Ruangrat, where the **post office** and the *Bangkok Bank* are also located.

■ **Transport.** Regular **buses** run north to Chumphon and Bangkok, south to Phuket. Boat trips to Ko Phayam and to the Surin Islands can be arranged through the Jansom Thara Hotel or directly from the port at Saphan Pla, 9km from Ranong. *THAI* has four **flights** each week to Bangkok (1hr).

The half-dozen small islands that constitute the **SURIN ARCHIPELAGO NATIONAL PARK** lie nearly 60km off the coast, closer to the nearest Burmese islands than to the Thai mainland. The park headquarters, where there are bungalows and a restaurant, is on Surin Nua, the largest island. Its southern neighbour, Surin Tai, is home to a small fishing community of Moken (Thai: Chao Le) fishing community, the semi-nomadic sea gypsies who inhabit many of these west coast islands.

The islands are covered with deciduous and evergreen forest and are surrounded by healthy coral reefs, which are among the very finest in Thai waters and are popular with snorkellers and scuba divers. Several species of turtle visit the islands, including the leatherback and Ridley's, and nearly 30 species of bird have been recorded. A visit is highly recommended and is best made between December and March or April. At other times of the year, especially during the southwest monsoon from May to October or November, the seas are often too rough.

The islands of the **Phayam archipelago** opposite the mouth of the Kra River estuary are home to communities of Moken and the site of cashew-nut plantations and a pearl farm. Day trips can be arranged at the Jansom Thara Hotel. Camping is permitted on the islands.

Road 4 heads south from Ranong c 50km to Kapoe district. Here a turning to the right leads to the 315 sq km **Laem Son National Park**, which comprises a coastline of mangrove forest and sandy beach, and a score of nearby islands. The park was established in 1983 and is home to nearly 50 bird species and dozens of crab-eating macaques. The park headquarters is at Bang Ben beach on the mainland, where there are park bungalows and a restaurant, and where it is possible to arrange boats to visit the other islands.

Beyond Kapoe the road passes through the market town of **Khura Buri**, where there is a park office and from where boats can be chartered to the Surin archipelago. The boats depart from the Phae Pla Chumphon pier in Ban Hin Lat, off to the right a short distance before Khura Buri.

At a junction c 50km south of Khura Buri, road 401 turns off left to Khao Sok National Park and Surat Thani (see Rte 49). Road 4 continues south through Takua Pa. The best hotel here is the *Amarin* at 7/5–8 T. Montri 2. Along the coast beyond Takua Pa, between the 75km and 57km stones, there is a string of beach resorts, some of which can arrange boat trips to the magnificent Similan archipelago, lying c 60km offshore.

Similan National Park. This archipelago, which consists of a chain of nine islands, established as the Similan National Park in 1982, contains some mature coral reefs composed of more than 200 species of hard coral. There are many fish and other marine organisms here, including manta rays and whale sharks. About 30 bird species can be found on the islands themselves, which are mostly covered with tropical rainforest. The best time to visit the islands, which are considered to provide some of the world's best scuba diving, is between December and April. The park can be reached by boat from Phuket (see Route 58), from the jetty in Thap Lamu, or by arrangement with some of the resorts along road 4 between Takua Pa and Thap Lamu. The trip from Phuket is the easiest to organise, but the most expensive.

To the right just beyond the 57km stone on road 4 is the entrance to **Khao Lak Lamru National Park**, which is set in lush forest and has several pleasant beaches and forest trails. There is a restaurant at the park headquarters.

6km further south, road 4147 turns off right to Thap Lamu jetty (5km) for boats to the Similan Islands. However, there is no regular service, and it is sometimes difficult to organise a private charter.

At **Thai Muang**, the next market town, is the 72 sq km **Khao Lampi-Hat Thai Muang National Park**, established in 1986 to protect some important turtle-nesting beaches. The park covers 72 sq km, consisting of a coastal strip and a hilly area inland, with several pleasant waterfalls, including Lampi Falls, 1500m along an earth road between the 33km and 32km stones. The turtles' nesting season lasts from November to February or March.

Road 4 continues south for 15km beyond Thai Muang as far as Khok Kloi, where road 402 forks right to the island province of **Phuket**, which is linked to the mainland by two bridges. The road runs the length of the island to Phuket town (c 45km), which is on the southeast coast (see p 415).

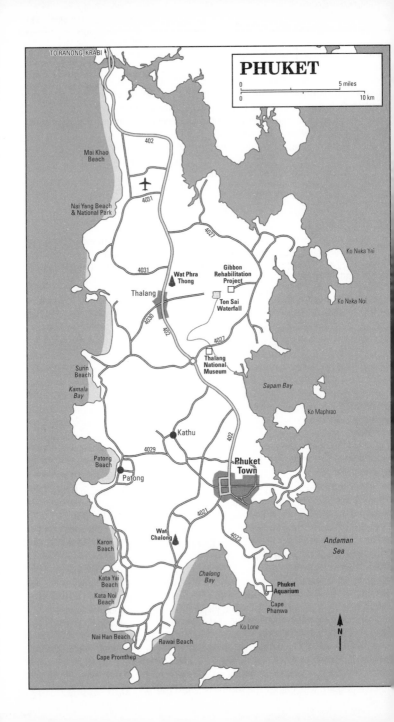

58 · Phuket

Phuket is the largest island off the coast of Thailand, being approximately the same size as Singapore. Its wealth is derived from tin, copra, rubber and more recently from tourism, as the fine sandy beaches along the west coast attract visitors all the year round, although the peak period is during the dry season between November and February. It has had the status of a province since 1933. The Malay name of the island is Ujong Salang, from which the name Junk Ceylon, by which it was formerly known to the Europeans, is derived. Phuket town, which is capital of the island, has a population of c 45,000.

■ **Information**. TAT and tourist police are at 73–5 T. Phuket (open daily 08.30–16.30). *Seng Ho* bookshop on T. Montri is the best source of English language publications.

■ **Hotels and services**. There are many hotels in the town. Among the best are the *Phuket Merlin* at 158/1 T. Yaowarat and the *Metropole* at 1 T. Montri. The *On On Hotel* at 19 T. Phangnga has cheap, adequate rooms. The TAT has a comprehensive list of accommodation. The *Bangkok Bank* is at 22 T. Phangnga, near the *Thai Farmers Bank*. The main **post office** is on the corner of T. Montri and T. Thalang and the **telecommunication centre** for international calls is on T. Phangnga.

■ **Land Transport**. **Buses** run frequently to Phangnga, Krabi, Surat Thani etc, and there are overnight air-conditioned services to Bangkok from Phuket bus terminus on T. Phangnga. **Share-taxis** can be hired to Krabi, Ranong, Surat Thani and Hat Yai from T. Phangnga. **Songthaeo** to most of Phuket's beaches can be found on T. Ranong. *Avis* and *Hertz* have desks in many of the large hotels and at the airport for **car rentals**. Cheaper rates are available from local agents in Phuket town. **Motorcycles** are available from numerous shops and agencies on T. Rasada in the town, and on Patong and Kata beaches. Since public transport is slow and infrequent, rentals are strongly recommended.

■ **Sea Transport**. Several companies operate **inter-island ferries** to the Phi Phi islands and the Similan and Surin archipelagos. **Flotilla sailing** and **yacht charters** are available from several companies in Phuket, including *Sunsail* (☎ (UK) 01705 219848; (USA) 305 524 7553), based at Sapam Bay on Phuket's east coast. Exhilarating trips by **sea canoe** into the magnificent limestone scenery of Phangnga Bay can be made by inflatable kayak with the reputable firm of *Sea Canoe Thailand*, which has an office in the *Pearl Village Hotel* on Nai Yang Beach.

■ **Flights**. THAI has up to 14 daily **flights** to Bangkok (1hr 20mins), two daily to Hat Yai (45mins), and less frequent services to Nakhon Si Thammarat (1hr 40mins), via Surat Thani (40mins) and to Narathiwat (1hr 20mins). The booking office is at 78 T. Ranong (open daily 08.00–17.00). *Bangkok Airways* flies daily to Ko Samui and Ranong; the booking office is on T. Yaowarat near the *Phuket Merlin Hotel*. **International services** from Phuket include *THAI* and *Malaysia Airlines* shared daily direct flights to Kuala Lumpur (1hr 15mins) and three flights a week to Penang (55mins). *SilkAir* has one or two daily flights to Singapore (1hr 40mins). *Dragonair* flies to Hong Kong three times a week (3hrs 25mins), and *China Airlines* has a direct service to Taipei (4hrs 20mins) five times a week. Several British **charter** companies fly direct from the UK to Phuket.

■ **Festival**. At the start of the ninth lunar month of the Chinese calendar, usually in October, a nine-day vegetarian festival is held to mark the start of the month during which Daoists abstain from eating meat in order to purify themselves and to earn merit. The festival is centred around several Chinese joss-houses in Phuket town, especially San Chao Chui Tui on Soi Phuton, off T. Ranong. The festival includes lively street processions and dancing, together with astounding acts of mortification and penance, including walking on hot coals and piercing the cheeks with sharp stakes, which apparently cause the penitents no pain.

History

The new Thai kingdom established in 1782 in Bangkok under the rule of Rama I met its first serious challenge in the Burmese invasion launched in 1785 by the Konbaung ruler, Bodawpaya (r. 1781–1819). He sent five armies simultaneously against the Thais—one from Mergui to Chumphon and Chaiya, one from Tavoy to Ratchaburi and Phetchaburi, one under Bodawpaya himself that was aimed at Bangkok and marched from Martaban across the Three Pagodas Pass to Kanchanaburi, and two more in the north to Tak and Kamphaeng Phet, and to Lampang and Phitsanulok. The first of these armies conquered Takua Pa and Takua Thung, and then marched south along the coast towards Thalang. At that time the governor of Thalang died after a long illness, so his widow and her younger sister, Chan and Suk, organised the defence of the island at Tapao harbour and at two strategic points behind Wat Phra Nang Sang in the centre of Thalang. For 11 months the Burmese invaders tried to take the town, but shortage of provisions eventually forced them to retreat to Burma. At the end of the war, to commemorate their victory, Rama I awarded the women the honorary titles of Thao Thep Krasatri and Thao Si Sunthorn. One important result of this invasion was that it prompted Rama I to strengthen Thai suzerainty over the Malay states of the peninsula—Patani, Kedah, Kelantan and Terengganu—by giving the ruler of Songkhla the title of Chao Phraya and making him responsible for Thai relations with these tributary states, directly answerable to Bangkok. There were further Burmese invasions subsequently, but none was successful, and by the beginning of the 19C peace had returned to Phuket.

Tin, which had been mined on the island since the 16C, was discovered in large quantities in Kathiu district in the late 18C, and before long several hundred tons were being mined annually. By the early 20C, production had reached more than 5000 tons a year. Chinese immigrants came to work the tin deposits and, as production boomed, Phuket town began to expand. In 1906 an Australian, Edward Thomas Miles, introduced the first tin dredger to the island. In 1903, the first rubber trees were introduced from the Malay States and the Straits Settlements.

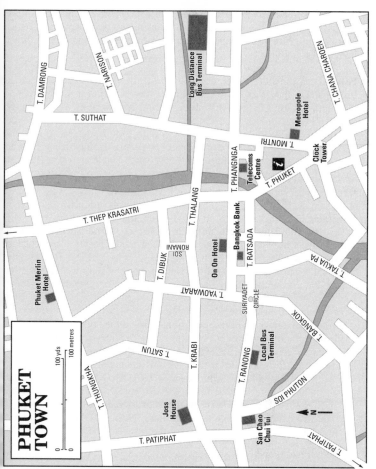

The centre of Phuket town has retained its charm, despite the enormous increase in traffic and much recent building in concrete and glass. There are still many fine examples of late 19C and early 20C **Chinese shop-houses** and some magnificent **mansions**, formerly the homes of wealthy merchants.

At the intersection of T. Thalang and T. Thep Krasatri, turn west along T. Thalang to the charming **Soi Romani**, which runs north from T. Thalang to T. Dibuk. T. Dibuk itself has a row of attractive shop-houses further to the west between T. Yaowarat and T. Satun. T. Krabi, a continuation of T. Thalang also to the west, has traditional shop-houses and, on the north side, a fine mansion set back from the road. On the northwest corner of the junction of T. Satun and T. Krabi are two especially fine Chinese mansions. Further along the north side, just before the junction with T. Patiphat is a Chinese joss-house, built in the mid-19C by immigrants who came from China to work in the burgeoning tin industry.

Turn left on to T. Patiphat and then left again on to T. Ranong. Almost immediately on the right are two more joss-houses, one of which, **San Chao Chui Tui,** plays a major role in the vegetarian festival held annually in September or October (see above).

Along the south side of T. Ranong is the **municipal market**, where piles of fresh fruit and vegetables overflow on to the pavement. T. Ranong is also the departure point for *songthaeo* to many of the island's beaches on the shores of the Indian Ocean.

Phuket town has numerous fine examples of early 20C architecture in colonial style, including the Provincial Court on T. Damrong, built in 1916, and the former Governor's Residence, now the seat of the provincial government.

Touring Phuket

Most visitors choose to stay at one of the island's many beach resorts on the west and south coasts rather than in the town itself. Until the road between Patong and Kamala beaches is improved, the island is best explored in two sections: a northern circuit taking in the National Museum, the small National Park, the Gibbon Rehabilitation Centre and the charming Butterfly Garden and Aquarium; and a southern circuit which takes in the south coast and the aquarium at Cape Phanwa. The following itineraries assume that the traveller has a privately chartered vehicle, as to rely on public transport would make the journeys slow, uncomfortable and tiring.

The northern circuit

The **Phuket Butterfly Garden and Aquarium**, on the northern outskirts of Phuket town, makes a pleasant first stop. Take T. Yaowarat north from the roundabout on T. Ranong and after 2.75km follow the sign to the right.

From the butterfly garden turn right towards the main highway, road 402, which heads north across the island towards **THALANG**. In the centre of the roundabout in Thalang are statues of the two sisters, Chan and Suk, who successfully defended Thalang in the Burmese invasion of 1785.

Turn east at the roundabout to **Thalang National Museum** (open Wed–Sun, 09.00–16.00), a few metres to the east. The museum has a small collection of regional artefacts. The displays, which are not well organised, include Indonesian *wayang* (shadow) puppets; southern Thai bamboo and rattan objects; early photographs of Phuket's rubber and tin industries; and tools of the Sakai, a nomadic proto-Malay people who live in the jungles near the Thai-Malaysian frontier. Of special note is a statue of Vishnu on the left side of the main hall. This is one of three figures found in Takua Pa district, partially embedded within the trunk of a large tree. One of the others is now in the Nakhon Si Thammarat National Museum (see p 388).

To the left of the main exhibition hall is a room with a series of dioramas, one of which records the exploits of the two sisters Chan and Suk against the Burmese in 1785.

From the museum turn east along road 4027, which bends round to the north to reach the **Gibbon Rehabilitation Project**. This is situated off to the left between the 8km and 9km stones in **Khao Phra Thaeo Wildlife Sanctuary**, an area of rainforest covering 233 sq km. The project attempts to retrain captive gibbons, most of them abandoned pets, to fend for themselves in the wild.

Road 4027 continues north before finally returning to the main highway. Turn north here and soon after turn west off the main road on to road 4031, passing the airport to reach **Hat Nai Yang National Park**. For most of the year there is little inducement to visit this coastal park, as much of the most accessible section near the airport is strewn with litter. However, between November and February, the northern stretch of coastline, which includes Mai Khao beach, is an important nesting site for the endangered leatherback and Ridley's turtles. On the edge of the park is the quiet and charming *Pearl Village Hotel*.

Follow road 4031 south through rubber plantations until it curves back east to rejoin the main highway a short distance north of Thalang. Turn south towards the centre of this rather congested market town, passing **Wat Phra Thong**, which is on the east side c 700m before the centre. In the *wihan* are the exposed head and shoulders of a partially buried image of the Buddha, covered with offerings of gold leaf. A local legend tells how a young water-buffalo herder once tethered one of his animals to a metal stake at this spot. The boy subsequently died, and his father had a dream which led him to dig at the spot where the buffalo had been tied. He discovered a solid gold image of the Buddha, but was unable to excavate it completely. Instead he built a *wat* around it. In the 18C some invading Burmese tried to steal the image, but they too were unable to remove it. The villagers later plastered over the image to protect the gold from further attempts at theft.

Turn east at the intersection in Thalang to reach **Ton Sai Waterfall**, in the west part of Khao Phra Thaeo Wildlife Sanctuary. Near the falls are some park bungalows and a restaurant.

Back in Thalang, continue west on road 4030, which heads southwest towards the coast. This road eventually leads to **Surin beach**, one of the quietest and most attractive coves on Phuket. In Surin is the island's largest mosque, evidence of the sizeable Muslim Malay population, most of whom still make their living from fishing.

To the south of Surin the sealed road continues to **Kamala Bay**, another agreeable and still little frequented beach where there are several good restaurants. Some villagers rent out bungalows here to supplement their income, and there are a few more expensive chalets. This is one of the most pleasant places to stay in Phuket. A very rough and extremely steep road, unsuitable for vehicles other than motorcycles or jeeps, heads south from Kamala, eventually reaching Patong beach.

The southern circuit

Head south from the roundabout on T. Ranong and turn left at the T-junction with road 4021. After 850m road 4023 forks left to **Phuket Aquarium** and **Cape Phanwa**, 10km to the southeast. The aquarium (open daily 08.30–16.00) is maintained by Phuket's Marine Biology Research Centre, which carries out research on the endangered species of marine turtle found along the Thai coast. It has quite a good collection of freshwater and pelagic fish on display. Nearby are several pleasant **seafood restaurants** with fine sea views. Just before the aquarium a steep road leads over a hill to the exclusive *Cape Phanwa (Panwa) Hotel*, which has its own funicular railway to take guests down to the beach.

Back on road 4021, continue south round Chalong Bay to a roundabout, from which the first exit leads down to the shore. The second leads in 5.5km to the uninteresting **Rawai beach** and then continues a further 3.5km to **Cape Promthep**, the southernmost tip of the island and a popular gathering place at sunset. The third exit leads directly to the main west coast beaches of Kata and Patong. However, the more circuitous route via Cape Promthep is recommended for these beaches.

The winding road beyond the cape climbs over a spur before descending to the attractive **Nai Han beach** and *Phuket Yacht Club*. Just before the beach, a road called Soi Naya to the right heads inland, reaching a T-junction after 2km. Turn left here, and after 500m turn left again for **Kata, Karon** and **Patong beaches** (Phuket town is straight ahead). The road to the beaches passes through a small rubber plantation and then climbs steeply up the ridge which runs behind the west coast. There are excellent views from this ridge road, which eventually descends after c 5km to Kata beach.

There are numerous hotels scattered about around **Kata Noi** and **Kata Yai**. The latter is dominated by a *Club Med* resort. Further north is Karon beach, which has another long string of hotels. On the three beaches there are altogether more than 70 different resort hotels and bungalows. North of Karon the road climbs over to Patong, passing on the way the luxurious *Meridien Phuket Hotel* in its private cove, Karon Noi.

Patong is the biggest, brashest and ugliest resort on the island, and here too the choice of accommodation, restaurants, bars and entertainment is enormous.

At the north end of Patong, road 4029 turns east across the island back to Phuket town. The road to Kamala beach (7.5km), which is very rough and steep in places, continues north along the coast.

59 · Phangnga, Krabi and environs

Roads 402 *and* 4, 97*km from Phuket town to Phangnga. Roads* 415 *and* 4, 85*km from Phangnga to Krabi.*

The coastal region of Phangnga and Krabi is outstandingly beautiful, with dozens of magnificent sandy beaches, picturesque islands, coral reefs and awe-inspiring karst seascapes. As a result, every year it attracts many thousands of tourists.

Road 402 from Phuket joins road 4 in the small market town of Khok Kloi, 9km north of the bridges linking Phuket with the mainland. Turn right towards Phangnga and follow the road past rubber and pineapple plantations to Takua Thung. Racks of latex sheets can be seen drying beside the road, in front of the neat rows of rubber trees. Along the route are several jetties where boats can be chartered for trips to see the magnificent drowned karst scenery of **PHANGNGA BAY**, which has had national park status since 1981. The green waters of the bay are dotted with scores of craggy limestone cliffs, rising sheer from the shallow seabed. Some contain caves with rock paintings, thought to date from the prehistoric or early historic period. Others hide mysterious lagoons in their interior, accessible only at low tide through natural tunnels. There are only 16 confirmed bird species in the bay, including the edible-nest swiftlet and black-nest swiftlet, although the low bird count may simply reflect the lack of a proper survey. Small mammals found on the islands in the bay include monkeys, fruit bats and lizards. Boats can be chartered from the various piers to **Phaya Nak Cave** and **Ko Khian**, both of which contain rock paintings, and further into the bay to **Ko Panyi**, where there is a Muslim village composed of houses on stilts built round a mosque on a rock, and where several large seafood restaurants cater to the hordes of tourists who pass through each day in the holiday season. To the south of Ko Panyi are **Ko Tapu** and **Ko Phing Kan**, two other islands included in most tour itineraries, but of little interest.

■ Another good way to see the bay's natural wonders is with the Phuket-based company, *Sea Canoes*, which runs excursions by inflatable canoe to some of the most spectacular parts of the bay. The TAT office in Phuket can provide information about the tours.

Continue on road 4 for 5km beyond Takua Thung to the Cave Temple of **Wat Tham Suwan Khuha**, which lies to the left beyond the 29km stone. In the large front chamber is a 12m reclining image of the Buddha and numerous other Buddha images. Against the walls of the cave can be seen the precarious bamboo poles which are used for the collection of edible birds' nests. At the back of the chamber up a flight of steps the cave is partially open to the sky. On the left are the engraved initials of several members of the Thai royal family, including King Chulalongkorn, who visited the cave in 1890 on his way south to the Malay States, and Vajiravudh, Prajadhipok and Bhumibol.

Road 4 continues south for 9km to Phangnga town. 5km before the town, road 4144 turns left to Tha Dan pier, one of the most popular starting points for boat trips to Phangnga Bay. Beyond the 4144 junction, road 4 skirts some limestone cliffs and passes the turning to Krabi (road 415) on the right before reaching the small provincial capital of **Phangnga** (pop. 11,000). There is little of interest here, but the simple hotels make a convenient base for visitors planning a dawn visit to Phangnga Bay. Beside the Tha Dan pier is a rather better hotel, the *Phangnga Bay Resort*.

Travellers bound for Krabi should take road 415 round the north side of the bay for 22km to the market town of Thap Put, where it rejoins road 4. Continue south for another 22km to an intersection in Ao Luk, where a turning to the right on to road 4039 leads after 1400m to the entrance on the left of **Bokkhorani National Park**. Here there is a pleasant arboretum and small waterfall, which make a suitable picnic spot.

▶ Several kilometres further along road 4039, a lane to the right winds for 2km through an oil-palm plantation to a small jetty at **Ban Bo Tho**, from where boats can be chartered for the short ride to the two caves of **Tham Lot** and **Tham Hua Khalok** (Tham Phi Hua To). This is a delightful excursion through mangroves, first reaching Tham Lot, which is in fact not a cave but a natural tunnel, with stalactites hanging down almost to the water, and then, a short distance further, Tham Hua Khalok, which consists of several adjoining caverns containing rock paintings that are possibly of prehistoric origin and include outline drawings of humans, fish, birds and hand prints. Piles of seashells on the cave floor indicate that the sea-level was once much higher than it is today.

13km further along road 4039 is the small fishing village of **Laem Sak**, from where boats can sometimes be chartered to other caves and islands, including **Ko Rang Nok**, an isolated limestone rock off the northeast corner of Ko Yao Yai which is a favourite nesting site for edible-nest swiftlets. Numerous rock paintings can also be seen here. ◄

Return to the Ao Luk intersection and turn south on road 4 towards Krabi. Travellers heading for the popular resorts at Ao Nang should turn right on to road 4034 c 4km before reaching Krabi town. **Ao Nang** has a pleasant beach and a string of bungalow resorts ranging in quality from basic to very comfortable. A short distance to the west is **Nopharat Thara beach**, the mainland part of **Hat Nopharat Thara-Mu Ko Phi Phi National Park**, established in 1983.

Since the late 1980s the supremely beautiful islands of the **PHI PHI ARCHIPELAGO** have been an immensely popular tourist destination. Sadly, the protection accorded by national park status counts for little on these small islands, which are in danger of being completely overwhelmed by the crowds of tourists flocking to their sandy beaches. **Phi Phi Don**, the largest of the islands, and the only one to be inhabited, now has dozens of bungalow resorts and restaurants, most of them offering boat tours and diving trips. The soaring limestone cliffs and azure waters attract a rich bird life, and there are many colourful reef fish and corals. **Phi Phi Le**, its uninhabited southern neighbour, has a cavern, popularly known as **Viking Cave** (Tham Wai King), which contains paintings of ships similar in form to caravels, that probably date from the Ayutthaya period. The cave, together with many others in the area, is a source of valuable edible birds' nests.

Ko Mai Phai and **Ko Yung**, two small islands to the north of Phi Phi Don are popular snorkelling and picnicking destinations for day-trippers.

Krabi

The once rather somnolent fishing port of Krabi (pop. 17,000) has been transformed since the late 1980s into an important tourism service centre, with numerous guest-houses, restaurants, travel agencies, vehicle rental agencies, banks and post office, and boat services to nearby islands and sandy beaches. During the holiday season from November to January, the numerous resort hotels in Krabi itself and nearby bays and islands are sometimes completely full. Inevitably, the huge number of visitors is putting ever greater pressure on the local population and environment; articles appear increasingly often in the local press expounding the problems of waste disposal, water pollution and the offensive behaviour of culturally insensitive tourists.

■ **Information**. For visitors planning to explore the islands and countryside around Krabi, the *Guide Map of Krabi* by V. Hongsombud, usually available in local shops, is highly recommended.

■ **Hotels and services**. The better accommodation is not in the town, but along the coast to the west at **Ao Nang** and **Ao Phra Nang**, two bays which have a wide range of resorts. The *Bangkok Bank* is at 135 T. Utarakit. Money changing facilities are available in the town and at Ao Nang. Travel agencies in the town can advise on bus and boat tickets.

■ **Land Transport**. The main **bus station**, 5km north of Krabi near the main highway (road 4), can be reached by a regular **songthaeo** shuttle service from the town centre. Frequent *songthaeo* also run from Krabi town centre to the beach resorts of Ao Nang, 18km to the west. **Motorcycle** and **jeep rentals** are available in Krabi and Ao Nang.

■ **Boat services from Krabi**. There are several boats daily to Ko Phi Phi Don and to Laem Phra Nang, a beautiful limestone cape to the west of the town.

■ **Boat services from Ao Nang**. There is a steady stream of small boats shuttling all day between Ao Nang and Laem Phra Nang. There are also daily services to the beautiful beaches on Ko Poda, Ko Thap and Ko Hua Khwan, c 7km off the coast.

▶ A short boat-ride upstream from the pier in Krabi brings the visitor to undisturbed stretches of mangrove, home to a rich variety of bird life, best seen in the early morning. Inland from the coast, a pleasant day trip can be made to the charming 50 sq km **Khao Phanom Bencha National Park**, which also has a wealth of bird life (more than 150 species) and flora, and some beautiful waterfalls and trails through the forest. Simple bungalow accommodation is available, but food is not. To get there, take road 411 north from Krabi town to rejoin road 4. Turn right at the junction in Ban Talat, where the two roads meet, and after 600m turn off left towards the park, a further 20km away. The park is difficult to reach by public transport.

A further 1.5km east along road 4 a turning left leads to **Tham Sua**, one of several cave temples in this area. Tham Sua is in a particularly delightful setting at the foot of limestone cliffs. The main cave is up to the left in the cliff face. Beyond this is a flight of more than 1200 steps leading up to the top of the cliff, where there is a Footprint of the Buddha and a magnificent view. Another flight of steps leads over a ridge into a wooded dell surrounded by natural limestone walls. Here are the monks' meditation cells, a series of small interlinked caves, and some enormous *bodhi* trees. ◀

▶ The area to the **northwest of Krabi** is of considerable natural beauty and well worth exploring, particularly by jeep or motorcycle, which can be rented in Krabi. The *Guide Map of Krabi* is invaluable for negotiating routes through the rubber plantations and lush jungle scenery. Tucked away down narrow lanes on the coast are unexpected bungalow resorts. Some, like the simple *Coconut Home* near **Ban Khao Thong**, with its amusing tree-houses, are of considerable charm. ◀

60 · Krabi to Trang and Satun

Roads 4 and 4046, 136km from Krabi to Trang. Roads 404, 416 and 406, 134km from Trang to Satun.

Road 4 turns southeast from Krabi towards Khlong Thom, from where a **detour** can be made to the lowland forest area that contains the **Khao Prabang Khram Wildlife Sanctuary**, home to more than 290 bird species, including the rare ground-dwelling **Gurney's pitta**. To reach the forest, turn left in Khlong Thom on to road 4038 and almost immediately fork right along a dirt track. From here it is 16km to the guard post, which stands in the forest beside a beautiful pool of crystal-clear water. There are walking trails in the vicinity, and rudimentary accommodation is available in Ban Bang Thieo. Public transport to the sanctuary is extremely difficult to find.

Beyond the 64km stone on road 4, turn right on to road 4206 towards the three islands of **Ko Klang**, **Ko Lanta Noi** and **Ko Lanta Yai**, which are separated from each other and from the mainland by narrow channels. Lanta Yai is the most interesting of the three, with its pleasant hilly scenery and beaches, and has several bungalow resorts along its west coast. In the main settlement, Ban Sala Dan, at the north end of the island there is an information office where maps can be obtained. Several neighbouring islands and a part of Ko Lanta Yai together comprise **Lanta Archipelago National Park**, established in 1990 in an attempt to protect the mangrove forests and coral reefs along the islands' coasts. Of particular note are the small, beautiful islands of Ko Rok Nok and Ko Rok Nai to the south of Ko Lanta Yai, and Ko Ngai to the southeast, which has several small resorts.

Continue south on road 4 and near the 45km stone turn left to **Ban Bo Muang**, from where there are direct ferries to Ko Lanta Yai. During the peak tourist season (Nov–Feb) there are also ferry services to Ko Lanta Yai from the pier in Krabi.

In Ban Khuan Kun, beyond the 39km stone, road 4046 leads off road 4 to the right towards **Sikao**, an attractive little market town with many wooden houses. Travellers bound directly for Trang can stay on road 4, but this alternative route on road 4046 is recommended for its pleasant scenery.

▶In Sikao, a **detour** to the right on to road 4162 leads to the coastal village of **Pak Meng**, from where there are boats to the nearby islands of **Ko Muk** and **Ko Kradan**, as well as to **Ko Ngai** (see above). All three are extremely beautiful and offer adequate accommodation. Parts of Ko Muk and Ko Kradan lie within the **Hat Chao Mai National Park**, established in 1981 to try to protect the dugongs which inhabit these coastal waters. The dugong is herbivorous, and its food supply of sea-grass is threatened by the local fishing trawlers, which cut wide swathes through the grass beds. The park comprises c 12 islands and a narrow coastal strip to the south of Pak Meng. Park bungalows are available at the headquarters on **Chang Lang beach**. The extremely rare **black-necked stork** may still be found on some of the islands in the park. ◀

From Sikao continue east on road 4046 to the provincial capital of **TRANG** (pop. 58,000), a busy, modern town with a large Chinese population, situated on the river of the same name. The province is an important rubber-growing region, but the town itself is of little interest except during the nine-day Chinese vegetarian festival held in September or October (see Rte 59). The wealth of Trang is derived principally from its rubber plantations, which account for the large number of Chinese immigrants. There is also, as in many southern Thai towns, a substantial Malay population.

■ **Hotels and services**. The *Trang Hotel* at 134/2–5 T. Wisetkun and the *Thamrin* at 138 T. Kantang are among the best hotels in the town. The *Bangkok Bank* is at 102 T. Phra Ram VI (Rama VI). There are several travel agencies in the town that can arrange transport to nearby islands and accommodation there.

■ **Transport. Buses** run regularly to Satun, Phatthalung, Krabi and Bangkok. From the **railway station** at the end of T. Phra Ram VI there are two overnight services to Bangkok. *THAI* has six **flights** a week to Phuket (40mins). The booking office is at 199/2 T. Wisetkun.

The direct route from Trang to Satun is along road 404, but a more scenic alternative is provided by road 4 (T. Phatthalung), which runs c 20km east to where, just before the 53km stone, a narrow road turns off right (south) through charming countryside to **Khlong Lamchan Waterfowl Park**. A quick detour can first be made on road 4 to the **Khao Chong Botanical Gardens**, in a beautiful forest setting c 3km east of that junction.

Return to the junction and turn south to Khlong Lamchan Waterfowl Park, on the right side after 1km and reached along a track through a rubber plantation. The road continues south, flanked to the east by wooded hills, which form the spine of the peninsula, as far as the Malaysian border. The road passes numerous cascades, including the impressive **Ton Te Falls** on the left near the 26km stone, before joining the main coastal route (road 416) in Thung Yao.

Visitors heading for Satun should turn left here towards Thung Wa. The road passes along a broad valley, with rugged limestone outcrops to the right and gently rolling hills to the left. In Langu, road 4052 forks left to **Pak Bara**, the port for boats to Phetra Archipelago National Park and Tarutao National Park, two marine parks with spectacular coral reefs and beaches. The **PHETRA ARCHIPELAGO**, established as a park in 1984, is made up of a large number of small islands scattered over 500 sq km of sea. Simple accommodation is available on some of the islands, including beautiful Ko Bulon Le.

The islands that constitute **TARUTAO NATIONAL PARK**, further to the south, are also reached from the pier at Pak Bara. This archipelago, which extends over 1490 sq km of sea, was established in 1974 as Thailand's first marine park. The habitats include coral reefs, tropical forests and mangroves, but there are significant variations between the islands. Ko Adang and Ko Rawi are composed of granite, while the largest island, Ko Tarutao, is entirely limestone and sandstone. The park is an important breeding ground for four species of sea turtle, including the giant leatherback, and is also home to monitor lizards, dusky lemurs and the endangered dugong. Bird life comprises more than 100 species, including white-bellied sea-eagles, ospreys, Pacific reef egrets and hornbills. For a while in the 1930s, Ko Tarutao was a detention centre for political prisoners. Today there is pleasant accommodation available on several of the islands, including Ko Tarutao, Ko Adang, Ko Rawi and Ko Lipe. A visit to either the Phetra or the Tarutao archipelagos is highly recommended. Both are populated by friendly Moken (Thai: Chao Le), the nomadic sea gypsies who live in many of the islands off the coasts of southwest Thailand, and by Muslim Malays.

Beyond Langu, road 416 continues southeast towards Satun, passing between rice fields on one side and limestone cliffs on the other. At Ban Chalung, turn right on to road 406 to Satun, or left to Thale Ban National Park.

▶The **detour** to **Thale Ban National Park** is a pleasant journey through forest scenery. After 6km, turn right off road 406 on to road 4184, which runs down to the Malaysian border. The park headquarters lie beside a small lake to the left after 21km. This park, which covers an area of 196 sq km, is in mountainous country covered with tropical evergreen forest. It contains many caves and waterfalls, and some good hiking trails. More than 200 bird species have been recorded. Beside the lake are bungalows and a restaurant, and camping is permitted. Near the park headquarters lives a group of the semi-nomadic Sakai people, who in recent years have come into conflict with the park authorities by hunting wild animals within the park boundary.

Beyond the park, road 4184 continues south to Wang Prachan and the Malaysian frontier (open daily 09.00–16.30). Taxis operate from Satun to the border, and travellers will be met by Malaysian taxis on the other side.◀

The small provincial centre of **SATUN** (pop. 19,000), the southernmost town on Thailand's west coast, has a predominantly Muslim population, clearly evident from the large number of mosques in the town. There is not much of interest except for **Kuden Palace** on T. Satun Thani. This large two-storeyed Chinese-style house was designed in the late 19C by an architect from Penang in Malaysia, and was the governor's residence and guest-house until the 1930s. In 1942 it became the Japanese army command headquarters, and after the war it was used as the city hall and district office. Restored in the early 1990s by the Fine Arts Department, it is now open to the public.

- **Hotels and services**. There are three acceptable hotels in Satun: the *Wang Mai Hotel* at 43 T Satun Thani, the *Rian Thong* at 124 T. Saman Pradit and the *Satun Thani* at 90 T. Satun Thani. The *Bangkok Bank* and *Thai Farmers Bank* are on T. Buriwanit and the **post office** is on T. Saman Pradit.

- **Transport**. Frequent **bus services** run to Trang and beyond. **Taxis** operate a regular service to the border town of Wang Prachan, passing through Thale Ban National Park. There are also fast **passenger boats**, which run down the coast to **Kuala Perlis**, just across the frontier in Malaysia. It is important to visit the immigration office on T. Buriwanit to complete exit formalities before embarking on these boats.

GLOSSARY

abhaya mudrā (Skt), gesture of dispelling fear, bestowing protection. The hand is raised with palm outwards and all fingers pointing upwards.

acroterion, pedestal supporting an ornament at the corners or peak of a roof, or the ornament itself.

Agastya, a Vedic seer, born of an urn, to whom the authorship of the *Rig Veda* is traditionally ascribed. His exploits are recounted in the *Purāṇas*, the *Mahābhārata* and the *Rāmāyaṇa*.

Agni, the Vedic god of fire and, with Indra and Surya, one of the three principal gods in the *Rig Veda*, cleanser of sin and mediator between gods and men.

akṣamala (Skt), rosary, meditation beads, an attribute of Shiva and Ganesha.

Airavata, white elephant with four tusks, usually three-headed, sometimes 33-headed, the mount of Indra.

Akshobya, 'Imperturbable', the transcendental Buddha of the eastern region of the universe. He performs the *bhūmisparśa mudrā*. His mount is an elephant.

Amitabha, 'Infinite Light', the transcendental Buddha of the western region of the universe. He performs the *dhyāna mudrā*. His mount is a peacock.

Amoghapasa, a form of Avalokiteshvara, usually portrayed with six arms, occasionally eight. In five hands he holds a noose, a lotus, a vase, a rosary and a jewel, the sixth arm being in *vara mudrā*.

amṛta (Skt), elixir of life or ambrosia produced by the Churning of the Sea of Milk.

Ananta, cosmic serpent who supports Vishnu while he sleeps before the rebirth of the world.

Anantasayin, epithet for Vishnu when sleeping on the back of Ananta.

Angkor, ancient city in Cambodia, capital under various names of the Khmer empire from the 9C until its conquest by the Thais in 1431–32.

antarāla (Skt), corridor in a Khmer temple connecting the *garbhagṛha* to the *maṇḍapa*.

antaravāsaka (Skt, Pali), undergarment of Buddhist monks, covering the lower part of the body.

antefix, triangular, leaf-shaped ornamental element projecting upwards from the corner or ridge of a roof, frequently used to decorate each level or storey of a Khmer or Khmer-style tower sanctuary. See *prasat, prang*.

ao (Thai), 'bay'.

apsarās (Skt, pl. *apsarasas*), celestial dancers who entertain the Hindu gods, consorts of the *gandharvas*.

arahat, arahant, arhat (Skt), 'worthy one', ascetic worthy of special reverence because advanced in spiritual achievement. In Buddhism it specifically denotes a liberated or enlightened person.

arogyasālā (Skt), 'house of the sick', institution, which may have been either a hospital or simply a dispensary, established in many places in the Khmer empire. In almost every case only the chapel survives, and these all date from the reign of Jayavarman VII (1181–c 1220).

āsana (Skt), 'seat', 'throne', leg positions or sitting postures of deities and Buddha images.

Ashoka, Buddhist ruler of the Maurya empire in north and central India (c 273–236 BC), traditionally believed to have sent Buddhist missionaries to Sri Lanka and Southeast Asia and considered to be the model of the universal ruler. See *cakravartin*.

asura (Skt), demon, enemy of the gods.

ātman, in the *Upaniṣads*, the inner self or essence of the individual and so identical with *brahman*.

Avalokiteshvara, the compassionate *bodhisattva*, also known as Lokeshvara, often depicted holding a lotus in his left hand and with an image of the Amitabha Buddha in his headdress.

avatar (Skt, *avatāra*), literally 'descent', manifestation or incarnation in human or animal form of a god on earth.

bai raka (Thai), leaf- or flame-shaped ornament on the crest of the barge-boards surrounding the gables of Thai temple buildings.

bai sema or **sima** (Thai), upright stone slabs placed round an *ubosot* at the cardinal and sub-cardinal points to demarcate consecrated ground. Sometimes double or triple if associated with a royal foundation, and set on a pedestal and/or under a canopy. See *luk nimit*.

ban (Thai), 'village', 'house'.

bang (Thai), village built near water.

baray (Khmer), artificial pond, reservoir.

bencharong (Thai), multi-coloured overglaze enamel ware originally imported from China.

Bhaisajyagura, in Mahayana Buddhism the Buddha of medicine and healing, to whom the *arogyasālās* were dedicated.

bhūmisparśa mudrā (Skt), gesture of calling the earth to witness the Buddha's victory over the devil Mara (see *Maravijaya*). The left hand is on the lap, the right hand is touching the ground with the back

of the hand outwards.

bodhi (Skt, Pali), perfect knowledge, enlightenment leading to the attainment of Buddhahood. See *sambodhi*. Also used to denote the peepul tree (*Ficus religiosa*), the tree beneath which the Buddha is believed to have achieved his Enlightenment after seven days of meditation.

bodhisattva (Skt), in Mahayana Buddhism person who has achieved Buddhahood, but chooses to remain in the world in order to assist others to achieve understanding. In Theravada Buddhism one who has reached the state preceding the final liberation and attainment of Buddhahood.

bot (Thai), see *ubosot*.

Brahma, creator of the universe and dispenser of the Vedas, with Vishnu and Shiva one of the Trinity (*Trimūrti*) of principal gods of Hinduism, born of the golden lotus that grew from Vishnu's navel when he awoke from cosmic sleep (see Ananta). He is four-faced and four-armed and his attributes are the sceptre, rosary, bow and alms bowl. His mount is a goose (*haṁsa*).

brahman (Skt), the universal, transcendental divine source or essence of reality. See *ātman*.

brāhman, brāhmana, brahmin (Skt), the priestly caste in India.

Brahmanism, the early religion of India based on Vedism and the authority of the priestly caste (*brāhman*) and later identified with Hinduism.

Buddha, 'Enlightened One', a being who has achieved supreme understanding of the nature of existence and has thus succeeded in passing out of the cycle of rebirths into *nirvāna* or extinction. There are an infinite number of Buddhas; the last one is the historical Buddha, Siddhartha Gautama or

Shakyamuni Buddha, who was born a prince of the Shakya clan in Kapilavastu in the Himalayas in 543 BC. The Buddha of the future is called Maitreya.

Buddhapāda (Skt, Pali), 'Footprint of the Buddha', symbolising his presence in a particular place, usually copied from the Footprint on Adam's Peak in Sri Lanka.

buri (Thai), 'town', 'city'.

busabok (Thai), open-sided structure, with a multi-tiered roof or canopy in the form of a mondop and standing on a square base with redented corners, used as a throne, shrine or reliquary. It is usually made of carved wood, often lacquered and gilded.

cakra (Skt), 'wheel', 'solar disc', one of the attributes of Vishnu, usually carried in his upper right hand. Also used in association with the figures of two deer as a symbol of the Buddhist doctrine and of the Buddha's first sermon in the Deer Park at Sarnath, when the Wheel of the Law (*Dharmacakra*) was set in motion.

Cakravala, in Hindu cosmology the concentric mountain ranges surrounding the cosmic mountain, Mount Meru.

cakravartin (Skt), 'Sovereign of the Wheel', universal monarch, world ruler.

cetiya (Pali), see *chedi*.

chadok (Thai), see *jātaka*.

Chakri, name of the present ruling dynasty of Thailand.

chat (Thai). See *chattra*.

chattra (Skt), 'parasol', symbol of high rank and protection against evil.

chedi (Thai), solid structure, usually hemispherical or bell-shaped and surmounted by a tapering spire, containing relics of the Buddha or the ashes of a deceased person. See *stūpa*.

cho fa (Thai), 'sky tassel', decorative horned finial at the apex of the gable of the roof of a Thai sacred or royal building.

Chola, dynasty and school of art in India (c 900–1287 AD).

corbel, method of constructing a vault by placing stones or bricks projecting slightly one above the other on opposite walls until they meet in the centre to form a false arch.

deva, devatā (Skt, Pali), god, deity.

devarāja (Skt), 'the god who is king', a Khmer religious cult, frequently but not invariably associated with the worship of Shiva in the form of a *liṅga*

Devi, consort of Shiva in her benevolent aspect. See Uma, Parvati, Durga.

Dharani, the earth, earth goddess.

dharma (Skt), moral and religious law or duty. In Buddhism the teachings of the Buddha, which are held to be the absolute and ultimate truth.

dharmacakra mudrā (Skt), gesture of setting the Wheel of the Law in motion at the first sermon in the Deer Park at Sarnath. The right hand, representing the wheel, is raised, with the thumb and forefinger joined at the tips and almost touching the same fingers of the left hand, which is turning the wheel.

dharmaśālā (Skt), term used to designate the travellers' rest houses built along the highways in the Khmer empire, mostly dating from the reign of Jayavarman VII (1181–c 1220).

dhyāna mudrā (Skt), gesture denoting deep meditation (*samādhi*), with both hands resting in the lap.

Dhyani Buddha, the transcendental Buddha deep in eternal meditation. In Mahayana Buddhism there are five Dhyani or Jina ('Conqueror') Buddhas presiding over the zenith and the four quarters of the universe: Vairocana (zenith),

Akshobya (east), Ratnasambhava (south) Amitabha (west), Amogasiddhi (north).

doi (Thai), 'mountain' (in north Thailand).

Durga, consort of Shiva in her terrible aspect and associated with death. Also known as Kali and as Mahishasuramardini, slayer of the buffalo demon. Mahisha.

dvārapāla (Skt), 'door guardian', figure of a deity placed at the entrance of a temple in order to keep away evil spirits. The figure on the right of the entrance is generally portrayed as benign, that on the left as ferocious.

Dvaravati, kingdom or group of kingdoms of predominantly Mon population that flourished in the central plains of Thailand between the 7C and the 11C.

Erawan, Thai name for Airavata.

Funan, Chinese name for an ancient Indianised kingdom in the lower Mekong basin which flourished between the 1C and the 6C. It was succeeded by Zhenla.

gajasiṁha (Skt), mythical lion with an elephant's head.

gaja (Skt), 'elephant'.

gamboge, yellow pigment obtained from the resin of trees of the genus *Garcinia*. These grow in Cambodia, from which the word derives.

gaṇa, an attendant of Shiva. The *gaṇas'* leader is Shiva's son, Ganesha.

gandharva (Skt), 'fragrance', celestial deity, often portrayed as a heavenly musician. Associated with the *apsarasas*.

Ganesha, 'Lord of the Ganas', son of Parvati and Shiva, god of wisdom and knowledge and destroyer of obstacles. Portrayed as an obese seated figure with an elephant's head.

garbhagṛha (Skt) 'womb house', innermost chamber or cella in a Khmer sanctuary.

garuḍa (Skt), mythical creature, king of the birds and enemy of the *nāgas*, remover of obstacles. One of the *garuḍas* (Garuda) is the mount of Vishnu. Usually represented with the torso and arms of a human and the beak, wings, legs and claws of an eagle.

gopura (Skt), entrance pavilion in a temple, sometimes surmounted by a tower. Commonly found in Khmer temples.

Govardhana, mountain lifted by Krishna to protect the cowherds and cattle from the rain sent by Indra.

haṁsa (Skt), sacred goose, the mount of Brahma and sometimes of Varuna, the guardian deity of the west. In Buddhism used to represent the flight of the doctrine.

Hanuman, general of the monkey army and Rama's ally in the *Rāmāyaṇa*.

hang hong (Thai), 'swan's tail', acroterion at the end of a barge-board or an eave.

hang yao (Thai), long-tailed boat.

Harihara, combination in a single person of Vishnu (Hari) and Shiva (Hara).

harmikā (Skt), box-like, cube-shaped element between the bell-shaped reliquary chamber and the ringed conical spire of a *chedi*, often with a balustrade. Thought to symbolise the throne of the Buddha and originally used as a reliquary.

hat (Thai), 'beach'.

Himaphan, Thai name for Himavanta.

Himavanta, forest at the foot of the cosmic mountain, Mount Meru, abode of the half-human, half-bird *kinnaras* and other mythical creatures.

hin (Thai), 'stone'.

Hinayana, 'Lesser Vehicle', pejorative term used for the Theravada doctrine of Buddhism.

hong (Thai), see *haṁsa*.

ho trai (Thai), scripture repository, library, in which the Pali texts and other holy scriptures are stored. Often built on stilts over water to protect the scriptures from insects.

ho rakhang (Thai), 'belfry'.

In, Thai name for Indra.

Indra, Vedic god of the sky, guardian of the east and president of the gods dwelling on the summit of Mount Meru.

Isuan, Thai name for Ishvara (Shiva).

jātaka (Skt, Pali), 'birth tale', story of the former lives of the Buddha, in which he achieved perfection in the practice of different virtues. Many of the tales are derived from Indian folklore. Of the 550 lives which the Buddha is said to have lived, the last ten (Thai, *Tosachat*) and, in north Thailand, some non-canonical tales are the most frequently depicted.

jaṭāmukuṭa (Skt), tall chignon worn by Shiva, by *riṣis* and by *bodhisattvas*.

Jayabuddha Mahanartha, name given to the Buddha images sent by command of Jayavarman VII to cities throughout the Khmer empire and thought to be portrait statues of him.

Jina Buddha, see Dhyani Buddha, Vajrasattva.

Kailasa, sacred mountain in the Himalayas, the abode of Shiva and of Kuvera.

kāla (Skt), demon mask frequently carved over temple entrances to protect the temple from evil spirits.

kalae (Thai), V-shaped structure at the end of the roof ridge of houses in northern Thailand.

kalaśa (Skt), pitcher, pot containing the water of immortality and symbolising wealth and prosperity, sometimes used as a finial to crown a temple.

Kali, see Durga.

kamphaeng (Thai), 'wall', 'rampart'.

khan tuai (Thai), bracket supporting a roof.

khao (Thai), 'hill', 'mountain'.

khon (Thai), a form of Thai classical theatre, performed by masked actors and dancers accompanied by a chorus and orchestra. Most of its themes are taken from the *Rāmāyaṇa*.

khlong (Thai), 'canal'.

khrut (Thai, Khmer), see *garuḍa*.

khuan (Thai), 'dam'

kinnara (m.), **kinnari** (f.) (Pali), mythical creature, half-human, half-bird dwelling in the Himavanta Forest. Often represented as a heavenly musician.

kīrttimukha (Skt), 'glory face', symbol of prosperity often used in the same way as the *kāla* motif and sometimes confused with it.

klong bucha (Thai), hollow wooden drum with drumheads attached by wooden pegs.

klong yao (Thai), long wooden drum shaped like an inverted goblet with a skin stretched over the bulbous top part.

ko (Thai), 'island'.

kranok (Thai), decorative flame motif used in Thai art.

Krishna, eighth incarnation of Vishnu, hero of the *Mahābhārata*.

ku (Thai), in north Thailand an altar or shrine for a Buddha image in the form of a *prang*.

Kurma, incarnation of Vishnu as a giant turtle that supported Mount Mandara in the Churning of the Sea of Milk.

kuti (Thai), monastic cell.

Kuvera, god of riches, guardian of the north, usually portrayed as an obese figure surrounded by pots of money and jewels. In Buddhism more often known as Vaishravana or Vessanava.

lai nam thang (Thai), *bencharong* ware made for the exclusive use of royalty.

lak muang (Thai), city foundation stone.

lakhon (Thai), classical Thai dance-drama.

Laksamana, Rama's brother in the *Rāmāyaṇa*.

lakṣaṇa (Skt), 'mark', 'symbol', 'sign', auspicious mark on the body of a Buddha, *bodhisattva* or *cakravartin*.

Lakshmi, consort of Vishnu, goddess of fortune and symbol of Vishnu's creative energy. Her attribute is the lotus.

lalitāsana, leg position in which the left foot is placed on the ground or on a stool or pedestal and the right leg is folded. Images of the Buddha in this position are usually seated on a lotus base.

liṅga (Skt), 'sign', 'symbol' 'emblem', symbolic representation of Shiva as a stylised phallus. Often divided into three parts: a cube at the base representing Brahma, an octagonal shaft representing Vishnu and a cylindrical section with a rounded top representing Shiva. See also *mukhaliṅga*.

Lokeshvara, see *Avalokiteshvara*.

luk nimit (Thai), large round stone buried under the eight *bai sema* surrounding an *ubosot*. A ninth stone is buried inside the *ubosot*, either in the centre or under the principal Buddha image.

mae nam (Thai), 'river', literally 'mother of waters'. Sometimes used by Western writers to denote the Chao Phraya River.

Mahābhārata, Hindu epic written between 400 BC and AD 200 that recounts the conflict between the Kaurava and Pandava dynasties. Its hero is Krishna.

Mahāparinirvāṇa, (Skt), complete extinction of the Buddha, his final death, after which he will have no further rebirths.

Maitreya, benevolent *bodhisattva*, residing in the Tushita Heaven, who will be the future Buddha.

makara (Skt), aquatic monster resembling a crocodile with scales and claws and an elephant's trunk, often shown spewing forth flowers, a *siṁha* or a *nāga*, and found in association with the *kāla* motif. Sometimes the mount of Varuna, the guardian deity of the west, and of the river goddess Ganga.

makuṭa (Skt), see *mukuṭa*.

maṇḍala (Skt), magic diagram representing the cosmos.

maṇḍapa (Skt), antechamber, pavilion or porch in front of a sanctuary, especially in a Khmer temple.

Mandara, mythical mountain used as a pivot in the Churning of the Sea of Milk. See *amṛta*.

Mara, force of evil and sensual pleasure, master of illusion. In Buddhist mythology the devil and tempter of the Buddha.

Māravijaya (Skt, Pali), the Buddha's victory over Mara, symbolised in Buddhist iconography by the *bhūmisparśa mudrā*.

men (Thai), **meru** (Skt), tall, conical wooden funerary tower erected for royal cremation ceremonies.

Meru, mythical cosmic mountain, axis of the world round which the continents and oceans are grouped, and abode of the gods. At its summit is the Tavatimsa Heaven. Also known as Sumeru. See *men*.

mokṣa (Skt), in Hinduism, final liberation from the cycle of rebirths.

Mon, people closely related to the Khmers, who inhabited large areas of lower Burma and central Thailand from the 6C to the 11C and developed a rich and influential Buddhist culture. See *Dvaravati*.

mondop (Thai), cube-shaped building with a multi-tiered pyramidal roof usually enshrining a Footprint of the Buddha or other sacred object or a collection of Buddhist scriptures.

muang (Thai), 'town', 'city', 'state'.

Mucalinda, king of the *nāgas* (*nāgarāja*), who protected the Buddha from the rain while he was deep in meditation after his Enlightenment by raising him out of the mud on his coils and spreading his many-headed hood over him.

mudrā (Skt), ritual hand gesture of a deity or of the Buddha.

mukhaliṅga (Skt), *liṅga* with the face of Shiva carved on the top section.

mukuṭa (Skt, Pali), 'crown', 'diadem'.

nāga (Skt, Pali), serpent deity dwelling in the subterranean and submarine regions, guardian of the treasures and enemy of the *garuḍas*.

naak (Thai), see *nāga*.

nakhon (Thai), 'city'.

nam tok (Thai), 'waterfall'.

Nandi, Nandin, sacred white bull, the mount of Shiva.

nang yai (Thai), shadow play performed with large cowhide puppets.

Narai, Thai name for Vishnu.

Narasimha (Skt), incarnation of Vishnu in the form of a creature with a man's body and a lion's head.

nibbāna (Pali), see *nirvāṇa*.

nirvāṇa (Skt), 'extinction', final liberation from the cycle of rebirths.

pa (Thai), 'forest'.

Pacceka (Skt), 'Silent' Buddha, a being who has attained Enlightenment, but has not preached the doctrine to mankind. Pacceka Buddhas dwell in the Himavanta Forest.

padma (Skt), 'lotus'.

Padmapani ('The One who Carries a Lotus'), a form of the *bodhisattva* Avalokiteshvara. Usually portrayed in the *tribhaṅga* position.

padmāsana (Skt), seat in the form of a lotus; 'lotus position', a leg position identical to the *vajrāsana*, in which the legs are folded with each foot resting sole upward on the opposite thigh.

pak nam (Thai), 'estuary'.

Pali, the sacred language of Theravada Buddhism, one of the Prakritic or popular languages and dialects derived from Sanskrit.

pandhāna (Skt), rectangular piece of cloth worn as a covering for the legs.

Parvati, 'Daughter of the Mountain', consort of Shiva.

paryankāsana (Skt), see *vīrāsana*.

patra (Skt), alms bowl.

phaniat (Thai), elephant kraal.

phanom (Thai), 'mountain', sometimes also used to designate a temple on a mountain site.

phanung (Thai), garment covering the lower half of the body, worn by both sexes. It is often worn pulled up between the legs and fastened to the belt at the back. See *sampot*.

phasin (Thai), ankle-length tubular skirt traditionally worn by Thai women.

phnom (Khmer), see *phanom*.

phra (Thai), 'venerable', 'lord', honorific title given to gods, kings, monks, Buddha images, religious and royal monuments, and sacred places.

Phra Malai, Buddhist monk who journeyed to Heaven and Hell and on his return preached to the faithful about his experiences. He is the subject of a Pali Buddhist tale, thought to be of Sri Lankan origin, translated into Thai and frequently illustrated in Thai mural paintings and manuscripts.

phra rabieng (Thai), gallery surrounding the inner courtyard of a *wat*, usually containing rows of Buddha images and often decorated with mural paintings.

Phrom, Thai name for Brahma.

Phuttha Bat (Thai), see *Buddhapāda*.

pi (Thai), double-reeded, oboe-like musical instrument.

piphat (Thai), Thai orchestra, consisting of metallophones, xylophones, drums and *pi*.

pom (Thai), 'fortress', 'bastion'.

pradakṣiṇā (Skt), 'toward the south', ritual circumambulation clockwise round a monument.

Prajnaparamita, 'Perfection of Wisdom', female form of the *bodhisattva* Avalokiteshvara, spiritual mother of all the Buddhas.

pralambapādāsana (Skt), leg position, sometimes called the European position, in which the legs hang downwards with knees apart as if seated on a chair.

prang (Thai), tower-sanctuary modelled on the Khmer *prasat*, with a distinctive corn-cob profile and usually set on a high square base.

prasat (Khmer, Thai), 'palace', 'temple'. In Khmer it generally designates only the tower-sanctuary in a temple complex, in Thai the whole temple.

pratu (Thai), 'door', 'gateway'.

quincunx, arrangement of five objects, of which one is at the centre and the other four are at the corners.

rabiang (Thai), roofed gallery surrounding a *prang* or other temple building.

Rahu, 'Seizer', one of the nine planets, a demon whose head was severed from his body by Vishnu's discus and who is therefore often depicted as a bodiless head and is believed to cause eclipses by trying to swallow the sun and the moon.

Rama, seventh incarnation of Vishnu, hero of the *Rāmāyaṇa*.

Ramakien, Thai version of the *Rāmāyaṇa*, written by King Taksin in the late 18C.

Rāmāyaṇa, Hindu epic, probably written in two parts between 500 BC and AD 200, that recounts the adventures of Rama and his wife, Sita.

Ratanakosin, 'Jewel of Indra', name given to the period since the transfer of the Thai court and capital to Bangkok and referring specifically to the legend that the Emerald Buddha was carved from an emerald in Indra's treasure.

Ravana, many-armed and many-headed demon who abducts Sita in the *Rāmāyaṇa*.

redentation, indentation of the corners of a building in a series of right angles.

reua hang yao (Thai), long-tailed boat.

Rig Veda, the earliest of the sacred texts of Hinduism, composed in Sanskrit c 1400 BC. It relates the struggles between Indra and the dragon Vritra.

riṣi (Skt), 'ascetic', 'hermit', usually portrayed as a bearded figure wearing animal skins and a *jaṭāmukuṭa* or with a stag's head or antlers.

rusi, russi (Thai), see *riṣi*.

sa (Thai), 'pond', 'reservoir'.

śakti (Skt), female creative force, hence spouse or consort of a male deity.

śāl (śāla) (Skt), tree (*Shorea robusta*) grasped by Queen Maya when she was giving birth to Prince Siddhartha, the future Buddha.

sala (Thai), open-sided pavilion used for meetings or as a shelter and resting place.

sala kan parian (Thai), preaching or study hall in a *wat*.

samādhi (Skt), deepest form of meditation. See *dhyāna mudrā*.

sambodhi (Skt), 'full enlightenment', supreme attainment of knowledge, characteristic of a Buddha.

samlo (Thai), three-wheeled vehicle.

sampot (Khmer), garment covering the lower half of the body, consisting of a rectangle of cloth tied in front with the edges between the legs and fastened to the belt at the back. See *phanung*.

samsāra (Skt), the cycle of life and rebirth which is undergone by all living beings and is brought to an end only by *nirvāṇa*.

samut (Thai), 'sea'.

Sangha (Pali), Buddhist monkhood, community of all Buddhist monks.

sanghātī (Skt), one of the three garments of the Buddhist monk, a shawl usually carried folded and placed over the left shoulder.

sankha (Skt), 'conch shell', an attribute of Vishnu. Its sound when blown symbolises the transience of the universe.

Sanskrit, the sacred language of Hinduism and Mahayana Buddhism.

saphan (Thai), 'bridge'.

Shiva, god of destruction and rebirth, with Brahma and Vishnu one of the Trinity (*Trimūrti*) of principal Hindu deities. His mount is Nandi. See *liṅga*.

sim (Lao), *ubosot* in northeast Thailand and Laos.

siṁha (Skt), mythical lion.

singha (Thai), see *siṁha*.

Sita 'Furrow', the wife of Rama in the *Rāmāyaṇa*, abducted by the demon Ravana and carried off to Lanka.

Shaivite, belonging to the cult of Shiva.

Shakyamuni, 'Sage of the Shakya Clan', a name of the historical Buddha.

Skanda, son of Shiva, god of war, represented as a youth with three or five locks of hair. His mount is a peacock.

soi (Thai), 'lane'.

Sri, 'Auspicious', a name of Lakshmi, the consort of Vishnu. also used as an honorific prefix (in Thai usually romanised as 'Si') added to the names of deities, important personages and places.

stela, stele, upright stone slab bearing an inscription.

stūpa (Skt), originally a burial mound or tumulus, later a reliquary built to house Buddhist relics, or a solid commemorative monument, usually in the form of a dome surmounted by tiered parasols. See *chedi*.

suan (Thai), 'garden', 'park'.

Sumeru, see Meru.

Surya, god of the sun, represented with a lotus in each hand.

takro (Thai), game similar to basket ball or volley ball played with a ball of woven rattan, which can be propelled with any part of the body except the hands.

talat (Thai), 'market'.

tam bun (Thai), 'make merit'.

Tantrism, esoteric form of Buddhism in which magical and erotic rites play an important part.

Tavatimsa, the heavenly abode of the 33 gods presided over by Indra at the summit of Mount Meru. The Buddha is said to have visited it in order to preach to his mother, who had died seven days after his birth. The length of his stay is believed to have been the same as the period of retreat observed by Buddhist monks during the rainy season (the so-called Buddhist Lent). The Buddha's descent from the Tavatimsa Heaven by a *nāga* staircase made of gold and silver and adorned with jewels, accompanied by Brahma, Indra and *gandharvas* is a favourite theme in Thai art.

tham (Thai), 'cave'.

thammat (Thai), 'pulpit'.

thanon (Thai), 'road', 'street'.

that (Thai, Lao), specially in northeast Thailand and Laos, a reliquary monument, generally set on a square base and terminating in a bulbous spire.

thep (Thai), 'angel', 'celestial being'.

Theravada, 'Teaching of the Elders', a traditional and conservative form of

Buddhism practised in Burma, Cambodia, Laos, Sri Lanka and Thailand. It places more emphasis on the efforts of the individual to attain enlightenment through his own merits than on the worship of the Buddha *bodhisattvas*.

thung (Thai), forest clearing.

Totsachat (Thai), 'Ten Births', the *jātakas* of the last ten lives of the Buddha.

Traibhūmi (Skt), in Buddhist cosmology the three worlds of desire (*kharmabhūmi*), forms or appearances (*rūpabhūmi*) and formlessness (*arūpabhūmi*).

Traiphum (Thai), see *Traibhūmi*.

tribhaṅga (Skt), 'thrice bent', triple flexion, a standing position found in some Indian and Southeast Asian statuary in which the head, chest and limbs are not aligned vertically, and one hip protrudes in a pronounced curve.

Trimūrti (Skt), the Hindu Trinity of Brahma, Vishnu and Shiva.

triśūla (Skt), 'trident', an attribute of Shiva.

tua lam yong (Thai), decorated gable board in the form of a nāga.

Tusita, a heaven far above Mount Meru, abode of the *bodhisattvas* awaiting their final existence on earth.

ubosot (Thai), a building in a Buddhist monastery in which the principal Buddha image is displayed and where ordination ceremonies are held. The consecrated ground on which it stands in demarcated by the *luk nimit* and *bai sema*.

Uma, see Parvati.

Upaniṣads, a group of Vedic and later philosophical and mystical writings from which the concept of *brahman* is derived.

ūrnā (Skt), hairy, white mole between the eyebrows of the Buddha, one of the *lakṣaṇas*, usually rendered as a round dot.

uṣṇīṣa (Skt), royal turban, headdress, the knob or flame-like protuberance on the top of the head of Buddha images symbolising the Buddha's perfect knowledge.

uthayan haeng chat (Thai), 'national park'.

uthayan prawatisat (Thai), 'historical park'.

uttarāsanga (Skt, Pali), outer robe of Buddhist monks, usually worn leaving the right shoulder bare.

vāhana (Skt), mount or vehicle of a god, e.g. *haṁsa* (Brahma).

Vairocana, 'Illustrious', the transcendental Buddha of the zenith. He performs the *dharmacakra mudrā*. His mount is a lion or dragon.

Vaishnavite, belonging to the cult of Vishnu.

Vaisravana, see *Kuvera*.

vajra (Skt), 'diamond', 'thunderbolt'.

vajrāsana (Skt), 'adamantine position', leg position in which the legs are crossed with each foot sole upwards on the opposite thigh. Associated with the Buddha's seat of Enlightenment under the *bodhi* tree. Also known as *padmāsana*.

Vajrasattva, 'Deity with a Thunderbolt', the supreme or primordial Buddha from whose meditations emerged the five Jina or Dhyani Buddhas.

vara mudrā, varada mudrā (Skt), gesture of bestowing charity and favours. The hands are as in the *bhūmisparśa mudrā*, but with the palm of the right hand outwards.

Varuna, guardian deity of the west. His mount is a *makara*.

vat (Khmer), see *wat*.

Vessanava, see *Kuvera*.

Vessantara Jātaka, last of the *jātakas*, very popular in Thailand. It relates the life of Prince Vessantara, the last previous life of the *bodhisattva* whose final rebirth was as Prince Siddhartha, the historical Buddha.

vidyādhara (Skt), 'bearer of wisdom', celestial being who has attained supreme wisdom, often portrayed flying above the head of a deity carrying a garland symbolising that wisdom.

virāsana (Skt), 'hero position', leg position in which one leg lies sole upwards over the other, usually the right over the left. Also known as *paryankāsana*.

Vishnu, Hindu god of re-creation, protection and preservation. He has ten incarnations, including Rama, 24 forms and 100 names. With Brahma and Shiva one of the Trinity (*Trimūrti*) of principal Hindu gods. His mount is Garuda.

vitarka mudrā (Skt), gesture of preaching, reciting doctrine. The left hand is in the lap, the right hand is raised with palm outwards, thumb and forefinger touching at the tips and the other three fingers pointing outwards. In some images this gesture is performed with both hands, in which case it refers to the Buddha's descent from the Tavatimsa Heaven.

wai (Thai), greeting or gesture of respect performed by placing the palms of the hands together in front of the face or chest as if in prayer.

wang (Thai), 'palace'.

wat (Thai), Buddhist monastery composed of several religious and secular buildings in a single enclosure, and so, by extension, any temple or place of worship.

wiang (Thai), 'town', 'city'.

wihan (Thai), a building in a Buddhist monastery containing one or more Buddha images, where merit-making ceremonies are performed. Originally used to denote the living quarters of Buddhist monks (Pali, *vihāra*).

yak (Thai), **yakṣa** (Skt), benevolent or malevolent demigod, often depicted as a giant guardian.

Yama, god of death and guardian deity of the south. His mount is a water buffalo.

yan lipao (Thai), a durable fern-like vine common in south Thailand, where it is used to weave baskets.

yoginī (Skt), female practitioner of yoga, demoness, sorceress.

yoni (Skt), female organ, symbol of the female principle, often found as a pedestal for the *linga*, which emerges from it to form a single symbol of divine procreative energy. It also sometimes functions as a receptacle and channel for ritual libations.

Zhenla, Chinese name for an Indianised state that flourished in Cambodia before the foundation of the kingdom of Angkor.

INDEX

This index is limited to topographical entries. Ayutthaya, Bangkok, Chiang Mai, Chiang Saen, Kamphaeng Phet, Lampang, Lop Buri, Nakhon Ratchasima (Khorat), Phetchaburi, Phuket, Si Satchanalai and Sukhothai have sub-indexes.

With only a few exceptions, Hindu and Buddhist monuments (Chedi, Prang, Prasat, Wat, etc), forts (Pom), mosques (Masayit), palaces (Wang), sites of ancient cities (Muang, Wiang) and islands (Ko) are listed under their Thai designations. Museums, markets and geographical locations are generally listed under their English designations preceded by their Thai names (e.g. Nang Bay, Narathat beach, Rusi beach, Rusi Cave, Chao Sam Phraya National Museum, Bokkhorani National Park, Bacho Waterfall).